ADVANCED MICROSOFT® VISUAL BASIC® 5

The Mandelbrot Set
(International) Limited

Microsoft®Press

Advanced Microsoft Visual Basic 5

Published by **Microsoft Press**
A Division of Microsoft Corporation
One Microsoft Way
Redmond, Washington 98052-6399

Library of Congress Cataloging-in-Publication Data pending.

Printed and bound in the United States of America.

1 2 3 4 5 6 7 8 9   QMQM   2 1 0 9 8 7

Distributed to the book trade in Canada by Macmillan of Canada, a division of Canada Publishing Corporation.

A CIP catalogue record for this book is available from the British Library.

Microsoft Press books are available through booksellers and distributors worldwide. For further information about international editions, contact your local Microsoft Corporation office. Or contact Microsoft Press International directly at fax (425) 936-7329.

Power Macintosh is a registered trademark of Apple Computer, Inc. ROOS is a trademark of The Mandelbrot Set (International) Limited. FoxPro, IntelliSense, Microsoft, MS-DOS, PowerPoint, SourceSafe, Visual Basic, Visual C++, Win32, Windows, and Windows NT are registered trademarks and ActiveX, Visual FoxPro, and Visual SourceSafe are trademarks of Microsoft Corporation. Java is a trademark of Sun Microsystems, Inc. Other product and company names mentioned herein may be the trademarks of their respective owners.

Companies, names, and/or data used in screens and sample output are fictitious unless otherwise noted.

Acquisitions Editor: Stephen G. Guty
Project Editors: Sally Stickney, Ron Lamb
Technical Editors: Jean Ross, Jim Fuchs

CONTENTS

CHAPTER 1

PETER J. MORRIS

ON ERROR GOTO HELL

A METHODICAL APPROACH TO ERROR HANDLING   2

CHAPTER **4**

ADAM MAGEE

KAREN FIELD

CHAPTER **5**

JON BURN

CHANGING YOUR APPROACH
TO VISUAL BASIC CODING

CHAPTER **6**

KEVIN HOUSTOUN

CHAPTER **7**

MARK PEARCE

CHAPTER **8**

PETER J. MORRIS

MINUTIAE

CHAPTER **9**

MARK MAYES

HOW DOES THE YEAR 2000 PROBLEM AFFECT VISUAL BASIC?   376

CHAPTER **10**

JON PERKINS

WELL, AT LEAST IT COMPILED OK!
THE VALUE OF SOFTWARE TESTING   426

CHAPTER 11

STEVE
DOLAN

CHAPTER **12**

SIMON JONES

So You Want to Add Another User!

CHAPTER **13**

VAUGHAN BRANT

Data Access Options

CHAPTER **16**

MARK
SEWELL

ALAN
INGLIS

HOW TO JUGGLE 30 BALLS BLINDFOLDED

MAKING ENTERPRISE DEVELOPMENT A SUCCESS 674

FOREWORD

The Microsoft Visual Basic product has always been about providing a state-of-the-art rapid applications development environment for Microsoft Windows. With the release of Visual Basic 5 Professional and Enterprise Editions, the Visual Basic product family has added functionality at the very highest level of the developer workspace, fully supporting the development of enterprise-wide, line-of-business applications in a programming environment that literally millions of developers have mastered. Visual Basic 5 provides the power and performance needed to create applications that run in Internet and intranet environments.

One of the companies that I see pushing the Visual Basic envelope most frequently is The Mandelbrot Set (International) Limited (TMS). Every time I hear from Peet Morris or Mark Sewell, I expect them to ask me some question that usually requires a bit of head scratching before I can give an answer. These guys are always pushing Visual Basic above and beyond its limits, whether it be through using RDO, doing multitier distributed applications, or using the *AddressOf* operator to do who knows what! They conceived and developed MicroHelp's Code Complete toolset and have established a strong reputation as one of the leading consulting firms specializing in Visual Basic development.

I first met Peet Morris from TMS at VBITS in Los Angeles three years ago. He came up to me after a midnight madness panel discussion with a question that now escapes me. But I do remember that his question made my brain hurt. I thought to myself, "This guy is definitely a dedicated Visual Basic developer if he can ask those sorts of questions at midnight after three hours of open panel discussions during VBITS!"

This book is not a beginner's guide to writing "Hello, world!" types of programs, nor is it a step-by-step linear guide to product features. Intended for the working professional, this volume explores in depth many of the topics that beginning books either ignore or gloss over. Drawing on the many and varied strengths of the experts at TMS, each chapter drills down into topics that are not often considered carefully in the course of day-to-day project development. The net effect is like going out to a pub and talking shop with these guys (and gals) over a couple of beers (which I have done on more than one occasion)—but without the morning-after side effects.

Life on the "bleeding edge" is hard, and TMS has often had to learn the "how" the hard way. This book is your chance to benefit from their combined experience. If you're working with Visual Basic and trying to push the envelope, I think you'll find a lot of very useful information here.

Scott Swanson
Development Manager
Visual Basic Component Team
Microsoft Corporation

PREFACE

When we first approached Microsoft Press with the idea of writing an advanced Visual Basic 5 book that was a bit different from the rest, we wondered what reaction we'd get. We were particularly keen on incorporating three features:

- The book was to be a focused collection of the writings and opinions of many individuals. Perhaps, healthily, some of these people would disagree with one another.

- By including material about advanced real-world issues, we wanted the book to be of real interest to corporate managers and developers who were trying to push the tool to its limits.

- Through content and a mix of engaging writing styles, we wanted the book to be entertaining and highly readable.

We expected each author to write about a subject he or she felt passionately about. The subject had to be relevant to real-world programming issues. It also had to be drawn from practical, real-life experience gained from developing and consulting in the trenches—you'll find no code describing how to flip a window upside down in this book!

Microsoft Press liked our ideas, and this book is the result.

At The Mandelbrot Set (International) Limited, or just plain TMS, we've been committed to Visual Basic since version 1.0—in fact, Peet Morris did the world's first public showing of the tool. We're also the British company behind two successful programmer toolkits for both Visual Basic 3 and 4, including Micro-Help's Code Complete. In our ISV position, we've been in on the early testing programs for Visual Basic and were the first site in Europe to have access to version 5—we've been using Visual Basic 5 for a long time!

What else do we do? We spend the bulk of our time on the road developing Visual Basic software and consulting for mostly blue-chip clients. Over the years, we've become familiar with all the issues around enterprise-level development with Visual Basic. From time to time, we also write articles for various Visual Basic–oriented publications, speak at events such as VBITS and TechEd, and run advanced Visual Basic training courses and seminars.

Because of our background and our experience, we're in a superb position to write authoritatively on Visual Basic 5, the most significant upgrade yet.

WHO SHOULD READ THIS BOOK?

This book is geared toward two broad audiences. *Technical managers* responsible for planning, designing, and supporting Visual Basic applications should read it with a view to understanding what they can and can't expect from the teams they are or will be managing and what capabilities Visual Basic 5 has. *Developers* responsible for designing, programming, and implementing Visual Basic applications within the corporate arena should study it to find out how other experts handle the common, yet often complex and frustrating, problems they are likely to encounter (or are already wrestling with).

WHAT IS COVERED IN THIS BOOK?

This book covers a wide range of Visual Basic topics. Here's a brief sample of the subjects discussed: error handling, designing distributed business objects, client/server issues, intranet and Internet topics, designing distributed applications, debugging, migration issues, the Year 2000 problem as it relates to Visual Basic 5, software testing, multimedia issues, data access options, security, reusability, successful enterprise development, coding conventions, and numerous other mission-critical aspects of Visual Basic development. There is really no start and end—just dip into whatever chapter takes your fancy. By the time you've finished reading this book, you'll understand how to make the most of this marvelous technology.

ACKNOWLEDGMENTS

Our sincere thanks to the following people:

The entire TMS authoring team. You sacrificed much personal time and effort to deliver high-quality work under tight deadlines.

The rest of TMS for supporting, and putting up with, the authoring team!

Jim Brown, Steve Guty, Sally Stickney, Jean Ross, Ron Lamb, Jim Fuchs, Bill (just call me Zephan) Teel, and everyone else at Microsoft Press (you know who you are) for getting such a high-quality job done.

From the Visual Basic team, Scott Swanson for suggesting to Microsoft Press that these Brits were the guys to do the book, and everyone else who has supported us. What a truly great product you've made—well done.

Lastly, Helen, William, Katie, Amy, Fiona, and Daniel, for all the love and support.

AND FINALLY

We hope you enjoy this book and get as much pleasure out of it as we did in writing it. If you'd like to contact any of the individual chapter authors, send an e-mail message to book_team@TheMandelbrotSet.com.

Peter J. Morris and Mark Sewell
Directors and Cofounders

The Mandelbrot Set
(International) Limited

Using the Companion CD

Complete sample applications and code used in this book are provided on the companion CD located at the back of the book. The files for the sample programs are contained in the CD's SAMPLES folder. They are organized according to the chapter in the book in which they are discussed. (For example, Chapter 1 samples are located in the \SAMPLES\CHAP01 folder.) You can browse these files on the CD, or you can install them on your hard drive. Installing them requires approximately 12 MB of disk space.

To install the sample files on your hard drive, place the CD in your CD-ROM drive and follow these steps:

1. Click on the CD-ROM drive in Windows Explorer.
2. Double-click SETUP.EXE in the root directory of the CD.

or

1. Select Run from the Start menu.
2. Type *d:\setup* in the Run dialog box (where *d* is the drive letter of your CD drive).

NOTE

If you try to browse the files on the CD without installing them and you're unable to read some of the files, your CD driver software probably doesn't support long filenames. If this is the case, you must run the setup program to install the sample files in order to browse them.

To uninstall the sample files, do the following:

1. Open the Control Panel, and select Add/Remove Programs.
2. On the Install/Uninstall tab, select Advanced Visual Basic 5.
3. Click Add/Remove.
4. Click Yes when prompted.

If you have trouble running any of the sample files, review the text in the appropriate chapter in the book. You can also refer to the README.TXT file in the root directory of the CD, and some of the chapter subfolders also have their own README.TXT files.

Also contained on the CD is an AVI file you can run from the CD to find out more about the authors and The Mandelbrot Set (International) Limited.

On Error GoTo Hell

A Methodical Approach to Error Handling

PETER MORRIS

Peet is a Director and a cofounder of The Mandelbrot Set (International) Limited (TMS), the author of *Windows: Advanced Programming and Design,* a part-time blues guitarist and pilot, and a former Microsoft employee. Peet is acknowledged industry-wide as a Windows and Visual Basic expert and is a frequent speaker at events such as VBITS and TechEd. As a developer/lecturer, he has taught Windows (SDK) API, Advanced Windows API, Visual Basic (all levels), OS/2 Presentation Manager, C, C++, Advanced C and C++, Pascal, Compiler-Theory, OWL, Smalltalk, and CommonView. For more about Peet, turn to page 320.

What is an error? The short answer is, "Something that's expensive to fix." Dealing with errors is costly in terms of both money and time. As you probably know already, your test cycle will be longer, more complex, and less effective if you don't build appropriate error handling into your code right from the start. For these reasons alone, you should do all you can to reduce and handle errors in order to reduce costs, deliver quality code, and keep to schedules.

One way to eradicate errors—a way that I'll dismiss immediately—is to write error-free code. I don't think it's generally possible to write such pristine code. A more realistic way to deal with errors effectively is to plan for them properly so that when they do occur:

- The application doesn't crash.
- The error's root cause (and thus cure) is relatively easy to determine.
- The error is as acceptable and as invisible to the user as is humanly possible.

So what must we do to put a good error handling scheme in place? It's a deceptively simple question with a deceptively big (subjective) set of answers. I think that acquiring and then using some fundamental knowledge is where we should start:

- Ensure that all your developers truly understand how Visual Basic raises and then dispatches and handles errors.

- Make sure that those same developers understand both the consequences of writing code that is hard to debug and the true costs of any unhandled error.

- Develop a suitable error handling strategy that's based on your understanding of the preceding two points and that takes into account your budget and line of business.

- Apply your strategy; demand self-discipline and team discipline.

Handling errors properly in Visual Basic is also a good idea because of the alternative: Visual Basic's default error handling rules are rather severe. Unhandled errors are reported, and then an *End* statement is executed. Keep in mind that an *End* stops your application dead—no form QueryUnload or Unload events, no class Terminate events, not much of anything in fact.

To help you develop an effective strategy for dealing with errors, I'll go over some concepts that I consider vital to the process. These are presented (in no particular order) as a series of tips. "Pick 'n mix" those you think will suit you, your company, and, of course, your development project. Each tip is empirical, and we have employed them in the code we write at The Mandelbrot Set (TMS). I hope they serve you as well as they have served us!

Tip 1: Inconsistent as it is, try to mimic Visual Basic's own error handling scheme as much as possible.

When you call a Visual Basic routine that can fail, what is the standard way that the routine signals the failure to you? It probably won't be via a return value. If it were, procedures, for one, would have trouble signaling failure. Most (but not all) routines raise an error (an exception) when they want to signal failure. (This applies to procedures, functions, and methods.) For example, *CreateObject* raises an exception if it cannot create an object—for whatever reason; *Open* does the same if it cannot open a file for you. (Not all routines raise such exceptions. For example, the *Choose* function returns Null [thus, it requires a Variant to hold its return value just in case it ever fails] if you index into it incorrectly.) In other words, if a routine works correctly, this fact is signaled to the caller by the absence of any error condition.

Routines such as *Open* work like this primarily so that they can be used more flexibly. For example, by not handling the error internally, perhaps by prompting the user in some way, the caller is free to handle errors in the most suitable way. The caller can also use routines in ways perhaps not thought of by their writers. Listing 1-1 is an example using *GetAttr* to determine whether the machine has a particular drive. Because this routine raises exceptions, we can use it to determine whether or not a disk drive exists.

LISTING 1-1

Using error handling to test for a disk drive

```
Public Function bDriveExists(ByVal sDriveAndFile As String) _
As Boolean
' ================================================================
'
' Module: modFileUtilities. Function: bDriveExists.
'
' Object: General
'
' Author - Peter J. Morris. TMS Ltd.
' Template fitted : Date - 01/01/97     Time - 00:00
'
' Function's Purpose/Description in Brief
'
' Determines whether the drive given in sDriveAndFile
' exists. Raises an exception if no drive string is given.
'
' Revision History:
'
' BY            WHY AND WHEN            AFFECTED
' Peter J. Morris. TMS Ltd. - Original Code 01/01/97, 00:00
'
' INPUTS - sDriveAndFile - holds the drive name, e.g., "C".
'          Later holds the name of the drive and the filename
'          on the drive to be created.
'
'
' OUTPUTS - Via return. Boolean. True if drive exists;
'           else False.
'
' MAY RAISE EXCEPTIONS
'
```

>>

LISTING 1-1

```
' NOTES: Uses formals as variables.
'        Uses delayed error handling.
'
' ==================================================================

' Set up general error handler.

On Error GoTo Error_General_bDriveExists:

    Const sProcSig = MODULE_NAME & "General_bDriveExists"

    ' ========== Body Code Starts ==========

    ' These are usually a little more public - shown local
    ' for readability only.
    Dim lErr As Long
    Dim lErl As Long
    Dim sErr As String

    ' Constants placed here instead of in typelib for
    ' readability only.
    Const nPATH_NOT_FOUND       As Integer = 76
    Const nINTERNAL_ERROR_START As Integer = 1000
    Const nERROR_NO_DRIVE_CODE  As Integer = 1001

    ' Always default to failure.
    bDriveExists = False

    If sDriveAndFile <> "" Then

        ' "Trim" the drive name.
        sDriveAndFile = Left$(sDriveAndFile, 1)

        ' Root directory.
        sDriveAndFile = sDriveAndFile & ":\"

        ' Enter error-critical section - delay the handling
        ' of any possible resultant exception.
        On Error Resume Next

        Call VBA.FileSystem.GetAttr(sDriveAndFile)

        ' Preserve the error context. See notes later on
        ' subclassing VBA's error object and adding your own
        ' "push" and "pop" methods to do this.
```

LISTING 1-1

>>

```
    GoSub PreserveContext

    ' Exit error-critical section.
    On Error GoTo Error_General_bDriveExists:

    Select Case nErr

        Case nPATH_NOT_FOUND:
            bDriveExists = False

        ' Covers no error (error 0) and all other errors.
        ' As far as we're concerned, these aren't
        ' errors; e.g., "drive not ready" is OK.
        Case Else
            bDriveExists = True

    End Select

Else

    ' No drive given, so flag error.
    Err.Raise nLoadErrorDescription(nERROR_NO_DRIVE_CODE)

End If

' ========== Body Code Ends ==========

Exit Function

' Error handler
Error_General_bDriveExists:

    ' Preserve the error context. See notes later on
    ' subclassing VBA's error object and adding your own "push"
    ' and "pop" methods to do this.
    GoSub PreserveContext

    ' **
    ' In error; roll back stuff in here.
    ' **

    ' **
    ' Log error.
    ' **
```

>>

LISTING 1-1

```
    ' Reraise as appropriate - handle internal errors
    ' further only.
    If (lErr < nINTERNAL_ERROR_START) Or _
       (lErr = nERROR_NO_DRIVE_CODE) Then

        VBA.Err.Raise lErr

    Else

        ' Ask the user what he/she wants to do with this
        ' error.

        Select Case MsgBox("Error in " & sProcSig & " " _
                        & CStr(lErr) & " " & _
                        CStr(lErl) & " " & sErr, _
                        vbAbortRetryIgnore + vbExclamation, _
                        sMsgBoxTitle)
            Case vbAbort
                Resume Exit_General_bDriveExists:

            Case vbRetry
                Resume

            Case vbIgnore
                Resume Next

            Case Else
                VBA.Interaction.MsgBox _
                                "Unexpected error" _
                                , vbOKOnly + vbCritical _
                                , "Error"

            End

        End Select

    End If

Exit_General_bDriveExists:

    Exit Function
```

LISTING 1-1

>>

```
PreserveContext:

    lErr = VBA.Err.Number
    lErl = VBA.Erl
    sErr = VBA.Err.Description

Return

End Function
```

Here are a few comments on this routine:

- It's a fabricated example, although I've tried to make sure that it works and is complete.

- It handles errors.

- It uses delayed error handling internally.

- It's not right for you! You'll need to rework the code and structure to suit your particular needs and philosophy.

- The error handler might raise errors.

- It doesn't handle errors occurring in the error handler.

- It uses a local subroutine, *PreserveContext*. This subroutine is called only from within this routine, so we use a *GoSub* to create it. The result is that *PreserveContext* is truly private and fast—and it doesn't pollute the global name space. (This routine preserves the key values found in the error object. Tip 11 explains a way to do this using a replacement *Err* object.)

Within *bDriveExists*, I've chosen to flag parameter errors and send the information back to the caller by using exceptions. The actual exception is raised using the *Raise* method of the Visual Basic error object (*Err.Raise*) and the return value of a function (*nLoadErrorDescription*). This return value is used to load the correct error string (typically held in string resources and *not* a database since you want to always be able to get hold of the string quickly). This string is placed into *Err.Description* just before the *Raise* method is applied to the error object. Reraising, without reporting, errors like this allows you to build a transaction model of error handling into your code. (See Tip 14 for more on this topic.)

The *nLoadErrorDescription* function is typically passed the error number (a constant telling it what string to load), and it returns this same number to the caller upon completion. In other words, the function *could* look something like this (omitting any boilerplate):

```
Public Function nLoadErrorDescription(ByVal nCode As Integer)

    ' Return the same error code we're passed.
    nLoadErrorDescription = nCode

    ' Load the error text for nCode from some source and assign it
    ' to Err.Description.
    Err.Description = LoadResString(nCode)

    Exit Function

End Function
```

In this example, we're using a string resource to hold the error text. In reality, the *routine* we normally use to retrieve an error string (and, indeed, to resolve the constant) is contained in what we call a ROOS—that's a Resource Only OLE Server, which we'll come back to in Tip 10.

A good error handler is often complex, so we must ask ourselves another question: What will happen if we get an error in the error handler? Well, if we're in the same local scope as the original error, the error is passed back up the call chain to the next available error handler. (See Tip 5 for more information on the call chain and this mechanism.) In other words, if you're in the routine proper when this second error occurs, it will be handled "above" your routine; if that's Visual Basic, you're dead! "OK," you say, "to handle it more locally, I must have an error handler within my error handler." Sounds good—trouble is, it doesn't work as you might expect. Sure, you can have an *On Error Goto xyz* (or *On Error Resume Next* or *On Error Resume 0*) in your error handler, but the trap will not be set; your code will not jump to *xyz* if an error occurs in your error handler. The way to handle an error in your error handler is to do it in another procedure. If you call another procedure from your error handler, that routine can have an error trap set. The net effect is that you *can* have error handling in your error handler just as long as another routine handles the error. The ability to handle errors in error handlers is fundamental to applying a transaction processing model of error handling to your application, a subject I'll explain further in Tip 14.

To recap, the reason *GetAttr* doesn't handle many (if any) internal errors is that to do so would take away its very flexibility. If the routine "told" you that the drive didn't exist, by using, say, a message box, you couldn't use it the way we did in *bDriveExists*.

If you're still not convinced, I'll be saying a little more on why raising errors is better than returning True or False later. But for now, let's think BASICA!

Tip 2: Use line numbers in your source code.

Line numbers!? Yup, just like those used in "real" Basic. Bear with me here—I'll convince you!

In older versions of Basic, line numbers were often used as "jump targets" as well as simply being mandatory. A jump target is a line number used with a *GoTo*, such as *GoTo 2000*. The *2000* identifies the start of a block of code to execute next. After *GoTo* came *GoSub* (and *Return*). Now you had a "Basic subroutine," albeit one with a strange name: *GoSub 2000*. You can think of the (line) number almost as an address (just as in C). These days, of course, Basic *is* Visual Basic and we use symbolic names for labeling such jump targets (real subroutines, just like those in C and other programming languages). Line numbers have become a peculiarity designed to allow nothing more than some level of backward compatibility with some other version of Basic.

Or then again, maybe not. In Visual Basic, *Erl*, a Visual Basic (undocumented in Visual Basic 4 and 5 but present in all versions of Visual Basic thus far) "global variable," gives you access to the line number of any erroring line of code. So by using line numbers and by using *Erl* in your error handlers, you can determine which line of code erred—wow! What happens to *Erl* if you don't use line numbers? Easy—it will always be 0.

Of course, you won't want to start typing line numbers in by hand. You need some automation. At TMS, we add line numbers to our code using an internal tool we originally developed for working with Visual Basic 2. It now works as an add-in under Visual Basic 5. There are tools on the market that can do the same for your code.

At TMS, we don't work with line numbers in our source code, however. We add them only when we're doing a ship build—that is, when we want to ship a binary to, say, beta testers or to manufacturing for an impending release. We use our internal tool to build a new version of the code, complete with line numbers, and then we make an executable from that. We store the line numbered source code in our source control system and ship the executable. We cross-reference the EXE version number (the Auto Increment option is just great here) to the source code stored in the source control system. Every time we do a new build for shipping, we create a new subproject whose name is the version number of the build and store the line numbered source code in it along with a copy of the binary image. If an error report comes in, we can easily refer back to the source code to find the erroring line (*very, very easy* if you're using Microsoft Visual SourceSafe). Typically, the error report will contain details of the module, routine, and line number of the error.

Listing 1-2 is a typical Click event, line numbers and all.

LISTING 1-2

Generic Click event with line numbers

```
Private Sub Command1_Click()
' ================================================================
' Module Type : Form
' Module Name : Form1
' Object      : Command1
' Proc Type   : Sub
' Proc Name   : Click
' Scope       : Private
' Author      :
' Date        : 01/01/97 00:00
'
' History     : 01/01/97 00:00: Peter J. Morris : Original Code.
' ================================================================

' Set up general error handler.
On Error GoTo Error_In_Command1_Click:

1   Dim sErrorDescription As String

2   Const sProcSig = MODULE_NAME & "Command1_Click"

        ' ========== Body Code Starts ==========

3   Debug.Print bDriveExists("")

        ' ========== Body Code Ends ==========
```

LISTING 1-2

>>

```
4  Exit Sub

' Error handler
Error_In_Command1_Click:

5  With Err
6     sErrorDescription = "Error '" & .Number & " " & _
      .Description & "' occurred in " & sProcSig & _
      IIf(Erl <> 0, " at line " & CStr(Erl) & ".", ".")
7  End With

8  Select Case MsgBox(sErrorDescription, _
                      vbAbortRetryIgnore, _
                      App.Title & " Error")

      Case vbAbort
9         Resume Exit_Command1_Click:
10     Case vbRetry
11        Resume
12     Case vbIgnore
13        Resume Next
14     Case Else
15        End

16  End Select

Exit_Command1_Click:

End Sub
```

Notice in Listing 1-2 that *sProcSig* is made up of the module name (*Form1*) and the routine name (*Command1_Click*). Notice also that the error handler examines *Erl to* "see" whether line numbers have been used. Figure 1-1 shows what's typically displayed when an error occurs using this kind of scheme.

FIGURE 1-1

*Error and
line number
information*

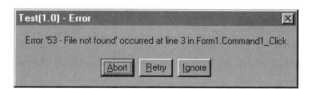

Of course, the actual code that makes up the error handler is entirely up to you. If you use this scheme, I recommend you have a module-level constant to hold your module name and use a routine-level constant to hold the routine name plus the module name:

Module Declaration Section

```
Private Const MODULE_NAME As String = "Form1."
```

Command1_Click Event

```
Const sProcSig As String = MODULE_NAME & "Command1_Click"
```

Tip 3: Raise exceptions when possible because return values *will* be ignored.

This tip supplements Tip 1: "Inconsistent as it is, try to mimic Visual Basic's own error handling scheme as much as possible." Since Visual Basic 4, a function can be called like a subroutine. (In Visual Basic 3 and earlier, it couldn't.) To demonstrate this, consider the following code fragments:

```
Sub Command1_Click ()

    Debug.Print SomeFunc()
    Call SomeFunc

End Sub


Function SomeFunc () As Integer

    SomeFunc = 42

End Function
```

The line *Call SomeFunc* is illegal in Visual Basic 3 but legal in Visual Basic 4 and later. (It's VBA!) In case you're wondering why this is so, the facility was added to VBA (Visual Basic for Applications) to allow you to write routines that were more consistent with some of Visual Basic's own routines, such as *MsgBox*, which acts sometimes like a function and sometimes like a statement (or a C type procedure if you're used to that language). (In Tip 4, you'll find out how to write your own *MsgBox* routine.)

A side effect of all this is that routines that return some indication of success or failure might now have that result ignored. As C and SDK programmers know only too well, this *will* cause problems! In Visual Basic 3, the programmer always had to use the return value. Typically, he or she would use it correctly. If a programmer can ignore a routine's returned value (say it's not a database handle but a True/False value—that is, either it worked or it failed), however, he or she usually will ignore it.

Exceptions, on the other hand, cannot easily be ignored (except by using *On Error Resume Next* or *On Error Resume 0*—both easy to test for and legislate against). Also, keep in mind that "newer" Visual Basic developers sometimes lack the necessary self-discipline to use and test return values correctly. By raising exceptions, you force them to test and then to take some appropriate action in one place: the error handler.

Another reason to use exceptions is that not using them can cause your code to become more difficult to follow—all those (un)necessary conditional tests to see that things have worked correctly. This kind of scheme, in which you try some code and determine that it didn't work by catching a thrown exception, is pretty close to "structured exception handling" as used in C++ and Microsoft Windows NT. For more on structured exception handling, see the Visual C++ 4.0 online help. (Select Contents, and follow this path: Visual C++ books; C/C++; Programming Techniques; Structured Exception Handling.)

Here's an example of a structured exception handling type of scheme:

```
Private Sub SomeWhere()

    If a() Then
        ⋮
        If b() Then
            ⋮
            If c() Then
                ⋮
            End If
        End If
    End If

End Sub
```

OK, I agree, this example is not too hard to figure out. But I'm sure you've seen far more complex examples of nesting conditionals and get the idea! Here's the same code using exceptions to signal errors in *a*, *b*, or *c*:

```
Private Sub SomeWhere()

' TRY
On Error Goto ????

    a()
        ⋮
    b()
        ⋮
    c()
        ⋮

' CATCH
????

    ' Handle exception here.

End Sub
```

Can you see the flow any easier here? What you cannot see is that to get to the call to *b*, *a* must function correctly—it's only implied by the presence of the error handler. By losing the *If*, you're losing some plain readability but you're also gaining some—the code is certainly less cluttered. Of course, sometimes code is clear just because you're used to it. Consider replacing *b*, for instance, with a call to *Open*. If you were to use the *If...Then* scheme to check for errors, you couldn't check for any errors in *Open* because you can't put conditional statements around a procedure. So it's easy for you to accept the fact that after *Open* is called, if an error occurs, the statement following *Open* will not run. It works the same with the *b* function. If an error occurs in the *b* function, the error routine rather than the statement that follows *b* will execute.

If you adopt this kind of error handling scheme, just make sure that you have projectwide collaboration on error codes and meanings. And by the way, if the functions *a*, *b*, and *c* already exist (as used previously with the *If* statements), we'll be using this "new" ability to ignore returned values to our advantage.

NOTE

Once again, if a routine's returned value can be ignored, a programmer will probably ignore it!

Tip 4: Automatically log critical *MsgBox* errors.

One way to log critical *MsgBox* errors is by *not* using the standard message box provided by VBA's *Interaction.MsgBox* routine. When you refer to an object or a property in code, Visual Basic searches each object library you reference in order to resolve it. Object library references are set up in Visual Basic's References dialog box. (Open the References dialog box by selecting References from the Project menu.) The up arrow and down arrow buttons in the dialog box move references up and down in a list so that they can be arranged in priority order. If two items in the list use the same name for an object, Visual Basic uses the definition provided by the item listed higher in the Available References list box. The three topmost references (Visual Basic For Applications, Visual Basic Runtime Objects And Procedures, and Visual Basic Objects And Procedures) cannot be demoted (or shuffled about). The caveat to all this prioritizing works in our favor—internal modules are always searched first.

Visual Basic 5 allows you to subclass its internal routines such as *MsgBox* and replace them with your own (through aggregation). Recall that in the code shown earlier (in Listing 1-1) some of the calls to *MsgBox* were prefixed with *VBA*. This explicitly scopes the call to VBA's *MsgBox* method via the Visual Basic For Applications type library reference. However, calls to plain old *MsgBox* go straight to our own internal message box.

A typical call to our new message box might look like this:

```
MsgBox "Error text in here", _
       vbYesNo + vbHelpButton + vbCritical, sMsgBoxTitle
```

vbHelpButton is not a standard Visual Basic constant but rather an internal constant. It's used to indicate to *MsgBox* that it should add a Help button. Also, by adding vbCritical, we're saying that this message (error) is extremely serious. *MsgBox* will now log this error to a log file.

To replace *MsgBox*, all you have to do is write a function (an application method really) named *MsgBox* and give it the following signature. (The real *MsgBox* method has more arguments that you might also want to add to your replacement: use the object browser to explore the real method further.)

```
Public Function MsgBox _
( _
    ByVal isText As String _
    , Optional ByVal inButtons As Integer _
    , Optional ByVal isTitle  As String _
)
```

Here's an example of a trivial implementation:

```
Public Function MsgBox _
( _
    ByVal isText As String _
    , Optional ByVal inButtons As Integer _
    , Optional ByVal isTitle   As String  _
)

    Dim nResult As Integer

    nResult = VBA.Interaction.MsgBox(isText, inButtons, isTitle)

    If Not IsMissing(inButtons) Then
        If (inButtons And vbCritical) = vbCritical Then
            Call LogError(isText, inButtons, isTitle, nResult)
        End If
    End If

    MsgBox = nResult

End Function
```

Here we're logging (implied by the call to *LogError*) the main message text of a message box that contains the vbCritical button style. Notice that we're using the VBA implementation of *MsgBox* to produce the real message box on screen. (You could use just *VBA.MsgBox* here, but we prefer *VBA.Interaction.MsgBox* for clarity.) Within your code, you use *MsgBox* just as you always have. Notice also that in our call to *LogError* we're logging away the user's response (*nResult*) too—"I'm sure I said 'Cancel'!"

Another good idea with any message box is always to display the application's version number in its title; that is, modify the code above to look like this:

```
sTitle = App.EXEName & "(" & App.Major & "." & _
                            App.Minor & "." & _
                            App.Revision & ")-"

nResult = VBA.Interaction.MsgBox(isText, inButtons, _
                            sTitle & isTitle)
```

Figure 1-2 shows the message box that results from this code.

Of course, you don't have to use VBA's *MsgBox* method to produce the message box. You could create your own message box, using, say, a form. We create our own custom message boxes because we often want more control over

the appearance and functionality of the box. For example, we often use extra
buttons (such as a Help button, which is what the vbHelpButton constant was
all about) in our message boxes.

Tip 5: Have an error handler in every routine.

Because Visual Basic nests routines into local address space, all errors happen
locally. An unhandled error in some routine that might be handled above that
routine, in another error handler, should be considered unhandled because it
will probably destabilize the application.

Let's go over that again, but more slowly. Visual Basic handles local errors. By
this, I mean that whenever an error handler is called it always thinks it's acting
upon an error produced locally within the routine the error handler is in. (Indeed, a bit of obscure and normally unused—because it's implied—syntax, *On
Local Error GoTo*, gives this little secret away.) So if we write some functions
named *SubA*, *SubB*, and *SubC* and arrange for *SubA* to call *SubB* and *SubB* in
turn to call *SubC*, we can spot the potential problem. (See Figure 1-3 on the
next page.) If *SubC* generates an error, who handles it? Well, it all depends. If
we don't handle it, Visual Basic will. Visual Basic looks up *Err.Number* in its
list of error strings, produces a message box with the string, and then executes
an *End* for you. If, as in Figure 1-3, *SubA* handles errors, Visual Basic will
search up through the call chain until it finds *SubA* (and its error handler)
and use that error handler instead of its own default error handler. Our error
handler in *SubA*, however, now *thinks* that the error happened locally to it;
that is, any *Resume* clause we might ultimately execute in the error handler
works entirely within the local *SubA* routine.

Your code always runs in the context of some event handler; that is, any entry point into your code must ultimately be in the form of an event handler.
So substituting *SubA* for, say, *Form_Load*, you could now write a catchall error
handler by providing an error handler in *Form_Load*. Now, when *SubC* generates its error (I'm assuming here that these functions are only ever called from
Form_Load), Visual Basic will find the local error handler in *Form_Load* and
execute it. Ultimately, this error handler will execute a *Resume* statement. For
argument's sake, let's say that it's *Resume Next*.

FIGURE 1-3

The call chain in action

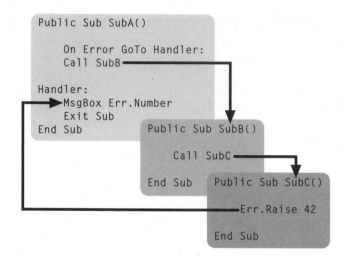

```
Public Sub SubA()

    On Error GoTo Handler:
    Call SubB

Handler:
    MsgBox Err.Number
    Exit Sub
End Sub
```

```
Public Sub SubB()

    Call SubC

End Sub
```

```
Public Sub SubC()

    Err.Raise 42

End Sub
```

The *Next* here means after the call to *SubB*. OK, so what's the problem? If a problem exists, it's buried inside *SubB* and *SubC*—we don't know what they did! Imagine this scenario. Maybe *SubC* opened some files or perhaps a database or two, and somewhere within *SubC*, it was also going to close them. What happens if the erroring code happened somewhere in between these two things—say, the files/databases got opened but were never closed? Again it depends, but loosely speaking, it means trouble.

 NOTE

> The situation described above could be worse, however. Maybe instead of *Resume Next* we simply used *Resume*, that is, try again. This will result in an attempt to open the same files again; and as we all know, this attempt may fail for many reasons—perhaps instead of using *FreeFile*, you used hard-coded file handle IDs, or maybe you opened the files last time with exclusive access.

Unfortunately, when Visual Basic fires an error handler, there's no easy way of telling whether the error handler was really local to the error. So there's no way to guarantee that you handled it properly. And of course, there's no way to install a global error handler that's called automatically by Visual Basic whenever an error occurs. There's no way around it: to write professional and robust applications, we must have error handlers *absolutely everywhere!*

Tip 6: Write meaningful error logs (to a central location if possible).

By way of an example, Listing 1-3 is a typical log file entry produced by our internal application template code. No explanation is provided because most of the entry is pretty obvious.

```
*****************************************************************************
* Error Entry Start. TEST. Created 04 February 1997 18:15
*****************************************************************************
The Application:
----------------
C:\TMS\TEMPLATE\TEST.EXE   Version 1.0.10
OS App Name C:\TMS\TEMPLATE\TEST.EXE

The Error:
----------
An error has occurred in C:\TMS\TEMPLATE\TEST.EXE - the TMS error code associated
with this error is 000053. If the problem persists, please report the error to TMS
support.  The error occurred at line 100.

The error probably occurred in frmMainForm.cmd1_Click.
The standard VB error text for this error is 'File not found'.

Active Environment Variables:
-----------------------------
TMP=C:\WINDOWS\TEMP
winbootdir=C:\WINDOWS
COMSPEC=C:\COMMAND.COM
PATH=C:\WINDOWS;C:\WINDOWS\COMMAND;C:\;C:\DOS
TEMP=C:\TEMP
DIRCMD=/OGN/L
PROMPT=$e[0m[$e[1;33m$p$e[0m]$_$g
CMDLINE=WIN
windir=C:\WINDOWS

Relevant Directories:
---------------------
Windows DIR C:\WINDOWS        - 16
System  DIR C:\WINDOWS\SYSTEM - 16
Current DIR C:\TMS\TEMPLATE   - 16
```

>>

LISTING 1-3   *Typical log file entry*

```
>>
```

```
Versions:
----------
Windows    - 3.95
DOS        - 7.0
Mode       - Enhanced
CPU        - 486 or Better
COPRO      - True
Windows 95 - True

Resources:
----------
Free Mem (Rough) 15,752 MB
Free GDI  (%) 79
Free USER (%) 69
Free Handles 103
*******************************************************************************
* Error Entry End. TEST
*******************************************************************************


*******************************************************************************
* Stack Dump Start. TEST. Created 04 February 1997 18:15
*******************************************************************************
Stack Frame: 001 of 003 AppObject    - Run          Called @ line 70 CheckStack
Stack Frame: 002 of 003 AppObject    - CheckStack   Called @ line 10 cmd1_Click
Stack Frame: 003 of 003 frmMainForm  - cmd1_Click
*******************************************************************************
* Stack Dump End. TEST
*******************************************************************************


*******************************************************************************
* DAO Errors Start. TEST. Created 04 February 1997 18:15
*******************************************************************************
No Errors
*******************************************************************************
* DAO Errors End. TEST
*******************************************************************************
```

The log files you write can be centralized; that is, all your applications can write to a single file or perhaps to many different files held in a central location. That "file" could be a Microsoft Jet database. Now if you log meaningful information of the same kind from different sources to a database, what have you got? Useful data, that's what! At TMS, we created a system like this once for a client. All the data gathered was analyzed in real time by another Visual Basic application and displayed on a machine in the company's support department. The application had some standard queries it could throw at the data ("How's application *xyz* performing today?") as well as a query editor that the company could use to build its own queries on the data. ("Show me all the Automation errors that occurred for user *abc* this year, and sort them by error code.") All the results could be graphed too, which, as is usual, allowed the true nature of the data statistics to become apparent.

After a little while, it wasn't just Support who accessed this database. User Education used it to spot users who were experiencing errors because of a lack of training, and developers would use it to check on how their beta release was running. Remember, users are generally bad at reporting errors. Most prefer to Ctrl+Alt+Delete and try again before contacting support. By logging errors automatically, you don't need the user to report the error (sometimes incorrectly or with missing information: "Let's see, it said something about…"); it's *always* done by the application, and *all* the necessary information is logged *automatically*.

Another issue involved in making error messages and error logs meaningful is to know who was using the application and as a result who will be viewing the errors. It's a good idea to display different error messages for different audiences. The best method for identifying the audience whenever an error occurs is to determine whether we're running in Visual Basic's design time Integrated Development Environment (IDE). Once this has been determined, we can log or output different error text and do some other stuff differently, depending on the result of that test. The reason we do this is that programmers, who would be the only people using Visual Basic's IDE, are not end users. A programmer doesn't mind seeing "Input past end of file," but users almost always do. If you know *how* you're running, you can easily switch messages.

The test we do internally to determine this involves a routine named *bInDesign*. Listing 1-4 on the next page is a comment- and explanation-free version (to save a little space).

By using *bInDesign*, we can do things a little differently at run time, depending on whether or not we're running in the IDE. We store the result of a single call to *bInDesign* in a property of the *App* object named *InDesign*. We replace the real *App* object with our own, also called *App*, and add this property at application start-up.

LISTING 1-4

bInDesign *determines whether the application is running in design mode*

```
Option Explicit

Private Const GWW_HINSTANCE As Integer = (-6)

Private Declare Function WinFindWindow Lib _
"user32" Alias "FindWindowA" _
(ByVal lpClassName As String, ByVal l As Long) As Long

Private Declare Function WinGetWindowLong Lib _
"user32" Alias "GetWindowLongA" _
(ByVal hwnd As Long, ByVal nIndex As Long) As Long


Public Function bInDesign() As Boolean

    If Forms.Count = 0 Then
        MsgBox "This routine cannot be called if " & _
               "no forms are loaded." _
               , vbOK Or vbCritical _
               , "Error"
    Else

        Dim hInstanceVB As Long
        Dim hVBMainWindow As Long

        ' Find the VB IDE's main window.
        hVBMainWindow = WinFindWindow("ThunderMain", 0)

        hInstanceVB = IIf( _
                        hVBMainWindow <> 0 _
                      , WinGetWindowLong(hVBMainWindow _
                                       , GWW_HINSTANCE) _
                      , 0 _
                      )

        bInDesign = IIf( _
                        hInstanceVB = WinGetWindowLong( _
                                        Forms(0).hwnd _
                                      , GWW_HINSTANCE _
                                      ) _
                      , True _
                      , False _
                      )

    End If

End Function
```

Another use of *App.InDesign* is to turn off your own error handling altogether. Now, I know that Visual Basic allows you to *Break On All Errors*, but that's rarely useful because you might have deliberate delayed error handling activated that you don't want to be ignored. Use *App.InDesign* to conditionally turn error handling on or off:

```
If Not App.InDesign Then On Error GoTo ...
```

The reason for this is that one of the last things you want within the IDE is active error handlers. Imagine you're hitting F8 and tracing through your code. I'm sure you know what happens next—you suddenly find yourself in an error handler. What you really want is for Visual Basic to issue a *Stop* for you on the erroring line (which it will do by default if you're using the IDE and hit an error and don't have an error handler active). The code above causes that to happen even when your error handling code has been added. Only if you're running as an EXE will the error trap become enabled.

Tip 7: Use assertions.

Assertions are routines (in Visual Basic) that use expressions to "assert" that something is or is not True. For example, you might have a line of code like this in your project:

```
nFile = FreeFile
```

So how do you know if it works? Maybe you think that it raises an exception if all your file handles are taken up. (The Help file doesn't tell you.) We wouldn't leave this to chance. What we'd do during both unit and system testing is use assertions to check our assumption that all is indeed well. We would have a line that looks like this following the line above:

```
Call Assert(nFile <> 0, "FreeFile")
```

This checks that *nFile* is not set to 0. Assertions are easy to use and extremely handy. They would be even better if Visual Basic had a "stringizing" preprocessor like the one that comes with most C compilers. Then *it* could fill in the second parameter for you with the asserted expression, like this:

```
Call Assert(nFile <> 0, "nFile <> 0")
```

Assertions should be removed at run time. They serve only for testing during development, a kind of soft error handler, if you will. (This removal could be done using the *App.InDesign* property described earlier.) If a line asserts regularly during development, we usually place a real test around it; that is, we test for it specifically in code. For the preceding example, we would replace

```
Call Assert(nFile <> 0, "FreeFile")
```

with

```
If nFile = 0 Then
    Err.Raise ????
End If
```

If an assertion doesn't assert regularly (or at all) during development, we remove the assertion. See Chapter 7 for more on writing and using assertions and on the *Debug* object's *Assert* method (which I haven't used here).

Tip 8: Don't retrofit blind error handlers.

The best error handlers are written when the routine they protect is being written. Tools that insert error handlers for you help but are not the answer. These tools can be used to retrofit semi-intelligent error handlers into your code once you're through writing—but is this a good idea? Your application will be error handler–enabled, that's for sure; but how *dynamic* will it be in its handling of any errors? Not very!

We rarely use any kind of tool for this purpose because in fitting a blind error handler there is little chance of adding any code that could recover from a given error situation. In other words, by fitting an error handler after the fact, you might just as well put this line of pseudocode in each routine:

```
On Error Condition Report Error
```

You're handling errors but in a blind, automated fashion. No recovery is possible here. In a nutshell, what we're saying is that a blind error handler is potentially of little real use, although it is of course better than having no error handling at all. Think "exception" as you write the code, and use automation tools only to provide a template from which to work.

Tip 9: Trace the stack.

As you saw in the log file in Listing 1-3 on page 21, we dump the VBA call stack when we hit an unexpected error because it can be useful for working out later what went wrong and why. We build an internal representation of VBA's stack (because VBA's stack is not actually available—shame), using two fundamental routines: *TrTraceIn* and *TrTraceOut*. Here they are in a typical routine:

```
Public Sub Testing()

' Set up general error handler.
On Error GoTo Error_General_Testing:

    Const sProcSig = MODULE & " General.Testing"
    Call TrTraceIn(sProcSig)

    ' ========== Body Code Starts ==========
    ⋮
    ' ========== Body Code Ends ==========

    Call TrTraceOut(sProcSig)
    Exit Sub

' Error handler
Error_General_Testing:
    ⋮
End Sub
```

These routines are inserted by hand or by using the same internal tool I mentioned earlier in Tip 2 that adds line numbers to code. Notice that *sProcSig* is being passed into these routines so that the stack can be built containing the name of the module and routine.

The stack frame object we use internally (not shown here) uses a Visual Basic collection with a class wrapper for its implementation. The class name we use is *CStackFrame*. As a prefix, *C* means class, and its single instance is named *oStackFrame*. We drop the *o* prefix if we're replacing a standard class such as *Err* or *App*.

Tip 10: Use a ROOS (Resource Only OLE Server).

A basic ROOS (pronounced "ruse") is a little like a string table resource except that it runs in-process or out-of-process as an Automation server. A ROOS provides a structured interface to a set of objects and properties that enables us to build more flexible error handling routines.

For example, the ROOS holds a project's error constants (or rather the values mapped to the symbols used in the code that are resolved from the object's type library). The ROOS also holds a set of string resources that hold the actual error text for a given error and the methods used to load and process errors at run time. To change the language used in error reports or perhaps the vocabulary being used (for example, user vs. programmer), simply use a different ROOS. (No more DLLs with weird names!)

Tip 11: Replace useful intrinsic objects with your own.

Our main ROOS contains a set of alternative standard object classes, *TMSErr* and *TMSApp*, for example. These are instantiated as *Err* and *App* at application start-up as part of our application template initialization. (All our Visual Basic applications are built on this template.) By creating objects like this, we can add methods, properties, and so on to what looks like one of Visual Basic's own objects.

For example, our error object has extra methods named *Push* and *Pop*. These, mostly for historical reasons, are *really* useful methods because it's not clear in Visual Basic 4 when *Err.Clear* is actually applied to the *Err* object—that is, when the outstanding error, which you've been called to handle, is automatically cleared. This can easily result in the reporting of error 0. Watch out for this because you'll see it a lot!

Usually, an error is mistakenly cleared in this way when someone is handling an error and from within the error handler he or she calls some other routine that causes Visual Basic to execute an *Err.Clear*. All sorts of things can make Visual Basic execute an *Err.Clear*. The result in this case is that the error is lost! These kinds of mistakes are really hard to find. They're also really easy to put in—lines of code that cause this to happen, that is!

The Visual Basic 4 Help file under Err Object includes this Caution about losing the error context. (Note the "may be" here.)

> If you set up an error handler using On Error GoTo and that handler calls another procedure, the properties of the Err object may be reset to zero and zero-length strings. To retain values for later use, assign the values of Err properties to variables before calling another procedure, or before executing Resume, On Error, Exit Sub, Exit Function, or Exit Property statements.

Actually, this problem never seemed to be the case in Visual Basic 4. Regardless, the good news is that Visual Basic 5 seems to have fixed this problem. Now *Err.Number* stays put. How do we know for sure? Because the Visual Basic 5 Help (again under Err Object) now just says this:

> The Err object's properties are reset to zero or zero-length strings
> ("") after any form of the Resume or On Error statement and after
> an Exit Sub, Exit Function, or Exit Property statement within an
> error-handling routine. The Clear method can be used to explic-
> itly reset Err.

Two things warrant mentioning, however. Keep in mind that if *Err.Number* is
set to a nonzero value when you call another routine, it will stay set as that
routine's code is executed (as long as you don't specifically reset it). Testing
Err.Number in a routine doesn't mean, unless you've previously reset it, that
the error occurred in the executing routine. Also, if you're mixing Visual Basic 4 and Visual Basic 5, remember that this behavior is apparently not consistent between the two environments—although as I've said, I've never
witnessed anything different in Visual Basic 4.

Of course, if you do reset *Err.Number* (perhaps by using *On Error GoTo* in the
called routine), when you return to the calling routine the error will be lost.
The answer, of course, is to preserve, or push, the error context to some kind
of error stack. We do this with *Err.Push*. It's the first line of code in the error
handler—*always*. (By the way, Visual Basic won't do an *Err.Clear* on the call
to *Err.Push* but only on its return—guaranteed.) Here's an example of how this
push and pop method of error handling looks in practice:

```
Private Sub Command1_Click()

    On Error GoTo error_handler:

    VBA.Err.Raise 42

    Exit Sub

error_handler:

    Err.Push
    Call SomeFunc
    Err.Pop
    MsgBox Err.Description
    Resume Next

End Sub
```

Here we're raising an error (42, as it happens) and handling it in our error
handler just below. The message box reports the error correctly as being an
Application Defined Error. If we were to comment out the *Err.Push* and *Err.Pop*

routines and rerun the code, the error information would be lost and the message box would be empty (as *Err.Number* and *Err.Description* have been reset to some suitable "nothing"), assuming the call to *SomeFunc* completes successfully. In other words, when we come to show the message box, there's no outstanding error to report! (The call to *Err.Push* is the first statement in the error handler. This is easy to check for during a code review.)

NOTE

> If we assume that Visual Basic itself raises exceptions by calling *Err.Raise* and that *Err.Raise* simply sets other properties of *Err*, such as *Err.Number*, our own *Err.Number* obviously won't be called to set *VBA.Err* properties (as it would if we simply had a line of code that read, say, *Err.Number = 42*). This is a pity because if it did call our *Err.Number*, we could detect (what with our *Err.Number* being called first before any other routines) that an error was being raised and automatically look after preserving the error context; that is, we could do an *Err.Push* automatically without having to have it appear in each error handler.

Of course, the implementation of this new error object is not important (and should be kept hidden). Needless to say, the implementation is easy. (TMS uses another Visual Basic collection and a *CErrorStack* wrapper.) Another Visual Basic object we replace with our own is the *Debug* object. We do this because we sometimes want to see what debug messages a built executable might be emitting.

As you know, "normal" *Debug.Print* calls are thrown away by Visual Basic (when your application is running as a binary executable); "special" *Debug-.Print* calls, however, can be captured even when the application is running as binary. Replacing this object is a little trickier than replacing the *Err* object because the *Debug* object name cannot be overloaded; that is, you have to call your new object something like *Debugger*. This new object can be designed to write to Visual Basic's debug window so that it becomes a complete replacement for the *Debug* object. Chapter 7 shows you how to write your own *Assert* method so that you can also replace the *Debug* object's *Assert* method.

Tip 12: Check DLL version errors.

Debugging and defensive programming techniques can be used even in post-implementation. We always protect our applications against bad dynamic links (with DLLs and with ActiveX components such as OLE Custom Controls, or OCXs) by using another internal tool.

One of the really great things about Windows is that the dynamic linking mechanism, which links one module into another at run time, is not defined as part of some vendor's object file format but is instead part of the operating system itself. This means, for example, that it's really easy to do mixed language programming (whereas with static linking it's really hard because you're at the mercy of some vendor's linker—you just have to hope that it will understand). Unfortunately, this same mechanism can also get you into trouble because it's not until run time that you can resolve a link. Who knows what you'll end up linking to in the end—perhaps to an old and buggy version of some OCX. Oops!

By the way, don't use a GUID to determine the version of any component. The GUID will almost always stay the same unless the object's interface has changed; it doesn't change for a bug fix or an upgrade. On the other hand, the object's version number should change whenever the binary image changes; that is, it should change whenever you build something (such as a bug fix or an interface change) that differs in any way from some previous version. The version number, not the GUID, tells you whether you're using the latest incarnation of an object or application.

Because it affects your application externally, this kind of versioning problem can be extremely hard to diagnose from afar (or for that matter, from anear)!

Tip 13: Use Microsoft's MSINFO32.EXE when you can.

When you're trying to help a user with some problem (especially if you're in Support), you often need to know a lot of technical stuff about the user's machine, such as what is loaded into memory or how the operating system is configured. Getting this information out of the user, even figuring out where to find it all in the first place, can be extremely time-consuming and difficult. (Asking the user to continually hit Ctrl+Alt+Delete in an attempt to bring up the Task List and "see" what's running can be a dangerous practice: *User:* "Oh, my machine's rebooting." *Support:* "What did you do?" *User:* "What you told me to do—hit Ctrl+Alt+Delete again!") Microsoft thought so too, so they provided their users with an application to gather this information automatically: MSINFO32.EXE (MS Info). The good news is that you can use this application to help your customers.

MS Info comes with applications such as Microsoft Word and Microsoft Excel. If you have one of those applications installed, you're almost certain to have MS Info installed too. It also ships with Visual Basic 5. If you haven't seen this applet before, choose About Microsoft Visual Basic from the Help menu and click the System Info button. You'll see a window similar to Figure 1-4.

The bottom line is that if your user is a Microsoft Office user or has an application such as Microsoft Excel installed, MS Info will be available. All you need to do then to provide the same information on the user's system is to run the same application!

GLOBALLY UNIQUE IDENTIFIERS (GUIDs)

A GUID (Globally Unique Identifier) is a 128-bit integer that can be used by COM (Component Object Model) to identify ActiveX components. Each GUID is guaranteed to be unique in the world. GUIDs are actually UUIDs (Universally Unique Identifiers) as defined by the Open Software Foundation's Distributed Computing Environment. GUIDs are used in Visual Basic mainly to identify the components you use in your projects (referenced under the References and Components options of the Project menu) and to help ensure that COM components do not accidentally connect to the "wrong" component, interface, or method even in networks with millions of component objects. The GUID is the actual name of a component, not the string you and I use to name it, nor its filename. For example, a component we've probably all used before is F9043C88-F6F2-101A-A3C9-08002B2F49FB. You and I most likely refer to this component as "Microsoft's Common Dialog Control," or more simply, COMDLG32.OCX. (I have two of these on my machine, both with the same GUID. Their versions are different, however. One is 5.00.3609, and the other is 5.00.3112. Which do you link with?)

To determine a component's GUID, you look in your project's .VBP file. You'll see something like this if you use the common dialog control:

```
Object={F9043C88-F6F2-101A-A3C9-08002B2F49FB}#1.1#0; COMDLG32.OCX
```

Visual Basic creates GUIDs for you automatically (for every ActiveX control you build). If you want to create them externally to Visual Basic, you can use either GUIDGEN.EXE or UUIDGEN.EXE, Microsoft utilities that come with the Visual C++ compiler, with the OLE SDK, and on the Visual Basic 5 CD. In Chapter 8, you'll also find a Visual Basic program to generate GUIDs.

FIGURE 1-4

*Running
MSINFO32.EXE
opens the
Microsoft
System
Information
application*

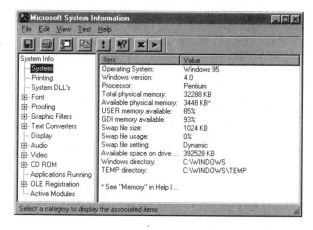

FIGURE 1-4

*Running
MSINFO32.EXE
opens the
Microsoft
System
Information
application*

To determine whether you've got this application to work with, look in the
following location in the Registry:

```
HKEY_LOCAL_MACHINE\SOFTWARE\Microsoft\SharedTools\MSInfo\Path
```

In the following example, we use the registration API in ADVAPI32.DLL to
retrieve the value of the Registry key. We can then check to see whether the
application really exists. If it does, *Shell* it!

Declaration Section

```
Option Explicit

Private Const REG_SZ                    As Long = 1
Private Const ERROR_SUCCESS             As Long = 0
Private Const HKEY_LOCAL_MACHINE        As Long = &H80000002
Private Const STANDARD_RIGHTS_ALL       As Long = &H1F0000
Private Const KEY_QUERY_VALUE           As Long = &H1
Private Const KEY_ENUMERATE_SUB_KEYS    As Long = &H8
Private Const KEY_NOTIFY                As Long = &H10
Private Const SYNCHRONIZE               As Long = &H100000
Private Const READ_CONTROL              As Long = &H20000
Private Const STANDARD_RIGHTS_READ      As Long = (READ_CONTROL)
Private Const KEY_READ                  As Long = _
                                          ((STANDARD_RIGHTS_READ _
                                          Or KEY_QUERY_VALUE _
                                          Or KEY_ENUMERATE_SUB_KEYS _
                                          Or KEY_NOTIFY) _
                                          And (Not SYNCHRONIZE))
```

>>

```
Private Declare Function WinRegOpenKeyEx Lib "advapi32.dll" _
Alias "RegOpenKeyExA" (ByVal hKey As Long, _
                       ByVal lpSubKey As String, _
                       ByVal ulOptions As Long, _
                       ByVal samDesired As Long, _
                       phkResult As Long) As Long

Private Declare Function WinRegQueryValueEx Lib _
"advapi32.dll" Alias "RegQueryValueExA" _
                       (ByVal hKey As Long, _
                       ByVal lpValueName As String, _
                       ByVal lpReserved As Long, _
                       lpType As Long, lpData As Any, _
                       lpcbData As Long) As Long

Private Declare Function WinRegCloseKey Lib "advapi32" _
Alias "RegCloseKey" (ByVal hKey As Long) As Long
```

Form Load Event

```
Private Sub Form_Load()

    Dim hKey    As Long
    Dim lType   As Long
    Dim Buffer As String

    ' Need some space to write string into - DLL routine
    ' expects us to allocate this space before the call.
    Buffer = Space(255)

    ' Always expect failure!
    cmdSystemInfo.Visible = False

    ' This will work if MS Info is installed.
    If WinRegOpenKeyEx( _
                HKEY_LOCAL_MACHINE _
                , "SOFTWARE\Microsoft\Shared Tools\MSInfo" _
                , 0 _
                , KEY_READ _
                , hKey _
                ) = ERROR_SUCCESS Then

        ' Read the Path value - happens to include the filename
        ' too, e.g.,
        ' "C:\Program Files\Common Files\Microsoft Shared\
        ' MSinfo\msinfo32.exe".
```

```
        If WinRegQueryValueEx( _
                        hKey _
                        , "Path" _
                        , 0 _
                        , lType _
                        , ByVal Buffer _
                        , Len(Buffer) _
                        ) = ERROR_SUCCESS Then

            ' Make sure we read a string back. If we did...
            If lType = REG_SZ Then
                ' Make sure the Registry and reality are in
                ' alignment!
                ' Note: Using FileAttr() means you're
                ' suffering from paranoia<g>.
                If Dir$(Buffer) <> "" Then
                    ' Put the path into the buttons tag
                    ' and make the button visible.
                    cmdSystemInfo.Tag = Buffer
                    cmdSystemInfo.Visible = True
                End If
            End If

        End If

        ' We open - we close.
        Call WinRegCloseKey(hKey)

    End If

End Sub
```

Button Click Event

```
Private Sub cmdSystemInfo_Click()

    ' If we got clicked, we must be visible and therefore
    ' must have our tag set to the name of the MS Info app -
    ' Shell it!
    Call Shell(cmdSystemInfo.Tag, vbNormalFocus)

End Sub
```

In the code above, as the form loads (maybe this is an About box?) it detects whether or not MS Info exists. If it does, the form makes a command button visible and sets its *Tag* property to point to the program. When the form becomes visible, the button either will or won't be visible. If it is visible, you have MS Info on your machine. When you click the button, it simply shells its *Tag*. For more information on the APIs used in this example, see the appropriate Win32 documentation.

It's possible via subclassing to provide an alternative internal class to replace CommonDialog, or whatever you want to call your one and only instance of a CommonDialog control. (You use only one, right?) We do this in our applications for two reasons. First, we use this alternative class to provide our users with both 16- and 32-bit versions of each dialog box, which is especially useful with the file type dialog boxes. Second, we use it to add a new type of dialog box to the control. Guess what it is. Here's a clue:

CommonDialog1.ShowMSInfo

Tip 14: Treat error handling like transaction processing.

When you hit an error, always attempt to bring the application back to a known and stable condition; that is, roll back from the error. To do this, you'll need to handle errors locally (to roll back within the scope of the erroring procedure) and more globally by propagating the error back up through each entry in the call chain.

Here's how you proceed. When your most local (immediate) error trap gets hit, make sure you clean up as required locally first. For example, make sure you close any files that you opened in this routine. Once done, and if this routine is not an event handler, reraise the error (in reality, you might raise some other error here) and repeat this process for each previous stack frame (a stack frame refers to an entry in the call chain); that is, continue this process for each preceding call until you get back up to an event handler. If you've cleaned up locally all the way through the stack and if you had an error handler for each entry in the complete stack frame (so you didn't jump over some routines), you should now have effectively rolled back from the error. It will seem as though the error never really happened! Note that by *not* reporting errors from anywhere other than an event handler, you will not have shown your user a stream of message boxes.

Localized error handling might need error handling itself. Look at the following code fragment:

```
On Error GoTo Error_Handler:

    Dim nFile As Integer

    nFile = FreeFile
    Open "c:\time.txt" For Output Access Write As nFile
    Print #nFile, Time$
    Close nFile

    Exit Sub

Error_Handler:

    ' Roll back!
    Close nFile

    Exit Sub
```

Imagine you've opened a file and are attempting to roll back in your error handler. How do you know whether or not you opened the file? In other words, did the error occur before or after the line of code that opens the file? If you attempt to close the file and it's not open, you'll cause an error—but if it's open, you don't want to leave it open as you're trying to roll back! I guess you could use *Erl* to determine where your code erred, but this implies that you're editing line numbered source code—yuck. (You'll recall from Tip 2 that we added line numbers only to the code for the final EXE, not to the code we're still editing.) Probably the best way to determine what did or did not get done is to limit the possibilities; that is, keep your routines small (so you've only a small problem domain) and different. Of course, that's not going to help us here. What we need to do is apply a little investigation!

Given this type of problem, you're probably going to have to test the file handle to see whether it points to an open file. In the code above, we would probably use *FileAttr(nFile, 2)* to determine whether or not the file *nFile* is open for writing. If the file is not open, *FileAttr* raises an exception (of course). And obviously, you can't handle this locally because you can't set an error trap from within an error trap unless your error handling is in another routine! (Refer to Tip 5 for details.)

Tip 15: Don't test your own software or write your own test plans.

Do you have dedicated testers where you work? Possibly not—not many companies do. Many companies say they "can't afford such a luxury." Well, in my opinion, they're a luxury that's really worth it (as many of the leading software development companies in the world already know).

Independent testers should (and often do) exhibit the following characteristics:

- Are impartial
- Are less informed about the usage and the type of input your code expects
- Are usually more knowledgeable about the usage and the type of input your code doesn't expect
- Are more likely than you to spend time trying to break code
- Are typically more leery of your interfaces and more critical of your coupling
- Are into doing you damage and breaking your code
- Are more informed than you about system limits
- Unlike you, actually want to find bugs in your software!

From time to time, Microsoft talks about its ratio of developers to testers: around 1:1. You do the math; for every programmer there's a tester. In fact, rumor has it that some developers occasionally get shifted to being testers. This could happen if a developer consistently develops very buggy software. Nothing like a shift to testing to improve one's knowledge and appreciation of what good solid code involves!

Tip 16: Stress test your applications.

Years ago, the Windows SDK (Software Development Kit) shipped with an applet named SHAKER.EXE. This applet simply ran around allocating and releasing memory blocks. When and what it actually allocated or released was random!

What was it for, then? Well, before the days of protect mode and virtual memory addressing, you could access any arbitrary memory location through a simple pointer (using C as a programming language, of course). Often, and erroneously, these pointers would be stored in nonrefreshed static variables as an application yielded control to the operating system. This access—or similar access—would cause the problems for which SHAKER.EXE was used to try to uncover.

In between handling one event and a subsequent one, Windows could move (as it can now) both your code and data around. If you'd used a static pointer to, say, point to some data, you'd quickly discover that it was no longer pointing to what you intended. (Modern virtual addressing methods make this problem go away.) So what was the point of SHAKER.EXE? It turned out that, back then, even though your application was being naughty and had stored a static pointer, you didn't know it most of the time; the Windows memory manager hadn't, between your handling of two events, moved your data around. The bottom line was that you didn't really know you had a problem until memory moved, and on your machine, that rarely, if ever, happened! Customers, however, did see the problem because they were running both your application and others and had loaded their systems to a point where the memory manager, to accommodate everyone, was starting to move memory blocks around. The whole thing, as someone at the time pointed out, was pretty much like attempting to hold a party in a small closet. Initially, everyone had plenty of room. As more people arrived and the closet filled up, however, some of the guests were bound to get their feet stepped on sooner or later! SHAKER.EXE literally shook the operating system on the developer's machine until something fell off!

OK, so why the history lesson? Basically, the lesson is a good one and one we can still use. In fact, an associated application, named STRESS.EXE, still ships in Visual C++. (See Figure 1-5.) (STRESS.EXE is available for Windows 95 only, not for Windows NT.)

FIGURE 1-5

*Stress me
(STRESS.EXE)*

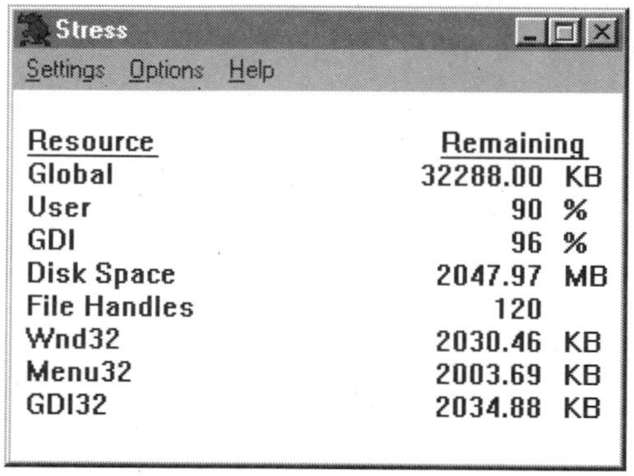

Resource	Remaining	
Global	32288.00	KB
User	90	%
GDI	96	%
Disk Space	2047.97	MB
File Handles	120	
Wnd32	2030.46	KB
Menu32	2003.69	KB
GDI32	2034.88	KB

Like SHAKER.EXE, STRESS.EXE is used to make the operating system appear more loaded/busy than it actually is. For example, by using STRESS.EXE you can allocate all of your machine's free memory, making it look really loaded.

Tools such as STRESS.EXE can present your code with a more realistic, perhaps even hostile, environment in which to work. Such conditions can cause many hidden problems to rise to the surface—problems you can fix at that point instead of later in response to a client's frustrated phone call. I'd certainly recommend using them.

Tip 17: Use automated testing tools.

See Chapter 10 for coverage of this broad and very important subject.

Tip 18: Consider error values.

Let's suppose you still want to return an indication of success from a function (instead of using exceptions). What values would you use to indicate whether or not something worked?

Normally, 0 (or False) is returned for failure, and –1 (True) for success. What are the alternatives? Some programmers like to return 0 for success and some other value for failure—the reason for failure is encoded in the value being returned. Other programmers prefer to return a negative value for failure that again encodes the reason.

By using the first alternative, we can quickly come up with some pretty weird-looking code:

```
If CreateThing() <> True Then ' It worked!
```

or

```
If Not CreateThing() Then ' It worked!
```

or

```
If CreateThing() = False Then ' It worked!
```

or

```
If CreateThing() = SUCCESS Then ' It worked!
```

SUCCESS, of course, is defined as 0.

To capture failure, you can't just do the same, though:

```
If Not CreateThing() Then ' It worked!
Else
    ' Failed!
    ' What do we do?
End If
```

Here the reason for failure is lost. We need to hold it in some variable:

```
nResult = CreateThing()

If nResult <> SUCCESS Then
    ' Failed!
    ' What do we do?
End If
```

All very messy, especially where the language lacks the ability to do an assignment in a conditional expression (as is the case in Visual Basic and is *not* the case in C).

Consider someone writing the test using implicit expression evaluation:

```
If CreateThing() Then
```

If this works, it returns 0, which causes the conditional *not* to execute any code in the body of the compound statement. Yikes! What code might not get executed all because I forgot to test against SUCCESS!

Because any nonzero value is evaluated as True (in an *If*), using a value other than 0 (say, a negative value) to indicate failure can be equally dangerous. The language conspires against you here (given that in any conditional expression you don't have to test against an explicit value and that nonzero means run the compound statement) not to use 0 as a code indicating success.

I'd advise sticking to True meaning success and False meaning failure. In the case of failure, I'd implement a mechanism such as the one used in C (*errno*) or perhaps Win32's *GetLastError*. The latter returns the value of the last error (easily implemented in a project—you could even add a history feature or automatic logging of errors).

Patterns of Cooperation in Bytes and Blood

Systems of Distributed Business Objects

LAWSON DAVIES

Lawson is a TMS Consultant who was born a Welshman six weeks after Sputnik. On his return from five years' working and walking in the Highlands of New Guinea, he abandoned the stressful life of an itinerant teacher, novelist, and social parasite to enter the safe, comfortable mainstream world of client/server development, where he has chilled out for the last eight years. His areas of special interest are primarily design, real ale, system architecture, Islay malts, database connectivity, distributed systems, and the oeuvres of Brian Eno and Gary Glitter.

Now I have to say that I am already on bad terms with the inanimate world. Even when making a cup of coffee or changing a lightbulb (or a fuse!), I think—what is it with objects? Why are they so aggressive? What's their beef with me? Objects and I, we can't go on like this. We must work out a compromise, a freeze, before one of us does something rash. I've got to meet with their people and hammer out a deal.

Martin Amis*

This chapter has a vision—the whole book probably shares it. What I want to do is architect, build, and deploy systems that are essentially swarms of business objects engaging in numerous unpredictable yet effective patterns of collaboration. The value of such objects is their ability to collaborate with other business objects and components to create structures that their developers never planned for or imagined. I'm trying to build objects that can be used and assembled in unpredictable combinations. I want to build components that can dynamically discover each other's services and behaviors at run time, and to do this I need to set up the minimum number of rules, constructs, constraints, metaphors, and prerequisites to allow for the maximum of recombinant potential. And I want to do all this with Visual Basic.

Herein lies the central paradox: rules enable you to build and assemble, but they also constrain your freedom. In this chapter, I'll show you how you can achieve this vision of a flexible, innovative collaboration of business objects using "the rules" of Visual Basic. Indeed, Visual Basic is the infrastructure on which the vision rests.

---

* From "Bujak and the Strong Force or God's Dice" in *Einstein's Monsters*.

VISUAL BASIC AND "THE SYSTEM THAT IS YET TO COME"

This "the system that is yet to come" stuff is all very messianic, very Gene Roddenberry, I suppose, especially when you appear to deflate this grand vision by tacking on at the end the much maligned (unjustly in my view) Visual Basic. Even those who have worked with Visual Basic from the beginning sometimes have trouble accepting the possibility, let alone the feasibility, of the notion that Visual Basic is capable of producing great things. People with a little Basic experience dating from "way back when" are frankly incredulous. I wouldn't have guessed in 1991 when I first found a copy of Visual Basic 1 on my desk that I would have been talking about building "big sky" distributed systems with "that bloody Basic."

Visual Basic has come a long way. In my more paranoid moments, I've imagined Gates, Allen, and maybe even Alan Cooper meeting with their Object Generals to plot the storming of development shops with a battering ram of practical object orientation—Visual Basic. But even then I didn't really see them having designs on the fully distributed world too—not until Visual Basic 4 Enterprise Edition anyway. I think this vision is becoming increasingly practicable with Visual Basic. I have some experience with it, scars and all, and I'm going to try to paint a picture in this chapter of what the options are and how you might make such a distributed, object-oriented system work. I'll concentrate on Visual Basic, although inevitably, because of the developments in the Microsoft Transaction Server (code name Viper) arena, Transaction Server will get mentioned too. You won't see as much code here as in some of the other chapters—after all, I'm going for the big picture. But I won't tell you about anything that can't be done, I'll try to explain how to do everything I bring up, and I'll also attempt to tell you what's impossible.

I OBJECT

So just what is a business object? Here are some definitions:

- An intellectual entity made manifest
- A real-world object reduced to bits and bytes
- A body where flesh is data and methods are its bones
- A template for things of a particular type
- An encapsulation of functionality and data capable of having identity

If you're in the car rental business, a business object might be a car or a contract; if you work in a bank, a customer and an account would certainly be two of your primary business objects. These business objects are full of business rules, rules that basically govern the way a business is run. The rules are usually represented in code as *Case* statements or nested *If*s that allow or disallow actions, modify elements, or perform methods differently depending on state.

Why Business Objects Are Cool

So what is so cool about having lots of instances of a number of types of different software objects (EXEs or DLLs) that have functionality, data, methods, and properties floating around a network? Good question.

Reuse

You'll have heard about this reuse "thang." Chapters within this very book look at it, and software pundits have been sky-writing the word "reuse" for decades. Reuse is important to companies who build a lot of software because it means that they don't have to build everything from scratch—an "old" component can be used in a new system. Reuse is what made cars a practical, affordable proposition for lots of people. (We won't debate the issue of how that has worked out.) Reuse is the idea of taking components and building systems from them. But you know all this—you read the magazines. The reasons for coveting reuse are numerous, but none are as key as these two: you can build systems quicker, and you can build them more complex. Both reasons can be used as cost arguments, so when you justify the costs for a project, the numbers could look a bit better if you factor in reuse. Then how come we're not all already reusing components and taking this process for granted? Well, you have to have built your components in the first place, of course. This is the first major hurdle to reuse, especially since many organizations that are project driven in their Information Systems (IS) efforts fail to take the long view, which involves spreading the cost of building some reusable components across more than one project. The second hurdle is to make it easy to reuse what you already have— but I'm not writing about repositories just now. To do reuse, you have to *do it*—it doesn't just happen like rain and taxes.

Scalability, or my daddy was a mainframe

Another justification you run into for business object building is the supposed central benefit of the three-tiered or *n*-tiered architecture. In essence, this architecture is a combination of manageability and scalability. Many people working with a range of software tools have found the problem of scalability a tough nut to crack. The hang-up is that as the numbers of users, or the size of the data being transferred and manipulated, or the transaction rate, or all of them increase, the system begins to creak, crack, and fall apart—the problem of crumbleware.

Visual Basic (until version 4 Enterprise Edition) was frequently the butt of scalability criticism and might even have been the origin of the term "fat client." Actually, if you do still build these "fat clients," the phrase "rich client" might come in useful. Lots of big-time consulting organizations would flame Visual Basic regularly, and yet people still used it. Here are three possible explanations:

- **The Samuel Beckett one:** People are bloody stupid apes.
- **The Conspiracy theory:** The developers want to put you off the scent.
- **The True explanation:** Writing good programs in Visual Basic is hard work that needs thought and commitment, and these qualities are not combined that often.

Do you remember the pre–Visual Basic days, when dinosaurs roamed the earth and digital watches seemed like a pretty neat idea? You would be put in charge of a project that had the goal of either getting each instance of the client application to do more work or getting more users working with the system. The idea was to get more out of the software. The PC that the client software (written in Visual Basic) was running on had finite resources. Visual Basic (even as far as version 4) was an interpreted rather than a compiled language. So you would recommend upgrading the client PCs, optimizing the client code, or moving some or all of the significant work elsewhere.

But none of these solutions is ideal, especially in a big corporate environment. You have 300 users of your software; you want to do another release. Just upgrading them all is hard enough anyway, but we'll come to manageability problems in a while. Your release is going to add significant new functionality, consume substantial resources, and demand prohibitively expensive hardware upgrades. Your budget for the upgrade project is rejected. You go back to the spreadsheets. Sadly, you don't know about the Visual Basic Code Profiler (you should, but you don't), so you take off the hardware budget for the upgrade and put in a new row for optimization work costs. Finger in the air stuff. You know that optimization is one of the unquantifiables. If only you knew about Visual Basic Code Profiler (VBCP). (VBCP is available on the Visual Basic 4 CD in the folder Tools\VBCP. On the Visual Basic 5 CD, it's in the folder

UNSUPPRT\VBCP.) You don't, so you only know how much you want to improve the application's performance. You don't know where the application is spending all its time, and you certainly don't know how to prove how much effort and cost you're going to expend to get the performance you want—if you ever do get it. So you put down a big figure, because you're realistic. Then you shave it a bit, because you're hopeful (a natural concomitant of developing software) and because you want to get your project into the feasibility stage. Your budget is rejected again, either because it's still too high or because you shaved off too much and management knew enough to know it and were morally honest enough to care.

How about moving the work to be done somewhere other than the client PC? You have a development shop of Visual Basic coders. Right now you have an architecture that has two tiers (by which I mean client talking directly to database server, as illustrated in Figure 2-1), and you have two types of machine, client PCs for the users and a big database server or a mainframe that you talk to for data.

FIGURE 2-1

A two-tier ("fat client") application

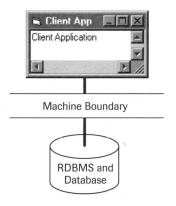

In order to upgrade, suddenly you're looking at new hardware and new skills, perhaps new people, and a complete redesign of the application. You've also just received an e-mail message from your manager saying that the other business areas love the prototypes you did and marketing now wants to launch a new product that needs the functionality. And it all has to be completed two months earlier than your original ballpark estimates projected.

This is the point at which a sane person would start looking for a lateral move into the business strategy unit where he or she could write white papers that no one would ever read and certainly never implement, at least until the optimal strategy had already changed. A bleak scenario? Possibly. Real? I think so.

Evaluating tools in the scales

So how do you avoid this predicament today? You could argue (many people do) that at the outset you should pick a new development tool that is lauded for its scalability. Such tools are often costly, and the learning curves for them are usually steep. The ability to produce new functionality and (let's face it) cool-looking screens in anything like a reasonable time is virtually never there, and worst of all, you can make the swap and find it's no more scalable than Visual Basic was. Also, keep in mind this Law of Tool Scalability: "You only ever discover that your tool doesn't scale properly fifteen minutes before it becomes absolutely critical that it does."

Visual Basic 4: Open the box, add water, and distribute

So what's the answer for scalable distributed applications? Some people—and I'll put my hand up, I was one—thought they had found it in Visual Basic 4 Enterprise Edition. Thanks to the class module and collections, we could make objects with properties and methods that could encapsulate data and functionality. I won't go into the object-oriented purity of an object's polymorphism and multiple inheritance from grandfather objects—objects so long forgotten that you couldn't tell whether your object instances had a full head of jet black hair into their nineties or were bald before they were twenty-five. Well, not until the First Law of Multiple Inheritance manifested itself: "When you need to know how a thing is going to behave, it's already too late." Thanks to Remote Automation and later DCOM, we could plonk the objects in a Windows environment somewhere other than the client PC—on a machine with more processors, more RAM, and more disk space—and use them (almost) as if they were on our machine and part of our good old "fat client." We *could* even deploy our existing skill sets to build them in good old Visual Basic. Nirvana, Valhalla, Ambrosia. (These are, incidentally, names I've never dared give to any system—so you may take them and use them without fear of my enforcing copyright.) Simply open the Visual Basic 4 Enterprise Edition box, add water, and distribute—now with the super new added ingredient: scalability.

The Visual Basic 4 vision, then, was of being able to take monolithic designs and even monolithic applications and slice them up for implementation. We wanted to build systems of cooperating components that could easily ("seamlessly" was always the irritating buzzword) combine to provide the means of carrying out a task, no matter where we wanted to deploy them—any platform anywhere that they would run best.

Some of us, of course, had already been applying a bit of common sense to our designs in the first place, even before Visual Basic 4 Enterprise Edition. We had been building our applications in a modular fashion, albeit they were compiled into one executable. Such visionary developers had fewer problems than many out there who didn't build modular applications, but we still didn't have the ability to build lots of separate executables or DLLs and deploy them where we would. Sure, we could build our applications in such a way that we had a number of cooperating executables all on the client. But organizing them and marshaling their resources for an application's tasks often appeared an unnecessary complication using anything other than OLE (now called ActiveX); and despite the best will in the world, OLE in previous versions of Visual Basic proved to be ponderous and heavy on resources. So this route was usually pursued only as a way of breaking up monolithic applications into functional pieces after they had reached the size where they didn't work sensibly or in some cases wouldn't even compile in Visual Basic anymore.

Centralization and manageability

I envisaged other benefits to this distributed modular approach. I once built software for a bank, and my immediate line manager there had responsibility not only for our development work but also for network management and desktop support throughout the corporate headquarters. I liked him, talked to him, and saw him harried to death by worrying about what was where on the networks, how things were to be deployed and upgraded, and how the hell we would move everybody to a new version of an ODBC driver for all the applications on a particular network server at the same time or start using the new interest rate calculation method on the same day across the board. Working with the betas of Visual Basic 4 Enterprise Edition, I imagined the brave new world of components. No longer would the ODBC driver be installed and upgraded on each user's PC. Now one module of Visual Basic code in the whole company would deal with interest rates. Now my manager would get home before his kids had gone to bed and wouldn't come in on a Sunday to read his e-mail backlog. Software should be fun. Now hardware, that's a different business—but software certainly should be.

Silver Bullet Syndrome Again

What we all should have known, however, is that all these cool business objects are never going to cooperate "seamlessly" or even seamfully without an underlying infrastructure. Through almost all of its history, Visual Basic had been a good tool for allowing application programmers to concentrate on the business functionality of the application they were trying to build and ignore the lower-level technicalities of what they were doing. The best Visual Basic programmers soon get into the Windows API(s) or data access complexities. But mostly, Visual Basic allowed implementers to focus on achieving functional complexity rather than forcing on them a high level of technical complexity. That sounds like a polite way of saying that it allowed a lot of people to behave like cowboys—still, let it stand. All silver linings have a cloud, however, and the ease and rapidity of Visual Basic's learning curve and its deceptively nontechnical approach of drawing windows on the screen soon led to deficiencies, usually structural, in systems. Such deficiencies are not troublesome when you have small systems, noncritical systems, or stand-alone systems. Even two-tier systems can live like this. But for big, critical corporate systems, structural inadequacies are the kiss of death. You'll probably find that most of the chapters of this book, one way or another, are aimed at fixing or avoiding these problems, whether it be through error handling, coding standards, project management, data access, or sound technical solutions to common technical problems in the Visual Basic environment.

GET AN INFRASTRUCTURE IF YOU WANT A LIFE

So why an infrastructure exactly? It is always a false economy in any significant system to do without an architecture—and who wants to work on insignificant systems? Let's look at some application models. I'm going to start at base level and work up, so please excuse the first few; even if you find them trivial and straightforward, they are the bases of the whole thing, and I want to be sure we all understand the foundation.

Three "Simple" Tiers

We'll skip desktop and two-tiered (client to data usually) systems and begin with a distributed, componentized system in its simplest form: three tiers (or more frequently encountered in real life as three layers masquerading as tiers). Figure 2-2 shows an example of a simple three-tiered application.

This model is essentially very simple. At the top level, we have a client for showing and manipulating information. Business-level logic is at the middle level. This logic comprises the rules about how you calculate information and what state this information has to be in before you can carry out particular operations on it. These rules are separated into three different kinds of business logic, corresponding to "real" world (at least to the business) objects; customer,

FIGURE 2-2

*A simple
tiered
application*

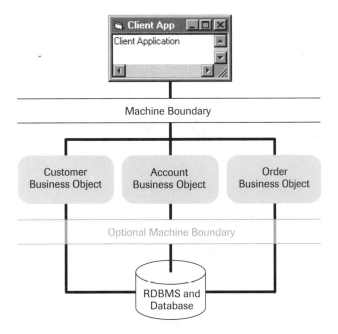

account, and order. Finally, we have an underlying RDBMS, which essentially holds the data that becomes the values of the properties in our three business objects. By building a system like this, we are in essence building a slim client—we hope. Nevertheless, the client has to coordinate all business object DCOM to communicate with our business objects. (The decision about whether to use Remote Automation or DCOM will depend on the operating systems we are working to—there is no 16-bit DCOM, nor is it in NT 3.51; in my humble opinion, no other excuses are acceptable for using the slower, less stable Remote Automation now.) We build the business objects themselves, which do all their own direct database access, as well as apply their individual business rules. We've also got to create and implement the database design.

So what's wrong with creating an architecture like this? Well, several things. First, by leaving coordination in the client, you are increasing the amount of work it does and the amount of code that's in it. Baby, your client is getting rich! That means you are really *layering* rather than *tiering*. Tiering is all about business objects working with each other cooperatively and horizontally within a tier, whereas layering is merely interacting vertically between layers. Bye-bye, vision. Second, you are building the same data access multiple times (in each individual business object) since you have only one RDBMS in your system. So long, reuse. Worst of all, you haven't thought about the resource implications if these are all the software components you're going to deploy (rather than all the functional components you're going to build). Farewell, scalability!

The distinction I'm trying to emphasize here is the difference between where business functionality lies and where infrastructure comes in. Actually, the data access layer here (basically the RDBMS and its underlying data) might not be strictly functional unless you're using triggers or stored procedures or something, but we'll let that pass.

Have we done anything right? Well, we have moved a lot of the logic to one central place since the hardware environment we're looking at now looks something like the setup in Figure 2-3.

FIGURE 2-3

*Physical
distribution
of a typical
tiered system*

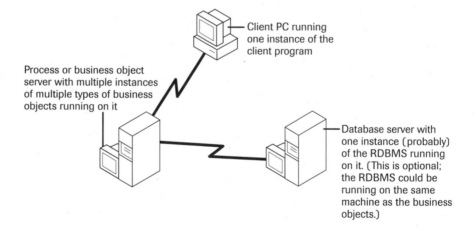

Client PC running
one instance of the
client program

Process or business object
server with multiple instances
of multiple types of business
objects running on it

Database server with
one instance (probably)
of the RDBMS running
on it. (This is optional;
the RDBMS could be
running on the same
machine as the business
objects.)

This hardware setup might make that logic code (please let it be processor and memory intensive) run faster, since it's on a bigger machine and is all in one place for those frequent occasions on which the rules of the business change. Beers all around, then? Hold on a minute! If we look more carefully at what we've done, we see that we've just lost a big cost justification here. We've moved from a situation in which all that business logic and data access that was using a lot of resources down on the client is now using comparable resources on the server. In fact, if you factor in having common infrastructural code, such as data access in all the servers, and logging, tracing, and error handling modules being in both the client and all the servers, we've probably got more code loaded now, using more resources. So we've moved the work to a different processor, made more work, and need more RAM, albeit in a different place. The cost is interesting too—this system is more complex and therefore more costly and slower to develop. And then there's the cost of the object server machine. Admittedly, we've gotten around some of the problems of idle resources being on the clients and resources not being used except at processing peaks; but we've still missed a few tricks.

One-to-one objects and instancing

In the preceding example, we made the assumption that throughout the life of the client application (that is, from start-up to shut-down), the application holds connections to three different types and at least three instances of business objects. So if we have 50 client applications running on desktop PCs, we have at least 150 instances of server-side business objects.

FIGURE 2-4

Setting a class's Instancing *property in Visual Basic 5*

The *counting instances* aspect depends partly on whether an object can be used by more than one user at a time. In Visual Basic 4 and Visual Basic 5, you can specify this by setting the class's *Instancing* property, as shown in Figure 2-4.

SingleUse Creatable If you picked *3 - SingleUse*, each client essentially got its own copy of the object. When the client application set its object reference to nothing, it closed down if nothing else was holding a reference to that server object instance since the OLE method is based on instance count, much like old-style DLLs.

MultiUse Creatable If you set the class's *Instancing* property to *5 - MultiUse*, you could have multiple client applications accessing one object. When a client application tries to create an instance of that class, it will first check to see whether there is already a running copy of the code; if there is, that code will supply the object. Excellent, dude! Only what about the data? If you've got two client applications running a single process, what about your global data? Who's seeing what? If one client changes the data, how is the other client's data affected? Well, we're safe, more or less. What we have is a separate copy of global data per thread. If your objects are on different threads, even if they are created in the same loaded code (as in a MultiUse instanced server's EXEs), they get their own copy of global data. If they are SingleUse EXEs, every client calling in to the top-level class loads a new instance of the code, and therefore the data (that is, what fills its properties) is obviously unique. If your objects are DLLs, they haven't got a thread of their own but are created on another process's thread, so you have more than one object on a thread. There is one risk, though. If you were to create a multithreaded EXE with a MultiUse instancing in its top-level class and use a thread pool to give round-robin creation to your threads (see the "Multiple threads of execution" section below), you could get two objects created on one thread with one copy of global data. You can't predict which thread an object will go on in this scenario unless you set the thread pool to 1.

Hang on though, we just said that MultiUse instanced objects *have only one set of loaded code!* Warning bells, alarms, dive, dive, dive! So this means that when client *A* calls in and wants to execute a long-running method at the same time client *B* calls in and wants to execute some method, the request that came to the server first is serviced and the second is blocked. This happens because there is only one set of loaded code; and since Visual Basic 5 is by default—as it is in Visual Basic 4—single threaded, only one process can run at a time. You have just been torpedoed by serialization and single-threadedness in Visual Basic 5, and the U.S.S. *Scalability* has gone down with all hands again.

So MultiUse Creatable looks like bad news when you're trying to build a scalable client/server system.

Multiple threads of execution: Gassed and hanged at the same time!

"If only we had multiple threads," you think. But what about that little frame on the General tab of the Project Properties dialog box, the one that says Unattended Execution? (See Figure 2-5.)

As you can see in Figure 2-5, that frame contains stuff about threads. When you want the project to run as a server, without any user interaction, you can set up threads. These are your options:

- Click Thread Per Object to create every instance of a MultiUse class on a unique thread. Each thread has a unique copy of all global variables and objects and will not interfere with any other thread since Visual

Basic 5 is thread-safe and serialized by ActiveX. This option is not without its hazards, however, since you can make reentrancy happen if you aren't careful. (See the Visual Basic Books Online for more information on reentrancy.)

- Click Thread Pool to ensure a maximum number of threads; and when you reach the maximum, new objects go on old threads. Thus, each instance of a class marked as MultiUse in the *Instancing* property will be created on a thread from the thread pool. Which thread is used is determined by which one's turn it is; and they are very strict about turns. (Even if several threads have no objects and the next thread has two objects on it, that thread will still get the next object created.) Each thread has its own copy of all global variables, but here multiple instances reside on a given thread and can potentially interfere with one another.

Multithreading really works best with multiple processors to make true scalability, but on a server, in my experience, it can be useful to ease the blocking problem.

FIGURE 2-5

That thread-ing stuff in a project's general properties

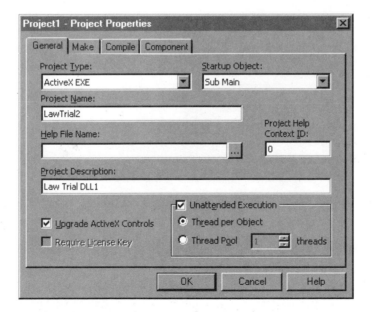

A SUMMARY OF INSTANCING AND THREADS

SingleUse, Single-Threading

As shown in Figure 2-6, in out-of-process, SingleUse, single-threaded servers, each client application starts a new instance of the server application, and all objects in that server application share one set of global data and one thread of execution. So to give exclusive use of an object and a thread, put only one SingleUse externally creatable class in the server. Having more than one class as SingleUse creatable in the server complicates the issue because you can't predict which client will have an object provided by which server, and therefore you can have more than one client trying to exercise requests in the same object and therefore thread at the same time. If a top-level object in a SingleUse, single-threaded component created another instance of itself, it would be provided by the same instance of the component rather than by a new one, even though if a client created another instance of that top-level object, that object would be provided by a new instance of the server component.

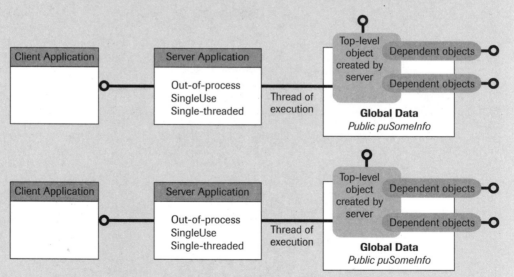

FIGURE 2-6   *Out-of-process, SingleUse, single-threaded servers*

MultiUse, Single-Threading

In out-of-process, MultiUse, single-threaded servers, multiple clients get top-level objects created by the same running instance of the server. All top-level objects share one thread and one copy of global data, and all dependent objects do likewise, as shown in Figure 2-7.

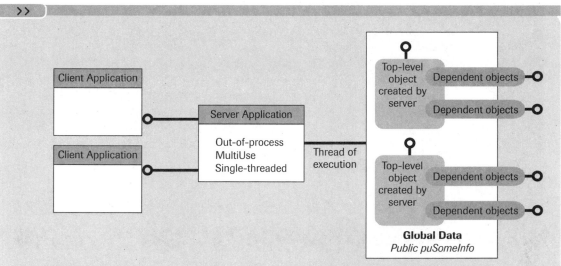

FIGURE 2-7   *Out-of-process, MultiUse, single-threaded servers*

MultiUse, Multithreading, Thread per Object

Multiple clients in MultiUse, thread per object servers (see Figure 2-8) get top-level objects created by the same running instance of the server. Each top-level object gets its own thread and its own copy of global data, and all dependent objects from a top-level object share that top-level object's thread

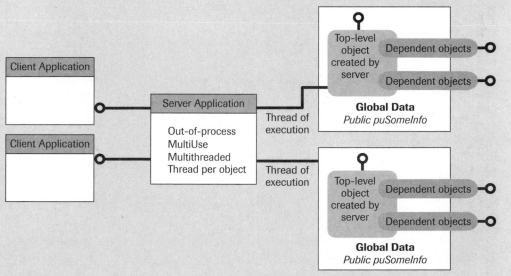

FIGURE 2-8   *Out-of-process, MultiUse, thread per object servers*

and global data. Top-level objects on different threads can communicate by holding references to each other's objects, but this will be almost as slow as if they were talking across a process boundary.

MultiUse, Multithreading Thread Pool

In MultiUse, thread pooling servers, multiple clients get top-level objects created by the same running instance of the server, as shown in Figure 2-9. As each top-level object is created, it gets assigned to the next thread in a strict round-robin sequence. Thus, where a server has a thread pool of two threads, the third object created will be assigned to the first thread, along with the first object created. Because each thread gets its own copy of global data, objects might end up sharing their global data, and objects on the same thread will be serialized and blocked in their calls. Now would be a good time to open Visual Basic Books Online and read all about Apartment Threading.

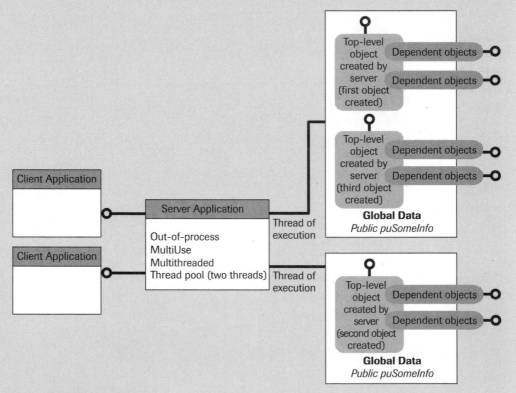

FIGURE 2-9   *Out-of-process, MultiUse, thread pooling servers*

Connection Duration: What a State We're In

The scenario of one client getting and holding for a prolonged period an object reference to an instance of a SingleUse instancing top-level class in an executable means that no blocking problems will occur. As we've already seen, however, this scenario would not support any hardware-saving argument that might be used to bolster the case for building a distributed *n*-tiered system. Because every client here has a corresponding server, the memory (RAM) that might have been put into client PCs will have to be put into a server machine to support the occurrences of each instance of a SingleUse creatable Garbage Server needed by each client. (See Figure 2-10.) In fact, this kind of configuration will probably cost more in memory since even the lightest and least fully functioned server executable uses large amounts of memory. You also need to consider the expense of the server machine. The issue is that each time a client requests a Garbage Server, one will be created (since it is a SingleUse instancing server), and thus eventually the object server will not have enough resources remaining to create new instances.

FIGURE 2-10

The SingleUse option for distributed servers

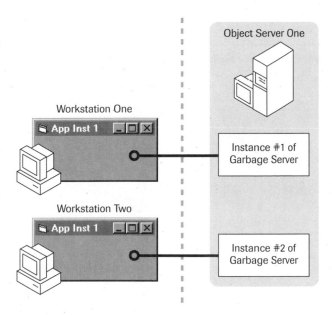

Admittedly, the reality is that if connections to objects are broken as soon as practicable (for instance, after every task) and if a task doesn't take a long time, or if asynchronous communications (notifications) between servers and clients for longer-running services are used, the ratio of servers to clients might be lower. Certainly that lower ratio is what we have to aim for, and as a result we might want to design our objects to be stateless (which we'll get into later).

Of course, if we can scale the hardware sufficiently to cope with additions of extra clients, scalability isn't a problem, just a cost. But if there is no control of the number of users that can be logged onto the server at one time, there

SIZE OF AN ACTIVEX PROCESS

Standard received wisdom says that an ActiveX server executable uses 500 KB of memory even for an empty server process that is running idle with all memory pages that can be being swapped out. I did a little experiment and made a server—a very simple three-class project with no fancy code, compiled as a SingleUse, multithreaded EXE—that is included on the companion CD (CHAP02\ServerEXE\LawTrialEXE.vbp). I compiled it and called it from a client (also included on the CD: CHAP02\ServerEXE\DataTestEXE.vbp). Running the server on Microsoft Windows NT Server 4, on a 64-MB RAM 200-MHz Pentium Pro, I found in the Windows NT Task Manager that the out-of-process server had memory usage of 2092 KB and virtual memory size of 432 KB with one client using it, and that each client had a memory usage of 2460 KB and 452 KB. (See Figure 2-11.)

Pretty hungry! People don't believe you when you tell them this. I then made the server into a DLL (CHAP02\ServerDLL\LawTrialDLL.vbp) and made a client (CHAP02\ServerDLL\DataTestDLL.vbp) for that and found that each client now had a memory usage of between 2180 KB and 2196 KB and a virtual memory size of 424 KB. (See Figure 2-11.) The minor discrepancy is almost certainly due to the number of elements created.

This seems to be a strong argument for procurator processes. (See the "Procurators or Process Managers" section on page 78.) I include the code on the companion CD, and you can test this yourself if you are running version 4 of

>>

is no control of the creation of objects, and eventually the objects can proliferate and choke the server machine that hosts them, unless some control is reestablished over how many objects can exist at any given time. We also get splatted by the problem of slow start-up of an object instance (which we've already talked about).

The next configuration that might suggest itself is one that involves merely a change in instancing for the Garbage Server, as shown in Figure 2-12. You might think we could move the server to having one instance of the code loaded even though we have multiple clients accessing and using it.

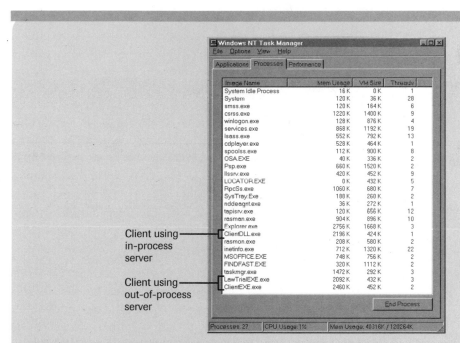

Client using in-process server

Client using out-of-process server

FIGURE 2-11   *Checking out memory usage in Windows NT 4 Server's Task Manager*

Windows NT, using the Task Manager, which is often handier than the Performance Monitor for quick tests such as this.

FIGURE 2-12

The MultiUse instancing option for distributed servers

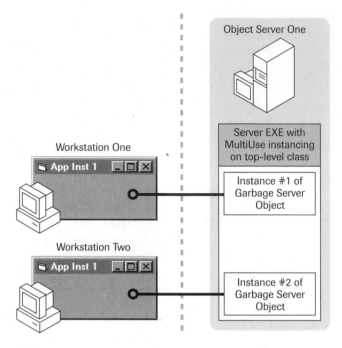

This configuration would appear to get around the number of loaded instances and memory usage problems on the server since each client gets its own instance; but that instance is provided by one loaded set of code, and each instance has its own copy of global data to work on. Remember this, because it means you can't use this model to share global data between clients.

Where many clients are requesting services from a server that is satisfying all those requests with a single-threaded application (as Visual Basic 4 had to do, and Visual Basic 5 can do), the issue is blocking. Even on a preemptive multitasking operating system such as Windows NT, when a request is being serviced by one loaded instance of code, another request cannot be serviced. This is because ActiveX has to handle the possibility that a thread might be interrupted before it has completed its work and that the process that gets the processor next might call the same server. It handles this by blocking—serializing requests so that any other request is accepted by the server but cannot be run until the outstanding request, which is in the works already, is satisfied.

If all requests were quickly turned around, the faster your server machine, the more requests it can get through, and the less of an issue blocking is. However, if the server machine is underpowered in relation to the peaks of requests made of it or if some of the requests are long running and others short, clients might have to wait for a long time to have their requests serviced. As you know, users don't like not knowing how long something is going to take, and they *really* don't like finding out that the same task can take different amounts of time on different occasions.

CHOICES FOR *N*-TIERED ARCHITECTURES

It's now common knowledge that initializing and loading an ActiveX server can take time and therefore affect performance. This is a real hassle for a distributed system that already has to contend with the overhead of network access. If the object instance were already initialized and loaded, however, you could avoid this performance effect; and let's face it, nobody's application can afford to give away performance in seconds. This is where *n*-tiered architectures come in.

Pool Management

Visual Basic 4 gave us the ability to distribute parts of an application, and Microsoft recommended using a pool manager to maintain pools of precreated objects that could be given out in response to client requests for service more or less instantaneously on demand. With Visual Basic 5, the requirement for some kind of infrastructure layer in a distributed system still remains.

The pool management idea is that a client application or component asks a pool manager for a reference to an object it wants to use. (See Figure 2-13 on page 64.) The pool manager checks its resource pool and either grants or denies the request. As we have seen, MultiUse instanced servers have blocking problems with a pool manager, so the natural choice is to create SingleUse instanced server object classes. The issue with this approach is that without a pool manager there is nothing to steward resources on the business object server machine; but the pool manager can be designed to do this.

FIGURE 2-13

A pool management model for tiered development

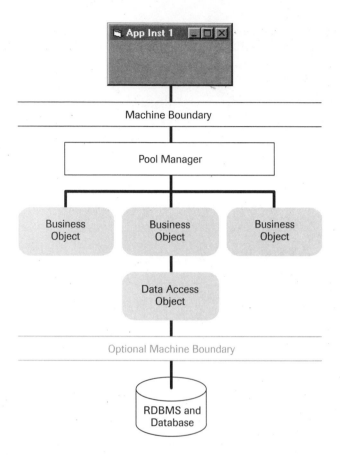

NOTE

For simplicity, I haven't shown the pool manager being used by one business object to get references to another business object or a data access object. I don't mean to imply this shouldn't happen—in fact, doing this is what distinguishes tiering from layering, as mentioned earlier.

Benefits of a nice clean pool

Using a pool, you can avoid the performance cost of ActiveX server creation for each client request since the pool would typically be created and restocked before a client needed a server; so when the clients request an object, it is already instantiated. You can manage server machine resources so that you don't create more business server processes on your server machine than its hardware can handle—again, a real possibility. Depending on your code, an algorithm based on the frequency of client requests, the potential number of clients, and the duration of server tasks can be used to derive the pool size to be created (or even adjusted, according to demand). The aim is that the pool should be significantly smaller than a one-to-one allocation of servers to clients, which means we're going to keep down the resource consumption. Users being the cantankerous and uncaring beasts they are, we can't realistically expect them to perfectly space their service requests, so we have to be prepared for both peaks and valleys of service. However, if we can keep down the connection time of a client to an object, we can expect that a pool size of perhaps 10 ActiveX servers could meet the normal needs of 100 clients. The pool manager will limit the number of servers of a specific type that can be created to a threshold that has been determined by the server administrator. So by restricting the number of server object processes running on it, we can avoid bringing our server machine to a grinding halt. This can be a very useful tuning parameter.

Goals in pool management design

A pool manager needs to be created in an extensible way to allow for the future deployment and management of a number of different kinds of servers, some not yet designed. It needs to be able to manage each type of server explicitly, rather than as a homogenous mass of instances whose specific type it doesn't know. A pool manager also needs to be designed to allow for extending and modifying any management algorithms as needed to cope with peaks of demand, changes in usage patterns, and so on. A useful addition is to make your pool manager capable of remote management through an ActiveX interface since invariably the business object server machine will be in the least convenient place—often in a locked room and well away from both those who use it and those who need to administer the objects on it.

Objects to be managed   A pool manager is an important corporate resource and has to be capable of managing different object server types. For it to do this, you have to make it capable of configuring itself to add new objects and to treat those objects the same regardless of their class. There is a proviso here: the pool manager does need to recognize what type or class it is so that calls for a particular class of object can be handled in the most convenient way. Unfortunately, to treat the instances of different classes or types of object as generically as possible, you have to break one of the unwritten laws of ActiveX object instantiation and sacrifice performance for generic code. So instead of instantiating in your pool manager with the typical:

```
Private oNewObject as ObscureObjectClass
Set oNewObject = New ObscureObjectClass
```

you would actually need to use the normally execrable:

```
Private oNewObject as Object
Set oNewObject = CreateObject(sClassname)
```

Although the first code example has all the advantages of early binding and we're even using the *New* keyword only when we explicitly want to create the object, we must use the second example because we want to add new classes to be managed without changing the references or recompiling the project. We also want to store the class names as text somewhere. (I have used the Windows NT Registry in the past, although the efficacy of this is debatable—but another time, huh?)

Pool manager administration

If you're going to build rules into a pool manager, you need to make it capable of remote dynamic rule alteration. It also makes sense to include extras such as server and object version information inquiry so that an object type or an instance of a type can be interrogated for its version information, how many instances of it are running, and so on via the pool manager.

In short, you can enable your pool manager to respond to queries with information about how it's running and what objects it's shepherding by using an ActiveX interface (that is, ActiveX methods and properties). Then it can be remotely interrogated, which would allow a *viewer utility* to be built that could be used remotely. Such a utility would allow administrators to monitor the system, for example.

Object instantiation

Deciding how your pool manager creates instances of objects is a key decision. Because the pool manager needs to be as free as possible to allocate an object at any time, without forcing requesters to wait until an instance has been created, how object instances are started becomes an important consideration. Let's go over some of the options for creating object instances.

Create objects during "idle" time For this option, we would notice when our pool of a certain object class was running low as we gave out object instances, but we would log this fact for future action and instantiate new object instances only when the pool manager was not being called on to do anything else. This strategy calls for careful management of the number of free objects in the pool so that you rarely have to start new ones in response to an immediate demand. Nevertheless, using this strategy is eventually going to restrict scalability since creating an instance of an out-of-process server is a lengthy business.

In-process object servers We could have our server objects provided by in-process object servers, which are in process to the pool manager. If we did this, the instantiation hit would be much lower. A drawback of this method is that it restricts being able to easily add new object types on the fly.

Call out to create For all additions to an object type's pool, the pool manager could call an *AddNew* method in another stand-alone application (an instantiator) by using an ActiveX callback or an event so that the pool manager would be informed when the object instance had been created and was available for use.

Call in to create We can make our instantiator a class within a multithreaded pool manager, in which case we can use a new thread to instantiate or to launch and use an instantiator.

Garbage collection: Take out the trash

A pool manager needs to have a garbage collection service that sweeps up the dead. Once an object instance has been given out for use, depending on the way you are doing this, the pool manager will probably have no further dealings with the object instance. It might not even be referencing the instance until the client has in some way returned the instance to the pool. But objects die—it happens. Sometimes it's the user's fault ("Always," you say? You must be a real developer!); sometimes your code is the cause; sometimes something outside your control happens. (I had one that died when a corrupt SQL Server database was read using RDO [Remote Data Objects].) Your pool manager needs to keep tabs on these objects.

It would be nice to ask the object directly if it is all right and still in use. Unfortunately, you run the risk that if the server instance is frozen and you try to call a method on it, your pool manager can be sucked into a similar black hole.

How you keep track of objects depends partly on the way you give out objects. Assume you make your pool manager hand out the object references but keep a reference to the object instance itself (as in the code in 1A and 1B in Figure 2-14). Your purpose is to keep the object instance alive when the client has finished with it or when the client application dies. Now, however, you need explicit garbage collection, since you can't rely on ActiveX to do it for you with its reference count. Because there are two references to the object instance—one held by the client and one held by your pool manager—releasing one of them will not allow the instance to die. If something goes wrong with the client application and it dies or sets its reference to nothing but is unable to tell the pool manager that it no longer requires the object instance, you have a problem. As far as the pool manager is concerned, the object instance it gave

FIGURE 2-14

The main options in passing object references via a pool manager

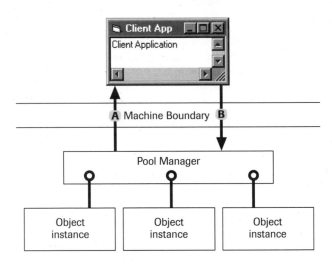

Passing the Parcel

Either 1
A: `Set oObject = oPoolMan.GetInstance(sObjectType, lObjectId)`
B: `bReturn = oPoolMan.ReturnInstance(sObjectType, lObjectId)`

or 2
A: `bReturn = oPoolMan.GetInstance(oObject, sObjectType)`
B: `bReturn = oPoolMan.ReturnInstance(oObject, sObjectType)`

or 3
A: `Set oObject = oPoolMan.GetInstance(sObjectType)`
B: `bReturn = oPoolMan.ReturnInstance(oObject, sObjectType)`

out to the client is still being used by the client. So it keeps it alive because it believes the instance is being used. In fact no client is now using it; but because the pool manager thinks it is being used, it won't release the instance back into the pool for reuse by other clients. If you do get errors, reboots, and so on (tell me you don't with a straight face, I dare you!), garbage will build up on your server machine.

Another way you can keep track of objects is simply to have your pool manager pass an object reference to the client and set its own object reference to nothing, as in 2A and 2B or 3A and 3B in Figure 2-14. Then you take the view that if something goes wrong in either client or server that stops the server instance from being able to complete its task, the client application will take one of these two actions:

- Set the object reference to nothing if it can
- Let the reference pass out of scope by dying or even having the machine reboot at the client end

Either way, the server instance's object reference will pass out of scope. Because of ActiveX's reference counting mechanism for keeping objects alive, when that final reference goes, the instance will also die.

A waste disposal system

A more complex arrangement would be to time how long the server instance has been out of the pool and in use and measure this time against an "I-am-worried" time. When the pool manager starts getting worried about the time, it starts looking to see whether the client is still out there. You can look for the client by using API network calls in Visual Basic 4, but since you cannot use callbacks and thus enumerated API calls, you have to write a little C DLL to do this. In Visual Basic 5, you can exploit the new capability to use callbacks. Obviously, the client then has to provide the pool manager with its machine ID. If the client exists, the pool manager has to take the view that the object instance is still required by that client. If the pool manager doesn't find the client, however, or if we've now had the instance booked out so long that it has reached a "This-can't-go-on" time, the pool manager might figure that something is wrong. When the pool manager decides this, it believes that the object instance isn't coming back anymore, so it takes action to clear out the dead/redundant object (using the previously stored process ID of the server instance, for example, to kill the process). The code for this example is in CHAP02\Listings\Listings.vbp (Kill.Bas) on the companion CD.

Pool managers and multiple machine management

The pool manager can be designed to manage a pool of objects of a number of object types across more than one physical machine. Several configurations are possible.

Single machine, mixed-object type pools   In mixed-class, single-machine pools, different pool managers on different server machines manage the same object types, and clients have a default server. If the default server is not available or cannot service a request for an object instance, by dynamically rewriting the client machine's Registry settings the client application can retry against a pool manager on its second-choice server. (See Figure 2-15.)

You can rewrite the Registry settings by setting a reference to RACREG32.DLL in your project and then using the methods *GetAutoServerSettings* and

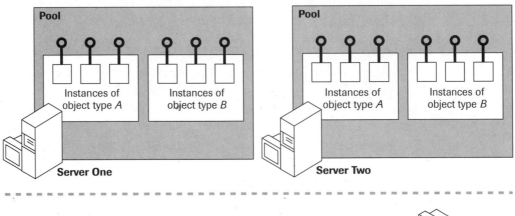

Client One
First-choice server: Server One
Second-choice server: Server Two

Client Two
First-choice server: Server Two
Second-choice server: Server One

Client Three
First-choice server: Server Two
Second-choice server: Server One

FIGURE 2-15   *Using a pool manager to manage mixed classes on a single server machine*

SetAutoServerSettings on a *RegClass* object for Remote Automation. *Set-DCOMServerSettings* and *SetNetOLEServerSettings* are also available for DCOM settings, but I have yet to locate "gets" for DCOM. (To retrieve Remote Automation settings, use *sPuReadAutomationSettings* in CHAP02\Listings \Listings.vbp (AutDCOM.Bas) on the companion CD.)

CAUTION

> Be careful of methods that change Registry Settings: they are not risk-free. Using the first beta of Visual Basic 5 to write to the Registry, I corrupted an unbacked-up Registry—luckily it was on my own test machine rather than on someone else's.

This pool configuration means that a pool manager will equate to a server machine and will be managing all ActiveX server instances of whatever class or type is running on that machine. Thus a pool manager will be capable of managing the load on a single server.

Single-machine, single-object type pools   In single-machine, single-object type pools, requests for different object types are made to different servers. (See Figure 2-16.) This pool configuration involves either using a lot of calls

FIGURE 2-16

Pool manager managing one class of object on one server machine

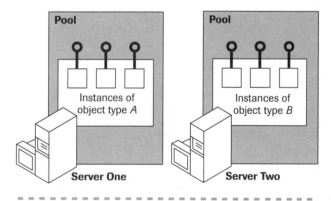

All clients get objects of type *A* from Server One's pool and objects of type *B* from Server Two's pool.

to change Registry settings or using Registry settings for different server machine pool managers (that is, pool managers that have separate GUIDS on all client machines).

Multimachine pools   In multimachine pools, the pool manager is on Server One, and all client Registry settings for the pool manager direct them to get pool manager references from Server One. (See Figure 2-17.) The pool manager itself, however, can create different kinds of objects on different machines and manage them as a single logical pool.

FIGURE 2-17

One pool manager used to manage different classes of objects on more than one server machine

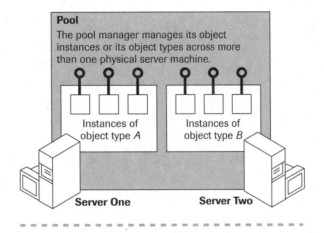

All clients get all object types from Server One's pool even though the object instances might reside on Server Two.

What pools need to know about object types

Any given object type will have a collection of running instances in one or more pools. Each object type will need to provide information for a pool manager to create and manage the right number of objects. Table 2-1 lists some properties you can use to set up a pool manager.

Bean counting for developers   The Threshold Maximum number can be derived by using the Frequency of client requests, the Potential Number Of

TABLE 2-1 **Things a Pool Manager Might Like to Know**

Characteristic	Notes
Threshold Minimum	The minimum number of objects of that type the pool manager must maintain.
Threshold Maximum	The maximum number of objects of that type the pool manager can start and have running at a given time whether free or servicing a request. This property can be set or derived from other properties, such as the capability of the server machine.
Frequency	The frequency of requests per minute expected for the server. This can be derived by logging requests over a period of time and creating and monitoring an average.
Potential Number of Clients	The maximum number of concurrent running client applications (although this might equate to users) that could potentially use this object type. If two different kinds of client application were in use, we could decide that client type A could have up to three instances of itself running on the same machine at any given time and would be available on 50 machines; client type B could have only one instance running at a time on any machine and would be installed on 70 machines. In this case, the potential number of clients is $3*50$ (for client A) + $1*70$ (for client B) = 220.
Average Duration of Server Task	The average length of time a server task is expected to run, based on the number of tasks that ran during a period and how long each ran from start to finish. This can be set or derived. For additional information, see the comments on mixed-duration tasks inVisual Basic 5 Books Online.
Logging Enabled	Enables/disables logging of statistics for the object type to derive some of the values above.
Garbage Collection	Enables/disables garbage checking for that object type or object instance. (See the "Garbage collection: Take out the trash" section on page 67.) You can extend this to have different methods of garbage collection if you want to be really flashy.

Clients, and the Average Duration Of Server Task to derive a linear allocation plan:

$$\text{Threshold Maximum} = \frac{\text{Potential Number of Clients} \times \text{Frequency}}{\text{Seconds per Minute} \div \text{Average Duration of Server Task}}$$

Characteristic	Values
Frequency of requests per client	5 requests per minute
Potential number of clients	100
Average duration of server task	3 seconds

$$\text{Threshold Maximum} = \frac{100 \times 5}{60 \div 3} = 25$$

At this point, you might want to put in a reality factor—an admission that not all your clients will be needing objects all the time. This step involves some risk, however, since if you wanted to truly scale to the maximum number of clients, you would be relying on probability to bail you out of any peaks. Although you can be aware of the maximum number you might ever need, you still have to consider this figure in the context of *all* server objects that might be running on your object server machine. After adding in the overhead of any other processes running there and comparing this figure to the capability of the machine, you'll have a fairly good idea of whether the memory will be adequate. Consider this scenario:

- You need a maximum *ever* of 150 objects running.
- Each of those objects needs 1 MB of memory.
- You also have other processes you need to run that perform optimally in around 64 MB.

Perhaps in this case 256 MB of RAM looks viable on your machine. Nevertheless, you'd probably go for a more dynamic strategy of precreating perhaps 50 of the 150 object instances you could need as your pool and monitoring usage to see if they are being used. You would create more of a type (up to the maximum of that type you are currently allowing) only when you are approaching your threshold minimum of free objects, in effect stocking up for expected demand.

Scheduling

Any scheduling algorithm you use to initialize, adjust, and manage pool sizes can be as simple or as complex as your requirements demand. It almost certainly will need to change to allow for changing circumstances during the lifetime of an installation; but better this than having to frequently restructure ActiveX servers for the same reasons. Custom factors used to manage pool sizes might include an awareness of peak load times and the urgency of certain tasks. Bearing in mind that a pool manager can need to be designed to manage many types of ActiveX server on the same host machines, this kind of complexity might require complex rules and schedules for creating new object types in a large and complex work environment.

Where regular peaks or troughs of service requirement can be identified—presumably based on experience noted from logging—events, particularly the creation and destruction of objects, can be made schedulable. An event can be created for an object type; an event can occur daily, weekly, monthly, or only once. Each of these occurrences equates to a derived date of next running of the event, and the event can be enabled or disabled. An event also has a time associated with it. An event can be either a create or a destroy event with an associated number of object instances.

Thus an object type being managed by the pool manager will have a collection of schedule events, which will be added to via an *AddScheduleEvent* routine. Each schedule event will have a method to delete itself. You can get into scheduling modifying events too, although changing the number of objects and toggling the enabled bit are the most likely changes you'll want to make. Otherwise, modifying is probably a complication you can do without; instead, just use delete of an old event and then create a new one.

Create events   Where a create event is scheduled, and its time and date mean that it should be run, after checking the current state and threshold limit defined for the object type, the pool manager will instantiate that number of object instances of that object type in addition to those already running.

Destroy events   Where a destroy event is scheduled, and its time and date mean that it should be run, the code will check the current state and threshold minimum for the object type, and the pool manager will destroy that number of free object instances of that object type.

Rule-based creates   A rule (for example, if the number of unused running object instances < 10, then add 5) can be used on a create or destroy event.

A possible pool manager object model

Figure 2-18 shows a COM-type object model for a pool manager that might support all this.

FIGURE 2-18

Possible object model for a pool manager

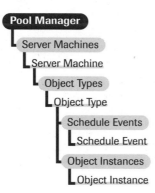

For the pool manager top-level class, which is the root of the pool manager application, I would suggest a 32-bit out-of-process server (unless you intend to use Microsoft Transaction Server). The pool manager class should be *Public* and MultiUse and compiled for Unattended Execution. As to the number of threads to use, I would personally use a thread pool based on how many processors I had and how I was going to carry out my creates. An OMT (Object Modeling Technique) class diagram for it might look something like Figure 2-19.

Pool manager persistent data storage   With all this information, the data that the pool manager will need to store must be kept somewhere. It can be kept in flat files in the same folder as the pool manager's executable, in the Registry, or in a database. Each storage location has its pros and cons. Flat files are easy to manage and change, but this is a double-edged sword because it's easy for *anyone* to change. The Registry is more secure, but it's slower, less friendly, and also a higher risk, considering you could disable your whole system with an incorrect Registry setting (although I have used the Registry quite successfully). A database, even a local .MDB, would appear to be adding unnecessary complication. Logically, storage for a pool manager might look like the example shown in Figure 2-20 on page 78.

FIGURE 2-19

A candidate pool manager class diagram

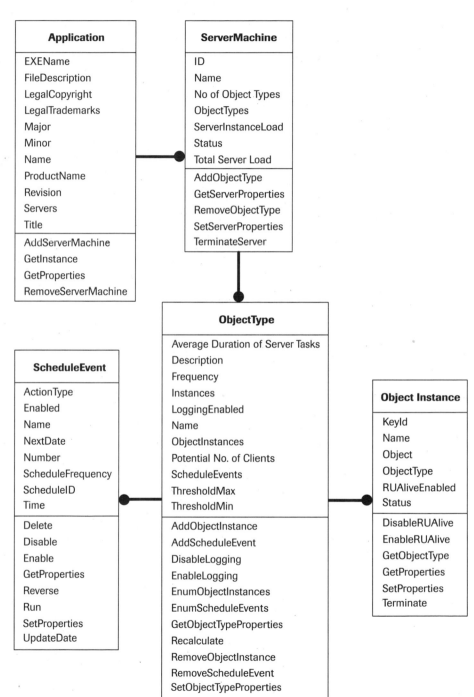

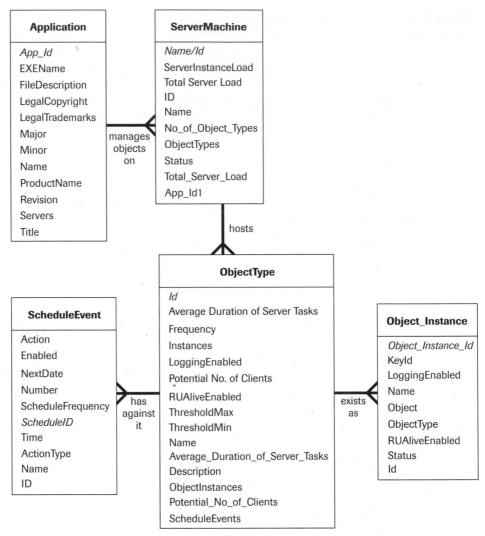

FIGURE 2-20   *An example of pool manager storage*

Procurators or Process Managers

An extension of the pool manager with in-process servers (essentially OLE or ActiveX DLLs) plugged into it is an out-of-process procurator or process manager component that can have in-process components attached to it. (See Figure 2-21.)

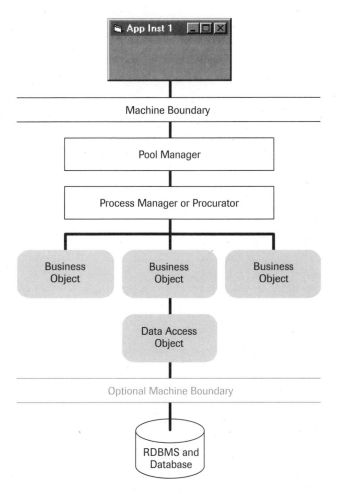

FIGURE 2-21

A tiered architecture with procurators or process managers

This object, or more realistically these objects, can be pool managed in their turn. If they were not, the procurators would go back into a one-to-one relationship with their clients (but might have references to all the other objects of the system) and would be able to create them from in-process calls to the DLLs that would supply them. The advantage over a pool manager managing multiple instances of SingleUse creatable business objects is that the number of individual processes—assuming you have more than one business object type—is smaller and thus requires less memory to run. If you have a lot of components, your system will probably be a little easier to manage too.

Certainly, performance will be enhanced, especially if you are genuinely tiering, by which I mean that your objects are talking to each other in your tiers rather than just talking between tiers (since all within-a-tier calls are going to be in process).

However, the procurator must know about all the components of the system and how to make them work. If a new component were added, the procurator process might well have to be recompiled. The procurator has the benefit of moving a lot of the management of the system from the client to the server, which makes for a thinner client—not to be sneezed at when the days

IN-PROCESS COMPONENTS AND THREADING

MultiUse, Multithreaded Server with Single-Threaded DLL

As you can see in Figure 2-22, in a MultiUse, multithreaded server with a single-threaded DLL, multiple clients get top-level objects created by the same running instance of the server. Each top-level object gets its own thread and copy of global data. Objects created in an in-process component are created on one of the server's threads.

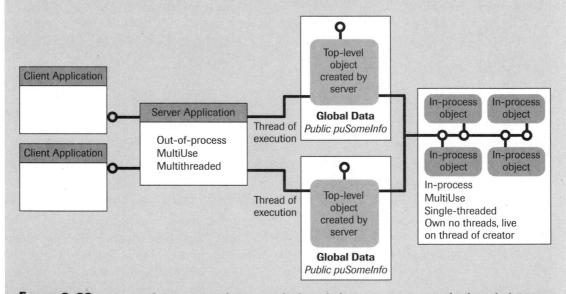

FIGURE 2-22 *An out-of-process, MultiUse, multithreaded server using a single-threaded DLL*

of intranet applications are upon us. The procurator process can also be used to hold state information for the client, especially where a number of separate server processes have to work cooperatively on the same object.

Queue Managers

So far we have been thinking mostly about synchronous communication between our client and server. This means that the client is effectively blocked, waiting for a response from a remote server (be it a business object or a pool manager), and cannot carry on with any other work while it waits.

MultiUse, Multithreaded Server with Multithreaded DLL

In Figure 2-23, you'll see an example of a MultiUse, multithreaded server with a multithreaded DLL. Multiple clients get top-level objects created by the same running instance of the server. Each top-level object gets its own thread and copy of global data. Objects created in an in-process component are created on the thread of their top-level creator.

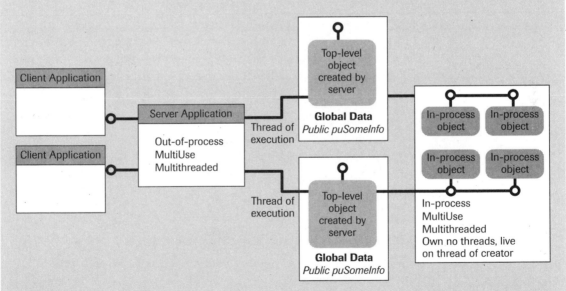

FIGURE 2-23 *An out-of-process, MultiUse, multithreaded server using a multithreaded DLL*

An asynchronous link lets the client do something else while its request is being processed. So it can request an object type to use, and while that object is being created or supplied, the client can carry on with some other work. Incidentally, identifying work to carry out asynchronously is often an art in itself. The Application Performance Explorer (APE) that ships with Visual Basic 5 Enterprise and Professional Editions implements a queue manager. The essential difference between a pool manager and a queue manager is that with a queue manager, requests from a client are never refused. If a business object cannot be provided immediately, the queue manager stores the request and, working on a first come–first served basis, services the request for an object when such an object is available. In this way, the server machine is providing the best service it is capable of, and the server objects are servicing requests as fast as they can. Returning information in this kind of a scenario is usually done through ActiveX callbacks to provide an asynchronous link.

Microsoft Transaction Server Model

It would be criminal indeed if I didn't mention this. I'm not going to go into it in any depth, however, partly because it would more than occupy this whole chapter to do it justice and partly because I have never deployed Microsoft Transaction Server (except on an in-house network, which doesn't represent a good scalability test). The facilities of Transaction Server (code name, Viper) are at least a partial match for the requirements you might have for a pool manager and an infrastructure to support distributed object systems written using Visual Basic. In fact, Transaction Server provides more, since it covers these areas as well:

- Just-in-time instantiation of components—it wants things provided to it as ActiveX DLLs
- Component packaging and deployment of systems
- Thread and process management
- Database connection pooling
- A mechanism for sharing data among components
- A very small amount of code in your components to call Transaction Server's methods

Figure 2-24 shows Transaction Server's model for a distributed, tiered application.

FIGURE 2-24

The Microsoft Transaction Server model for a distributed, tiered application

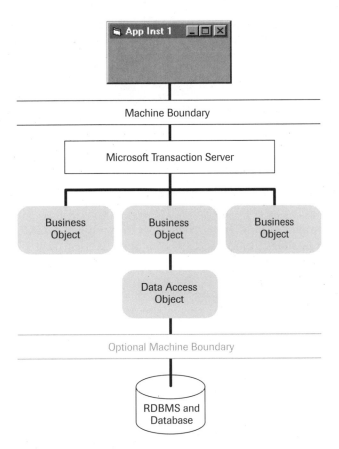

There! I said I would mention it! If you're using Visual Basic to create distributed applications, you really have to look at this product. Transaction Server will radically reduce the infrastructure effort you have to make to deploy distributed applications with Visual Basic.

A Final Parting Word

I feel I need to emphasize that your tiers can be many more than the typical three you will have seen drawn in many of the illustrations in this chapter. It is a point often missed by newcomers to distributed, tiered architectures: a tier and a machine are not necessarily synonymous; and the typical user services, business logic, and data services tiering could be increased extensively depending on the needs of the application. Also keep in mind that tiers and physical machines need not be in any one-to-one relationship. However, the machines that distribute components, other than the database server itself, need to have Windows NT (preferably Windows NT Server 4.0) present to run successfully.

NOW BUILD YOUR SYSTEM

When they come to you and say, "That Visual Basic builds remote server applications now, doesn't it? So it won't be any trouble for you to throw together a system to …" try to give them an idea of the architecture and design work and the planning and implementing of an infrastructure that has to be put in to build a cooperative distributed system of business objects. I have attempted to lay out such a system in this chapter. We all need to be aware that there's more to it than just taking some functionality and splitting it up into a few bits. Unfortunately, if you want to make scalable applications with Visual Basic, your objects have to be structured to support them; you also have to do some of that thinking stuff and a little bit of experimentation.

With regard to the experimentation, I have included some of my own experiments as code on the companion CD. They each come with their own README.TXT files that explain what you have to do and what each experiment intends to prove. If you want to do larger, more real-world experiments, the APE that ships with Visual Basic 5 Enterprise and Professional Editions is an excellent place to start and is well worth taking the trouble to come to grips with so that you can customize it successfully. Good luck, and happy remote instantiation.

Empowering Your Users' Reports with Visual Basic 5

Clive is a TMS Associate who works predominantly with financial organizations in London. He is currently a development team leader for a leading financial fund asset management company. His experience includes seven years of design, development, and testing of software systems. Clive has spent the last three years developing multiuser Visual Basic and Microsoft Access systems against a variety of databases. He is a Microsoft Certified Professional. Clive enjoys most sports, especially skiing, golf, and wind surfing.

CLIVE HUBBARD

In this chapter, we'll explore various methods for solving complex reporting issues. You'll see that by using report formats suited to your company's particular needs, you'll be able to reduce training costs, development overhead, and the user's need to maintain detailed knowledge of a myriad of applications and tools.

The rapid advancement in hardware and software technology ensures that application development is in a continuous state of evolution. We've quickly progressed from monolithic character-based applications to state-of-the-art WYSIWYG ones. You need look no further than the advances in word processor offerings to see how the style, flexibility, and complexity of commercial applications have evolved in the space of a decade.

Custom development has followed suit, thanks to the availability of powerful languages and a vast array of software tools the developer can use. While frequenting the local bar, I've occasionally heard drunken tales of how easily users are impressed with the bells and whistles they are given in a typical application demonstration. Enthusiastically, the developer in question might boast that he was able to awe his users simply by whipping together a couple of screens incorporating some clever graphics and a smattering of code. Such tales might contain a certain amount of truth; however, it's unlikely that you would ever hear a developer make such claims about a user's reporting requirement. In fact, a discussion of user reports is likely to sober up even the most hardened developer with painful flashbacks: the numerous times a report had to be redeveloped because it didn't quite match the user's requirement; a user's scorn because of the inability to control the positioning of page breaks; worst of all, the inevitable user question, "I was able to produce this report in Microsoft Excel; why can't you create an application to do the same?"

This chapter aims to help you avoid some of these unpleasant experiences by illustrating ways of using the latest technologies in Microsoft Visual Basic 5 to your reporting advantage.

NOTE

This chapter does not deal with the production of reports from Crystal Reports. For information on this product, refer to the relevant user guide.

REPORTING ISSUES

The success or failure of a custom-developed report will almost always be judged on how well it matches the requirement, how easy it is to use, and how much time it took to deliver the solution, as well as on the quality and accuracy of the output. Examining a traditional method of producing custom reports might help highlight why it is so difficult to meet user expectations.

The same data is usually reported in two formats: on screen and on paper. On screen, the data is often displayed in text fields or other controls on a form; when sent to a printer, the data appears on paper (although don't forget that most applications provide a Print Preview feature, in which data appears on screen in the same format that is sent to the printer). Independent methods must be provided for the selection, display, and processing of the output for the screen output and for the printer output. The different methods are often necessary because of the limitations of the software and hardware technology used. As a result, applications are designed to have separate menu options, toolbars, and selection criteria for essentially the same output information. The biggest complication is that because two methods of programming are required for one logical process, the opportunity for errors to creep into the solution doubles. The net result of this dual programming is a disjointed view of the user requirement, forcing the user to think nonintuitively.

User requirements, application complexity and training requirements, technology, and development schedules all contribute to the challenge of developing reports. Each of these issues is discussed briefly in the following sections to help identify alternative approaches for your development projects.

User Requirements

A user's expectations often center around the capabilities of another application he or she is more familiar with, usually a commercially available word processor or spreadsheet. Expectations turn into requirements, making it an arduous task for the developer to explain to a user why the report being developed is not as flexible or functionally rich as the likes of Microsoft Word or Microsoft Excel. Although the reasons can be explained in terms of cost, resource requirements, and schedule, they do not temper the user's perception of what a custom application should be able to do. You need to be aware of the advantages these commercial products offer. Table 3-1 highlights the output characteristics of Excel and Word that separate such applications' output from custom-developed output.

TABLE 3-1

OUTPUT CHARACTERISTICS OF WORD AND EXCEL COMPARED WITH THOSE OF A CUSTOM APPLICATION

Report Characteristic	Word and Excel	Custom
Content	Flexible	Predefined
Layout	Flexible	Fixed
Format and style	Flexible	Fixed
Output	Editable	Read-only
Integration with application	Seamless	Separate

This problem of trying to create flexible custom reports is improving with each new release of report-writing tools such as Microsoft Access's report writer, Crystal Reports, and others. It remains a reality, however, that most reports based on information stored in a database or from other data sources will require the help of a developer. Building reports remains a task too complex for the average user.

You are unlikely to be given the go-ahead to reinvent Word and Excel from within your custom development, so as the old saying goes, "If you can't beat 'em, join 'em." Luckily, you won't need to sell your soul to the developers at Microsoft to achieve this. Long ago, Microsoft identified this problem of custom developers wanting to use features included in Microsoft products. Now through ActiveX technology, Microsoft has provided us with the capability to manipulate and control components of Word, Excel, and other applications.

Application Complexity and Training

Once a user masters an application, he or she often has a natural resistance to working with other products that apply alternative techniques or methods for similar activities. To avoid resistance to the report application you're developing, it is therefore crucial to provide reporting within an environment familiar to the user. User training is expensive; by adopting an approach the user already knows, you can help reduce the need for training, cut down on costs, and improve user acceptance of new applications.

Technology

Report writer tools rarely have a common set of methods and properties. They are implemented in different ways and often have a built-in dependency on a specific database source for the report content. These limitations are a nonissue when you're dealing with basic report formats, but they do pose a problem when you need to generate complicated reports. It is an unfortunate reality that to produce complex reports developers expend considerable effort in manipulating the internal logic of a report writer. For reports not suited to report writers, it is necessary to rely on components exposed by other applications to achieve the required result.

Most Microsoft software vendors support the use of COM (Component Object Model), and the higher-level architecture ActiveX is gaining acceptance on Windows-based computers. Briefly, an *Automation server* is an application that exposes programmable objects. An *Automation client* is a controlling application that accesses those objects. An *ActiveX type library* describes programmable objects. *ActiveX control creation* refers to a class of application that can generate visual objects for embedding in other applications' objects (forms, reports, documents, and so on). *ActiveX control capable* refers to a class of application that accepts ActiveX controls (on a local PC or on the Internet). *ActiveX document creation* refers to a class of applications that generate visual objects in the form of a document for use with other applications. *ActiveX document capable* refers to the class of applications that can display ActiveX documents.

The ActiveX components mentioned ensure that a consistent method is used to communicate with the public components of applications. Even with this level of commonality, however, considerable differences still exist in the implementation of core components in applications. This variation makes programming difficult for a developer because he or she must know the specific limitations and quirks in any given application before successfully incorporating it as a common component in report production.

Commercial applications and core component technology are becoming easier to integrate with every new release; for now, however, you need to be aware of the differences in the applications used for reporting. Table 3-2 shows you how various applications support ActiveX controls.

TABLE 3-2   IMPLEMENTATION OF ACTIVEX CONTROLS

ActiveX Component	Visual Basic 4	Visual Basic 5	Excel 5/7	Excel 97	Word 6/7	Word 97	Access 7	Access 97	Internet Explorer 3
Automation client	✓	✓	✓	✓		✓	✓	✓	
Automation server	✓	✓	✓	✓	✓	✓	✓	✓	
Type library support	✓	✓	✓	✓		✓	✓	✓	
Control creation		✓							
Control capable		✓		✓		✓		✓	✓
Document creation*				✓					
Document capable*				✓					

*Visual Basic user document

Microsoft Visual Basic for Applications (VBA) is one of the key mechanisms used to make specific functionality within applications available, both internally as the core basic language and externally as a public interface for other applications. Although we would expect the implementation of VBA to be common across all applications, the *Find* command example here clearly shows that presumption to be incorrect:

Component	Version	Internal Basic Language
WordBasic	7	`EditFind .Find = "test",...`
Excel VBA	7	`Cells.Find(What:="test",...)`

Word VBA	97	`With Selection.Find`
		`    .Text = "test."`
		`End With`
		`Selection.Find.Execute`

Excel VBA	97	`Cells.Find(What:="test",...)`

The basic functionality of the *Find* command is equivalent in Word and Excel and should have a common format and parameter-naming convention. In version 7 (Microsoft Office 95), Word was based on an older macro-style Basic, and Excel had a partial implementation of the object technology (properties and methods). In Office 97, the situation improves slightly. The command has the same name in both applications; however, Word leapfrogs ahead by supporting a purer implementation of the object technology.

Similar issues exist in the public implementation of the application's Basic language, as shown here:

Component	Version	Basic Language Used Within Visual Basic
WordBasic	7	`objWord.Selection.Find.Text = "test"`
Excel VBA	7	`ObjExcel.Find(What:= "test") or` `Excel.Selection.Find(What:= "test")`
Word VBA	97	`objWord.Find.Text = "test" or` `Word.Find.Text = "test"`
Excel VBA	97	`ObjExcel.Find(What:= "test") or` `Excel.Selection.Find(What:= "test")`

In version 7, Excel provides positional and named parameter references (*What:=*) from within Visual Basic. Word 7 provides only positional parameter referencing, *.Find* being the first parameter in the *EditFind* procedure. Excel provides full VBA support from within Visual Basic, including early binding (*Excel.Selection.Find*), whereas Word provides only late binding and no VBA support. In the 97 versions, the differences are resolved, and both applications support positional and named parameter references and early and late binding.

Differences also exist in instancing, as shown here:

Component	Version	Instancing
WordBasic	7	CreateObject("Word.basic")
Excel VBA	7	CreateObject("Excel.Application")
Word VBA	97	CreateObject("Word.Application")
Excel VBA	97	CreateObject("Excel.Application")

In version 7, a new instance of Excel is created each time *CreateObject* is executed; in Word, only a single instance occurs. This inconsistency is rectified in Office 97, in which both applications produce multiple instances of the application object when called more than once.

Even if your organization is using only Office 97, you should wrap the most commonly used Basic commands in a Visual Basic 5 class, as illustrated in "The Control Object Layer" section on page 98. This ensures that the developer is provided with a common language syntax; it also helps avoid major code rewrites every time a new version of VBA is released.

Development Schedules

Software development is a costly business. If you continually reengineer a solution because of changing requirements, you are failing to provide a suitable solution. If users are able to manipulate their own reports, they will rely less on developers, which will reduce development overhead. The key to developing successful solutions is to provide as much flexibility within the application as possible.

Consider the following scenario. A user makes a request to add a report based on an existing report to the company's reporting application. The modifications requested are to remove all references to stock information and the company identifier, to add a footnote, and to disable stock and company identifier fields on the selection screen.

The modifications, which to the user appear trivial, generate considerable work for an information systems department. The company reporting application must be modified, the modifications need to be tested, the design document adjusted, a code review performed, and a change control request made to release the application into the live environment.

All told, the user request generates at least one to two days of work for most information systems departments. If the application supported user-defined report templates and criteria selection, the effort involved would be dramatically reduced. If no development work were required, a twenty-minute explanation on how to create the new template would be the only task—potentially saving days worth of work for a basic report. It stands to reason that the time savings would increase with more complicated report requests.

IDENTIFYING THE NEED FOR ADVANCED REPORTING

One of the key areas of concern I have with custom development is the trend toward over-engineered solutions. There's no point in developing complex reports unless you have to. If your user is happy with a fixed-format report and doesn't continually request changes, you should just leave the standard report as is.

The need for advanced reporting is driven by the nature of the requirement and the user's work environment. A user who produces a stock list once a month for internal viewing has a fixed, well-defined report requirement. In contrast, a user in the same company who provides ad hoc marketing information to external clients, the CEO, and other managers is unlikely to be able to pin down the requirements to one set of reports.

An example of a traditional report requirement is an application that generates payroll checks. The report that produces the check has fixed data content, report format, and report layout. The report requirement probably won't change over time, and you'd certainly not make it possible for your users to edit the end result. In direct contrast, an advanced report would be required to generate quoted company details (company information with relevant stock prices and stock levels) published in a range of formats from within Microsoft Excel, Word, and Microsoft Internet Explorer without forcing a user to cut and paste information from each separate application.

SELECTING THE RIGHT APPROACH

On the surface, providing complex reporting facilities seems to be a straightforward process:

1. Note the user requirement.
2. Create a new ActiveX business object.
3. Create a report template in an Excel workbook.

4. Insert VBA code to reference the ActiveX business object.

5. Repeat this process for each new user request.

This approach is not recommended, however, because it causes a major maintenance headache.

As with all facets of development, if you take enough time up front in analysis and design, you'll derive a suitable approach to act as a framework for further development and won't be restricted to the specifics of developing for one user request. A technique I find useful in evaluating a requirement is to break down the requirement according to the mechanisms and methods needed to produce the result:

1. Gather the right data.

2. Retrieve the data.

3. Filter the data.

4. Manipulate the data.

5. Present and store the report result.

The following sections describe what's involved in each of these steps.

Data Encapsulation

The single most important aspect of any successful report development is ensuring that data and retrieval logic is encapsulated into business objects. If the user is unaware of a physical database behind the scenes, you have achieved the right mix of data and business logic. This mix makes it much simpler for users and developers to select and manipulate data, allowing you to cut down on excess coding and to ensure a uniform approach to data retrieval no matter what technology is being used. Both an ActiveX control displaying stock price information in a Visual Basic form and an embedded ActiveX EXE document displaying stock level information in Internet Explorer should use the same business object internally.

Methods of Data Retrieval

Many software components are involved in retrieving data from a database and presenting it in a useful report format. The components can range from proprietary database drivers and ODBC (open database connectivity) DLLs to the software used to display and print the report. Each component introduces its own level of complexity and detailed knowledge requirements. The techniques presented in this chapter hide this complexity by providing three distinct components: a business object, the control application, and the report output medium.

By using this object-based approach, you reduce data retrieval to the mechanics of deciding which components should obtain the data and control the report output production. Of the three components available, the control application and the report output medium are best suited for controlling report production. The developer then decides how to split the control between the two components depending on user preference and the nature of the requirement.

It might be appropriate to provide a solution that appears as though it originated from the output report medium familiar to the user, for example, Microsoft Excel. Or if more than one medium is to be used, say, the user requires the report to be produced in Excel and Word from one application, you might want to have a controlling application place data into the output report medium. Table 3-3 shows three available data retrieval techniques.

TABLE 3-3

Technique	Control Component	Example
	DATA RETRIEVAL TECHNIQUES	
Push	The control application processes data directly into the output medium component.	ReportInExcelAndWord (See page 141.)
Pull	No control application exists; the output medium component is powerful enough to process data directly.	ReportInExcel (See page 147.)
Combined	The push and pull techniques are combined.	

The ReportInExcelAndWord example illustrates the push technique with no code in the receiving application, using Visual Basic as the controlling application to place data into Excel and Word. The ReportInExcel example illustrates the pull technique, with partial code in Excel that pulls data into a worksheet. An example of the push technique with partial code in the receiving application would be a Visual Basic application that creates a text file and passes control to an Excel VBA macro to read the file and populate a worksheet.

Office 97 Considerations

You can effectively use all three techniques described in Table 3-3 in Office 97 because of the introduction of a common VBA development environment. You can even develop fully functional applications from within Word and Excel without using Visual Basic 5 at all. This raises a pertinent question: do we need Visual Basic 5 in the first place if all the functionality required is available in the report output application? The answer is not a clear-cut yes or no, although a number of fundamental issues sway my opinion toward yes.

Implementing a fully functional system within a document or a spreadsheet is not ideal for version control; most source control applications rely heavily on the fact that the source is based in a text format that can be easily read for differences and stored in a compressed format. If an application is contained within a document or a spreadsheet, all the benefits of source control are lost because the contents of a document or spreadsheet are stored in a binary format along with other nonrelated details that are difficult to decipher.

The ability to store source code separately from the resultant program is critical in ensuring that only one copy of the source code exists and that it is locked away from the prying eyes of users and other developers. Releasing a Word application to ten users results in the proliferation of ten copies of source code, providing ample opportunity for users and developers alike to adjust the code in one copy and not in the others.

Finally, VBA code held within Word and Excel is interpreted rather than compiled as with Visual Basic 5, which negates many of the possible performance improvements.

Each VBA component has a place—if used in moderation, the VBA development environment within Word and Excel is ideal for prototypes and small-scale reporting systems. The larger, more complex systems that involve more than one component work best as Visual Basic 5–developed applications, which allow for source control, version control, and performance improvements.

User Criteria Selection

Two formats are available for user selection: predefined criteria selection screens (Figure 3-1 on the following page), which are best suited to beginning and intermediate users; and free-format criteria selection (Figure 3-2), which is for advanced users. Free-format criteria selection can be placed in a text box or into the report output medium.

FIGURE 3-1

Predefined criteria selection

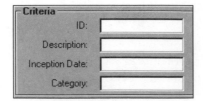

FIGURE 3-2

Free-format criteria selection

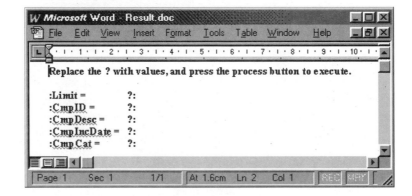

The Control Object Layer

The control object layer acts as the glue that holds together the business object and the code that populates the data into the report object. You must cater to the control object layer to ensure that the business and report objects remain independent of each other. The control object layer might exist in a number of formats—everything from a Visual Basic 5 class module to an ActiveX document. The ReportInExcel example later in this chapter (see page 147) illustrates the use of an ActiveX DLL as a control object layer.

Report Format Storage

Any file that can be read by Word, Excel, Internet Explorer, and other applications is a potential candidate for reporting purposes. Table 3-4 lists some of the possible file formats. Any one of these file formats can be read into an application and used for reporting, immediately providing you with a range of report, edit, display, print, and storage applications that don't require you to write a single line of code.

All the basic formatting for color, font, graphics, shapes, and drawings can be defined with a report editor and saved in one of the file formats listed in Table 3-4. In Word, we can produce a table in the 3D Effects 3 format provided

Table 3-4 — File Formats Useful in Reporting

File Extension	Template Extension	File Type	Some Applications That Can Read the Format
XLS	XLT	Excel workbook	Excel, Word
DOC	DOT	Word document	Word
TXT	None	Text file (tab delimited)	Excel, Word, Write, Notepad
PRN	None	Text file (space delimited)	Excel, Word, Write
RTF	None	Rich text file	Word
CSV	None	Text file (comma delimited)	Excel, Word, Write
WRI	None	Windows write	Word, Write
HTM	None	HTML document	Internet Explorer, Word, Excel
VBD	None	Visual Basic document	Internet Explorer

with the Table AutoFormat option. Inserting the field descriptors recognized by the control layer object will produce the following report template:

	Heading 1	Heading 2	Heading 3
:Item1:	:Item1Value1:	:Item1Value2:	:Item1Value3:
:Item2:	:Item2Value1:	:Item2Value2:	:Item2Value3:
Total	Total 1	Total 2	Total 3

You can design report templates in any format you want; unfortunately, the user can easily overwrite templates that aren't in DOT or XLT format with the results of the report process. To restrict user access to templates, you need to add some code to your application to open the template and to save it immediately as a new result file before the user has the opportunity to edit it. The following lines of VBA code will create a copy of the Word template:

```
' Use the cmUtils DLL (VBActiveXDLL) to open the Word template.
    cmUtils.OutputMedium = cmToWord
    cmUtils.OpenOutputMedium objOutput, _
        App.Path & "\" & sDocTemplate & _
        sDocWordTmpltExtension

' Determine the next available result filename.
    sFileName = App.Path & "\" & _
        sDocResult & sDocWordExtension

' Loop through until we have a valid file.
    nPos = 1
    On Error Resume Next
```

>>

>>

```
' Remove the existing result file.
    Kill sFileName
    Do Until Err.Number = nErrorNone _
        Or Err.Number = nErrorFileNotFound

' We were unable to remove the file, so
' it must be in use. Try the next available file.
        sFileName = App.Path & "\" & _
            sDocResult & nPos & _
            sDocWordExtension
        nPos = nPos + 1

' Try to remove it.
        Kill sFileName
    Loop
    On Error GoTo 0

' We have a valid file; now copy the template to
' the result file.
    objOutput.FileSaveAs sFileName

' The user can now use the copied report template.
    objOutput.AppShow
```

You can define field descriptors in a variety of ways: as bookmarks in Word; as defined named ranges in Excel; as invisible or normal text with special control characters delimiting the text. Choosing an appropriate format depends on your requirements. If Word is the only output report format you'll use, bookmarks are an obvious choice. Plain text delimited with special characters is the most usable field descriptor because it can be stored in most file formats, is easy to read, is easy to search for, and can be added to easily by a user.

In all the examples provided in this chapter, I've used plain text with a colon (:) to delimit the beginning and end of a field descriptor. For example, :CmpID: is identifiable as the company identifier. Providing total flexibility is no longer a problem. Figure 3-3 illustrates the power of this technique.

The report in Figure 3-3 was created using the following criteria:

```
:FilterStart:
:Limit = 3:
:CmpStockID = 3:

:StockNoOfUnits > 1000:
:StockDateOfChange >= #01/01/1996#:
:StockDateOfChange <= #04/30/1996#:
:FilterEnd:
```

FIGURE 3-3

Advanced report result

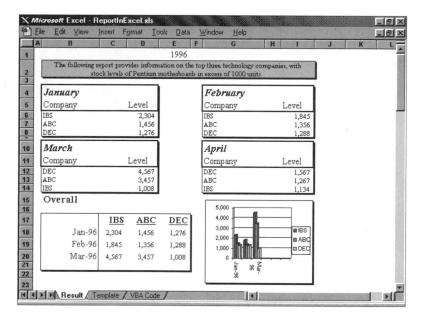

For this example, the code was entered into the report before execution. This example is fully illustrated in the ReportInExcel example later in this chapter. (See page 147.)

COMPONENTS AT OUR DISPOSAL

Visual Basic provides us with the ability to create a range of components that are useful in the reporting process. Figure 3-4 on the next page displays some of the possible roles the various components can play in generating reports with Office 95 and Visual Basic 5. Microsoft Access is included in the business object layer because of the ease with which it can manipulate data objects (for example, a view on Microsoft SQL Server that represents business information). Reports or queries in Access can then be used to extract information from the data object and put it into a range of report output formats, normally Access reports.

Compare the lines between the control layer and the output medium layer in Figure 3-4 and in Figure 3-5. Figure 3-5 represents an improvement in integration between components, the result of common integration of ActiveX components in Office 97.

FIGURE 3-4

Using ActiveX components for reporting in Office 95

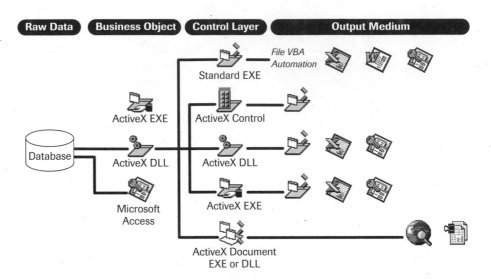

FIGURE 3-5

Using ActiveX components for reporting in Office 97

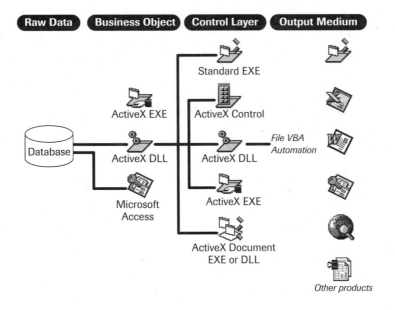

You might wonder why Microsoft Access is excluded from the control layer given that it is just as capable as Visual Basic 5 of producing report results. It's because Access requires considerable memory and computer resources to run even the most basic application. This penalty isn't worth it when only a few Access features will be used in the implementation of a control layer.

ActiveX EXEs and DLLs

ActiveX controls allow developers to assemble software components that encapsulate business logic and data. ActiveX EXE and DLL components are well suited to building business objects because they are designed to provide services (public methods and properties) to a whole range of client components. An application that uses a component's code, by creating objects and calling their properties and methods, is referred to as a *client.*

An ActiveX EXE is classified as an out-of-process component because it runs in its own process space, separate from the application using it. Because an ActiveX EXE executes in its own process space, you can use a single occurrence of an object with many other applications at once, much in the same way that Data Access Objects (DAO) are used throughout a range of applications. The downside is performance degradation caused by the extra overhead undertaken in communicating with external processes. (Look back at Figure 3-5 to see how an ActiveX EXE component interacts with its clients.)

An ActiveX DLL is classified as an in-process component that coexists in the same process space as the application using it. Sharing process space with the application, an ActiveX DLL executes methods and properties more quickly than its EXE counterpart because no extra communication overhead is needed to reference it. ActiveX DLLs do have disadvantages, however; many restrictions are imposed on the way they can be designed and used. (Refer to Visual Basic Books Online for further details.) The real benefit of an ActiveX DLL is in providing common control functionality for its host application. Stripping text out of a string and replacing it with new text is an example of a common method well suited for DLL use. Most of the examples provided later in this chapter use the CommonMethodsAndProperties ActiveX DLL, which provides a range of methods and properties to act as a link between the business object and the actual report generation utilities.

A new feature in Visual Basic 5 is the ability to compile applications to native code, which can result in substantial gains in speed over the interpreted versions of the same application. Unfortunately, this new feature provides little or no improvement for the type of EXE and DLL created in this chapter. The examples here make intensive use of COM, string manipulation, VBA run-time libraries, and inline processes. In all these situations, the code is already optimized by being in a precompiled format, so no benefits can be gained from compiling the code that calls these components.

You can, however, use this new compile feature to enhance the performance of routines that use computationally intensive algorithms as well as those that manipulate arrays or classes set up as data collections. Visual Basic Books Online contains a section called "Compiled vs. Interpreted Applications" that provides some general guidelines regarding native-code compilation.

NOTE

> Visual Basic ActiveX DLLs are not referenced in the same manner as traditional DLLs. The *Dim* statement is used instead of the *Declare* statement.

ActiveX Controls

ActiveX controls, formerly called OLE controls, are standard user interface elements that allow you to assemble forms and dialog boxes rapidly. ActiveX controls also add functionality to Web pages on a company's intranet or on the Internet.

An ActiveX control is an in-process component that runs within the application process. Controls are ideal components to wrap up common reporting functionality. For example, using the RTF file format, you can wrap the open, close, print, and execute actions of a report into a control with a rich text box.

TIP

> When designing controls for the Internet, keep the executable code size as small as possible. This restriction is less relevant for an intranet because of the higher communication bandwidth available.

ActiveX Documents

ActiveX documents are Visual Basic forms that can appear within Internet browser windows. ActiveX documents offer built-in hyperlinks, document view scrolling, and menu capabilities. ActiveX documents can contain insertable objects, such as an ActiveX control. They can also display message boxes and normal Visual Basic forms.

ActiveX documents are powerful components that offer a user document interface to otherwise standard Visual Basic forms. They provide an ideal opportunity for the developer to move reporting onto an intranet, in a format that millions of people are accustomed to, without having to learn an Internet programming language such as Java.

VBA Used in Conjunction with ActiveX Automation

A key aspect of ActiveX is its ability to facilitate application integration. Applications are provided with the mechanisms to define a set of standard interfaces through which one application accesses the services of another.

By using Automation, an ActiveX component or application can provide a public set of commands and functions that other applications can use, in the form of methods and properties. Methods allow a client component to perform an action on an object, such as underline a word. Properties return information about the state of an object, such as whether or not a word is underlined.

ILLUSTRATED EXAMPLES

On the companion CD, you'll find a folder named CHAP03 with subfolders containing all the illustrated examples for this chapter. To run the examples provided, you'll need to have Microsoft Office Professional for Windows 95 or higher and Visual Basic 5 installed on your computer. Follow the instructions provided with each example to ensure that all Registry and object library references that the examples need to work are available. Be sure to run the file CHAP03\RegisterFiles.bat after you create the Business Data Object EXE and the Control Layer DLL.

Creating a Business Data Object

Our objective in this example is to ensure that the database is hidden from the developer and the user. We'll achieve this by encapsulating the physical database data content and structure within a business object with methods and properties. To do this, we need to create an ActiveX EXE, which fronts the Company Stock.mdb sample database. We'll use the resulting ActiveX EXE throughout all the examples in this chapter, demonstrating the reuse of common components and the ease with which a developer or user can learn to utilize a number of methods and properties rather than the underlying data structure and SQL to retrieve the data.

Folder:	CHAP03\Business Object
Dependencies:	Microsoft DAO 3.5 Object Library
Project Name:	CompanyStock.vbp
Instructions:	Load Visual Basic 5, and open the CompanyStock.vbp file. Select Make CompanyStock.exe from the File menu to register the component.

Our first step is to make sure we have the right methods and properties exposed for the developer to use. To do this, we analyze the table relationship diagram in Figure 3-6 and identify the user requests (which are assumed here). I've come up with the following set of public objects for the ActiveX component:

Classes

CompanyDetails (object)

Companies (collection)

Company (data item)

Stocks (collection)

Stock (data item)

CFields (collection)

CField (data item)

Public Methods

BuildCompanyCriteria

BuildCompanyList

GetCompanyList

RemoveCompanyList

GetStockList

Item (companies and stocks)

Public Properties

DataPassFormat

Count (companies and stocks)

Public Constants

csPassByProperties

csPassByVariant

csPassByFile

FIGURE 3-6

Table relationship diagram for Company Stock.mdb

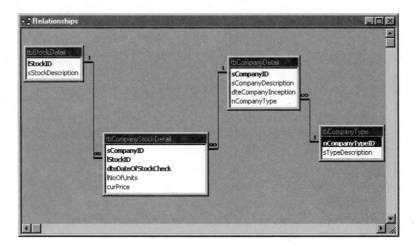

CompanyDetails

This class is the public container for two collection classes: Companies and CFields. Methods provided are broken down into these five categories: *BuildCompanyCriteria*, *BuildCompanyList*, *GetCompanyList*. *RemoveCompanyList*, and the standard *Item* method. The only public properties of this class are *DataPassFormat*, which determines how the data will be retrieved from the ActiveX EXE, and *Count*. The public constants csPassByProperties, csPassByVariant, and csPassByFile define the available retrieval methods.

BuildCompanyCriteria creates a filter for the selection of company and stock details based on the information provided in its parameters. *BuildCompanyList* creates a data list of company and stock details. *GetCompanyList* physically retrieves the data list into the calling component. *RemoveCompanyList* frees up the data list, ready for the next selection. *Item* selects Company or CField data details, based on the key parameter value, and *Count* tells us how many Company or CField details are available.

FIGURE 3-7

Company Stock business object class hierarchy

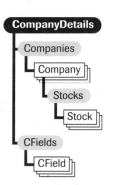

I haven't mentioned the Stocks collection class so far because of the way I've structured the hierarchy of the business object. (See Figure 3-7.) The Stocks class belongs to the Company class, which allows individual stock items to be held in separate Stocks collections per Company class. This logic determines that the Company class is the best location for the *GetStockList* method. No public *RemoveStockList* or *BuildStockList* methods are provided in this example. Again, this was a design decision I made to enforce the structure of the business object. Stocks data items can be added only through the holding object: *CompanyDetails*.

Companies, Company

Companies and Company are the collection class and the data item class for company details, respectively. As mentioned above, the Company class contains further structure information by holding a reference to the Stocks collection.

Stocks, Stock

Stocks and Stock are the collection class and the data item class for stock details, respectively.

CFields, CField

CFields is the collection class and CField is the data item class for the field descriptors associated with the business object. A number of details are stored in the CField object: *ReportFieldName*, *SQLFieldName*, *TableName*, and *TableShortName* provide a common source for mapping information. For example, the report field descriptor :CmpID: is mapped to the sCompanyID field in the physical table tbCompanyDetail in the database. Although this information is made public, it is not generally used by calling components other than to determine the range of report field descriptors available.

Retrieving information from the business object

To retrieve information from the business object, you declare a reference to the ActiveX component. Make sure you include *As New* to ensure the component is loaded and initialized automatically in the declare statement. In the following example, *csCompDet* becomes the object reference to the *CompanyDetails* business object:

```
Private csCompDet As New CompanyDetails
```

The method of data transfer is determined by setting the *DataPassFormat* property. In this example, we use the Properties data pass format provided by the ActiveX component:

```
csCompDet.DataPassFormat = csPassByProperties
```

The *DataPassFormat* property is built into the business object to provide three methods for the client applications to retrieve data: using properties and methods, using a variant array, and using a text file. The different methods are required for performance reasons for low-, medium-, and high-volume data transfer, respectively. (The ReportInGrid example on the CD illustrates these techniques in greater detail.)

To build a list of company details, we provide our criteria through optional parameters. Here we limit the number of company details returned to *txtNoOfItems* and to the criteria selected on the company description in the text field *txtCriteria(1)*:

```
csCompDet.BuildCompanyList _
    (Limit:=txtNoOfItems, CompanyDescription:=txtCriteria(1))
```

And finally, we retrieve the result by using the *Count* property on the Companies collection to retrieve the company description:

```
For nPos = 1 To csCompDet.Companies.Count
    griDisplay.AddItem _
    csCompDet.Companies.Item(nPos).Description
Next nPos
```

Compare this approach with the following code, which demonstrates the level
of coding detail required from the developer using the same example but
accessing the database directly rather than through an object. The developer
needs to know the following additional details: location and name of the database; how to open the database; names of the physical table and the fields; how
to construct the SQL statement; and how to open a recordset and monitor for
the end of the file.

```
Dim wsDefault As Workspace
Dim db       As Database
Dim rs       As Recordset
Dim sSQL     As String

Set wsDefault = CreateWorkspace("", "admin", "", dbUseJet)
Set db = wsDefault.OpenDatabase("Company Stock.mdb")

sSQL = ""
sSQL = sSQL & "Select DistinctRow "
sSQL = sSQL & "Top " & txtNoOfItems & "sCompanyDescription "
sSQL = sSQL & "From tbCompanyDetail "
sSQL = sSQL & "Where sCompanyDescription " & txtCriteria(1)

set rs = dbDatabase.OpenRecordSet(sSQL, dbOpenSnapshot)
If rs.RecordCount > 0 Then
    rs.MoveFirst
    Do Until rs.Eof
        griDisplay.AddItem rs!sCompanyDescription
        rs.MoveNext
    Loop
End If
rs.Close
Set rs = Nothing
:
```

Creating the *Company Stock* business object (ActiveX EXE)

Having identified the public objects required, we now need to set up a Visual
Basic project to implement them. When developing ActiveX EXE components,
I find it easier to define and code the object in a layered approach from top to
bottom, then bottom to top, adding detail each time I iterate through the cycle.
Adopting this technique, you'd create the business object in the following
manner.

Define the top-level business entity within the business object. In this case, it's Company Details. I create a class named CompanyDetails (plural, because it can contain many different company details). This class acts as the primary public interface and will hold the structure of the object.

Work out your key data components, and add two classes for each data component. The first class holds the data item, and the other acts as a collection for the first, allowing for the addition of more than one data item. In this example, I add six classes: Company, Companies, Stock, Stocks, CField, and CFields. It is good practice to name the collection class in the plural form of the data item class because this is the de facto standard Microsoft uses.

Now define the structure of the object from the structure in Figure 3-7 on page 107. I adopt a hierarchical class approach because a company rather than the set of companies owns stock. The Company class has a public reference to the Stocks class. Stocks contains a private collection of the Stock class. The Companies class contains a private collection of the Company class. The CField class contains a private collection of the CField class, and the CompanyDetails class has a public reference to the Companies and CFields classes. To accomplish this hierarchy, the following code is added to each class Declaration section:

Class	Declaration Details
CompanyDetails	`Public Companies As New Companies` `Public Fields As New CFields`
Companies	`Private colCompany As New Collection`
Company	`Public Stocks As New Stocks`
Stocks	`Private colStock As New Collection`
Stock	(Nothing added)
CFields	`Private colField As New Collection`
CField	(Nothing added)

We now consider how to create instances of the classes. This is easy to do because the only class that the user can create is the top level of the hierarchy, CompanyDetails, which we set to GlobalSingleUse. The other classes are set to PublicNotCreatable. This ensures that a separate instance of the *CompanyDetails* object is created each time it is used. The other classes are visible to the developer but cannot be created independently of the *CompanyDetails* object.

Let's now look at the public methods and properties in each class by working our way back up the class structure, starting with CField:

Class	Properties	Methods
CField	SQLFieldName ReportFieldName, TableName, TableShortName	
Stock	ID, DateOfChange, Description, NoOfUnits, Price	
Company	ID, Description, InceptionDate, Category	GetStockList
CFields	Count	Item
Stocks	Count	Item
Companies	Count	Item
CompanyDetails	DataPassFormat	BuildCompanyCriteria, BuildCompanyList, GetCompanyList, RemoveCompanyList

In the collection classes CFields, Stocks, and Companies, the *Add*, *Remove*, and *RemoveAll* methods are restricted to use within the project by the *Friend* statement. This is an intentional design feature to ensure that items can be added or removed only by the business object rather than by the calling applications, which can lead to unpredictable results. The *Friend* statement is ideal for this purpose because it ensures that a function is global to the object functions and subroutines but hidden from the public interface for the object.

All that is left now is to define the public properties. The *DataPassFormat* property allows the object to pass information back to the caller in a number of different formats. In the following code (found on the companion CD in CompanyDetails.cls), this property has been implemented using *Property Get* and *Property Let* procedures, with a predefined range of values in the form of global constants:

```
' The three methods for passing data
' Place this code in the Declaration section of
' the CompanyDetails class.
```

```
' We can now refer to related constant values using a single name by
' grouping them in an enumerator; we can expose them publicly in type
' libraries.
Public Enum Constants
    csPassByProperties = 1
    csPassByVariant = 2
    csPassByFile = 3
End Enum

' Return the current setting.
Public Property Get DataPassFormat()
    DataPassFormat = nPassByProperties
End Property

' Validate and set the data pass format.
Public Property Let DataPassFormat(ByVal Method As Variant)
    If Method <> csPassByProperties And _
        Method <> csPassByVariant And _
        Method <> csPassByFile Then
        Err.Raise vbObjectError + 1, _
        "CompanyStock.CompanyDetails", "Invalid Method"
    Else
        nPassByProperties = CInt(Method)
    End If

End Property
```

The last important point is to ensure that you have terminated a class in a structured fashion. Never use an *End* statement, and always close all references to objects. In the following code, notice that all database objects and collections items are closed or removed before termination:

```
' Close all references and objects.
Private Sub Class_Terminate()
    On Error Resume Next
    Companies.RemoveAll
    Set Companies = Nothing
    Set dbDatabase = Nothing
    Set wsDefault = Nothing
End Sub
```

TIP

When developing ActiveX servers, use the project group capabilities of Visual Basic 5 for testing. Once the first project is set up, add another project by selecting Add Project from the File menu. Remember to set the second project, your test harness, as the start-up project.

The rest of the coding is straightforward. Pertinent methods are listed in Table 3-5.

TABLE 3-5

ADDITIONAL METHODS OF THE BUSINESS OBJECT

Method	Description
BuildPortionOfCriteria	Extracts information out of the criteria string.
InsertItemIntoCriteria	Adds criteria information to an SQL string.
LoadCompanyList	Executes the SQL and loads the data into the classes.
BuildCompanyList	Creates the SQL needed. The parameters are all passed as string arrays, held in variants, allowing us to determine whether a field descriptor has been used more than once.
GetCompanyList	Illustrates three methods of passing information to the calling program. The ReportInGrid example (see page 129) shows the timing differences between the different methods.

Creating the Control Layer

The objective of this example is to ensure that the common code we need for all our examples is encapsulated into classes with public methods and properties. The reason for this encapsulation is to provide the developer with the ability to easily manipulate both the business object and the reporting tool.

Folder:	CHAP03\Common Utilities
Dependencies:	Microsoft Excel 5.0 Object Library
Project Name:	VBActiveXDLL.vbp
Instructions:	Load Visual Basic 5, and open the VBActiveXDLL.vbp file. Select Make VBActiveXDLL.dll from the File menu to register the component.

You need to be aware of the restrictions that are placed on ActiveX DLL and EXE development. In the examples provided, I have split the functionality in the control layer into two discrete objects: an add-in class module to handle RTF object manipulation and an ActiveX DLL for Word and Excel. The reason for this split has to do with one of the "evils" of OLE programming: you should not pass references to private objects to an external component. In a number of the examples, a rich text box control is manipulated by the common methods and properties. The rich text box control is an ActiveX control, private to the Visual Basic form in which it is contained. It is poor programming practice to pass the reference to the control to an ActiveX DLL because the control is not designed for external use and the DLL could potentially crash your system if the form were unloaded while the DLL held a reference to the control.

Two classes are created for this example, with almost identical code. The first, VBCommonMethodsAndProperties.cls, contains the code to control rich text boxes. This class module is used within a Visual Basic project by adding the CLS file in the same way you would any other common file. The CommonMethodsAndProperties.cls class contains code to control Excel and Word. (Both fully support Automation, allowing them to be called from external ActiveX components.) In this case, we wrap the class in a DLL named VBActiveXDLL.dll.

Implementing a class module within Visual Basic is important because it ensures that the parent application can control error handling and housekeeping, thus preventing the problems associated with a DLL in an inconsistent state.

Creating a control layer object (ActiveX DLL and class module)

We first identify what common code will be useful when dealing with the business object and reporting tools. In this example, I've chosen the *OutputMedium* property and the methods described in Table 3-6. The developer can set the

TABLE 3-6   METHODS IN THE ACTIVEX DLL

Method	Description
Report Component Methods	
OpenOutputMedium	Automatically opens the report component and provides the developer with a reference to the report component. Some of the components do not need to be opened; for example, a rich text box preexists on a form.
PrepareOutputMedium	Prepares the report component for data population.
PopulateCell	Populates a predefined cell with data. A cell in this example references a descriptor in an object that will be replaced with data.
DeleteRow	Removes a row within a report component.
InsertCopyRow	Duplicates a row within a report component.
Business Object Methods	
ExtractCriteria	Extracts text from the report component that contains the report criteria.
StripData	Extracts data from the variant that holds data delimited by control characters.

OutputMedium property to indicate which report component will be used. In this example, we have three possibilities: Word, Excel, and rich text box.

Using the *OutputMedium* property and these methods, a developer can create detailed reports without having detailed knowledge of the business object or the report component being used. The following code uses the control layer object to produce a report in Microsoft Excel.

```
Sub Example()
' Set up the variables required; objOutput is a global object.

Dim cmUtils    As New CommonMethodsAndProperties
Dim csCompDet As New CompanyDetails
Dim vFrom      As Variant
Dim vList      As Variant
Dim nPos       As Integer

' Indicate that Excel should be used, with a particular template.
    cmUtils.OutputMedium = cmToExcel
    cmUtils.OpenOutputMedium objOutput, "Template.xlt"

' Grab any criteria held within the template.
    vFrom = cmUtils.ExtractCriteria(objOutput, _
    ":FilterStart:", ":FilterEnd:")

' Pass this on to the business object to build the criteria.
    csCompDet.BuildCompanyCriteria vFrom, _
    vNoOfItems, vCompanyID, vCompanyDescription, _
    vCompanyInceptionDate, vCompanyCategory

' Tell the business object to build the result set.
    csCompDet.BuildCompanyList Limit:=vNoOfItems, _
    CompanyID:=vCompanyID,_
    CompanyDescription:=vCompanyDescription, _
    CompanyInceptionDate:=vCompanyInceptionDate, _
    CompanyCategory:=vCompanyCategory

' Get the result set.
    vList = csCompDet.GetCompanyList

' Prepare Excel for the data load.
    cmUtils.PrepareOutputMedium objOutput

' Loop through all company details, and populate the cells.
    For nPos = 1 To UBound(vList, 1)
        cmUtils.InsertCopyRow objOutput, ":CmpID:"
```

>>

```
        cmUtils.PopulateCell objOutput, ":CmpDesc:", "" & _
            cmUtils.StripData(vList(nPos), 2, Chr(9))
        ⋮
    Next nPos

' Delete the remaining row, a result of the InsertCopyRow method.
    cmUtils.DeleteRow objOutput, ":CmpID:"

' Now prepare Excel for viewing the result.
    cmUtils.PrepareOutputMedium objOutput

End Sub
```

The control layer simplifies the task considerably for the developer, especially when dealing with products that don't have common object structures or code syntax, as the following code (used to find a string) demonstrates:

Rich Text Box

```
obj.SelStart = 0
obj.SelLength = 0
vFoundValue = obj.Find(striFind)
```

Microsoft Excel

```
obj.Range("A1").Activate
vFoundValue = obj.Cells.Find(What:= striFind)
```

Microsoft Word

```
obj.StartOfDocument
obj.EditFind striFind
```

It is far easier for the developer to remember one syntax rather than all three of these. For example, use *v = cs.Find Text:=striFind*, where the *cs* references the common ActiveX DLL containing the *Find* property.

Because VBCommonMethodsAndProperties.cls and CommonMethodsAndProperties.cls are similar in content, I concentrate on the latter, which is wrapped into an ActiveX DLL project. The project consists only of the CommonMethodsAndProperties class, which is set to GlobalMultiUse to ensure that we have only one DLL in existence for the application using it.

In the Declaration section, I set up two public properties, using *Public* and *Enum* to reference the type of report object we're working with. I use *nOutputMedium* with the *Property Get* and *Property Let* routines to hold the current report type. The *Class_Initialize* routine ensures that the Excel report type is the default.

```
Option Explicit

Private nOutputMedium As Integer

Public Enum Constants
    cmToWord = 1           ' Produce output in Word.
    cmToExcel = 2          ' Produce output in Excel.
End Enum

Private Sub Class_Initialize()
    OutputMedium = cmToExcel
End Sub

Public Property Get OutputMedium()
    OutputMedium = nOutputMedium
End Property

Public Property Let OutputMedium(ByVal Method As Variant)
    nOutputMedium = CInt(Method)
End Property
```

The *OpenOutputMedium* method activates a user-selected object, in this case
Word or Excel. In the Word section of the code, no error trap is required
around the opening of a document because only one instance of Word.basic
for Word 6/7 can exist at any one time. If no instance exists, one is automatically created, ensuring that no further checks are necessary to see whether we
need to create the object.

```
Sub OpenOutputMedium(obj As Object, _
    Optional sFileName As String)

    Select Case OutputMedium
        Case cmToWord
            If sFileName <> "" Then
                Set obj = CreateObject("Word.basic")
                obj.Fileopen sFileName
            Else
                Set obj = CreateObject("Word.basic")
            End If
        Case cmToExcel
            On Error Resume Next
            Set obj = GetObject(, "Excel.application")
            If Err > 0 Then
                Set obj = CreateObject("Excel.application")
            End If
            Err.Clear
```

```
        On Error GoTo 0

        If sFileName <> "" Then
            obj.Workbooks.Open filename:=sFileName
        End If
    End Select
End Sub
```

The *PrepareOutputMedium* routine is necessary to help with performance problems. It toggles the report object window between minimum (or as small as is feasible) and maximum states to avoid excessive screen refresh.

```
Public Static Sub PrepareOutputMedium(obj As Object)

Dim blnOnOff As Boolean

    blnOnOff = Not blnOnOff ' Toggle true/false
    Select Case OutputMedium
        Case cmToWord
            If blnOnOff = False Then
                obj.DocMaximize
                obj.StartOfDocument
            Else
                ' We must not minimize the window because we will
                ' lose focus to it.
                If obj.DocMaximize() Or obj.DocMinimize() Then
                    obj.DocRestore
                End If
                ' Make 1/20 of the application size to help keep
                ' screen refreshes of the active document to a
                ' minimum. An error would occur if
                ' Word had the document minimized.
                obj.DocSize (Val(obj.AppInfo$(6)) * _
                0.05), Val(obj.AppInfo$(7) * 0.05)
            End If

        Case cmToExcel
            If blnOnOff = False Then
                obj.ActiveWindow.WindowState = xlMaximized
                obj.Range("A1").Activate
            Else
                obj.ActiveWindow.WindowState = xlMinimized
            End If
    End Select

End Sub
```

The *InsertCopyRow* routine is used to copy a row that is identified by the contents of *striFind*. This routine provides us with a useful technique for copying the style of a row while preserving the original row, which will be populated with data. In the Word section of the *Case* statement, I've checked whether or not a table is being used. This is necessary because the statements to copy a row in a table are different from those to copy to a standard line of text.

```vb
Public Sub InsertCopyRow(obj As Object, striFind As String)

Dim nFoundPos As Integer

    Select Case OutputMedium

        Case cmToWord
            obj.StartOfDocument
            obj.EditFind striFind
            nFoundPos = obj.GetSelStartPos()

            ' Find out whether we are in a table.
            On Error Resume Next
            obj.TableSelectTable
            If Err > 0 Then
                ' No - copy line.
                obj.EndOfLine 1
                obj.EditCopy
                obj.EndOfLine
                obj.InsertPara
            Else
                ' Yes - reset selection point.
                obj.SetSelRange nFoundPos, nFoundPos
                obj.TableSelectRow
                obj.EditCopy
            End If
            obj.EditPaste

        Case cmToExcel
            obj.Range("A1").Activate

            obj.Cells.Find(What:=striFind, _
                After:=obj.ActiveCell, LookIn:=xlFormulas, _
                LookAt:=xlPart, SearchOrder:=xlByRows, _
                SearchDirection:=xlNext, MatchCase:=False).Activate

            nFoundPos = obj.ActiveCell.Row
            obj.Rows(nFoundPos & ":" & nFoundPos).Select
            obj.Selection.Copy
```

>>

119

```
                                    obj.Rows(nFoundPos + 1 & ":" & nFoundPos _
                                        + 1).Select
                                    obj.Selection.Insert Shift:=0
                           End Select

                   End Sub
```

The *DeleteRow* routine deletes the row identified by the contents of *striFind*. Again, we need to check whether or not we are in a table when using Word.

```
Public Sub DeleteRow(obj As Object, striFind As String)

Dim nFoundPos As Integer

    Select Case OutputMedium
        Case cmToWord
            obj.StartOfDocument
            obj.EditFind striFind
            nFoundPos = obj.GetSelStartPos()

            ' Find out whether we are in a table.
            On Error Resume Next
            obj.TableSelectTable
            If Err > 0 Then
                ' No - delete line.
                obj.EndOfLine 1
                obj.EditClear
            Else
                ' Yes - reset selection point.
                obj.SetSelRange nFoundPos, nFoundPos
                obj.TableDeleteRow
            End If
        Case cmToExcel
            obj.Cells.Find(What:=striFind, _
                After:=obj.ActiveCell, LookIn:=xlFormulas, _
                LookAt:=xlPart, SearchOrder:=xlByRows, _
                SearchDirection:=xlNext, _
                MatchCase:=False).Activate

            nFoundPos = obj.ActiveCell.Row
            obj.Rows(nFoundPos & ":" & nFoundPos).Select
            obj.Selection.Delete Shift:=xlUp
    End Select

End Sub
```

The *PopulateCell* routine finds a field descriptor and replaces it with the contents of *striReplace*. Notice that the routine always searches from the start of the object. This ensures that the first occurrence of the field descriptor is detected; keep in mind that there will always be two or more field descriptors while rows are being added to a report. The second occurrence of the descriptor is needed to keep the format and location of the cells that require population while the first copy is overwritten with text.

```
Sub PopulateCell(obj As Object, striFind As String, _
    striReplace As String)

Dim nFoundPos     As Integer
Dim nFoundLength As Integer

    Select Case OutputMedium

        Case cmToWord
            obj.StartOfDocument

            obj.EditFind striFind, _
                striReplace, 0, 0, 0, 0, 0, 0, 1

        Case cmToExcel
            obj.Range("A1").Activate

            obj.Cells.Find(What:=striFind, _
                After:=obj.ActiveCell, LookIn:=xlFormulas, _
                LookAt:=xlPart, SearchOrder:=xlByRows, _
                SearchDirection:=xlNext, MatchCase:=False).Activate

            nFoundPos = obj.ActiveCell.Row
            obj.Rows(nFoundPos & ":" & nFoundPos).Select

            obj.Selection.Replace What:=striFind, _
                Replacement:=striReplace, LookAt:=xlPart, _
                SearchOrder:=xlByRows, MatchCase:=False
    End Select

End Sub
```

The *StripData* routine shown on page 122 is used to extract text between the *niPos − 1* and *niPos* occurrences of the contents of *sCompare*.

```
Public Function StripData(ByVal viData As Variant, _
    ByVal niPos As Integer, ByVal sCompare As String) _
    As Variant

Dim nStartPos As Integer
Dim nEndPos   As Integer
Dim nPos      As Integer

    nEndPos = 0
    For nPos = 1 To niPos
        nStartPos = nEndPos + 1
        nEndPos = InStr(nStartPos + 1, viData, sCompare)
    Next nPos

    If nEndPos = 0 Then nEndPos = Len(viData) + 1

    StripData = Mid(viData, nStartPos, nEndPos - nStartPos)

End Function
```

The *ExtractCriteria* routine extracts text from the report object identified by the contents of *sCriteriaStart* and *sCriteriaEnd*. These fields are used to determine the start and end points of the selection criteria entered by the user. You need to know where the criteria are located because you might have more than one set of criteria per report. The following routine is designed to extract the criteria entered in report output medium:

```
Public Function ExtractCriteria(obj As Object, _
    ByVal sCriteriaStart As String, _
    ByVal sCriteriaEnd As String) As Variant

Dim nFoundStartPos As Integer
Dim nFoundEndPos   As Integer
Dim sRTFText       As String
Dim vTempCriteria  As Variant

    vTempCriteria = ""

    Select Case OutputMedium

        Case cmToWord
            obj.StartOfDocument
            obj.EditFind sCriteriaStart, "", _
                0, 0, 0, 0, 0, 0, 1
            nFoundStartPos = obj.GetSelStartPos()
            obj.StartOfDocument
            obj.EditFind sCriteriaEnd, "", 0, 0, 0, 0, 0, 0, 1
```

```
            nFoundEndPos = obj.GetSelEndPos()
            vTempCriteria = _
                obj.GetText$(nFoundStartPos, nFoundEndPos)

            obj.SetSelRange nFoundStartPos, nFoundEndPos
            obj.EditClear

        Case cmToExcel
            obj.Range("A1").Activate
            obj.Cells.Find(What:=sCriteriaStart, _
                After:=obj.ActiveCell, LookIn:=xlFormulas, _
                LookAt:=xlPart, SearchOrder:=xlByRows, _
                SearchDirection:=xlNext, MatchCase:=False).Activate

            nFoundStartPos = obj.ActiveCell.Row
                obj.Cells.Find(What:=sCriteriaEnd, _
                After:=obj.ActiveCell, LookIn:=xlFormulas, _
                LookAt:=xlPart, SearchOrder:=xlByRows, _
                SearchDirection:=xlNext, MatchCase:=False).Activate

            nFoundEndPos = obj.ActiveCell.Row
                obj.Rows(nFoundStartPos & ":" & _
                nFoundEndPos).Select

            obj.Selection.Copy
            vTempCriteria = Clipboard.GetText
            obj.Selection.Delete Shift:=xlUp
            obj.CutCopyMode = False
            obj.Range("A1").Activate
    End Select

    ' Now remove the Start and Criteria statements
    ' if they still exist.
    If vTempCriteria & "" <> "" Then
        If InStr(vTempCriteria, sCriteriaEnd) > 0 Then
            vTempCriteria = Left(vTempCriteria, _
                Len(vTempCriteria) - Len(sCriteriaEnd))
        End If
        If InStr(vTempCriteria, sCriteriaStart) > 0 Then
            vTempCriteria = Right(vTempCriteria, _
                Len(vTempCriteria) - Len(sCriteriaStart))
        End If
    End If

    ExtractCriteria = vTempCriteria

End Function
```

Creating Reports in Microsoft Access

The report writer provided with Microsoft Access is by far one of the most powerful and flexible report writers around. It does, however, have some major drawbacks:

- A report cannot be separated from an Access MDB file, which means that considerable memory overhead is required to load and display a report.

- The VBA interface contained within Access 97 and Access 7 allows you to manipulate other Access objects through the *Application* object. For example, by using the *OpenReport* method of the Access *DoCmd* object, you can open an Access report from Visual Basic 5. The *DoCmd* object syntax is very similar to the *DoCmd* statement used in earlier versions of Access. This *DoCmd* object could use some reworking for the next release of Access to provide a more intuitive object model with improved functionality. Access 2 has no VBA interface, and communication through the use of Dynamic Data Exchange (DDE) is crude and problematic at best. Also bear in mind that DDE is being phased out, and many applications no longer support this method of communication.

- All reports are based on bound data, which for complex reporting dealing with disparate data can be a problem.

- Creating reports on the fly within another application is difficult, and the user requires detailed knowledge about designing reports in Access to create a report without assistance.

Knowing these limitations helps us to define a suitable environment for using the Access report writer. In situations in which reports are reasonably well defined and have a common data content, it is easy to create a range of reports within an MDB file based on queries. It is possible to execute the reports from within other applications by using the publicly exposed method *OpenReport*, which opens a report in a selected view mode (normal, design, or preview). It also allows you to filter by using a query or an SQL WHERE statement without the word WHERE included.

With the *OpenReport* method, it is a relatively simple task to wrap Access into an environment familiar to the user and to provide a range of user reports that don't require any detailed knowledge of Access to create. You'll also find it relatively easy to build identification into reports so that you can determine which reports should be accessed, depending on your user's requirement. In this example, I make an obvious assumption that all reports available within the Access database will be based on the same query.

Microsoft Access as a report tool

In this example, I use a Visual Basic 5 front end to interrogate a user-selected Microsoft Access database for all the reports it contains. A user can then select a report by name and filter it according to the criteria selected on screen. (See Figure 3-8.) The result is viewable on screen in Print Preview mode or is printable to paper.

Folder:	CHAP03\ReportInAccess
Dependencies:	Company Stock.mdb
	Microsoft Common Dialog Control 5.0
	Microsoft Windows Common Controls 5.0
	Microsoft DAO 3.5 Object Library
Project Name:	ReportsInAccess.vbp
Instructions:	Load Visual Basic 5, and open the ReportsInAccess.vbp file. Press Ctrl+F5 to run.

FIGURE 3-8

Report selection utilizing the Microsoft Access report writer

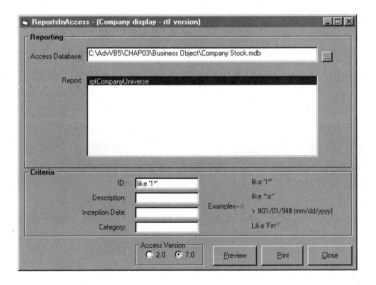

The starting point for this example is in the Company Stock.mdb database, where a query is designed to support the example's report requirement. The qryUniverseOfCompanies query is created with all possible fields available for report use. No filtering is performed within the query because we will use the WHERE clause option of *OpenReport*. (This ensures that the user has total flexibility over what data will be returned in the report.) Two macros are also created: *OpenReport*, which supports the alternative method of opening Access 2 MDB files where no Access VBA object model is available for communication with Access; and *CloseReport*, which exits the Access application when the user closes the report.

The *OpenReport* and *CloseReport* macros contain the following functions and commands:

- *OpenReport*: *Runcode* macro command with the *Function Name* argument set to *CustomOpenReport*, a customized function that reads the command line to determine what parameters the calling program has passed to Access. The parameters for this command include all the parameters used in the *OpenReport* method in VBA.

- *CloseReport*: *Quit* macro command with default settings.

The rptCompanyUniverse report is then designed with two key properties set: *Record Source* set to qryUniverseOfCompanies, and *On Close* set to the macro *CloseReport*. These settings ensure that the right data is being used with the report and that the Access application will terminate when the user quits the report. This feature is important if you consider the problems that can occur if the user has free rein over the database window, which in this example is hidden behind the report.

Now we are left with the task of providing the user with the tools to gain access to this report. Two components are included in ReportsInAccess.vbp: the module modReportsInAccess, which loads the main form on start-up; and the main form frmReportsInAccess, which provides the user with an interface for reporting. Within frmReportsInAccess, a private variable is defined to hold the database filename in which the report resides:

```
Private fm_sDatabaseFileName As String
```

In the *cmdOpenDatabase_Click* procedure, we determine what reports are available in the Access database. Two points are critical:

1. The Reports collection provides details only on open reports.
2. The document container is unsupported in Access VBA for other applications.

Because of these two points, it is impossible to determine what reports are available to access the system MSysObjects table held within the Access database. This table provides details of all objects within an Access database, from tables to reports. Reports are identified by the Type data column having the value

−32764. (To view systems tables with Access, you need to select Options from the Tools menu and enable the View System Objects option. Here is the code in the *cmdOpenDatabase_Click* routine to retrieve the report names into a list box:

```
' Define the variables required to access the database.
Dim ws As Workspace
Dim db As Database
Dim rs As Recordset

' Find the database the user wants.
    dlg.Filter = "Database (*.mdb)|*.mdb"
    dlg.InitDir = App.Path
    dlg.ShowOpen
    If dlg.filename & "" <> "" Then
        fm_sDatabaseFileName = dlg.filename
    End If
    txtDatabase = fm_sDatabaseFileName

    Me.MousePointer = vbHourglass

    ' Make sure that we have a filename to work with.
    If txtDatabase <> "" Then
        lstReports.Clear

        ' Open a Jet workspace, and get the database.
        Set ws = CreateWorkspace("", "Admin", "", dbUseJet)
        Set db = ws.OpenDatabase(fm_sDatabaseFileName)

        ' Read the system table to find all reports.
        Set rs = _
        db.OpenRecordset _
        ("Select Name From MSysObjects " & _
            "Where Type = -32764 Order By Name", _
            dbOpenSnapshot, dbReadOnly)

        ' Load any reports into the list box.
        If rs.RecordCount > 0 Then
            rs.MoveFirst
            Do Until rs.EOF
                lstReports.AddItem rs!Name
                rs.MoveNext
            Loop
            lstReports.ListIndex = 0
        End If
```

>>

```
        ' Close all objects.
        rs.Close
        Set rs = Nothing
        db.Close
        Set db = Nothing
        ws.Close
        Set ws = Nothing
    End If

    Me.MousePointer = vbDefault
```

The code used to activate the report is split into two different methods: the Access 2 method, which fires a *Shell* command to load Access and execute the *OpenReport* macro created earlier to display the report; and the Access VBA method, which uses the *DoCmd.OpenReport* method to display the report. The code to place a report into Print Preview follows:

```
Private Sub cmdPreview_Click()

' Create an Access object.
Dim objAccess As Object

    Me.MousePointer = vbHourglass

    ' Make sure a report is selected.
    If lstReports.ListIndex <> -1 Then

        ' Which Access method has been selected?
        Select Case optAccessVersion(0).Value
          Case True 'Access 2.0
                ' Provide the parameters in string format
                ' delimited by |.
                ' /X executes an Access macro.
                ' /Cmd provides additional string data on the
                ' command line.
                Shell "Msaccess.exe " & fm_sDatabaseFileName _
                    & " /X OpenReport /Cmd " & lstReports & _
                    "|2|" & sBuildWhereClause, vbMaximizedFocus

          Case False ' Access 7/97

                ' Get the Access database application object.
                Set objAccess = _
                    GetObject(fm_sDatabaseFileName)

                ' With the application object, open the report
                ' and maximize it within Access's MDI parent
                ' window.
```

```
With objAccess.Application
        .DoCmd.OpenReport lstReports, acPreview, _
              , sBuildWhereClause

        .DoCmd.Maximize
    End With
    ' Close the object.
    Set objAccess = Nothing
End Select
End If

Me.MousePointer = vbDefault
```

This example provides a simple solution for accessing Access reports from within other component applications. Given the drawbacks mentioned earlier, though, I don't recommend that you attempt to provide too much reporting to your users via the Access report writer.

Creating Reports in Visual Basic

Both grid and rich text box controls are useful for basic reporting and are easy to implement and control. The examples in the following sections demonstrate the difference between fixed- and free-format data selection and report production.

Grid control as a report tool

In this example, data is populated into an unbound grid control. The data selection is based on the user-entered contents of text boxes in the form's predefined Criteria section. Three business object data retrieval methods are included to illustrate the differences in syntax and performance of each method.

Folder:	CHAP03\ReportInGrid
Dependencies:	CompanyStock.exe
	Microsoft Rich TextBox Control 5.0
	Microsoft Common Dialog Control 5.0
	Microsoft Windows Common Controls 5.0
	Microsoft FlexGrid Control 5.0
Project Name:	ReportInGrid.vbp
Instructions:	Ensure that CompanyStock.exe has been registered in the Registry. (Refer to page 105 on creating the EXE.) Load Visual Basic 5, and open the ReportInGrid.vbp file. Press Ctrl+F5 to run. The application will look similar to Figure 3-9 on the next page.

FIGURE 3-9

Standard report using a grid

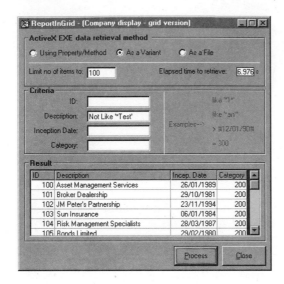

The hardest part of this example is formatting the form, frmReportInGrid, with controls to hold the selection criteria, the method of data retrieval, and the report result (grid). Once you've set these controls up, simply add the lines of code documented in this section for a fully functional Company Details viewer.

In the module modReportInGrid, the routine *Sub Main()* is linked as the start-up object in the ReportInGrid Project Properties dialog box. This routine contains a single line of code to display the form.

In the form frmReportInGrid Declarations section, we add one line of code to create a new instance of the *CompanyDetails* business object:

```
Private csCompDet As New CompanyDetails
```

The *New* statement ensures that the object is created automatically at run time.

In the *Form_Load* event, code is entered to inform the business object of the default method of data retrieval. In the *Form_Unload* event, basic housekeeping is performed to ensure that no trailing reference to the business object is left.

```
Private Sub Form_Load()
    ' Default to the data pass method.
    optCommMethod(csCompDet.DataPassFormat).Value = True
End Sub

Private Sub Form_Unload(Cancel As Integer)
    Set csCompDet = Nothing
End Sub
```

Setting *csCompDet* to *Nothing* doesn't necessarily mean that the object is destroyed. It ensures only that the current reference to the object is removed. Only when the last reference to the object is removed will the object destroy itself.

Now place the following code in the option box event *optCommMethod_Click*:

```
Private Sub optCommMethod_Click(Index As Integer)
    csCompDet.DataPassFormat = Index
End Sub
```

In the *cmdProcess_Click* event, I link the Index value of the option box controls to the methods of passing data: csPassByProperties, csPassByVariant, and csPassByFile.

Apart from closing the form and initializing the grid with the correct number of rows and columns, we only have to add the code to retrieve the company details and to populate the return result into the grid:

```
csCompDet.BuildCompanyList Limit:=txtNoOfItems, _
    CompanyID:=txtCriteria(0), _
    CompanyDescription:=txtCriteria(1), _
    CompanyInceptionDate:=txtCriteria(2), _
    CompanyCategory:=txtCriteria(3)
```

In the code above, the *BuildCompanyList* method is invoked, which in turn builds up the appropriate SQL from the selection criteria parameters passed. This method also executes the SQL and creates the result in memory, with the business object ready for retrieval by the calling application.

Pass by parameter, data retrieval The first method of data retrieval (csPassByProperties) uses the public methods and properties of the *CompanyDetails* object (*csCompDet*):

```
For nPos = 1 To csCompDet.Companies.Count
    griDisplay.AddItem csCompDet.Companies.Item(nPos).ID
Next nPos
```

This format is easy to read and understand. Unfortunately, it is exceptionally slow compared with the other methods, making it impractical to use with high-volume data. The poor performance is a result of the overhead associated with cross-process-boundary communication; the Visual Basic application and the *CompanyDetails* object reside in different processes. Each time the calling application makes a reference to a property or method, the program must communicate (cross boundaries), which requires setting up stack space, pointer references, and communication handshaking. In the preceding code, this would occur for each pass through the loop.

Pass by variant, data retrieval   This method (csPassByVariant) addresses the performance issues in the previous method, and it returns the data as a variant:

```
vList = csCompDet.GetCompanyList
For nPos = 1 To csCompDet.Companies.Count
    griDisplay.AddItem vList(nPos)
Next nPos
```

This method cuts down cross-process-boundary communication significantly. With the *GetCompanyList* method, cross-process-boundary communication is required only once. It's up to you, however, to place the data into the variant and to strip it out at the other end. I've intentionally stored the data in the variant as a single-dimension array with each value containing multiple values delimited by tabs. This type of storage allows us to pass the relevant array value to the grid, which in turn automatically splits the data according to the tabs.

Pass by file, data retrieval   Oddly enough the fastest method (csPassByFile) of the lot, retrieving data from a disk drive, is quicker in some cases than retrieving the data from memory structures. Again, cross-process communication is a factor; here the physical data is transferred to and from the disk from separate processes rather than across a process boundary:

```
nFile = FreeFile
Open csCompDet.GetCompanyList For Input As nFile
Do Until EOF(nFile)
    Input #nFile, sDetail
    griDisplay.AddItem sDetail
Loop
Close nFile
```

This method poses a security risk, however, by creating a public file on the network. It also requires you to trap all file error situations to ensure that the method is stable. For these reasons, I don't recommend this method unless you need to retrieve high volumes of data and it's not practical to hold the information in memory.

Rich text box control as a report tool

In this example, we progress from using a grid to a rich text box, which allows us greater flexibility in criteria selection and report formatting. This example provides users with the ability to type their criteria requirements within the same object that presents the result. This capability is useful for advanced users who often want to maintain total control over the report.

Folder:	CHAP03\ReportInRichTextBox
Dependencies:	CompanyStock.exe
	Microsoft Rich TextBox Control 5.0
	Microsoft Common Dialog Control 5.0
	Microsoft Windows Common Controls 5.0
	Microsoft FlexGrid Control 5.0
	VBCommonMethodsAndProperties class
Project Name:	ReportInRichTextBox.vbp
Instructions:	Ensure that CompanyStock.exe has been registered in the Registry. Load Visual Basic 5, and open the ReportInRichTextBox.vbp file. Press Ctrl+F5 to run.

The interface and the reporting medium here are totally different from the preceding example, and yet the code is very similar. This is possible because we have used the components approach. This approach allows all parts of the reporting process to be independent of each other. Making minor code changes in specific code components can completely change the look and functionality of a program. In this example, we're no longer using a fixed-selection screen or a grid. The project consists of three objects:

- The form frmReportInRichTextBox, which contains a rich text box and three buttons.

- The module modReportInRichTextBox, which includes the *Sub Main()* routine that displays the form.

- The class module VBComMethAndProp (discussed earlier in the "Creating the Control Layer" section), which contains all the methods and properties needed to control the rich text box control.

In the frmReportInRichTextBox Declarations section, we add constants to hold information about the report template to use, two lines of code to create a new instance of the *CompanyDetails* business object, and an in-process instance of the *VBComMethAndProp* object:

```
Private Const sRtfTemplate = "Company List Template"
Private Const sRtfResult = "rtfResult"
Private Const sRtfExtension = ".rtf"

Private cmvbUtils As New VBComMethAndProp
Private csCompDet As New CompanyDetails
```

In the *Form_Load* event, we enter code to inform the business object of the default method of data retrieval and code to let the common utilities know what control is being used for reporting. In the *Form_Unload* event, basic housekeeping is performed to ensure that no trailing reference to either of the objects remains.

```
Private Sub Form_Load()
    ' Use only the pass by variant method.
    csCompDet.DataPassFormat = csPassByVariant

    ' Use rich text box utilities.
    cmvbUtils.OutputMedium = cmvbToRtfControl

    ' Load the example template.
    cmdReload_Click
End Sub

Private Sub Form_Unload(Cancel As Integer)
    Set csCompDet = Nothing
    Set cmvbUtils = Nothing
End Sub
```

The command button cmdReload is used to load a template and ensure that the user never overwrites it. The following code is placed in the Click event of cmdReload:

```
Private Sub cmdReload_Click()

Dim sFileName As String
Dim nPos      As Integer

' Open the template, and immediately save it as a result file.
    cmvbUtils.OpenOutputMedium rtfDisplay, App.Path & "\" & _
        sRtfTemplate & sRtfExtension
    sFileName = App.Path & "\" & sRtfResult & sRtfExtension

    nPos = 1
    On Error Resume Next
    Kill sFileName
    Do Until Err.Number = nErrorNone Or Err.Number = _
        nErrorFileNotFound
        sFileName = App.Path & "\" & sRtfResult & nPos & _
            sRtfExtension
        nPos = nPos + 1
        Kill sFileName ' Try again.
    Loop
```

```
On Error GoTo 0
rtfDisplay.SaveFile sFileName, rtfRTF

End Sub
```

In the *cmdProcess_Click* event, include code to extract the user-entered criteria and to populate the return result:

```
' Call the common method to extract the criteria.
sFrom = cmvbUtils.ExtractCriteria(rtfDisplay, ":FilterStart:", _
    ":FilterEnd:")

' Build the criteria, and place it into the variant parameters.
csCompDet.BuildCompanyCriteria sFrom, _
    vNoOfItems, _
    vCompanyID, _
    vCompanyDescription, _
    vCompanyInceptionDate, _
    vCompanyCategory, v1, v2, v3, v4, v5

' Build the company list from the criteria given.
csCompDet.BuildCompanyList Limit:=vNoOfItems, _
    CompanyID:=vCompanyID, _
    CompanyDescription:=vCompanyDescription, _
    CompanyInceptionDate:=vCompanyInceptionDate, _
    CompanyCategory:=vCompanyCategory

' Retrieve the result into a variant array.
vList = csCompDet.GetCompanyList
```

Now that the result is available, we add more code to the *cmdProcess_Click* event to prepare and populate the rich text box with the result.

```
' Prepare the rich text box.
cmvbUtils.PrepareOutputMedium rtfDisplay

' Loop through the result set, and populate each row with data.
For nPos = 1 To UBound(vList, 1)
    ' Copy the row containing the field descriptor CmpID.
    cmvbUtils.InsertCopyRow rtfDisplay, ":CmpID:"

    ' Populate the fields if they exist.
    cmvbUtils.PopulateCell rtfDisplay, ":CmpID:", "" & _
        cmvbUtils.StripData(vList(nPos), 1, Chr(9))
' And so on
:
Next nPos
```

>>

```
' We're left with one too many rows; delete it.
cmvbUtils.DeleteRow rtfDisplay, ":CmpID:"

' Show the result.
cmvbUtils.PrepareOutputMedium rtfDisplay
```

Figure 3-10 shows the example in action. The user now has the ability to modify the report (a copy of the template) in any number of ways, such as altering the criteria, moving or deleting a column, changing the color of a heading, or adding narrative text.

FIGURE 3-10

Report template in rich text box format

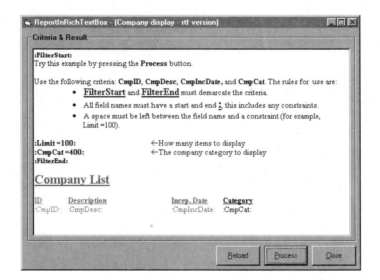

Once the Process button is pressed, the program extracts the criteria, calls the business object to retrieve the data, and then populates the output using the common VBComMethAndProp class. Figure 3-11 shows the result of the report after processing. In the examples used, the criteria section is removed to provide a clearer result. You don't have to remove it; in fact, in many cases you should leave it so you know what selection was used to produce a specific result.

Rich text control wrapped into an ActiveX control for reporting

In this example, we attempt to simplify the developer's task further by encapsulating the previous example into an ActiveX control, with a number of buttons providing load, save, execute, and print functionality.

FIGURE 3-11

*Report
result after
execution*

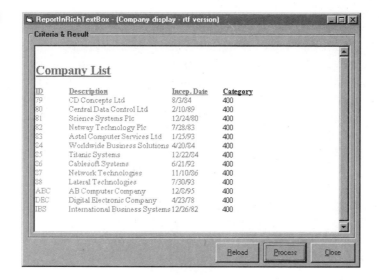

Folder:	CHAP03\ReportInOCXControl
Dependencies:	CompanyStock.exe
	Microsoft Rich TextBox Control 5.0
	Microsoft Common Dialog Control 5.0
	Microsoft Windows Common Controls 5.0
	Microsoft Windows Common Controls-2 5.0
	Microsoft Picture Clip Control 5.0
	Microsoft FlexGrid Control 5.0
	VBCommonMethodsAndProperties class
Project Name:	ReportInOcxControl.vbg
Instructions:	Ensure that CompanyStock.exe has been registered in the Registry. Load Visual Basic 5, and open the ReportInOcxControl.vbp file. Press Ctrl+F5 to run.

Before developing ActiveX controls, you must be sure you know the content and functionality of each control you plan to use. The easiest way to test an ActiveX control is by setting up a group project with the control and test code in separate projects, as shown in Figure 3-12 on the following page. It's a different story when a control has already been released to other developers in OCX format. Every subsequent iteration of the control will require a developer to rereference a project to the latest version of the control by adding the new control into the control's component bar. (See Figure 3-12.)

NOTE

When a control OCX is modified, the associated CLSID Registry key changes. As a result, the reference in the Visual Basic project to the control becomes invalid; so the next time you try to open the project, you receive a "Cannot load…" error message. The control is then converted to a picture box on the form, and you have to manually add the new version of the control back into the project and onto the form. To avoid these problems, any time you modify a control, it's a good idea to increment the control's version number and store the control under a separate directory while leaving the previous version of the control intact. By doing this, your Visual Basic project can continue to reference the previous version until you're ready to change the reference to the new version, thus saving yourself the problems of error messages and picture boxes.

FIGURE **3-12**

*ActiveX
control under
development*

Component bar   Test code project

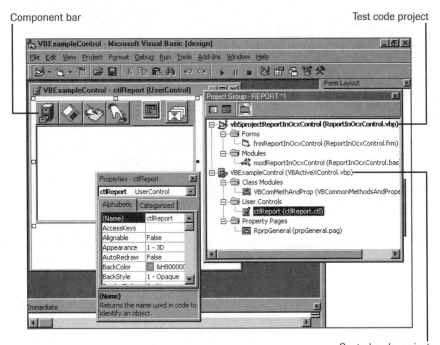

Control code project

The project group ReportInOcxControl.vbg consists of two projects: VBActiveXControl.vbp and ReportInOcxControl.vbp. The VBActiveXControl project creates the ActiveX control, and the ReportInOcxControl project tests the control in design mode.

The VBActiveXControl project consists of three objects: a user control, ctlReport, which contains the previous example wrapped up with an improved interface and enriched functionality; a class module, VBComMethAndProp (Visual Basic Common Methods and Properties), the same module used in the previous example; and a property page, RprpGeneral, which holds the default template. You'll notice that there's no normal module: we don't need one because a user control requires no start-up object.

Only a few pieces of code in this example were not covered in the previous example. One of these is the *UserControl_Resize* event. A developer might want to size the control according to the form used, so it is necessary to ensure that the rich text box embedded inside the user control is kept in proportion to the size of the control. The following code ensures this:

```
' Set the toolbar (tbr) to the top of the form.
tbr.Top = 1

' Set the control to sit below the toolbar.
rtfDisplay.Top = tbr.Height

' Size the height and width of the control to the form.
rtfDisplay.Width = UserControl.Width
rtfDisplay.Height = UserControl.Height - tbr.Height
```

It is useful to call this code from the *UserControl_Initialize* event of the user control to ensure that the control appears in the correct format when first viewed on a form. The Declarations section includes a public variable that provides a link to the property page:

```
Public DefaultTemplate As String
```

This variable is referenced in the *UserControl_Initialize* event with the following line of code:

```
rtfDisplay.filename = DefaultTemplate
```

The property page includes code to monitor whether the value has changed. This information is trapped in the text field holding the default template value and in the two events *PropertyPage_ApplyChanges* and *PropertyPage_SelectionChanged*:

```
Private Sub txtDefaultTemplate_Change()
    Changed = True
End Sub
```

>>

```
Private Sub PropertyPage_ApplyChanges()
    SelectedControls(0).DefaultTemplate = _
        txtDefaultTemplate.Text
End Sub

Private Sub PropertyPage_SelectionChanged()
    txtDefaultTemplate.Text = _
        SelectedControls(0).DefaultTemplate
End Sub
```

The ReportInOcxControl project consists of two objects: a form, named frmReportInOcxControl, which contains the ActiveX control; and a module, modReportInOcxControl, which includes the *Sub Main()* routine that displays the form. The only lines of code required in this example load and unload the form:

```
Sub main()
    frmReportInOcxControl.Show
End Sub

Private Sub cmdClose_Click()
    Unload frmReportInOcxControl
End Sub
```

All the rest is handled internally by the ActiveX control, which provides a tremendous benefit for the developer, who can now reuse the control in a range of projects without needing to know the detail behind it. Figure 3-13 shows the ActiveX control in use.

FIGURE 3-13

ActiveX control embedded in a Visual Basic form

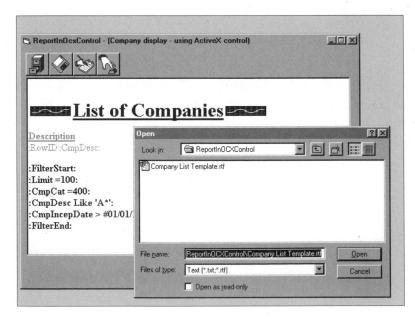

Using Visual Basic Automation with Word and Excel

Word provides a powerful report environment for narrative-based reports. In Word you can insert data in the form of text, tables, and graphs between passages of text, creating a professional-looking report—a feat nearly impossible in standard report writers. The example provided here examines the use of a table, or plain text, within a Word document.

NOTE

> Word 6/7 is not an Automation client, and it provides only limited Automation Server capabilities.

Excel provides a very powerful report environment for grid and calculation-based reports. With Excel you can insert data into cells for manipulation with formulas. Excel is the ultimate grid control, providing full control over every cell and allowing for embedded graphs and other objects. The example provided populates a two-dimensional table of company details.

Pushing data into Word or Excel

This example demonstrates how to use Visual Basic as a controlling application to push data into Word and Excel.

Folder:	CHAP03\ReportInExcelAndWord
Dependencies:	CompanyStock.exe
	VBActiveXDLL.dll
	Microsoft Common Dialog Control 5.0
	Microsoft Windows Common Controls 5.0
Project Name:	ReportInExcelAndWord.vbp
Instructions:	Ensure that CompanyStock.exe and VBActiveXDLL.dll have been registered in the Registry. Load Visual Basic 5, and open the ReportInExcelAndWord.vbp file. Press Ctrl+F5 to run.

This example is an extension of the techniques adopted in the rich text box example. The report output medium is Word and Excel, and the same template techniques are used to allow the user to select or create a range of report results.

The project consists of two objects: a form, frmReportInExcelAndWord, which contains three command buttons and two option buttons (and which controls the activation of Word and Excel with the correct template and the execution of the report); and a module, modReportInExcelAndWord, which includes the *Sub Main()* routine that displays the form.

In the frmReportInExcelAndWord Declarations section, we add constants to hold information about the report template to use:

```
Private Const sDocTemplate = "Company List Template"
Private Const sDocResult = "Result"
Private Const sDocWordExtension = ".doc"
Private Const sDocExcelExtension = ".xls"
Private Const sDocWordTmpltExtension = ".dot"
Private Const sDocExcelTmpltExtension = ".xlt"
```

Two forms of each application's output are used: the standard document format (XLS, DOC) and the template equivalent (XLT, DOT).

Two lines of code create a new instance of the *CompanyDetails* business object and an in-process instance of the *CommonMethodsAndProperties* (ActiveX DLL) object:

```
Private cmUtils    As New CommonMethodsAndProperties
Private csCompDet As New CompanyDetails
```

Two lines of code create a reference to the application object being used and to a variable that indicates which method the user has selected:

```
Private nOutputMedium As Integer
Private objOutput      As Object
```

In the *Form_Load* event, we enter code to inform the business object of the default method of data retrieval and code to ensure that no output medium is selected yet. In the *Form_Unload* event, basic housekeeping is performed to ensure that no trailing reference to the objects remains.

```
Private Sub Form_Load()
    ' Use only the pass by variant method.
    csCompDet.DataPassFormat = csPassByVariant
    nOutputMedium = -1 ' No value
End Sub

Private Sub Form_Unload(Cancel As Integer)
    Set csCompDet = Nothing
    Set cmUtils = Nothing
    Set objOutput = Nothing
End Sub
```

The command button cmdReload is used to load a template and ensure that the user never overwrites it. The following code is placed in the *cmdReload_Click* event to ensure that the correct object is created and the relevant template is loaded and saved as an output result file:

```
Private Sub cmdReload_Click()

Dim nPos      As Integer
Dim sFileName As String

' Which output medium has the user selected?
    Select Case nOutputMedium
        Case cmToWord

' Indicate to the common utils object that Word is selected.
            cmUtils.OutputMedium = cmToWord

' Prepare the object.
            cmUtils.OpenOutputMedium objOutput, App.Path & "\" _
                & sDocTemplate & sDocWordTmpltExtension
            sFileName = App.Path & "\" & sDocResult & _
                sDocWordExtension

' Make sure we have a unique output result file.
            ' See example code on the CD.
            ⋮
            objOutput.FileSaveAs sFileName
            objOutput.AppShow

        Case cmToExcel
' Indicate to the common utils object that Excel is selected.
            cmUtils.OutputMedium = cmToExcel

' Prepare the object.
            cmUtils.OpenOutputMedium objOutput, App.Path & "\" _
                & sDocTemplate & sDocExcelTmpltExtension
            sFileName = App.Path & "\" & sDocResult & _
                sDocExcelExtension

' Make sure we have a unique output result file.
            ' See example code on the CD.
            ⋮
            objOutput.activeworkbook.SaveAs sFileName
            objOutput.application.Visible = True

' No output method is active; report error.
        Case Else
            MsgBox "Please select an output medium"
    End Select
End Sub
```

Figure 3-14 and Figure 3-15 show the format of the output result file once the Activate button (cmdReload) is clicked.

FIGURE 3-14

Word template used by Visual Basic application

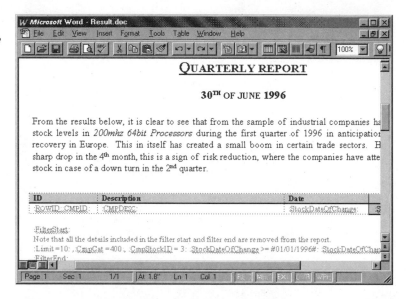

FIGURE 3-15

Excel template used by Visual Basic application

The command button cmdProcess is used to populate the active object document with data extracted from the business object. The criteria for the report reside within the object document and are retrieved in the same fashion as in the earlier rich text box example. Here's a sample of the code:

```
    ⋮
' Extract the criteria from the object document.
    vFrom = cmUtils.ExtractCriteria(objOutput, _
        ":FilterStart:", ":FilterEnd:")
    csCompDet.BuildCompanyCriteria vFrom, v1, v2, v3, v4, _
        v5, v6, v7, v8, v9, v10

    csCompDet.BuildCompanyList v1, v2, v3, v4, v5, v6, _
    v7, v8, v9, v10

' Get the result back into a variant.
    vCompanyList = csCompDet.GetCompanyList

' Prepare the output medium for data population.
    cmUtils.PrepareOutputMedium objOutput

' Loop through the return variant array, and populate the data.
    On Error Resume Next
    For nPos = 1 To UBound(vCompanyList, 1)
        cmUtils.InsertCopyRow objOutput, ":RowID:"
        cmUtils.PopulateCell objOutput, ":RowID:", ""

        vStockList = csCompDet.Companies.Item(nPos).GetStockList

        cmUtils.PopulateCell objOutput, ":CmpID:", "" & _
            cmUtils.StripData(vCompanyList(nPos), 1, Chr(9))
        ' And so on
        ⋮
        For nPos1 = 1 To UBound(vStockList, 1)
            If nPos1 > 1 Then
                cmUtils.InsertCopyRow objOutput, ":RowID:"
                cmUtils.PopulateCell objOutput, ":RowID:", ""
                cmUtils.PopulateCell objOutput, ":CmpID:", ""
                ' And so on
                ⋮
        Next nPos1
    Next nPos

' A trailing row is left; remove it.
    cmUtils.DeleteRow objOutput, ":RowID:"
    On Error GoTo 0

' Display the result.
    cmUtils.PrepareOutputMedium objOutput
    ⋮
```

Figure 3-16 shows the format of the output result file in Word once the Process button (cmdProcess) is clicked. The Excel worksheet appears as in Figure 3-17.

FIGURE 3-16

Word report result

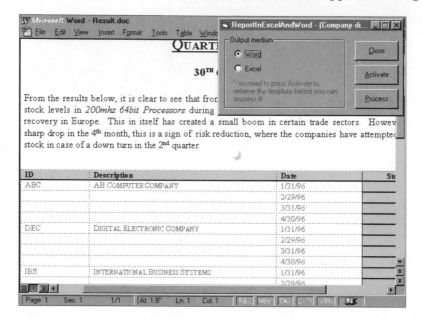

FIGURE 3-17

Excel report result

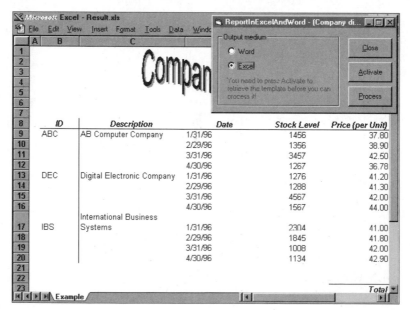

Reporting with Microsoft Excel VBA

This example demonstrates the preferred technique for data population into Microsoft Excel. Data is pulled rather than pushed into Excel using Excel VBA code linked to a toolbar. This example is considerably faster than the previous example because the control object layer resides inside the Excel process, removing the need for some of the cross-process-boundary communication.

Folder:	CHAP03\ReportInExcel
Dependencies:	CompanyStock.exe
	VBActiveXDLL.dll
Project Name:	ReportInExcel.xls (also in ReportInExcel '97.xls)
Instructions:	Ensure that the CompanyStock.exe and VBActiveXDLL.dll have been registered in the Registry. Load Excel, and open the ReportInExcel.xls file, shown in Figure 3-18. Follow the instructions given.

FIGURE 3-18

Reporting from within Excel using a toolbar

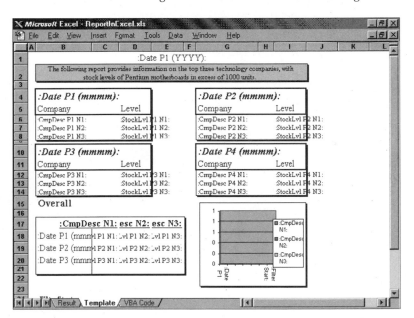

A workbook is created, with a worksheet named Template and a module named VBA Code that contains a routine named *Process.* The module would normally be hidden from the user; for this example, however, we'll leave it visible.

> When ReportInExcel.xls is opened in Excel 97, the VBA Code module is not visible. All the code that had been in that module is now available in the VBA Editor. (Select Visual Basic Editor from the Macro submenu of the Tools menu.)

The worksheet is a standard template example, in the same format as used in the previous examples. The module consists of code similar to that used in the earlier Word and Excel example but with a number of key differences.

Excel 5/7 can reference the Visual Basic objects only as follows:

```
Set cmUtils = _
    CreateObject("VBActiveXDLL.CommonMethodsAndProperties")
Set csComDet = CreateObject("CompanyStock.CompanyDetails")
⋮
csComDet.DataPassFormat = 2
```

Notice that no *Dim* statement is used to create an instance of the object. This is because of the limited support within Excel 5/7 for Visual Basic–created objects and the lack of a New command. The *CreateObject* function describes the Visual Basic ActiveX object being referenced in the following format: VBProjectEXEName.ClassName.

Another difference is the lack of support in Excel 5/7 for named constants: csPassByVariant has to be replaced with its value of 2.

Excel 97 resolves these issues. You can simply refer to the objects as shown here:

```
Private cmUtils   As New CommonMethodsAndProperties
Private csCompDet As New CompanyDetails
⋮
csComDet.DataPassFormat = csPassByVariant
```

You also need to make some minor amendments to ensure that the right worksheet is selected:

```
⋮
' Delete any previous result sheet.
    Application.DisplayAlerts = False
    On Error Resume Next
    Sheets("Result").Select
    If Err = 0 Then
        ActiveWindow.SelectedSheets.Delete
    End If
    On Error GoTo 0
    Application.DisplayAlerts = True
```

```
' Now copy the template to a result sheet.
   Sheets("Template").Select
   ActiveSheet.Copy Before:=Sheets(1)
   sSheetName = ActiveSheet.Name
   Sheets(sSheetName).Select
   ActiveSheet.Name = "Result"
⋮
```

As with the previous example, the code used to access the business object remains the same. The major difference in this example is in the way we manipulate the output data. As mentioned before, Excel provides a powerful environment for reporting, and I've used some of its capabilities to illustrate this.

A graph is embedded with predefined named ranges (for example, Template!POne, Template!PTwo) so all that is required to display the graph is the population of the relevant cells. Two extra routines are included with the VBA code to handle specific tasks: *PopulateDates(vCompanyList)* reformats all :Date...: descriptors into the relevant data and display format, and *PopulateCompanies(vCompanyList)* populates all the :CmpDesc...: and :StockLvl...: descriptors with the relevant data.

PopulateDates contains search and replace code that is easily implemented in Excel.

```
' Process all dates by taking the first available date range for
' the first company.

   ' Populate into the date array.
   vStockList = csComDet.Companies.Item(1).GetStockList

   ReDim adData(1 To UBound(vStockList, 1))
   For nPos = 1 To UBound(vStockList, 1)
       adData(nPos) = _
       CDbl(Format(cmUtils.StripData(vStockList(nPos), _
           3, Chr(9)), "0"))
   Next nPos

   Range("A1").Select

   On Error Resume Next
   Err = 0
   Do Until Err <> 0
       Cells.Find(What:=":Date*:", After:=ActiveCell, _
           LookIn:=xlFormulas, LookAt:=xlPart, _
           SearchOrder:=xlByRows, _
           SearchDirection:=xlNext, _
           MatchCase:=False).Activate
```

```
                            vValue = ActiveCell.Value

                            ' Once  the descriptor is found, find out its details.
                            nStartPos = InStr(vValue, ":Date")
                            nEndPos = InStr(nStartPos + 1, vValue, ":")
                            vOldValue = Mid$(vValue, nStartPos, nEndPos)

                            ' Holds the period offset
                            nPos = Val(Mid$(vOldValue, 8, 1))

                            ' Holds the date format
                            sFormat = Mid$(vOldValue, 11)
                            sFormat = Left$(sFormat, Len(sFormat) - 2)

                            ' If there is no offset, use today's date.
                            If nPos = 0 Then
                                    dOutDate = Now()
                                Else
                                    dOutDate = adData(nPos)
                            End If

                            ' Preserve the rest of cell's contents
                            ' when populating back.
                            ActiveCell.Value = Mid$(vValue, 1, nStartPos - 1) & _
                                Format(CVDate(dOutDate), sFormat) & _
                                Mid$(vValue, nEndPos + 1)

                            Cells.FindNext(After:=ActiveCell).Activate
                        Loop
```

PopulateCompanies contains sort, search, and replace code, which is easy to implement in Excel:

```
    ' Constant holding raw data start row
    nPos2 = RawDataRowStart

    ' Loop through all companies.
    For nPos = 1 To UBound(viCompanyList, 1)

        ' Get this company's stock list.
        vStockList = csComDet.Companies.Item(nPos).GetStockList

        ' Loop through all stock details, and populate the raw data
        ' area.
        For nPos1 = 1 To UBound(vStockList, 1)
            Cells(nPos2, 1).Value = _
                cmUtils.StripData(viCompanyList(nPos), 1, Chr(9))
```

```
            ' And so on
        ⋮
        nPos2 = nPos2 + 1
    Next nPos1

Next nPos

' Select the raw data area.
Range(Cells(RawDataRowStart, 1), Cells(nPos2, 3)).Select

' Sort by date and then by level.
Selection.Sort Key1:=Range("B" & RawDataRowStart), _
    Order1:=xlAscending, Key2:=Range("C" & RawDataRowStart), _
    Order2:=xlDescending, Header:=xlGuess, OrderCustom:=1, _
MatchCase:=False, Orientation:=xlTopToBottom

' Loop through the raw data result.
Range("A1").Select
For nPos = 100 To nPos2 - 1
    On Error Resume Next
    Err = 0
    Do Until Err <> 0
        ' This looks complicated but isn't; populate the
        ' descriptor Pn Nn with the right cell value.

        cmUtils.PopulateCell objOutput, ":CmpDesc P" & _
            Int((nPos - RawDataRowStart) / _
            UBound(viCompanyList, 1)) + 1 & " N" & _
            (nPos - RawDataRowStart) Mod UBound(viCompanyList _
            , 1) + 1 & ":", Cells(nPos, 1).Value

        cmUtils.PopulateCell objOutput, ":StockLvl P" & _
            Int((nPos - RawDataRowStart) /  _
            UBound(viCompanyList, 1)) + 1 & " N" & _
            (nPos - RawDataRowStart) Mod UBound(viCompanyList _
            , 1) + 1 & ":", Cells(nPos, 3).Value
    Loop

    ' Populate nonperiod descriptors.
    cmUtils.PopulateCell objOutput, ":CmpDesc N" & _
        (nPos - RawDataRowStart) Mod UBound(viCompanyList, 1) _
        + 1 & ":", Cells(nPos, 1).Value

Next nPos

' Delete the raw data area, and you're done!
Rows(RawDataRowStart & ":" & nPos2 - 1).Delete
```

OFFICE 97 CONSIDERATIONS

This example works, as is, with Excel 97. The performance improves considerably, however, if you convert the Excel workbook to 97 format and rewrite parts of the code into the new VBA standard. The ReportInExcel '97.xls file on the companion CD illustrates some of these benefits. Note that the existing VBActiveXDLL.dll file refers to the Microsoft Excel 5.0 Object library, not the Microsoft Excel 8.0 Object library. To use the new object library, you'll need to recompile VBActiveXDLL.dll with the correct Excel reference.

To use the example, simply create a toolbar that includes a button that links to the *Process* routine, and then hide the code module. Select Toolbars from the View menu. (These instructions are for Excel 5/7; Excel 97 will work a little differently.) Type *ReportInUserDocument* in the Toolbar Name text box, and press the New button. Drag an icon of your choice onto the newly created toolbar. Right-click the icon in the new toolbar, and select Assign Macro. Select the ReportInExcel.xls!'[VBA Code].Process' macro, and press the OK button. The example is now ready to be executed.

Creating Reports in Internet Explorer

This example demonstrates the ability to use standard Visual Basic 5 forms and code in an ActiveX user document accessible from Internet Explorer.

Visual Basic ActiveX document used for reporting

This example introduces the concepts of a user document usable within a Web browser. As with previous examples, I rely heavily on the business object and, in this case, the VBComMethAndProp class to provide the infrastructure for the reporting requirement. The two methods of selecting criteria are included, allowing advanced users to bypass the limitations of field text boxes. The output is presented in a rich text box, with an RTF document storing the output format.

Folder:	CHAP03\ReportInUserDocument
Dependencies:	CompanyStock.exe
	VBCommonMethodsAndProperties class
	Microsoft Rich TextBox Control 5.0
	Microsoft Windows Common Controls-2 5.0

Project Name: VBActiveXDocDll.vbp

Instructions: Ensure that the CompanyStock.exe has been registered in the Registry. Load Visual Basic 5, and open the VBActiveXDocDll.vbp file. Press Ctrl+F5 to run, and then load Internet Explorer 3. Enter the path to usrDocExample.vbd (\Program Files\DevStudio\VB by default) into Internet Explorer's Address box, and hit Enter. Your screen should look similar to Figure 3-19.

FIGURE 3-19

Visual Basic ActiveX document

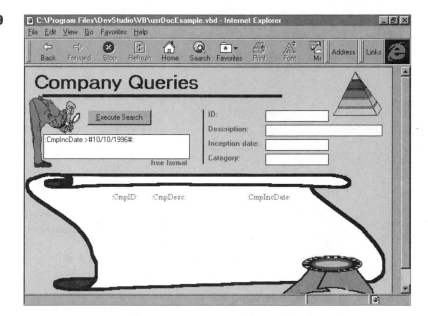

The project consists of two objects: a user document, usrDocExample, which contains the controls required to support a Web browser page; and the common class module VBComMethAndProp.

User documents are powerful objects capable of wrapping up standard Visual Basic 5 forms into documents that are usable with Internet Explorer 3 and Office Binder. In the user document usrDocExample, we first add a shape control to allow for a scrollable window within the Web browser. With a scrollable window, you now have the capability of creating extended forms that are larger than the physical size of the screen. You can add the rest of the controls within the boundaries of the shape control.

In the Declarations section of the user document, we add constants to hold information about which report template to use and the object references to VBComMethAndProp and CompanyDetails:

```
Private Const sRtfTemplate       As String = "Company List Template"
Private Const sRtfResult         As String = "rtfResult"
Private Const sRtfExtension      As String = ".rtf"
Private Const nErrorNone         As Integer = 0
Private Const nErrorFileNotFound As Integer = 53

Private cmvbUtils As New VBComMethAndProp
Private csCompDet As New CompanyDetails
```

The *UserDocument_Initialize* and *UserDocument_Terminate* events hold code to initialize the objects, load the template output format, and close the object references:

```
Private Sub UserDocument_Initialize()
    ' Use only the pass by variant method.
    csCompDet.DataPassFormat = csPassByVariant

    ' Use rich text box utilities.
    cmvbUtils.OutputMedium = cmvbToRtfControl

    ' Load the example template.
    cmvbUtils.OpenOutputMedium rtfDisplay, App.Path & "\" _
        & sRtfTemplate & sRtfExtension

End Sub

Private Sub UserDocument_Terminate()
    Set csCompDet = Nothing
    Set cmvbUtils = Nothing
End Sub
```

The population of the rich text box is the same as in the ReportInRichTextBox example. (See page 133.) The way we select the criteria differs only in how the text control data is loaded into the *sFrom* variable:

```
' Open the output template format.
cmvbUtils.OpenOutputMedium rtfDisplay, App.Path _
    & "\" & sRtfTemplate & sRtfExtension

    ' Wrap up the criteria selection
    ' for the criteria the user has selected.
    If txtSelection & "" = "" Then
```

```
        ' Basic criteria
        sFrom = ":FilterStart: "
        If txt(0) & "" <> "" Then
            sFrom = sFrom & ":CmpID " & txt(0)
        End If
        ' And so on
        ⋮

        sFrom = sFrom & " :FilterEnd:"
    Else
        ' Advanced criteria
        sFrom = ":FilterStart: " & txtSelection & " :FilterEnd:"
    End If

' Build the criteria.
    csCompDet.BuildCompanyCriteria sFrom, v1, v2, v3, v4, _
        v5, v6, v7, v8, v9, v10

' Build the list.
    csCompDet.BuildCompanyList v1, v2, v3, v4, v5, _
        v6, v7, v8, v9, v10

' Get the list.
    vList = csCompDet.GetCompanyList
```

To see the user document in action, you need to have Internet Explorer 3 or above installed on your computer. In design mode, the user document can be run but has no visible interface, so you need to open Internet Explorer and select Open on the File menu to locate the usrDocExample.vbd file, which is normally inserted in the Visual Basic directory when you run VBAActivex-DocDll. (You can also find this file on the companion CD.) It is now possible to debug the project while viewing the result. When you're happy with the document result, you'll need to close Internet Explorer before creating the user document DLL.

Performance Tips

One negative aspect of the reporting methods proposed in this chapter is the time it takes to generate a report. As mentioned earlier, the primary cause of this time hit is the overhead of cross-process-boundary communication. For example, pushing data from Visual Basic into Word crosses at least two process boundaries, possibly more, depending on how your data is retrieved. This situation is improving with each new release of Office and with the improvements in ActiveX and the COM architecture—and, of course, the lightning performance packed into the latest Pentium Pro computers doesn't hurt.

Many of us, however, are stuck with earlier versions of Office and less powerful computers. If you fall into this category, you'll need to take into account the performance issues. Here are a few tips for improving performance:

- Ensure that the foreground and background tasks obtain an equal share of the processor's time. In Windows NT 3.51 and Windows NT 4, it is possible to do this by setting the multitasking of foreground and background activities to be equally responsive. The option is available in the control panel under system properties.

- Don't display the report as it is being created; this will reduce the overhead of displaying each change made to the screen before the instruction is completely processed.

- Where possible, try to run the code within the reporting tool. Generating the output is normally far slower than retrieving the data. If you're able to run the output code within the same process, you'll be able to reduce some of the overhead.

- Employ intelligent code. For example, if you're finding field descriptors, it might be quicker to read the cells within a range individually rather than to use the Find command.

- Place data into the clipboard or into a file to be read into the report tool. Doing this might be faster than populating data line by line.

- Turn off functionality within the reporting tool (such as the automatic Re-Calc facility in Excel) that could slow down the process when generating a report.

SOME FINAL THOUGHTS

I hope this chapter has provided you with an insight into the capabilities of Microsoft Office applications as a component in producing user reports. We still have a ways to go before we can view all the applications as one common model, with objects containing uniform properties and methods. Even with Visual Basic 5 and Office 97, I recommend that you develop a control object layer to hide the inconsistency between products. This layer will help you future-proof your code by ensuring that only a small portion of code (rather than hundreds of individual programs) requires a rewrite. Also keep in mind that backward compatibility is rarely supported for more than two versions of a VBA object. This can lead to a mammoth task of upgrading old code, which in reality will require a complete rewrite—case in point being the numerous Excel 4 macros still in use.

Over time, as COM and ActiveX gain greater acceptance and Microsoft further restructures its Office applications, we can expect to see the task of developing user reports become increasingly easier, with less ambiguity and duplication in objects and their methods and properties—perhaps to the extent that the developer becomes redundant (although I think not!).

Transferring Information Over the Internet

Adam is a TMS Developer with six years' experience in Microsoft Windows software development. He specializes in Visual Basic and Microsoft Access and is a Microsoft Certified Solution Developer. His areas of expertise include database programming, object-oriented development, and the software development process. When not coding till dawn, he enjoys the odd glass of amber nectar.

ADAM MAGEE

Karen is TMS's Director of Business Development and expert on groupware and Internet/intranet development initiatives. She has lectured worldwide on the deployment and integration of groupware and Internet/intranet technologies. Karen's knowledge of Microsoft Windows spans 10 years, during which time she has worked on development initiatives and trained Windows developers in the United States and Europe. Karen has an MBA in information systems management and has held a variety of senior positions involving both technical and business management.

KAREN FIELD

Just as Visual Basic has rapidly matured into the de facto standard for corporate programming projects, the Internet has become the lingua franca for computer interoperation worldwide. It seems only natural, then, that these two technologies in conjunction are a potentially powerful tool for the wired business world. The superior rapid-development capabilities of Microsoft Visual Basic, linked with the globally pervasive framework of the Internet, let developers create powerful business solutions.

This chapter examines the potential of Visual Basic and the Internet from a business perspective and takes a look at one of the core uses for the Internet—information transfer. You'll see how easy it is to incorporate this capability to transfer information into your software through the use of the Internet Transfer Control.

A BRIEF OVERVIEW OF THE INTERNET

No matter who you talk to today, a majority of people will have at least heard of the Internet phenomenon. Technology that was once confined within the walls of academia has come kicking and screaming into the world of twentieth century commerce. Even more astonishing has been the rate at which many forward-thinking visionaries in the business community have embraced and exploited this technology. The adoption of Internet and associated World Wide Web technologies by the business community has been greatly influenced by the direction and strategies emanating from every key software vendor in the industry. Indeed, it is difficult to find any vendor today who has not Internet-enabled or Web-enabled any products.

OK, before we tackle the business benefits, let's go over the jargon and technology components that make up the Internet and the World Wide Web. If you've heard it all before, you can move on to the "Compelling Business Reasons in the Internet Revolution" section on page 164.

First question, then—just what is the Internet? The Internet is the largest network in the world. It provides a means by which computers all over the globe can communicate between networks on different platforms and in different environments and allows users throughout the world to access and share information. Originally developed by the U.S. government as a way of linking geographically separate Department of Defense computers, it has grown phenomenally over the last few years, from a tiny 300 connected networks in 1988 to over 100,000 today.

The structure of the Internet is such that no particular company or government "owns" it. It has been cultivated by the cooperation of connecting networks and the collaborative development and adoption of standards. Today the growth and the structure of the Internet are regulated by a cooperative body called the Internet Engineering Task Force (IETF). The standards that define the technical details of the Internet are recorded in publicly available specification documents known as Requests For Comment (RFCs).

One of the strengths of the Internet as a tool for communication is that it was designed to withstand a nuclear attack. (It's harder to imagine a more rigorous design criterion.) The Internet has no central backbone—it stretches around the globe in spiderweb fashion. When you connect from one computer to another via the Internet, the path that is used to connect you (the links from one computer to another) is not fixed but is dynamically determined as you transfer data. Thus, the data being transferred between two computers can take many different routes.

Protocols and Standards

Internet communications and data exchange are facilitated by the development of standard communication protocols. Central to the operation of the Internet is the fundamental language that all connected computers "speak." The dialect of the Internet is TCP/IP (Transmission Control Protocol/Internet Protocol). This protocol allows any computer connected to the Internet to be uniquely identified and allows any such computer to send information to or receive information from any other Internet-connected computer.

At the heart of TCP/IP is the concept that each computer has a unique address. This address is a 32-bit number represented as four 8-bit components (for example, 103.205.67.88). This number is referred to as an IP number. Public IP numbers are regulated by an Internet body—InterNIC—to ensure that there are no clashes between computers connected to the Internet.

IP numbers don't mean much to the average user, so a Domain Name Service (DNS) can be used to translate the 32-bit number into something a little more readable. This readable version of an IP number is called a domain name. The IP number 103.27.56.45 could be referred to as *mycompany.com* or *myuniversity.edu*. The DNS does the job of maintaining the lists of IP numbers and domain names. Most Domain Name Services are managed by Internet Service Providers (ISPs) or network administrators and are not something that individual users have to worry about.

One of the most common uses for the Internet has been to access files stored on a remote computer. The standard Internet protocol for remote file access is File Transfer Protocol (FTP). This allows remote users to connect to a computer and to browse and retrieve files that have been made publicly available.

World Wide Web

Fundamentally, the Web is a set of protocols that operate over the Internet and that can be extended to operate over private, internal networks. Three essential technologies define the World Wide Web today and set out to characterize the communication between a Web client (an individual user's computer) and a Web server (the computer containing files that individual users access) connected over a TCP/IP network.

The first is the Internet standard protocol referred to as Hypertext Transfer Protocol (HTTP), which was developed in the late 1980s. HTTP is different from FTP in that it was designed to provide a standard way of viewing documents as well as transferring them from one computer to another. The second technology of the Web is often referred to as the language of the Web—Hypertext Markup Language (HTML). HTML is the document format for Web documents or pages. Traditional word processors use a proprietary method for representing document attributes such as spacing and fonts. HTML uses directives, or tags, to specify format, leaving the actual formatting to the client. HTML is a subset of Standard Generalized Markup Language (SGML), providing codes used to format hypertext linking between documents. The HTML standard is guarded closely by the World Wide Web Consortium (W3C), which is headed by Tim Berners-Lee, the founder of the World Wide Web.

HTML documents can contain references to drawings, pictures, sound, and other multimedia content. HTML documents can also refer to other documents by a Uniform Resource Locator (URL). A URL is the location of a particular Internet resource. A possible URL for an HTML document might be *http:// www.mycompany.com/sales/august.html*.

The ability of an HTML document to contain a reference, or link, to another HTML document creates a collection of interlinked documents. This collection of documents is referred to as the World Wide Web. But keep in mind that the World Wide Web is not the Internet. It is merely an application that uses the features that the Internet provides.

The ease of use and practical nature of the World Wide Web have been the main force behind the explosion of Internet use over the last decade. Over 50 million documents exist on the World Wide Web, and the number of documents continues to increase dramatically.

Web protocols (specifically HTTP and HTML) have gone through at least three phases to date and continue to metamorphose. The first phase provided no more than the ability to publish information by means of a hypertext model. Each section of the document could point to other sections in different documents on the same or different servers at different locations on different platforms—navigation was totally ad hoc and nonlinear.

Of course, "static" publishing was OK, but it didn't take long for developers to recognize the potential for "dynamic" publishing. Some information is static, but certain elements are real-time. This provision is referred to as "dynamic" publishing—the need to tie static information in with live data. The Web also allows for "interactive," or "active," publishing. An interactive site can canvass input from the user by means of, for example, a form containing fields, and the data collected can then be processed and a response can be created dynamically. If you want to use the Web to collect customer information, you can write a Web application that creates an appropriate fill-in form and puts the data gathered into tables. If your customers are having trouble finding specific information within your organization, write a Web application that provides an interface that lets users search your data.

Interactive Web sites are seen as a key to providing support for electronic commerce and transaction processing. This, of course, will require programming beyond HTML and Common Gateway Interfaces (CGI).

WEB BROWSER

A Web browser, in its simplest terms, is any program that implements Web client protocols. This client application enables the client computer to gain access to a Web server or other Internet Services such as FTP. From a user perspective, this is the true window on the World Wide Web. It interprets and displays Web pages. Soon the browser will be in an integrated environment in which applications such as electronic mail systems use Web protocols to access database servers that also happen to implement Web protocols. Hence, it will be the protocols that both determine and limit what can be done on the Web.

Figure 4-1 shows just how these protocols fit together.

FIGURE 4-1

How client protocols fit together

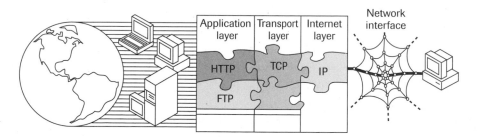

When is the Internet not the Internet? When it is an intranet. (Well, at least it isn't another acronym.) The term "intranet" is widely used to describe the application of Internet technologies in internal corporate networks. Businesses are using intranets today to share information more effectively and as a vehicle to integrate their existing infrastructure and legacy systems, thus taking advantage of the Internet browser paradigm. Intranets are based on technology that already exists in many enterprises. To access an intranet, at a minimum you'll need to install TCP/IP and a Web browser on the client computer and have a Web server. A connection to the Internet is helpful as well.

Transaction-oriented business applications are the lifeblood of businesses. The corporate intranet offers great potential for adding value to and extending the reach of legacy systems and permits new ways of creating, presenting, searching, and managing that key corporate asset called information. It is not surprising, therefore, to see the swarm of activity from vendors to provide both client and server support in their product offerings.

Because intranets and the Internet are so closely related, you need to consider how they interact and how they are typically utilized. The framework put in place should divide the business use of networks between internal (intranet) and external (Internet), and between informative and transactional use.

COMPELLING BUSINESS REASONS IN THE INTERNET REVOLUTION

Some say that the Internet is the most important technology since the dawn of the PC revolution in the 1980s. It offers the world of commerce not only a means of leveraging existing investments made in LAN and PC technology but also new and exciting ways for those organizations to use the Web as the basis for a much broader range of business applications that extend their communication and information-sharing capabilities.

Some pundits contend that your organization will not survive into the twenty-first century without a presence on the Internet. Phrases such as "increased competitive advantage" and "a thousandfold return on any investment you make when you deploy this technology" are indeed compelling. Couple this with the ability to provide greater flexibility in global communications both inside and outside the enterprise (based on common infrastructure standards), and an environment that supports the accessibility and dissemination of that elusive corporate asset—information—appears to clinch the deal. As the Internet and associated Web technologies continue to mature into an effective platform for businesswide communication and information sharing, the level of sophistication and functionality will unquestionably increase. Tempted, or still skeptical? In either case, read on.

So just how easy is it? Well, to meet this challenge, you need to provide an integrated, platform-independent environment that provides access to information, irrespective of time and place. It's relatively easy to provide Internet access (subject to your IP network being in place and that you don't forget the additional demand that will be placed on your server technology and communications bandwidth), and it is relatively easy to put up your first Web site to supplement the front-office publicity vehicle providing paper-based promotional activities. The reality, of course, is that this will be yet another technology fad unless it is driven by a well-defined strategy and it identifies some clear business benefits up front. Companies need to at least understand the basics and determine exactly what this technology can do for them. Despite how this technology develops in the future, the business potential of the Internet and associated technologies appears to be here to stay, and the one thing you can be sure of is that your competitors are at least exploring the potential.

Strategies that are driving the adoption of this technology are in line with key factors driving business. These factors apply to every organization: the need to increase the competitive edge, to reduce time to market for new products and services, and to increase revenues while driving down the cost of operations. This technology also offers completely new business opportunities that were never possible before. Other factors that drive deployment are based on threat. Web technology really does level the playing field; entry into existing markets becomes less expensive and easier as barriers, including geography and currency, are blown into cyberspace. Your organization could well be competing against an almost virtual organization, one that does not have the mature overheads and inflexible IT infrastructures of overweight dinosaurs.

Benefits can be realized at many different levels across the enterprise: corporate, business unit, and departmental or functional. Each of these areas has a fundamental need for effective communications, information sharing, and collaboration throughout the organization, both vertically and horizontally, from the start of the supply chain through to delivery of finished goods or services.

This may well include both suppliers and customers as part of the process. Let's also consider initiatives such as Business Process Reengineering (BPR). Yes, I know, most office processes were never designed in the first place, so how can they be reengineered? However, BPR is all about breaking down the silos, those departmental barriers that have been reinforced more often than not by the technology solutions of the past. BPR attempts to extend the private network to the public network and integrates suppliers, customers, and partners into the workflow. Organizations are preparing to extend their corporate vision beyond the boundaries of the enterprise itself, integrating suppliers, customers, and partners as part of the end-to-end value chain. The vision is one of teams or workgroups delivering against business objectives—access in a timely manner to quality information for the new knowledge worker is the key element. This in turn will improve the speed and quality of decision making within and beyond the organization.

You might have read examples of what the leading companies are doing with the technology. In case you haven't, let's take a look at what organizations are doing currently. Early use of the technology tends to be evolutionary and generally falls into two categories: message-centric, in which the Internet technology is used for managing message transfer and file transfer between different locations; and document-centric, in which the technology is used to place corporate product and service information, policies, and standard office procedures on Web servers for access by both internal and external users.

What do we mean by "information" when we talk about the need to track down information quickly? We are *not* talking about structured data—all that wonderful stuff found inside our production and transactional databases. We are talking about unstructured information—all that ad hoc, rich information that our business communities use on a day-to-day basis, the real value-added information that continues to elude the business users. This information is scattered around the organization, sitting on those islands of isolation—personal computers. There is no version control and no easy way to retrieve the definitive source without sifting through tons of information. No wonder productivity within the office environment has declined during the past few years. Here is a key corporate asset that is generally little understood and, for the majority, is never really managed.

During the past year, the Internet and the World Wide Web developments have provided a range of technologies to assist in the publication of rich information in electronic form, not only in an effective and user-friendly way but in a way that offers a mechanism for providing a centralized repository and common navigation system that all can use. These technologies usually manifest themselves in an intranet within the organization. The intranet created a lot of interest in 1996, and it appears to be the most practical corporate use so far for Internet technologies. Intranets permit internal company information to be accessed from any platform and to be distributed cost effectively. Intranets provide many benefits to enterprises. Use of the browser paradigm simplifies internal information management and improves internal communication. Similarly, Web navigation and search engines make it easier for people to find and analyze information. Just as a World Wide Web presence informs customers, an internal Web presence can be used to inform and educate employees. Integrating Internet technologies with an enterprise infrastructure and legacy systems—whether they are client/server or mainframe applications—provides yet another opportunity for leveraging existing technology investments.

Businesses and software vendors are looking to the Internet as the ultimate in client/server networking. Businesses are defining the real value of the Internet as the connection between platform-independent desktop browser software and Web-enabled applications that are the front end for database servers. The Internet is additionally proving to be an ideal environment for exploiting the synergies among the many maturing but often proprietary technologies such as groupware, workflow, and document management.

The Groupware Perspective

Groupware as a collaborative tool provides an easily accessible, widespread platform for gathering and sharing information and for capturing ideas. So why not consider using a corporate intranet instead? You can capture corporate know-how with an intranet in much the same way you do with groupware, and you can set up newsgroups and discussion databases so that users can access them using Web tools.

The Workflow Perspective

A workflow perspective offers similar benefits. Many business activities are structured. Enterprises do not expect people to collaborate on processing an expense claim form; rather, the enterprise defines specific policies about how an expense claim form is to be routed through an organization so that it is properly approved, is auditable, and is secure. Many people are involved, but the enterprise's policies specify the *coordination* required between personnel to meet a defined objective. The successful completion of a predefined business process depends on the coordination of people in completing a set of structured tasks in a particular sequence and within expected time constraints. Historically, this has been the domain of workflow automation systems, which focus on highly structured business processes that exhibit *predefined, conditional* workflow. If you implement a workflow system on your own, you tend to define forms, specify the routing logic, specify triggering actions that occur when certain conditions are met, specify how data is to be accessed or modified, and provide some auditable tracking capability.

The Document-Management Perspective

Electronic documents are corporate resources that should be leveraged for business applications whenever possible. The Web is document-based, so one of the greatest challenges is not in creating documents but in managing them. These documents can take the form of HTML documents, text, multimedia, spreadsheets, presentation graphics, and so on. Before you rush into any plans for an electronic document management system (EDMS), let's first understand what characterizes an EDMS. A document-management system should be able to deal with long-term access to documents. Key features include the following:

- Document-change tracking (version control)
- Access control (security)
- Search facilities (full-text retrieval)
- Backup and archiving

In addition, they generally include an integrated workflow capability, imaging, and document manufacturing. The Web offers some of these capabilities, but they generally require some sophisticated programming to achieve a total solution. However, many of the leading EDMS suppliers today provide access to documents by means of a Web browser.

The Internet Challenge

The bad news is that most of the challenges you face are not related to technology. Before we move on to the good news, let's consider a couple of stoppers. First let's talk about some challenges related to information resource management and business practices. You need to identify the businesswide information needs; otherwise, you will be providing just another source of confusion. Providing tools that ease access to the right information at the right time is also important. After all, any benefits from information availability can be negated immediately if the *people* in your business spend all their time trying to track down the information. From a people perspective, issues are generally related to culture and current working practices. They include motivation to share, to use, and to add value to what is there already. Most people have become accustomed to the information push paradigm, in which information is constantly being thrown at them. The Internet and Web is very much a pull paradigm, in which users are expected to go out and get information.

The ability to customize rapid application development is a basic requirement for any future application strategies, particularly since IT functions worldwide are now expected to develop, deploy, and support technology solutions to meet business needs in a timely manner. To have this ability, you need an architecture that is robust, flexible, and responsive to the ever-changing needs of the whole enterprise.

The good news is that we are seeing a plethora of tools and products to assist with the complexities of delivering real business solutions on the Internet and the Web. Visual Basic 5 is just one product that offers the potential of enabling existing applications to access the Internet, integrating existing applications with Web sites, integrating other popular Internet protocols, and offering developers a rapid application development (RAD) tool to merge client/server and Internet technologies.

Internet Transfer Control Specifics

With the release of Visual Basic 5, Microsoft has included an ActiveX control that makes developing applications for communicating with Internet servers an achievable task for Visual Basic mortals. The Internet Transfer Control provides support for accessing both FTP and HTTP servers. The HTTP protocol lets you connect to World Wide Web servers and retrieve HTML files. The FTP protocol lets you send any kind of files to and receive any kind of files from an Internet FTP server.

The Internet Transfer Control is actually an OLE interface to an underlying Windows dynamic-link library (DLL) named WININET.DLL. This DLL is part of the Win32 Application Programming Interface (API) specification. This makes the Internet Transfer Control an interface to a core part of the Windows architecture, which might be reassuring to those concerned about the shelf life of the components with which they choose to develop.

Previously, developing Internet-based applications involved a tortuous descent into the arcane and complex world of TCP/IP, Windows Sockets, and esoteric C source code. With the inclusion of the Internet Transfer Control in Visual Basic 5, this is no longer the case.

Required Software

Before we look in detail at how the Internet Transfer Control works, you need to be sure you have a few other components installed on your computer or that you have access to them.

The TCP/IP protocol must be installed on your computer. This protocol comes with both Windows 95 and Windows NT. If you don't have this protocol installed, you can install it from your Windows setup media. (If you're not sure whether you have TCP/IP, you can check by opening the Start menu; choosing Settings, Control Panel, and then Network; and looking in the list box at the top of the screen on the Configuration tab.)

Life on the Internet is not much fun unless you have a remote computer with which you can communicate. This remote computer should be running an FTP or HTTP server (preferably both) that you have a private account on. You can use public FTP and HTTP servers, but in most cases you'll be limited to read-only communication. A better way is to set up your own FTP or HTTP server. This is easy with Microsoft Windows NT Server because both an FTP and an HTTP server are included with the operating system.

If you don't have access to a remote computer capable of running the requisite server software, fear not. A number of FTP and HTTP servers are available both commercially and via shareware, and provided you have installed TCP/IP on your PC, you can run them on the same machine that you use to develop with the Internet Transfer Control. Microsoft Personal Web Server can be downloaded for free from *http://www.microsoft.com* and contains both an FTP and an HTTP server.

Installing the Internet Transfer Control

The Internet Transfer Control is installed as part of the standard Visual Basic 5 installation procedure. To enable the Internet Transfer Control as part of your Visual Basic 5 toolbox, make sure you have selected the Microsoft Internet Transfer Control from the Project/Components menu in the design environment.

RETRIEVING A FILE FROM THE INTERNET

This chapter is focused on moving information across the Internet. So, what do we mean by "moving information"? More important, what benefit is there in a business making use of this technology?

At a practical level, moving information means copying a document from one location to another. On a corporate intranet, moving information might mean information being transferred between different internal departments. The information might be a Microsoft Excel spreadsheet containing the latest sales figures or a text file of client information updates that are produced weekly by the company mainframe. Both these documents are stored in an HTTP server. The two departments can be in the same building or on opposite sides of the earth. The Internet Transfer Control can be used to create a solution that automatically ensures the latest copy of these files is available, perhaps checking for new copies daily, avoiding the need for someone to manually perform the transfer.

On the wider Internet, a company might want to retrieve the latest pricing information from a major supplier who has made the information available on the Internet. A medical supplies company in Sydney might update its price lists with information from its supplier in London. (A lot of companies are now disseminating information in this manner.) Again, the fact that a system automates this process would mean that the company can be confident that it always has the latest available information at hand, saving unnecessary rework later.

A boat rental company might want to retrieve the latest weather conditions for its particular geographical region from its local meteorological office by means of an FTP server. The boat rental company would then be able to print out the latest meteorological report for its customers, providing timely and important information.

All these scenarios have one thing in common—they involve copying a file from one location on the Internet to another. Let's look at how using the Internet Transfer Control makes this task easy to achieve by means of the *OpenURL* method.

Retrieving a File with *OpenURL*

The *OpenURL* method is used to retrieve a document from an Internet URL and put a copy on a local computer. The URL that is supplied as a parameter to the *OpenURL* call can be the location of the latest sales figures spreadsheet mentioned previously. In this case, *OpenURL* will retrieve the spreadsheet from the location specified in the URL and will put a copy on the computer that executed the *OpenURL* method. All you have to specify is the URL of the document you are requesting, as shown here:

```
vntData = icMain.OpenURL("ftp://ftp.mycompany.com/public/sales.xls")
```

A couple of points about *OpenURL* are worth mentioning. The *OpenURL* method occurs synchronously—that is, execution in your code does not continue until the Internet Transfer Control has completed the transfer. If the spreadsheet you were requesting was quite large and you were accessing the Internet via a slow link (say, maybe, from a modem connection in a regional office), retrieving the document might take quite some time. Until the document was received in its entirety, the program would be unable to do anything else.

Second, transmission is one-way only. *OpenURL* can receive only documents. In the previous example, you can retrieve the latest sales information with *OpenURL*, but you don't have the capability to send any information back. To send information, you must use the *Execute* method, which is covered in detail later in this chapter.

The following code example gives an overview of the use of the *OpenURL* method. (This method is discussed in more detail later.) The code snippet here should give you a good idea about what is involved with using the *OpenURL* method.

```
' Retrieve latest software update from ftp.mycompany.com.

Dim bFile() as Byte          ' Retrieving a binary file.

' Retrieve the file.
bFile() = icTransfer.OpenURL _
    ("ftp://ftp.mycompany.com/upgrade/software.exe", _
    icByteArray)

' Write file to disk.
Open "C:\INTERNET\software.exe" For Binary Access Write As #1
Put #1, , bFile()
Close #1
```

In this example, the *OpenURL* method accepts a URL and a data type parameter. This parameter is either a string or a byte array that determines in what format the data will be retrieved.

If you're going to write the file to disk, a byte array is all you need. It doesn't matter whether you are retrieving a text file or an executable—they will both be written to disk in the same format in which they existed on the remote computer.

However, if you want to display the contents of the file in a text box—say, for instance, if it's an HTML file or a text file—it's easier to retrieve the document directly as a string than to have to jump through hoops to convert the byte array to a string.

What this parameter does mean, however, is that you have to know in advance what type of document you are retrieving and what you want to do with it once you have it.

HTTP Transfer Limitations

When you receive an HTML document via the *OpenURL* method, you don't receive any of the embedded objects in these documents. These include graphic images (JPG and GIF), sounds, video files, and other multimedia content. What you do receive is the raw HTML source. Displaying raw HTML in a text box won't give you the same results as viewing the file in a Web browser.

For best results in viewing the full content of an HTML file, you should use either Microsoft Internet Explorer or the Microsoft Web Browser ActiveX control.

Retrieving the Contents of a Directory

If the URL you have specified is not a file but a directory, the data returned by *OpenURL* will be the contents of the directory. For instance, requesting *http://www.mycompany.com/files/* or *ftp://ftp.mycompany.com/files* will return the contents of the files directory.

The format of the returned directory is determined by the protocol of the transfer. In both of the preceding cases, the directory is returned in HTML format. For an HTTP transfer, the directory will be bare-bones HTML, simply listing the directory's contents. An FTP transfer will return the directory structure with additional FTP server information such as welcome messages.

In practice, this means that you can't just grab the real contents of a directory structure using *OpenURL*. Any data that is returned as a directory listing is wrapped in all the HTML formatting codes. If you want to display the directory entries—say, in a text box—you'll have to parse the returned text for the individual directory entries.

It seems strange that an FTP operation will return results in HTML, but it does. An alternative to retrieving the HTML-wrapped directory entries from an FTP or HTTP server is the use of the *Execute* method of the Internet Transfer Control, as described later in this chapter.

STYLES OF DIRECTORY STRUCTURE RETURNED BY *OpenURL*

Two types of directory content are returned by the *OpenURL* call: HTTP style and FTP style. In both cases, extra processing of the returned text is required to strip away the extraneous HTML information and retrieve the actual directory names.

HTTP Style

```
<head>
<title>/test1/ - </title>
</head>
<body>
<H1>/test1/ - </H1>
<hr>
<pre>  21/01/97    22:19              5
<A HREF="/test1/hello.txt">hello.txt</A><br></body>
```

FTP Style

```
<!DOCTYPE HTML PUBLIC "-//IETF//DTD HTML//EN>
<HTML>
<HEAD>
<TITLE>FTP root at www.mycompany.com</TITLE>
</HEAD>
<BODY>
<H2>FTP root at www.mycompany.com</H2>
<HR>
<H4><PRE>
Windows 95 FTP Service.
</PRE></H4>
<HR>
<PRE>
07/02/96 06:31                 43 <A HREF="/~FTPSVC~.CKM">~FTPSVC~.CKM</A>
01/08/97 08:04                 15 <A HREF="/hello.txt">hello.txt</A>
</PRE>
<HR>
</BODY>
</HTML>
```

Notice the extra information provided by the FTP server (in this case, Microsoft Personal Web Server), such as FTP server name ("www.mycompany.com") and welcome message "Windows 95 FTP Service."

Handling Unreliable Connections

The Internet is not the most reliable of places: connections can be instantly dropped for no apparent reason, and connections that before were blindingly fast can drop to a mind-numbingly slow crawl. Add to this the size of files that are transferred in today's computing environments (Microsoft Word files with even a few embedded bitmaps can easily exceed one megabyte in size), and you have a very unstable environment for transferring files.

Because the *OpenURL* method is synchronous, execution of your code will not continue until the remote computer has processed the call. If the connection is disrupted or the remote computer is taking a long time to process the request, your code will not resume executing, effectively freezing your program. This can lead to very frustrated users.

To prevent this from occurring, you can set a maximum time (in seconds) for the Internet Transfer Control to wait for a response. The *RequestTimeOut* property is used for this purpose. If no data is received from the remote computer in this period, a time-out error will be generated in the *StateChanged* event. (The *StateChanged* event is explained later in this chapter.) An error message can then be displayed informing the user that because of a problem with the Internet connection, the file cannot be retrieved at this time (neatly avoiding any criticism of your code).

Getting Information About the Connection

When you access a document using the Internet Transfer Control via *OpenURL*, after the call has been made the URL that has been supplied as the first parameter is parsed and the various components of the URL are stored in the corresponding properties of the Internet Transfer Control. This feature is a nice time-saver because you can display the various elements of the URL as separate entities without having to parse the URL yourself. The component parts can then easily be assigned to variables or displayed in form controls.

Likewise, it is possible to create a URL string by assigning the various sub properties the required values. The URL property will then contain the complete concatenated URL.

The properties that contain the various properties of the URL are *Protocol*, *RemoteHost*, and *Document*.

All of the preceding properties are read/write, but they will be modified by an *OpenURL* operation to reflect the components of the new URL. Sometimes what you supply as a URL will actually be changed by the server. In the case of the HTTP protocol, sometimes the server will automatically jump you from the location of one HTML document to another. (Maybe a file location has changed, and the Web server includes an automatic link to the new file.) In this case, the URL that is returned in the URL *RemoteHost* and *Document* properties will be different from the one that you supplied to the *OpenURL* method. Watch out for this potential "gotcha" in your applications.

Accessing a Password-Protected Server

Because the Internet is open to all sorts of nefarious cyber lowlifes, security is often an issue when connecting to an Internet server. The most common form of security involves supplying a user name and valid password to the server. The *UserName* property and the *Password* property are used to supply a user name and password to a remote server that requires such information.

Most public HTTP sites don't have any security limitations, so these two properties can be left blank for most HTTP operations. FTP servers, however, nearly always require you to log on. Public FTP servers allow an anonymous logon, in which the user name is "anonymous" and the password is the user's e-mail address.

The Internet Transfer control provides default values for these properties. In most cases, these default values are all you will require to access an Internet server. However, if the server does require a specific password or the default values do not work, you can manually set these properties to allow you to log on.

Accessing the Internet from a Secure Network

A common type of situation occurs when the PC you are using to access the Internet is connected to it via what is known as a proxy server. A proxy server acts as an intermediary between you and the Internet. It is often used as a security barrier between an internal network (or intranet) and the outside Internet world. The proxy server prevents any unwanted access to your internal network by ensuring that all access to and from the Internet is channeled through a single point. The proxy server can then discard information that it does not deem safe. This is a common occurrence in business networks and when access is via an ISP.

If this is the case, you will have to let the Internet Transfer Control know that you have access to the Internet by way of a proxy server. If you don't notify the Internet Transfer Control, there is a strong chance that when the Internet Transfer Control attempts to connect to the outside world, the proxy server will deny access. (It actually depends on how strictly the proxy server enforces security.)

The *AccessType* property is used to inform the Internet Transfer Control of the existence of a proxy server. There are two options for this property: Direct and Proxy. If Proxy is selected, you need to supply the address of the proxy server in the *Proxy* property.

Putting It All Together

OpenURL provides an easy way to transfer information across the Internet. Let's put it to work in a fictional corporate example. MyCompany deals with four major suppliers. All four suppliers have started distributing their price lists on the Internet. These price lists are stored in an FTP server as comma-delimited text files.

So far, these price lists have been manually downloaded by an Internet-savvy salesperson, George. George has imported these lists into Microsoft Excel spreadsheets and distributed the results to his colleagues. This activity has begun to take a fair amount of George's time as the number of price lists has increased.

George approaches one of the IT officers and asks whether there is a way to improve this process. Sarah, the IT officer, thinks it would be better to import the lists into a Microsoft Access database, which would be shared among the sales staff. The best solution would be for her to somehow automate this task so that it would be easy to retrieve the latest price lists daily.

Sarah thinks she should be able to code up a Visual Basic application, using the Internet Transfer Control that she can run on the department's Windows NT application server.

This application will retrieve the latest price lists from all the FTP sites that George has been connecting to and transfer them to an Access database, thus saving George a lot of work and ensuring that timely and accurate price lists are distributed to the sales force.

The Visual Basic project IntSales.VBP in CHAP04\IntSales, shown running in Figure 4-2, demonstrates a sample application that performs this action (without actually transferring the files to Access).

FIGURE 4-2

Sample application using the OpenURL *method*

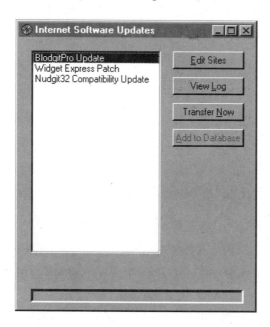

Technical Details

Let's have a look at some of the technical details of the *OpenURL* example. The code that does the transfer is quite simple. The only thing that needs special attention is writing the received file to disk. The core transfer routine is as follows. The database recordset containing site information is named *m_rstSites*.

```
Do Until m_rstSites.EOF

    ' Get file information.
    sURL = m_rstSites("URL")
    sFile = m_rstSites("SaveAs")

    ' Retrieve file as byte array.
    bFile() = icMain.OpenURL(sURL, icByteArray)

    ' Delete any previously existing files.
    If Dir$(sFile) <> "" Then
        Kill sFile
    End If
```

```
' Try to open file.
iFileHandle = FreeFile
Open sFile For Binary Access Write As iFileHandle

Put iFileHandle, , bFile()
Close iFileHandle

m_rstSites.MoveNext
```

Loop

Summing Up the *OpenURL* Method

The *OpenURL* method provides a remarkably simple interface for retrieving any files or documents from across the Internet. Unfortunately, it is limited by the fact that it is receive-only and does not automatically transfer the non-HTML portions of a Web page. However, as we have seen in the corporate example, we can use this technology to create real-life, effective solutions.

COMPLETE TRANSFER CONTROL

While *OpenURL* provides a simple interface, it is limited in a number of ways, as mentioned previously. The *Execute* method of the Internet Transfer Control provides the developer with an enhanced programming model for control of Internet file transfers. The *Execute* method's main strengths are that it executes asynchronously and that it allows files to be transmitted as well as received.

Asynchronous communication means that once a transfer has been initiated, program execution returns to the calling code. This provides a number of major advantages. First, it allows an easy way to manage and monitor large transfers (or small transfers over a slow connection). Transfer progress can be tracked and displayed, partial contents of files can be retrieved, and transfers can be interrupted at the user's request.

Second, the *Execute* method provides the ability to fully exploit the features of a particular server. FTP servers provide a complete set of commands that can be used not only to send and receive files but also to manage the file structure of the remote service. HTTP servers allow headers, or summary information, about particular documents to be retrieved.

Third, although the *Execute* method is more complex to use than *OpenURL*, it provides much better capabilities for exploiting the full potential of the

Internet. *OpenURL* provides you with the ability to retrieve a file—that's all. *Execute* opens your applications to smart ways of operating. Whether you're automatically posting new documents to Web servers or administering a remote FTP server, there is not much in the way of information transfer that the Internet Transfer Control does not let you do.

In the IntSales example, there was no way to determine whether the MyCompany staff already had the most current copy of the relevant price list. Using the *Execute* method would have allowed them to use the capabilities of an FTP server to check the time stamp of a file and decide whether they really needed to download the latest copy of the file, thus saving valuable Internet connect time.

Execute, StateChanged, and GetChunk

The *Execute* method works by sending a command to a remote server located on the Internet. The command might be a request to receive a file, to send a file, or even to delete a directory on the remote computer. The particular server you are talking to defines what commands you can send—the Internet Transfer Control does not define these commands. An FTP server has a complete set of commands that let you do more than transfer files to and from the server—they also let you manage files on the remote computer in a fashion similar to what you might remember from the days of the good old MS-DOS command line.

On the other hand, HTTP servers define a set of commands that let you not only send files to and receive files from the remote server but also transmit header information that describes the various properties of documents stored on the server. This allows summary information about documents to be retrieved without your having to transfer the entire document itself.

Once the server has received the particular command that had been transmitted by the *Execute* method, it sends a response to your program to let you know what action it has taken. The server's action is in response to the command it has received. The server can respond to the command by returning some data, performing an internal operation, or even closing the connection. The remote computer informs the calling code of the action it is taking by triggering the *StateChanged* event of the Internet Transfer Control. The *StateChanged* event provides a parameter that indicates the particular action the remote computer has just performed. Once this event is triggered, you can take appropriate action in your code depending on what action the remote server is performing.

The most important action you need to take in response to a *StateChanged* event is to retrieve any data that is waiting. Data is retrieved by using the *GetChunk* method. The *GetChunk* method will return, as the name indicates, a "chunk" of data. The size of a chunk is defined when you make the *GetChunk* call. A chunk is commonly 1024 bytes. This means that if you've requested a file that is 30 KB, you'll have to invoke the *GetChunk* method roughly 30 times to retrieve all the required data.

The following is the syntax for the *Execute* command. The *URL* and *operation* parameters are required for all types of servers; the *data* and *requestheaders* parameters are required only for HTTP transfers.

```
IcMain.Execute url operation data requestheaders
```

The process of issuing an *Execute* method, waiting for the *StateChanged* event, and then acting on the *StateChanged* event by using repeated *GetChunk* method invocations to retrieve data is the standard procedure for using the Internet Transfer Control via the *Execute* method. Be aware that some actions the server can take result in no data being returned to the calling program (closing a connection or transmitting a file), so the *GetChunk* method in these cases is not used.

The following section describes using the *Execute* method with an FTP server. The *StateChanged* and *GetChunk* methods are explained in detail after the discussion of the *Execute* method.

Execute Method

As previously mentioned, the FTP protocol supports a powerful set of commands that let you not only send and receive files but also browse and maintain the file structure of the remote computer. These features make transferring files using the FTP protocol a tremendously useful tool.

In an FTP transfer, the *data* and *requestheaders* parameters are ignored. Using the *Execute* method for an FTP transfer involves supplying an FTP command string for the *operation* parameter.

The syntax of the operation string for an FTP transfer is as follows:

```
operation file1 file2
```

The *file1* and *file2* parameters are optional and depend on the type of command that is employed.

A lot of the FTP commands will be familiar to you if you have experience with MS-DOS. The similarity between the functionality of MS-DOS and Windows makes understanding the FTP protocol a lot easier.

The FTP protocol supports numerous commands. Check the documentation of the particular FTP server to which you are connecting to find out the complete set of commands it supports. All FTP servers support a core set of commands. Some of the more useful commands are detailed in the following table.

Command	Operation
CD *file1*	Changes to the directory specified by *file1*.
CLOSE	Closes the current FTP connection.
DIR *file1*	Displays the directory entry for *file1*. (Wildcard characters are permitted and follow the syntax used by the remote computer.) If no file is specified, the entire directory is returned.
GET *file1* *file2*	Transfers *file1* from the remote computer to the local file *file2*.
PWD	Returns the name of the current directory on the remote computer.
SEND *file1* *file2*	Copies a local file, specified by *file1*, to the remote host, specified by *file2*.

StateChanged Event

After a command has been sent to a remote computer by means of the *Execute* method, any response from the remote computer is via the *StateChanged* event. The *StateChanged* event indicates what action the remote computer has performed via the *State* event parameter.

```
Private Sub icMain_StateChanged(ByVal State As Integer)
```

Depending on the value of the *State* variable, your application can perform tasks such as displaying status messages, updating progress meters, and handling any error information that comes back from the remote computer.

Most of the actions that the *StateChanged* event indicates via the *State* variable are simple status messages. In most messages, those actions can be ignored by your program. All of the values for the *StateChanged* status variable are defined in the Internet Transfer Control online help.

The actions indicating that data is present to be retrieved from the remote computer are *icResponseReceived* and *icResponseCompleted*. The *icResponseReceived* state indicates that data has been returned from the remote computer but the command is still executing. The *icResponseCompleted* state occurs after the entire command has completed. In practice, the *icResponseCompleted* command is used to initiate any pending data transfer.

Triggering of the *StateChanged* event does *not* mean that any information has been transferred from the remote computer to the Internet Transfer Control. It simply indicates that data is ready to be transferred. The actual transfer of the data is performed by using the *GetChunk* method, which is covered later in this chapter.

The *icResponseReceived* state also occurs when the action does not involve any data being returned. When you're in the process of connecting to a remote computer, certain information is received from the remote computer as part of the connection process. These *icResponseReceived* states do not result in any data being ready to be transferred.

The *icResponseComplete* state indicates that the operation is finished. If the operation was an FTP *send*, the *icResponseCompleted* state will indicate that the file has been transferred to the remote computer.

The other important state that can be returned is *icError*. In this case, the properties *ResponseCode* and *ResponseInfo* will contain further information about the error that has occurred.

GetChunk Method

The *GetChunk* method is used to receive data from the Internet Transfer Control after an *icResponseReceived* or *icResponseComplete* state is triggered in the *StateChanged* event.

```
object.GetChunk( size [,datatype] )
```

The *size* parameter indicates the size in bytes of the chunk to receive. The *datatype* parameter indicates whether the data being returned is a string or a byte array.

Although the *size* parameter can be set to any particular length, it is commonly set to 1024 bytes. If the connection is extremely slow or unreliable, a lower number will give a finer granularity of file transfer, which might be helpful. Likewise, a fast, reliable link (across a local area network, for instance) could benefit from a higher size setting. However, in most cases, it is advisable to stick with the default.

ResponseCode and *ResponseInfo* Properties

If an error has occurred during use of the Internet Transfer Control, the *ResponseCode* and *ResponseInfo* properties will contain further information about the error.

The *ResponseCode* property contains a number indicating the error number returned from the remote computer. The *ResponseInfo* property holds a string description corresponding to the error number.

```
Sub InternetErrorHandler()
    Msgbox "ErrorCode: " & icMain.ResponseCode & _
        " : " & icMain.ResponseInfo
End Sub
```

StillExecuting Property and *Cancel* Method

The *StillExecuting* property indicates whether the Internet Transfer Control is still processing a command. This property returns either True (the Internet Transfer Control is busy) or False (the Internet Transfer Control is ready to receive the next operation).

The *Cancel* method can be used to forcibly close the current connection. Before the *Cancel* method is used, it is wise to check the *StillExecuting* property first to ensure that it is free to accept the request.

The *Cancel* method can be used to let the user directly cancel a transfer. You might also use the *Cancel* method to halt transfers after a certain amount of information has been received—maybe retrieving only the first 100 characters of a number of text documents in order to provide a preview function.

The *RequestTimeOut* property as detailed in reference to the *OpenURL* method also applies when using the *Execute*, *StateChanged*, and *GetChunk* operations.

Putting It All Together

In the previous example, you saw how MyCompany used the *OpenURL* method to retrieve some known files from an FTP server. Sarah, the IT officer who implemented the sales price list application, is pleased with how easy it was to automate the process and is thinking of using the Internet Transfer Control to help her with another routine task that she often has to perform involving transferring files across the Internet.

With so many different applications in use across the company network, it has become a painful chore to continually download the latest set of updates for each application. Each supplier of software to MyCompany has made available the latest set of updated files and information. Unlike in the previous example, however, the individual files are not specified. Each set of files exists in a directory. The idea is to retrieve the entire contents of each directory for each particular site. This way, Sarah can be sure that she has the latest and greatest set of files for the many applications she has to maintain.

Sarah decides that by using the *Execute* method, she can retrieve the contents of each directory by using the FTP command DIR. Each file can then be individually retrieved by the GET command. Some of the FTP servers will have password protection, so she also needs a way of supplying user name and password information. Again, like the sales price list application, the remote site information is stored in an Access database to provide centralized administration of the process. Error messages will also be logged to this database to ensure that any errors in the transfer process are recorded.

Sarah also knows that by using the *Execute* method, she will be able to easily modify this application so that at a later stage she can use it as the basis for distributing files from MyCompany to other Internet sites.

The Visual Basic project IntSoft.VBP in CHAP04/IntSoft contains an example project that performs this task. (See Figure 4-3 on page 186.)

Technical Details

Let's look at some of the technical aspects of the Internet Software Update application (IntSoft.VBP).

The connection information is stored in an Access database. This makes it easy to administer the details of the various sites from which you want to retrieve software. Using the Visual Basic data-bound grid also makes it easy to maintain this information. The application loops through the individual site entries in the database and processes them one at a time.

The user name and password details stored in the database are supplied to the Internet Transfer Control. The Internet Transfer Control manages default values for the properties, so it doesn't matter whether or not there are values for

FIGURE 4-3

Sample application using the Execute *method*

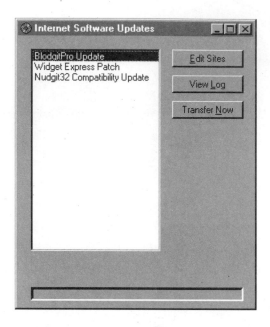

these fields. You simply assign values to the Internet Transfer Control and continue. (In the following examples, the Internet Transfer Control is named *icMain* and the recordset containing site information is *m_rstSites*.)

```
' Supply UserName/Password to Internet Transfer Control.
' The control will provide default properties if UserName
' or Password is NULL.
If Not IsNull(m_rstSites("UserName")) Then
    icMain.UserName = m_rstSites("UserName")
Else
    icMain.UserName = ""
End If

If Not IsNull(m_rstSites("Password")) Then
    icMain.Password = m_rstSites("Password")
Else
    icMain.Password = ""
End If
```

The next step is to connect to the remote computer using the user name and password you have supplied. This is achieved using the FTP USER command.

```
' Log onto the FTP site using the FTP 'USER' command.
icMain.Execute sURL, "USER " & icMain.UserName & " " & icMain.Password
zsWaitForResponse
```

Remember that any errors raised in the logon process will be reported by the *icError* state in the *StateChanged* event. Once you have logged on, you can then change to the appropriate directory by using the FTP CD command. The CD command performs exactly the same function as it does in MS-DOS. Note that when specifying the directories on the FTP server, you use forward slashes (/), but backward slashes (\) are still used for the local filename.

```
icMain.Execute sURL, "CD " & m_rstSites("Directory")
zsWaitForResponse
```

After you have successfully changed to this directory, you can retrieve the filenames it contains. Executing the command to retrieve the filenames is easy. Actually parsing the returned results is a bit more difficult. To retrieve the contents of the directory, send an FTP DIR command.

```
icMain.Execute sURL, "DIR"
zsWaitForResponse
```

After the DIR command is executed, any existing data is returned to you by the remote computer. You are notified of this by means of the *icResponse-Completed* state in the *StateChanged* event. In this event, you make a call to retrieve the data by means of the *GetChunk* method. One of the nice things about the directory structure returned by an FTP DIR command is that it has none of the extra formatting that accompanies a directory listing retrieved by the *OpenURL* method. This makes it a lot easier to retrieve the individual filenames.

```
Function zsGetText() As String
' Retrieve any text data that the remote sever has returned to us.
    Dim vChunk As Variant
    Dim sData  As String
    Dim bDone  As Boolean

    bDone = False
    vChunk = icMain.GetChunk(256)
    Do Until bDone
        sData = sData & vChunk
        vChunk = icMain.GetChunk(256)
        If Len(vChunk) = 0 Then
            bDone = True
        End If
    Loop
    zsGetText = sData
End Function
```

After executing the DIR command, you have retrieved the directory listing as a string. The problem is that the string contains all the filename entries, separated by carriage return and line feed characters. This string needs to be passed to a function that will retrieve the individual directory entries and build an array containing each file in the directory. A function that performs this task is as follows:

```
Sub zsGetFileList(asFiles, sDirectory)

' This function will fill the array 'asFiles' with the directory
' entries that have been returned as part of the sDirectory string.

    Dim i          As Integer
    Dim iLastIndex As Integer

    iLastIndex = 0

    Do Until Len(sDirectory) = 0
        For i = 1 To Len(sDirectory)
            If Mid$(sDirectory, i, 1) = Chr$(13) Then
                If Len(sDirectory) <= 2 Then
                    sDirectory = ""
                    Exit For
                End If
                ReDim Preserve asFiles(iLastIndex)
                asFiles(iLastIndex) = Left$(sDirectory, i - 1)
                iLastIndex = iLastIndex + 1
                sDirectory = Mid$(sDirectory, i + 2)
                Exit For
            End If
        Next
    Loop

End Sub
```

So now you have an array with each of the directory entries as an element of the array. All you have to do now is loop through this array and perform an FTP GET command to retrieve the files. An interesting fact about using the GET command with the Internet Transfer Control is that the actual control takes care of retrieving the files to your local machine. Normally you retrieve any data that has been sent to you by using the *GetChunk* method. But when a GET command is issued, the Internet Transfer Control will automatically save the files to the location you have specified in the command parameters.

```
' Loop through each file in the directory.
For i = 0 To UBound(asFiles)
    ' Retrieve current file.
    icMain.Execute sURL, "GET " & asFiles(i) & " " & sFileName
    zsWaitForResponse
Next
```

Now that you have retrieved all the files in the directory, you loop around to the next site from the database and continue.

What is *zsWaitForResponse*? The trick to using the *Execute* method is knowing how to handle the asynchronous mode of operation. The Visual Basic code needs to know when to sit and wait for the remote server to return a response. This process involves issuing a command and then waiting for the Internet Transfer Control to indicate (via the *StillExecuting* property) that it has finished processing the command.

The *zsWaitForResponse* line is a call to a piece of code that will wait until the remote computer has finished processing the last command issued before continuing. The *DoEvents* command is used to yield execution while the remote computer is processing the results.

```
Sub zsWaitForResponse()

' After executing an FTP command, we have to wait for it to complete
' before we undertake any further processing.

Do Until Not icMain.StillExecuting
    DoEvents
    ' We can do other things here.
Loop

End Sub
```

Summary

The *Execute* method provides a powerful way to move information across the Internet. What else is there that you could achieve with the *Execute* command and, more important, the Internet Transfer Control in general?

The examples in this chapter have focused mainly on FTP servers because these are still the most common servers in use today for transferring files. HTTP servers with the ability to send and retrieve not only the files but summary information about these files provide features that you can use to build more advanced applications based on these servers.

The Internet Transfer Control is a great tool that lets you exploit the benefits of transferring information across the Internet:

- Geographical distance is no longer a concern when you need to move information between two locations.

- The types of computers or software being used are no longer a concern when you transfer files from one company to another.

- The type of network being used to connect two computers doesn't prevent you from sending information from one to another.

The availability of these features of the Internet, combined with the tremendous ease of use of the Internet Transfer Control in the Visual Basic environment, means that you have at your disposal a powerful tool for creating effective business applications.

Changing Your Approach to Visual Basic Coding

JON BURN

Jon, a TMS Associate, has been programming under Microsoft Windows since the mid-1980s. He always found C programming tough, so the introduction of Visual Basic made his job a lot easier. He's been a fan ever since. Jon has worked on some retail software, such as the PagePlus DTP package, and a lot of custom software in the corporate environment. He has also taught programming and written various articles about it. He believes that if you're going to program, you might as well do it right. Thinking about what is right keeps him from getting too comfortable. Jon spends as much time as possible at home with his wife and two sons.

Microsoft Visual Basic 5 extends the object-oriented direction of Visual Basic 4. The benefits of object-oriented programming are well documented, but what modifications should you make to your programming style to get the most out of it? The Basic programming language is by design an all-purpose language, and it is still easy to write code in a non-object-oriented manner.

In this chapter, we will look at four standards, or rules, that you can apply in modifying your coding style and improving the quality of your code. We will look at how a disciplined, standards-based approach can make a genuine impact on the quality of your code. At the same time, these rules should enable you to quickly adopt a more object-oriented style of coding, more in keeping with the spirit and direction of Visual Basic 5.

STANDARDS

Time is tight, and whoever is paying you is shouting at you to hand over the program yesterday. Unfortunately, too often no one is also asking, "How good is the code?" If that question isn't being asked, the people who are paying you likely are going to end up spending a lot more than they bargained for. Although it is usual to blame management and the process for this—and often rightly so—there comes a time when we have to acknowledge that we programmers are also culprits. If no one ever asks you to monitor the quality of the code you write, it should be no surprise that the innards of the code can sometimes get a bit messy. That's when standards matter.

Standards have two principal characteristics:

- They force you to maintain a methodical and disciplined approach to your coding, whatever the pressure to take shortcuts.

- They constantly remind you that the internal quality of your code matters.

The very decision to use standards (and along with them a review process for making sure that they are adhered to) will affect how programmers approach coding. By making it clear that the standards are mandatory rules, not mere guidelines, you will ensure that those working on a project will realize that meeting the standards is an integral part of their job rather than a tacked-on step undertaken if they happen to have the time. Because standards are not guidelines, they should not be flexible. If a standard says, "We recommend that you place error handlers in all your event code," you might do so some of the time. But you are most likely to omit the error handlers when you are under the most pressure, and therefore they will be absent from your most error-prone code.

What the standards actually say is also important, of course. Traditionally, coding standards have focused on the following topics:

- Naming
- Layout
- Commenting
- Coding dos and don'ts, such as inclusion of error handling

The emphasis is on writing code that's shareable—that is, code that other programmers can read easily, and code that is in a familiar style. Shareable code is also beneficial even if you're the only person to work with it. When you return to it in three months, you'll find that you can pick it up and work with it again rather than gaze at it in incomprehension.

Another goal of traditional coding standards is to assist in making the code more robust. Error handling will be mandatory, *GoTo* statements will be prohibited, and so on. Program elements, files, functions, variables, and constants will all have to follow naming conventions. These requirements aid in the organization of your project. Also, prefixing elements to indicate the data type, as in Hungarian notation, is commonplace.

If you program in Visual Basic for a living and you and your organization are not enforcing any coding standards, you are slipping dangerously behind the competition.

Some Drawbacks of Standards

These types of coding standards are worthy and undoubtedly help in team or corporate environments. But they do not by themselves ensure that the code is of high quality.

Some people use the term "quality" loosely and subjectively, often in an effort to justify their particular point of view. It is necessary to be clear about what you mean by quality. Bertrand Meyer enumerates several key criteria of quality code in his book *Object-Oriented Software Construction* (Prentice-Hall, 1997). Most important are *correctness, robustness,* and *extensibility.* Correctness is the ability of the code to perform to its specification—that is, its behavior in known conditions. Robustness is its behavior in unknown conditions. Extensibility is the ease with which the code can be modified to accommodate new and changed requirements.

Unfortunately, traditional coding standards don't measure the extent of any of these quality attributes. It's perfectly feasible to write some incorrect, flaky, hard-to-modify code that adheres to the coding standards. In fact, writing such code is all too easy.

After all that building up, you might think that I'm about to reveal some magic ingredient that will instantly render all your code fabulously elegant and guaranteed bug free. I'm afraid not. What I will talk about are some rules that I treat as coding standards, which, together with the new object-oriented features of Visual Basic 5, take me a bit further in the right direction.

The Restrictive Property of Standards

Choosing to follow—or being forced to follow—a new set of standards is a bit like driving a new car. After a short period of acclimatization, you fall into line with the new ways of working, and it starts to feel pretty natural again. At least that applies to naming, commenting, and layout issues.

Programmers tend to resist standards more when the standards address specific language issues—such as, "Don't use the *GoTo* statement." This reaction occurs because language standards are always *restrictive*—they state which parts of the language you should *not* use. Maybe the standards are taking away your right to use a part of the language that the authors put in for a reason.

I've heard it argued that Visual Basic consists of a core 5 percent of the product that you should use and 95 percent of extra fluff that you can do without. The theory is that you can get by with a minimalist syntax that reduces the learning curve, is easier to read, and is more likely to stay compatible with future versions of Visual Basic. Some examples of fluff that you could cut out with no loss might be given, such as the redundant *While…Wend* statements.

Yet, many others' philosophy, including my own, is to learn about and use as much of the language as one possibly can. Although I can agree with the minimalist sentiment as far as *While…Wend* is concerned, I disagree with the overall percentages. Surely almost all of the features of Visual Basic add some value, and therefore you should learn about them and use them. Don't worry about the possibility that they will disappear from future versions of Visual Basic—judging by past practice, Microsoft will not even take out the useless features, let alone the good ones.

Standards That Change the Way You Program

Meaningful, substantive standards—standards that can genuinely improve program quality—are radical and modern, but I believe that they are in tune with the future direction of the development of the Visual Basic language.

For those of you in a hurry, I'll tell you the ending. Here are the standards. The rest of this chapter discusses the background to these and has plenty of interesting gems in it. But if you want, you can just go ahead and use these standards for a while. If you find that you're thinking more, typing less, and producing better code as a result, why waste time on the theory—it's the practice that counts.

- **Rule 1: Do not use global variables.** And I mean *no* globals! No exceptions are allowed. You can always accomplish the same result without a global variable. Later in this chapter, I explain why globals are bad, and I provide some examples of when Visual Basic programmers typically would use globals but needn't. By global, I mean a variable with global scope. So I count as global anything prefixed with the *Global* keyword, or a *Public* variable in a regular module (BAS file).

- **Rule 2: Do not use user-defined types.** By this, I mean anything with the *Type* keyword. I don't mean user-defined classes—you should have lots of those. The one exception to this is when you are calling into a DLL that requires a structure. Use them for this purpose alone.

- **Rule 3: Do not pass function parameters by reference.** Prefix all of your function parameters with *ByVal*. What a pity this isn't the default parameter-passing convention—it would have saved a lot of typing.

- **Rule 4: Do not use first-class data types—use Variants.** This rule is the most controversial. I'm aware that this one challenges the perceived wisdom, but it is the one that pays the most dividends. You should replace all variables of type integer, long, single, double, byte, date, string, Boolean, and currency with Variants. Trust me.

RULE 1: DO NOT USE GLOBAL VARIABLES

Global variables have long been frowned upon. They are the ultimate in short-term programming. Easy to define and use initially, they always create more problems than they solve in the long term.

The most obvious bad thing about them is that they increase the likelihood of bugs. Whether you are reading the variable or setting its value, you have to make assumptions. It may have been modified in some distant part of the program, leading you astray. Then again, if you modify it, the change might break some code elsewhere.

Global variables make code hard to change. When you revisit some code, whether yours or someone else's, the existence of globals makes it far harder to have full confidence in the effect of your modifications. Suppose you were making a small modification to a routine that contained some global variable. Because global variables can by definition be used throughout the program, it is necessary to sweep through the whole program, examining each instance of that variable's use to see if it is affected by your change. This review is time-consuming and error-prone.

THE SHACKLES OF BACKWARD COMPATIBILITY

Other chapters of this book concentrate on migration issues in detail, and of course some bits of code always need modification in moving from one version of Visual Basic to the next. But as a general principle, Microsoft has attempted to keep the language backward compatible. I guess it would be seen as a marketing weakness if reviews were to be printed with comments such as, "The next version of Visual Basic will break *all* of your code."

Fair enough, but this backward compatibility comes at a high price. The language will become more and more bloated with irrelevant and contradictory features until some stuff is pulled out and other stuff is put in. Some examples of what I mean follow.

The Use of + for String Concatenation

This misconceived experiment with operator overloading was considered bad form even back in the days of Visual Basic 2, when the string concatenation operator & was first introduced. Yet in Visual Basic 5 it is still supported. In particular, since version 4 brought in extensive implicit type conversion between numerics and strings, this issue has become even more important. It is easy to find examples of how you can be tripped up. Can you be confident of what the following will print?

```
Debug.Print "56" + 48
Debug.Print "56" + "48"
Debug.Print "56" -- "48"
```

What *should* happen is that adding to strings should have the same effect as subtracting from, multiplying, or dividing strings—that is, it should generate a type mismatch error. Unfortunately, this is not the case. The only argument for why it stays in there, causing bugs, is backward compatibility.

ReDim Bypassing the *Option Explicit* Directive

See if you can spot the bug in the following code:

```
Option Explicit
' Declare an array of players.
Dim FootballTeam() As Players
' Do stuff...
' Redimension to have 12 elements.
ReDim FootbalTeam(12)
```

ReDim does not require an array name to have been already explicitly declared, even if *Option Explicit* is set. If you have an existing array and you attempt to

>>

resize it with *ReDim* but you make a typing mistake and misspell the name of the array, you get a new array with the misspelled name. It is this type of common bug that *Option Explicit* was designed to trap and flag at compile time.

DefType

In my job reviewing program code, I've seen at least 50 different individuals' Visual Basic code—not one of them has ever used a *DefInt*, a *DefLng*, or one of the other types. Does anyone use this stuff? Is it just me, or does it seem a bizarre concept that a variable's type is defined by the first letter in the name?

Type Declaration Characters

Why should we have to remember that % is an integer or # a double? There are no type declaration characters for newer data types such as Boolean or date. Those who designed Visual Basic must have run out of punctuation or decided it was a bad idea. Type declaration characters are hangovers from pre–Visual Basic forms of Basic, but now we are just left with an inconsistent mess.

Zero-Based or One-Based Collections

If you are iterating through the Forms or the Controls collection, you step from 0 through Count −1; but if you are stepping through a standard Collection, you step from 1 through Count.

```
Dim i, colThings As New Collection
colThings.Add "Fred"

For i = 0 To Forms.Count - 1
    ' Iterate through Forms collection.
    Debug.Print Forms(i).Name
Next i
For i = 1 To colThings.Count
    ' Iterate through colThings collection.
    Debug.Print colThings(i)
Next i
```

Redundant Keywords

Redundant keywords such as *Let* and *While...Wend* don't do any harm, but they clutter your code.

That's enough griping. Visual Basic's designers are obviously aware of all of these flaws and inconsistencies. Why don't they fix them? Backward compatibility.

So what's new? Global variables have long been understood to hinder code reliability and readability, but Visual Basic has tended to encourage the use of global variables. For example, consider how you would typically solve these everyday problems.

Example 1:
Return Values from a Modal Dialog Box

As a simple example, consider a File Open dialog box. You need to know whether the user clicked OK or Cancel, and if the user clicked OK, you also need the name of the file selected.

The calling pseudocode might look something like this:

```
frmFileOpen.Show vbModal  ' Puts up file open dialog
' Returns here when form is unloaded
If okpressed Then
    filename = ???
End If
```

The two main questions are these:

1. How do you return the OK or Cancel result?
2. How do you return the filename?

One approach might be to store these in global variables, but I have already discounted this approach.

Another approach is a workaround that was used a lot on older versions of Visual Basic. Its merit is that it does avoid globals, but it's clumsy. The trick is not to unload the form but simply to hide it. That way, you can still read the values of controls on the form, such as the filename.

This approach has two drawbacks, however. One is that you still cannot "read" whether the user clicked OK or Cancel because these are events, not controls. You might use the *Tag* property of the form here, but this is still very error-prone and limited. Sometimes you end up with several sets of information that all need to be stored in the *Tag* property. The second drawback is that the calling function is left with the job of cleaning up the mess. It must determine when it is safe to unload the form, and it must remember to do so. This is another thing waiting to go wrong.

A better approach comes from treating the form like a class. Forms can have *Public* variables, property procedures, and methods in the same way classes do. These are accessible even after the form is unloaded. So in this example, we simply store the state in two *Public* variables as follows. *Form frmFileOpen* looks like this:

```
Option Explicit
' Public interface for frmFileOpen is two Variants, one to hold the
' okpressed state and another to hold the filename.
Public okpressed
Public filename

Private Sub cmdCancel_Click()
    okpressed = False
    Unload Me
End Sub

Private Sub cmdOK_Click()
    filename = txtFname ' Place content of text box in filename.
    okpressed = True
    Unload Me
End Sub
```

The calling program uses this approach:

```
frmfileopen.Show vbModal
' Form is now genuinely unloaded here.
If frmfileopen.okpressed Then
    MsgBox frmfileopen.filename
End If
```

It's quite readable, and I think you'll agree it's an improvement.

This looks like the end of the story, but it isn't. What we have here are *disguised* global variables! It is possible to access *frmfileopen.filename* from anywhere in the program and read from or write to its value.

The following line is legitimate anywhere. In all important respects, it is still just like a global!

```
frmfileopen.filename = "Fred"
```

NOTE

This will not reload the form, and it is quite unlike referring to the text box directly, as in:

```
frmfileopen.txtFname = "Fred"
```

This will cause the form to be reloaded.

We can mitigate this to some extent by making the values read-only. This is done by using a *Public Property Get* but no corresponding *Public Property Let*. You also have to store the values in a private *Form* level variable, which is a little clumsy. If you use the Class Builder, it will create all this for you.

```
Option Explicit
Private m_okpressed
Private m_filename


' Public interface for frmFileOpen is two property gets,
' one to read the okpressed state and another to read the filename.
Public Property Get filename()
    filename = m_filename
End Property
Public Property Get okpressed()
    okpressed = m_okpressed
End Property


Private Sub cmdCancel_Click()
    m_okpressed = False
    Unload Me
End Sub


Private Sub cmdOK_Click()
' Place content of text box in private filename variable.
    m_filename = txtFname
    m_okpressed = True
    Unload Me
End Sub
```

The *frmfileopen.filename* variable is now a global read-only variable, which is much safer. The only way it can be changed is by opening the form, changing the contents of the text box, and clicking OK.

We are treating forms as classes, and this is allowing us to use them more powerfully than before. However, we still have no control over the scope of the form. The real reason these variables are still global is that although the form name *frmfileopen* is a class name, it is also the name of a *single global instance* of that class. When the program loads this form for the first time, it creates an instance of the form class, which is global in scope and has the name of the class itself. This cleverly allows older code to run while making forms, in effect, classes. Once again, this is at the expense of the purity of the language.

To get around the scope issue, we can explicitly create an instance of the form and use that instead, as follows:

```
' Uses a second (nonglobal) instance of the form.
Dim f As frmfileopen
Set f = New frmfileopen

f.Show 1
' The form is now genuinely unloaded here.
If f.okpressed Then
    MsgBox f.filename
End If
' f terminate event occurs when f goes out of scope, after
' which properties cannot be accessed.
```

The *f.filename* variable has the same scope as the form *f*, which in this instance is local to the procedure in which this bit of code is run. There is now no chance of side effects, and the code is much more robust.

Example 2: Keep the INI File Read Operation in One Place

This example demonstrates some themes similar to those in Example 1. In the past, you might have done one of the following:

- Read your INI file at the beginning of your program and stored the values in global variables.
- Read your INI file "on demand." Wherever a value from an INI file is required, the file is opened and the value read there and then.

The second option has some advantages, especially if you're also writing back to the INI file from within your program, because you'll always get the latest value. Moreover, the performance degradation is negligible. Visual Basic has always handled text file input/output blindingly fast, so for any normal-size INI files, you won't notice the overhead that the file access imposes each time.

The downside is that there is no centralization. Not only does this cause administrative problems—that is, quickly finding out what is in your INI file—but it also is another example of the disguised global variable.

You can centralize INI file handling best by utilizing a class, as shown in the example on the following page.

Class Name: IniFile

```
Option Explicit
' Contains all properties in the INI file.
' We use the Get/Let properties to read/write
' the INI file entries.

Private Function IniFileName()
' If there is no command line, the INI file
' will be myapp.ini in the same dir as the EXE.
    If Command$ = "" Then
        If Right(App.Path, 1) = "\" Then
            IniFileName = App.Path & "myapp.ini"
        Else
            IniFileName = App.Path & "\myapp.ini"
        End If
    Else
        IniFileName = Command$
    End If
End Function

Public Property Get StyleFile()
' Read value from INI file.
    StyleFile = GetSetting(IniFileName(), "GENERAL", "StyleFile")
End Property

Public Property Let Color(newLongColor)
' Write new value to INI file, and store as RGB string;
' e.g., convert 16711680 to 0, 0, 255 (blue).
    Dim RGBColor
    RGBColor = LongToRGB(newLongColor)
    SaveSetting IniFileName(), "OPTIONS", "Color", RGBColor
End Property

Public Property Get Color()
' Read value from INI file, and convert from RGB string to long;
' e.g., convert 0, 0, 255 to 16711680 (blue).
    Dim RGBColor
    RGBColor = GetSetting(IniFileName(), "OPTIONS", "Color")
    If RGBColor = "" Then
        Color = RGB(255, 255, 255)
    Else
        Color = RGBToLong(RGBColor)
    End If
End Property
```

This code segment demonstrates various advantages of using a class-based approach:

- The private function *IniFileName* encapsulates the logic for where the INI file is located.

- We can have read-only INI file entries, such as *StyleFile*.

- We can include conversions as the data is read or written. In this instance—with the *Color* property—RGB colors, which are used as longs within the program, are stored as more user-friendly strings of the form 0,0,255 in the INI file.

- Defaults can be added where the INI file entry is missing. In this case, the default color is RGB(255, 255, 255).

- In addition to this, all INI file reading and writing is centralized, and there are no global variables.

When using this class, the code will look like this:

```
Dim ini As New iniFile
ini.Color = RGB(0, 255, 0)
```

You can access the INI file properties only where you have an *iniFile* object in scope—in this case, the *ini* object reference variable is local to this function.

As with the previous modal form example, you have to get used to creating new instances of the objects that you want to use, which is a rather new way of programming for Visual Basic users. It would be possible, of course, to create a global *ini* file object and reference it throughout your program; but though that would save a little bit of typing, it would take us back to the original problem.

Coding standards for Visual Basic have tended to be wishy-washy when it comes to globals. They are discouraged rather than prohibited. In the world of standards, this is ineffectual—you have to either say you can use something or say you can't. There is no middle ground. Improvements in the Visual Basic language now mean that there are no longer any reasons to use globals. Whenever you find yourself writing a bit of code that "requires" a global variable, stop! Think about it, and find an alternative way of writing it.

RULE 2: DO NOT USE USER-DEFINED TYPES

Visual Basic is becoming more object-oriented, and that is good. But it is not a goal in itself. The object-oriented approach exists to provide genuine benefits—principally *reuse* and *extensibility*.

Reuse

Reuse means not just reusing your code but reusing other people's code too. The gains in productivity should be immense, but in practice, information systems departments struggle to get it working. The use of third-party components in VBX/OCX form—user interface widgets, in particular—is widespread. But reusing in-house code—your own code—remains the exception rather than the rule. (See Chapter 15 for much more information about reuse.)

The reasons for this lack of reuse are part organizational and part cultural. But fundamentally they all come down to the simple reason that often the code you're thinking of reusing doesn't do the new task exactly right. It does too little, it does too much, or it is in some way not quite right. Instead, you end up coding your own version. Sound familiar?

Extensibility

We all change our code, and most of us change other people's code. Since Visual Basic became the most popular tool for creating applications for Windows some time ago, the software development life cycle has changed for good. Visual Basic programs are not analyzed, designed, and coded in an ordered, sequential fashion. All the traditional phases intermingle because Visual Basic is used for everything from prototyping to analyzing requirements, and the code is rapidly modified thereafter. The tool's productivity makes this route irresistible, but the downside is that it becomes difficult to prevent your code from degenerating when you continually revisit it. Extensible code is code that can be easily enhanced. The use of classes is key to achieving this.

Classes

Why does the use of classes in your Visual Basic code help make your code more reusable and extensible? What advantages do classes have over traditional BAS files, functions, variables, and so on?

Classes provide the framework for clearly defining and separating what is on the *inside* and the *outside*. The outside of any class is its interface. This is the contract that your class promises to abide by, and the code that utilizes your class can rely on that interface being present.

From the point of view of the Class Builder, the interface also lets *you* know what your clients are relying on. So provided that you keep the interface in place, you can extend the class without breaking any existing code. It's quite simple.

Use classes all the time

If you picture yourself creating your entire program out of these classes, the interaction of each part with the others becomes tightly controlled and the extensibility of the entire program is enhanced. Your program becomes far better structured and designed. In short, you have better-quality code.

How do you and your Visual Basic development group progress toward creating programs full of classes? The question, "What should be in my classes?" is a frequent one, and there is no simple catchall answer. In the textbooks, the examples are often too "real-world." Classes such as *Flea* or *Tyrannosaurus* make good examples to demonstrate concepts in the manuals because they directly map to real-world objects. Unfortunately, most of my programs seem to be concerned with more mundane problem areas—usually it involves taking some data from one place and putting it somewhere else. Does this mean that the problem is not suitable for an object-oriented approach? Not at all!

To discipline myself to use classes in these situations, I adopt the following rule: Do not declare any user-defined types. Wherever you have a user-defined type, replace it with a class.

Comparing Classes with User–Defined Types

The most obvious first thing to check is whether it is *possible* to replace user-defined types (UDTs) with classes. This should be fairly evident. Create a class, and give it a property for each of the members of the user-defined type. That's all you need to do.

Consider the following simple structure, a point:

```
Type Point
    x
    y
End Type
```

This should be rewritten as a class as follows:

```
Class Point
Public x
Public y
```

Simple usage comparisons are shown on the following page.

Using a Class

```
' Create a point.
Dim p As New Point
' Give it some values.
p.x = 17
p.y = 23

Dim p1 As Point
' Can get second references;
' can be useful.
Set p1 = p
```

Using a User-Defined Type

```
Dim p As Point
' Give it some values.
p.x = 17
p.y = 23

Dim p1 As Point
' Can copy points;
' can be useful.
p1 = p
```

Notice that when we move from UDTs to classes, we trade the ability to simply copy a point for the ability to obtain a second reference to an object. If you need to copy a point, you'll have to write your own copy method.

UDTs Are Not Self-Describing

One seemingly trivial difference between the two examples is that with the UDT case, you would need to have had the definition of *Point* visible to your code, either in that module or as a *Public Type* in another module. The class, on the other hand, comes as part of the Automation framework, which means you need only have a reference to the binary implementation of the class for it to work. The accompanying type library will describe to the calling code that the *Point* class has two properties, *X* and *Y*.

Suppose you were developing a library of code that handles point manipulation:

Using a Class

Calling function needs a reference to the library. Built-in type library enables calling function to use *Point* class.

Using a User-Defined Type

Need to ship a BAS file, which the calling function must include in its source code to understand *Point* UDT.

Automation is concerned with *binary* integration of components, not source code integration. Out-of-process and Remote Automation components interact with one another through the same mechanism as does code utilizing classes *within* a single program. It is clear that UDTs do not fit into this approach because of their inability to describe themselves at a binary level.

This explains why the newer features of Visual Basic tend not to support UDTs. For example, Visual Basic 5 will not let you do the following:

- Have a UDT as a public property of a class or a form
- Pass a UDT as a *ByVal* parameter to a subroutine or a function
- Have a UDT as a parameter to a public method of a class or a form
- Have a UDT as the return type of a public method of a class or a form
- Place a UDT into a Variant

However, you can do all these things with classes. For this reason alone, you should use classes instead of UDTs.

Use of Property *Let/Get*

Another way of writing the *Point* class is to have explicit property *Let* and *Get* functions for the *x* and *y* members, as follows:

Class Point

```
Private m_x, m_y

Public Property Let x(newValue)
    m_x = newValue
End Property

Public Property Get x()
    x = m_x
End Property

Public Property Let y(newValue)
    m_y = newValue
End Property

Public Property Get y()
    y = m_y
End Property
```

This is a lot of typing—is it worth it? The advantage of writing the *Point* class in this way is that it is better encapsulated. You can intercept every reference to *x* or *y*, every time it is read or written to. In this simplest of cases, this is not required.

On the negative side, you have unnecessary typing, work, and storage (*m_y* and *m_x*). In this case, I would stick with the initial definition using *Public x* and *Public y*. Remember that a public variable in a class or form is not a global variable, unlike a public variable in a module. In particular, it does *not* have global scope. It has no scope of its own but can be referenced only as a property of an object. Therefore, it has the scope of the object it belongs to. Contrast this with public variables declared in a module—these are always bad. (See the earlier discussion.)

Validation and Protection

Property *Let*/*Get* allows you to validate the property in a way that would not be possible with a UDT. In this example, we have a property that can have a discrete set of values. The traffic light can be red, green, or yellow. The constants are defined using an *Enum*, but this is not sufficient to ensure that the traffic light values fall into this range. You can perform the validation using a Property *Let* instead.

```
Public Enum TrafficLight
    RedLight
    GreenLight
    YellowLight
End Enum
```

Class TLight

```
Private m_TopLight As TrafficLight
Public Property Let TopLight(newValue As TrafficLight)
    ' You can validate the assignment to TopLight.
    ' Note that Enum will NOT do any checking for you.
    Select Case newValue
        Case RedLight, GreenLight, YellowLight
            m_TopLight = newValue
        Case Else
            ' Raise type mismatch.
            Err.Raise 13
        End Select
End Property
Public Property Get TopLight() As TrafficLight
    TopLight = m_TopLight
End Property
```

With the following code, only the last line will generate an error:

```
Dim tl As New TLight
Dim col As TrafficLight
```

```
col = RedLight
t1.TopLight = col

' Enums do not validate...
col = 1234      ' This works.
' ...but classes do validate.
t1.TopLight = col ' This gets an error.
```

Rule 3: Do Not Pass Function Parameters by Reference

I use this rule to force myself not to be lazy when defining functions.* Passing parameters by reference is a sign that I'm getting lazy, and the alarm bells start to ring. Passing parameters by reference is indicative of bad design, as I'll explain, but there are some lesser reasons not to pass parameters by reference that have to do with introducing bugs, as I'll also mention.

Bad Design

Passing parameters by reference is a sign that you don't have the relationships between your functions correct. To try to decide what constitutes a function, I think of the mathematical definition. The mathematical model of a function is of the form:

$$x = f(a,b,c,...)$$

where the function acts on a,b,c, and so on to produce a result x. Both sides of the equal sign are the same value. You can use either x or $f(a,b,c...)$ interchangeably.

In a Visual Basic program, this is not quite the case because the function *does* something as well, but it is still most useful to think of the return value x as the *result* of what that function f does. But if x contains the result, the result cannot be also in a,b, or c. In other words, only x is changed by the function. This is my simplistic conceptual model of a function, and it is at odds with the notion of passing by reference.

---

* In this instance, I use the term *function* in its most generic sense. Hence, this chapter applies to both functions and subroutines, as well as to property procedures and anything else that takes parameters.

Passing a parameter by reference indicates one of the following:

Functions are trying to do more than one task

This is going to lead to larger functions than need be, functions that are more complex than need be, and functions that are not as useful as they could be. You should break down the functions so that each one does only one task, as in the mathematical model.

A new class needs to be defined

If the function needs to return two related values, say an X and a Y value for a coordinate, create a class to hold the object that these values relate to, and return that. If the values are not sufficiently related to be able to define a class, you are almost certainly doing too much in the one function. As an example, this

```
GetCenter(f As Form, ByRef X, ByRef Y)
```

would be better written as

```
Set p = GetCenter(f As Form)
```

where p is an object of class *Point*.

Functions return some data and some related meta-data

By *meta-data,* I mean a description of the data returned. If you use only self-describing data types, this won't be an issue. For example, functions that return an array or a single element, depending on some argument, should return a Variant, which can hold either, and the caller can use *IsArray* to determine what sort of data is returned.

Functions return some data and an indication of the function's success

It is quite common to use the return value of a function to return True, False, or perhaps an error code. The actual data value is returned as a parameter by reference. For example, consider this code fragment:

```
bRet = GetFileVersion(ByRef nVersion, filename)
```

Here the version of *filename* is returned by reference, provided the file was found correctly. If the file was not found, the function will return False and *nVersion* will not be accurate.

You have a couple of alternatives.

- **Raise errors.** This has always been the Visual Basic way. (For example, Visual Basic's own *Open* works in this way.)

- **Return a Variant and use the *CVErr* function to create a Variant of subtype *vbError* holding the error condition.** The caller can then use *IsError* as follows:

```
nVersion = GetFileVersion(filename)

If IsError(nVersion) Then
    ' nVersion is unreliable; take some action...
Else
    ' nVersion is reliable; use it...
End if
```

Error raising and trapping is not to everyone's taste, so the second option might have some appeal for you.

Side Effects

Instances of parameters unexpectedly changing their value result in bugs and are a lesser form of the global variable issue. To put it at its simplest, parameters changing their values are a side effect, and side effects trip up programmers.

If I call the function

```
Dim a, b
a = f(b)
```

it is immediately apparent to me that a is likely to change, and probably b will not. But I cannot guarantee that without looking at the source code for the function f. This makes me place passing parameters by reference into the same category as user-defined types—they are not self-describing and do not fit well into the Automation framework.

It is particularly unfortunate that the default parameter-passing convention is *ByRef*, because it means that you have to do extra typing to implement this rule. Because of backward compatibility, I think there is no chance of this being changed.

Variant Bug Potential

Variants are extremely useful, as I will discuss in the next section, but they do not work well with passing parameters by reference and can give rise to some hard-to-spot bugs. Of course, I am therefore willing to avoid passing by reference rather than forgo Variants.

The problem is illustrated in the example on the following page.

```
Private Sub f(ByVal x As Variant)
    x = 6.4
    Debug.Print x       ' Shows 6.4
End Sub

Private Sub g(x As Variant)
    x = 6.4
    Debug.Print x       ' Shows 6
End Sub

Private Sub Form_Load()
    Dim i As Integer
    i = 3
    f i
    g i
End Sub
```

The problem, as you can see, is that in the subroutine g, you might reasonably expect that after assigning 6.4 to g, which is declared in the parameter list as a Variant, *Debug.Print* would show 6.4. Instead it shows only 6.

Note that the only difference between functions *f()* and *g()* is that the parameter is passed *ByVal* in *f()* and *ByRef* in *g()*.

When the function *f* is called, the actual parameter *i* is of type integer. Thus, in *f* the formal parameter *x* is created as a Variant of subtype integer and is initialized with the value 3. In other words, the subtype of the Variant *within* the function is defined by the type of the variable with which the function was actually called. When it is then set to the value 6.4, because *x* is a Variant it can accept this value and converts to a Variant of subtype double with the value 6.4. That much is straightforward.

When function *g* is called, Visual Basic has a bit of a problem. It is passing an integer by reference, so it cannot allow noninteger values to be placed in it. So instead of the integer being converted to a Variant, it remains an integer. Thus, even in the function *g* itself, where *x* is declared as a Variant, *x* is really an integer, and the assignment *x = 6.4* will result in an implicit *CInt* call and *x* ends up with the value 6. Not so straightforward.

Functions such as *f()* are powerful because they can perform the same task no matter what the data type of the actual parameters is. They could even perform different tasks depending on the types of the actual parameter, although this can be confusing.

Functions such as *g()* lead to bugs. Avoid them by avoiding passing by reference.

RULE 4: DO NOT USE FIRST-CLASS DATA TYPES—USE VARIANTS

Rule 4 states that you should not declare any variables to be first-class data types—that is, integer, long, single, double, byte, date, string, Boolean, or currency. Instead, you should declare only Variants. To implement this would be a big step for many Visual Basic programmers and is certainly at odds with the conventional wisdom. Let's start off by discussing some of the reasons why a lot of the current thinking insists that Variants are *bad* things and should be avoided.

First let's take a quick overview of Variants.

Variants

Variants were first introduced in version 2 of Visual Basic as a flexible data type that could hold each of the simple data types. This data type was extended substantially with Visual Basic 4 to include objects and arrays in particular and a little further with Visual Basic 5 to include the decimal data type. I find it interesting that the decimal data type is the first data type that is not available as a first-class data type—it is available only within a Variant.

A variety of functions will convert and test for these subtypes. Table 5-1 on page 216 shows the development of the Variant through the versions.

Comparing Variants with Simple Data Types

Every journal article on optimizing Visual Basic includes a mention of how Variants are slower than underlying first-class data types. This should come as no surprise. For example, when iterating through a sequence with a Variant of subtype integer, the interpreted or compiled code must decode the structure of the Variant every time it wants to use it instead of accessing an integer value directly. There is bound to be an overhead to doing this.

Plenty of authors have made a comparison using a Variant as a counter in a *For* loop, and yes, a Variant integer takes about 50 percent more time than an integer. This margin decreases as the data type becomes more complex, so a Variant double is about the same as a double, whereas, surprisingly, a Variant currency is quicker than a currency. Table 5-2 on page 216 sums up these results.

TABLE 5-1   **THE EVOLUTION OF VARIANTS**

Type	Visual Basic Name	Visual Basic Version	Convert Function	Test Function
0	Empty	2		IsEmpty
1	Null	2		IsNull
2	Integer	2	CInt	IsNumeric
3	Long	2	CLng	IsNumeric
4	Single	2	CSng	IsNumeric
5	Double	2	CDbl	IsNumeric
6	Currency	2	CCur	IsNumeric
7	Date	2	CVDate / CDate	IsDate
8	String	2	CStr	
9	Object	4		IsObject
10	Error	4	CVErr	IsError
11	Boolean	4	CBool	
12	Variant	4	CVar	
13	Object	4		
14	Decimal	5	CDec	IsNumeric
17	Byte	4	CByte	
8192	Array	4		IsArray
16384	ByRef	Never?		

TABLE 5-2   **TEST RESULTS FOR ITERATING THROUGH A *FOR* LOOP 1 MILLION TIMES***

Data Type	Native Data Type	Variant Equivalent
Integer	328 ms	502 ms
Long	319 ms	591 ms
Single	805 ms	1051 ms
Double	805 ms	1049 ms
Currency	805 ms	632 ms

* Visual Basic 5 was used in design mode on a 120-Mhz Cyrix 686.

Is this significant? Almost always it is not. The amount of time that would be saved by not using Variants would be dwarfed by the amount of time spent in loading and unloading forms and controls, painting the screen, talking to databases, and so on.

When optimizing, you benefit by looking at the bigger picture. If your program is too slow, you should reassess the whole architecture of your system, concentrating in particular on the database and network aspects. Then look at the user interface and algorithms. If your program is still so locally computation-intensive and time-critical that you think significant time can be saved by using integers rather than Variants, you should be considering writing the critical portion in C++ and placing this in a DLL.

Taking a historical perspective, machines continue to grow orders of magnitude faster, which allows software to take more liberties with performance. Nowadays, it is better to concentrate on writing your code so that it works, is robust, and is extensible. If you need to sacrifice efficiency to do this, so be it—your code will still run fast enough anyway.

Memory Doesn't Matter

A Variant data type takes up 16 bytes of memory and is structured as shown in Figure 5-1.

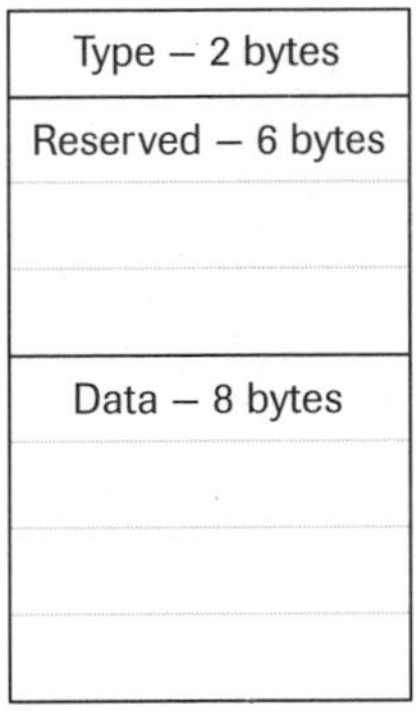

FIGURE 5-1

The structure of a Variant

| Type – 2 bytes |
| Reserved – 6 bytes |
| |
| |
| Data – 8 bytes |
| |
| |
| |

A common argument against Variants is that they take up more memory than do other data types. In place of an integer, which normally takes just 2 bytes of memory, a Variant of 16 bytes is taking eight times more space. The ratio is less, of course, for other underlying types, but the Variant always contains some wasted space.

The question is, as with the issue of performance discussed in the previous section, how significant is this? Again, I think not very. If your program has some extremely large arrays—say, tens of thousands of integers—an argument could be made to allow integers to be used. But they are the exception. All your normal variables in any given program are going to make no perceptible difference whether they are Variants or not.

I'm not saying that using Variants improves performance or memory. It doesn't. What I'm saying is that the effect Variants have is not a big deal—at least, not a big enough deal to outweigh the reasons for using them.

Type Safety

A more complex argument is the belief that Variants are poor programming style—that they represent an unwelcome return to the sort of dumb macro languages that encouraged sloppy, buggy programming.

This argument maintains that restricting variables to a specific type allows various logic errors to be trapped at compile time, an obviously good thing. Variants, in theory, take away this ability.

Example 1:
Assignment between incompatible variables

Consider the following code fragment:

```
Dim i As Integer, s As String
s = "Hello"
i = s
```

What happens? Well, it depends on which version of Visual Basic you run. In Visual Basic 3, you get a *Type mismatch* error at compile time. In Visual Basic 5, there are no errors at compile time, but you get the dialog box shown in Figure 5-2 when the program encounters the *i = s* line of code.

FIGURE 5-2

The dialog box that appears when i = s *is encountered*

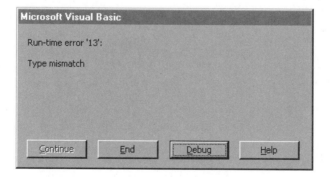

The difference is that the error occurs at run time instead of being trapped when you compile. Instead of you finding the error, your users do. This is a *bad* thing.

The situation is further complicated because it is not the fact that *s* is a string and *i* is an integer that causes the problem. It is the actual *value* of *s* that determines whether the assignment can take place.

This code succeeds, with *i* set to 1234:

```
Dim i As Integer, s As String
s = "1234"
i = s
```

This does not (you might have thought that *i* would be set to 0):

```
Dim i As Integer, s As String
s = ""
i = s
```

These two examples demonstrate why you get the error only at run time. At compile time, the compiler cannot know what the value of *s* will be.

The behavior is exactly the same with this piece of code:

```
Dim i As Integer, s As String
s = ""
i = CInt(s)
```

In other words, a hidden call to the *CInt ()* function takes place. The rules that determine whether *CInt ()* will succeed are the same as the rules that determine whether the plain *i = s* will succeed. This is known as *implicit type conversion,* although some call it "evil" type coercion.

If you don't use Variants, you should use some form of Hungarian notation to help you identify possible mismatches.

This code, on the other hand, succeeds in all versions of Visual Basic:

```
Dim i As Variant, s As Variant
s = "Hello"
i = s
```

Do you think I'm sidestepping the issue? I don't. Using Variants all but eliminates run-time type mismatch errors. The important point is that you have to go into it wholeheartedly. If you use only some Variants, you'll find you get even more type problems. Use *all* Variants, and you will get the reward.

Example 2: Function parameters and return types

Consider the following procedure:

```
Sub f(ByVal i As Integer, ByVal s As String)
End Sub
```

This procedure is called by this code:

```
Dim i As Integer, s As String
s = "Hello"
i = 1234

Call f(s, i)
```

You'll notice that I put the parameters in the wrong order.

With Visual Basic 3, you get a *Parameter Type Mismatch* error *at compile time,* but in Visual Basic 4 and 5, the situation is the same as in the previous example—*run-time* type mismatches, depending on the *values* in *s* and whether the implicit *CInt()* could work.

To summarize, from Visual Basic 4 on, there is no advantage to declaring variables to be of specific types in trapping logic errors. Instead, you leave open the possibility of run-time errors that appear only when your application ships.

Flexibility

Some time ago, while I was working for a big software house, I heard this (presumably exaggerated) anecdote about how the company had charged a customer $1 million to upgrade the customer's software. The customer had grown in size, and account codes required five digits instead of four. That was all there was to it. Of course, the client was almost certainly being ripped off, but there are plenty of examples in which a little lack of foresight proves very costly to repair. The Year 2000 problem is a prime example.

If you were negotiating a contract, the basic rules of business would dictate that you should try to obtain as much as possible and commit to as little as possible yourself. In the same way, if you view each class you write—even each function—as a contract, you should be making as few unnecessary commitments as possible in that code.

So if you need to pass the number of, let's say, biscuits as a parameter to a function, why commit to only allowing fewer than 32,768 biscuits (the maximum value of an integer)? At some point, you might need to allow for half a biscuit too, so you wouldn't want to restrict it to integer or long. You'd want to allow floating-point inputs. You could at this point declare the parameter to be of type double because this covers the range and precision of integer and long as well as handling floating points. But even this approach is still an unnecessary commitment. Not only might you still want the greater precision of currency or decimal, you might also want to pass inputs such as *An unknown number of biscuits.*

The solution is to declare the number of biscuits as a Variant. The only commitment that is made is about the meaning of the parameter—that it contains a number of biscuits—and no restriction is placed on that number. As much flexibility as possible is maintained, and the cost of those account code upgrades will diminish.

```
Function EatBiscuits(ByVal numBiscuits As Variant)
    ' Code in here to eat a number of biscuits
End Function
```

Suppose we want to upgrade the function so that we can pass *An unknown number of biscuits* as a valid input. The best way of doing this is to pass a Variant of subtype Null. Null is specifically set aside for the purpose of indicating *not known*.

If the parameter had not been a Variant, you would have had some choices:

- Add another parameter to indicate that the number is unknown. A drawback of this approach is that a modification would be required everywhere this function is called. That way lies the million-dollar upgrade. If the parameter were *Optional*, you would get away with this approach, but only the first time.

- Allow a special value to indicate *unknown*—perhaps −1 or maybe −32768. We might create a constant of this value so that the code reads a little better—*Const bisNotKnown = −1*—and use that. This approach leads to bugs. Sooner or later, you or another programmer will forget that −1 is reserved and use it as an ordinary value of the number of biscuits, however unlikely that may seem at the time you choose the value of the constant.

FLEXIBILITY AND CLASSES

It is standard to view the interfaces from the classes as a contract in the same way. In this case, the same contract flexibility principles apply.

In effect, you should make only those properties and methods *Public* that you have to. Avoid the temptation to think, "I'll also put this stuff in, in case they like it." It will only turn out to be a burden to you in the future. It is easy to add properties and methods, but it is much harder to take them out. (See also the sidebar entitled "The Shackles of Backward Compatibility" on page 198.)

I have noted that you can and should use Variants instead of integers, strings, and so on, and this is possible because a Variant can be a string or an integer. In the same way, if a class hierarchy exists in your design, you should declare variables to be of the parent class. In other words, declare your parameters and other interface variables to be of type *Animal* rather than *Flea* or *Tyrannosaurus* if it is the case that the *Animal* interface sufficiently defines the functionality that you utilize within your function.

If the parameters are Variants, you avoid these unsatisfactory choices when modifying the functions. In the same way, parameters and return types of class methods, as well as properties, should all be declared as Variants instead of first-class data types.

A New Style of Coding

I have extolled the virtues of using Variants and the flexibility that they give. To be more precise, they allow the *interface* to be flexible. By declaring the number of biscuits to be a Variant, you make it unlikely that the data type of that parameter will need to be modified again.

This flexibility of Variants has a cost to it. What happens if we call the function with an input that does not make sense?

```
N = EatBiscuits("Ugh")
```

Inside the function, we are expecting a number—so what will it make of this? You must assert your preconditions for the function to work. If, as is the case here, the input must be numeric, be sure that this is the case:

```
Function EatBiscuits(ByVal input As Variant) As Variant
    If IsNumeric(input) Then
        ' Do stuff...
    Else
        ' Return error.
    End If
End Function
```

You might think about using *Debug.Assert* in this instance, but it is no help at run time because all the calls to the *Assert* method are stripped out in compilation. So you would still need to implement your own checks anyway.

To use Variants safely, you need to modify your coding style to this more defensive style. If you do this, you can take advantage of their flexibility and write robust code at the same time.

Using the Variant as a General "Numeric" Data Type

Don't get sidetracked by irrelevant machine-specific details. Almost all the time, we want to deal with numbers. For example, consider your thought process when you choose between declaring a variable to be of type integer or type long. You might consider what the likely values of the variable are going to be, worry a little bit about the effect on performance or memory usage, and maybe check to see how you declared a similar variable somewhere else so that you can be consistent. Save time. Get into the habit of declaring all these variables as Variants.

NOTE

All variables in my code are either Variants or references to classes. Consequently, a lot of code starts to look like this:

```
Dim Top    As Variant
Dim Left   As Variant
Dim Width  As Variant
Dim Height As Variant
```

After a time, I started to take advantage of the fact that Variants are the default, so my code now typically looks like this:

```
Dim Top, Left, Width, Height
```

I see no problem with this, but your current Visual Basic coding standards will more than likely prohibit it. You might think about changing them.

Underused Variant Abilities

Flexibility is the fundamental reason to use Variants. But the built-in flexibility of Variants is not advertised enough, and consequently they tend to be underused. The use of *Empty*, *Null*, and Variant arrays in particular are still not very common in the Visual Basic programmer community.

Empty and *Null*

Any uninitialized Variant has the *Empty* value until something is assigned to it. This is true for all variables of type Variant, whether *Public*, *Private*, *Static*, or local. This is the first feature to distinguish Variants from other data types—you cannot determine whether any other data type is uninitialized.

As well as testing for *VarType* zero, a shorthand function exists—*IsEmpty()*—which does the same thing but is more readable.

In Visual Basic 3, once a Variant was given a value, the only way to reset it to *Empty* was to assign it to another Variant that itself was empty. In Visual Basic 5, you can also set it to the keyword *Empty*, as follows:

```
v1 = Empty
```

I like *Empty*, although I find it is one of those things that I forget about and sometimes miss opportunities to use. Coming from a C background, where there is no equivalent to Empty, doesn't help either. But it does have uses in odd places, so it's worth keeping it in the back of your mind. File it under miscellaneous.

Of course, *Null* is familiar to everyone as that database "no value" value, found in all SQL databases. But as a Variant subtype, it can be used to mean *no value* or *invalid value* in a more general sense—in fact, in any sense that you want to use it. Conceptually, it differs from *Empty* in that it implies you have *intentionally* set a Variant to this value for some reason, whereas *Empty* implies you just haven't gotten around to doing anything with the Variant yet.

As is the case with *Empty*, you have an *IsNull()* function and a Null keyword that you can use directly.

Visual Basic programmers tend to convert a variable with a Null value—read, say, from a database—to something else as quickly as possible. I've seen plenty of code in which Null is converted to empty strings or zeros as soon as it's pulled out of a recordset, even though this usually results in information loss and some bad assumptions. I think this stems from the fact that the stuff we want to do with data items—such as display them in text boxes or do calculations with them—often results in the all too familiar error 94—"Invalid use of Null."

This is exacerbated by the fact that Null propagates through expressions. Any arithmetic operator (+, −, *, /, \, Mod, ^) or comparison operator (<, >, =, <>) that has a Null as one of its operands will result in a Null being the value of the overall expression, irrespective of the type or value of the other operand. This can lead to some well-known bugs, such as:

```
v = Null
If v = Null Then
    MsgBox "Hi"
End if
```

In this code, the message "Hi" will *not* be displayed because as *v* is Null, the value of the expression *v = Null* is itself Null. And Null is treated as *False* in *If...Then* clauses.

The propagation rule has some exceptions. The string concatenation operator *&* treats *Null* as an empty string "" if one of its operands is Null. This explains, for example, the following shorthand way of removing Null when reading values from a database:

```
v = "" & v
```

This will leave *v* unchanged if it is a string, unless it is Null, in which case it will convert it to "".

Another set of exceptions is with the logical operators (And, Eqv, Imp, Not, Or, Xor). Here Null is treated as a third truth value, as in standard many-valued logic. Semantically, Null should be interpreted as *unsure* in this context, and this helps to explain the truth tables. For example:

```
v = True And Null
```

gives *v* the value Null, but

```
v = True Or Null
```

gives *v* the value True. This is because if you know A is true but you are unsure about B, you are unsure about A and B together, but you are sure about A or B. Follow?

By the way, watch out for the Not operator. Because the truth value of Null lies halfway between True and False, Not Null must evaluate to Null in order to keep the logical model consistent. This is indeed what it does.

```
v = Not Null
If IsNull(v) Then MsgBox "Hi"   ' You guessed it...
```

That's about all on Null—I think it is the trickiest of the Variant subtypes, but once you come to grips with how it behaves, it can add a lot of value.

Arrays

Arrays are implemented in Visual Basic 5 using the Automation data type named *SAFEARRAY*. This is a structure that, like Variants and classes, allows arrays to be *self-describing*. The *LBound* and number of elements for each dimension of the array are stored in this structure. All access to these arrays is through an extensive set of API calls. You do not get or set the array elements directly, but you use API calls. These API calls make use of the *LBound* and number of elements to make sure they always write within the allocated area. This is why they are *safe* arrays—attempts to write to elements outside the allowed area are trapped within the API and gracefully dealt with.

The ability to store arrays in Variants was new to Visual Basic 4, and a number of new language elements were introduced to support them such as *Array()* and *IsArray()*.

To set up a Variant to be an array, you can either assign it to an already existing array or use the *Array* function. The first of these creates a Variant whose subtype is the array value (8192) operated on by OR with the type of the original array. The *Array* function, on the other hand, always creates an array of Variants—*VarType 8204*.

The following code shows three ways of creating a Variant array of the numbers 0,1,2,3:

```
Dim v   As Variant
Dim a() As Integer
Dim i   As Integer

' Different ways to create Variant arrays
' 1. Use the Array function.
v = Array(0, 1, 2, 3) ' Of little practical use
v = Empty

' 2. Create a normal array, and assign it to a Variant.
' Iterate adding elements using a normal array...
For i = 0 To 3
    ReDim Preserve a(i) As Integer
    a(i) =  i
Next i

' ...and copy array to a Variant
v = a
' or
v = a()
' but not v() = a()

v = Empty

' 3. Start off with Array, and then ReDim to preferred size,
' avoiding use of intermediate array.
For i = 0 To 3
    ' First time we need to create array
    If IsEmpty(v) Then
        v = Array(i)
    Else
    ' From then on, ReDim Preserve will work on v.
        ReDim Preserve v(i)
    End If
    v(i) = i
Next i
```

Notice that the only difference between the last two arrays is that one is a Variant holding an array of integers and the other is a Variant holding an array of Variants. It can be easy to get confused here, so look at the following:

```
ReDim v(5) As Variant
```

This code is creating an array of Variants, but this array is *not* a Variant array. What consequence does this have? Well, with Variant arrays, you can utilize array copying. The manuals make surprisingly little of this great feature, and you've probably just stumbled on it by accident if you've discovered it at all. Array copying is supported for Variant arrays only because, as we've already seen, Visual Basic calls into the Automation API. At the Automation level, the function *VariantCopy* calls another Automation API named *SafeArrayCopy* if the variant is of subtype *VT_ARRAY*. When *SafeArrayCopy* copies an array, all elements are copied in their entirety, even if they are arrays themselves. In other words, a copy of the array and all its elements is made. The *SafeArrayCopy* function must have been written recursively because each element of the array is subject to the same rules. So where the element of an array is itself an array, that whole array is copied too. This is called a *deep copy*. In short, every part and subpart of our Variant "structure" is faithfully copied, however deep the nesting.

This code sample demonstrates the difference between a Variant array and an array of Variants:

```
ReDim v1(5) As Variant  ' Array 1 - an ordinary array of Variants
Dim v2 As Variant
v2 = Array(1,2,3) ' Array 2 - a Variant array of Variants

v2 = v1  ' Ok
v1 = v2  ' Syntax error (cannot assign to nonbyte array)
```

So Variants can contain arrays, and they can be arrays of Variants. As mentioned, if those contained Variants are just ordinary Variants—which they are—they can themselves be arrays, perhaps of Variants, which can be arrays too, and so on and so forth.

Just how deep can these arrays be nested? I don't know if there is a theoretical limit, but in practice I have tested at least 10 levels of nesting. This odd bit of code works fine:

```
Dim v As Variant, i As Integer

' Make v an array of two Variants, each of which is an array
' of two Variants, each of...and so on
For i = 0 To 10
    v = Array(v, v)
Next i

' Set a value...
v(0)(0)(0)(0)(0)(0)(0)(0)(0)(0)(0) = 23
```

How do these compare to more standard multidimensional arrays? Well, on the positive side, they are much more flexible. The contained arrays—corresponding to the lower dimensions of a multidimensional array—do not have to have the same number of elements. Figure 5-3 explains the difference pictorially.

FIGURE 5-3

The difference between a standard two-dimensional array (top) and a Variant array (bottom)

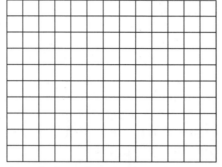

A standard two-dimensional array is a rectangle.

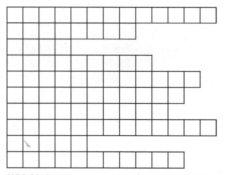

With Variant arrays, you need not waste space.

These are sometimes known as *ragged arrays*—and they were not possible to construct until Visual Basic 4. As you can see from Figure 5-3, we do not have all the wasted space of a standard multidimensional array. However, you have to contrast that with the fact that the Variant "trees" are harder to set up.

This ability of Variants to hold arrays of Variants permits some interesting new data structures in Visual Basic. One obvious example is a tree. In this piece of code, an entire directory structure is folded up and inserted in a single Variant:

```
Private Sub Form_Load()
    Dim v As Variant
    v = GetFiles("C:\") ' Places contents of C: into v
End Sub
```

```vb
Public Function GetFiles(vPath As Variant) As Variant
    ' NB cannot use recursion immediately because Dir
    ' does not support it, so get array of files first.
    Dim vDir As Variant, vSubDir As Variant, i

    vDir = GetDir(vPath)

    ' Now loop through array, adding subdirectory information.
    If Not IsEmpty(vDir) Then
        For i = LBound(vDir) To UBound(vDir)
            ' If this is a dir, then...
            If (GetAttr(vDir(i)) And vbDirectory) = vbDirectory Then
                ' replace dir name with the dir contents.
                vDir(i) = GetFiles(vDir(i))
            End If
        Next i
    End If

    GetFiles = vDir

End Function

Private Function GetDir(ByVal vPath As Variant) As Variant
    ' This function returns a Variant that is an array
    ' of file and directory names (not including "." or "..")
    ' for a given directory path.
    Dim vRet As Variant, fname As Variant

    ' Add \ if necessary.
    If Right$(vPath, 1) <> "\" Then vPath = vPath & "\"

    ' Call the Dir function in a loop.
    fname = Dir(vPath, vbNormal & vbDirectory)
    Do While fname <> ""
        If fname <> "." And fname <> ".." Then
            vRet = AddElement(vRet, vPath & fname)
        End If
        fname = Dir()
    Loop

    ' Return the array.
    GetDir = vRet
End Function
```

```
Public Function AddElement(vArray As Variant, vElem As Variant) As Variant
' This function adds an element to a Variant array
' and returns an array with the element added to it.

    Dim vRet As Variant ' To be returned

    If IsEmpty(vArray) Then
        ' First time through, create an array of size 1.
        vRet = Array(vElem)
    Else
        vRet = vArray
        ' From then on, ReDim Preserve will work.
        ReDim Preserve vRet(UBound(vArray) + 1)
        vRet(UBound(vRet)) = vElem
    End If

    AddElement = vRet

End Function
```

This is just an indication of the kinds of things you can do with Variant arrays. They are particularly useful when creating out-of-process object applications. If you have done this, you'll know how slow it is every time you cross a process boundary. I have found the ability to return arrays inside Variants invaluable in enabling the passing of a lot of information across a process boundary in one move.

Typeless Visual Basic

In Visual Basic 5, the question, "Is this variable of the correct type?" has become, "Does this variable reference an instance of a class that supports this interface?" Although we are dealing with Variants, there are similarities between the way you program with Variants and the way you program with classes. You can think of a Variant as a little class that contains just one property—its value. As is the case with a class, your access to that property is not direct—there is a layer of encapsulation. As a user of a class, you are not concerned with the *implementation* of the class so much as its *behavior*. Likewise, you can ignore the underlying implementation of a Variant and concern yourself with its behavior. In classes, the definition of the behavior is its *interface*. With Variants, we might think of the subtypes as various interfaces. To see whether the Variant supports them, we can use the set of *Is...* functions to check to see that the interface is supported.

For example, to see if a Variant is an array, we can use *IsArray()*. Good defensive programming should test with *IsArray* before using functions such as *UBound* on a Variant. If you get into this habit, you will find your code is more robust.

Conclusion

It is possible to continue coding with Visual Basic 5 in the same way you did with Visual Basic 3 and earlier versions. But if you do that, you're missing a great opportunity to write better code. It's a fact of life that if you embrace the object-oriented features of Visual Basic 5, you'll leave some old coding styles and practices behind. You'll find yourself coding in a new way. Give it a try.

Migration Issues in Visual Basic 5

Changes from Earlier Versions of Visual Basic

Kevin is a TMS Associate who spends part of his time developing, distributing, and supporting a range of Microsoft Windows–based software packages for niche markets. His first product was an office automation system for real estate agents selling and renting residential property. He originally wrote this product in Visual Basic 3 but has since ported it to 16-bit Visual Basic 4 and, more recently, to Visual Basic 5. He spends his remaining time advising companies on using Visual Basic. Kevin's hobbies are best not listed in any book liable to be read by the easily offended.

KEVIN HOUSTOUN

Microsoft Visual Basic has been with us for quite a long time now. Initially intended as a tool for rapidly knocking out small systems and prototypes, Visual Basic has been improved and improved, until it is now the preferred choice for developing large enterprise-wide systems. These systems are often fundamental to the survival of the businesses developing them.

Features added to each new version reflect this shift, or perhaps Visual Basic's role has changed to reflect the new features. With each version of Visual Basic, there has been a key improvement, although picking one feature as the key new feature is a matter of opinion. In Visual Basic 5, the key improvement is the ability to create ActiveX controls. The key improvements in other versions are listed at the top of the following page.

Version	Key Improvement
1	Visual Basic introduced
2	Integrated Development Environment (IDE) improved
3	Jet DAO added
4	Building of ActiveX server components allowed
5	Building of ActiveX controls allowed

Since the introduction of Visual Basic 4, the most significant improvement has been the addition of the capability to break down systems into components, or objects, that can be assembled into complete systems. This improvement allows complex systems to be built of many simpler components. Systems based on simpler components can be more easily maintained and integrated than their larger, monolithic predecessors.

With more code written in Visual Basic than in any other computer language, it is the facility to build components that represents Visual Basic's most underused strength. Interestingly, a lot of Visual Basic 3 code is still being written. For example, approximately one third of The Mandlebrot Set's clients are still developing in Visual Basic 3. With Visual Basic version 1 through version 3, it was difficult to write anything other than monolithic applications. With Visual Basic 4 and 5, it is relatively easy to write your application as a series of components.

Microsoft estimates that there are over 3 million Visual Basic programmers in the world; in 1996, Visual Basic overtook COBOL as the language with the most code written in it. Of this huge amount of code, some will wither and die, but a lot of it must be maintained. The best way to do this is for the code to exist in a series of small, simple-to-understand components.

The remainder of this chapter looks briefly at some of the new features in Visual Basic 5 and explains why you should seriously consider converting all your programs, not just your Visual Basic programs, to Visual Basic 5. It discusses the pitfalls you might experience en route. The chapter goes on to consider differing strategies for migrating your systems to a Visual Basic 5 development environment and illustrates by means of a small sample suite of programs some of the difficulties you might face and some possible solutions to these problems.

Why Convert Your Program to Visual Basic 5?

There are many reasons why you should convert from earlier versions of Visual Basic to Visual Basic 5. Some are technical, some motivational, and some personnel-related, but all of the reasons have one thing in common: they all enable you and your people to develop better applications faster. In this section, I will look at the reasons to convert. I have split the reasons into three areas: language features, improvements to the Integrated Development Environment (IDE), and other, less easily categorized, reasons.

Language Features

The following are some of the language features that make Visual Basic 5 worth moving to.

ActiveX Controls technology (new in Visual Basic 5)

Visual Basic 5 includes everything you need to create complete, stand-alone ActiveX controls from scratch. However, it is much more likely that these features will be used as discussed below.

Subclassing and customizing an existing ActiveX control   Developers can take advantage of more than 2000 commercially available ActiveX controls. An existing control can be subclassed, customized, and then compiled, creating a custom version of the same control. An example of this is using a multiline text box as a postal address box by limiting it to a number of lines of a certain length. The compiled result will be a custom ActiveX control featuring this new functionality.

Aggregating multiple ActiveX controls into a composite control   Developers can take advantage of the many commercially available ActiveX controls by aggregating multiple controls into an ActiveX control project, customizing their look and behavior, and then compiling the group of controls together into a single control. The resultant control could then be inserted into a Web page or a client/server application to "wrap," or contain, all of the user interface elements of that application. Microsoft anticipates that this will be a popular way for developers to share interfaces and code, thus gaining valuable reuse capabilities. An example of this is adding a second text box to the multiline example just mentioned to capture the postal code and then using the resultant composite control. The compiled result will be a custom ActiveX control featuring this new functionality.

Early binding (new in Visual Basic 4)

Early binding was introduced in Visual Basic version 4 and is better than late binding for several important reasons. Before talking about those reasons, though, let's be sure that you understand the difference between early and late binding.

With early binding, you declare the object type prior to using the object. For example, to early bind to an object, you would use something like this:

```
Dim ObjTest As Test.CTest
```

With late binding, the object type is declared when the object is created, something like this:

```
Dim ObjTest As Object
Set ObjTest = CreateObject("Test.CTest")
```

Here are some reasons you should use early binding:

- Early binding checks all of the code against the syntax stored in the type library when you compile the executable or the Visual Basic code. Syntax errors are detected during compilation. This is not true with late binding or ActiveX control binding.

- Early binding is insensitive to the localized version of the products you are using. Late binding and control binding are sensitive to the localized version. For example, if a user is running the French version of Microsoft Word and a type library was not used, the French version's commands will be required. So the *FicheOuvert* method will have to be used instead of the *FileOpen* method.

- Because control type and function checking is done at compile time and not at run time, the performance of early binding is significantly faster than the performance of late binding or control binding.

Remote Data Object (new in Visual Basic 4)

Essentially a programmer-friendly wrapper to the ODBC API, Remote Data Object (RDO) allows Microsoft SQL Server back ends to be accessed with nearly the programmatic simplicity normally associated with Jet. This grouping of controls into a composite control also eases the transition from single-user, local database applications to multiuser, three-tier client/server applications.

Automation server creation (new in Visual Basic 4)

Visual Basic 4 added the ability to create Automation servers to Visual Basic. This capability was the first step in the path away from monolithic programs to modular, component-based applications.

Remote Automation servers (new in Visual Basic 4)

Remote Automation servers allow you to build comprehensive, scalable solutions out of a series of ActiveX components, which can be installed on the appropriate machines. Processing can be distributed across multiple machines, and hardware can be centrally allocated to specific resource-intensive components.

Common programming capability across all Visual Basic host environments (new in Visual Basic 5)

A new version of Visual Basic for Applications (version 5) now in Microsoft Excel, Word, Microsoft PowerPoint, Microsoft Access, and Microsoft Project is also at the heart of Visual Basic 5. The IDE has been fully redesigned and standardized for greater consistency across all of these host applications.

Wizards (new in Visual Basic 5)

Visual Basic 5 comes with a series of wizards to guide you through creating applications, ActiveX controls, and ActiveX documents, and many other common programming tasks.

Callbacks (the *Addressof* feature) (new in Visual Basic 5)

Callbacks let developers use callback Windows API functions such as the *EnumWindows* and *EnumChildWindows* functions, which iterate through Windows. There are other callback functions to iterate through fonts, GDI objects, clipboard formats, printer jobs, and resources.

Typed optional parameters (new in Visual Basic 5)

Optional parameters to subroutines and function calls were introduced in Visual Basic 4, finally allowing our own code functions to emulate Visual Basic's built-in functions. In Visual Basic 5, these parameters can be typed, thereby restoring good programming practices.

User-definable events (new in Visual Basic 5)

The *RaiseEvent* statement allows classes to trigger events. You can use this feature to allow background tasks to communicate with foreground tasks, informing them of their progress.

You can also create nonvisual timer objects that generate events. Since these objects don't need to be attached to a form, they are now much easier to wrap up into modular, independent classes. And since objects can now raise events, any non–user interface object can be written as a class and doesn't need to be implemented on a form module.

Combining this with thread-safe multithreading and ActiveX callbacks allows for the implementation of techniques such as background printing. Previously, you could do this only with lots of smoke-and-mirrors trickery.

Data Access Objects 3 (new in Visual Basic 4)

The new 32-bit Data Access Objects (DAO) version 3 is faster than its 16-bit predecessor. Microsoft provides performance benchmarks showing that Jet version 3 is between 1.4 and 17.79 times faster than Jet version 2. Full details of these benchmarks can be found in Chapter 13 of the *Jet Database Engine Programmer's Guide*.

The new 32-bit DAO supports full or partial replication of databases. This is great for writing applications for mobile users (such as salespeople) who want to access their database even when away from the corporate LAN.

Long strings (new in Visual Basic 4)

With any of the 32-bit versions of Visual Basic, strings and byte arrays can exceed the 16-bit 32 KB limit. This improves file handling, allowing almost any file to be read or written with a single disk command, as shown here:

```
nFileNo = FreeFile
Open sFile For Binary As #nFileNo
ReDim byteArray(LOF(nFileNo))
Get #nFileNo, , byteArray
```

Once loaded into a byte array, the data can be manipulated at will using the string-handling functions. For details, see the code example in the section "Unicode and the byte data type" later in this chapter.

Objects and collections (new in Visual Basic 4)

Objects and collections are now familiar to anyone using Visual Basic 4. They provide a much more natural way of modeling data structures and can lead to many improvements in the structuring of code.

New language keywords

Features such as *GetSetting*, *SaveSetting*, and property procedures, all of which were introduced in Visual Basic 4, allow you to control from Visual Basic many features previously available only either from the Windows API or from special custom controls such as SpyWorks and MsgBlaster. New object properties such as the *StartUpPosition* property on the form object and the logging properties on the *App* object provide welcome new functionality.

Conditional compilation

Conditional compilation was added in Visual Basic 4 to allow the use of a common code base between the 16-bit and 32-bit versions, but it also offers a number of other advantages. For example, conditional compilation can be used

NOTE

If you want to maintain a code base that allows for conditional compilation under both Visual Basic 5 and 16-bit Visual Basic 4, it is worth knowing that although 16-bit Visual Basic 4 will not read Visual Basic 5 project files, it will read Visual Basic 5 form code and class modules. In 16-bit Visual Basic 4, you might need to remove the version number from the beginning of the text files. Thus, a program designed and written to compile and run under either 16-bit or 32-bit Visual Basic 4 can be compiled under either 16-bit Visual Basic 4 or 32-bit Visual Basic 5, provided you don't save the changes to the project file. Any new Visual Basic 5 properties generate an error when the forms are loaded, but in many cases you can ignore this error. This can be illustrated by experimenting with the CALLDLLS sample program from the Visual Basic 4 installation. The beginning of a Visual Basic 5 form module opened as a text file looks something like this:

```
VERSION 5.00
Begin VB.Form Form1
    Caption     =   "Form1"
    ClientHeight =   2640
```

The first line might need to be removed, and the text file might need to be saved to allow the module or form to load into 16-bit Visual Basic 4.

to exclude certain features from demonstration versions of programs. (Leaving out printing and saving capabilities will render a large number of programs useless for all purposes other than demonstration.)

Improvements to the IDE

The Integrated Development Environment (IDE) of Visual Basic for Applications (VBA) is a substantially improved programming environment. Improvements to the IDE since Visual Basic 4 include the following.

Improved Add-In model

Although the Add-In model in Visual Basic 4 was a great boon, it lacked important capabilities. There was no way to move between modules within a project, although you could send keystrokes to the project window. There was no access to the code in modules. Again, you could work around this either by using the *InsertFile* method on the *Component* or *FormTemplate* objects to add code immediately after the declarations section or by directly manipulating the text files and then reloading them. However, you can modify Visual Basic 5 to work the way you want it to; you can enforce corporate styles, add comment templates, and add standard error handlers. Or you can specify your ideal development environment and then build it by writing add-ins and modifying the IDE with personalized toolbars.

IntelliSense

IntelliSense technology has now been brought to the developer, making it easier and faster than ever to write syntactically correct code in Visual Basic 5. IntelliSense features provide developers with instant syntax reference and object model assistance to reduce programming time and assure syntactically correct code.

Multiproject support

The new IDE lets you manage multiple projects within a single instance of the IDE. Multiproject support lets you load multiple ActiveX controls and their test hosts (and debugs them in a single session).

Drag-and-drop between code windows

The editor now includes support for code drag-and-drop within and across code windows. Dragging sections of code and dropping them into newly declared procedures, functions, properties, or methods is a fast way to refine your code structure as you realize that a piece of functionality can be reused throughout a project.

Enhanced Project window

The enhanced Project window provides better navigation through project components and improves management of the programmer's workspace. The components in each of the projects loaded into Visual Basic are now arranged in hierarchical structures of forms, modules, class modules, user controls, and property pages.

Enhanced Properties window

The enhanced Properties window lets you arrange properties by categories or by alphabetical order. This approach lets you set and view related groups of object properties without scrolling up and down the window.

New debugging tools

New debugging tools help you track program execution, monitor the status of global and local variables, and rapidly track down bugs. The Watch and Immediate windows are now independent of each other, and a new window—the Locals window—shows the values of all locally scoped variables in the current procedure or function.

New Form Layout window

The new Form Layout window lets you visually set the start-up position of forms and preview the form screen locations at varying monitor resolutions. This window demonstrates, at design time, the effects of the new *StartUpPosition* form property.

Enhanced Object Browser

The enhanced Object Browser supports browsing and searching for properties and methods across object model libraries. The facility to search the methods and properties of objects lets you rapidly become familiar with new components.

MDI development environment

The new MDI development environment makes it much easier to track which instance of Visual Basic you are using when you have many projects open—for example, when you are debugging an add-in.

Customizable development environment

The VBA environment now includes command bars, a new type of menu/toolbar system. This new system offers dockable and free-floating toolbars that are fully customizable, including the ability to let you create and modify custom toolbars. Developers can modify any built-in menu bars and shortcut menus. For example, the undocked toolbar shown in Figure 6-1 contains numerous buttons.

FIGURE 6-1

The new IDE with a custom toolbar

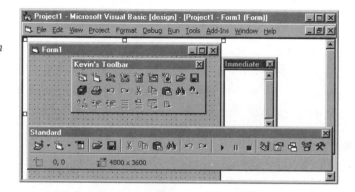

Other Reasons to Move to Visual Basic 5

Visual Basic 5 offers a number of other, miscellaneous reasons to upgrade from earlier versions.

Access 32-bit operating systems

Visual Basic 5 creates programs that run under and use the full features of the latest operating systems, such as Microsoft Windows 95 and Microsoft Windows NT 4.

Windows NT is rapidly gaining popularity for its stable development environment. Although 16-bit programs run as quickly under Windows 95 as they did under Windows 3.x (albeit with higher memory requirements), they don't run as quickly under Windows NT, where they need to run in a virtual Windows machine (NTVDM). Generally, 32-bit Visual Basic 4 programs run significantly faster than 16-bit Visual Basic 4 programs under Windows NT. Visual Basic 5 is the best tool with which to develop applications to run under 32-bit operating systems. There is little point in doing 16-bit development unless you are targeting 16-bit operating systems.

TIP

> If you're writing 16-bit programs under Windows NT, run Visual Basic in a separate address space. Click the Run In Separate Memory Space check box in the Program Item Properties dialog box in Program Manager when using Windows NT 3.51 or in the shortcut properties if you're using Windows NT 4. If your program then crashes, you can kill the 16-bit NTVDM session from PView (Process Viewer) in Windows NT 3.51 or earlier versions and from Task Manager in Windows NT 4.

Support for the Power Macintosh range is hinted at throughout the Visual Basic documentation, and this support would provide another market for your Visual Basic programs.

Avoid name space problems

Visual Basic 3 and to a lesser extent 16-bit Visual Basic 4 suffer from a name space problem. They are both given only 64 KB pages in memory for the names of variables, constants, and procedures. Many large corporate projects ran into this limitation, and many solutions were tried. VB Compress and MicroHelp's Code Analyst, written by The Mandelbrot Set (TMS), let programmers remove unused variables, constants, procedures, and functions. Programs were written to truncate variable, constant, and procedure names. Coding strategies were changed to the detriment of code maintainability. This issue disappears with 32-bit Visual Basic 4 and Visual Basic 5.

Compile and improve performance

Visual Basic 5 can compile your code to native Intel code. With this, you lose platform independence, but you gain some speed. Without compiling, you still get improved performance. Visual Basic 5's form drawing is much faster than Visual Basic 4's. The p-code interpreter has been more tightly optimized.

Use ActiveX documents

ActiveX documents are Visual Basic 5 applications that run in the environment of your Web browser. Many Visual Basic desktop-based forms for information gathering and retrieval could be remodeled as ActiveX document applications. These ActiveX documents are essentially normal Visual Basic programs running within a Web browser that can capture data and process it with all the sophistication of your existing Visual Basic programs using the Internet as a delivery and transport medium. A sample ActiveX document is shown in Figure 6-2 on the following page.

FIGURE 6-2

An ActiveX document running in Microsoft Internet Explorer 3 that is based on a sample Visual Basic 3 program

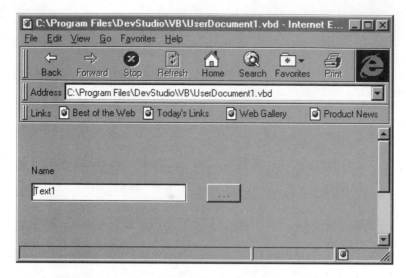

Solve the Year 2000 problem

Visual Basic 5 has improved the way Visual Basic handles dates over the millennium boundary. See Chapter 9 for detailed information on Visual Basic and the Year 2000 problem.

Boost morale

Programmers like to work with the latest release of a language. They like to learn about new features and how to use them. Happy programmers work harder and more efficiently.

See queries in Crystal Reports

Although you don't need to upgrade to Visual Basic 5 to get the latest version of Crystal Reports, the version that ships with Visual Basic 5 (and Visual Basic 4) has a great new feature: the ability to see queries. You simply construct a Jet query to do joins instead of using links in Crystal Reports. The old way of getting information from queries was by means of a temporary table.

Crystal Reports still doesn't let you see parameter queries, but why not write your own ActiveX object to run reports? At TMS, ours takes a collection of parameters—each made up of a parameter object containing the parameter name and value—and writes the results to a temporary table. The report is then run against this table. The alternative is to generate the SQL and save it as a query. Thus, the same Crystal Reports query for totaling account balances could be used with several different reports.

```
Const PRINT_REPORT As Integer = 1
Dim qd            As QueryDef
Dim sDate         As String

sDate = Format$(InputBox$(""))
Set qd = PubDB.CreateQueryDef("qryReport", _
    "Select Name From Names " & _
    & "Where DateAdded > " & sDate)
DB.QueryDefs.Append qd
rptctl.Action = PRINT_REPORT
```

Maintain Visual Basic legacy code

As mentioned earlier in this chapter, in June 1996, Visual Basic replaced COBOL as the computer language with the largest code base in written applications. As a result, there will undoubtedly be more demand for Visual Basic programmers to maintain systems than there will be for COBOL programmers, and more Visual Basic programmers will be required than are available. One way to lower your requirements for Visual Basic programmers is to create systems out of discrete components that can be easily maintained.

A strategy for maintaining your Visual Basic applications in a changing environment is needed. One strategy is to create lots of simple components that together form a complex system. That means usingVisual Basic 4 and later versions.

REASON NOT TO CONVERT TO VISUAL BASIC 5

With Visual Basic 5, Visual Basic becomes a 32-bit–only development tool. The 16-bit build of Visual Basic 4 was the last tool created that you can use to develop Visual Basic programs for the Windows 3.x platform. I understand that the 16-bit build of Visual Basic 4 will be maintained in much the same way Microsoft Visual C++ version 1.5 has been maintained to provide a 16-bit C++ compiler.

About the only valid reason I can think of not to convert to Visual Basic 5 is if you want to develop programs that will run on all three popular Windows platforms, Windows 3.x, Windows 95, and Windows NT. However, even if this is the case, you cannot ignore these issues completely because you still have to face the shell and Microsoft Office issues discussed later in this chapter if your program is ever run under Windows 95 or Windows NT Version 4.

CONVERTING YOUR PROGRAM TO VISUAL BASIC 5

Plan your move, and allocate resources to both performing the move and learning about Visual Basic 5's new features. Visual Basic 5 can be used as a *better* version of 32-bit Visual Basic 4, but you will receive greater benefit from the new technology if your developers are familiar with the intricacies of Visual Basic 5 and the opportunities to improve your product that it presents.

> Many projects created in previous versions of Visual Basic will load straight into Visual Basic 5 and compile, provided you have saved the files in text format. Visual Basic 5 will not read Visual Basic 3's binary format, so ensure that the project has Save As Text checked for all forms in the Form File Save As dialog box.

Differences

A number of the differences between Visual Basic 3 and the 32-bit varieties of Visual Basic might cause you problems.

Data Access Objects

The varying versions of the Data Access Objects (DAO) are not completely compatible with each other. Since Visual Basic 3 was launched, DAO has been through versions 1.1, 2, 2.5, 3.0, and 3.5. Most of the compatibility difference occurred in the transition from 2.5 to 3.0. See Appendix B for a listing of the old syntax and its replacements.

ActiveX controls have
replaced OCXs, which replaced VBXs

Since Visual Basic 4, Visual Basic has used OCXs rather than VBXs. The 16-bit version of Visual Basic 4 can use either, provided the controls are 16-bit. When you port a project to Visual Basic 5 or 32-bit version 4, you need to replace any VBXs with equivalent ActiveX controls. With the VBXs supplied by Microsoft, this is not a problem. However, with third-party OCXs, it may present a serious problem. Some vendors have taken the opportunity of rewriting their controls for the 32-bit world and ActiveX to redesign the way the controls work, and the new ActiveX control might not be completely compatible with the old VBX. Controls that are completely compatible with a preceding VBX add an entry to the VB.INI file and will port automatically.

When Visual Basic 4 came out, many third-party controls either were not available or were extremely unreliable. Those same controls can now be used with Visual Basic 5, but they have benefited from more than a year's use. Most have been through several bug-fix releases. These controls are now far more stable than they were a year and a half ago.

TIP

If you buy your controls from a distributor, particularly outside the United States, check to see that you have the latest release from the supplier's Web site or CompuServe forum because the inventory held by distributors is often several versions behind.

There are at least four ways to deal with controls that do not upgrade automatically. You can probably use the method that involves the least amount of work for your project.

- You can simply import the project and then manually change the picture boxes that have replaced the controls that have not upgraded.

NOTE

If you load a file into Visual Basic that references a control with a class name not loaded into your current Visual Basic session, Visual Basic replaces the control with a PictureBox control that has the same dimensions as the original control, pops up an error message, and writes an entry into a file named *formname.log*.

- You can use a text editor to search the original Visual Basic code files, saved as text, for all occurrences of unsupported controls and replace them with the class names of controls that are upgradable.

- You can use 16-bit Visual Basic 4 as a staging post. Import your Visual Basic project, keeping the VBXs that cannot be upgraded. These VBXs can then, according to their functionality, be wrapped up in 16-bit ActiveX servers or replaced by cutting and pasting their code into their nearest OCX equivalents. For large projects with many forms, it may be worth writing a 16-bit Visual Basic 4 add-in to perform this largely mechanical function. It is relatively easy to write a program to iterate through all the controls on a form and replace them on a new form with an alternate control. While you're replacing the control's properties, design-time values can be remapped, and event code can be moved. The only procedure in this kind of process that requires any smoke-and-mirrors programming is navigating through the modules in a form. For this, it's necessary to resort to the Visual Basic *SendKeys* function.

TIP

> If Visual Basic 4 is the currently active application, using *SendKeys* to send Ctrl+V, Ctrl+R, Down Arrow, and Enter will make the second form in the project window the active form. This form can then be manipulated from the VBIDE's properties and methods. This technique of using *SendKeys* to control applications is extremely unreliable, however, and you should use it only as a last resort.

- You can write your own ActiveX control that replicates the functionality you require. This may be a relatively straightforward exercise, or it may be a complete project in its own right. For example, writing your own masked edit control can be quite simple, while creating your own grid control may take a little longer.

Windows API

The world of Windows has changed. Under 32-bit Windows NT and Windows 95, the machine registers are 32-bit. The system therefore deals mostly with 32-bit data. Most API calls return a 32-bit value, which Visual Basic considers to be a long. Under Windows 3.*x*, these registers are 16-bit and API calls return 16-bit values. Visual Basic considers these integers. Most code will return longs into integer variables if the code is imported straight into Visual Basic 4 or 5. This can be rectified by changing the variable type. If the code base is to be used under 16-bit Visual Basic 4 and Visual Basic 5, use conditional compilation constants.

```
#IF WIN16 THEN
    Dim intRet As Integer
#ELSE
    Dim lngRet As Long
#ENDIF
```

```
        ' Version-independent code here

#IF WIN16 THEN
        intRet = SendMessage( ... )
#ELSE
        lngRet = SendMessage( ... )
#ENDIF
```

Alternatively, you can just use a long under both versions, though this is less elegant and slightly less efficient. If the syntax for the API call is the same under both Win16 and Win32, however, the code will be significantly simpler.

Furthermore, the 32-bit Windows API is case-sensitive, whereas the 16-bit API is not. You can use aliasing to get around this, as shown here:

```
Declare Function WinGetVersion Lib "kernel32" Alias "GetVersion" () As Long
```

With this declaration, if *WinGetVersion* is inadvertently changed to *WinGETVersion*, the program will still compile. Without the aliasing *GETVersion*, it would produce the error message shown in Figure 6-3.

FIGURE 6-3

The error message pro duced when a DLL call is capitalized

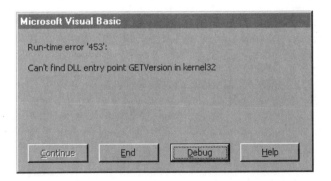

The Crescent division of Progress Software supplies an excellent program, Migrate, which replaces most 16-bit Windows API declarations with 32-bit Windows API declarations. It could only be improved by adding conditional compilation code. Fortunately, Progress Software ships the declarations with its replacements in a Microsoft Access database, and the new Visual Basic 5 Add-In structure lets you write a simple add-in that allows this change. Use the basic add-in framework that forms the Visual Basic IDE sample, and add something like the code on the following page to the part of the program that does the work.

```
Dim Proj              As VBProject
Dim VBComp            As VBComponent
Dim VBCode            As CodeModule
Dim lCount            As Long
Dim lOffset           As Long
Dim sLine             As String
Dim sReplacementLine  As String
Dim sAPIName          As String
Dim nDeclareStart     As Integer
Dim nAPINameStart     As Integer
Dim nAPINameLength    As Integer
Dim dbAPIs            As Database
Dim snpAPIs           As Recordset
Set dbAPIs = OpenDatabase("G:\Was on VB5\Migrate\Upwizard.MDB")
                         ' Or wherever your database is located
Set snpAPIs = dbAPIs.OpenRecordset("Win32Decl", dbOpenSnapshot)
Set Proj = VBInstance.ActiveVBProject
With Proj
    For Each VBComp In .VBComponents
        If VBComp.CodeModule.Find("Declare", 0, 0, _
            VBComp.CodeModule.CountOfLines, 255) = True Then
            Set VBCode = VBComp.CodeModule
            For lCount = 1 To VBCode.CountOfDeclarationLines
                nDeclareStart = InStr(VBCode.Lines(lCount + _
                    lOffset, 1), "Declare")
                If nDeclareStart > 0 Then
                    ' Replace code here.
                    sLine = VBCode.Lines(lCount + lOffset, 1)
                    nAPINameStart = InStr(nDeclareStart + _
                        Len("Declare "), sLine, " ")
                    nAPINameLength = InStr(nAPINameStart + _
                        1, sLine, " ") - nAPINameStart
                    sAPIName = Mid$(sLine, nAPINameStart + _
                        1, nAPINameLength - 1)
                    snpAPIs.FindFirst "Name like '" & _
                        sAPIName & "'"
                    If snpAPIs.NoMatch Then
                        sReplacementLine = "#IF WIN16 THEN" _
                            & vbCrLf & vbTab & sLine & _
                            vbCrLf & "#ELSE" & vbCrLf & _
                            vbTab & _
                            "' TODO - 32-bit eqv API needed" & _
                            vbCrLf & "#ENDIF" & vbCrLf
                    Else
```

```
                sReplacementLine = "#IF WIN16 THEN" & _
                    vbCrLf & vbTab & sLine & vbCrLf & _
                    "#ELSE" & vbCrLf & vbTab & _
                    snpAPIs!FullName & vbCrLf & _
                    "#ENDIF" & vbCrLf
            End If
            Call VBCode.ReplaceLine(lCount + lOffset, _
                sReplacementLine)
            lOffset = lOffset + 5
        End If
    Next lCount
    End If
    Next VBComp
End With
snpAPIs.Close
dbAPIs.Close
```

NOTE

A modified version of the Visual Basic 5 Sample Add-In program is included in the samples for this chapter on the companion CD to illustrate this point. It is saved as the project MyAddIn.Vbp and contains the code described in the following text. The sample can be easily modified to do other tasks, such as inserting default error handlers. Run this add-in against the Visual Basic 3 CALLDLLS.MAK sample to see what it does.

It's worth remembering that many Windows API calls haven't changed apart from the library in which they are now declared. One easy way to incorporate library name changes is to use a type library for the Windows API. Then the type library can be changed as you move from 32-bit to 16-bit without any need to change code. Such a Windows API type library comes with Bruce McKinney's excellent *Hardcore Visual Basic* (Microsoft Press, 1995). You can obtain updates for all the *Hardcore Visual Basic* programs from the Microsoft Press Web site at *mspress.microsoft.com/mspress/brucem/hardcore.htm*.

For the curious, the Microsoft Knowledge Base article Q137095, "How to Provide Constants for Use with an OLE Server" (*www.microsoft.com/Kb*), explains how type libraries are created.

Help is at hand

The Migrate program automatically converts API declarations and reports many of the other Visual Basic 3 oddities. It's cool, and it works.

String types

Visual Basic 3's string type was the HLSTR (High Level String). This consisted of a pointer to a block of memory containing the length of the string and a pointer to the string itself.

Since Visual Basic 4, the string type has been the BSTR, which is a pointer to the start of the string—the string itself is null-terminated. The string is also immediately preceded in memory by 4 bytes containing the string's length.

If you have written or been supplied with a DLL to be used with Visual Basic 3, and if that DLL handed back strings and those strings contained nulls, your DLL might not work with Visual Basic 4 and later versions. Such DLLs still hand back the same string, but Visual Basic 4 treats the null as the terminator for the string, thereby truncating your data at the first null.

A useful side effect of this change concerns strings used in user-defined types returned from or passed into DLLs. Since these strings are now null-terminated, user-defined types can be declared as follows:

```
Private Type TOpenFileName
    lStructSize  As Long
    hwndOwner    As Integer
    hInstance    As Integer
    lpstrFilter  As String
    ⋮
End Type
```

Unicode and the byte data type

Visual Basic 3 was not Unicode or Double-Byte Character Set (DBCS)–aware. Unicode stores each character in the character set in 2 bytes instead of 1. DBCS is a mixture—if the first character is in a certain range, the following byte also forms part of that character. These systems are used for displaying character sets in regions of the world where more than 256 characters are used—in Asia, for example. Since Visual Basic 4, the language has converted strings to Unicode for internal manipulation. If you're using Visual Basic under a version of Windows that uses DBCS, any information that is read in as a string can be translated into its equivalent Unicode string that maps to the DBCS byte pair. Because of this effect, any existing code that reads binary data (File I/O) using the string data type might need to be converted to use the byte data type. Visual Basic's internal Unicode strings are translated to ANSI strings when you are writing to a file or passing the string to a DLL. Additionally, code written to use Visual Basic strings as a way to manipulate binary data might need to be rewritten.

For example, the following code runs fine under Visual Basic 3 and 16-bit Visual Basic 4, but it will not work properly under 32-bit Visual Basic 4 or Visual Basic 5.

```
Type TData
    nAge  As Integer
    sName As String * 20
End Type
Type TStringBuffer
    sString As String * 22
End Type

Sub Main ()
    Dim nFileNo     As Integer
    Dim nNoRecords  As Integer
    Dim nRecord     As Integer
    Dim sTestString As String
    Dim udtData     As TData
    Dim udtString   As TStringBuffer

    nFileNo = FreeFile
    Open "TESTFILE.TST" For Binary As #nFileNo
    nNoRecords = 2
    Put #nFileNo, , nNoRecords
    udtData.nAge = 69
    udtData.sName = "Kevin"
    Put #nFileNo, , udtData
    udtData.nAge = 25
    udtData.sName = "Clive"
    Put #nFileNo, , udtData
    Close nFileNo
    nFileNo = FreeFile
    Open "TESTFILE.TST" For Binary As #nFileNo
    sTestString = Space(LOF(nFileNo) - 2)
    Get #nFileNo, , nNoRecords
    Get #nFileNo, , sTestString
    For nRecord = 1 To nNoRecords
        udtString.sString = Mid$(sTestString, _
            ((nRecord - 1) * 22) + 1, 22)
        LSet udtData = udtString
        MsgBox Trim$(udtData.sName) & " is " _
            & CStr(udtData.nAge)
    Next
    Close nFileNo
End Sub
```

The code that reads the data in needs to be rewritten thus:

```
Type TData
    nAge        As Integer
    sName(20) As Byte
End Type
Type TStringBuffer
    sString As String * 22
End Type
Sub Main()
    Dim nFileNo      As Integer
    Dim nNoRecords  As Integer
    Dim nRecord      As Integer
    Dim sTestString As String
    Dim bytArray()  As Byte
    Dim udtData      As TData
    Dim udtString    As TStringBuffer
    nFileNo = FreeFile
    Open "TESTFILE.TST" For Binary As #nFileNo
    ReDim bytArray(0 To LOF(nFileNo) - 2)
    Get #nFileNo, , nNoRecords
    Get #nFileNo, , bytArray
    sTestString = bytArray
    For intRecord = 1 To nNoRecords
        udtString.sString = MidB(sTestString, _
            ((nRecord - 1) * 22) + 1, 22)
        LSet udtData = udtString
        MsgBox Trim$(StrConv(udtData.sName, _
            vbUnicode)) & " is " & CStr(udtData.nAge)
    Next
    Close nFileNo
End Sub
```

TIP

Most DLLs that accept strings have two versions—one that handles Unicode and one that handles ANSI. When calling the API from Visual Basic, it is best to use the ANSI version because Visual Basic converts strings to this form when handing strings to DLL calls.

The conversion to using the *Byte* data type is accomplished as follows:

16-Bit Visual Basic Implementation

```
nFreeFile = FreeFile
Open sFileName For Binary As #nFreeFile
Dim sTemp As String * 128
Get #nFreeFile, , sTemp
```

32-Bit Visual Basic Implementation

```
nFreeFile = FreeFile
Open sFileName For Binary As #nFreeFile
Dim bTemp(0 To 127) As Byte
Get #nFreeFile, , bTemp()
```

To manipulate binary data using string functions, do the following:

- Put the binary data into a byte array using functions such as *Get*.

- Assign the byte array to a string. The data is not translated in any way—it is merely copied into the string. Note that strings in binary format are not usable in the normal sense because internal strings in Visual Basic under 32-bit Windows are assumed to be Unicode and double-byte for most operations.

- Use the "B" functions to manipulate the binary data in the string.

- Assign the contents of the string back to the byte array in order to write them back to the file.

The following functions manipulate strings of binary data:

Function	What It Does
AscB	Returns the value corresponding to the first byte in a string of binary data
InStrB	Returns the position of the first occurrence of one byte array within a string of binary data
MidB	Returns the specified number of bytes from a string of binary data
LeftB/RightB	Returns the specified number of bytes from the right or left side of a string of binary data
ChrB	Takes a byte and returns a binary string containing the byte

ODBC API

The ODBC API has been updated to 32-bit. Generally, the declarations and use are the same except that the DLL is now named ODBC32.DLL. Thus, the connect declaration has changed from

```
Declare Function SQLAllocConnect Lib "odbc.dll" (ByVal henv&, _
    phdbc&) As Integer
```

to

```
Declare Function SQLAllocConnect Lib "odbc32.dll" (ByVal henv&, _
    phdbc&) As Integer
```

You could convert your code to use the 32-bit DLL directly. However, why not convert it to use Remote Data Objects (RDO) instead? RDO represents a thin wrapper around the ODBC API and provides performance comparable to a programming model similar to the Jet DAO. RDO is fast, flexible, and powerful.

Long filenames

Windows 3.x and all 16-bit programs follow the 8.3 filename convention. Windows 95 and all 32-bit programs use filenames of up to 255 characters. They can include spaces and other characters that were never used in 8.3 filenames. This can cause problems depending on what your program does with filenames. If your interaction with filenames doesn't involve manipulating those filenames, you shouldn't have too many problems. If, on the other hand, you do manipulate those filenames, watch out for the following assumptions, all true with 8.3 filenames and now all false.

- Single extension of at most three characters. Filenames such as TEXTUAL.FILE.IN.TXT can now exist.

- No spaces in the name.

- No section of the name longer than eight characters.

Any code that makes any of these assumptions is likely to run into trouble when running under 32-bit Visual Basic 4 or Visual Basic 5.

One solution is to write an ActiveX server to convert all dialog boxes to 8.3 internally but display long filenames to the users. Your 8.3 filename code can then run unmodified. Another option is to use the Win32 functions *GetFullPathName* and *GetShortPathName* to convert your filenames as required. A third option is to rewrite the code.

Shell changes

The desktop user interface has changed with the move from Windows 3.x to Windows 95. The desktop area that was at your program's disposal under Windows 3.x was fixed. Under Windows 3.x, a maximized window covers the full screen at the current resolution; under the Windows 95 shell, a maximized window either covers the full screen (if the task bar is set to *AutoHide*) or covers the full screen minus the area occupied by the task bar in its current configuration. The size of a maximized window also depends on the setting of the Always On Top property of the task bar.

If you also consider the Microsoft Office 95 toolbar or other dockable toolbars, in the worst case the size of a maximized window might be just under half of the full screen. Controls that were accessible to users with your program running under Windows 3.*x* may now have disappeared.

Under any operating system with the new Windows 95 shell, the maximized desktop area is unpredictable. The user can resize the task bar, and the remaining visible desktop area is the maximized area. You must be careful to ensure that controls are not placed in an area that would have been visible under the old Windows interface but that is visible only under certain configurations of the new Windows 95 shell. There are at least two approaches to this problem. Either place code in the forms *Resize* event procedure to reposition the controls appropriately, or use a control such as VideoSoft's VS Elastic to automatically reposition the controls. (Also, see the *SystemParametersInfo* API function and the SPI_GETWORKAREA parameter.)

TIP

> If you want your users to start using the Windows 95–style interface, with either Windows NT 4 or Windows 95, you need to consider the issue of the available maximized desktop area for your legacy applications that are not being ported to Visual Basic 5.

Registry and INI files

When you load your 16-bit Visual Basic 4 program that uses *GetSettings* and *SaveSettings* into Visual Basic 5, you might wonder where your INI file values have gone. They are now stored under the Registry entry called *HKEY_CURRENT_USER\Software\VB* and *VBA Program Settings\appName\ section*, which would contain an entry such as *key: REG_SZ: value*. These keys and values can be created and modified by running RegEdit under Windows 95 and Regedt32 under Windows NT.

Replacing calls to the Windows API to manipulate INI file settings with the Visual Basic Settings functions can cause odd effects. Any 32-bit Visual Basic application will automatically look in the Registry for configuration information. To get around these calls when replacing a 16-bit Visual Basic 3 or Visual Basic 4 program with a 32-bit one, subclass the stock Visual Basic 5 *GetSettings* with the following:

```
#If Win32 Then
    Declare Function GetPrivateProfileString Lib "kernel32" _
        Alias "GetPrivateProfileStringA" _
        (ByVal lpApplicationName As String, _
        ByVal lpKeyName As Any, ByVal lpDefault As String, _
```

>>

```
            ByVal lpReturnedString As String, ByVal nSize As Long, _
            ByVal lpFileName As String) As Long
#End If

    Public Function GetSetting(ByVal Appname As String, _
        ByVal Section As String, ByVal Key As String, _
        ByVal Default As String) As String
    ' This function uses the program's INI file
    ' and copies its values to the Registry.
    Dim sValue As String
#If Win16 Then
    GetSetting = VBA.GetSetting(Appname, Section, Key, Default)
#Else

    lRet = GetPrivateProfileString(Section, Key, Default, _
        sValue, nSize, Appname)
    Call SaveSetting(Appname, Section, Key, sValue)
#End If
```

Additionally, you might have to run applications in a mixed Visual Basic 3 or 16-bit Visual Basic 4 environment when porting a suite of programs to 32-bit versions over a period of time. This means that you might need to update both the Registry and the INI files. Again, you can do this by subclassing the *GetSettings* function and the *SaveSettings* function. Either replace *GetSettings* or write code that updates both the Registry and the INI file entries.

Strategy for dealing with differing APIs

Your own 16-bit DLLs cannot be called in Visual Basic 5 directly. You can either rewrite the functions as 32-bit versions, write them as compiled Visual Basic 5 DLLs, or create a thunking layer around them by writing a 16-bit Visual Basic 4 ActiveX server that calls your original 16-bit libraries.

Microsoft Office has changed

With your users running your Visual Basic 3 application under Windows 3.x, if you are using Microsoft Office Components as Automation servers to provide output you know which version of Office you are using. As soon as your users move to the 32-bit operating systems, they could be using 16-bit versions of Microsoft Office, Microsoft Office 95, or Microsoft Office 97. Although the differences among these programs acting as Automation servers are small, they might cause problems for programs that have not been built to expect the changes.

Changes between Microsoft Office 3.*x* and Microsoft Office 95

While porting programs from Word 6.*x* to Word 7, I've noticed the following problems:

- The Word template directory has moved, and Word 7 will not find old templates correctly. Hence, you get an Automation error when you execute the statement WP.FileNew "MyTmplt".

- Word.AppShow is needed if you want users to see what is happening.

One solution to these problems is to wrap objects in your own ActiveX wrapper. If the underlying application's implementation changes your ActiveX wrappers, internals might need to change but your ActiveX object's public properties and methods will not need to change. The only change to your main application is the need to install and register a new ActiveX server.

Office conversion issues

After Office 95 is loaded, a shortcut to the old Word templates is created in the templates directory of the Office 95 root directory. If the old version of Office is then removed, this shortcut becomes invalid and causes problems with creating new documents. To rectify this problem, simply delete the shortcut from the templates directory.

When you set visible properties of toolbars via Automation, the Not Visible value in Office 4.3 maps to the Visible value in Office 95, turning off all the toolbars in Office 4.3 and turning on all the toolbars in Office 95.

When you change from 16-bit versions of Word to 32-bit versions of Word, the caption displayed in the title bar has changed to include the word *Microsoft* and to exclude the filename extension. Take care to ensure that ported programs do not try to locate an instance of Word using the *FindWindow* API call with the wrong title string.

TIP

You need to consider the Automation incompatibility issue for your legacy applications that are not being ported to Visual Basic 5 if you want your users to start using either Windows NT 4 or Windows 95. They might be using Office 3.*x*, Office 95, or Office 97.

Summary of Changes from a Previous Version of Visual Basic to Visual Basic 5

The following table shows the changes you need to consider when you convert from a previous version of Visual Basic to Visual Basic 5.

Possible Pitfall	Visual Basic 3	16-Bit Visual Basic 4	32-Bit Visual Basic 4
DAO	Changed	Changed	Changed
Windows 3.x APIs no longer available	Unchanged	Unchanged	Changed
Shell changes	If moving from Windows 3.x to Windows 95 or Windows NT 4	If moving from Windows 3.x to Windows 95 or Windows NT 4	If moving from Windows 3.x to Windows 95 or Windows NT 4
New ODBC API library	Changed	Changed	Unchanged

Moving from 32-Bit Visual Basic 4 to Visual Basic 5

Visual Basic 5's relationship to 32-bit Visual Basic 4 is a bit like Visual Basic 3's relationship to Visual Basic 2—a good product that got even better. In Visual Basic 3, the changes were mainly the addition of databases and bound controls. In Visual Basic 5, the changes are improved performance, native code compilation, control creation, and lots of other ActiveX technology. These changes, however, have little or no effect on an existing project written in 32-bit Visual Basic 4 because 32-bit Visual Basic 4 would not have used them. Containment classes written in Visual Basic 4 can now be migrated to true ActiveX controls in Visual Basic 5.

Moving from 16-Bit Visual Basic 4 to Visual Basic 5

In addition to the issues in moving from 32-bit Visual Basic 4 to Visual Basic 5, also be prepared to deal with the following issues.

There might be VBXs used in your 16-bit applications that do not have equivalent 32-bit controls. These controls will need to be replaced with functionally equivalent ActiveX controls. You might need to rewrite part of your application to allow for changes in the way a control works. An example of this was Apex's move from TrueGrid VBXs to DBGrid OCXs. These two versions of a grid control were incompatible.

TIP

> The version of DBGrid that ships with Visual Basic 5 has little in common with the TrueGrid unbound programming model. Since the release of version 4.0d of True DBGrid and True DBGrid standard, this problem has been reduced by introducing a series of events named *ClassicRead*, *ClassicWrite*, *ClassicAddNew*, and *ClassicDelete*, which follow the old TrueGrid unbound programming models. These new events make it much easier to convert your applications that used TrueGrid in unbound mode to use TrueDBGrid. TrueDBGrid Standard Edition is a slightly improved version of the DBGrid that shipped with Visual Basic 4.

On crossing the divide between 16-bit and 32-bit Visual Basic programming, you leave all your 16-bit API calls behind. Any code that calls the Windows API, the ODBC API, and any of your own APIs will need attention. The attention required may be limited—as with many Windows API calls and ODBC API calls, all you need to do is change the declaration of the procedure or function. However, the problem can be more complex when you've used Windows 3.*x* API calls that have no 32-bit equivalent. See Appendix C for a list of the Windows 3.11 API calls that don't have Windows 32 equivalents.

Moving from Visual Basic 3 to Visual Basic 5

When you move from Visual Basic 3 to Visual Basic 5, in addition to the issues involved in moving from Visual Basic 4 to Visual Basic 5, also be prepared to deal with the following issues.

DAO changes

Changes in DAO can be dealt with in the short term by using the DAO compatibility layer that recognizes methods such as *CreateDynaset* and maps them to the appropriate new methods such as *OpenRecordSet*. The DAO compatibility layer is automatically added to a project that uses DAO when it is first imported into Visual Basic 5. If it is not in your project, however, you can add it from the References dialog box. This will get your program working without any major changes to the code, but once you move it, you can ease future development if you rewrite the few areas affected. Generally, this involves a one-line change for each place where a recordset is created. See Appendix B for a list of old and new methods.

Type coercion

The behavior of type checking has changed between Visual Basic 3 and later versions of Visual Basic. Under Visual Basic 3, if you handed an integer type into a function expecting a string, you got a compile-time error. Under later versions of Visual Basic, the integer is converted to a string at run time and the program continues. This does not present a problem when porting a program from Visual Basic 3, but it does mean that programmers can make a new type of error. The new behavior can manifest itself as hard-to-fix bugs—functions expecting a specific data type to stop working correctly. The problem can be addressed by using explicit variable typing and not using the & and + operators to concatenate and add, respectively.

How to Take Advantage of New Features Without Rewriting Your Whole Project

Once you have moved your code, you have a Visual Basic 3 or Visual Basic 4 project in the Visual Basic 5 design environment. How do you then take advantage of Visual Basic 5's new features without completely rewriting your project? To start with, you already have significantly better performance without rewriting any code.

The next thing to do is identify any areas of your project that can be easily converted to take advantage of the new features. Controls with containment classes—that is, classes in which a control is handed in and its behavior is modified by the class—can easily be converted to ActiveX OCXs. Multiline address boxes are an obvious candidate for this treatment.

Change your user-defined types into classes and collections. Write methods to save your objects and collections. Construct forms that take the classes and display them.

Can you identify areas of functionality used in many executables across a system? One client, a major bank, recognized that the Visual Basic 3 system they were building was running out of resources and performing slowly under Windows NT. They didn't have time to convert the whole project to 32-bit Visual Basic 4 prior to their target delivery date, but they couldn't complete the system in Visual Basic 3. They converted one part of the system in trouble (the part had poor performance and a shortage of name space) to 32-bit Visual Basic 4.

NOTE

> The 16-bit versions of Visual Basic have a single 64-KB memory segment to store the data that makes up global variables and constants. Large Visual Basic 3 applications often exceeded this, preventing the program from compiling. The 16-bit version of Visual Basic 4 made better use of the same amount of memory, and 32-bit Visual Basic 4 has limitless name space for all practical purposes.

This part of the system represented approximately 100 form modules and 50 BAS modules. It took two programmers about three days to do the conversion, and it only took this long because all the forms contained TrueGrids for which there is no ActiveX OCX equivalent. A single component, consisting of several forms and a few BAS modules, was used in many places throughout the system. This component was built as a separate ActiveX out-of-process server and was called from the 32-bit Visual Basic 4 and 16-bit Visual Basic 3 code. This technique freed up precious name space in the Visual Basic 3 applications and helped the project meet its ship date.

THE SAMPLE PROGRAMS

The sample programs, contained on the accompanying CD, are completely stripped-down programs that illustrate solely the points being made in this chapter and consequently appear contrived. Because these programs have limited functionality and were never intended for real-world use, they don't contain any error handling. Error handling has been omitted to keep the listings short and uncluttered.

Program 1 (SAMPLE1.MAK) consists of a text box for user input, shown in Figure 6-4, and a button to bring up a screen to gather more information about that entry. This information is stored in an INI file. The information recorded by this program is considered relevant to the work of the current workstation's normal user.

FIGURE 6-4

A sample user-details dialog box produced by SAMPLE1.MAK

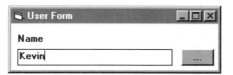

Program 2 (SAMPLE2.MAK) gathers the same information as Program 1 but for other people. It stores the information in an access database, shown in Figure 6-5. The information, along with the name of the user who captured it, can be printed out in a Word document.

FIGURE 6-5

A sample address form produced by SAMPLE2.MAK

Program 3 (SAMPLE3.MAK) demonstrates using an out-of-process ActiveX server in a Visual Basic 3 program, and AddressServer (AddressServer.Vbp) is the Visual Basic 5 out-of-process ActiveX server used in this example.

Data.mdb is the database file used by these programs, and its location should be set in the file SAMPLE.INI, which should be placed in the Windows directory.

The SAMPLE1.MAK and SAMPLE2.MAK programs share a common form— frmAddress—and some common subroutines and constants contained in Common.Bas. The frmAddress form uses an API call to ensure that users type in only five-line addresses.

SAMPLE1.MAK comprises frmUser.frm, Common.Bas, and frmAddre.Frm. SAMPLE2.MAK comprises frmName.frm, Common.Bas, and frmAddre.Frm.

Other changes made to the code to gradually move all systems to Visual Basic 5 in a controlled manner are illustrated throughout this chapter.

The other sample included is a program named SETTINGS.VBP (in the 16BitServer directory), which is a simple 16-bit ActiveX server that can be called from Visual Basic 5 to read and write to INI files. This illustrates two points—first, 16-bit Visual Basic 4 can be used as a way of thunking 16-bit APIs into 32-bit programs; and second, SETTINGS.VBP stands as an illustration of the "Where has my INI file data gone?" problem.

DIFFERING STRATEGIES FOR CONVERSION TO VISUAL BASIC 5

Real-world Visual Basic projects are rarely a single program. Given plenty of resources and no other work, we could convert all our programmers to Visual Basic 5 the day the eagerly awaited installation CD arrived. After a short period of learning about the new features, we could convert all our programs to use Visual Basic 5 and implement lots of new code to take advantage of all the new features. There is one intractable problem with this strategy: users still want systems delivered on time and under budget.

Move the Entire Project to Visual Basic 5

You could easily move your entire project to Visual Basic 5. Just open every project in Visual Basic 5 and compile. If your application doesn't use Windows API calls, Jet, ODBC, or any VBXs that don't have a 32-bit equivalent, you shouldn't have any problems.

Move Entire Programs Within the Project to Visual Basic 5

When moving entire programs to Visual Basic 5, you will face the problem of having two parts of the same system use different sources of configuration information, the Registry and the INI files. The solution is to write configuration information to both. Write a simple ActiveX server that writes to both the Registry and the INI file, and use this server from all systems within the project. All this server needs to do if written in Visual Basic 5 is call the standard Visual Basic *GetSetting* call to read from the Registry and the *GetPrivateProfileString* API call to write to the INI file.

Move Areas of Common Functionality Within Programs to Visual Basic 5

An ActiveX EXE server can be called from any Visual Basic program. ActiveX DLL servers can be used in process by 32-bit Visual Basic 4 and Visual Basic 5 programs. Areas of common functionality can be identified and placed in separate component programs. These can be compiled as either DLLs or EXEs, according to the client application. If you use EXEs, these programs can be run from any program. There is a small problem with running these servers out of Visual Basic 3 clients. While Visual Basic 3 is waiting for a return from a synchronous call in the ActiveX server, it doesn't receive any Windows messages.

The practical consequence of this is that if the server displays a dialog box, the Visual Basic 3 application will not repaint itself until the call has returned, as shown in Figure 6-6.

FIGURE 6-6

An illustration of the refresh problem in Visual Basic 3

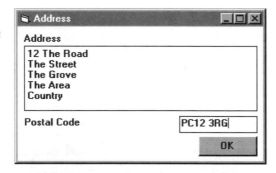

There are a number of workarounds to this problem: You can either make the dialog box nonmovable by removing the move item from the system menu, or you can make the server an asynchronous server and poll a programmer-defined property until it completes its processing. Another workaround is to port your Visual Basic 3 code to the 16-bit version of Visual Basic 4, which processes Windows messages when waiting for a server to return control.

As an example of this, the form FRMADDRE.FRM remains unchanged and is added to a Visual Basic 5 ActiveX.EXE program and the following code is added to the class:

```
Public Sub Show
    Dim frmNew As New frmAddress
    Load frmNew
    frmNew.txtAddress.Text = sAddress
    frmNew.txtPostalCode.Text = sPostalCode
    frmNew.Show Visual Basic Modal
    sAddress = frmNew.txtAddress.Text
    sPostalCode = frmNew.txtPostalCode.Text
    Unload frmNew
    Set frmNew = Nothing
End Sub
```

Set the class instancing to *5 - Multiuse*, and compile the project.

In the original Visual Basic 3 program, you replace the code behind the cmdAddress button with the following code:

```
Sub cmdPopUpAddressForm_Click ()

    Dim objAddress As Object
    Set objAddress = CreateObject("AddressServer.CAddress")

    objAddress.strAddress = spuAddress
    objAddress.strPostalCode = spuPostalCode

    objAddress.Show

    spuAddress = objAddress.strAddress
    spuPostalCode = objAddress.strPostalCode

    Set objAddress = Nothing
End Sub
```

Move Common Functionality to Visual Basic 5 ActiveX/OCX Controls

Since Visual Basic 5 allows the easy creation of ActiveX controls, it is possible to convert parts of your 32-bit Visual Basic 4 program to Visual Basic 5 ActiveX controls and then use these controls from within 32-bit Visual Basic 4. However, given the ease with which 32-bit Visual Basic 4 programs can be ported to Visual Basic 5, this doesn't seem worth the effort. However, this strategy may be useful if you haven't yet gotten a copy of Visual Basic 5 since the Control Creation Edition can be downloaded for free at any time from *www.microsoft.com*. Using this, you can write ActiveX controls that can be used in any ActiveX host environment (Visual Basic 4, Access 7, and so on), and you can gain useful experience with the new Visual Basic 5 design environment. These ActiveX controls can be packaged in thin 32-bit Visual Basic wrappers, compiled as ActiveX EXE servers, and used from Visual Basic 3 and 16-bit Visual Basic 4.

Insulating Your Projects from Further Change

Visual Basic 4 and later versions let you write your projects as a series of ActiveX components. Visual Basic 5 lets you move further down this route with the ability to add and create your own controls.

This approach has many advantages, including increasing the amount of code reuse. (See Chapter 15 on code reuse.) Its major advantage from a maintenance programming perspective is that each component deals with differing parts of the environment that your program has to operate in. When a part of that environment changes, if the elements of your program that communicate with the part of the environment are contained in a small component, your rework and testing is limited.

Future versions of ActiveX components such as Word will change. How will these changes affect your existing applications? At this stage, you cannot know. How can you insulate your applications from these changes? By wrapping up any code that performs tasks with these ActiveX servers. For instance, one application I worked on had three servers, one a wrapper to talk to Crystal Reports, one to talk to Microsoft Word, and one to talk to a U.S. Robotics Palm Pilot (not via ActiveX). When these applications change their ActiveX wrappers, the inner workings might need to change but their public interfaces will not.

To do your printing, you might rely on Crystal Reports for your reports displaying statistical information. Additionally, you can use Word to display well-presented views of the data for a single object. At the time this book went to press, there are two versions of Word that you are likely to find on a user's machine, and there will soon be three. Word 6, Word 7, and Word 8. Word 8 promises a new, more-structured ActiveX verb structure. This is different from Word 6's and 7's flat ActiveX models. And again, there are differences between Word 6 and 7. There are at least two ways you can work around this. You can choose to test the version and act accordingly; or you can, as we do at TMS, wrap your calls to Word in an ActiveX server, which exposes a few methods to your core application and installs an appropriate version of the ActiveX server. To maintain your application, all you need to do is modify the internals of your ActiveX server to allow for changes in components you are dependent on. Your front-end program can then call your servers without modification.

MOVING FROM VISUAL C++ TO VISUAL BASIC

No, this is not a joke. Large object-oriented projects started before the advent of Visual Basic 4 often used Visual Basic 3 as a front end to display information held in objects written in Visual C++ and stored on a back-end server database. Improvements to Visual Basic since then mean that it is possible to write these business objects in Visual Basic. Although Visual Basic still doesn't support inheritance, it's easier to fake it by using encapsulation of objects, and Visual Basic 5's *Implements* method makes this more natural still.

The advantages of this are that you have only one programming language on the project and that it's easier to obtain resources for long-term maintenance and to take action because you are maintaining Visual Basic code with a larger pool of potential programmers. The downside is that you cannot convert Visual C++ code straight to Visual Basic 5 code. However, serious consideration should be given to whether this approach is phased in.

CONCLUSION

It's easy to move to Visual Basic 5, and there are many advantages. The code can be compiled to native code for extra speed or compiled to p-code to minimize executable size for Internet downloading. The primary justification for staying with 16-bit Visual Basic 4 is the large number of Windows 3.x users.

Staying in Control

Effective Weapons in the War Against Bugs

MARK PEARCE

Mark is a TMS Associate who has been programming professionally for the past 18 years, working mainly in the banking industry. In recent years, Mark has concentrated on the design and development of effective client/server systems. His interest in zero-defect software comes from a previous incarnation as a professional chess player, where one mistake can lose a significant sum of money and ruin a wonderful game. Mark's current ambitions in life are to run a sub-2.30 marathon, juggle a Mills Mess for more than 1.5 seconds, and experience the perfect kiss—preferably all simultaneously.

At least one statement in this chapter is wrong (but it may be this one).

Peter Van Der Linden (paraphrased)

Program bugs are highly ecological because program code is a renewable resource. If you fix a bug, another will grow in its place. And if you cut down that bug, yet another will emerge; only this one will be a mutation with long, poisonous tentacles and revenge in its heart, and it will sit there deep in your program, cackling and making elaborate plans for the most terrible time to strike.

Every week seems to bring Visual Basic developers more powerful but also more complex language features, custom controls, APIs, tools, and operating systems. The phrase "technological downpour," coined by a Microsoft executive, strikes a chord with both developers and their managers. In the midst of all this technological chaos, the deadlines become tougher and our tools often refuse to cooperate with one another. If whatever we build lasts at least until we've finished building it, we consider it an unexpected bonus. Yet we are expected to sculpt stable Microsoft Visual Basic code that gives our users more flexible, less costly, and easier-to-use systems.

From this chapter's point of view, the key word is "stable." It's no use being able to churn out ever larger and more capable systems with these new, improved, wash-whiter-than-white tools if all that we succeed in doing is producing more defects. Developers often take a casual attitude toward bugs. They know them intimately, including their origin and often their species as well. A typical programmer looks at bugs in the same manner as an Amazonian tribe member looks at the surrounding insect-infested jungle—as an inevitable fact of life. The typical user is more like a tourist from the big city stranded in the same jungle. Enveloped by hordes of disgustingly hairy creepy-crawlies with too many legs and a nasty habit of appearing in the most unexpected places, the user often becomes upset—which is hardly surprising. This different perspective is one that software developers need to take on board if they expect to meet user expectations.

AN EXPENSIVE TALE

Production bugs are expensive, often frighteningly so. They're expensive in monetary terms when it comes to locating and fixing them. They're expensive in terms of data loss and corruption. And they're expensive when it comes to the loss of user confidence in your software. Some of these factors can be difficult to measure precisely, but they exist all the same. If we examine the course of a typical production defect in hard monetary terms alone, we can get some idea of the magnitude of costs involved when developers allow bugs into their master sources.

Enter Erica, a foreign exchange dealer for a major investment bank, who notices that the software she is using to measure her open U.S. dollar position seems to be misreporting the value of certain trades. Luckily she spots the defect quickly, before any monetary loss is incurred. Being distrustful of the new software, she has been keeping track of her real position on her trade blotter, so the only real cost so far is the time she has had to devote to identifying the problem and proving that it exists. But in that time, she has lost the opportunity to make an advantageous currency trade. Defect cost so far: $5,000.

Peter, a long-time programmer in the bank's Information Systems (IS) department, is given the task of finding and fixing the defect. Although Peter is not very familiar with the software in question, the original developer's highly paid contract ended a week ago, and he's lying on a beach in Hawaii. Peter takes a day to track down the bug (a misunderstanding about when Visual Basic triggers the *LostFocus* event of a text box) and another day to fix the program, test his fix, and run some regression tests to ensure that he has not affected any other part of the program. Defect cost so far: $6,000.

Sally is asked to check Peter's work and to write up the documentation. She notices that the same problem occurs in four other programs written by the Hawaii-resident contractor and tells Peter to fix those programs too. The fixes, testing, and documentation take another three days. Defect cost so far: $9,000.

Tony in the Quality Assurance (QA) department is the next person to receive the amended programs. He spends a day running the full set of QA standard tests. Defect cost so far: $10,000.

Finally, Erica is asked to sign off the new release for production. Because of other pressing work, she performs only the minimal testing needed to convince herself that she is no longer experiencing the same problem. The bug fix now has all the signatures necessary for production release. Total defect cost: $11,000.

But wait: statistics show that some 50 percent of bug fixes lead to the introduction of at least one new bug, which brings the statistical cost of this particular bug to over $16,000! This amount doesn't include the overhead costs of production support and implementation.

This example of a typical defect found in a production environment illustrates that the financial expenses involved in finding and fixing software bugs are often large. A commonly accepted figure in the information technology (IT) industry is that this kind of problem costs an order of magnitude more at each stage of the process. In other words, if the bug in our particular example had been found by the programmer during development, it might have cost $16 to fix. Found by a tester, the cost would have been around $160. Found by a user before it had gone into production, the cost might have been $1,600. Once the problem reaches production, the potential costs are enormous.

The most expensive bug ever reported (by Gerald Weinberg in 1983), the result of a one-character change in a previously working program, cost an incredible $1.6 billion. The jury is still out on the true cost of the millennium date bug, but current estimates are in the region of $600 billion worldwide. (See Chapter 9 for an in-depth treatment of the Year 2000 problem.) Intel spent $200 million to compensate PC owners for the now notorious Pentium bug. In 1992, a fly-by-wire passenger plane crashed during an air show, killing eleven people. The crash was traced to a bug in the software controlling the plane's flight systems. A total failure caused by bugs in a new software system installed to control the dispatch of London ambulances was judged to have directly contributed to at least one patient's death. In 1996, a London brokerage house had to pay more than $1 million to its customers after new software failed to handle customer accounts properly. The list goes on and on.

Most bugs don't have such life-or-death effects; still, the need for zero-defect or low-defect software is becoming increasingly important to our civilization. We have everything from nuclear power stations to international banking systems controlled by software, making bugs both more dangerous and more expensive. This chapter is about techniques that help to reduce or eliminate bugs in production code, especially when writing Visual Basic 5 programs.

WHAT ARE WE TRYING TO ACCOMPLISH?

The aim of this chapter is to teach you different methods of catching bugs during Visual Basic 5 program development and unit testing, before they can reach the master source files. As programmers, we are in a unique position. First, we can learn enough about bugs and their causes to eliminate large classes of them from our programs during initial development. Second, we are probably the only people who have sufficient knowledge of the internal workings of our programs to unit-test them effectively and thereby identify and remove many bugs before they ever reach our testers and users. Developers tend to be highly creative and imaginative people. The challenge is to impose a certain discipline over that talent in order to attack the bug infestation at its very source. Success in meeting this challenge will give us increased user confidence, less user support calls and complaints, shorter product development times, lower maintenance costs, shorter maintenance backlogs, and increased developer confidence—not to mention an ability to tamper with the reality of those developers who think that a zero-defect attitude to writing code is nonproductive.

A Guided Tour

In the first part of this chapter, we'll take a look at some of the more strategic issues involved in the high bug rate currently experienced by the IT industry and at some of the latest ideas that leading software companies such as Microsoft and Borland use to tackle those issues. Although these ideas aren't all directly related to writing code, Visual Basic developers and their managers need to understand them and the issues behind them. As Visual Basic 5 becomes more and more the corporate tool of choice in the production of large-scale projects, we are faced with attempting to produce complex, low-defect systems within reasonable schedules and budgets. Without a firm strategic base on which to build, the game will be lost even before we start designing and coding.

We'll also examine the role that management and developer attitudes play in helping to produce fewer bugs. One of the key ideas here is that most program bugs that reach production can be avoided by stressing the correct software development attitudes. Several studies have shown that programming teams are successful in meeting the targets they set, provided these targets are specific, nonambiguous, and appropriately weighted in importance for the project being tackled. The attitudes of developers are driven by these targets, and we'll look at ways of reinforcing the attitudes associated with low bug rates.

Then it will be time to get our hands dirty. Maybe you remember those medieval maps that used to mark large empty regions with the phrase "Here Be Dragons." We're going to aim for their Visual Basic 5 equivalent, boldly venturing into the regions labeled "Here Be Nasty Scaly Six-Legged Hairy Bugs" and looking at some issues directly related to Visual Basic coding. We'll see where some of the more notorious and ravenous bugs are sleeping and find out how we can avoid waking them—or at least how we can avoid really upsetting them. At this point, we'll sometimes have to delve into rather technical territory. This journey into technical details is unfortunately inevitable when peering at creatures worthy of some of H. R. Giger's worst creations. Once you come out on the other side unharmed, you should have a much better appreciation of when and where Visual Basic developers have to be careful.

In the final section of this chapter, we'll look at some tools that can aid the bug detection and prevention processes in several ways. Microsoft seems to have established a virtual monopoly on the term "Wizard" to describe an add-in or utility designed to help programmers with some aspect of code development. So casting around for a suitable synonym, I came up with "Sourcerer" (thanks, Don!) instead, or perhaps Sourceress. Three such tools are demonstrated and explained.

The Three Sourcerers

The first tool is the Assertion Sourcerer, an add-in that supplements Visual Basic 5's new *Debug.Assert* statement and allows you to implement assertions even in compiled modules, ideal for testing distributed components. Next comes the Metrics Sourcerer, also an add-in. It uses a couple of fairly simple measurements to estimate the relative complexity of your Visual Basic 5 project's procedures, forms, and classes. Several studies have shown that the longer and more complex a procedure, the more likely it is to have bugs discovered in it after being released to production. The final utility is the Instrumentation Sourcerer, yet another add-in. It adds instrumentation code to your Visual Basic 5 project to track all user interactions with your application's graphical interface. This tool can be invaluable in both tracking a user's actions leading up to that elusive program bug and showing exactly how different users use your application in the real world.

Some Final Thoughts Sections

Throughout this chapter, many short sections end with a recommendation (marked as **Some Final Thoughts**) culled from both my own experiences and those of many other people in the IT industry. Acting on these suggestions is probably less important than understanding the issues behind them, as discussed in each section. These recommendations are just opinions, candidly stated, with no reading between the lines required.

SOME STRATEGIC ISSUES

Before we take a closer look at Visual Basic 5, we need to examine several more general factors: priorities, technological progress, and overall project organization. Without understanding and controlling these factors, the best developers in the world aren't able to avoid producing defects. These issues are not really Visual Basic 5–specific—their effect is more on the whole development process. To extend the bug/beastie analogy onto even shakier ground, these are the real gargoyles of the bug world. Their presence permeates a whole project, and if left unrecognized or untamed they can do severe and ongoing damage.

Priorities: The Four-Ball Juggling Act

Software development is still much more of an art than a science. Perhaps one area in which we can apply a discipline more reminiscent of normal engineering is that of understanding and weighing the different aspects of a project. In almost any project, four aspects are critical:

1. The features to be delivered to the users
2. The hardware, software, and other budgets allocated to the project
3. The time frames in which the project phases have to be completed
4. The number of known defects with which the project is allowed to go into production

Balancing these four factors against one another brings us firmly into the realm of classical engineering trade-offs. Concentrating on any one of these aspects to the exclusion of any of the others is almost never going to work. Instead, a continuous juggling act is required during the life of most projects. Adding a new complicated feature might affect the number of production bugs. Refusing to relax a specific project delivery date might mean reducing the number of delivered features. Insisting on the removal of every last bug, no matter how trivial, might significantly increase the allocated budgets. So the users, managers, and developers make a series of decisions during the life of a project about what will (or won't) be done, how it will be done, and about which of these four aspects takes priority at any specific time.

The major requirement here from the zero-defect point of view is that all the project members have an explicit understanding about the relative importance of each of these aspects, especially that of production bugs. This consensus gives everybody a framework on which to base their decisions. If a user asks for a big new feature at the very end of the project, he or she then has no excuse for not being aware of the significant chance of production bugs associated with the new feature or of the budget and schedule implications involved in preventing those bugs from reaching production. Everybody will realize that a change in any one of these four areas nearly always involves compromises in the other three.

A recent project I was involved in inherited a legacy Microsoft SQL Server database schema. We were not allowed to make any significant structural changes to this database, which left us with no easy way of implementing proper concurrency control. After considering our project priorities, we decided to do without proper concurrency control in order to be able to go into production on the planned date. In effect, we decided that this major design bug was acceptable given our other constraints. Knowing the original project priorities made it much easier for us to make the decision based on that framework. Without the framework, we would have spent significant time investigating potential solutions to this problem at the expense of the more important project schedules. When pointed out in black and white, our awareness of the project's priorities seems obvious. But you'd be surprised at the number of projects undertaken with vague expectations and unspecified goals. Much too often, there is confusion about exactly which features will be implemented, which bugs will be fixed, and how flexible the project deadlines and budgets really are.

Some Final Thoughts Look at your project closely, and decide the priorities in order of their importance. Determine how important it is for your project to go to production with as few bugs as possible. Communicate this knowledge to all people involved in the project, including the users. Make sure that everyone has the framework in which to make project decisions based on these and other priorities.

Progress Can Be Dangerous

Avalanches have caused about four times as many deaths worldwide in the 1990s as they did in the 1950s. Today, in spite of more advanced weather forecasting, an improved understanding of how snow behaves in different climatic conditions, and the use of sophisticated radio-locating transmitters, many more people die on the snow slopes. In fact, analysis shows that the technological progress made over the last four decades has actually contributed to the problem. Skiers, snowboarders, and climbers are now able to roam into increasingly more remote areas and backwoods. The wider distribution of knowledge about the mountains and the availability of sophisticated instruments have also given people increased confidence in surviving an avalanche. While many more people are practicing winter sports and many more adventurers have the opportunity to push past traditional limits, the statistics show that they have paid a heavy price.

In the same way that technological progress has ironically been accompanied by a rise in the number of deaths caused by avalanches, the hot new programming tools now available to developers have proved to be a major factor in the far higher bug rates that we are experiencing today compared to five or ten years ago. Back in the olden days of Microsoft Windows programming (about five years ago), the only tools for producing Windows programs were intricate and difficult to learn. Only developers prepared to invest the large amounts of time required to learn the complex data structures and numerous application programming interface (API) calls that Windows programming needed could hope to produce something that even looked like a normal Windows program. Missing the exact esoteric incantations and laying on of hands, software developed by those outside an elite priesthood tended to collapse in a heap when its users tried to do anything out of the ordinary—or sometimes just when they tried to run it. Getting software to work properly required developers to be hard-core in their work, to understand the details of how Windows worked and what they were doing at a very low level. In short, real Windows programming was often seriously frustrating work!

With the introduction of Microsoft Visual Basic and other visual programming tools, a huge amount of the grunt work involved in producing Windows programs has been eliminated. At last, someone who hasn't had a great deal of training and experience can think about producing applications that have previously been the province of an elite group. It is no longer necessary to learn the data structures associated with a window or the API calls necessary to draw text on the screen. A simple drag-and-drop operation with a mouse now performs the work that previously took hours.

The effect has been to reduce dramatically the knowledge levels and effort needed to write Windows programs. Almost anybody who is not a technophobe can produce something that resembles, at least superficially, a normal Windows program. Although placing these tools into the hands of so many people is great news for many computer users, it has led to a startling increase in the number of bug-ridden applications and applications canceled because of runaway bug lists. Widespread use of these development tools has not been accompanied by an equally widespread understanding of how to use them properly to produce solid code.

What is necessary to prevent many types of defects is to understand the real skills required when starting your particular project. Hiring developers who understand Visual Basic alone is asking for trouble. No matter how proficient programmers are with Visual Basic, they're going to introduce bugs into their programs unless they're equipped with at least a rudimentary understanding of how the code they write is going to interact with all the other parts of the system. In a typical corporate client/server project, the skills needed cover a very broad range besides technical expertise with Visual Basic. Probably the most essential element is to understand how to design the application architecture properly and then to be able to implement the architecture as designed. In addition, any potential developer needs to understand the conventions used in normal Windows programs. He or she must understand the client/server paradigm and its advantages and disadvantages, know an appropriate SQL dialect and how to write efficient stored procedures, and be familiar with one or more of the various database communication interfaces such as VBSQL, Jet, ODBC, and RDO. Other areas of expertise might include knowledge about the increasingly important issue of LAN and WAN bandwidth and an understanding of 16-bit and 32-bit Windows architecture together with the various flavors of Windows APIs.

Some Final Thoughts You don't hire a chainsaw expert to cut down trees— you hire a tree surgeon who is also proficient in the use of chainsaws. So to avoid the serious bugs that can result from too narrow an approach to programming, hire developers who understand client/server development and the technical requirements of your specific application, not those who just understand Visual Basic.

Dancing in Step

One of the most serious problems facing us in the battle against bugs is project size and its implications. As the size of a project team grows linearly, the number of communication channels required between the team members grows factorially (in fact, almost exponentially once the numbers reach a certain level). Traditionally, PC projects have been relatively small, often involving just two or three people. Now we're starting to see tools such as Visual Basic 5 being used in large-scale, mission-critical projects staffed by ten to twenty developers or more. These project teams can be spread over several locations, even over different continents, and staffed by programmers with widely varying skills and experience.

The object-oriented approach is one attempt to control this complexity. By designing discrete objects that have their internal functions hidden and that expose clearly defined interfaces for talking to other objects, we can simplify some of the problems involved in fitting together many pieces of code produced by multiple developers into a workable application.

However, programmers still have the problems associated with communicating what each one of hundreds of properties really represents and how every method and function actually works. Any assumptions a programmer makes have to be made clear to any other programmer who has to interact with the first programmer's objects. Testing has to be performed to check that none of the traditional implementation problems that are often found when combining components have cropped up. Where problems are found, two or more developers must often work together for a while to resolve them.

In an effort to deal with these issues, which can be a major cause of bugs, many software companies have developed the idea of working in parallel teams that join together and synchronize their work at frequent intervals, often daily. This technique enables one large team of developers to be split into several small teams, with frequent builds and periodic stabilization of their project. Small teams traditionally have several advantages over their larger counterparts. They tend to be more flexible, communicate faster, have less likelihood of misunderstandings, and exhibit more team spirit. An approach that divides big teams into smaller ones but still allows these smaller groups to synchronize and stabilize their work safely helps to provide these small-team advantages even for large-team projects.

What is the perfect team size? To some extent, the optimum team size depends on the type of project; but studies typically show that the best number is three to four developers, with five or six as a maximum. Teams of this size are easier to control and communicate more effectively.

Having said this, I still think you need to devise an effective process that allows for the code produced by these small teams to be combined successfully into one large application. You can take several approaches to accomplish this combination. The process I recommend for enabling this "dancing in step," which is similar to the one Microsoft uses, is described here:

1. **Create a master copy of the application source.** This process depends on there being a single master copy of the application source code, from which a periodic (often daily) test build will be generated and released to users for testing.

2. **Establish a daily deadline after which the master source cannot be changed.** With nobody permitted to change the master source code after a certain time each day, developers know when they can safely perform the synchronization steps discussed in detail in the rest of these steps.

3. **Check out.** Take a private copy of the code to be worked on from the master sources. You don't need to prevent more than one developer from checking out the same code because any conflicts will be dealt with at a later stage. (See step 8.)

4. **Make the changes.** Modify the private copy of the code to implement the new feature or bug fix.

5. **Build a private release.** Compile the private version of the code.

6. **Test the private release.** Check that the new feature or bug fix is working correctly.

7. **Perform pretesting code synchronization.** Compare the private version of the source code with the master source. The current master source could have changed since the developer checked out her private version of the source at the start of this process. The daily check-in deadline mentioned in step 2 ensures that the developers know when they can safely perform this synchronization.

8. **Merge the master source into the private source.** Merge the current master source into the private version of the source, thus incorporating any changes that other developers might have made. Any inconsistencies caused by other developers' changes have to be dealt with at this stage.

9. **Build a private release.** Build the new updated private version of the source.

10. **Test the private release.** Check that the new feature or bug fix still works correctly.

11. **Execute a regression test.** Test this second build to make sure that the new feature or bug fix hasn't adversely affected previous functionality.

12. **Perform pre-check-in code synchronization.** Compare the private version of the source code with the master source. Because this step is done just prior to the check-in itself (that is, before the check-in deadline), it will not be performed on the same day that the previous pre-testing code synchronization (which occurs after the check-in deadline; see step 7) took place. Therefore, the master source might have changed in the intervening period.

13. **Check in.** Merge the private version of the source into the master source. You must do this before the daily check-in deadline mentioned in step 2 so that other developers can perform their private code synchronization and merges safely after the deadline.

14. **Observe later-same-day check-ins.** It is essential that you watch later check-ins that day before the deadline to check for potential indirect conflicts with the check-in described in step 13.

15. **Generate a daily build.** After the check-in deadline, build a new version of the complete application from the updated master sources. This build should be relatively stable, with appropriate punishments being allocated to project members who are responsible for any build breaks.

16. **Test the daily build.** Execute some tests, preferably automated, to ensure that basic functionality still works and that the build is reasonably stable. This build can then be released to other team members and users.

Although the above process looks lengthy and even somewhat painful in places, it ensures that multiple developers and teams can work simultaneously on a single application's master source code. It would be significantly more painful to experience the very frustrating and difficult bugs that traditionally arise when attempting to combine the work of several different teams of developers.

Some Final Thoughts Split your larger project teams into smaller groups, and establish a process whereby these groups can merge and stabilize their code with that of the other project groups. The smaller teams will produce far fewer bugs than will the larger ones, and an effective merging process will prevent most of the bugs that would otherwise result from combining the work of the smaller teams into a coherent application.

SOME ATTITUDE ISSUES

One of the major themes of this chapter is that *attitude* is everything when it comes to writing zero-defect code. Developers aren't stupid, and they can write solid code when given the opportunity. Provided with a clear and unambiguous set of targets, they are usually highly motivated and very effective at meeting those targets. If management sets a crystal-clear target of zero-defect code and then does everything sensible to encourage attitudes aimed at fulfilling that target, the probability is that the code produced by the team will have few defects. So given the goal of writing zero-defect code, let's look at some of the attitudes that are required.

Swallowing a Rhinoceros Sideways

The stark truth is that there is no such thing as zero-defect software. The joke definition passed down from generation to generation (a generation in IS being maybe 18 months or so) expresses it nicely: "Zero defects [noun]: The result of shutting down a production line." Most real-life programs contain at least a few bugs simply because writing bug-free code is so difficult. As one of my clients likes to remind me, if writing solid code were easy, everybody would be doing it. He also claims that writing flaky code is much easier—which might account for the large quantity of it generally available.

Having said this, it is really part of every professional developer's job to aim at writing bug-free code. Knowing that bugs are inevitable is no excuse for any attitude that allows them the slightest breathing space. It's all in the approach. Professional programmers know that their code is going to contain bugs, so they bench-test it, run it through the debugger, and generally hammer it every way they can to catch the problems that they know are lurking in there somewhere.

If you watch the average hacker at work, you'll notice something interesting. As soon as said hacker is convinced that his program is working to his satisfaction, he stops working, leans back in his chair, shouts to his boss that he's ready to perform a production release, and then heads for the soda machine. He's happy that he has spent some considerable time trying to show that his program is correct. Now fast-forward this hacker a few years, to the point where he has become more cynical and learned much more about the art of programming; what do you see? After reaching the stage at which he used to quit, he promptly starts working again. This time, he's trying something different— rather than prove his program is correct, he's trying to prove that it's incorrect.

Perhaps one of the major differences between amateur and professional developers is that amateurs are satisfied to show that their programs appear to be bug-free, whereas professionals prefer to try showing that their programs still contain bugs. The amateurs mostly haven't had enough experience to realize that when they believe their program is working correctly, they are perhaps just halfway through the development process. After they've done their best to prove a negative (that their code doesn't have any bugs), they need to spend some time trying to show the opposite.

Some Final Thoughts Find developers who are (a) intelligent, (b) knowledgeable, (c) willing to learn, and (d) good at delivering effective code. Find out whether they are also (e) aware that writing bug-free code is so difficult that they must do everything possible to prevent and detect bugs. Don't hire them without this final magical factor. It's true that (a) through (d) are all wonderful qualities, but they are meaningless without (e).

Looping the Loop

One of the most effective ways of restraining soaring bug rates is to attack the problem at its source—the programmer. Programmers have always known about the huge gap between the quality of code produced by the best and by the worst programmers. Industry surveys have verified this folklore by showing that the least effective developers in an organization produce more than twenty times the number of bugs as the most effective developers produce. It follows that an organization would benefit if its better programmers produced the majority of new code. With that in mind, some corporations have introduced the simple but revolutionary idea that programmers have to fix their own bugs—and have to fix them as soon as they are found.

This sets up what engineers call a negative feedback loop, otherwise known as evolution in action. The more bugs a programmer produces, the more time he or she is required to spend on fixing those bugs. At least four benefits rapidly become apparent:

1. The more bugs a programmer produces, the less chance he or she has of working on new code and therefore of introducing new bugs. Instead, the better programmers (judged by bug rate) get to write all the new code, which is therefore likely to have less bugs.

2. Programmers soon learn that writing buggy code is counterproductive. They aren't able to escape from the bugs they've introduced, so they begin to understand that writing solid code on the first pass is more effective and less wasteful of time than having to go back to old code, often several times in succession.

3. Bug-prone developers start to gain some insights into what it's like to maintain their own code. This awareness can have a salutary effect on their design and coding habits. Seeing just how difficult it is to test that extremely clever but error-prone algorithm teaches them to sympathize more with the maintenance programmers.

4. The software being written has very few known bugs at any time because the bugs are being fixed as soon as they're found. Runaway bug lists are stomped before they can gather any momentum. And the software is always at a point where it can be shipped almost immediately. It might not have all the features originally requested or envisioned, but those features that do exist will contain only a small number of known bugs. This ability to ship at any point in the life of a project can be very useful in today's fast-changing business world.

Some people might consider this type of feedback loop as a sort of punishment. If it does qualify as such, it's an extremely neutral punishment. What tends to happen is that the developers start to see it as a learning process. With management setting and then enforcing quality standards with this particular negative feedback loop, developers learn that producing bug-free code is very important. And like most highly motivated personalities, they soon adapt their working habits to whatever standard is set. No real crime and punishment occurs here; the process is entirely objective. If you create a bug, you have to fix it, and you have to fix it immediately. This process should become laborious enough to teach developers how to prevent that type of bug in the future or how to detect that type of bug once it has been introduced.

Some Final Thoughts Set a zero-defect standard and introduce processes that emphasize the importance of that standard. If management is seen to concentrate on the issue of preventing bugs, developers will respond with better practices and less defects.

Back to School

Although Visual Basic 5 is certainly not the rottweiler on speed that C++ and the Microsoft Foundation Classes (MFC) can be, there is no doubt that its increased power and size comes with its own dangers. Visual Basic 5 has many powerful features, and these take a while to learn. Because the language is so big, a typical developer might use only 10 percent or even less of its features in the year he or she takes to write perhaps three or four applications. It has become increasingly hard to achieve expertise in such a large and complex language. So it is perhaps no surprise to find that many bugs stem from a misunderstanding of how Visual Basic implements a particular feature.

I'll demonstrate this premise with a fairly trivial example. An examination of the following function will reveal nothing obviously unsafe. Multiplying the two maximum possible function arguments that could be received (32767 * 32767) will never produce a result bigger than can be stored in the long variable that this function returns.

```
Private Function BonusCalc(ByVal niNumberOfWeeks As Integer, _
    ByVal niWeeklyBonus As Integer) As Long

BonusCalc = niNumberOfWeeks * niWeeklyBonus

End Function
```

Now if you happened to be diligent enough to receive a weekly bonus of $1,000 over a period of 35 weeks…well, let's just say that this particular function wouldn't deliver your expected bonus! Although the function looks safe enough, Visual Basic's intermediate calculations behind the scenes cause trouble. When multiplying the two integers together, Visual Basic attempts to store the temporary result into another *integer* before assigning it to *BonusCalc*. This, of course, causes an immediate overflow error. What you have to do instead is give the Visual Basic compiler some assistance. The following revised statement works because Visual Basic realizes that we might be dealing with longs rather than just integers:

```
BonusCalc = niNumberOfWeeks * CLng(niWeeklyBonus)
```

Dealing with these sorts of language quirks is not easy. Programmers are often pushed for time, so they sometimes tend to avoid experimenting with a feature to see how it really works in detail. For the same reasons, reading the manuals or online help is often confined to a hasty glance just to confirm syntax. These are false economies. Even given the fact that sections of some manuals appear to have been written by Urdu swineherders on some very heavy medication, those pages still contain many pearls. When you use something in Visual Basic 5 for the first time, take a few minutes to read about its subtleties in the manual and write a short program to experiment with its implementation. Use it in several different ways within a program, and twist it into funny shapes. Find out what it can and can't handle.

Some Final Thoughts Professional developers should understand the tools at their disposal at a detailed level. Learn from the manual how the tools *should* work, and then go beyond the manual and find out how they really work.

Yet More Schoolwork

Visual Basic 4 introduced the concept of object-oriented programming using the Basic language. Visual Basic 5 takes this concept and elaborates on it in several ways. It is still possible to write Visual Basic 5 code that looks almost exactly like Visual Basic 3 code or that even resembles procedural COBOL code if you want to be committed to an institution for the very silly. The modern emphasis, however, is on the use of relatively new ideas in Basic, such as abstraction and encapsulation, which aim to make applications easier to develop, understand, and maintain. Any Visual Basic developer unfamiliar with these ideas first has to learn what they are and why they are useful and then has to understand all the quirks of their implementation in Visual Basic 5. The learning curve is not trivial. For example, understanding how the *Implements* statement produces a virtual class that is Visual Basic 5's way of implementing polymorphism can require some structural remodeling of one's thought processes. This is heavy-duty object-oriented programming in the 1990s style. Trying to use it in a production environment without a clear understanding is a prime cause of new and unexpected bugs.

Developers faced with radically new concepts usually go through up to four stages of enlightenment. The first stage has to do with reading and absorbing the theory behind the concept. The second stage includes working with either code examples or actual programs written by other people that implement the new concept. The third stage involves using the new concept in their own code. Only at this point do programmers become fully aware of the subtleties involved and understand how *not* to write their code. The final stage of enlightenment arrives when the programmer learns how to implement the concept correctly, leaving no holes for the bugs to crawl through.

Some Final Thoughts Developers should take all the time necessary to reach the third and fourth stages of enlightenment when learning new programming concepts or methodologies. Only then should they be allowed to implement these new ideas in production systems.

Eating Humble Pie

Most developers are continually surprised to find out how fallible they are and how difficult it is to be precise about even simple processes. The human brain is evidently not well equipped to deal with problems that require great precision to solve. It's not the actual complexity but the type of complexity that defeats us. Evolution has been successful in giving us some very sophisticated pattern-recognition algorithms and heuristics to deal with certain types of complexity. A classic example is our visual ability to recognize a human face even when seen at an angle or in lighting conditions never experienced before. Your ability to remember and compare patterns means that you can recognize your mother or father in circumstances that would completely defeat a computer program. Lacking your ability to recognize and compare patterns intelligently, the program instead has to use a brute-force approach, applying a very different type of intelligence to a potentially huge number of possibilities.

As successful as we are at handling some sorts of complexity, the complexity involved in programming computers is a different matter. The requirement is no longer to compare patterns in a holistic, or all-round, fashion but instead to be very precise about the comparison. In a section of program code, a single misplaced character, such as "+" instead of "&," can produce a nasty defect that often cannot be easily spotted because its cause is so small. So we have to watch our P's and Q's very carefully, still retaining our ability to look at the big picture but also ensuring that every tiny detail of the picture is correct. This endless attention to detail is not something at which the human brain is very efficient. Surrounded by a large number of potential bugs, we can sometimes struggle to maintain what often feels like a very precarious balance in our programs.

A programmer employed by my company came to me with a bug that he had found impossible to locate. When I looked at the suspect class module, the first thing I noticed was that one of the variables hadn't been declared before being used. Like every conscientious Visual Basic developer, he had set *Require Variable Declaration* in his Integrated Development Environment (IDE) to warn him about this type of problem. But in a classic case of programming oversight, he had made the perfectly reasonable assumption that setting this option meant that all undeclared variables are always recognized and stomped on. Unfortunately, it applies only to new modules developed from the point at which the flag is set. Any modules written within one developer's IDE and then imported into another programmer's IDE are never checked for undeclared variables unless that first developer also specified *Require Variable Declaration*. This is obvious when you realize how the option functions. It simply inserts *Option Explicit* at the top of each module when it is first created. What it doesn't do is act globally on all modules. This point is easy to realize when you stop and think for a moment, but it's also very easy to miss.

Some Final Thoughts Learn to be humble when programming. This stuff is seriously nontrivial (a fancy scientific term for swallowing a rhinoceros sideways), and arrogance when trying to write stable code is counterproductive.

Getting Our Hands Dirty

Steve Maguire, in his excellent book *Writing Solid Code* (Microsoft Press, 1995), stresses that many of the best techniques and tools developed for the eradication of bugs came from programmers asking the following two questions every time a bug is found:

- How could I have automatically detected this bug?
- How could I have prevented this bug?

In the following sections, we'll look at some of the bugs Visual Basic 5 programmers are likely to encounter, and I'll suggest ways of answering both of the above questions where appropriate. Applying this lesson of abstracting from the specific problem to the general solution can be especially effective when carried out in a corporate environment over a period of time. Given a suitable corporate culture, in which every developer has the opportunity to formulate general answers to specific problems, a cumulative beneficial effect can accrue. The more that reusable code is available to developers, the more it will be utilized. Likewise, the more information about the typical bugs encountered within an organization that is stored and made available in the form of a database, the more likely it is that the programmers with access to that information will search for the information and use it appropriately. In the ideal world, all this information would be contributed both in the form of reusable code and in a database of problems and solutions. Back in the real world, one or the other method may have to suffice.

Some Final Thoughts Document all system testing, user acceptance testing, and production bugs and their resolution. Make this information available to the developers and testers and their IS managers. Consider using an application's system testing and user acceptance bug levels to determine when that application is suitable for release to the next project phase.

In-Flight Testing: Using the *Assert* Statement

One of the most powerful debugging tools available, at least to C programmers, is the *Assert* macro. Simple in concept, it allows a programmer to write self-checking code by providing an easy method of verifying that a particular condition or assumption is true. Visual Basic programmers have had no structured way of doing this—until Visual Basic 5. Now we can write statements like this:

```
Debug.Assert 2 + 2 = 4

Debug.Assert bFunctionIsArrayHealthy

Select Case iUserChoice
    Case 1
        DoSomething1
    Case 2
        DoSomething2
    Case Else
        ' We should never reach here!
        Debug.Assert nUserChoice = 1 Or nUserChoice = 2
End Select
```

Debug.Assert operates in the development environment only—conditional compilation automatically drops it from the compiled EXE. It will take any expression that evaluates to either TRUE or FALSE and then drop into break mode at the point the assertion is made if that expression evaluates to FALSE. The idea is to allow you to catch bugs and other problems early by verifying that your assumptions about your program and its environment are true. You can load your program code with debug checks; in fact, you can create code that checks itself while running. Holes in your algorithms, invalid assumptions, creaky data structures, and invalid procedure arguments can all be found in flight and without any human intervention.

The power of assertions is limited only by your imagination. Suppose you were using Visual Basic 5 to control the space shuttle. (We can dream, can't we?) You might have a procedure that shuts down the shuttle's main engine in the event of an emergency, perhaps preparing to jettison the engine entirely. You would want to ensure that the shutdown had worked before the jettison took place, so the procedure for doing this would need to return some sort of status code. To check that the shutdown procedure was working correctly during debugging, you might want to perform a different version of it as well and then verify that both routines left the main engine in the same state. It is fairly common to code any mission-critical system features in this manner. The results of the two different algorithms can be checked against each other, a practice that would fail only in the relatively unlikely situation of both the algorithms having the same bug. The Visual Basic 5 code for such testing might look something like this:

```
' Normal shutdown
Set nResultOne = ShutdownTypeOne(objEngineCurrentState)

' Different shutdown
Set nResultTwo = ShutdownTypeTwo(objEngineCurrentState)

' Check that both shutdowns produced the same result.
Debug.Assert nResultOne = nResultTwo
```

When this code was released into production, you would obviously want to remove everything except the call to the normal shutdown routine and let Visual Basic 5's automatic conditional compilation drop the *Debug.Assert* statement.

You can also run periodic health checks on the major data structures in your programs, looking for uninitialized or null values, holes in arrays, and other nasty gremlins:

```
Debug.Assert bIsArrayHealthy CriticalArray
```

Assertions and *Debug.Assert* are designed for the development environment only. In the development environment, you are trading program size and speed for debug information. Once your code has reached production, the assumption is that it's been tested well and that assertions are no longer necessary. Also, experience shows that a system loaded with assertions can run from 20 to 50 percent slower than one without the assertions, which is obviously not suitable in a production environment. But because the *Debug.Assert* statements remain in your source code, they will automatically be used again whenever your code is changed and retested in the development environment. In effect, your assertions are immortal—which is as it should be. One of the hardest trails for a maintenance programmer to follow is that left by your own assumptions about the state of your program. Although we all try to avoid code dependencies and subtle assumptions when we're designing and writing our code, they invariably tend to creep in. Real life demands compromises, and the best-laid code design has to cope with some irregularities and subtleties. Now your assertion statements can act as beacons, showing the people who come after you what you were worried about when you wrote a particular section of code. Doesn't that give you a little psychic frisson?

Another reason why *Debug.Assert* is a very important new tool in your fight against bugs is the inexorable rise of object-oriented programming. A large part of object-oriented programming is what I call "design by contract." This is where you design and implement an object hierarchy in your Visual Basic program, and expose methods and properties of your objects for other developers (or yourself) to use. In effect, you're making a contract with these users of your program. If they invoke your methods and properties correctly, perhaps in a specific order or only under certain conditions, they will receive the services or results that they want. Now you are able to use assertions to ensure that your methods are called in the correct order, perhaps, or that the class initialization method has been invoked before any other method. Whenever you want to confirm that your class object is being used correctly and is in an internally consistent state, you can simply call a method private to that class that can then perform the series of assertions that make up the "health check."

One situation in which to be careful occurs when you're using *Debug.Assert* to invoke a procedure. You need to bear in mind that any such invocation will never be performed in the compiled version of your program. If you cut and paste the following code into an empty project, you can see clearly what will happen:

```
Option Explicit
Dim mbIsThisDev As Boolean

Private Sub Form_Load()
mbIsThisDev = False

' If the following line executes, the MsgBox will display
' True in answer to its title "Is this development?"
' If it doesn't execute, the MsgBox will display false.

Debug.Assert SetDevFlagToTrue
MsgBox mbIsThisDev, vbOKOnly, "Is this development?"


Unload Me
End Sub

Private Function SetDevFlagToTrue() As Boolean

SetDevFlagToTrue = True
mbIsThisDev = True

End Function
```

When you run this code in the Visual Basic environment, the message box will state that it's true that your program is running within the Visual Basic IDE because the *SetDevFlagToTrue* function will be invoked. If you compile the code into an EXE, however, the message box will show FALSE. In other words, the *SetDevFlagToTrue* function is not invoked at all. Offhand, I can't think of a more roundabout method of discovering whether you're running as an EXE or in the Visual Basic 5 IDE.

When should you assert?

Once you start using assertions seriously in your code, you need to be aware of some pertinent issues. The first and most important of these is when you should assert. The golden rule is that assertions should not take the place of either defensive programming or data validation. An assertion is normally used only to detect an illegal condition that should never happen if your program is working correctly. To return to the control software of our space shuttle, consider this code:

```
Sub InsertIntoEngine(ByVal vntiAnObject As Variant)

Debug.Assert TypeName(vntiAnObject) = Object
' The insert into engine code goes here.

End Sub
```

Asserting procedure arguments like this is fine, but only provided the assertion is in addition to some proper argument validation that handles nasty situations, such as trying to insert a nonobject into the engine. In other words, don't ever let assertions take the place of normal validation as we did in this example. Instead you might want to say something like this:

```
Sub InsertIntoEngine(ByVal vntiAnObject As Variant)

If TypeName(vntiAnObject) <> "Object" Then
    Debug.Assert TypeName(vntiAnObject) = "Object"
    Err.Raise vbObjectError + mgInvalidObjectError
Else
    ' The insert into engine code goes here.
End If

End Sub
```

If the *InsertIntoEngine* routine was on a critical path and you weren't allowed to generate any errors, you could avoid an engine accident by coding defensively instead:

```
Sub InsertIntoEngine(ByVal vntiAnObject As Variant)

If TypeName(vntiAnObject) <> "Object" Then
    Debug.Assert TypeName(vntiAnObject) = "Object"
    Exit Sub
Else
    ' The insert into engine code goes here.
End If

End Sub
```

Be aware that defensive programming like the above is dangerous if you don't include the assertion statement. Although using defensive programming to write what might be called nonstop code is important for the prevention of user data loss as a result of program crashes, it can also have the unfortunate side effect of hiding bugs. Without the assertion statement, a programmer who called the *InsertIntoEngine* routine with an incorrect argument would not necessarily receive any warning of a problem. Whenever you find yourself programming defensively, include an assertion statement.

Explain your assertions

Perhaps the only thing more annoying than finding an assertion statement in another programmer's code and having no idea why it's there is finding a similar assertion statement in your own code. Document your assertions. A simple one- or two-line comment will normally suffice—you don't need to write a dissertation. Some assertions can be the result of quite subtle code dependencies, so in your comment try to make it clear why you're asserting something, not just what you're asserting.

Beware of Boolean coercion weirdness

The final issue with *Debug.Assert* is Boolean type coercion. Later in this chapter, we'll look at Visual Basic's automatic type coercion rules and where they can lay nasty traps for you. For now, you can be content with studying the following little enigma:

```
Dim nTest As Integer
nTest = 50
Debug.Assert nTest
Debug.Assert Not nTest
```

You will find that neither of these assertions fire! Strange, but true. The reason has to do with Visual Basic coercing the integer to a Boolean. The first assertion says that *nTest = 50*, which, because nTest is nonzero, is evaluated to TRUE. The second assertion calculates *Not nTest* to be −51, which is also nonzero and again evaluated to TRUE.

However, if you compare *nTest* and *Not nTest* to the actual value of TRUE (which is −1) as in the following code, only the first assertion fires:

```
Debug.Assert nTest = True
Debug.Assert Not nTest = True
```

Some Final Thoughts *Debug.Assert* is a very powerful tool for bug detection. Used properly, it can catch many bugs automatically, without any human intervention. (See the discussion of an Assertion Sourcerer on page 314 for a utility that supplements *Debug.Assert*.)

How Sane Is Your Program?

A source-level debugger such as that available in Visual Basic is a wonderful tool. It allows you to see into the heart of your program, to watch data as it flows through your code. Instead of taking a "black box," putting input into it, and then checking the output and guessing at what actually happened between the two, you get the chance to examine the whole process in detail.

Back in the 1950s, many people were still optimistic about the possibility of creating a machine endowed with human intelligence. In 1950, English mathematician Alan Turing proposed a thought experiment to test whether a machine was intelligent. His idea was that anybody who wanted to verify a computer program's intelligence would be able to interrogate both the program in question and a human being via computer links. If after asking a series of questions, the interrogator was unable to distinguish between the human and the program, the program might legitimately be considered intelligent. This experiment had several drawbacks, the main one being that it would be very difficult to devise the right type of questions. The interrogator would forever be devising new questions and wondering about the answers to the current ones.

This process is remarkably similar to what happens during program testing. A tester devises a number of inputs (equivalent to asking a series of questions) and then carefully examines the output (listens to the computer's answers). And like Turing's experiment, this type of black-box testing has the same drawbacks. The tester simply can't be sure whether he or she is asking the right questions or when enough questions have been asked to be reasonably sure that the program is functioning correctly.

What a debugger allows you to do is dive below the surface. No longer do you have to be satisfied with your original questions. You can observe your program's inner workings, redirect your questions in midflight to examine new issues raised by watching the effect of your original questions on the code, and be much more aware of which questions are important to ask. Unlike a psychiatrist, who can never be sure whether or not a patient is sane, using a source-level debugger means that you will have a much better probability of being able to find out about the sanity of your program.

Debugging windows

Visual Basic 5's source-level debugger has some improvements over the Visual Basic 4 version. Instead of having just a single Debug window, you now have three debugging windows as part of the IDE:

- The Immediate window is a drop-in replacement of the old Debug window, with all the familiar abilities such as being able to execute single-line statements or subroutines.

- The Locals window is rather cool. It displays the name, value, and data type of each variable declared in the current procedure. It can also show properties. You can change the value of any variable or property merely by clicking on it and then typing the new value. This can save a lot of time during debugging.

- The Watches window also saves you some time, allowing you to watch a variable's value without having to type any statements into the Immediate window. You can easily edit the value of any Watch expression you've set or the Watch expression itself by clicking on it, just as you can in the Locals window.

Debugging hooks

One technique that many programmers have found useful when working with this type of interactive debugger is to build debugging hooks directly into their programs. These hooks, usually in the form of functions or subroutines, can be executed directly from the Immediate window when in break mode. An example might be a routine that walks any array passed to it and prints out its contents, as shown here.

```
Public Sub DemonstrateDebugHook()

Dim saTestArray(1 to 4) As Integer
saTestArray(1) = "Element one"
saTestArray(2) = "Element two"
saTestArray(3) = "Element three"
saTestArray(4) = "Element four"

Stop

End Sub
```

>>

```
Public Sub WalkArray(ByVal vntiArray As Variant)
Dim nLoop As Integer

' Check that we really have an array.
Debug.Assert IsArray(vntiArray)

' Print the array type and number of elements.
Debug.Print "Array is of type " & TypeName(vntiArray)
nLoop = UBound(vntiArray) - LBound(vntiArray) + 1
Debug.Print "Array has " & CStr(nLoop) & " elements"

' Walk the array, and print its elements.
For nLoop = LBound(vntiArray) To UBound(vntiArray)
    Debug.Print "Element " & CStr(nLoop) & " contains:" _
        & vntiArray(nLoop)
Next nLoop

End Sub
```

When you run this code, Visual Basic will go into break mode when it hits the *Stop* statement placed in *DemonstrateDebugHook*. You can then use the Immediate window to type:

```
WalkArray saTestArray
```

This debugging hook will execute and show you all the required information about any array passed to it.

NOTE

> The array is received as a Variant so that any array type can be handled and so that the array can be passed by value. Whole arrays can't be passed by value in their natural state. These types of debugging hooks placed in a general debug class or module can be extremely useful, both for you and for any programmers who later have to modify or debug your code.

Exercising all the paths

Another effective way of utilizing the debugger is to step through all new or modified code to exercise all the data paths contained within one or more procedures. You can do this quickly, often in a single test run. Every program has code that gets executed only once in a very light blue moon, usually code that handles special conditions or errors. Being able to reset the debugger to a particular source statement, change some data to force the traversal of another path, and then continue program execution from that point gives you a great deal of testing power.

```
' This code will work fine - until sTest is empty.
If Len(sTest) > 0 And Left$(sTest, 1) = "0" Then
    DoSomething
Else
    DoSomethingElse
End If
```

When I first stepped through this code while testing another programmer's work, the *sTest* string was 2 bytes long. I stepped through to the *End If* statement—everything looked fine. Then I used the Locals window to edit the *sTest* variable and change it to a null string, set the debugger to execute the first line again,...and of course the program crashed. (Visual Basic doesn't short-circuit this sort of expression evaluation. No matter what the length of *sTest*, the second expression on the line will always be evaluated.) This ability to change data values and thereby follow all the code paths through a procedure is invaluable in detecting bugs that might otherwise take a long time to appear.

Peering Inside Stored Procedures

One of the classic bugbears of client/server programming is that it's not possible to debug stored procedures interactively. Instead, you're forced into the traditional edit-compile-test cycle, treating the stored procedure that you're developing as an impenetrable black box. Pass in some inputs, watch the outputs, and try to guess what happened in between. Now Visual Basic 5 introduces something that's rather useful: a Transact-SQL (T-SQL) interactive debugger.

There are a few constraints. First of all, you must be using the Enterprise Edition of Visual Basic 5. Also, the only supported server-side configuration is Microsoft SQL Server 6.5. Finally, you also need to be running SQL Server Service Pack 1 or 2. (Service Pack 2 is included on the Visual Basic 5 Enterprise Edition CD.) When installing Visual Basic 5, select Custom from the Setup dialog box, choose Enterprise Features, and click Select All to ensure that all the necessary client-side components are installed. Once Service Pack 2 is installed, you can install and register the T-SQL Debugger interface and Remote Automation component on the server.

The T-SQL Debugger works through a UserConnection created with Microsoft UserConnection, which is available on the Add ActiveX Designer submenu of the Project menu. Once you've created a UserConnection object, just create a Query object for the T-SQL query you want to debug. This query can be either a user-defined query that you build using something like Microsoft Query or a stored procedure.

The T-SQL Debugger interface is similar to most language debuggers, allowing you to set breakpoints, change local variables or parameters, watch global variables, and step through the code. You can also view the contents of global temporary tables that your stored procedure creates and dump the resultset of the stored procedure to the output window. If your stored procedure creates multiple resultsets, right-click the mouse button over the output window and select More Results to view the next resultset.

Some Final Thoughts The combination of these two powerful interactive debuggers, including their new features, makes it even easier to step through every piece of code that you write, as soon as you write it. Such debugging usually doesn't take nearly as long as many developers assume and can be used to promote a much better understanding of the structure and stability of your programs.

Jumping out of the Loop

One psychological factor responsible for producing bugs and preventing their detection is an inability to jump from one mind-set to another. For example, in our push to examine what are often subtle details, we often overlook the obvious. The results of a study performed a decade ago showed that that 50 percent of all errors plainly visible on a screen or report were still overlooked by the programmer. The kind of mistake shown in the preceding sentence ("that" repeated) seems fairly obvious in retrospect, but did you spot it the first time through?

One reason for this tendency to overlook the obvious is that the mind-set required to find gross errors is so different from the mind-set needed to locate subtle errors that it is hard to switch between the two. We've all been in the situation in which the cause of a bug has eluded us for hours, but as soon as we explained the problem to another programmer, the cause of the error immediately became obvious. In this type of confessional programming, the other developer often doesn't even have to say a single word, just nod wisely. The mental switch from an internal monologue to an external one is often all that we need to force us into a different mind-set, and we can then reevaluate our assumptions about what is happening in the code. Like one of those infuriating magic pictograms, the change of focus means that what was hidden before suddenly becomes clear.

Some Final Thoughts If you're stuck on a particularly nasty bug, try some lateral thinking. Use confessional programming, explaining the problem to a colleague. Perhaps take a walk to get some fresh air. Work on something entirely different for a few minutes, returning later with a mind that's fresh to the problem. Or you can go so far as to picture yourself jumping out of that mental loop, reaching a different level of thought. All of these techniques can help you avoid endlessly traveling around the same mental pathways.

The Events from Hell

Visual Basic's *GotFocus* and *LostFocus* events have always been exasperating to Visual Basic programmers. They don't correspond to the normal *KillFocus* and *SetFocus* messages generated by Windows; they don't always execute in the order that you might expect; they are sometimes skipped entirely; and they can prove very troublesome when you use them for field-by-field validation.

If these two events have caused problems in previous versions of Visual Basic, you might legitimately ask why Microsoft didn't find a way of "fixing" their behavior in Visual Basic 5. The reason they were left alone has to do with Visual Basic being designed to protect the developer as much as possible from the underlying environment and to be reasonably GPF-proof. If *GotFocus* and *LostFocus* really did correspond to *KillFocus* and *SetFocus*, trying to do something like show a message box in a *GotFocus* or *LostFocus* event would be walking straight into GPF territory. It appears that the Visual Basic team made a decision to "post" these events rather than "send" them. Under the ever-useful principle of least astonishment, most programmers would prefer not to have events whose order is difficult to predict or that disappear entirely, but that's what we have to live with.

To demonstrate some of the problems with these two events, I wrote a simple application. This project contains a single window with two text box controls, an OK command button, and a Cancel command button. (See Figure 7-1.)

FIGURE 7-1

Simple interface screen hides events from hell

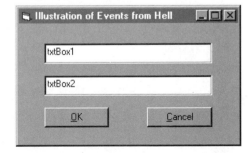

Both command buttons have an accelerator key; the OK button's *Default* property is set to TRUE (that is, pressing the Enter key will click this button), and the Cancel button's *Cancel* property is set to TRUE (that is, pressing the Esc key will click this button). The *GotFocus* and *LostFocus* events of all four controls contain a *Debug.Print* statement that will tell you (in the Immediate window) which event has been fired. In this manner, we can easily examine the order in which these events fire and understand some of the difficulties with using them.

When the application's window is initially displayed, focus is set to the first text box. The Immediate window shows the following:

```
Program initialization
txtBox1_GotFocus
```

Just tabbing from the first to the second text box shows the following events:

```
txtBox1_LostFocus
txtBox2_GotFocus
```

So far, everything is as expected. Now we can add some code to the *LostFocus* event of *txtBox1* to simulate a crude validation of the contents of *txtBox1*, something like this:

```
Private Sub txtBox1_LostFocus

Debug.Print "txtBox1_LostFocus"
If Len(txtBox1.Text) > 0 Then
    txtBox1_SetFocus
End If

End Sub
```

Restarting the application and putting any value into *txtBox1* followed by tabbing to *txtBox2* again shows what looks like a perfectly normal event stream:

```
txtBox1_LostFocus
txtBox2_GotFocus
txtBox2_LostFocus
txtBox1_GotFocus
```

Normally, however, we want to inform the user if a window control contains anything invalid. So in our blissful ignorance, we add a *MsgBox* statement to the *LostFocus* event of *txtBox1* to inform the user that something's wrong:

```
Private Sub txtBox1_LostFocus

Debug.Print "txtBox1_LostFocus"
If Len(txtBox1.Text) > 0 Then
    MsgBox "txtBox1 must be empty!"
    txtBox1_SetFocus
End If

End Sub
```

Restarting the application and putting any value into *txtBox1* followed by tabbing to *txtBox2* shows the first strangeness. We can see that when the message box is displayed, *txtBox2* never receives focus—but it does lose focus!

```
txtBox1_LostFocus
txtBox2_LostFocus
txtBox1_GotFocus
```

Now we can go further to investigate what happens when both text boxes happen to have invalid values. So we add the following code to the *LostFocus* event of *txtBox2*:

```
Private Sub txtBox2_LostFocus

Debug.Print "txtBox2_LostFocus"
If Len(txtBox2.Text) - 0 Then
    MsgBox "txtBox2 must not be empty!"
    txtBox2_SetFocus
End If

End Sub
```

Restarting the application and putting any value into *txtBox1* followed by tabbing to *txtBox2* leads to a program lockup! Because both text boxes contain what are considered to be invalid values, we see no *GotFocus* events but rather a continuous cascade of *LostFocus* events as each text box tries to claim focus in order to allow the user to change its invalid contents. This problem is a well-known one in Visual Basic, and a programmer usually gets caught by it only once.

At this point, removing the *MsgBox* statements completely only makes the situation worse. If you do try this, your program goes seriously sleepy-bye-bye. Because the *MsgBox* function no longer intervenes to give you some semblance of control over the event cascade, you're completely stuck. Whereas previously you could get access to the Task Manager to kill the hung process, you will now have to log out of Windows to regain control.

These are not the only peculiarities associated with these events. If we remove the validation code to prevent the application from hanging, we can look at the event stream when using the command buttons. Restart the application, and click the OK button. The Immediate window shows a normal event stream. Now do this again, but just press Enter to trigger the OK button rather than clicking on it. The Debug window shows quite clearly that the *LostFocus* event of *txtBox1* is never triggered. Exactly the same thing happens if you use the OK button's accelerator key (Alt+O)—no *LostFocus* event is triggered. Although in the real world you might not be too worried if the Cancel button swallows a control's *LostFocus* event, it's a bit more serious when you want validation to occur when the user presses OK.

There are several more or less satisfactory methods of overcoming the problems with these two events. Possibly the best strategy is to ignore them altogether and instead use a tool such as MsgBlaster or SpyWorks to intercept the Windows messages that correspond to these events (*SetFocus* and *KillFocus*). This makes performing activities such as field-by-field validation relatively trivial.

Some Final Thoughts Never rely on *GotFocus* and *LostFocus* events actually occurring or occurring in the order you expect.

Evil Type Coercion

A programmer on my team had a surprise when writing Visual Basic code to extract information from a SQL Server database. Having retrieved a recordset, he wrote the following code:

```
Dim vntFirstValue As Variant, vntSecondValue As Variant
Dim nResultValue1 As Integer, nResultValue2 As Integer

vntFirstValue = Trim(rsMyRecordset!first_value)
vntSecondValue = Trim(rsMyRecordset!second_value)

nResultValue1 = vntFirstValue + vntSecondValue
nResultValue2 = vntFirstValue + vntSecondValue + 1
```

He was rather upset when he found that the "+" operator concatenated the two variants but added the final numeric value. If *vntFirstValue* contained "1" and *vntSecondValue* contained "2", *nResultValue1* had the value 12 and *nResult-Value2* had the value 13.

To understand exactly what's going on here, we have to look at how Visual Basic handles type coercion. Up until Visual Basic 3, type coercion was relatively rare. Although you could write Visual Basic 3 code like

```
txtBox.Text = 20
```

and find that it worked without giving any error, almost every other type of conversion had to be done explicitly by using statements such as *CStr* and *CInt*. Starting with Visual Basic 4, and continuing in Visual Basic 5, performance reasons dictated that automatic type coercion be introduced. Visual Basic no longer has to convert an assigned value to a Variant and then unpack it back into whatever data type is receiving the assignment. It can instead invoke a set of hard-coded coercion rules to perform direct coercion without ever involving the overhead of a Variant. Although this is often convenient and also achieves the laudable aim of good performance, it can result in some rather unexpected results. Consider the following code:

```
Sub Test()

Dim sString As String, nInteger As Integer
sString = "1"
nInteger = 2
ArgTest sString, nInteger

End Sub

Sub ArgTest(ByVal inArgument1 As Integer, _
            ByVal isArgument2 As String)
' Some code here
End Sub
```

In Visual Basic 3, this code would give you an immediate error at compile time because the arguments are in the wrong order. In Visual Basic 4 and Visual Basic 5, you won't get any error because Visual Basic will attempt to coerce the string variable into the integer parameter and vice versa. This change is not a very pleasant one. If *inArgument1* is passed a numeric value, everything looks and performs as expected. As soon as a nonnumeric value or a null string is passed, however, a run-time error occurs. This means that the detection of certain classes of bugs has been moved from compile time to run time, which is definitely not a major contribution to road safety.

The table at the top of the following page shows Visual Basic 5's automatic type coercion rules.

Source Type	Coerced To	Apply This Rule
Integer	Boolean	0=False, nonzero=True
Boolean	Byte	False=0, True=255
Boolean	Any numeric	False=0, True=−1 (except Byte)
String	Date	String is analyzed for MM/dd/yy and so on
Date	Numeric type	Coerce to Double and use DateSerial(Double)
Numeric	Date	Use number as serial date, check valid date range
Numeric	Byte	Error if negative
String	Numeric type	Treat as Double when representing a number

Some Final Thoughts Any Visual Basic developer with aspirations to competence should learn the automatic type coercion rules and understand the most common situations in which type coercion's bite can be dangerous.

Arguing safely

In Visual Basic 3, passing arguments was relatively easy to understand. You passed an argument either by value or by reference. Passing *ByVal* was safer because the argument consisted only of its value, not of the argument itself. Therefore, any change to that argument would have no effect outside the procedure receiving the argument. Passing *ByRef* meant that a direct reference to the argument was passed. This allowed you to change the argument if you needed to do so.

With the introduction of objects, the picture has become more complicated. The meaning of *ByVal* and *ByRef* when passing an object variable is slightly different than when passing a nonobject variable. Passing an object variable *ByVal* means that the type of object that the object variable refers to cannot change. The object that the object variable refers to is allowed to change, however, as long as it remains the same type as the original object. This rule can confuse some programmers when they first encounter it and can be a source of bugs if certain invalid assumptions are made.

Type coercion introduces another wrinkle to passing arguments. The use of *ByVal* has become more dangerous because Visual Basic will no longer trigger certain compile-time errors. In Visual Basic 3, you could never pass arguments to a procedure that expected arguments of a different type. Using *ByVal* in Visual Basic 5 (or Visual Basic 4) means that an attempt will be made to coerce each *ByVal* argument into the argument type expected. For example, passing a string variable *ByVal* into a numeric argument type will not show any problem unless the string variable actually contains nonnumeric data at run time. This means that this error check has to be delayed until run time. (See the earlier section dealing with type coercion for an example and for more details.)

If you don't specify an argument method, the default is that arguments are passed *ByRef*. Indeed, many Visual Basic programmers use the language for a while before they realize they are using the default *ByRef* and that *ByVal* is often the better argument method. For the sake of clarity, I suggest defining the method being used every time rather than relying on the default. I'm also a firm believer in being very precise about exactly which arguments are being used for input, which for output, and which for both input and output. A good naming scheme should do something like prefix every input argument with "i" and every output argument with "o" and then perhaps use the more ugly "io" to discourage programmers from using arguments for both input and output. Input arguments should be passed *ByVal,* whereas all other arguments obviously have to be passed *ByRef*. Being precise about the nature and use of procedure arguments can make the maintenance programmer's job much easier. It can even make your job easier by forcing you to think clearly about the exact purpose of each argument.

One problem you might run into when converting from previous versions of Visual Basic to Visual Basic 5 is that you are no longer allowed to pass a control to a DLL or OCX using *ByRef*. Previously, you might have written your function declaration like this:

```
Declare Function CheckControlStatus Lib "MY.OCX" _
        (ctlMyControl As Control) As Integer
```

You are now required to specify *ByVal* rather than the default *ByRef*. Your function declaration must look like this:

```
Declare Function CheckControlStatus Lib "MY.OCX" _
        (ByVal ctlMyControl As Control) As Integer
```

This change is necessary because DLL functions now expect to receive the Windows handle of any control passed as a parameter. Omitting *ByVal* causes a pointer to the control handle to be passed rather than the control handle itself, which will result in undefined behavior and possibly a GPF.

The meaning of zero

Null, IsNull, Nothing, vbNullString, "", vbNullChar, vbNull, Empty, vbEmpty... Visual Basic 5 has enough representations of nothing and zero to confuse the most careful programmer. To prevent bugs, programmers must understand what each of these Visual Basic keywords represents and how to use each in its proper context. Let's start with the interesting stuff.

```
Private sNotInitString As String
Private sEmptyString As String
Private sNullString As String
sEmptyString = ""
sNullString = 0&
```

Looking at the three variable declarations, a couple of questions spring to mind. What are the differences between *sNotInitString*, *sEmptyString,* and *sNull-String*? When is it appropriate to use each declaration, and when is it dangerous? The answers to these questions are not simple, and we need to delve into the murky depths of Visual Basic's internal string representation system to understand the answers.

After some research and experimentation, the answer to the first question becomes clear but at first sight is not very illuminating. The variable *sNotInit-String* is a null pointer string, held internally as a pointer that doesn't point to any memory location and that holds an internal value of 0. *sEmptyString* is a pointer to an empty string, a pointer that does point to a valid memory location. Finally, *sNullString* is neither a null string pointer nor an empty string but is just a string containing 0.

Why does *sNotInitString* contain the internal value 0? In earlier versions of Visual Basic, uninitialized variable-length strings were set to an empty string internally. Ever since the release of Visual Basic 4, however, all variables have been set to 0 internally until initialized. Developers don't normally notice the difference because, inside Visual Basic, this initial zero value of uninitialized strings always behaves as if it were an empty string. It's only when you go outside Visual Basic and start using the Windows APIs that you'll receive a shock. Try passing either *sNotInitString* or *sEmptyString* to any Windows API function that takes a null pointer. Passing *sNotInitString* will work fine because it really is a null pointer, whereas passing *sEmptyString* will cause the function to fail. Of such apparently trivial differences are the really nasty bugs created.

```
Private Declare Function FindWindow Lib "user32" Alias _
    "FindWindowA" (ByVal lpClassName As Any, _
                    ByVal lpWindowName As Any) As Long


Dim sNotInitString As String
Dim sEmptyString As String
Dim sNullString As String

sEmptyString = ""
sNullString = 0&

Shell "Calc.exe", 1
DoEvents
' This will work.
x& = FindWindow(sNotInitString, "Calculator")

' This won't work.
x& = FindWindow(sEmptyString, "Calculator")

' This will work.
x& = FindWindow(sNullString, "Calculator")
```

Now that we've understood one nasty trap and why it occurs, the difference between the next two variable assignments becomes clearer.

```
sNullPointer = vbNullString
sEmptyString = ""
```

It's a good idea to use the former assignment rather than the latter, for two reasons. The first reason is safety. Assigning *sNullPointer* as here is the equivalent of *sNotInitString* in the above example. In other words, it can be passed to a DLL argument directly. However, *sEmptyString* must be assigned the value of *0&* before it can be used safely in the same way. The second reason is economy. Using "" will result in lots of empty strings being scattered throughout your program, whereas using the built-in Visual Basic constant vbNullString will mean no superfluous use of memory.

Null and *IsNull* are fairly clear. The only hazard here is a temptation to compare something with Null directly, because Null will propagate through any expression that you use. Resist the temptation and use *IsNull* instead.

```
' This will always be false.
If sString = Null Then
    ' Some code here
End If
```

Continuing through Visual Basic 5's representations of nothing, vbNullChar is next on our travels. This constant is relatively benign, simply CHR$(0). When you receive a string back from a Windows API function, it is normally null-terminated because that is the way the C language expects strings to look. Searching for vbNullChar is one way of determining the real length of the string. Beware of using any API string without doing this first, because null-terminated strings can cause some unexpected results in Visual Basic, especially when concatenated.

Finally, two constants are built into Visual Basic for use with the *VarType* function. vbNull is a value returned by the *VarType* function for a variable that contains no valid data. vbEmpty is returned by *VarType* for a variable that is uninitialized. Better people than I have argued that calling these two constants vbTypeNull and vbTypeEmpty would better describe their correct purpose. The important point from the safety point of view is that vbEmpty can be very useful for performing such tasks as ensuring that the properties of your classes have been initialized properly.

The Bug Hunt

Two very reliable methods of finding new bugs in your application are available. The first involves demonstrating the program, preferably to your boss. Almost without exception, something strange and/or unexpected will happen, often resulting in severe embarrassment. Although this phenomenon has no scientific explanation, it's been shown to happen far too often to be merely a chance occurrence.

The other guaranteed way of locating bugs is to release your application into production. Out there in a hostile world, surrounded by other unruly applications and subject to the vagaries of exotic hardware devices and unusual Registry settings, it's perhaps of little surprise that the production environment can find even the most subtle of weaknesses in your program. Then there are your users, many of whom will gleefully inform you that "your program crashed" without even attempting to explain the circumstances leading up to the crash. Trying to extract the details from them is at best infuriating, at worst impossible. So we need some simple method of trapping all possible errors and logging them in such a way as to be able to reconstruct the user's problem. (For details on error handling, refer to Chapter 1.) Here we'll examine the minimum requirements needed to trap and report errors and help your user retain some control over what happens to his or her data after a program crash.

The first point to note about Visual Basic 5's error handling capabilities is that they are somewhat deficient when compared with those of most compiled languages. There is no structured exception handling, and the only way to guarantee a chance of recovery from an error is to place an error trap and an error handler into *every* procedure. To understand why, we need to look in detail at what happens when a run-time error occurs in your program.

Your program is riding happily down the information highway, and suddenly it hits a large pothole in the shape of a run-time error. Perhaps your user forgot to put a disk into drive A, or maybe the Windows Registry became corrupted. In other words, something fairly common happened. Visual Basic 5 first checks whether you have an error trap enabled in the offending procedure. If it finds one, it will branch to the enabled error handler. If not, it will search backward through the current procedure call stack looking for the first error trap it can locate. If none are found, your program will terminate abruptly with a rude error message, which is normally the last thing you want to happen. Losing a user's data in this manner is a fairly heinous crime and is not likely to endear you to either your users or the technical support people. So at the very least you need to place an error handler in the initial procedure of your program.

Unfortunately, this solution is not very satisfactory either, for two reasons. Another programmer could come along later and modify your code, inserting his or her own local error trap somewhere lower in the call stack. This means that the run-time error could be intercepted, and your "global" error trap might never get the chance to deal with it properly. Instead, your program has to be happy with some fly-by-night error handler dealing with what could be a very serious error. The other problem is that even if, through good luck, your global error trap receives the error, Visual Basic 5 provides no mechanism for retrying or bypassing an erroneous statement in a different procedure. So if the error was something as simple as being unable to locate a floppy disk, you're going to look a little silly when your program can't recover. The only way of giving your user a chance of getting around a problem is to handle it in the same procedure in which it occurred.

There is no getting away from the fact that you need to place an error trap and error handler in every single procedure if you want to be able to respond to and recover from errors in a sensible way. The task then is to provide a minimalist method of protecting every procedure while dealing with all errors in a centralized routine that is clever enough to be able to discriminate between the different types of errors, interrogate the user about which action to take, and return control back to the procedure where the problem occurred. The other minimum requirement is to be able to raise errors correctly to your clients when you are writing ActiveX components.

Adding the following code to every procedure in your program is a good start:

```
Private Function AnyFunction() As Integer

On Error GoTo LocalError
' Normal procedure code goes here.

Exit Function
LocalError:
If Fatal("Module.AnyFunction") = vbRetry Then
    Resume
Else
    Resume Next
End If

End Function
```

This code can provide your program with comprehensive error handling, provided the *Fatal* function is written correctly. *Fatal* will receive the names of the module and procedure where the error occurred, log these and other error details to a disk log file for later analysis, and then inform the program's operator about the error and ask whether it ought to retry the statement in error, ignore it, or abort the whole program. If the user chooses to abort, the *Fatal* function needs to perform a general cleanup followed by *Reset* and *End* statements. If the user makes any other choice, the *Fatal* function returns control back to the procedure in error, communicating what the user has chosen. The code needed for the *Fatal* function can be a little tricky. You need to think about the different types of error that can occur, including those raised by ActiveX components. You also need to think about what happens if an error ever occurs within the *Fatal* function itself. (Again, see Chapter 1 for a more detailed analysis of this type of error handling.) Here I'll examine a couple of pitfalls that can occur when handling or raising Visual Basic 5 errors that involve the use of vbObjectError.

When creating or using ActiveX components, you often need to either propagate errors specific to the component back to the client application or handle an error raised by the component. The accepted method for propagating errors is to use *Error.Raise*. To avoid clashes with Visual Basic 5's own range of errors, you add your error number to the vbObjectError constant. Be careful, however, about raising any errors within the range vbObjectError through vbObjectError + 512. Visual Basic 5 remaps some error messages between vbObjectError and vbObjectError + 512 to standard Automation run-time errors. This can result in unexpected behavior, so user-defined errors should always be greater than vbObjectError + 512. This little beauty has caught many programmers, and it always causes confusion when encountered.

When using a universal error handler to deal with many different types of problems, always bear in mind that you might be receiving errors that have been raised using the constant vbObjectError. You can use the *And* operator (*Err.Number And vbObjectError*) to check this. If *True* is returned, you should subtract vbObjectError from the actual error number before displaying or logging the error. Because vbObjectError is mainly used internally for interclass communications, there is seldom any reason to display it in its natural state.

SOME VISUAL BASIC 5 TOOLS

We now turn to a discussion of the three Sourcerers mentioned at the beginning of the chapter. These tools—the Assertion Sourcerer, the Metrics Sourcerer, and the Instrumentation Sourcerer—will help you detect and prevent bugs in the programs you write.

Registering the Three Sourcerers

All three Sourcerers we're going to discuss are available in the CHAP07 folder on the companion CD. These Sourcerers are designed as Visual Basic 5 add-ins, running as ActiveX DLLs. To register each Sourcerer in the Microsoft Windows 95 or the Microsoft Windows NT system Registry, load each project in turn into the Visual Basic 5 IDE and compile it. One more step is required to use the add-ins, which is to inform Visual Basic 5 itself about each add-in. This is done by creating an entry in VBAddin.INI under a section named [Add-Ins32]. This entry takes the form of the project connection class name, for example, VB5Assert.Connect=0 for the Assertion Sourcerer. To perform this automatically for all three Sourcerers, just load, compile, and run the BootStrap project available in the CHAP07 folder on the companion CD. This will add the correct entries in the VBAddin.INI file.

Assert Yourself: The Assertion Sourcerer

Although *Debug.Assert* fulfills its purpose very well, certainly improvements to it would be welcome. It would be nice if you had the ability to report assertion failures in compiled code as well as source code. Because one of the aims of the Enterprise Edition of Visual Basic 5 is to allow components to be built and then distributed across a network, it is quite likely that others in your organization will want to reference the in-process or out-of-process ActiveX DLLs that you have built using Visual Basic 5. Ensuring that assertion failures in compiled Visual Basic 5 programs were reported would be a very useful feature, enabling better testing of shared code libraries and allowing the capture of assertion failures during user acceptance testing. This kind of functionality cannot be implemented using *Debug.Assert* because these statements are dropped from your compiled program. Additionally, because you cannot drop from object code into Visual Basic's debugger on an assertion failure, you are faced with finding some alternative method of reporting the assertion failures.

Step forward the Assertion Sourcerer. This add-in supplements *Debug.Assert* with the functionality mentioned above. When you have registered the Sourcerer in the Registry and used the Add-In Manager to reference it, you can select Assertion Sourcerer from the Add-Ins menu to see the window shown in Figure 7-2.

FIGURE 7-2

The Assertion Sourcerer dialog box

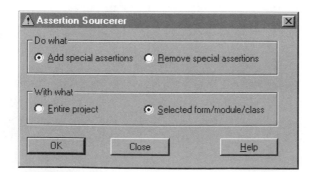

The standard assertion procedure, which supplements the *Debug.Assert* functionality, is named *BugAssert*. It is part of a small Visual Basic 5 module named DEBUG.BAS, which you should add to any project in which you want to monitor run-time assertion failures. You can then specify which of your *Debug.Assert* statements you want converted to run-time assertions; the choices are all assertions in the project or just those in the selected form, class, or module.

The Assertion Sourcerer works in a very simple manner. When you use the Assertion Sourcerer menu option on the Add-Ins menu to request that assertion calls be added to your project, the Assertion Sourcerer automatically generates and adds a line after every *Debug.Assert* statement in your selected module (or the whole project). This line is a conversion of the *Debug.Assert* statement to a version suitable for calling the *BugAssert* procedure. So

```
Debug.Assert bTest = True
```

becomes

```
Debug.Assert bTest = True
BugAssert bTest = True, "bTest = True," _
          "Project Test.VBP, module Test.CLS, line 53"
```

BugAssert's first argument is just the assertion expression itself. The second argument is a string representation of that assertion. This is required because there is no way for Visual Basic to extract and report the assertion statement being tested from just the first argument. The final argument allows the *BugAssert* procedure to report the exact location of any assertion failure for later analysis. The *BugAssert* procedure that does this reporting is relatively simple. It uses a constant to not report assertion failures, to report them to a *MsgBox*, to report them to a disk file, or to report them to both. The complete DEBUG.BAS module looks like this:

```
Option Explicit

' Output flags determine output destination of assertions and
' messages
Private Const mnDebug As Integer = 3
Private Const mnLogfile As Integer = 1
Private Const mnMsgBox As Integer = 2

' Display appropriate error message.
Sub BugAssert(ByVal vntiExpression As Variant, _
              Optional siExpression As String)
```

>>

```
If mnDebug Then
    If vntiExpression Then Exit Sub
    If IsMissing(siExpression) Then siExpression = ""
    BugMessage "Assertion failed: " & siExpression
End If

End Sub

Sub BugMessage(ByVal siMsg As String)
Dim nLogFile As Integer

' Print message to disk debug file.
If mnDebug And mnLogfile Then
    nLogFile = FreeFile
    Open App.EXEName & ".DBG" For Append Shared As nLogFile
    Print #nLogFile, siMsg
    Close #nLogFile
End If

' Show message as dialog box.
If mnDebug And mnMsgBox Then
    MsgBox siMsg
End If

End Sub
```

Before compiling your executable, you'll need to set the constant mnDebug in the DEBUG.BAS module. Now, whenever your executable is invoked by any other programmer, assertion failures will be reported to the location(s) defined by this constant. Before releasing your code into production, you can tell the Assertion Sourcerer to remove all *BugAssert* statements from your program.

Complete source code for the Assertion Sourcerer is supplied on the CD accompanying this book in CHAP07\AstSrce so that you can modify it to suit your own purposes.

Some Final Thoughts You can use the Assertion Sourcerer as a supplement to *Debug.Assert* when you want to implement assertions in compiled Visual Basic code.

Size Matters: The Metrics Sourcerer

Take any production system and log all the bugs it produces over a year or so. Then note which individual procedures are responsible for the majority of the defects. It's common for only 10 to 20 percent of a system's procedures to be responsible for 80 percent of the errors. If you examine the characteristics of these offending procedures, they will usually be more complex or longer (and sometimes both!) than their better-behaved counterparts. Keeping in mind that the earlier in the development cycle that these defects are detected the less costly it is to diagnose and fix them, any tool that helps to predict a system's problem areas before the system goes into production could prove to be very cost-effective. Step forward the Metrics Sourcerer. (See Figure 7-3.) This Visual Basic 5 add-in analyzes part or all of your project, ranking each procedure in terms of its relative complexity and length.

FIGURE 7-3

The Metrics Sourcerer dialog box

Defining complexity can be fairly controversial. Developers tend to have different ideas about what constitutes a complex procedure. Factors such as the difficulty of the algorithm or the obscurity of the Visual Basic keywords being employed can be considered useful to measure. The Metrics Sourcerer measures two rather more simple factors: the number of decision points and the number of lines of code that each procedure contains. Some evidence suggests that these are indeed useful characteristics to measure when you're looking for code routines that are likely to cause problems in the future. The number of decision points is easy to count. Certain Visual Basic 5 keywords— for example, *If...Else...End If* and *Select Case*—change the flow of a procedure, making decisions about which code to execute. The Metrics Sourcerer contains an amendable list of these keywords that it uses to count decision points. It then combines this number with the number of code lines that the procedure contains, using a user-amendable weighting to balance the relative importance of these factors. The final analysis is then output to a text file, viewable by utilities such as WordPad and Microsoft Word. (By default, the filename is the name of your project with the extension MET.) You might also want to import the text file into Microsoft Excel for sorting purposes. There's no point in taking the output of the Metrics Sourcerer as gospel, but it would certainly be worthwhile to reexamine potentially dangerous procedures in the light of its findings.

Another factor that might be useful to measure is the number of assertion failures that each procedure in your program suffers from. This figure can be captured using the Assertion Sourcerer. Combining this figure with the numbers produced by the Metrics Sourcerer would be a very powerful pointer toward procedures that need more work before your system goes into production.

Some Final Thoughts Use the Metrics Sourcerer as a guide to the procedures in your programs that need to be examined with the aim of reducing their complexity. Very economical to execute in terms of time, the Metrics Sourcerer can prove to be extremely effective in reducing the number of bugs that reach production.

A Black Box:
The Instrumentation Sourcerer

When a commercial airliner experiences a serious incident or crashes, one of the most important tools available to the team that subsequently investigates the accident is the plane's black box (actually colored orange), otherwise known as the flight data recorder. This box provides vital information about the period leading up to the accident, including data about the plane's control surfaces, its instruments, and its position in the air. How easy would it be to provide this type of information in the event of user acceptance or production program bugs and crashes?

The Instrumentation Sourcerer, shown in Figure 7-4, walks through your program code, adding a line of code at the start of every procedure. This line invokes a procedure that writes a record of each procedure that is executed to a log file on disk. (See Chapter 1 for an in-depth examination of similar techniques.) In this way, you can see a complete listing of every button that your user presses, every text box or other control that your user fills in, and every response of your program. In effect, each program can be given its own black box. Because of the interactive nature of Windows programs, with users able to pick and choose their way through the different screens available to them, it has traditionally been difficult to track exactly how the user is using your program or what sequence of events leads up to a bug or a crash. The Instrumentation Sourcerer can help you to understand more about your programs and the way they are used.

Configuration options allow you to selectively filter the procedures that you want to instrument. This might be useful if you want to document certain parts of a program, such as Click and KeyPress events. You can also choose how much information you want to store. Just as in an aircraft's black box, the

Figure 7-4

*The Instru-
mentation
Sourcerer
dialog box*

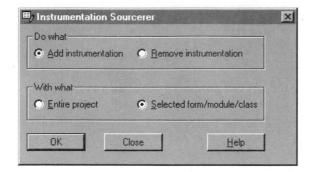

amount of storage space for recording what can be a vast amount of information is limited. Limiting the data recorded to maybe the last 500 or 1000 procedures can help you to make the best use of the hard disk space available on your machine or on your users' machines.

Some Final Thoughts The Instrumentation Sourcerer can be useful in tracking the cause of program bugs and crashes, at the same time providing an effective record of how users interact with your program in the real world.

FINAL THOUGHTS

Is it possible to write zero-defect Visual Basic 5 code? I don't believe it is—and even if it were, I doubt it would be cost-effective to implement. However, it is certainly possible to reduce the number of production bugs drastically. You just have to *want* to do it and to prepare properly using the right tools and the right attitudes. From here, you need to build your own bug lists, your own techniques, and your own antidefect tools. Although none of the ideas and techniques described in this chapter will necessarily prevent you from creating a program with a distinct resemblance to a papcastle (something drawn or modeled by a small child that you are supposed to recognize), at least your programs will have presumptions toward being zero-defect papcastles.

Final disclaimer: All the bugs in this chapter were metaphorical constructs. No actual bugs were harmed during the writing of this work.

Minutiae

PETER MORRIS

You first met Peet on page 2. Here is the rest of his story. Recently Peet was the technical lead on MicroHelp's Code Complete suite of Visual Basic 4 programmer's tools (which was written by TMS), and he cowrote TMS's other Visual Basic toolkit, *TMS Tools*. Peet was a member of the ANSI X3J11 and X3J16 standards groups (C and C++) and is a founding member of the IEEE P1201.1/2 (API and UI) standards groups. He's also a member of the IEEE computer society and the ACM. In the rare moments he's not working, his time is almost exclusively the property of his baby son, Daniel.

As you can probably guess from its title, this chapter is going to cover a rather broad range of information about Visual Basic. Think of this chapter as a Visual Basic programmer's smorgasbord. You'll learn about such topics as the advantages and disadvantages of compiling to p-code and to native code. You'll get some hints on how to optimize your applications beyond just writing excellent code. And you'll also receive up-to-the-minute information on such scintillating subjects as types and type libraries. So let's begin!

Perhaps it's bad form to start off so early in the chapter with a disclaimer. Well, you may scold me if you wish, but here's the disclaimer anyway: Some of the code in this chapter is, for good reason, written in C. Wherever I've used C, I've endeavored to make the code as readable and easy to follow as possible. I have not, however, included a C tutorial. To learn more about C code, you'll need to refer to an appropriate text.

STUFF ABOUT THE COMPILER

In this section, we'll examine applications compiled to native code. We won't deal much with p-code (the normal Visual Basic situation, which seems to have changed very little from Visual Basic 4 to Visual Basic 5) aside from a brief introduction and some comparisons with native code.

As you've probably discovered already, Visual Basic 5 applications can now be "properly" compiled. In other words, as well as producing p-code executables (still), Visual Basic 5 can now provide a native code binary. Which compile option you choose is up to you. I suspect that most corporate developers will want to know more about this new compiler process than they ever wanted to know about p-code.

A Little About P-Code

P-code applications are usually smaller (and slower) than native code applications. With p-code, an interpreter compresses and packages your code. Then, at run time, this same interpreter expands and, of course, runs your application. P-code applications are usually ported more easily to different processors.

The term p-code was derived from the term "pseudocode" because p-code consists of a RISC-like set of instructions for a "make-believe" processor. At run time, this processor, usually known as a stack machine (because it uses a stack for practically all its operations), is simulated by the built-in interpreter. (Just so you know, a "normal" processor uses registers and a stack primarily to pass values to and from function calls.) Because of its imaginary nature, the processor's instruction set never needs to change; instead, each instruction is mapped, via a lookup table, to a real instruction on any given processor. Logically, then, all that's required to move code from one processor to another is this mapping—code generation remains largely unaffected.

With p-code, typical size reduction from native code is more than 50 percent. For example, when the VisData sample that is included on the Visual Basic 5 CD is compiled to p-code, it's less than half the size it would be if compiled to native code (425 KB vs. 868 KB). Additionally, compiling to p-code is a lot faster than compiling to native code—around seven times faster. (Some of the reasons for the speed of p-code compiling will become evident later in the chapter.) My machine (a 200-MHz Pentium Pro) took just over a minute to compile VisData to native code and less than 10 seconds to compile it to p-code!

You'll need to keep this compile-time difference in mind during your development and testing phases.

A native code compiler was, I think, one of the most requested features, so I'm not surprised to find that Microsoft put it in Visual Basic 5. Personally, however, I think that native code compilation, for many reasons (and forgetting for a second that it typically executes faster) is a backward step. I'm still convinced that p-code is ultimately a superior technology compared to native code generation.

Generating Code

You select the code generation model you want via the somewhat hidden dialog box shown in Figure 8-1. You get to this dialog box by clicking Options on the Make Project dialog box.

FIGURE 8-1

Visual Basic's compiler options dialog boxes

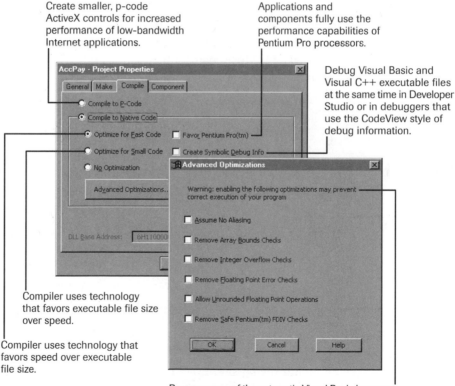

Create smaller, p-code ActiveX controls for increased performance of low-bandwidth Internet applications.

Applications and components fully use the performance capabilities of Pentium Pro processors.

Debug Visual Basic and Visual C++ executable files at the same time in Developer Studio or in debuggers that use the CodeView style of debug information.

Compiler uses technology that favors executable file size over speed.

Compiler uses technology that favors speed over executable file size.

Remove some of the automatic Visual Basic language protective features from executable files to further enhance performance, but first make sure the code doesn't need the features you're removing.

As you can see in Figure 8-1, some extra compilation options and advanced optimization choices become available when you select Compile To Native Code. I'll discuss some of these options a little later.

When you compile to native code, the Visual Basic 5 native code generator/ compiler, C2.EXE, is run once for each code component in the project. For example, if a project has a form, Form1; a module, Module1; and a class, Class1; then C2.EXE is run once to compile each component. Each invocation's options are the same depending on which you selected in the dialog box; that is, the options you select are used to compile the entire project. In case you're interested, C2 runs as a multithreaded, Win32, 32-bit console process.

Each time the native code compiler is run, a hidden process (described as 16-bit by the Windows 95 Task Manager) is started and the code generator/compiler, also run as a hidden process, is run attached to this process. (In Windows 95, this process is run from the file WINOA386.MOD, with a process description of "Non-Windows application component for 386 enhanced mode." This file is not required if you're running under Windows NT.) As each invocation of C2 terminates, the instance of WINOLDAP (the module name given to WINOA386.MOD) in which it was run is also terminated. You should now start to see why this process might be slower than selecting p-code generation (which is an internal process and doesn't use C2). Here's what the command-line arguments of a typical run look like (with no optimizations):

```
C2 -il C:\WINDOWS\TEMP\VB819310 -f Form1 -W3 -Gy -G5 -Gs4096 -dos
-Zl -FoC:\TEMP\Form1.OBJ -Qifdiv -ML -basic
```

These flags are explained in Table 8-1. Some of them are described in more detail here as well:

- **-il** This flag is undocumented, but "intermediate language" is a good guess for what "il" stands for. Files produced when this flag is set are <Signature>GL, SY, EX, IN, and DB. I have no idea what these files contain. In the command-line example in Table 8-1, the following files (long filenames shown) are generated temporarily while the application is being built:
  - VB819310GL
  - VB819310SY
  - VB819310EX
  - VB819310IN
  - VB819310DB

TABLE 8-1   COMMAND–LINE FLAGS FOR THE C2 COMPILER

Flag	Explanation
-il C:\WINDOWS\TEMP\VB819310	Undocumented but also used for a C program; probably used to "name" intermediate language files
-f Form1	The input file to be compiled
-W3	Warning level 3
-Gy	Enables function-level linking
-G5	Optimize for Pentium
-Gs4096	Turn off stack probes
-dos	Undocumented but also used for a C program
-Zl	Removes default library name from OBJ file
-FoC:\TEMP\Form1.OBJ	Name of output file
-Qifdiv	Performs Pentium FDIV erratum fix
-ML	Creates a single-threaded executable file
-basic	Undocumented but appears to be a new flag for Visual Basic compilation

- **-G5** The option optimizes the generated code to favor the Pentium processor. Here's what the Microsoft Developer Network (MSDN) says about the same Visual C++ 4.2 flag: "Use this option for programs meant only for the Pentium. Code created using the /G5 option does not perform as well on 80386- and 80486-based computers as code created using the /GB (Blend) option." Interestingly, by default, the -G5 switch is always used—even when you compile on a 486 machine.

- **-Gs[*size*]** If a function requires more than *size* stack space for local variables, its stack probe is activated. A stack probe is a piece of code that checks whether the space required for passed parameters and local variables is available on the stack before any attempt to allocate the space is made. -Gs0 is the same as -Ge, turn stack probes on; -Gs4096 is the default.

- **-ML** This option places the library name LIBC.LIB in the object file so that the linker will use LIBC.LIB to resolve external symbols. This is the compiler's default action. LIBC.LIB does not provide multithread support, by the way.

Don't bother to scan your Visual Basic 5 documentation for information about these flags because you won't find any—they are all undocumented. If you have a set of documentation for the Visual C++ compiler, however, you might be in luck. Why? Because it seems that C2 is taken from the Visual C++ compiler. In fact, you'll soon see why I'm pretty sure that C2.EXE is the C2 from Visual C++. Nevertheless, the above interpretation of the flag meanings is mine alone. Microsoft doesn't document how its C++ compiler works beyond describing CL.EXE (the front end to the C compiler).

Visual Basic itself evidently provides the compiler's first pass, unlike Visual C++ (in which in terms of compilers, CL.EXE is seemingly analogous to VB5.EXE), and the first pass (the parser and some of the optimizer) in C and C++ is apparently provided by C1.EXE (C) and C1XX.EXE (C++). C2.EXE appears to be in Visual Basic what it is in Visual C++—the code generator and optimizer (the part of it to do with generation).

How do I know? First, the way C2.EXE is driven is similar to the way the "real" C2.EXE, supplied with the Visual C++ compiler, is driven. Here's the input to the C2 component of Visual C++ 5 (directive/invocation provided by CL.EXE) for a simple one-file C application named TEST.C:

```
MSC_CMD_FLAGS=-il C:\WINDOWS\TEMP\a54497 -f test.c -W 1 -G4
-Gs4096 -dos -Fotest.obj -ML -Fdvc50.idb
```

I gathered this information using the same tool I used on Visual Basic 5's C2. I'll discuss the tool more fully a little later. For now, let's forget the how and concentrate on the what.

Can you see the similarities? (For a more detailed explanation of these flags, see MSDN or Visual C++ itself.)

Second, I looked back on our prerelease Visual Basic 5 CDs and examined the evolution of this component, comparing what I found there with the C2.EXE file supplied with Microsoft's Visual C++ 4.2 and 5 products. The results of my examination of the component's version information are shown in Table 8-2.

As you can see from Table 8-2, the C2.EXE file in the Visual Basic alpha release had the same description as that of the real thing in Visual C++—this was later changed. (On the alpha and beta 1 CDs, the file C23.ERR was also supplied. This file [also supplied with Visual C++ 4.2], which contains error message text as used by the C compiler, has been removed from the packing list for the release version of Visual Basic 5 and for Visual C++ 5.)

Third, replacing the C2 of Visual C++ with that of Visual Basic 5 worked; that is, once I copied the file MSPDB41.DLL to the SharedIDE folder so that Visual

TABLE 8-2   **THE EVOLUTION OF THE C2 COMPILER**

Application	Compiler Version Number	Compiler Description	Compiler Product Name
Visual C++ 4.2	10.20	Microsoft 32-Bit C/C++ Compiler 80x86 Back End	Microsoft Visual C++
Visual C++ 5	11.00	Microsoft 32-Bit C/C++ Compiler 80x86 Back End	Microsoft 32-Bit C/C++ Optimizing Compiler
Visual Basic 5, last alpha	11.00	Microsoft 32-Bit C/C++ Compiler 80x86 Back End	Microsoft 32-Bit C/C++ Optimizing Compiler
Visual Basic 5, betas, RC1*, and the marketing beta	11.00	Microsoft 32-Bit Visual Basic Compiler 80x86 Back End	Microsoft 32-Bit Visual Basic Optimizing Compiler
Visual Basic 5, release	11.00	Microsoft 32-Bit Visual Basic Compiler 80x86 Back End	Microsoft 32-Bit Visual Basic Optimizing Compiler

* RC1 stands for Release Candidate 1, the first version of the product that Microsoft believes is up to release standards. Depending on what comes back from the testers, this version might be the one that goes on sale.

C++ 5 could find it, a step that is not necessary if you compile from a DOS box rather than from the Visual C++ IDE, I could build C applications (such as the application shown in Listing 8-2 beginning on page 336) using Visual Basic's C2.EXE with Visual C++ 5. (You can also use Visual Basic 5's C2 with Visual C++ 4.2.) The reverse process also worked; I was able to compile and run a program in Visual Basic 5 using the C2 from Visual C++ 5. (This scenario does *not* work with Visual C++ 4.2, however, probably because of the -basic flag.)

The Differences

The C2 and C1 as invoked by Visual C++ are passed their input (as shown on page 326) via an environment variable named MSC_CMD_FLAGS, whereas the C2 that comes with Visual Basic 5 is passed its arguments on the command line. In Visual Basic–speak, C2's arguments are in Command$ rather than in Environ$. (The C program for obtaining this information is shown in Listing 8-2.) However, the fact that C2 is interchangeable between Visual Basic 5 and Visual C++ 5 means that the way variables are passed is not an issue. But when I tried this same test using the C2 of Visual C++ 4.2 with Visual Basic 5, I received an error: 1007. If you look up this error in Visual C++, you'll see that it means you have an unrecognized flag; so it seems as though we started Visual C++ 4.2's C2 in Visual Basic 5 with at least one unknown flag, probably -basic. The C2 of Visual C++ 5 does have a -basic flag, which seems to confirm my suspicion that Visual Basic 5 ships with what is essentially the same C2.EXE as Visual C++ 5.

If C2.EXE is the same (with some small modifications), it follows that at some future time we might be able to use Visual Basic to generate, just as we can do with Visual C++, binaries for platforms such as Apple's Power PC, Macintosh, and so on.

Just before this chapter went to press, Microsoft published the Visual Basic 5 Evaluators Guide. Some interesting references to the Alpha chip seemed to confirm, at least partially, my suspicion about the interchangeable compilers:

> Run-time scalability: "Using version 5.0, developers can use the power of RISC processor architectures with native compiled code for Alpha processors."

> Cross-platform capabilities: "Using version 5.0, developers can use the power of RISC processor architectures with native compiled code for Alpha applications and components."

> The system requirements for Visual Basic 5, Enterprise Edition, include a PC with a 486DX/66 MHz or higher processor (Pentium or higher processor recommended), or any Alpha processor running Microsoft Windows NT Workstation.

Interesting—is Visual Basic for Applications (VBA) destined to become *the* portable language?

The Logger

The C application in Listing 8-2 (and on the CD) can be used to replace the real C2.EXE file. To replace it, follow these steps:

1. Rename Visual Basic's C2.EXE to C3.EXE.

2. If you want to rebuild the application, make sure the first real line of code in this file reads as here:

    ```
    strcat(&carArgs[0], ".\\C3 ");
    ```

3. Copy the EXE (OUTARGS.EXE) to C2.EXE. Your original C2.EXE is now C3.EXE, so no damage is done.

    ```
    copy outargs.exe c2.exe
    ```

4. Use Visual Basic 5 as you normally would.

After you have carried out these steps the following will happen: When Visual Basic 5 runs (to compile to native code), it will run C2.EXE. C2.EXE, really our OUTARGS program, will log the call made to it to the file C2.OUT. (C2 logs to a file based on its own name, <EXEname>.OUT; because our program is named C2.EXE, the log file will be C2.OUT.) Information logged includes the parameters that have been passed to it. C2.EXE will then shell C3.EXE (the "real" C2), passing to it, by default, all the same parameters that it was passed. The net effect is that you have logged how C2 was invoked.

Listing 8-1 is a typical C2.OUT log.

Listing 8-1

*Typical
C2.OUT
log file*

```
********** Run @ Wed Jan 1 00:00:00 1997

* EXE file...

        C2

* Command Line Arguments...

1       -il
2       C:\WINDOWS\TEMP\VB819310
3       -f
4       Form1
5       -W
6       3
7       -Gy
8       -G5
9       -Gs4096
10      -dos
11      -Z1
12      -FoC:\TEMP\Form1.OBJ
13      -QIfdiv
14      -ML
15      -basic
:
* 'Real' program and arguments...

        .\C3 -il C:\WINDOWS\TEMP\VB819310 -f Form1 -W 3 -Gy -G5
        -Gs4096 -dos
        -Z1 -FoC:\TEMP\Form1.OBJ -QIfdiv -ML -basic

********** Run End
```

The Visual Basic team seems to have added a space between the -W and the 3, possibly causing C2 to interpret this as two separate switches. Since C2 doesn't error or complain, I'm assuming that it knows what to do with the space.

By further altering the code, you can change, add, or remove compiler switches. For example, you can add the following code to the argument processing loop to replace, say, -G5 with, say, -GB, the "blend" switch mentioned earlier in our discussion of -G5 on page 325.

```
if(0 == strcmp(argv[nLoop], "-G5"))
{
    (void)strcat(&carArgs[0]    , "-GB ");

    continue;
}
```

This replacement C2 (OUTARGS.EXE) doesn't like long filenames that include spaces. Each "gap" would cause the next part of the name to be passed to C3 as a separate command-line argument. To fix this, either alter the C code to quote delimit each path or copy your test Visual Basic sample to, say, C:\TEMP before attempting to use it; that is, remove any long pathname. (Leave the re-named outargs C2.EXE in the same folder as the real, now renamed, C3.EXE.)

To restore the "real" program, simply copy over C2.EXE with C3.EXE:

```
copy c3.exe c2.exe
```

The Linker

As I've already said, C2 compiles each component to an object file. When all the components are compiled, they are linked using LINK.EXE. Table 8-3 on page 332, which is based on the Visual C++ online help, lists the command-line arguments you might find in a typical run when creating an EXE containing a single form, class, and module. The only native code option switched on for this run was Create Symbolic Debug Info. This information was captured using the OUTARGS program.

Again, LINK.EXE is taken from the Visual C++ 4.2 compiler. At the time of writing, its version number was 4.20.6164—exactly the same version as that supplied with Visual C++ 4.2. See the Visual C++ documentation or MSDN for more information about these linker switches.

Why these switches?

I have no idea why some of these switches are used explicitly (on the compiler also), particularly since some are set to the default anyway. Perhaps some of the reasons for using these switches will become documented at some later date.

NOTE

> The Visual Basic 5 CD contains, in TOOLS\UNSUPPRT\TYPLIB, what appears to be the C/C++ compiler as supplied with Microsoft's Visual C++ 4.1 (CL version 10.10, C1 version 10.10). I copied CL, C1, C2, and LINK off the CD and into a directory on my hard disk and successfully compiled the OUTARGS.C program shown earlier. It appears as if Visual Basic 5 might ship complete with the C compiler too!

Library and object files

From Table 8-3, you'll notice that VBAEXE5.LIB is linked with our own OBJ file (created from our files and modules). The library contains just one component (library files contain object files), NATSUPP.OBJ. (NATSUPP might stand for "native support.") You can find this object by using *DUMPBIN /ARCHIVEMEMBERS VBAEXE5.LIB*. (DUMPBIN.EXE is the Microsoft Common Object File Format [COFF[1]] Binary Dumper.) NATSUPP.OBJ can be extracted for further examination using the Microsoft Library Manager, LIB.EXE:

```
lib /extract:e:\vbadev\r5w32nd\presplit\vbarun\obj\natsupp.obj
vbaexe5.lib
```

The reason for including the path to the OBJ file is that the library manager expects us to specify exactly the name of the module—including its path. (This path is embedded in the library file when the object file is first put into it and is discovered using *DUMPBIN /ARCHIVEMEMBERS*.) In other words, the object file probably "lived" at this location on someone's machine in Redmond! Similarly, we can use *DUMPBIN /ALL vbaexe5.lib* to tell that the source code for this object file was named NATSUPP.ASM and was in the directory e:\vbadev\rt\win32. It was assembled using Microsoft's Macro Assembler, Version 6.11d, and it seems as though it was created on "Fri Dec 06 11:17:38 1996." Interestingly, it doesn't contain any code—just data—although what looks like a jump table (a mechanism often used to facilitate calls to external routines) appears to be included. To call a routine, you look up its address in the table and then jump to it, as shown in Table 8-4 on page 333.

---

1. For a more detailed description of the COFF file format, see the MSDN library or *Windows 95 System Programming Secrets*, by Matt Pietrek (IDG Books, 1995).

TABLE 8-3 COMMAND–LINE SWITCHES FOR THE LINKER

Switch	Explanation
C:\TEMP\Form1.OBJ	Form OBJ file
C:\TEMP\Module1.OBJ	Module OBJ file
C:\TEMP\Class1.OBJ	Class OBJ file
C:\TEMP\Project1.OBJ	Project OBJ file
C:\PROGRAM FILES\ DEVSTUDIO\VB\VBAEXE5.LIB	Library of Visual Basic OBJs
/ENTRY:__vbaS	Sets the starting address for an executable file or DLL. The entry point should be a function that is defined with the *stdcall* calling convention. The parameters and the return value must be defined as documented in the Win32 API for *WinMain* (for an EXE) or *DllEntryPoint* (for a DLL). This entry point is in the <project name>.obj file—here it will be in project1.obj. Note that neither Sub Main nor Form_Load is mentioned.
/OUT:C:\TEMP\Project1.exe	The output file—the EXE!
/BASE:0x400000	Sets a base address for the program, overriding the default location for an executable file (at 0x400000) or a DLL (at 0x10000000). The operating system first attempts to load a program at its specified or default base address. If sufficient space is not available there, the system relocates the program. To prevent relocation, use the /FIXED option. The default is 0x400000. The BASE generated for a Visual Basic 5 OLE DLL is 0x11000000—something that's different from the default at last.
/SUBSYSTEM:WINDOWS,4.0	Tells the operating system how to run the EXE file. (Options include CONSOLE | WINDOWS | NATIVE | POSIX.)
/VERSION:1.0	Tells the linker to put a version number in the header of the executable file or DLL. (This option has nothing to do with a VERSIONINFO resource.) The major and minor arguments are decimal numbers in the range 0 through 65535. The default is version 0.0. Visual Basic uses the Major and Minor settings in the Options dialog box, available from the File menu's

TABLE 8-3

>>

Switch	Explanation
	Make EXE option, for these values. This switch is used to document the image version as shown by DUMPBIN.EXE (another Microsoft Visual C++ tool).
/DEBUG	Creates debugging information for the executable file or DLL. The linker puts the debugging information into a program database (PDB). It updates the PDB during subsequent builds of the program.
/DEBUGTYPE:CV /DEBUGTYPE:{CV | COFF | BOTH}	Generates debugging information in one of three ways: Microsoft format, COFF format, or both. CV is CodeView; COFF is Common Object File Format.
/INCREMENTAL:NO	Specifies whether incremental linking is required.
/OPT:REF	Excludes unreferenced packaged functions from the executable file. Packaged functions are created using the -Gy flag at compile time. (See Table 8-1 on page 325.) Packaged functions have several uses (not mentioned here) and are created automatically, sometimes by the compiler. For example, C++ member functions are automatically packaged.
/MERGE:.rdata=.text /MERGE:from=to	Combines the first section (from) with the second section (to), naming the resulting section "to". If the second section does not exist, LINK renames the section "from" as "to". The /MERGE option is most useful for creating VxDs and for overriding the compiler-generated section names.

TABLE 8-4

CONTENTS OF NATSUPP.OBJ

Name	Size	Content
.text	0	Readable code
.data	4	Initialized readable writable data
.debug$S	140	Initialized discardable readable data
.debug$T	4	Initialized discardable readable data

The sections are as follows:

- **.text** is where all the general-purpose code created by the compiler is output. (It's 0 bytes big, which probably means no code!)
- **.data** is where initialized data is stored.
- **.debug$S** and **.debug$T** contain, respectively, CodeView Version 4 (CV4) symbolic information (a stream of CV4 symbol records) and CV4 type information (a stream of CV4 type records), as described in the CV4 specification.

As well as statically linking with this library file, other object files reference exported functions in yet another library file, MSVBVM50.DLL. This is a rather large DLL installed by the Visual Basic 5 Setup program in the WINDOWS\SYSTEM directory. (The file describes itself as Visual Basic Virtual Machine and at the time of writing was at version 5.00.3724.) Using *DUMPBIN /EXPORTS MSVBVM50.DLL* yields some interesting symbolic information. For example, we can see that it exports a number of routines, 600 in fact. Some interesting-looking things, possibly routines for invoking methods and procedures, are in here as well: MethCallEngine and ProcCallEngine. Additionally, there are what look like stubs, prefixed with rtc ("run-time call," perhaps?), one for apparently all of the VBA routines: *rtcIsArray*, *rtcIsDate*, *rtcIsEmpty*, … *rtcMakeDir*, … *rtcMsgBox*, … *rtcQBColor*, and so on. And like most DLLs, some cryptic yet interesting exports, such as *Zombie_Release*, are included.

In addition to this symbolic information, the DLL contains a whole bunch of resources, which we can extract and examine using tools such as Microsoft's Visual C++ 5. Of all the resources the DLL contains, the one that really begs examination is the type library resource. If we disassemble this using OLEVIEW.EXE, we can see its entire type library in source form. (Do not confuse OLEVIEW.EXE with OLE2VW32.EXE, which is another Microsoft tool located on the Visual Basic 5 CD in \TOOLS\OLETOOLS.)

The type library contains all sorts of stuff as well as the definitions of methods and properties, such as *vbNullChar*. In the following code, \0 is C-speak for the integral value 0 and \r\n means carriage return and line feed:

```
⋮
[entry(0x00000001), helpcontext(0x0010aa32)] const LPSTR vbNullString = "";
[entry(0x00000002), helpcontext(0x0010aa32)] const LPSTR vbNullChar = "\0";
[entry(0x00000003), helpcontext(0x0010aa32)] const LPSTR vbCrLf = "\r\n";
[entry(0x00000004), helpcontext(0x0010aa32)] const LPSTR vbNewLine = "\r\n";
⋮
```

> From type libraries such as this, we can gather information about help context IDs. Such information will come in handy should you ever want to provide help on someone else's objects. By using these context IDs and, of course, the right help file, you can link F1 to another help file (other than your own).

It turns out that MSVBVM50.DLL is probably the run-time support DLL for any Visual Basic 5 native and p-code executable; that is, it acts like MFC42.DLL does for a non–statically linked MFC application. (MFC stands for Microsoft Foundation Classes, Microsoft's C++/Windows class libraries.) We can confirm this by dumping a built native code executable. Sure enough, we find that the executable imports routines from the DLL. (By the way, the setup wizard also lists this component as the Visual Basic Runtime.) I wasn't surprised to find out that a VBRUN500.DLL doesn't ship with Visual Basic 5!

By dumping other separate object files, we can gather information about what is defined and where it is exported. For example, we can use *DUMPBIN /SYMBOLS MODULE1.OBJ* to discover that a function named *Beep* will be compiled using Microsoft's C++ name decoration (name mangling) regime and thus end up being named ?Beep@Module1@@AAGXXZ. Presumably, this function is compiled as a kind of C++ anyway; that is, in C++ it is defined as (private: void __stdcall Module1::Beep(void)). Or better yet, we can use *DUMPBIN /DISASM MODULE.OBJ* to disassemble a module.

The same routine—*Beep*—defined in a Class, Class1 for example, looks like this:

```
?Beep@Class1@@AAGXXZ (private: void __stdcall Class1::Beep(void))
```

Maybe now we can see why, since Visual Basic 4, we've had to name modules even though they aren't multiply instantiable. Each seems to become a kind of C++ class. According to the name decorations used, *Beep* is a member of the C++ Classes Class1 and Module1.

The Logger Code

As promised, here's the C code source for the spy type application we used earlier. The application in Listing 8-2 on the next page is written in C because it seemed to want to work correctly only as a Win32 console application, not as a windowed Windows application. (So I couldn't write it in Visual Basic—even Visual Basic 5!) You can find this file on the companion CD in the CHAP08 folder. A compiled executable made from this file is in CHAP08/Release.

LISTING 8-2

*The
OUTARGS
logger appli-
cation*

```c
/****************************************************************

  Small C applet used to replace Visual Basic 5 compiler apps
  so as to gather their output and manipulate their
  command-line switches.

  See notes in main text for more details.

****************************************************************/

#include < stdio.h   >
#include < string.h  >
#include < time.h    >
#include < windows.h >

int main
(
    int    argc       // Number of command-line arguments
   ,char * argv[]     // The arguments themselves
   ,char * env []     // Environment variables
)
{
    /* ************************************************************
    ** General declares.
    */
    #define BUFF 2048                        // Change to const if you
                                             // prefer C++.

    auto FILE *       stream;                // File to write to

    auto struct tm * tt;                     // Time stuff for time of
                                             // write
    auto time_t      t;                      // ----- " " -----

    auto char        carBuff[255];           // Used for holding output
                                             // filename

    auto char        carArgs[BUFF];          // Holds command line
                                             // arguments for display
    auto int         nLoop;                  // Loop counter


    /* ************************************************************
    ** Used by CreateProcess.
    */
```

LISTING 8-2

```c
static  STARTUPINFO           sui = {sizeof(STARTUPINFO)};
// Filled in by CreateProcess()
auto    PROCESS_INFORMATION    pi;
auto    long                   l   = 0;



/* ***************
** Code starts ...
*/


// Change according to what real (renamed) application you
// want to start.
(void)strcat(&carArgs[0], ".\\C3 ");

// Get the system time, and convert it to ASCII string.
(void)time(&t);
tt = localtime(&t);

// Going to need to append to our EXE name, so write to
// temp buffer.
(void)strcpy(&carBuff[0], argv[0]);

// Now append .OUT - should contain ???.OUT after this, where ???
// could be APP.EXE or just APP depending on how this program is
// run.
(void)strcat(&carBuff[0], ".OUT");

// Write to EXEName.OUT file (append mode)...
if(NULL != (stream = fopen(&carBuff[0], "a")))
{
    // Write out the time.
    (void)fprintf(stream, "********** Run @ %s\n", asctime(tt));

    // Output name of EXE file.
    (void)fprintf(stream, "* EXE file...\n\n");
    (void)fprintf(stream, "\t%s\n", argv[0]);

    /* ****************************************************
    ** Output command line arguments
    ** (exclude our EXE name argv[0]).
    */

    (void)fprintf(stream, "\n* Command Line Arguments...\n\n");

    for(nLoop = 1; nLoop < argc; nLoop++)
```

>>

LISTING 8-2

```
    {
        (void)fprintf(stream,"%d\t%s\n", nLoop, argv[nLoop]);

        // Append to arguments buffer.
        (void)strcat(&carArgs[0]    , argv[nLoop]);
        (void)strcat(&carArgs[0]    , " ");
    }


/* ******************************
** Output environment variables.
*/

(void)fprintf(stream, "\n* Environment Variables...\n\n");

for(nLoop = 0; NULL != env[nLoop]; nLoop++)
{
    (void)fprintf(stream, "%d\t%s\n", nLoop, env[nLoop]);
}


/* ********************************************************
** Output name and arguments of other application to start.
*/

(void)fprintf(stream,
        "\n* 'Real' program and arguments...\n\n");
(void)fprintf(stream, "\t%s\n", &carArgs[0]);

(void)fprintf(stream, "\n********** Run End\n\n\n");

    // All done, so tidy up.
    (void)fclose(stream);
}


/* ********************************************************
** Execute the real (renamed) EXE as if it had been executed
** directly by Visual Basic
*/

sui.dwFlags     = STARTF_FORCEONFEEDBACK | STARTF_USESHOWWINDOW;
sui.wShowWindow = SW_SHOWNORMAL;

// Creating a process whose main thread will be realtime-class
// privileged - we need this to execute without any yielding.
if (TRUE == CreateProcess(
                      NULL
                     ,&carArgs[0]
```

LISTING 8-2

`>>`

```
                                 ,NULL
                                 ,NULL
                                 ,TRUE
                                 ,REALTIME_PRIORITY_CLASS
                                 ,NULL
                                 ,NULL
                                 ,&sui
                                 ,&pi
                                 )
    )
    {
        // EXEcuted OK, so now wait for the process to complete.
        // Assume CreateProcess() worked OK.
        (void)WaitForSingleObject(pi.hProcess, INFINITE);

        // Get its exit code for returning to Visual Basic.
        (void)GetExitCodeThread(pi.hThread, (LPDWORD)&l);

        (void)CloseHandle(pi.hProcess);

        // Return exit code.
        return l;
    }

    return 0;
}
```

STUFF ABOUT OPTIMIZATION

This section deals with how best to optimize your applications. Notice that the word "code" didn't appear in the preceding sentence. To correctly optimize the way we work and the speed with which we can ship products and solutions, we need to look beyond the code itself. In the following pages, I'll describe what I think are the most effective ways to optimize applications.

Choosing the Right Programmers

In my opinion, there's a difference between coding and programming. Professional programming is all about attitude, skill, knowledge, experience, and last but most important the application of the correct algorithm. Selecting the right people to write your code will *always* improve the quality, reuse, and, of course, execution time of your application.

Profiling Your Code

Once you've written your code, you should profile it. When optimizing code, you must make sure that you optimize the right bit—not just the slow stuff but the frequently used slow stuff! A *profiler* is a tool that is used to time code. An *execution profile* is the result of running such a tool. You can use the output of the profiler to identify where execution time is being spent. If you're already using Visual Basic 4, you should know that VBCP is the name given to the Visual Basic Code Profiler add-in. The VBCP is also included with Visual Basic 5 and is an extremely powerful tool that helps you track down important and frequently hit slow code.

Using Mixed-Language Programming

Correctly written Visual Basic code can easily outperform poorly written C code. This is especially true with Visual Basic 5. (Visual Basic 5 native code is faster than p-code.) Whatever language you use, apply the correct algorithm.

At times, of course, you might have to use other languages, say, to gain some required speed advantage. One of the truly great things about Windows (all versions) is that it specifies a linkage mechanism that is defined at the operating system level. In MS-DOS, all linkages were both early and defined by the language vendor. The result was that mixed-language programming was something only the very brave (or the very foolish) would ever have attempted. It used to be impossible, for example, to get some company's FORTRAN compiler to produce object files that could be linked with other object files generated by another company's C compiler. Neither the linker supplied with the FORTRAN compiler nor the one that came with the C compiler liked the other's object file format. The result was that mixed-language programming was almost impossible to implement. This meant, of course, that tried-and-tested code often had to be ported to another language (so that the entire program was written in one language and therefore linked).

Trouble is that these days we've largely forgotten that mixed-language programming is even possible. It is! Any language compiler that can produce DLLs can almost certainly be used to do mixed-language programming. For example, it's now easy to call Microsoft COBOL routines from Visual Basic. Similarly, any language that can be used to create ActiveX components can be used to create code that can be consumed by other, language-independent, processes.

At The Mandelbrot Set (International) Limited (TMS), when we really need speed—and after we've exhausted all the algorithmic alternatives—we invariably turn to the C compiler. We use the existing Visual Basic code as a template for writing the equivalent C code. (We have an internal rule that says we must write everything in Visual Basic first—it's easier, after all.) We then compile and test (profile) this code to see whether the application is now fast enough. If it's not, we optimize the C code. Ultimately, if it's really required, we get the C compiler to generate assembly code, complete with comments (/Fc and /FA CL.EXE switches are used to do this), and discard the C code completely. Finally, we hand-tune the assembly code and build it using Microsoft's Macro Assembler.

Controlling Your Code's Speed

Don't write unnecessarily fast code. What I mean here is that you shouldn't produce fast code when you don't need to—you'll probably be wasting time. Code to the requirement. If it must be fast, take that into account as you code—not after. If it's OK to be slow(er), then again, code to the requirement. For example, you might decide to use nothing but Variants if neither size nor execution speed is important. Such a decision would simplify the code somewhat, possibly improving your delivery schedule. Keep in mind that each project has different requirements: code to them!

Putting On Your Thinking Cap

The best optimizations usually happen when people really think about the problem.[2] I remember once at TMS we had to obtain the sine of some number of degrees many times in a loop. We used Visual Basic's *Sin* routine to provide this functionality and ultimately built the application and profiled the code. We found that about 90 percent of all our recalculating execution time was spent inside the *Sin* routine. We decided therefore to replace the call to Visual Basic's routine with a call to a DLL function that wrappered the C library routine of the same name. We implemented the DLL, rebuilt, and retested. The results were almost identical. We still spent most of the time inside the *Sin* routine (although now we had another external dependency to worry about— the DLL!). Next we got out the C library source code for *Sin* and had a look at how we might optimize it. The routine, which was coded in assembly language, required detailed study—this was going to take time! At this point, someone said, "Why don't we just look up the required value in a previously built table?" Brilliant? Yes! Obvious? Of course!

---

2. See the book *Programming Pearls*, by Jon Bentley (Addison-Wesley, 1986), for more on this approach.

Staying Focused

Don't take your eyes off the ball. In the preceding example, we lost our focus. We got stuck in tune mode. We generated the lookup table and built it into the application, and then we rebuilt and retested. The problem had vanished.

"Borrowing" Code

Steal code whenever possible. Why write the code yourself if you can source it from elsewhere? Have you checked out MSDN and all the sample code it provides for an answer? The samples in particular contain some great (and some not so great) pieces of code. Unfortunately, some programmers have never discovered the VisData sample (VB\samples\VisData) let alone looked through its source code. Let's see if I can tempt you to browse this valuable resource. VISDATA.BAS contains the following routines. Could they be useful?

ActionQueryType	*MsgBar*
AddBrackets	*NewLocalISAM*
AddMRU	*NewMDB*
CheckTransPending	*ObjectExists*
ClearDataFields	*OpenLocalDB*
CloseAllRecordsets	*OpenQuery*
CloseCurrentDB	*OpenTable*
CompactDB	*RefreshErrors*
CopyData	*RefreshTables*
CopyStruct	*SaveINISettings*
DisplayCurrentRecord	*SetFldProperties*
DupeTableName	*SetQDFParams*
Export	*ShowDBTools*
GetFieldType	*ShowError*
GetFieldWidth	*ShutDownVisData*
GetINIString	*StripBrackets*
GetODBCConnectParts	*StripConnect*
GetTableList	*StripFileName*
HideDBTools	*StripNonAscii*
Import	*StripOwner*
ListItemNames	*stTrueFalse*
LoadINISettings	*UnloadAllForms*
MakeTableName	*vFieldVal*

There's more! The BAS files in the SETUP1 project (VB\setupKit\setup1) contain these routines—anything useful in here?

AbortAction	DllEnableLogging
AddActionNote	DllLogError
AddDirSep	DllLogNote
AddHkeyToCache	DllLogWarning
AddPerAppPath	DllNewAction
AddQuotesToFN	DLLSelfRegister
AddURLDirSep	EnableLogging
AllocUnit	EtchedLine
CalcDiskSpace	ExeSelfRegister
CalcFinalSize	ExitSetup
CenterForm	Extension
ChangeActionKey	fCheckFNLength
CheckDiskSpace	fCreateOSProgramGroup
CheckDrive	fCreateShellGroup
CheckOverwritePrivateFile	fDllWithinAction
CommitAction	FileExists
ConcatSplitFile	fIsDepFile
CopyFile	fNTWithShell
CopySection	FSyncShell
CountIcons	fValidFilename
CreateIcons	fValidNTGroupName
CreateOSLink	fWithinAction
CreateProgManGroup	GetAppRemovalCmdLine
CreateProgManItem	GetClsidFromActXFile
CreateShellLink	GetDefMsgBoxButton
DecideIncrementRefCount	GetDepFileVerStruct
DetectFile	GetDiskSpaceFree
DirExists	GetDrivesAllocUnit
DisableLogging	GetDriveType
DiskSpaceFree	GetFileName
DllAbortAction	GetFileSize
DllAddActionNote	GetFileVersion
DllChangeActionKey	GetFileVerStruct
DllCommitAction	GetLicInfoFromVBL
DllDisableLogging	GetLongPathName

>>

>>

GetPathName
GetRemoteSupportFileVerStruct
GetShortPathName
GetTempFilename
GetUNCShareName
GetWindowsDir
GetWindowsSysDir
GetWinPlatform
IncrementRefCount
InitDiskInfo
intGetHKEYIndex
intGetNextFldOffset
IsDisplayNameUnique
IsNewerVer
IsUNCName
IsValidDestDir
IsWin32
IsWindows95
IsWindowsNT
IsWindowsNT4WithoutSP2
lmemcpy
LogError
LogNote
LogSilentMsg
LogSMSMsg
LogWarning
MakePath
MakePathAux
MoveAppRemovalFiles
MsgError
MsgFunc
MsgWarning
NewAction
OpenConcatFile
OSfCreateShellGroup
OSfCreateShellLink
OSfRemoveShellLink
OSGetLongPathName

PackVerInfo
ParseDateTime
PerformDDE
ProcessCommandLine
PromptForNextDisk
ReadIniFile
ReadProtocols
ReadSetupFileLine
ReadSetupRemoteLine
RegCloseKey
RegCreateKey
RegDeleteKey
RegEdit
RegEnumKey
RegisterAppRemovalEXE
RegisterDAO
RegisterFiles
RegisterLicense
RegisterLicenses
RegisterTLB
RegisterVBLFile
RegOpenKey
RegPathWinCurrentVersion
RegPathWinPrograms
RegQueryNumericValue
RegQueryRefCount
RegQueryStringValue
RegSetNumericValue
RegSetStringValue
RemoteRegister
RemoveShellLink
ReplaceDoubleQuotes
ResolveDestDir
ResolveDestDirs
ResolveDir
ResolveResString
RestoreProgMan
SetFileDateTime

SetFormFont

SetMousePtr

SetTime

ShowLoggingError

ShowPathDialog

SrcFileMissing

strExtractFilenameArg

strExtractFilenameItem

strGetCommonFilesPath

strGetDAOPath

strGetDriveFromPath

strGetHKEYString

strGetPredefinedHKEYString

strGetProgramsFilesPath

StripTerminator

strQuoteString

strRootDrive

strUnQuoteString

TreatAsWin95

UCase16

UpdateStatus

WriteAccess

WriteMIF

VB5STKIT.DLL, which contains some of the routines in the preceding list, is used by SETUP1.EXE, which the setup wizard includes for you on your distribution disks. It seems reasonable to me, then, to include it in your list of dependencies so that it gets installed on your customer's machine. (It's actually in the bootstrap, so it gets copied across anyway.) This all means that you can use the routines in this DLL in your own applications. (Keep in mind, however, that they're documented only through their use in the SETUP1 source.)

Calling on All Your Problem-Solving Skills

Constantly examine your approach to solving problems, and always encourage input and criticism from all quarters on the same. Think problems through. And *always* profile your code!

It would be nice if VBCP included some way to time Visual Basic's routines. For example, how fast is *Val* when compared with its near functional equivalent *CInt*? You can do some of this profiling using the subclassing technique discussed in Chapter 1 (replacing some VBA routine with one of your own—see Tip 11), but here's a small example anyway:

Declarations Section

```
Option Explicit

Declare Function WinQueryPerformanceCounter Lib "kernel32" _
    Alias "QueryPerformanceCounter" (lpPerformanceCount As _
    LARGE_INTEGER) As Long
Declare Function WinQueryPerformanceFrequency Lib "kernel32" _
Alias "QueryPerformanceFrequency" (lpFrequency As LARGE_INTEGER) _
    As Long
```

```
Type LARGE_INTEGER
    LowPart     As Long
    HighPart    As Long
End Type
```

In a Module

```
Function TimeGetTime() As Single

    Static Frequency    As Long
    Dim CurrentTime     As LARGE_INTEGER

    If 0 = Frequency Then
        Call WinQueryPerformanceFrequency(CurrentTime)
        Frequency = CurrentTime.LowPart / 1000
        TimeGetTime = 0
    Else
        Call WinQueryPerformanceCounter(CurrentTime)
        TimeGetTime = CurrentTime.LowPart / Frequency
    End If

End Function
```

Replacement for *Val*

```
Public Function Val(ByVal exp As Variant) As Long

    Dim l1 As Single, l2 As Single
    l1 = TimeGetTime()
    Val = VBA.Conversion.Val(exp)
    l2 = TimeGetTime()
    Debug.Print "Val - " & l2 - l1

End Function
```

The *TimeGetTime* routine uses the high-resolution timer in the operating system to determine how many ticks it (the operating system's precision timing mechanism) is capable of per second (*WinQueryPerformanceFrequency*). *TimeGetTime* then divides this figure by 1000 to determine the number of ticks per millisecond. It stores this value in a static variable so that the value is calculated only once.

On subsequent calls, the routine simply returns a number of milliseconds; it queries the system time, converts that to milliseconds, and returns this value to the calling program. For the calling program to determine a quantity of time passing, it must call the routine twice and compare the results of two calls.

Subtract the result of the second call from the first, and you'll get the number of milliseconds that have elapsed between the calls. This process is shown in the "Replacement for *Val*" code on the facing page.

With this example, one can imagine being able to profile the whole of VBA. Unfortunately, that isn't possible. If you attempt to replace certain routines, you'll find that you can't. For example, the *CInt* routine cannot be replaced using this technique. (Your replacement *CInt* is reported as having an illegal name.) According to Microsoft, for speed, some routines were not implemented externally in the VBA ActiveX server but were kept internal—*CInt* is one of those routines.

Using Smoke and Mirrors

The best optimization is the perceived one. If you make something look or feel fast, it will generally be perceived as being fast. Give your users good feedback. For example, use a progress bar. Your code will actually run slower (it's having to recalculate and redraw the progress bar), but the user's perception of its speed, compared with not having the progress bar, will almost always be in your favor.

One of the smartest moves you can ever make is to start fast. (Compiling to native code creates "faster to start" executables.) Go to great lengths to get that first window on the screen so that your users can start using the application. Leave the logging onto the database and other such tasks until after this first window is up. Look at the best applications around: they all start, or appear to start, very quickly. If you create your applications to work the same way, the user's perception will be "Wow! This thing is usable *and* quick." Bear in mind that lots of disk activity before your first window appears means you're slow: lots after, however, means you're busy doing smart stuff!

Because you cannot easily build multithreaded Visual Basic applications (see Chapter 14 to see some light at the end of this particular tunnel), you might say that you'll have to block sometime; that is, you're going to have to log on sometime, and you know that takes time—and the user will effectively be blocked by the action. Consider breaking out the logging on into a separate application implemented as an out-of-process ActiveX server, perhaps writing this server to provide your application with a set of data services. Use an asynchronous callback object to signal to the user interface part of your application when the database is ready to be used. When you get the signal, enable those features that have now become usable. If you take this approach, you'll find, of course, that the data services ActiveX server is blocked—waiting for the connection—but your thread of execution, in the user interface part of the application, is unaffected, giving your user truly smooth multitasking. The total effort is minimal; in fact, you might even get some code reuse out of the ActiveX server. The effect on the user's perception, however, can be quite dramatic.

Using the Compiler to Optimize Your Code

The effect of the optimizer (project properties dialog box settings) on how C2.EXE and LINK.EXE are driven is summarized in Table 8-5 (for building a standard EXE). Because most switches have no effect on these two EXEs, we must assume that they are being acted on within VB5.EXE itself. (It seems to contain the compiler's first pass.)

TABLE 8-5

THE COMPILER EFFECT

Optimization Option	C2.EXE Effect	LINK.EXE Effect
Optimize For Small Code	None	None
Optimize For Fast Code	None	None
Favor Pentium Pro	/G6 (from G5)	None
Create Symbolic Debug Info	/Zi	/DEBUG/DEBUGTYPE:CV
Assume No Aliasing	None	None
Remove Array Bounds Checks	None	None
Remove Integer Overflow Checks	None	None
Remove Floating Point Error Checks	None	None
Allow Unrounded Floating Point Operations	None	None
Remove Safe Pentium FDIV Checks	/Qifdiv Removed	None

Obviously, -G6 means favor the Pentium Pro. Even the Visual C++ 4.2 compiler doesn't implement this. But of course, Visual Basic 5's C2 is taken from Visual C++ version 5!

As I've said before, compiled code is faster than p-code, so of course, one "easy" optimization everyone will expect to make is to compile to native code. Surely this will create faster-executing applications when compared with a p-code clone?

Using the *TimeGetTime* routine (discussed fully earlier on page 346), we do indeed see some impressive improvements when we compare one against the other. For example, the following loop code, on my 200-MHz machine, takes 13.5 milliseconds to execute as compiled p-code and just 1.15 milliseconds as native code—almost 12 times faster (optimizing for Favor Pentium Pro and Fast Code). If this kind of improvement is typical, "real" compilation is, indeed, an easy optimization.

```
Dim n As Integer
Dim d As Double

For n = 1 To 32766
    ' Do enough to confuse the optimizer.
    d = (n * 1.1) - (n * 1#)
Next
```

In case you're interested, this same code compiled as p-code under Visual Basic 4 (32-bit) executed in 12.75 milliseconds.

Microsoft claims that Visual Basic 5 produces native code applications that run up to 20 times faster than applications built with earlier versions of Visual Basic. The CPU-intensive benchmarks in Figure 8-2 show that for compute-intensive operations, Visual Basic 5 is 20 to 60 times faster than Visual Basic 4.

FIGURE 8-2

CPU-intensive benchmark results— Visual Basic 5 vs. Visual Basic 4

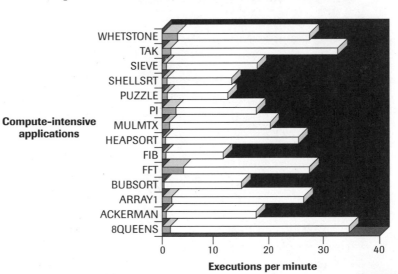

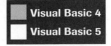

We discovered one disappointing native code negative in conducting our tests, although this drawback might affect very few people. At TMS, we often use *GoSub* to write local subroutines—that is, subroutines that don't pollute the global name space and that are called very fast. The idea is that you might expect to have a *GoSub* simply resolve to a push/jmp instruction sequence. Because you don't have the ability to use passed arguments to the subroutine, you might also expect to see a saving here on not having to push a set of arguments. (You use local variables for holding passed information.) Well, in the past, all of this was simply dandy. With Visual Basic 5 in Native Code mode, however, *GoSub* calls run *really* slowly. Our advice is not to use them in Visual Basic 5 if you're going to compile to native code.

STUFF ABOUT TYPES

Code reuse is mostly about object orientation—the effective packaging of components to suit some plan or design. This section examines the mechanisms that exist in Visual Basic to effectively bring about code reuse. In particular, we'll look at how we can extend the type system in Visual Basic.

Visual Basic as an Object-Oriented Language

People often say that Visual Basic is not properly object oriented. I would answer that if you're comparing it with C++, you're both right and wrong. Yes, it isn't C++; it's Visual Basic!

C++ is a generic, cross-platform programming language designed around a particular programming paradigm that is, subjectively, object oriented. It is based on and influenced by other programming languages such as Simula, C, and C with Objects[3] and is also "committee driven" (by the ANSI X3J16 standards group).

Visual Basic has evolved—and has been influenced too—according to system considerations, not primarily to different languages. It was designed to be platform specific; there's not an implementation for a CRAY supercomputer, for example. Visual Basic's object orientation, then, is not primarily language based. In other words, its object-oriented language constructs are not there to implement object orientation directly but rather to best utilize the object-oriented features of the operating system—in Windows, of course, this means ActiveX.

---

3. See *History of Programming Languages,* edited by Thomas J. Bergin and Richard G. Gibson Jr. (Addison-Wesley, 1996), for more on the evolution of C++.

ActiveX itself, however, is not a language definition but a systems-level object technology built directly into a specific range of operating systems. It is not subject to committees either, although you might consider this to be a negative point. Additionally, I think I'd call the object orientation offered by both ActiveX and Visual Basic "commercial," whereas I'd probably call C++ "academic." I have nothing against C++ or any other programming language. Indeed, I'm a proponent of mixed-language programming and use C++ almost daily. What I am against, however, is a comparison of Visual Basic with C++. These two languages are as different as COBOL and FORTRAN, and both were designed largely to solve different problems and to cater to different markets. This all said, I'm still keen to model the world realistically in terms of objects, and I also want to encourage both high cohesion and loose coupling between and within those objects. (Here's a quick tip for the latter: Use ByVal—it helps!) Whether or not I achieve this cohesion and coupling with Visual Basic and ActiveX is the real question.

Cohesion and coupling

Before going any further, let me take a moment to define the terms *cohesion* and *coupling.* A component is said to be cohesive if it exhibits a high degree of functional relatedness with other related components. These related components (routines typically) should form cohesive program units (modules and classes). Every routine in a module should, for example, be essential for that module to accomplish its purpose. Generally, there are seven recognized levels of cohesion (none of which I'll cover here). Coupling is an indication of the strength of the interconnections and interactions exhibited by different program components. If components are strongly coupled, they obviously have a large dependency on each other—neither can typically work without the other, and if you break one of the components, you'll invariably break the others that are dependent on it. In Visual Basic, tight coupling typically comes about largely through the overuse and sharing of public symbols (variables, constants, properties, and routines exported by other units). Components that are highly cohesive yet loosely coupled are more easily shared. If code reuse is an issue, consider rigorously promoting both of these simple philosophies.

What are your intentions?

Having an object implies intention; that is, you're about to do something with the object. This intention should, in turn, define the object's behavior and its interfaces. Indeed, a strong type system implies that you know what you'll do with something when you pick it up. After all, you know what you can do with a hammer when you pick one up! A sense of encapsulation, identity, and meaning is an obvious requirement. To add both external and procedural meaning to an object, you need to be able to add desirable qualities such as methods and properties. What does all this boil down to in Visual Basic? The class, the interface, and the object variable.

Classes are essentially Visual Basic's way of wrappering both method, which is ideally the interface, and state—that is, providing real type extensions (or as good as it gets currently). A real type is more than a description of mere data (state); it also describes the set of operations that can be applied to that state (method). Unfortunately, methods are currently nonsymbolic. One feature that C++ has that I'd love to have in Visual Basic is the ability to define symbolic methods that relate directly to a set of operators. With this ability, I could, for example, define what it means to literally add a deposit to an account using the addition operator (+). After all, the plus sign is already overloaded (defined for) in Visual Basic. For example, the String type supports addition. Also, a solution will have nothing to do with ActiveX; the ability to define symbolic methods is a mere language feature.

Visual Basic "inheritance"

Visual Basic lacks an inheritance mechanism (definitely more of an ActiveX constraint) that is comparable with that of C++. To reuse another object's properties in Visual Basic, you must use something else—either composition or association.

NOTE

> By the way, C++ type of inheritance is often used badly; that is, an object that inherits from other objects exports their public interfaces. The result is that top-level objects are often bloated because they are the sum of all the public interfaces of the objects they are derived from—a sort of overprivileged and overfed upper class!

Composition is the process whereby an object is made up of other objects. Inheritance is a "kinda" (is a kind of) relationship, whereas composition is a "hasa" (has a) relationship. Obviously, then, we can describe an instance of a car as something that "hasa" engine (unless it's been removed, of course), not as a "kinda" engine. Building from this example, in Visual Basic, we exhibit composition by having a member (probably a private member) of class Car defined as being an object of class Engine.

Consider Scenario 1:

Class CCar

```
Private Engine As New CEngine
```

Somewhere Else

```
Dim Car As CCar        ' Initialize event will create "Engine."
Car.Start              ' Start is a public method of CCar.
```

Association has to do with associating an object pointer—in Visual Basic an object variable—with an instance of an object class. Now consider Scenario 2:

Class CCar

```
Public Engine As CEngine
```

Somewhere Else

```
Dim Car As CCar        ' Initialize event will create "Engine."
Car.Engine.Start       ' Start is a public method of CEngine.
```

The classic question given both possibilities is, of course, "Do you start the car or the engine?" (You could use a Public Engine and composition, and then you could export the engine to be started externally—but that begs the question.) I'll let you decide between the car and the engine! In this second scenario, it's because we don't have inheritance that we're having to make the whole of the engine public so that we can "push" its starter. Making the engine public, however, might be undesirable; that is, maybe you don't want your consumers to be able to access the engine directly—maybe that kind of access would invalidate their warranty, or maybe the engine has other methods that you wouldn't want published. To export the *Start* method more directly without also exposing the engine, you need Scenario 1; that is, you'd really have a *Car.StartEngine* method trigger *Engine.Start*. (This is called forwarding.) Of course, a Car must now "know" about its internal composition and export the starter—not a good situation. You could have a car simply Implement the engine, but that's not very clean either.

Another problem with association (actually, it's just as easy in Visual Basic to do this via composition) as compared to inheritance is that it's easier to accidentally negate the reference to the engine. For example, maybe you have the means to change the type of engine in your car. To do this, you first destroy

The placing of the *New* keyword is not as important (semantically) in Visual Basic as it would be in, say, C++; that is, an object declared using *New* doesn't change the type of the reference being declared—it's still an object variable, not necessarily the thing itself. In other words, even though we're implying that *Dim o As New Thing* and *Dim o As Thing* (*New*'ed later) are different, they are in fact the same. This sameness is an advantage because it means that an object that is composed of a New Engine can also exhibit associative behavior. If you like, the *Engine* object variable is simply being associated during Car construction.

the current engine by setting the current reference to *Nothing*. Next, you create a new engine and reset the pointer to point to it. Historically (pre-Implements), because of the typing requirements of Visual Basic, the object variable being set must be of type Object since an object variable of type CEngine1 cannot be set to point to ("hold" in Visual Basic—the same thing) an instance of CEngine2. This, of course, also means that your engine could get set to point to a form or to some other object type. If the *Set Engine = New CEngine2* code never executes, maybe you encounter an error, it means that Engine now points to *Nothing*—which doesn't have a starter! This is one of the problems fixed by the Implements keyword. For more information on Implements, see Visual Basic Books Online.

The Object type is effectively typeless since it is polymorphic with any other object type. You might say that it Implements everything! You can access any object type via an object variable of type Object, yet it will respond according to the type of object it is (points to—same thing) rather than to the reference you have to it. For example, *o.Start*, where *o* is of type Object, is perfectly legal if *o* has previously been set to point to an object of type Engine—Visual Basic doesn't complain by saying that the class Object doesn't support the *Start* method. You're going to get the same effect with Implements. The difference is that with Implements you should never find the method missing!

Object orientation *is* modeling the requirements. Defining the requirements therefore dictates the object model and implementation method you'll employ. You can build effective sets of objects in Visual Basic, but you cannot do today all of what is possible in C++. As I said earlier, Visual Basic and C++ are two different things, and you should learn to adapt to and utilize the strengths of each as appropriate.

Using Collections to Extend the Type System

You can also extend the type system ("type" meaning mere data at this point) in other ways. At TMS, we often use a *Collection* object (as in the following code) to represent objects that are entirely entities of state; that is, they have no methods. (You cannot append a method to a collection.)

```
Dim KindaForm As New Collection

Const pHeight As String = "1"
Const pWidth  As String = "2"
Const pName   As String = "3"

    ⋮

With KindaForm
    .Add Key:=pHeight, Item:=Me.Height
    .Add Key:=pWidth, Item:=Me.Width
    .Add Key:=pName, Item:=Me.Name
End With

    ⋮

With KindaForm
    Print .Item(pHeight)
    Print .Item(pWidth)
    Print .Item(pName)
End With
```

Here we have an object named *KindaForm* that has the properties *pHeight*, *pWidth*, and *pName*. In other words, an existing Visual Basic type (with both properties and method) is being used to create a generic state-only object. If you're using classes to do this, you might want to consider using *Collection* objects as shown here instead.

You can add functional members to a *Collection* object with just one level of indirection by adding an object variable to the collection that is set to point to an object that has the necessary functionality defined in it. Such methods can act on the state in the other members of the collection.

So what's the difference between using a collection and creating a user-defined type? Well, a collection is more flexible (not always an advantage) and has support for constructs such as For Each:

```
For Each v In KindaForm
    Print v
Next
```

The advantage of user-defined types is that they have a known mapping. For example, they can be used as parameters to APIs, sent around a network, and passed between mainframe and PC systems—they are just byte arrays. (See Chapter 5 for more on user-defined types—they're one of Jon Burn's favorite things!) Obviously, a state-only *Collection* object doesn't mean much to a mainframe system, and passing *KindaForm* as "the thing" itself will result in your only passing an object pointer to a system that cannot interpret it. (Even if it could, the object would not be available because it's not transmitted with its address.)

Adding to *VarType*

Another "byte array" way to extend the type system is to add new Variant types. In Visual Basic 4, the following subtypes were available via the Variant:

Visual Basic Name	*VarType*	Description
vbEmpty	0	Uninitialized (default)
vbNull	1	Contains no valid data
vbInteger	2	Integer
vbLong	3	Long integer
vbSingle	4	Single-precision floating-point number
vbDouble	5	Double-precision floating-point number
vbCurrency	6	Currency
vbDate	7	Date
vbString	8	String
vbObject	9	Automation object
vbError	10	Error
vbBoolean	11	Boolean
vbVariant	12	Variant (used only for arrays of Variants)
vbDataObject	13	Non-Automation object
vbByte	17	Byte
vbArray	8192	Array

In Visual Basic 5, we have one addition (and a great deal of scope for adding more—a lot of gaps!):

vbDecimal	14	Decimal value

With some limitations, we can add to this list. For example, we could, with only a small amount of effort, add a new Variant type of 42 to represent some new entity by compiling this C code to a DLL named NEWTYPE.DLL:

```c
#include "windows.h"
#include "ole2.h"
#include "oleauto.h"

#include <time.h>

typedef VARIANT * PVARIANT;

VARIANT  __stdcall CVNewType(PVARIANT v)
{
    // If the passed variant is not set yet...
    if(0 == v -> vt)
    {
        // Create new type.
        v->vt = 42;

        // Set other variant members to be meaningful for this
        // new type...
        // You do this here!
    }

    // Return the variant, initialized/used variants unaffected by
    // this routine.
    return *v;
}


int  __stdcall EX_CInt(PVARIANT v)
{
    // Sanity check - convert only new variant types!
    if(42 != v->vt)
    {
        return 0;
    }
    else
    {
        // Integer conversion - get our data and convert it as
        // necessary.
        // Return just a random value in this example.
        srand((unsigned)time(NULL));

        return rand();
    }
}
```

This code provides us with two routines: *CVNewType* creates, given an already created but empty Variant (it was easier), a Variant of *VarType* 42; *EX_CInt* converts a Variant of type 42 to an integer value (but doesn't convert the Variant to a new Variant type). "Converts" here means "evaluates" or "yields." Obviously, the implementation above is minimal. We're not putting any real value into this new Variant type, and when we convert one all we're doing is returning a random integer. Nevertheless, it is possible! Here's some code to test the theory:

```
Dim v As Variant

v = CVNewType(v)

Me.Print VarType(v)
Me.Print EX_CInt(v)
```

This code will output 42 and then some random number when executed against the DLL. The necessary DLL declarations are as follows:

```
Private Declare Function CVNewType Lib "NEWTYPE.DLL" _
(ByRef v As Variant) As Variant
Private Declare Function EX_CInt    Lib "NEWTYPE.DLL" _
(ByRef v As Variant) As Integer
```

Again, we cannot override Visual Basic's *CInt* (see page 347), and so I've had to name my routine something other than what I wanted to—in this case, *EX_CInt* for "external" CInt. I could, of course, have overloaded *Val*:

```
Public Function Val(ByRef exp As Variant) As Variant

    Select Case VarType(exp)
        Case 42:   Val = EX_CInt(exp)
        Case Else: Val = VBA.Conversion.Val(exp)
    End Select

End Function
```

Here, if the passed Variant is of type 42, I know that the "real" *Val* won't be able to convert it—it doesn't know what it holds after all—so I convert it myself using *EX_CInt*. If, however, it contains an old Variant type, I simply pass it on to VBA to convert using the real *Val* routine.

Visual Basic has also been built, starting with version 4, to expect the sudden arrival of Variant types about which nothing is known. This assertion must be true because Visual Basic 4 can be used to build ActiveX servers that have methods. In turn, these can be passed Variants as parameters. A Visual Basic 5 client (or server) can utilize these servers. A Visual Basic 5 client, then, might surprise a Visual Basic 4 server! In other words, because a Visual Basic 5 executable can pass in a Variant of type 14, Visual Basic must be built to expect unknown variant types, given that the Variant type is likely to grow at every release. You might want to consider testing for this in your Visual Basic 4 code.

Having said all this and having explained how it could work, I'm not sure of the real value currently of adding a value to *VarType*. This is especially true when, through what we must call a feature of Visual Basic, not all the conversion routines are available for subclassing. In other words, why not use a user-defined type or, better still, a class to hold your new type instead of extending the Variant system?

Another limitation to adding to *VarType* is due to the way we cannot override operators or define them for our new types. We have to be careful that, unlike an old Variant, our new Variant is not used in certain expressions. For example, consider what might happen if we executed *Me.Print 10 + v*. Because *v* is a Variant, it needs to be converted to a numeric type to be added to the integer constant 10. When this happens, Visual Basic must logically apply *VarType* to *v* to see what internal routine it should call to convert it to a numeric value. Obviously, it's not going to like our new Variant type! To write expressions such as this, we'd need to do something like *Me.Print 10 + Val(v)*. This is also the reason why, in the *Val* substitute earlier, I had to pass *exp* ByRef. I couldn't let Visual Basic evaluate it (which it would have to do using ByVal), even though it's received as a Variant.

Variants also might need to be destroyed correctly. When they go out of scope and are destroyed, you might have to tidy up any memory they might have previously allocated. If what they represent is, say, a more complex type, we might have to allocate memory to hold the representation.

Microsoft does not encourage extending the Variant type scheme. For example, 42 might be free today, but who knows what it might represent in Visual Basic 6. We would need to bear this in mind whenever we created new Variant types and make sure that we could change their *VarType* values almost arbitrarily—added complexity that is, again, less than optimal!

All in all, adding to *VarType* is not really a solution at the moment. If we get operator overloading and proper access to VBA's conversion routines, however, all of this is a little more attractive.

NOTE

The code to create Variants needs to be written in a language such as C. The main reason is that Visual Basic is too type safe and simply won't allow us to treat a Variant like we're doing in the DLL. In other words, accessing a Variant in Visual Basic accesses the type's value and storage transparently through the VARIANT structure or user-defined type. To access its internals, it's necessary to change the meaning of variant access from one of value to one of representation.

Pointers

A common criticism of Visual Basic is that it doesn't have a pointer type. It cannot therefore be used for modeling elaborate data types such as linked lists. Well, of course, Visual Basic has pointers—the object variable can be treated as a pointer. Just as you can have linked lists in C, so can you have them in Visual Basic.

Creating a linked list

Let's look at an example of a circular doubly linked list where each node has

FIGURE 8-3

A node in the list

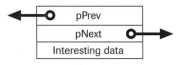

a pointer to the previous and next elements in the list, as shown in Figure 8-3. Notice in the code that we have a "notional" starting point, *pHead*, which initially points to the head of the list.

The Node Class

```
Option Explicit

' "Pointers" to previous and next nodes.
Public pPrev As Node
Public pNext As Node

' Something interesting in each node -
' the creation number (of the node)!
Public nAttribute As Integer

Private Sub Class_Initialize()

    Set pNext = Nothing
    Set pPrev = Nothing

End Sub
```

```vb
Private Sub Class_Terminate()

    ' When an object terminates, it will already have
    ' had to set these two members to Nothing;
    ' this code, then, is slightly redundant.
    Set pNext = Nothing
    Set pPrev = Nothing

End Sub
```

The Test Form

```vb
Option Explicit

Private pHead    As New Node
Private pV       As Node


Public Sub CreateCircularLinkedList()

    Dim p         As Node
    Dim nLoop     As Integer
    Static pLast  As Node       ' Points to last node created -
                                ' pHead if first node.

    pHead.nAttribute = 0
    Set pLast = pHead

    ' 501 objects in list - the pHead object exists
    ' until killed in DeleteList.

    For nLoop = 1 To 501
        Set p = New Node
        p.nAttribute = nLoop
        Set pLast.pNext = p
        Set p.pPrev = pLast
        Set pLast = p
    Next

    ' Decrement reference count on object.
    Set pLast = Nothing

    ' Join the two ends of the list, making a circle.
    Set p.pNext = pHead
    Set pHead.pPrev = p

    Exit Sub

End Sub
```

>>

```vb
Public Sub PrintList()

    Debug.Print "Forwards"
    Set pV = pHead

    Do
        Debug.Print pV.nAttribute
        Set pV = pV.pNext
    Loop While Not pV Is pHead

    Debug.Print "Backwards"
    Set pV = pHead.pPrev

    Do
        Debug.Print pV.nAttribute
        Set pV = pV.pPrev
    Loop While Not pV Is pHead.pPrev

End Sub


Public Sub DeleteList()

    Dim p As Node

    Set pV = pHead

    Do
        Set pV = pV.pNext
        Set p = pV.pPrev

        If Not p Is Nothing Then
            Set p.pNext = Nothing
            Set p.pPrev = Nothing
        End If

        Set p = Nothing
    Loop While Not pV.pNext Is Nothing

    ' Both of these point to pHead at the end.
    Set pV = Nothing
    Set pHead = Nothing

End Sub
```

The routines *CreateCircularLinkedList*, *PrintList*, and *DeleteList* should be called in that order. I have omitted building in any protection against deleting an empty list. To keep the example as short as possible, I've also excluded some other obvious routines, such as *InsertIntoList*.

In Visual Basic, a node will continue to exist as long as an object variable is pointing to it (because a set object variable becomes the thing that the node is set to). For example, if two object variables point to the same thing, an equality check of one against the other (using *Is*) will evaluate to True (an equivalence operator). It follows, then, that for a given object all object variables that are set to point to it have to be set to *Nothing* for it to be destroyed. Also, even though a node is deleted, if the deleted node had valid pointers to other nodes, it might continue to allow other nodes to exist. In other words, setting a node pointer, *p*, to *Nothing* has no effect on the thing pointed to by *p* if another object variable, say, *p1*, is also pointing to the thing that *p* is pointing to. This means that to delete a node we have to set the following to *Nothing*: its *pPrev* object's *pNext* pointer, its *pNext* object's *pPrev* pointer, and its own *pNext* and *pPrev* pointers (to allow other nodes to be deleted later). And don't forget the object variable we have pointing to *p* to access all the other pointers and objects. Not what you might expect!

It's obvious that an object variable can be thought of as a pointer to something and also as the thing to which it points. Remember that *Is* should be used to compare references, not =. This is why we need *Set* to have the variable point to something else; that is, trying to change the object variable using assignment semantically means changing the value of the thing to which it points, whereas *Set* means changing the object variable to point elsewhere.

Linked lists that are created using objects appear to be very efficient. They are fast to create and manipulate and are as flexible as anything that can be created in C.

Addresses

Visual Basic 5 (with VBA) is also able to yield real pointers, or addresses. Three undocumented VBA methods—*VarPtr*, *ObjPtr*, and *StrPtr* (which are just three different VBA type library *Declare* statements pointing to the same entry point in the run-time DLL)—are used to create these pointers. You can turn an object into a pointer value using *l* = *ObjPtr(o)*, where *o* is the object whose address you want and *l* is a long integer in which the address of the object is put. Just resolving an object's address doesn't AddRef the object, however. You can pass this value around and get back to the object by memory copying *l* into some dummy object variable and then setting another object variable to this dummy (thus adding a reference to the underlying object):

```
Call CopyMemory(oDummy, l, 4)
Set oThing = oDummy
```

CopyMemory should be defined like this:

```
Private Declare Sub CopyMemory Lib "kernel32" Alias _
"RtlMoveMemory" (pDest As Any, pSource As Any, ByVal ByteLen As Long)
```

The really neat thing here is that setting *l* doesn't add a reference to the object referenced by the argument of *ObjPtr*. Normally, when you set an object to point to another, the object to which you point it (attach it, really) has its reference count incremented, meaning that the object can't be destroyed, because there are now two references to it. (This incrementing also happens if you pass the object as a parameter to a routine.) For an example of how this can hinder you, see the discussion of the linked list example on page 360.

By using *VarPtr* (which yields the address of variables and user-defined types), *StrPtr* (which yields the address of strings), and *ObjPtr*, you can create very real and very powerful and complex data structures.

Here's the short piece of code I used to discover that *VarPtr, ObjPtr,* and *StrPtr* are all really pretty much the same thing (that is, the same function in a DLL):

```
Private Sub Form_Load()

    ' VB code to dump or match up an external
    ' server method with a DLL entry point. Here it's
    ' used to dump the methods of the "_HiddenModule".

    ' Add a reference to 'TypeLib Information' (TLBINF32.DLL),
    ' which gives you TLI before running this code.

    Dim tTLInfo  As TypeLibInfo
    Dim tMemInfo As MemberInfo
    Dim sDLL     As String
    Dim sOrdinal As Integer

    Set tTLInfo = _
        TLI.TLIApplication.TypeLibInfoFromFile("MSVBVM50.DLL")

    For Each tMemInfo In _
        tTLInfo.TypeInfos.NamedItem("_HiddenModule").Members
```

```
With tMemInfo
    tMemInfo.GetDllEntry sDLL, "", sOrdinal

    ' labDump is the label on the form where the
    ' output will be printed.
    labDump.Caption = labDump.Caption & _
            .Name & _
            " is in " & _
            sDLL & _
            " at ordinal reference " & sOrdinal & _
            vbCrLf
End With

    Next

End Sub
```

The code uses TLBINF32.DLL, which can interrogate type libraries (very handy). Here I'm dumping some information on all the methods of a module (in type library parlance) named _HiddenModule. You'll see that this is the module that contains *VarPtr, ObjPtr,* and *StrPtr,* which you can discover using OLEVIEW.EXE to view MSVBVM50.DLL:

```
module _HiddenModule {
        [entry(0x60000000), vararg, helpcontext(0x000f6c9d)]
        VARIANT _stdcall Array([in] SAFEARRAY(VARIANT)* ArgList);
        [entry(0x60000001), helpcontext(0x000f735f)]
        BSTR _stdcall _B_str_InputB(
                        [in] long Number,
                        [in] short FileNumber);
        [entry(0x60000002), helpcontext(0x000f735f)]
        VARIANT _stdcall _B_var_InputB(
                        [in] long Number,
                        [in] short FileNumber);
        [entry(0x60000003), helpcontext(0x000f735f)]
        BSTR _stdcall _B_str_Input(
                        [in] long Number,
                        [in] short FileNumber);
        [entry(0x60000004), helpcontext(0x000f735f)]
        VARIANT _stdcall _B_var_Input(
                        [in] long Number,
                        [in] short FileNumber);
        [entry(0x60000005), helpcontext(0x000f65a4)]
        void _stdcall Width(
                        [in] short FileNumber,
                        [in] short Width);
```

>>

```
    [entry(0x60000006), hidden]
    long _stdcall VarPtr([in] void* Ptr);
    [entry(0x60000007), hidden]
    long _stdcall StrPtr([in] BSTR Ptr);
    [entry(0x60000008), hidden]
    long _stdcall ObjPtr([in] IUnknown* Ptr);
};
```

Or you can use OLE2VW32.EXE:

```
'==================================================================
' Type Info: _HiddenModule, TypeInfo Version 0.000
' GUID: {CF1C2C60-0D25-1069-9427-00DD0111BF30}
' LCID: 0X00000009
' TypeKind: module
' Help: C:\WINDOWS\SYSTEM\VBA.HLP (Help ID: 0X00000000)
'------------------------------------------------------------------

' Function: Array
' Help: C:\WINDOWS\SYSTEM\VBA.HLP (Help ID: 0X000F6C9D)
'
Declare Function Array (ParamArray ArgList As Variant) _
As Variant

' Function: _B_str_InputB
' Help: C:\WINDOWS\SYSTEM\VBA.HLP (Help ID: 0X000F735F)
'
Declare Function _B_str_InputB (ByVal Number As Long, _
ByVal FileNumber As Integer) As String

' Function: _B_var_InputB
' Help: C:\WINDOWS\SYSTEM\VBA.HLP (Help ID: 0X000F735F)
'
Declare Function _B_var_InputB (ByVal Number As Long, _
ByVal FileNumber As Integer) As Variant

' Function: _B_str_Input
' Help: C:\WINDOWS\SYSTEM\VBA.HLP (Help ID: 0X000F735F)
'
Declare Function _B_str_Input (ByVal Number As Long, _
ByVal FileNumber As Integer) As String

' Function: _B_var_Input
' Help: C:\WINDOWS\SYSTEM\VBA.HLP (Help ID: 0X000F735F)
'
Declare Function _B_var_Input (ByVal Number As Long, _
ByVal FileNumber As Integer) As Variant
```

```
' Function: Width
' Help: C:\WINDOWS\SYSTEM\VBA.HLP (Help ID: 0X000F65A4)
'
Declare Sub Width (ByVal FileNumber As Integer, _
ByVal Width As Integer)

' Function: VarPtr
' Help: C:\WINDOWS\SYSTEM\VBA.HLP (Help ID: 0X00000000)
'
Declare Function VarPtr (ByRef Ptr As Variant) As Long

' Function: StrPtr
' Help: C:\WINDOWS\SYSTEM\VBA.HLP (Help ID: 0X00000000)
'
Declare Function StrPtr (ByVal Ptr As String) As Long

' Function: ObjPtr
' Help: C:\WINDOWS\SYSTEM\VBA.HLP (Help ID: 0X00000000)
' Declare Function ObjPtr (ByVal Ptr As LPUNKNOWN) As Long
```

When you run the Visual Basic code beginning on page 364, you'll see this output:

```
Array          is in VBA5.DLL at ordinal reference 601
_B_str_InputB  is in VBA5.DLL at ordinal reference 566
_B_var_InputB  is in VBA5.DLL at ordinal reference 567
_B_str_Input   is in VBA5.DLL at ordinal reference 620
_B_var_Input   is in VBA5.DLL at ordinal reference 621
Width          is in VBA5.DLL at ordinal reference 565
VarPtr         is in VBA5.DLL at ordinal reference 644
StrPtr         is in VBA5.DLL at ordinal reference 644
ObjPtr         is in VBA5.DLL at ordinal reference 644
```

This output shows the method name together with the DLL and ordinal reference (into the DLL) that implements its functionality. If you use *DUMPBIN /EXPORTS* on MSVBVM50.DLL like this:

```
dumpbin /exports msvbvm50.dll > dump
```

and then examine the dump file, you'll see that the routine at ordinal 644 is in fact *VarPtr*. In other words, *VarPtr, ObjPtr,* and *StrPtr* all do their stuff in the MSVBVM50.DLL routine *VarPtr!*

Matching the code output to the dump, we see this:

```
Method Name    DLL Routine Name
Array          rtcArray
_B_str_InputB  rtcInputCount
```

>>

```
_B_var_InputB     rtcInputCountVar
_B_str_Input      rtcInputCharCount
_B_var_Input      rtcInputCharCountVar
Width             rtcFileWidth
VarPtr            VarPtr
StrPtr            VarPtr
ObjPtr            VarPtr
```

I haven't explained what the other routines do—you can discover that for yourself.

STUFF ABOUT TYPE LIBRARIES

In this section, we'll take a quick look at type libraries—not those created by Visual Basic (because they're free) but those created by hand. You'll see how to use these hand-made type libraries as development tools and as aids that will help you ensure that your coding standards are correctly applied.

A type library is where Visual Basic records the description of your ActiveX server's interfaces. Put another way, a type library is a file, or perhaps a part of a file, that describes the type of one or more objects. (These objects don't have to be ActiveX servers.) Type libraries do not, however, store the actual objects described—they store only information about objects. (They might also contain immediate data such as constant values.) By accessing the library, applications can check the characteristics of an object—that is, the object's exported and named interfaces.

When ActiveX objects are exported and made public in your applications, Visual Basic creates a type library for you to describe the object's interfaces. You can also create type libraries separately using the tools found on the Visual Basic 5 CD in TOOLS\UNSUPPRT\TYPLIB.

Type libraries can be written using a language called Object Description Language (ODL) and compiled using MkTypLib. A good way to learn a little more about ODL is to study existing type libraries. You can use the OLEVIEW tool mentioned earlier to disassemble type libraries from existing DLLs, ActiveX servers, and controls for further study.

As I just said, the object information described by a type library doesn't necessarily have anything to do with ActiveX. Here are a couple of handy examples to show you how you might use type libraries.

Removing *Declare* Statements

You might have noticed that throughout this book we generally prefix Windows API calls with *Win* to show that the routine being called is in Windows, that it's an API call. You've also seen how to make these calls using *Alias* within the declaration of the routine. (*Alias* allows you to rename routines.) Here *BringWindowToTop* is being renamed *WinBringWindowToTop*:

```
Declare Function WinBringWindowToTop Lib "user32" Alias _
"BringWindowToTop" (ByVal hwnd As Long) As Long
```

However, we could use a type library to do the same thing. Here's an entire type library used to do just that:

APILIB.ODL

```
// The machine name for a type library is a GUID.
[uuid(9ca45f20-6710-11d0-9d65-00a024154cf1)]

library APILibrary
{
    [dllname("user32.dll")]

    module APILibrary
    {
        [entry("BringWindowToTop")] long stdcall
            WinBringWindowToTop([in] long hWnd);
    };
};
```

MAKEFILE

```
apilib.tlb : apilib.odl makefile
    mktyplib /win32 apilib.odl
```

The MAKEFILE is used to create the TLB file given the ODL file source code. To run MAKEFILE, invoke NMAKE.EXE. If you don't have NMAKE.EXE, simply run MkTypLib from a command prompt like this:

```
mktyplib /win32 apilib.odl
```

The type library contains a description of an interface in APILibrary named WinBringWindowToTop. Once you have compiled the library, run Visual Basic and go to References on the Project menu. Click the Browse button to find the APILIB.TLB file, and then select it, as shown in Figure 8-4.

FIGURE 8-4

*Visual Basic's
References
dialog box*

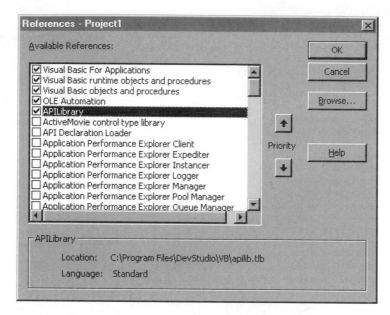

Click OK and press F2 to bring up Visual Basic's Object Browser, which is shown in Figure 8-5.

FIGURE 8-5

*APILibrary
displayed in
Visual Basic's
Object
Browser*

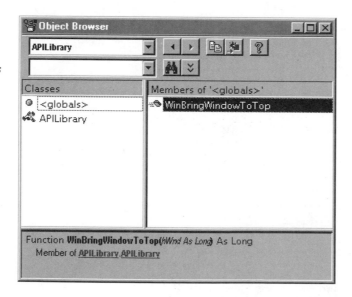

In Figure 8-5, notice that the method *WinBringWindowToTop* seems to be defined in a module and a server, both named APILibrary. Notice also that we have access to the syntax of the method. (The ToolTip Help in Visual Basic will also display correctly for this method.) To use the method (which is really a function in USER32.DLL), all we have to do is enter code. No DLL declaration is now required (and so none can be entered incorrectly).

```
Call WinBringWindowToTop(frmMainForm.hWnd)
```

Another useful addition to a type library is named constants. Here's a modified APILIB.ODL:

```
[uuid(9ca45f20-6710-11d0-9d65-00a024154cf1)]

library APILibrary
{

[dllname("user32.dll")]

module WindowsFunctions
{
    [entry("BringWindowToTop")] long stdcall
        WinBringWindowToTop([in] long hWnd);
    [entry("ShowWindow"     )] long stdcall
        WinShowWindow       ([in] long hwnd, [in]
    long nCmdShow);
};

typedef
[
        uuid(010cbe00-6719-11d0-9d65-00a024154cf1),
        helpstring
        ("WinShowWindow constants - See SDK ShowWindow for more.")
] enum
{
    [helpstring("Hides the window; activates another"        )]
            SW_HIDE          = 0,
    [helpstring("Maximizes the window"                       )]
            SW_MAXIMIZE      = 3,
    [helpstring("Minimizes the window; activates next window")]
            SW_MINIMIZE      = 6,
    [helpstring("Activates the window"                       )]
            SW_RESTORE       = 9,
    [helpstring("Activates/displays (current size and pos)"  )]
            SW_SHOW          = 5,
    [helpstring("Sets window state based on the SW_ flag"    )]
            SW_SHOWDEFAULT   = 10,
```

>>

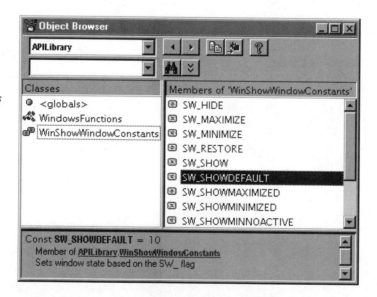

```
    [helpstring("Activates window - displays maximized"    )]
            SW_SHOWMAXIMIZED  = 3,
    [helpstring("Activates window - displays minimized"    )]
            SW_SHOWMINIMIZED  = 2,
    [helpstring("Displays  window minimized"               )]
            SW_SHOWMINNOACTIVE = 7,
    [helpstring("Displays  window to current state."       )]
            SW_SHOWNA         = 8,
    [helpstring("Displays  window (current size and pos)"  )]
            SW_SHOWNOACTIVATE = 4,
    [helpstring("Activates and displays window"            )]
            SW_SHOWNORMAL     = 1,
} WinShowWindowConstants;

};
```

The library (APILibrary) now contains two sections, WindowsFunctions and WinShowWindowConstants, as shown in Figure 8-6.

FIGURE 8-6

APILibrary with named constants displayed in Visual Basic's Object Browser

The long numbers [uuid(9ca45f20-6710-11d0-9d65-00a024154cf1)] used in the ODL file are GUIDs (Globally Unique IDs). (See Chapter 1, page 32, for more detailed information on GUIDs.) The Visual Basic 5 CD contains, in the directory \TOOLS\IDGEN, the UUIDGEN.EXE and GUIDGEN.EXE utilities required for generating GUIDs. Just for your interest, here's a small Visual Basic program that'll generate IDs for you. No matter how many times you run this program (which outputs a GUID for each button click), it will never produce the same GUID twice!

Declaration Section

```
Option Explicit

Private Type GUID
    D1          As Long
    D2          As Integer
    D3          As Integer
    D4(8)       As Byte
End Type

Private Declare Function WinCoCreateGuid Lib "OLE32.DLL" _
Alias "CoCreateGuid"(g As GUID) As Long
```

CreateGUID

```
Public Function CreateGUID() As String

    Dim g           As GUID
    Dim sBuffer     As String
    Dim nLoop As Integer

    Call WinCoCreateGuid(g)

    sBuffer = PadRight0(sBuffer, Hex$(g.D1), 8, True)
    sBuffer = PadRight0(sBuffer, Hex$(g.D2), 4, True)
    sBuffer = PadRight0(sBuffer, Hex$(g.D3), 4, True)
    sBuffer = PadRight0(sBuffer, Hex$(g.D4(0)), 2)
    sBuffer = PadRight0(sBuffer, Hex$(g.D4(1)), 2, True)
    sBuffer = PadRight0(sBuffer, Hex$(g.D4(2)), 2)
    sBuffer = PadRight0(sBuffer, Hex$(g.D4(3)), 2)
    sBuffer = PadRight0(sBuffer, Hex$(g.D4(4)), 2)
    sBuffer = PadRight0(sBuffer, Hex$(g.D4(5)), 2)
    sBuffer = PadRight0(sBuffer, Hex$(g.D4(6)), 2)
    sBuffer = PadRight0(sBuffer, Hex$(g.D4(7)), 2)

    CreateGUID = sBuffer

End Function
```

PadRight0

```
Public Function PadRight0( _
                    ByVal sBuffer As String _
                    , ByVal sBit As String _
                    , ByVal nLenRequired As Integer _
                    , Optional bHyp As Boolean _
                    ) As String

    PadRight0 = sBuffer & _
                sBit & _
                String$(Abs(nLenRequired - Len(sBit)), "0") & _
                IIf(bHyp = True, "-", "")

End Function
```

Command1_Click Event Handler

```
Private Sub Command1_Click()

    Print CreateGUID

End Sub
```

Notice that the optional Boolean argument in *PadRight0* is set to False if it is missing in Visual Basic 5; that is, it is never actually missing. (See *IsMissing()* in the Visual Basic 5 online help.) In Visual Basic 5, an optional argument typed as anything other than Variant is never missing. An integer is set to 0, a string to "" a Boolean to False, and so on. Bear this in mind if you really need to know whether or not the argument was passed. If you do, you'll need to use *Optional Thing As Variant* and *IsMissing()*. Even in Visual Basic 4 an object is never really missing; rather, it is set to be of type vbError (as in *VarType* will yield 10). I've no idea what the error's value is.

How **D**oes the **Y**ear **2**000 **P**roblem **A**ffect **V**isual **B**asic?

Mark is a TMS Associate specializing in client/server developments for corporate clients. He has 15 years' experience in IT and has been using Visual Basic since its introduction. Mark is heavily involved with the Year 2000 problem and its potential effect on Visual Basic applications. Having reviewed hundreds of thousands of lines of Visual Basic code, Mark says that he never again wants to see a date string in Visual Basic code as long as he lives! Mark is a Microsoft Visual Basic Certified Professional.

CHAPTER

9

What, you might ask, is the Year 2000 topic doing in a Visual Basic book? Isn't the Year 2000 problem (or the Millennium Bug, as the media like to call it—even though the new millennium doesn't actually begin until 2001) a mainframe problem for COBOL programmers to fix? I'll answer both these questions in this chapter. So even if you've never heard of the Year 2000 (frequently referred to as Y2K) issue, read on. If you've heard of it but always assumed that it wasn't a problem in Visual Basic, also read on: you might be in for a surprise.

THE PROBLEM

When the clock strikes midnight on New Year's Eve, 1999, millions of computer programs throughout the world will interpret the date January 1, 2000, as 01/01/00, ignoring the century part (the digits "20"). As a result, the majority of those programs will assume that the date is January 1, 1900. For a program to interpret the date January 1, 2000, correctly, it would need to view this date as 01/01/2000.

January 1, 1900! We were expecting a new year that would inspire such twenty-first-century hopes as witnessing long-distance space travel, experiencing matter transportation (beam me up, Scotty!), and possibly monitoring the first time travelers. What we will be faced with instead are millions of computer programs that will fling us backward in history, to 1900—a time that had barely seen the introduction of the motor car and the radio. Televisions and, more important, computers were still just a spark in someone's imagination.

Can you imagine what kind of effect such a step backward could have? Try to picture the world without computers! How would you go about your everyday life with no computers? Consider the following scenario, which, although pessimistic, is not beyond the realm of possibility.

You have to return to work on Tuesday, January 4, 2000. You need to drive to work, but your car's gas tank is nearly empty, so you drive to the gas station. Unfortunately, the gas station has no gasoline to sell you because no one ordered a delivery for 100 years ago! So you take the train, which is delayed because the engineer had trouble finding enough gasoline to get to work too. You arrive at work a few hours late. When you get there, you discover that the office has been burgled; the computer-controlled security system opened all the front doors on Saturday, believing that it was Monday, January 1, 1900.

You finally get to your desk and power up your PC. Everything on it seems to be working normally, and you thank your lucky stars that the Millennium Bug didn't strike your personal computer. When you try to call up a list of all unpaid invoices that need to be paid this month, the computer doesn't return anything. (After all, how many invoices do you have for January 1900?) So you postpone paying the invoices and move on to checking the delivery orders from your suppliers. That batch of widgets that should have arrived today hasn't turned up, so you call the dispatcher from the delivery company, who tells you that the phone lines have been burning up with disgruntled clients who haven't received today's order. He closes with, "I don't know what could've gone wrong. The computer handles all our scheduling, and we've never had this problem before!"

In the afternoon, you receive an e-mail message from the payroll department explaining that you won't be paid this month because, according to the computer, you haven't started working for the company yet. Panicky, you call the bank to arrange a quick loan; the loan officer asks for your birth date and then puts you on hold. She comes back on the phone and says that your request for a loan has been declined because the computer says the birth date you gave is not valid.

How Does the Year 2000 Problem Affect Visual Basic?   Chapter

9

On your way home, you decide to get some cash from the bank to tide you over. Unfortunately, the bank has experienced a wild rush by customers in situations similar to yours and has run out of cash. In desperation, you try the automatic teller machine—but it's out of operation because of "computer problems."

After a week or so, your company is unable to pay its invoices or its staff (despite last-ditch attempts to run the accounting department manually). More important, the company's customers are also unable to pay their way. Your company crashes, and you lose your job.

The national economy is just as bleak. The stock market has lost all confidence in the ability of companies to survive and suffers a massive crash, losing billions.

OK, all of this doom and gloom probably sounds way over the top; but I have a theory when it comes to the concept of chance: "If it can happen, eventually it will happen." In other words, in the interest of your company's survival, don't leave anything to chance when it comes to preparing for the year 2000. The best possible outcome would be that all rogue Y2K programs are fixed by the turn of the century and that any problems are confined to minor glitches that companies can handle internally. The worst-case scenario would be that some internal security mechanism at a nuclear silo would fail and the bombs would start flying, causing mass destruction and another world war.

I apologize if I've thoroughly depressed you! But I want to make sure you understand that the Year 2000 problem has implications for all developers, regardless of whether we program in COBOL, Visual Basic, or some other language. I'll spend the rest of this chapter preparing you to deal with the Y2K problem as it relates to Visual Basic.

How Does the Y2K Problem Affect Visual Basic?

For a while now, people have assumed that mainframe/legacy programs and applications built using COBOL were the only areas likely to be affected by the Y2K problem. Let's look at a bit of history to see why this assumption came about.

During the 1960s and 1970s, data storage space was not inexpensive. In an effort to conserve space, the practice of storing dates without the century part became accepted. This resulted in dates being represented in formats such as DDMMYY, MMDDYY, and YYMMDD.

At the time, developers understood the consequences of not storing the century part of a date; they just didn't really believe that those COBOL programs would still be around by the year 2000. But the fact is that in many companies those thirty-year-old programs are still alive and kicking—even worse, in many cases they are the fundamental, central components for systems that have grown into enormous core business applications.

It's probably fair to say that only about 3 percent of the world's business applications are written in Visual Basic, and thus it's understandable that the main focus of Y2K attention is on COBOL and other such older, more widely used languages. However, this still leaves hundreds of thousands of Visual Basic applications that are critical to the functionality and survival of many companies. Ignoring the Y2K threat from Visual Basic applications on the basis of the fact that they make up only a fraction of potentially lethal languages is rather like putting a new application into production having tested only 95 percent of its functionality: "It should be OK; we've tested most of it."

Another popular myth is that applications written in Visual Basic and other modern programming languages are automatically Year 2000 compliant. This assumption is based on the fact that modern languages (including Visual Basic) have intrinsic date-handling functions and specific data types for dates that when used correctly will yield Year 2000–compliant results.

On the face of it, it's reasonable to assume that Visual Basic is a Y2K-friendly language. In all fairness to Microsoft, Visual Basic is very good at handling dates. The Microsoft TechNet document *How the Year 2000 Affects Microsoft Product Date Fields* has this to say on the subject:

> By design, Microsoft products support dates well into the next century. However, even with Microsoft products it is possible for applications to perform incorrectly if developers have not used built-in date formats and functions.

So there you have it, the bottom line: Visual Basic applications will perform past the turn of the century as long as the applications have been coded with the date problem in mind. Unfortunately, the shortsightedness of the last couple of decades within the mainframe fraternity has spilled over into the PC systems of today. The symptoms of this shortsightedness are plain to see. Look around— how many PC systems can you find that accept a date from the user that includes the century part? Not many! A two-digit input date is often a user requirement simply to cut down on the number of keystrokes.

How Does the Year 2000 Problem Affect Visual Basic? CHAPTER

9

In addition to the user input problem, other external interfaces to a Visual Basic application, such as the system clock, external databases, and command-line arguments, can provide incorrectly formatted dates that will not function correctly as of the year 2000. Let's look at a simple example of how such interfaces could affect date processing.

Consider the following scenario. In a Visual Basic 3 application, a user enters a date into a text box (*txtEndDate*). The entered date is used to calculate the number of days remaining until a loan expires and subsequently to calculate the total repayment amount for the loan based on a daily payment of five dollars. Assume that the current date is July 10, 1996. (To simplify the example, the code does not validate anything.) In addition to the text box, the application's form contains a command button (*cmdCalculate*). The *cmdCalculate_Click* event looks like this:

```
Dim lDaysRemaining As Long
Dim lTotalPayment  As Long

' Calculate the number of days between today and the end
' date.
lDaysRemaining = DateDiff("d", Now, txtEndDate)

' Multiply the number of remaining days by five units to get
' the total.
lTotalPayment = lDaysRemaining * 5

' Display the number of days remaining.
MsgBox "Days remaining until expiration: " & lDaysRemaining

' Display the total amount to repay.
MsgBox "Total to pay: " & lTotalPayment
```

Try running this program under Visual Basic 3. First of all, enter 1/1/2026 into the text box, and then click the command button. If the system date on your machine is July 10, 1996, you should see that the loan has 10,767 days to run and that you have a total of $53,835 to pay.

If you enter 1/1/26 into the text box (that is, no century part), however, the number of days until the loan expires will be incorrectly calculated as –25,758 and the total repayment figure will be –$128,790.

NOTE

This example is designed to run in version 3 of Visual Basic, not version 5. If you run this example in version 5, the days will be calculated correctly whether or not you enter the century. I don't mean to imply, however, that all date processing will work in Visual Basic 5. For a more detailed discussion of the differences among versions of Visual Basic, refer to the section "The Technical Issues" later in this chapter.

It goes without saying that this example is extremely simplified, and I would certainly hope that nobody ever writes code like this! However simplistic, though, this example does prove a significant point I raised earlier: yes, Visual Basic is Year 2000 compliant, but *only* when the programmer fully understands the techniques involved in processing dates.

So in answer to the people presuming that the Y2K issue affects only mainframe and COBOL programs, I have this to say: The example just described is only the tip of the iceberg in terms of the possible nightmares Visual Basic applications could face if their developers ignore the potential for Y2K problems.

In their publication *So You Think the Year 2000 Is Just a Mainframe Problem?* the Gartner research group has this to say:

> Many organizations with a comprehensive strategy for dealing with the date crisis in mainframe applications have forgotten the hundreds, perhaps thousands, of PC applications built by end users in business units. These applications represent the core technology for business decision making and often contain suspect dates. Further, these PC applications may well pass an invalid date to a previously corrected mainframe program and re-infect the application.

> These PC applications are a ticking time bomb, just waiting for the day a date calculation for a maturity date, a due date, a payment date, or the like extends beyond Jan. 1, 2000. Although the present time is 1996, enterprises do not have 3.5 years to fix this problem: Of those applications that users insist "will be rewritten before 2000," a significant percentage contain dates that are forecasts in nature and thus extend into or beyond 2000. Enterprises must start now to deal with this impending crisis. They cannot afford to wait until all the mainframe and legacy applications are repaired and then tackle the other stuff.

I guess the question you really need to ask yourself is, "Can I be 100 percent certain that every single line of code, throughout all my Visual Basic applications, in all my systems, will manipulate dates correctly?" As you are no doubt aware from your experience with application tests, it takes only a single line of code to bring a system to its knees. Are you prepared to take that gamble?

What Should I Do, and When Should I Do It?

Having reached this point, I'm assuming that you acknowledge the Year 2000 issue coupled with Visual Basic applications as a realistic potential problem and that you're wondering what your next step should be. Besides asking, "What should I do?" you also need to rephrase the question and ask, "When should I do it?" In all truthfulness, it's probably too late already. If you make a good start soon, however, you might be able to catch up.

Don't panic if you haven't started yet—but don't delay either. Start planning your Year 2000 conversion *now!* To begin, think about the projects in your company. How many have actually been delivered on time and within budget? My guess is that more of your projects have missed their deadlines than have achieved them. With this reality in mind, perhaps you should consider performing a risk assessment exercise to prioritize your applications, starting with the applications that are fundamental to your company and working down from there.

One factor critical to the success of your conversion efforts is the availability of information systems (IS) personnel. Some sources predict that near the end of the century, the number of people available for technical positions will be very low. If every company that takes the Y2K issue seriously is working at the same time to address the problem, your company won't exactly find an abundant pool from which to choose highly skilled staff. If your Visual Basic applications handle dates of any kind, delaying your conversion project could prove to be your biggest—and last—mistake!

Simply modifying the code in your applications is just one step. You should also consider the other tasks that will impact your IS department's workload, including developing test scripts, program specifications, user documentation, help files, databases, flat files, and so on.

Think about the conversion realistically. At the moment, how long does it take to implement a major change in your current system? Exactly! The impact of the Y2K conversion project on your business will not be trivial. Application changes need to be designed, coded, tested, and implemented. All of this activity will strain your company's resources. Finding the right people for the job (if you can) will take time.

Depending on the nature of your business, you might hit the Y2K problem well before the end of the century. If your company deals with long-term data such as insurance, mortgages, and so on, you might have already experienced difficulties. So don't imagine that starting your conversion in the middle of 1999 will give you enough time to fix your Visual Basic applications.

What's My Next Step?

At this point, the Y2K issue separates into two areas: nontechnical and technical. You probably have the most experience in the technical area, which involves drilling down and fixing problems. Undoubtedly, programmers find this area more interesting than the nontechnical area. The nontechnical, or management, side of the issue includes doing the initial analysis, planning the conversion, and allocating resources for the project. Although you might consider the nontechnical side of things drawn out and dull, this area is an absolutely essential part of the whole Y2K effort. As you'll soon discover, fixing Y2K problems is not going to be cheap. Your entire effort must be planned and budgeted as accurately as possible.

Because the management issues of the Y2K problem will need to be dealt with before the programmers can get to work, let's start there.

THE MANAGEMENT ISSUES

Although this book can never replace (and doesn't pretend to) the many excellent articles available on project management, the following findings might help you deal with the specific topic of planning and managing a Year 2000 project.

Without a doubt, the most difficult challenge that will confront you will be convincing people of the gravity of the Y2K issue. I'm guessing here, but I suspect that you're not the person responsible for initiating projects, allocating resources, and generally spending the money. In fact, you might be several positions down the ladder, in which case the challenge of being taken seriously is even greater.

If you are "just a Visual Basic programmer" (no offense), you are faced with two alternatives. You can simply ignore the problem and hope that someone else within your organization deals with it. Or you can be proactive and at the forefront of bringing the issue to the attention of senior management. If you ignore the problem and it is not resolved, it is conceivable that the finger of blame could come pointing your way when the you-know-what hits the fan.

On the other hand, if you choose to convey this problem to your superiors, it is possible that no end of recognition, praise, pay raises, and promotions will be showered upon you. In short, it's your choice—you can be the villain or the hero.

Getting the Ball Rolling

Having covered the personal motivation factor, let's turn next to the issue of getting the project started. To begin with, you need to alert your superiors to this problem using the normal chain of command. If the powers that be are unwilling to accept the problem as realistic, your task changes to one of converting the nonbelievers. This could be a daunting task. The Year 2000 problem will drain the resources of even the largest company; the problem is far from straightforward. Worse still, nobody wants to explain to senior management that this project will cost millions of dollars and have no perceived benefit to the company other than keeping it alive!

One statistic that might do the trick comes from the Gartner research group and states, "Enterprises that delay dealing with the Y2K crisis in user-developed applications will see up to 60 percent of those applications fail or deliver erroneous results by the year 2000 (0.9 probability)."

If statistics don't help, there can be no more persuasive argument than actual proof. Why not build a very small applet that accepts and processes date values. Enter dates with two digits for the year (similar to what we did in the previous example), and show the results to your superiors. Build an example that clearly demonstrates how a noncompliant Visual Basic application could influence the running of your company's business.

If management still isn't convinced, find an actual Y2K bug in the source code of an existing Visual Basic application within your organization. Change the system dates or input date data to create a Y2K error. Run the application with your superiors watching. If this demonstration doesn't convince them of the seriousness of the issue, I'm afraid very little else will.

One other argument your superiors might listen to is the potential legal implications of an application failing because of a Y2K bug. Some cynics have suggested that the whole Y2K thing is nothing more than a gigantic money spinner for consultants, vendors, and the like. Although I disagree strongly with this opinion (Y2K is a real problem, believe it!), I can see one sector that will definitely jump on the bandwagon when investors start to lose money by the bucket load. You can bet your bottom dollar that the lawyers will be hot on the heels of any company that fails to ensure against a major catastrophe by not checking its mission-critical applications for Y2K compliance.

If a bank goes down because of crippled computer systems caused by the Y2K bug, who will be to blame? In past failures, it has been fashionable to fire the project manager and be done with it. Because of the possibility of immense losses, however, some industry analysts have suggested that laws will be changed in the future to punish the management of companies that neglected to take any action to fix a problem that was considered common knowledge. Companies will not be allowed to claim ignorance. The Y2K problem is receiving more and more media coverage every day.

If none of the preceding suggestions get your managers' attention, as a last resort, go for the satirical approach. Attach the following list in strategic locations around your office.

You're not working on the Year 2000 problem because...

- It's not your problem.
- You still believe in Santa Claus.
- You're using client/server applications.
- Your company can't afford it (but it can afford to go under).
- The New Year's holiday is always over a long weekend—that should give you enough time to fix the problem.
- You're moving to a paper-based office.
- How could two little digits cause so much trouble?
- Your horoscope doesn't mention anything about it.
- There are no programmers left; they're all working on the Y2K problem.
- You have company standards that deal with this sort of thing.
- You never work over the New Year's holiday.
- Your standards and QA wouldn't allow anything bad to happen.
- You deleted the Visual Basic code for your applications from your hard disk.
- You'll have a support person go in over the weekend just in case.
- You can't admit to having released software that doesn't work properly.
- You believe that the world will come to an end in 1999.
- Things are too busy at the moment.
- Your applications will have been replaced by the year 2000.
- You don't use third-party controls.

How Does the Year 2000 Problem Affect Visual Basic?   Chapter

9

- Microsoft will fix the problem.

- All your software is written by outside vendors, so the Y2K stuff won't be a problem.

- Year 2000 problem—what Year 2000 problem?

- You just can't be bothered.

- You hate this company anyway; let them suffer.

- You get a buzz from all the doom and gloom.

- The whiz kids are bound to come up with a silver bullet that will fix everything.

- You're waiting until your competition starts working on the problem.

- You're looking for a new job.

- Nobody has asked you to look into it yet.

- All your resources are tied up writing new applications.

- The Year 2000 crisis should help to strengthen your team awareness.

- You can't bear the thought of all that work.

- It's all hype.

- You've still got over two years left, so what's the rush?

- You've always thought that your company relied too much on computers anyway.

- It's a PC problem; the software won't be affected.

- You're trying to get into a more relaxed lifestyle.

- You'll get around to it any day now.

- You don't use many dates in your applications.

- You can't face telling your manager about the problem.

- You're playing it by ear.

- You'll be retired before the year 2000.

- All your applications are brand-new, so it won't be a problem.

- You've never liked New Year's Eve parties anyway.

- The Year 2000 sounds so far in the future.

- You work only with fancy buzzwords; this problem isn't attractive enough.

- It's just a job.

- You haven't heard of this problem, so it can't be true.

- You wrote your software and can't bear to admit it has a problem.
- If anything goes wrong, you'll bring in a contractor to fix it.
- You don't really need to invoice your customers for a few months.
- You don't do maintenance.
- You're planning to look into this next year.
- You believe the Y2K problem has been invented by consultants.

OK, so let's say that you've convinced management that the problem is real, and they have agreed to look into the Y2K issue. The next step is to plan your company's approach to fixing the problem. No manager will agree to allocate resources to a project unless it has a clearly defined plan that includes cost estimates, staffing requirements, and time constraints.

Having and using a solid plan will help to keep project staff and senior management focused on the tasks at hand. Any issues or slips will be noticed immediately, so the deadline should remain intact. Don't underestimate the power of planning. In the Year 2000 projects that have been completed so far, estimates suggest that about a fifth of the effort involved was in project management.

At this point, it's worth mentioning that it's imperative to appoint a Year 2000 task group or coordinator/project manager at the earliest stage. Attempting to deal with the Year 2000 problem from hundreds of directions not only will duplicate many hours of work but also might impact other divisions of the IS department outside your own. By running the project from a central location, you can group all issues and tasks under one umbrella, even if this means one person overseeing the entire IS department. Also, because the Year 2000 problem affects systems of all origins (mainframe, PC, database, and so on), a central overseer can coordinate any system integration or data sharing that might occur between systems.

In short, don't try to take on the world by yourself! It's possible that your Visual Basic applications interact with outside systems. It's also highly likely that you have no control over these external systems and therefore you are powerless to initiate any Year 2000 tests or changes within these projects. Again, get a coordinator to oversee this interaction.

Because project management is an area that most Visual Basic programmers don't come across every day, I'll try to keep the planning issues as simple and straightforward as possible. I could break down the plan into a zillion stages with billions of subtasks, but in the interest of sanity, I'll take a four-stage

How Does the Year 2000 Problem Affect Visual Basic?   Chapter

9

approach: analysis, modification, testing, and implementation. At the highest level imaginable, analysis involves figuring out what needs to be done; modification does it; testing ensures that it works; and implementation puts it back into production.

Let's take a more detailed look at each of these stages.

Stage 1: Analysis

The first task of the analysis stage should be to create an issues list. To begin with, this list can be a huge pot containing all unknown entities. Try to make the issues list a global, dynamic document so that anybody and everybody can add issues, questions, and observations to it at will. No matter how hard you try, you'll probably never think of every possible Year 2000–related issue, but the people doing the actual work will be aware of various situations and scenarios that you might never have thought of. The best way to get the ball rolling is to create the issues list yourself and then make it public. As time goes by, you can resolve or delete certain issues or convert issues to tasks.

Issues to get you started

Consider whether the following areas in your company will be affected by the Year 2000 problem.

Off-the-shelf applications   You should review off-the-shelf applications and systems that have been purchased externally. In particular, consider any third-party custom controls (VBXs, OCXs, DLLs, and so on) that might include date processing. Calendar controls are an obvious concern here.

Internally built applications   It's possible that your company has hundreds of small in-house applications for a variety of purposes. These applications are potentially dangerous because they might have been built "on the quick" and therefore might not have been subject to the usual quality control measures.

Operating systems   Regardless of the operating systems currently used within your company (Microsoft Windows 3.x, Windows 95, Windows NT, and so on), you still need to be certain that the Year 2000 problem will not adversely impact the operating system's performance. So check it out!

Databases   Your Visual Basic applications might interact with any number of external databases—local Jet databases, shared Jet databases, client/server databases, and so on. You need to ensure that any data processing that includes date values in these databases will function as expected into the year 2000.

BIOS for PC systems   I'll cover this topic a little more in a bit. For now, be aware that certain makes of PC will reset the clock date to 1980 if they are turned off before the turn of the century and then back on again after the turn of the century.

Costs of fixing the Y2K problem   Nobody knows for sure exactly how much the Y2K problem will cost to fix. Because of the likely shortage of available staff and the time involved, however, the costs are likely to double each year between now and 2000. In other words, it will cost you twice as much to fix the problem if you put it off until next year as it would if you were to begin fixing the problem now.

Most estimates making the rounds at the moment tend to consider the number of lines of code (LOC) in an application when estimating costs. At the time I wrote this chapter, between $0.50 and $1.50 per LOC was considered an acceptable estimate. So obtaining a detailed inventory of your applications will obviously help you answer the following questions so that you can better estimate the costs involved in fixing the Y2K problem:

- Does your company have enough staff available to physically check every line of code in every application in every system?
- How will you coordinate testing across your entire company's systems when most of the systems will have been changed?
- Which, if any, applications use special dates?

Some applications use special dates to indicate certain processing boundaries, such as 00/00/00 or 12/31/99. Watch for these dates, and consider their use after 1999—that is, will they still be valid?

The Y2K day-of-the-week problem   What is the Year 2000 day-of-the-week problem? This problem could affect some programs that calculate the day of the week. January 1, 2000, is a Saturday; if the Visual Basic application incorrectly defines the date as January 1, 1900, any application that relies on the day of the week will interpret this day as a Monday.

Dates in keys   Some database tables and data files use a date as the key for a record. For example, a table of appointments keyed on Customer Surname and Date would have data in the format "Smith010198," indicating that customer Smith has an appointment on January 1, 1998. If the date format of a database table or file doesn't include the century digits, all sorts of problems can occur when a user is attempting to retrieve records based on a date past December 31, 1999. Again, be sure to look for the use of dates as keys.

How Does the Year 2000 Problem Affect Visual Basic? Chapter

9

2000 as a leap year Some programmers have been known to calculate the occurrence of leap years incorrectly by not following the rule stating that when the year is the last year of a century (the year xx00) and divisible by 400, it is a leap year. See the "Leap Years" section on page 409 for a more detailed discussion of this problem.

Tools for testing Many good testing tools are available. You might save time and money by investing in a testing tool that permits automated testing, including regression tests, based on test scripts.

Key analysis tasks

Having initiated the issues list, your next step is to complete the key tasks of the analysis stage. The following subsections cover some essential tasks and also some nonessential tasks (depending on your company's situation). Draw up a list of tasks similar to those mentioned here, and execute each task in turn. Try to be rigid about sticking to the tasks. Such strictness will ensure that any deviation from the plan or any possible time slip will be noticed immediately.

Define Visual Basic date standards and rules Your company might already enforce certain programming standards. These standards probably don't cover the Year 2000 issue. With this in mind, create a standards document that deals only with the date processing within a Visual Basic application. This document can be circulated to all programmers working on the Y2K effort and used as a constant reference when they are fixing coding problems. For details and ideas about what this document should contain, see the section "The Technical Issues" later in this chapter.

Create a testing strategy Depending on the number of applications throughout your company, you could be facing possibly tens or even hundreds of conversions. In an attempt to reduce the duplication of effort, you should produce a testing strategy detailing all known conditions that could be affected by the Year 2000 problem. Refer to "The Technical Issues" section later in this chapter for ideas about what such a strategy should include.

Create a system inventory A detailed inventory is one of the best tools for estimating effort. Armed with the exact number of systems and their related metrics, you should be able to produce a detailed estimate of the effort required to fix Y2K problems.

The inventory should include such items as systems; Visual Basic projects within systems; modules (form, module, class, and so on), third-party custom controls, and DLLs used within Visual Basic projects; the number of lines of code in each project; the location of all necessary files; and so forth.

The inventory is really the main starting block for managing the conversion project. Without a detailed record of all systems in use, any attempt at estimating the required effort will be distorted.

Identify date-critical applications   Using the system inventory as a starting point, examine the program specifications or code for each Visual Basic project and identify those business-critical projects whose functionality relies on the accurate processing of date values. The likelihood here is that all your Visual Basic projects will use dates at some time or other; however, you might be able to reduce your workload by omitting projects that have absolutely no date processing from the conversion effort.

Examine external interfaces   In addition to the Visual Basic project information in the inventory, you should examine the interactions with external data sources. Any external data source accessed from a Visual Basic application should be added to the inventory. These sources include local databases, shared databases, client/server databases, data files, and so on.

Identify required skill sets   Your Visual Basic system might have been developed using programming techniques for which skills are not commonly available, such as OLE and DDE. So be sure to identify the Visual Basic programming skill set that will be a minimum requirement to work on your systems.

Complete a pilot project   Plan and implement a pilot conversion project on an existing Visual Basic application. This rehearsal will help to establish cost, time, and other resource estimates for future planning.

For this pilot project, try to use a typical Visual Basic project that represents the norm within your company. Obviously, don't pick the largest and most complex Visual Basic application to convert; the feedback data from this exercise would be misleading.

Produce estimates   Using the feedback data from the pilot project coupled with the data retrieved from the system inventory, calculate the estimated time and cost of completing the conversion project across all systems. If possible, calculate the time and cost per system, application, module, and line of code. All of this data will assist management in allocating resources to the project.

Also consider the other significant factors, aside from the number of occurrences of Date data types in the source code, that can affect cost estimates. You need to consider the ability of your staff, the availability of the original specification and analysis documents for each application, the learning curve involved if the Visual Basic application is being fixed by somebody unfamiliar with the business aspect of an application, and many other weighty factors.

How Does the Year 2000 Problem Affect Visual Basic?   Chapter

9

You also must consider the complexity of your Visual Basic source code when attempting to add time estimates for each application. You might have two applications with the same number of lines of code; however, one application might have such complex functionality and logic that it would require twice the work-hours to fix as the other application would.

Create a conversion schedule   Using the data and metrics collated so far in this stage of the project, define an overall schedule for the project that has clearly defined goals. As appropriate, ensure that the plan interacts with any planned maintenance releases.

The schedule should include the planned start and end dates for each Visual Basic project and, if applicable, should be broken down to module level. If staff availability data is on hand at this stage, add this information to the schedule as well.

Produce an analysis document   During the analysis stage of the project, you must be vigilant about documenting your findings. Without documentation, you will soon start to lose direction.

Bear in mind the possibility that somebody else might pick up your work at a later stage. If you haven't documented anything, you run the risk that your work will be duplicated or, worse yet, that certain tasks will be skipped.

Stage 2: Modification

The modification stage must be applied individually to each Visual Basic application. The first task of this stage is to identify which areas of the application require modification. This is not as easy as it sounds. You might be faced with the daunting task of finding potential problems in an application of 20,000 lines of code. You might have an easier time finding a needle in a haystack! So to start with, make a pass of the entire application while performing the following tests.

Identify possible Y2K noncompliant code

Without a doubt, this challenge will be your hardest. The only way to be 100 percent certain that you have identified all possible Y2K bugs is to scan every single line of code looking for date-type code. You're searching for any piece of code that even remotely looks like it could be involved with dates, including variables that are acted on by date functions and other variables that the values of those variables are assigned to. For a complete list of code items to look for, refer to "The Technical Issues" section later in this chapter.

Having identified all date-type code, you should then do a second pass on the code you found, looking for Y2K noncompliant logic. Without physically scanning every single line of code, you cannot (dare not!) go back to your manager and say, with hand on heart, that you can guarantee that every possible problem has been identified and fixed. The net result of this task should be a list of locations pointing to each line of Y2K noncompliant code.

You should do this job properly or not at all. What's the point of doing things halfheartedly, anyway? Remember my theory: "If it can happen, eventually it will happen." So do the job, and do it right.

Identify possible Y2K noncompliant database columns

The thing to look for here is columns in your database that either display externally or store internally dates with only two digits for the year part. Obviously, the date format depends on the makeup and structure of your database.

Be aware that it is possible for a database to store dates internally as four digits for the year part but to display them (via *Select* statements) with two digits. If this is the case, you might need to include some type of format function within the *Select* statement, depending on the style of your database.

The net result (output) of this task should be a list of database columns accessed by your Visual Basic application that might store the date incorrectly.

Identify possible Y2K noncompliant data file record fields

This task is almost identical to the preceding one. Identify which files are accessed by your Visual Basic application, and examine the files for date fields that are Y2K noncompliant. Finally, produce a list of all incorrectly formatted fields.

Identify dates in keys

While performing the preceding two tasks, you should also look out for record fields and table columns that have date values as part of the key. This technique is common in data entities used for storing time-related activities such as deliveries and appointments. For example, you might have a table that stores the details for appointments. The table might have a combination of surname and date as its key, in which case the value of a key might look like this: MAYES010196. If the date part is stored as shown here, with two digits for the year, the effect of accessing this table will be disastrous in the year 2000. So compile a list of any database tables or files that use a Y2K noncompliant date within the key.

How Does the Year 2000 Problem Affect Visual Basic? CHAPTER

9

Identify dates in hard-copy reports

Many applications produce hard-copy reports. It is a common requirement to include the date and sometimes the time in the header of a report. If the date used in a report uses only two year digits, changing the format to four year digits could have the residual effect of wrapping the printed text over a new line. You need to keep this potential problem in mind if you change the display format of years on reports from two to four. It's possible that you'll need to reformat the entire report to allow for the new length of the date field. So compile a list of all hard-copy reports that display a date containing only two digits in the year part of the date.

Identify Y2K noncompliant data input fields

Without a doubt, data input fields will be the most common area for finding potential Y2K bugs. Not many forms that I've seen require the user to enter four-digit years. In fact, in my experience, users will simply not stand for having to enter four-digit years.

You can solve this problem in one of two ways. Either you can write a function that will internally convert the user input to a four-digit year, or you can insist that all dates are input with four digits for the year.

Any function that you write to convert user input to a four-digit year will at some time need to guess the required date. It is impossible to know for sure what a user's intention was when he or she entered data into a date field. How is the application to know that 01/01/00 should be interpreted as January 1, 2000, and not January 1, 1900? As I said, you can guess the intentions, but you can't be positive. With this in mind, I would opt for the second solution: forcing the user to enter a four-digit year in all date fields. This choice might not be popular with the users, but I'm sure that a system crash on their return to work after the New Year's holiday in the year 2000 would be even less popular!

So produce a list of all input fields within your application that accept a date from the user. Bear in mind that it's not only date fields that can accept date input. Many applications use calendars to accept dates from the user. If your application uses a calendar utility, you should list this utility along with the list of date data input fields.

Produce an application detail report

Your last step in the modification stage will be to produce a report that displays all the information gathered from the previous tasks. The conversion programmer can use this report as a checklist when physically converting the application code, databases, utilities, and so on.

Convert the Visual Basic code using the defined Y2K standards

Having identified all possible problem areas, you now need to rectify these problems. In theory, since you've done most of the mule work already, this next task should be relatively simple (if only!).

Here are the tasks required when physically converting the application:

- Change all applicable reports to use a four-digit year.
- Change database columns that use a two-digit year.
- Change data file record fields that use a two-digit year.
- Redesign the key of any database table or data file record that has a two-digit year in the key.
- Change all input fields that use a two-digit year.

Although the main testing is left until the next project stage, all changes should be tested to ensure that the application continues to work as expected. Test data might need to be created or amended in order to carry out this first-time, one-off (one-time runthrough) testing.

Stage 3: Testing

Without a doubt, the testing stage is the most important of the four stages. Even if you don't convert any code, you should, at the very least, test all your Visual Basic applications to ensure that they are Y2K compliant.

If you have made changes, perform regression testing where possible, using the original test scripts for each application. If you don't have access to the original test scripts, you should attempt to test the functionality of the entire application, regardless of whether certain functionality uses date processing. This step is necessary because various changes at any level of the application could have a domino effect (for any number of reasons) on any other application functionality. Testing just the changes is not good enough.

Ensure that all test conditions and the results from all testing are well documented. Don't settle for second best!

The testing tasks and issues described in the following subsections might help you formulate your testing plan.

Test third-party controls

As I mentioned earlier, calendar controls are at the top of the hit list for potential Y2K horror stories. There are too many commercial calendar controls for this book to cover individually, and I wouldn't be surprised if many of the existing calendars are updated to new versions fairly soon.

On the subject of external vendors releasing new versions of their products in order to satisfy Year 2000 compliance, it's worth noting that many companies will simply not upgrade their existing production applications to use the newer version of a product. This refusal to upgrade often has a history; simply plugging a brand-new version of a component into a previously built application has at times proven to be unsuccessful and far from seamless—unlike advertised. One reason for these upgrading problems is the need to write code that effectively works around bugs or quirks that might exist in certain versions of a component.

I've seen situations in which version 1.0 of a component had bug X that required work-around code to achieve the original specification. When version 2.0 of the product was released and plugged into the original application, bug X no longer existed, and as a result, the original work-around code introduced new bugs into the application.

This scenario might sound strange, but I've seen it happen in large companies. No doubt, other consultants have seen similar situations. The net result of such scenarios is that many companies will leave existing applications untouched even when a new, Year 2000–compliant version of a component is released.

In addition to the wave of upgraded, bigger, better, faster components to hit the market every week, some component manufacturers will probably be working hard at developing Year 2000–compliant products for release very soon. While the motives for these gallant acts of global concern are possibly not the purest, it is worth pointing out that the legal arguments as to who is actually responsible for some Year 2000 problems are likely to last for years.

Your application's use of calendars will have been identified in the previous project stage. So if your application uses a calendar, and even if you have a new Year 2000–compliant version of that calendar, give it a real good hammering. Test all conceivable scenarios, and leave no stone unturned.

In Appendix D, you'll find a table that shows the life expectancy of various Microsoft products and the date formats used within them.

Test external interfaces

Depending on the nature of your system, your Visual Basic programs might read data that has been provided by another set of programs. Your system might even save data that will be read and used by another system. If either of these conditions applies to your system, besides testing your own applications with their own set of preprepared data, you should also strongly consider running your Year 2000 tests in conjunction with the tests being run on other systems that rely on your system or that your system relies on.

The reason for such tests should be obvious. For example, suppose that as part of your analysis and conversion you decide to change the data structure of certain dates that are stored in a database. You insert preprepared test data into the database to test your newly converted Visual Basic system (having restructured the data types), and everything comes up roses. But if no one has changed the structure of the date fields in the system supplying the dates to the database, your system will be expecting one format of date but will receive another! The same goes for systems that your system is supplying data to.

In short, communicate with the developers working on the systems providing your input, and communicate with the developers working on the systems relying on your output. (Your newly appointed Year 2000 coordinator should facilitate this communication.) Finally, test all systems side by side.

In the big world of corporate IS, you can usually count the systems that are completely autonomous on one hand. So bang your heads together and get it right!

Test data and conditions

Testing for the Year 2000 won't be like any testing you've done before. Here's why: in order to be 100 percent certain that your business can survive into the year 2000, you'll need to execute three completely separate system tests dealing with three sets of test data, and more than likely (depending on the size of your organization), each of these three tests will be in a different testing environment.

Regression test of today's production environment   Having made changes to your current system, your next task is to test that all programs function as expected for the current time frame. In other words, your business can continue to use its Visual Basic applications with no unexpected side effects.

How Does the Year 2000 Problem Affect Visual Basic?   Chapter

9

In effect, this test will ensure that the systems work exactly the same as they did when they were originally built. This test might sound counterproductive to begin with, but it's no good announcing to the world that all your applications are Year 2000 compliant if they come crashing to their knees now!

Future date testing   Having verified that your system functions correctly in the present, you'll need to create a second set of test data that will test your system's ability to cope with dates on either side of the year 2000. The particulars for this test will depend entirely on the business nature of your applications.

For example, let's suppose that your Visual Basic application maintains car insurance policies, which typically have a life cycle of 12 months. You'll need to set your system clock to some time in 1999 and run your tests, this time looking specifically for the application's ability to process car insurance policies that will expire in the year 2000.

Your business might have a shorter future date requirement, such as a long-term car parking system that has a maximum life cycle of 6 months. In this case, you would need to ensure that the system date is set to at least August 1999 so that you can adequately test processing into the year 2000.

And the list goes on. Make sure you thoroughly understand the future date capabilities and scope of your system. Then run your system so that it is forced to process future dates that are at least in the year 2000, if not later.

Running your system in the future   The final test involves gauging the ability of your applications to function in and beyond the year 2000. Set your system date to some time beyond 2000, and run your original test scripts. Don't forget that if your system processes historical information, you should have test conditions in which you've set your system clock beyond 2000 and you then force your applications to look at dates before 2000.

Leap years   Include in all three of your system tests conditions that will force your application to process the last two days in February and the first two days in March. The year 2000 is a leap year, which means that February 29, 2000, is a valid date. Don't be caught out by this one. I've seen much debate from mathematicians and rocket scientists on the correct way to calculate leap years, and I've naturally researched the subject myself thoroughly enough to conclude that 2000 is a leap year. In fact, I nearly had a fight with my neighbor the other day because he wouldn't accept that February has 29 days in the year 2000!

The point I'm trying to make here is that if superhumans and neighbors can disagree on the number of days in February 2000, so can programmers! It's possible that during the development of your Visual Basic applications, a programmer might have manually calculated (incorrectly) that the year 2000 is *not* a leap year, so be sure to test for it.

Recommended system dates   If you're lucky (or wise), you'll have already built automated testing procedures that don't require too much manual intervention. Otherwise, somebody is going to get very sore fingers! In a perfect world, I would suggest running your complete system test against the following system date years:

> 1997, 1998, 1999, 2000, 2001, 2002, 2007

Change your system date

Before we get into the techniques involved in changing your system date, be warned! Some system resources and functions are date and time sensitive and might be switched on or off when you change the system date. Before changing your system date, make sure that you understand all of the consequences. Better still, consult an expert first.

The tests you carry out with regard to the system date serve dual purposes. Not only are you testing the ability of your applications to function correctly in the year 2000 and beyond, but you are also testing how well your hardware will cope with the change. Although the hardware issue is outside the scope of this chapter, it's still an important concern, because without the hardware... Say no more!

In many cases, your system date will come from one of three places: as a date value in your database, from the clock on your server, or from the clock on your PC. Retrieving the current system date from the database is a very wise move. If your Visual Basic applications do this, resetting your system date is simply a matter of changing the value in the database. That's all there is to it. But you'll still need to test the ability of your machines to function in the year 2000, and we'll look at the steps involved with that in a moment.

If your applications retrieve the system date from the PC's clock and the PC is connected to a network, chances are that your workstation retrieves its system

How Does the Year 2000 Problem Affect Visual Basic? Chapter

9

date from the server. In this case, you should definitely consult your network administrator about changing the system date. There is one way of changing the system date without being affected by the network, and that is to disconnect the PC from the network. If you disconnect your PC, however, you will probably defeat the whole purpose of the exercise, especially with regard to testing the hardware.

If your system date is retrieved only from the PC's clock, consider the fact that on some older PCs you might not be able to set the clock beyond the year 2000. This is because the BIOS doesn't know about centuries. Whatever the case, you should run the following two tests on your PC to judge both your application's functionality and your hardware's capabilities.

System clock automatic update test   In most cases, when the clock rolls over to start the year 2000, most of us will be popping party balloons, singing, and hugging loved ones (or with my track record, lying at the bottom of the garden caressing an empty bottle of vodka!). I expect very few office PCs will actually be turned on over the New Year's holiday (although it has been suggested that companies should leave them on just in case), and even fewer Visual Basic applications will be running. In the spirit of completeness, however, you should test to find out whether your PC's clock will actually roll over. To do so, follow those steps:

1. Using the DOS DATE function, set the PC's date to 12/31/1999.
2. Using the DOS TIME function, set the PC's clock to 11:58:00.00.
3. Keep the power on.
4. Wait until the clock passes midnight.
5. Check the date to ensure that it is 01/01/2000.
6. Test your Visual Basic application (if appropriate).
7. Turn off the power.
8. Wait for a while.
9. Turn on the power.
10. Check the date to ensure that it is still 01/01/2000.
11. Just for good measure, test your Visual Basic application again (if appropriate).

System clock automatic update test after a power down The more likely scenario is that all office workers will go home on Friday evening, December 31, 1999, having switched off their machines, and will return on Tuesday, January 4, 2000. To ensure that the PC's clock will have successfully moved on to the correct date while the power was down, do this test:

1. Using the DOS DATE function, set the PC's date to 12/31/1999.
2. Using the DOS TIME function, set the PC's clock to 11:58:00.00.
3. Turn off the power.
4. Wait for at least three minutes.
5. Turn on the power.
6. Check the date to ensure that it is January 1, 2000.
7. Test your Visual Basic application (if appropriate).

There are countless more tasks and issues concerned with testing for Year 2000 compliance. I hope the issues I've raised will set you on your path toward creating the perfect test plan. The important thing is to be sensible about testing. Consider all possible scenarios, and don't cut corners.

Stage 4: Implementation

It's crunch time! Now you can find out how effective your analysis, modification, and testing really were. I know what you're thinking: "How much trouble can two little digits really cause?" Well, how many smooth, trouble-free implementations have you ever been involved in? If you've experienced more than two implementations and never had a problem, you're either the world's luckiest person or you're walking around with tight underpants over your trousers and a big red "S" on your shirt!

In all seriousness, don't expect simply to put the software back into the production environment and have a fully functional system on the first try. It goes without saying that the earlier you can get the software up and running, the more time you'll leave yourself to fix those annoying problems that always seem to crop up just as you thought it was safe to go back in the water.

Although the whole point of this conversion project is to make your applications Year 2000 compliant, you should put that aside to begin with and concentrate on ensuring that your users can continue to use the software without incident. It's quite possible that during the conversion you might have changed some

How Does the Year 2000 Problem Affect Visual Basic?   Chapter

9

input fields to accept four-digit centuries instead of two-digit centuries. In fact, from the user's perspective, this is probably all that's changed. The important thing is to communicate to the users any visible changes in the applications. Before committing your software to the production environment, be sure to consider some of the following issues that, depending on the size and context of your applications, might need to be communicated to the users.

Version change announcement

All major version changes should follow an announcement to the users regarding the changes in functionality, features, and user interface. You might not consider that changes to date data input fields warrant a major version change; however, just wait until your date field input validation fails on the users and they don't know why! Ensure that the users are aware of the changes to the system, especially the user interface changes.

Of course, it's possible that no user interface elements have changed, including date data input fields. If this is the case, the implementation should be transparent from the user's perspective—perhaps a formal announcement isn't warranted. It's my guess, however, that the whole Year 2000 issue will gain much more media attention in the near future, and you might consider it important to assure your users that their software is now Year 2000 compliant.

Documentation

If your applications rely on user documentation, you'll need to update the relevant sections on date input fields. Don't forget to update any screen shots.

Training and training material

If you already have a formal training program in place for your existing system, you'll need to update any training material that refers to dates. It might also be a good idea to build into the training a section covering the use of four-digit years. This can't do any harm and might even save a fair amount of user frustration later on. Keep in mind that users do use other software and that other software might allow them to enter short format dates even if yours doesn't.

Help files

As with user documentation, your help files will need to be brought in line with the new user interface. Again, don't forget to update any screen shots.

Some Final Words on Management Issues

No matter how large or small your system is, planning, managing, and coordinating the Year 2000 conversion project will be a big job for somebody. At times, it will be a real headache. How do you convert all that software across all those systems and departments and still manage to coordinate the code changes alongside ongoing maintenance work and possibly together with existing enhancements? Let me rephrase—it could be a nightmare! But as long as you remember to plan your work and work your plan, you should keep on the straight and narrow.

One last thing to consider before we move on to the technical side of the problem is the worst-case scenario. What do you do if it all goes horribly wrong? Any system worth its salt has an effective contingency plan. You have to ask yourself, "How can my business survive if I can't use the system?" You might be in a position to revert to a paper-based solution temporarily, until show-stopping bugs or system crashes are fixed. Then again, you might not. What will you do then? It's never pleasant to think of the worst possible situation; nevertheless, if you give it some thought now, at least you'll be prepared should your worst nightmare come true.

THE TECHNICAL ISSUES

Now it's time to explore the technical issues involved with the Visual Basic language and various other date handling issues—the nuts and bolts of the Year 2000 problem. The structure of this section will be less apparent than that of the last because the areas that need to be addressed cover a much wider scope. In addition to examining the Visual Basic date type intrinsic functions, you'll need to cross-reference those functions against each of the last three major releases of Visual Basic (versions 3, 4, and 5), and where appropriate, you'll need to cross-reference again against the various data types that those functions will act on (String, Variant, Date, and so on).

Data Types

Without a doubt, the single most contributing factor to a Visual Basic application that is Year 2000 noncompliant will be the incorrect usage of data types. Regardless of how many applications I review, I'm still never quite prepared for the total lack of understanding displayed by experienced

How Does the Year 2000 Problem Affect Visual Basic?   CHAPTER

9

programmers who assign date values to the String data type and process all their dates using only strings. You'd think that people would have gotten the message when Microsoft introduced the V_DATE(7) Variant data type, which is used specifically for maintaining dates. And later, when the fully fledged Date data type was made available, did people do the right thing and stop using the String date type? No! People continue to use string variables to maintain dates.

Finding and replacing the date strings in your Visual Basic applications should be your number one priority. As you'll see later, anyone who has taken the time to research and use the Date data type [and Variant(7)] will now be reaping the benefits of their foresight because these data types are far more prepared for the change of the century than are strings. Those of you who continued to use strings after Variants and dates became available now have a lot of work to do.

Let's look at some of the reasons why strings continue to be used over their date and Variant cousins.

Variant ignorance is rampant

Now is not the time to point the finger of blame. However! It's quite possible that your programmers just aren't aware that they shouldn't be storing dates as strings. With this in mind, let's take a whirlwind tour of the correct data types to use.

In Visual Basic 3, the Variant data type can be used to store dates of all shapes and sizes. Once a Variant contains a valid date, its VarType (the type of data that it contains) has the value 7 (or constant V_DATE in Visual Basic 3, vbDate in versions 4 and 5).

Date variants exhibit a unique behavior in that they expose their value externally in the format of a short date, but internally they store the value as a double-precision number. For example, try the following snippet of code in Visual Basic 3, and check out the two values for one variable:

```
Dim vDate As Variant
Dim sDate As String
vDate = CVDate("2/2/1996")
sDate = "2/2/1996"
MsgBox "As a Date, I look like: " & vDate
MsgBox "But internally, I look like: " & CDbl(vDate)
MsgBox "Adding 1, I look like this: " & vDate + 1
' This line will error.
MsgBox "But the string...: " & sDate + 1
```

Notice that the *CDbl* function shows the internal representation of the Variant date variable. This internal representation is the reason you're able to accomplish simple arithmetic on the variable without having to subject it to any special conversion. If you want the last line of code above to work, you'll need to convert the string to a date using the *CVDate* function.

Visual Basic versions 4 and 5 move the whole date-handling process one stage ahead by using the Date data type. This is not a Variant of type 7 but an actual data type in its own right. The Date data type is similar to the Variant(7) data type in the way that it exposes its external value as a date but internally processes itself as a double-precision number.

A few points about both Variant dates and Date data types are noteworthy. When the value of a date is exposed externally, it takes on the formatting characteristics of the short date format used by your system. For example, the standard short date format is MM/dd/yy. If you assign the value *3/17/1964* to a date variable (my birthday—all cards, cash, and so on accepted!) and then examine the variable, it has the external value *03/17/64*. In other words, the year part of the date is displayed as a two-digit date, even though I explicitly assigned a four-digit year to the variable. Because the short date format of my system uses only two-year digits, this is how the Date data type will look regardless of the format of the value assigned to it. This thinking that the Date data type won't store dates correctly could be another reason why programmers have not used it. Remember that internally the value is stored as a double, so it always knows which century it's in.

The internal double value is actually the number of days since December 31, 1899, with the value 1 representing December 31, 1899; 2 representing January 1, 1900; and so on. If you move backward in time, the value starts counting down to a negative number. So if you try the code

```
Dim vDate As Variant
vDate = CDbl(CVDate("1/1/1899"))
MsgBox vDate
```

in Visual Basic 3, the value displayed will be –363 (locale permitting).

In Visual Basic 3, you should use the CVDate function to convert an expression to a Variant of type V_DATE(7). In Visual Basic 4 and 5, however, you can use the CDate function, which will convert an expression to a Date data type and not a Variant of type Date. This difference is subtle but useful to know.

Similarly, the *DateValue* function will return the Variant date value of an expression, not the Date data type value.

How Does the Year 2000 Problem Affect Visual Basic? Chapter

9

Most dates are stored or start as strings

Another popular reason for using strings to store date values is that most dates start life as a string and, in some cases, are displayed externally as strings. This flawed logic maintains that if the data type of a date value is a string, it should be maintained as such.

An example of this logic is accepting dates from a text box. The default data type of any value in a text box is String. So when assigning a text box date value to a variable, many programmers inadvertently assign the value to a string variable. The same excuse is given for dates stored on disk files and for some databases that expose dates as strings.

For all the previous examples, the correct technique is to convert or assign the string value to a date or Variant(7) variable at the earliest opportunity.

Performance freaks advise against Variants

Most articles that discuss such topics as improving performance and tuning code preach that using Variants is bad. In most cases, this is good advice because a Variant takes up more storage space than other dedicated data types do and often requires more processing muscle to move the data around.

The downside to this advice is that it puts many people off using Variants for life. I once asked a programmer why he had used a string to store a date instead of a Variant(7) and was told that his project recently went through a "firefighting" exercise to tune the code, and all Variants had been converted to their "real" data types. The fact that the date value in question was used only about nine times in the whole program didn't occur to him.

The point to remember here is that the Variant(7) and Date data types were introduced to provide more efficient and, above all, more accurate date handling. If somebody gives you a lighter, will you continue to rub sticks to make fire?

COBOL habits die hard!

COBOL is the language in which the majority of the Year 2000 problems will originate. This is simply because it's the language in which most of the business applications throughout the world today were written.

Many Visual Basic programmers will have come to Visual Basic from the mainframe/COBOL environment, in which there are only two real data types: strings and numbers. In COBOL, you can declare a date much the same way that you would declare a user-defined type of strings in Visual Basic (mm, dd, yy, and so on).

This isn't "have a go at COBOL" time. Rather, I bring this up because I've known programmers to use strings over Variants and dates because "that's the way I've always done it." This really brings us full circle to my original point about ignorance. Many programmers are simply unaware that the Variant(7) and Date data types are out there and ready to be used.

DateValue and *CDate* are not the same

DateValue and *CDate* (or *CVDate* in Visual Basic 3) are extremely useful functions for processing any type of date data in Visual Basic. The differences between the two functions are not always clear, however. Both functions accept date expressions as an argument and return a Variant(7) or a Date data type that is stored internally as a date serial number (or double-precision number). I'm often asked which function should be for which purpose.

As far as I can tell (and please correct me if you know better), there are two main differences between the conversion functions: how they deal with time and the types of input expressions they can process.

Time   *CDate* (or *CVDate*) will convert the time portion of a date expression whether it's included with a date or the expression consists of just a time value on its own. *DateValue* will ignore the time portion unless the time is invalid, in which case *DateValue* will raise an error.

Converted expressions   The *DateValue* function expects its input to look like dates, whereas *CDate* or *CVDate* will convert any expression that could be considered a date. The main expression that springs to mind here is the date serial number. As you learned earlier, a Variant(7) or date variable has an internal representation of its date value. That internal representation is sometimes called a date serial number. This serial number can be broken into two parts: the whole number and the fraction. Any value to the left of the decimal point is interpreted as the number of days passed since December 31, 1899. Any number to the right of the decimal point represents the time as a fraction of the 24-hour clock. For example, the value 0.5 represents noon. If you pass the *DateValue* function a value of 1, you'll get a "Type Mismatch" error. However, the *CDate* and *CVDate* functions will return *12/31/89* (depending on the locale setting on your computer).

These differences are subtle, but they might help you understand the programmer's intentions when converting your existing Visual Basic code.

How Does the Year 2000 Problem Affect Visual Basic? Chapter

9

Leap Years

Many words have been written offering the correct formula for calculating whether or not a particular year is a leap year. I don't intend to add fuel to the debate other than to demonstrate the following formula, which as it happens is the correct and only formula that should be used.

Before showing the code, it's worth mentioning that given the correct date, Visual Basic will figure it all out for you anyway. I can think of only a few rare cases that would genuinely require a separate leap-year algorithm. In the spirit of completeness, however, here goes.

The magic numbers are 4, 100, and 400. The golden rule for calculating a leap year has three parts:

1. If the year is divisible by 4, it's a leap year.

2. But—if the year is also divisible by 100, it's not a leap year.

3. Double but—if the year is also divisible by 400, it is a leap year.

The code to represent this formula in a function would look something like this:

```
Function bIsLeapYear(ByVal inYear As Integer) As Boolean
    bIsLeapYear = ((inYear Mod 4 = 0) _
            And (inYear Mod 100 <> 0) _
            Or (inYear Mod 400 = 0))
End Function
```

So now you have the proof. The year 2000 *is* a leap year. The year 1900 was *not* a leap year. The year 1600 was a leap year.

With respect to the people who know a lot more about this subject than I do, there are some issues regarding dates earlier than 1600 and later than 3000. I suggest that if you're genuinely interested in dates spanning that wide a range, you consult your local expert.

Date Window

Visual Basic 5 improves on the internal date processing of versions 3 and 4 by employing what is sometimes referred to as a *date window* or *date windowing technique.* In a nutshell, when presented with a date consisting of only two digits for the year, Visual Basic will assume that any year greater than 29 is in the 1900s and any date below 30 is in the 2000s. For example, given the year 97, because it's greater than 29, Visual Basic will assume the date to be (and convert it to) 1997. On the other hand, given the year 12, because it's less than 30, Visual Basic will assume it represents 2012.

This is definitely a step in the right direction for many corporations and will go a long way toward minimizing the impact of the year 2000 on Visual Basic applications. Before porting all your existing applications to Visual Basic 5 and forgetting about the whole Y2K issue, however, you should bear in mind the implications that a fixed date window, such as 1930, can have.

Obviously, depending on the nature of your applications and the scope of any date processing that your applications might handle, I'd be very cautious before committing a Visual Basic application to be Year 2000 compliant without thoroughly investigating each line of code and testing the application to the hilt. Consider the example in Listing 9-1, which isn't necessarily a business application but nonetheless demonstrates the dangers of presuming the context of an application and not supplying a user-defined, sliding-date–range window. This code is used to determine whether the user can afford his or her dream home at retirement age. The subject could just as easily be a pension plan, an insurance policy, an application, and so on. Enter the information required as you are prompted. Try this a number of times using different dates with two-digit years, both before and after 20 (1/1/18, 1/1/42). This sample is available on the companion CD in CHAP09\DateTest.bas.

LISTING 9-1

Using Visual Basic 5's date window in calculating retirement information

```
' ************************************************************************
' *
' * Purpose - To retrieve details concerning the user's planned
' *           savings, interest rate, retirement date, and the
' *           cost of the dream retirement home.  After this is
' *           done, a function will be called to determine
' *           whether the user can afford the dream retirement
' *           home.
' *
' *           Finally, a message will be displayed
' *           indicating whether the home can be afforded.
' *
' * Author - Mark Mayes (TMS)
' *   Date - 09/09/1996
' *
' * Inputs - None
' * Outputs - None
' * Returns - None
' *
```

How Does the Year 2000 Problem Affect Visual Basic?   Chapter

9

Listing 9-1

>>

```
' *    Notes - The point of this program is to demonstrate the
' *            use of VB5's date window. Any two-digit year
' *            greater than '29' is interpreted as being in the
' *            twentieth century; that is, 34 is treated as 1934.
' *            Any date less than 30 is interpreted as
' *            being in the twenty-first century; that is,
' *            12 is treated as 2012.
' *
' *            When running this program, experiment with
' *            entering different retirement dates. Vary the
' *            number of year digits from two to four, and enter
' *            various dates either side of "30," be it 1930 or
' *            2030.
' *
' *            Please note that because this is a simple demonstration,
' *            there is absolutely NO validation of user input in the
' *            program, so it is VERY easy to break!
' ****************************************************************
Sub Main

Dim fMonthlySavings As Single    ' The amount to be saved
Dim fAPR             As Single   ' The annual % rate
Dim dteRetirementDate As Date    ' The retirement date
Dim curCostOfHome    As Currency ' Retirement home cost
Dim fSavings         As Single   ' Amount that will be
                                 ' saved

' Retrieve from the user the amount that can be saved each
' month.
fMonthlySavings = InputBox("Monthly Savings")

' Retrieve from the user the annual percentage rate on the
' savings.
fAPR = InputBox("Enter the expected annual percentage rate.")

' Retrieve from the user the date of retirement.
dteRetirementDate = InputBox("What is your retirement date?")

' Retrieve from the user the cost of the dream retirement home.
curCostOfHome = InputBox("How much is the retirement home?")

' Call the function to establish whether the home can be
' afforded.
```

>>

LISTING 9-1

```
If mbCanIAffordIt(fMonthlySavings, _
                  fAPR, _
                  dteRetirementDate, _
                  curCostOfHome, _
                  fSavings) Then
    ' The home CAN be afforded, so display a happy message.
    MsgBox "Whoopee! - As you will have saved " _
        & Format(fSavings, "Currency") _
        & ", you CAN afford your dream retirement home."
Else
    ' The home can NOT be afforded, so display a sad message!
    MsgBox "Boohoo! - As you will have saved only " _
        & Format(fSavings, "Currency") _
        & ", you CAN'T afford your dream retirement home."
End If
End Sub




' ******************************************************************
' *
' * Purpose - Based on the input parameters, calculate
' *           whether the user's savings over the specified
' *           period of time will cover the cost of the
' *           desired item.
' *
' *  Author - Mark Mayes (TMS)
' *    Date - 09/09/1996
' *
' *  Inputs - ifMonthlySavings - The monthly savings
' *           ifAPR            - The APR on the savings
' *           idteEndDate      - The date when saving ceases
' *           icurCostOfItem   - The cost of the desired item
' *
' * Outputs - iofSavings       - The total amount that will
' *                                 have been saved
' *
' * Returns - True if the desired item can be afforded.  False
' *           otherwise.
' *
' *   Notes - I'm not a financial whiz kid!!!  The interest
' *           calculations are probably all wrong.  However,
```

LISTING 9-1

>>

```
' *            the point of the function is to watch for the
' *            date calculations.
' *
' *            Please note that because this is a simple demonstration,
' *            there is absolutely NO validation of user input in the
' *            program, so it is VERY easy to break!
' ******************************************************************
Private Function mbCanIAffordIt(ByVal ifMonthlySavings _
                               As Single, _
                               ByVal ifAPR As Single, _
                               ByVal idteEndDate As Date, _
                               ByVal icurCostOfItem _
                               As Currency, _
                               ByRef iofSavings As Single) _
                               As Boolean

    Dim nNumberOfPayments As Integer ' Calculated payments

    ' Establish whether a positive APR was entered.
    If ifAPR > 0 Then
        ' Yes, we have an APR, so convert it to a monthly
        ' percentage rate.
        ifAPR = (ifAPR / 100) / 12
    End If

    ' Calculate the number of monthly payments remaining until
    ' saving ceases.

    ' Notice that we are attempting to force the end date to a
    ' four-digit year.
    nNumberOfPayments = DateDiff("m", Now, _
                                Format(idteEndDate, _
                                       "dd/mm/yyyy"))

    ' Calculate the total amount that will be saved.
    iofSavings = FV(ifAPR, nNumberOfPayments, _
                    -ifMonthlySavings)

    ' Set the return code of this function depending on whether
    ' or not the total savings meet or exceed the cost of the
    ' desired item.
    mbCanIAffordIt = iofSavings >= icurCostOfItem

End Function
```

Needless to say, the code in Listing 9-1 won't win any prizes for its complexity, but it does demonstrate the very real danger attached to the date window used in Visual Basic 5. So don't assume that all your troubles are over. You'll still need to check all your applications before giving them the Year 2000–compliant seal of approval.

How OLEAUT32.DLL affects the date window

The date window functionality in Visual Basic 5 is actually due to the mechanics of version 2.2 of a file named OLEAUT32.DLL. (At the time of this writing, the latest version of this floating around The Mandelbrot Set was 2.20.4054, which describes itself as "Microsoft OLE 2.20 for Windows NT(TM) and Windows 95(TM) Operating Systems.") This is a system file that comes with Windows and is also distributed by applications that use the DLL, including Visual Basic 5. The earlier version (2.1) of the file is installed with Windows 95 and does not contain the date window functionality.

One very important point to consider regarding the version of this file is the question of compatibility. As it stands, Visual Basic 4 doesn't include any date window functionality when using version 2.1 of the file. However, if your version of this file is overwritten by a newer version, your Visual Basic 4 applications will all of a sudden start to display this windowing behavior. This change in behavior occurs because the file is a system file, and as such its functionality is not exclusive to Visual Basic. The Microsoft Knowledge Base article "Years 01–29 Default to Year 2000 When Typed as M/D/YY" (Article ID: Q155669) refers to this exact problem and points out that the new version of OLEAUT32.DLL is installed with Microsoft Internet Explorer 3 and Microsoft Windows NT 4.

I don't know what the outcome of this version compatibility issue will be, but for the time being, consider the following highly likely scenario: On machine A, which has version 2.1 of OLEAUT32.DLL, you develop a Visual Basic 4 application that includes some work-around code to deal with dates and centuries. Now you distribute your new application, and it is installed on machine B, which just happens to have version 2.20.4049 of OLEAUT32.DLL because the user recently installed Microsoft Internet Explorer 3. Your Visual Basic 4 application will now start to make assumptions about the context of dates and centuries that you were not prepared for.

Let's hope that this possible conflict is cleared up by the time this book is published. If not, remember that you've been warned.

Writing your own date window

In implementing the date window at the year 1930, Microsoft has attempted to satisfy the likely date requirements of most corporate Visual Basic applications. Despite the obvious good intentions of this solution, however, it's only a second guess at your business functionality and cannot possibly be all things to all people.

In addition, the windowing technique employed by Visual Basic 5 is a fixed window, which never changes, as opposed to a more dynamic sliding-window technique, which in addition to moving with the times will permit a wider future or historic date range than the 100 years offered by the static system in some flavors of the algorithm. Consider some of the disadvantages of the fixed window:

- Should your application need to process dates beyond a 100-year range, the fixed-window technique will not adequately calculate the desired date. In general, people are leading healthier lifestyles (discounting myself, of course!), and the average age expectancy is creeping up all the time. It's not unreasonable to expect your applications to deal with records of people who exceed the age of 100. Consider how a fixed-window technique would affect your applications under these circumstances.

- Without a doubt, any application using a fixed-window technique that is still around in a few decades (don't you dare say, "Remember what they said in the 1970s") will require manual code changes to continue functioning correctly. Suppose your particular Visual Basic application keeps going for another forty years. How will programmers in the year 2037 relate to Visual Basic? Will there still be programmers in the year 2037? Or will they have developed an organically engineered plug-in-person component by then?

- If it's only your processing that changes and not your data, any system that your fixed-window application supplies data to must make the same windowing assumptions that your application does. To a certain extent, this is also true of a sliding-window technique, but at least this disadvantage is more manageable under those conditions.

To be certain that your application will function as expected for the entire range of dates needed by your business, ideally you should develop your own sliding date window functions.

Intrinsic Date Functions

In the remainder of this chapter, we'll explore each of Visual Basic's intrinsic date-handling functions and any possible Year 2000 issues that could arise through their use. You might want to use this list as a conversion programmer's reference or checklist when executing your Year 2000 conversions.

Date quirks

Before looking at each intrinsic function, I'll address a few quirks common to most of Visual Basic's date functions.

Regional settings The first of these funnies involves exceptions in the way that Visual Basic determines whether or not a given date is valid. The format of the date argument must adhere to a predefined set of rules. This exception is true regardless of your regional settings. For example, suppose your long date format defined in the regional settings looks something like "ddd, dd MMMM, yyyy." This means that any date used as an argument to Visual Basic's *Format* function with the format *Long Date* will end up looking something like "Sun, 06 October, 1996". So far, everything is perfectly valid and aboveboard. Now try using this formatted date as an argument to one of Visual Basic's intrinsic date functions, such as *CVDate* or *CDate*, and see what happens. You will receive an error 13, "Type Mismatch." In short, Visual Basic does not like overcustomized dates.

How Does the Year 2000 Problem Affect Visual Basic?   Chapter

9

As far as I've been able to tell, if your long date format in the regional settings has a value for weekday (that is, Monday or Mon), or if there is any value in the date separator field in the Date property page of the Regional Settings Properties property sheet (such as a comma or a slash), Visual Basic will not recognize any date expression formatted as a long date. As an example of this, try changing your long date format to "ddd, dd MMMM, yyyy" and running the following line of code:

```
MsgBox CDate(Format(Now, "Long Date"))
```

Visual Basic will give you an error 13 because it does not recognize the date as valid even though your system settings do recognize the date format.

The following long date formats will be recognized in Visual Basic:

Long Date Format	Example Date
MMMM dd, yyyy	October 06, 1996
MMM dd, yyyy	Oct 06, 1996
dd-MMM-yyyy	06-Oct-1996
dd MMMM yy	06 October 96

The following long date formats will *not* be recognized in Visual Basic:

Long Date Format	Example Date
ddd, MMMM dd, yyyy	Sun October 06, 1996
ddd MMM dd, yyyy	Sun Oct 06, 1996
dddd dd-MMM-yyyy	Sunday 06-Oct-1996
dddd dd MMMM yy	Sunday 06 October 96

Obscure regional settings   While researching the various date functions and their relation to the system settings, I came across two quirks, which both appear to be unique to Visual Basic 3. The *CVDate* and *DateValue* functions do not like any regional setting in the order year, month, day. If your short date regional setting is in this order and your long date setting isn't (or vice versa), Visual Basic 3 will not recognize as a valid date any date expression in the long date format.

This quirk can be additionally demonstrated by trying the *IsDate* function on a long date expression while the regional settings reflect the conditions above. For example, try the test on the following page.

1. Change your short date setting in your regional settings so that the order of parts is YMD.

2. Change the order of the long date regional setting to anything but YMD.

3. Try the following line of code:

```
MsgBox "The date is " & CVDate(Format$(Now, "Long Date"))
```

You should get a "Type Mismatch" error. If you try the *DateValue* function, you'll receive an "Illegal Function Call" error. If you try the *IsDate* function on the date expression above, it will return FALSE.

Another problem along the same lines is the use of a medium date format when the short date regional settings order is YMD. Visual Basic will not recognize as a valid date any date expression in the medium date format when your short date regional settings order is YMD. If you alter your regional settings to the above condition, the following line of code will error with a "Type Mismatch:"

```
MsgBox "The date is " & CVDate(Format$(Now, "Medium Date"))
```

As with the previous quirk, the *DateValue* function will error with "Illegal Function Call" and the *IsDate* function will return FALSE.

Documentation   This issue is slightly sillier; nonetheless, I have met people who were confused by the wording of certain documentation. Some documentation indicates that certain intrinsic Visual Basic functions will convert an expression to a date. Don't be misled by this statement; most functions will return a value but will not alter the original value (used as an argument) in any way. This should really go without saying, but for the benefit of people who take the documentation literally, it's worth keeping in mind. For instance, consider the following example:

```
Dim dteStartDate As Date
Dim sUserEntry As String
sUserEntry = "9/10/96"
dteStartDate = CDate(sUserEntry)
```

The argument to the *CDate* function (*sUserEntry*) is not converted, and its value does not change. Instead, the result of the *CDate* function is assigned to the *dteStartDate* variable.

CDate and *CVDate*

These two functions each return a value that can be interpreted as a date. It is preferable to "convert" any dates that might be held as strings using these functions.

How Does the Year 2000 Problem Affect Visual Basic?   CHAPTER

9

Compatibility   As mentioned previously, the *CDate* function is available only in Visual Basic 4 and 5. For Visual Basic 3, you should use the *CVDate* function. *CVDate* is provided in Visual Basic 4 and 5 for backward compatibility, although you'll probably want to steer clear of this because of the return type.

Return value   Both the *CDate* and *CVDate* functions will return a value that can be interpreted as a date. The difference is that *CDate* will return an actual Date data type, whereas *CVDate* will return a Variant(7) data type that represents a date. Because the Date data type is available in Visual Basic 4 and 5, it should always take precedence over a Variant(7); hence the use of *CDate* in Visual Basic 4 and 5 over *CVDate*.

A variable declared as a Date or Variant(7) data type that has been assigned the result of a *CDate* or *CVDate* function is unique in that it actually holds two values. To the outside world, the value is exposed as a normal date in the short date format of the system settings. Internally, however, the value is stored as a double-precision number of which the integer portion represents the number of days since December 31, 1899, and the fractional portion represents the time of the converted expression as a fraction of the 24-hour clock.

Arguments   Any expression that constitutes a valid date according to the locale settings can be used as an argument to *CDate* or *CVDate*. (See "Regional settings" at the beginning of this section.) In addition to expressions that look like dates to the naked eye, *CVDate* and *CDate* will also accept date serial numbers such as 2 (January 1, 1900) and 36525 (December 31, 1999). Date expressions that include a time value can also be passed to *CVDate* or *CDate* as an expression.

Y2K issues   In Visual Basic 3, if your date argument is not a serial number and includes only a two-digit year, *CVDate* will always assume the twentieth century. In Visual Basic 4, if your date argument is not a serial number and includes only a two-digit year, *CDate* will assume the current century (unless you have a new version of OLEAUT32.DLL—see "How OLEAUT32.DLL affects the date window" on page 414). For example, try the following piece of code in Visual Basic 3 or 4:

```
Dim sMessage As String

sMessage = "Day One of the new century has a date serial of "
MsgBox sMessage & CDbl(CVDate("1/1/0"))
```

The date serial will be calculated as 2, which represents the second day since December 31, 1899—that is, January 1, 1900, and *not* January 1, 2000, as you might expect.

If you change the system date on your PC to some time after the change of the next century, Visual Basic 4 will interpret "1/1/0" as January 1, 2000, but the result for Visual Basic 3 will not change. Although the Visual Basic 4 example appears to be an improvement, depending on the nature of your business, it could cause just as much havoc with your system if your system processes historical dates.

If your Visual Basic application is written in Visual Basic 3, the implications of this issue should be obvious. When your application receives a short date–formatted date for the Year 2000 or beyond, the date will be interpreted as the 1900s instead of the 2000s. Three remedies to this problem are possible:

1. **Convert your application to Visual Basic 5.** Although this solution would solve your problem, you need to consider the logistics of converting an entire system to a newer version of the language. In addition, consider the hard-coded, static 1930 window used by Visual Basic 5, which is covered in the "Date window" section.

2. **Accept only four-digit century dates.** This would be the best all-round solution, although it might also involve considerable changes to the user interface. More important, it could invoke a negative reaction from the users of your system.

3. **Use a windowing function on the short date.** This solution is possibly the easiest to implement both technically and politically. Read the "Writing your own date window" section for a more thorough discussion of the sliding-window technique.

DateValue

This function is similar to the *CVDate* and *CDate* functions. For a discussion of the main differences between these functions, see the "*DateValue* and *CDate* are not the same" section. The *DateValue* function will return a value that can be interpreted as a date. It is preferable to "convert" any dates that might be stored as strings using this function.

Return value   The return values for these functions are described in the "*CDate* and *CVDate*" section (under "Return value") on page 418.

How Does the Year 2000 Problem Affect Visual Basic? Chapter

9

Arguments   The normal argument for this function is a string variable with a date string value, although in Visual Basic 4 and 5, you can use any valid date expression.

Y2K issues   The Y2K issues for these functions are covered in the "*CDate* and *CVDate*" section (under "Y2K issues") on page 419.

Other issues   In Visual Basic 3, if you try to use *DateValue* on a short date that is in the wrong international format, you'll get an error 5: "Illegal function call." For example, in the U.K., the short date format is dd/mm/yy; if I try to use *DateValue* on a U.S. formatted short date such as the following, the code will error:

```
MsgBox DateValue("12/31/99")
```

Date

Used as a function, *Date* returns the current system date.

Return value   The return value of the *Date* function is either a Variant(7) or a Date, depending on the data type of the variable to which the function is being assigned. The *Date$* function will return the system date as a string formatted "mm-dd-yyyy" regardless of your international settings.

Arguments   The *Date* function has no arguments.

Y2K issues   No obvious Y2K issues occur as a result of using the *Date* function.

Format

Under Format Function, the Visual Basic 5 Help file says that the *Format* function "Returns a Variant(String) containing an expression formatted according to instructions contained in a format expression." In the current context, the *Format* and *Format$* functions are used to "convert" a date to a different date format.

Return value   The return type of the *Format* function depends on the data type of the receiving variable and the particular formatting being applied to the expression argument.

Arguments   Visual Basic versions 4 and 5 have some extra "first day of the week" type arguments that are not relevant to Y2K issues. The main arguments of the *Format* function are *Expression*, which is any valid expression, and *Format*, which is the formatting that should be applied to *Expression*.

Y2K issues   In Visual Basic 3, if you use a short date as an expression, Visual Basic will assume the 1900s, even if the system date is past the year 2000. For example, the following code will display "January 01, 1900" (depending on your locale):

```
MsgBox Format("1/1/0", "Long Date")
```

Visual Basic 4 on the other hand will assume the current century. As I've mentioned before, this is no real advantage for applications that process historical dates.

Now

The *Now* function returns the current system date and time.

Return value   The data type of the return value depends on the type of variable that *Now* is being assigned to. Under normal circumstances, *Now* returns a Date or a Variant(7), but you can assign the return value to a string variable.

Arguments   The *Now* function has no arguments.

Y2K issues   There are no real Y2K issues with the *Now* function. In large client/server or corporate systems, however, wherever possible you should try to retrieve the system date from a central source such as a row on a lookup table. Retrieving the system date from a central source will help when running system tests against different dates.

DateAdd

The *DateAdd* function is used widely in Visual Basic to perform arithmetic on dates. Using a mixture of arguments, you can add any number of time intervals (day, month, year) to any valid date.

Return value   As with most functions, the *DateAdd* function's return value depends on the data type of the variable that it is being assigned to. The default return type is a Variant(7).

Arguments   The *DateAdd* function has three arguments: *interval*, *number*, and *date*. The *interval* argument represents the time interval, such as day, month, or year. The *number* argument represents the actual number of intervals to add. This can be a negative number if you want to subtract a time interval. The *date* argument is the date expression on which to perform the calculation. So, for example, the following code will display the date of Christmas Day:

```
MsgBox DateAdd("d", 1, "12/24")
```

How Does the Year 2000 Problem Affect Visual Basic?   Chapter

9

Notice that I omitted the year part of the date to demonstrate how Visual Basic will assume the current year.

Y2K issues   If you try the code example above in Visual Basic 3 with your system date set to the year 2000, the message box function will display "12/24/100." So wherever possible, try to provide a year for the date.

As with most other date functions, the Year 2000 problems for the *DateAdd* function start to happen when short dates are interpreted. Try the following code example in Visual Basic 3 and 4, and watch how Visual Basic jumps a hundred years:

```
MsgBox Format$(DateAdd("d", -1, "1/1/0"), "Long Date")
```

This example is simply subtracting one day from the first day of the new year. However, the result is "December 31, 1899". Notice that the result is the same even if you use a double for your date literal (#1/1/0#) instead of a string.

DateDiff

As with *DateAdd*, the *DateDiff* function is used widely in Visual Basic to perform arithmetic on dates. The *DateDiff* function will return the number of time intervals between two given dates.

Return value   The return value for the *DateDiff* function is the number of specified time intervals between the two given dates. This function always returns a number.

Arguments   Visual Basic 4 and 5 have some extra "first day of the week" type arguments that are not relevant to the Y2K topic. The main arguments of the *DateDiff* function are *interval*, which is the time period in question (that is, day, month, year, and so on), and *date1* and *date2*, which are the two dates being compared. So for example, the following code will display the number 1, indicating that given December 24, there is only one day remaining until Christmas Day:

```
MsgBox "Days until Xmas = " & DateDiff("d", "12/24", "12/25")
```

Again, notice that I omitted the year part of the date to demonstrate how Visual Basic will assume the current year.

Y2K issues   Yep, you guessed it! *DateDiff* in Visual Basic 3 and 4 doesn't like date expressions formatted as short dates. The following code example tells me that there are 36,523 days between December 31, 1999, and January 1, 2000, instead of the one day that I would have expected. Admittedly, I didn't enter four-digit years; but your users probably won't either!

```
Msgbox "Difference = " & DateDiff("d", "1/1/0", "31/12/99")
```

DatePart

The *DatePart* function allows you to retrieve a specified time period from a given date. For example, if you want to know what quarter of the year a given date is in, the *DatePart* function will tell you.

Return value   The return value for the *DatePart* function depends entirely on the specified time period. For example, if you're looking for the weekday for a given date, the return value will be somewhere between 1 and 7. If you're looking for the quarter of a given date, however, the return value will be somewhere between 1 and 4. The return value is always a number.

Arguments   Visual Basic 4 and 5 have some extra "first day of the week" type arguments that are not relevant to the Y2K topic. The main arguments of the *DatePart* function are *interval*, which is the time period in question (that is, day, month, year, and so on), and *date*, which is the date being sought. So for example, the following code will display the number 4, indicating that Christmas Day is in the fourth quarter:

```
MsgBox "Xmas in Quarter " & DatePart("q", "12/25/96")
```

Y2K issues   It's the usual story. In Visual Basic 3 and 4, given a short date, Visual Basic will interpret the date as the 1900s. Check the following code, which reports that the year part of a date is 1900:

```
MsgBox "The year is " & DatePart("yyyy", "1/1/0")
```

IsDate

The *IsDate* function is used to tell whether an expression represents a valid date.

Return value   The return value of the *IsDate* function will always be either True or False, depending on whether or not the date expression is valid.

Arguments   The *IsDate* function has only one argument, *Expression*, which represents the date to be tested.

Y2K issues   In addition to the usual short date problem, which affects most of the Visual Basic intrinsic date functions, be sure to check for quirks in international settings, date formats, and so on.

Day, Month, Weekday, and Year

The *Day*, *Month*, *Weekday*, and *Year* functions extract and return a time portion from a given date. In many ways, these functions are similar to the *DatePart* function, which extracts a given time period from a date expression. Of these functions, probably only the *Year* function will be affected by the Year 2000 issue.

Date statement

The *Date* statement is used for setting the system date on your machine. By now, it should be fairly obvious that in addition to the various date formatting quirks associated with Visual Basic, assigning a date expression formatted as a short date to the system date will cause problems when crossing over to the year 2000. However, because of the limitations of the *Date* statement, you are somewhat protected from this problem.

Using the *Date* statement, you are limited by your system as to the dates that can be assigned. On MS-DOS systems, the earliest date that can be set is January 1, 1980, and the latest date is December 31, 2099. Using Windows NT, the earliest date that can be set is January 1, 1980, and the latest date is December 31, 2079. So if you attempt to set your system date to #1/1/0# using the *Date* statement, Visual Basic will interpret this date as January 1, 1900, and return an "Invalid Procedure Call" error.

THE FUTURE

Having looked at the managerial and technical issues associated with the Year 2000 problem and its impact on Visual Basic applications, it's fairly plain to see that this is a messy business! It is my hope that even if you gained only a few insights from this chapter, you will now appreciate the following realities:

- The Year 2000 issue *can* affect Visual Basic applications.
- To fix the Y2K problem, you need to start working on it *now*.
- To deal with the problem efficiently, you *must* plan your work thoroughly.
- Using strings to handle dates is taboo.
- Using short dates with only two-year digits is simply asking for trouble.

Above all, even if you decide not to convert your Visual Basic code to be Year 2000 compliant, I would urge you to at least test your systems using both future system dates and processing that deals with dates crossing the year 2000.

The future of your company could very well depend on the ability of its systems to handle processing into the year 2000. Don't let your company become one of the "Companies that didn't make it through the year 2000" statistics that are bound to be published in 2001.

"**W**ell, at **L**east **I**t **C**ompiled **OK!**"

The Value of Software Testing

Quiet Please

Tests In Progress

JON PERKINS

Jon is a TMS Associate who has been developing applications with Visual Basic since version 1. He now specializes in writing three-tier, client/server applications with Visual Basic and Microsoft SQL Server. He is also a Microsoft Certified Professional Solution Developer. His interests include New Age philosophy, cooking, reading, gardening, and do-it-yourself projects. Jon lives in the Northamptonshire countryside with his wife and their two cats, Solomon and Micha.

It is my belief that software development is one of the most complex tasks that humans are called on to perform. And like many other human endeavors, developing software is not an exact science—even though it should be. Accountants, who arguably put as much mental effort into their work as developers do, at least have the benefit of being reasonably sure that the fruits of their labor are correct, because one set of figures balances with another. Software developers do not have precise debits and credits to verify the accuracy of their work, and so to trust that their software performs as intended, they must undertake the arduous process of testing each unit of code.

Although software development has formal guidelines that lay down techniques for drawing up logic tables, state tables, flow charts, and the like, the commercial pressures that are frequently placed on a development team often mean that a system must be ready by a certain date no matter what. Some people might argue with this observation, but it happens nevertheless. When a new computer system was implemented at the London Ambulance Service in October 1992, the number of system failures that occurred during its first few days quickly resulted in the staff abandoning it and reverting to a completely manual system. Different financial and managerial factors led up to this, but at the end of the day, the system failed because the testing process had not been conducted properly.

One of the biggest headaches for a software developer is time or, rather, the lack of it. When your project lead sits you down and asks you to estimate the amount of time that it will take to code up an application from a design specification that he or she has given you, it is difficult to know beforehand what problems will arise during the project. You are also faced with a bit of a dilemma between giving yourself enough time to code it and not wanting to look bad because you think that the project might take longer than the project lead thinks it will. The logical part of your mind cuts in and tells you not to worry because it all looks straightforward. However, as the development cycle proceeds and the usual crop of interruptions comes and goes, you find that you are running short of time. The pressure is on for you to produce visible deliverables, so the quality aspect tends to get overlooked in the race to hit the deadline. Code is written, executed once to check that it runs correctly, and you're on to the next bit. Then, eventually, the development phase nears its end—you're a bit late, but that's because of (insert one of any number of reasons here)—and you have two weeks of testing to do before the users get it. The first week of the two-week test period is taken up with fixing a few obvious bugs and meeting with both the users and technical support over the implementation plan. At the beginning of the second week, you start to write your test plan, and you realize that there just isn't time to do it justice.

I dread to think how many systems have been developed under these conditions. I'm not saying that all development projects are like this, and the problems are slightly different when there is a team of developers involved rather than an individual, but it's an easy trap to fall into. The scenario I've described indicates several problems, most notably poor project management. Even more detrimental to the quality of the final deliverable, however, is the lack of coordinated testing. The reason I tie in testing with the project management function so strongly is that a developer who is behind schedule will often ditch the testing to get more code written. This is human nature, and discipline is required (preferably from the developer) to follow the project plan properly rather than give in to deadline urgency. The discipline I'm talking about is writing a proper test plan beforehand and then striving to write code that can be easily tested. The project management process should ensure that the creation of the test suite is also proceeding along with the actual development.

It's very easy to think of the debugging process as being synonymous with the testing process. Certainly, the distinction between the two processes blurs on small systems at the unit testing stage (defined a bit later). Other chapters in this book cover the debugging side of the software development process, which should allow the distinction to become more apparent.

In this chapter, I'll start by covering the formalities—that is, the various phases of testing that a good development project will undergo. I'll then outline a few tips that I think will help with the testing of a Visual Basic program, and I'll finish up with a discussion of test environments. I've also included a few Microsoft Word 97 templates on the CD that accompanies this book. Although most companies will have their own in-house versions of these templates, I've included them as starting points for people who do not already use them. Each template should be self-explanatory as to its usage. Note that I have kept the templates generic—different businesses have different requirements and audit standards, so they can be modified as necessary. Just copy them to the Templates subdirectory in your Microsoft Office installation, start up Word, and select the New command from the File menu. The templates should appear under the General tab.

THE PURPOSE OF TESTING

Testing verifies that a software deliverable conforms precisely to the functional and design specifications that have been agreed to with the users. That's a formal definition. However, testing is also used in the detection of bugs—not to prove that there are none, but to locate any that are present. It is a sad fact that we all inadvertently code bugs into our applications. The trick is to reduce the number of bugs in a deliverable to as few as possible so that the system is completely operable. In an ideal world, we would continue to hone and refine the application ad nauseum until it was bug free, but the users can't wait that long, unfortunately. As a general rule, bugs are found and eliminated exponentially—that is, it gets harder to track down bugs as time goes by, but that doesn't mean that they aren't there. When the product is released, they will pop up from time to time, but the user's perception will hopefully be that the application is stable and robust.

THE FORMAL TEST CYCLE

Before we get our teeth too deeply into the Visual Basic way of programming, I think it's worth reviewing the different levels of testing that apply to all software development projects regardless of the programming language or target platform.

The nature of testing is so varied in its requirements that it is difficult to give generalized definitions. What is appropriate for a small (one-person or two-person) application is totally unsuitable for a large (twenty-person) development, whereas the amount of formality that accompanies a large project would slow down the delivery of a small application by a wholly unreasonable amount. With this in mind, I have tried where appropriate to illustrate the relative scale that is necessary at each stage.

Unit/Component Testing

Unit testing is a test of a simple piece of code—in our case a subroutine, a function, an event, or a *Property Get/Let/Set*. In formal terms, it is the smallest piece of code testable. It should be nonreliant on other units of code that have been written for this development project because they will almost certainly be only partly tested themselves. However, it is acceptable to call library routines (such as the Visual Basic built-in functions) since you can be highly confident that they are correct. The idea is to confirm that the functional specification of the unit has been correctly implemented. An example of a unit would be a single user-defined calculation.

Sometimes it is necessary to comment out one piece of code to get another piece to work. This might be necessary during the main development cycle when, for example, the underlying code might be dependent on something that has not yet been written or that contains a known bug. If you have to comment out a piece of code, add a *Debug.Print* statement just before or after it to highlight the fact that you have done so. It's inevitable that you'll forget to remove the leading apostrophe from time to time, and adding a *Debug.Print* statement should save your having to find out the hard way.

Component-level testing is the next level up from unit testing. A component can have fairly straightforward functionality, but it is just complex enough to warrant breaking down the actual implementation into several smaller units. For example, a logical process could be specified that calculates the monthly salary for an individual. This process might consist of the following operations:

- Extract from the database the number of hours worked in the month.
- Calculate the amount of gross pay.
- Optionally, add a bonus amount.
- Make all standard deductions from this amount.

Each operation will probably have different requirements. For example, the database extraction will need error handling to allow for the usual group of possibilities (user record not found, database service not available, and so on). The calculations will need to prevent numeric type errors (divide by zero, mainly), and if they are remote components, they will have to raise fresh errors. Therefore, the entire component (for example, *CalcMonthlySalary*) will consist of four smaller units (*GetHoursForEmployee*, *CalcGrossPay*, *GetBonusAmount*, and *CalcDeductions*), but *CalcMonthlySalary* will still be small enough to qualify as a unit (for testing purposes).

To test a defined unit, a series of scenarios should be devised that guarantees every line of code will be executed at some time (not necessarily in the same test). For example, if a function includes an *If..Then..Else* statement, at least two test scenarios should be devised, one to cover each path of execution. If it is a function that is being tested, defining the expected result of the test is generally easier because the return value of the function can be tested for correctness or reasonableness. However, if you are testing a subroutine, you can check only the effect(s) of calling the routine because there is no return value. I generally have a bias toward writing routines as functions where this is reasonable. For some operations, particularly GUI manipulation, it is not so necessary or beneficial because an error should generally be contained within the routine in which it occurred.

In a small system, the developer would likely perform this level of testing. In a larger system, the initial test would still be performed by the developer, but a more formal version of the test would most likely be conducted by a separate individual.

Integration Testing

Integration testing is the next level up. It is concerned with confirming that no problems arise out of combining unit components into more complex processes. For example, two discrete functions might appear to test successfully in isolation, but if function B is fed the output of function A as one of its parameters, it might not perform as expected. A possible cause might be incorrect or insufficient data validation. Using the previous example of the calculation of the single net salary figure, the actual system might implement a menu or command button option to calculate the salaries for all employees and produce a report of the results. It is this entire routine that would qualify as an integration test.

As with unit testing, it is important to write test plans that will execute along all conceivable paths between the units. Integration testing, by its nature, will probably be performed by a dedicated tester except for small projects.

System Testing

System testing is concerned with the full build of an application (or application suite). At this level, the emphasis is less on bug hunting per se and more on checking that the various parts of the system interact with each other correctly. The level of testing that would be conducted at this phase would be more systemwide—for example, correct initialization from the Registry, performance, unexpected termination of resources (for example, database connections being terminated when other parts of the system still expect them to be there), logon failures, error recovery and centralized error handling (if appropriate), correct GUI behavior, and correct help file topics, to name just a few.

A system test is conducted on a complete build of the application under construction or at least on a specified phase of it. Ideally, it should be in the state in which the end user will see it (for example, no test dialog boxes popping up and no "different ways of doing things until we code that part of the interface"). Therefore, it should be as complete as is possible. In my opinion, the testing cycle should also include the system installation task and not just the execution of the application. If you are developing software for corporatewide use, it is highly unlikely that you will be performing the installations. Most large corporations have dedicated installation teams, and these people are still end users in that they will be running software that you have generated. On the other hand, if you are developing commercial software, the setup program is the first thing the "real" user will see. First impressions count. The Application Setup Wizard has matured into a very useful tool, but you should still test its output.

User Acceptance Testing

User acceptance testing happens when a tested version of the specified deliverable is made available to a selected number of users who will have already received training in the use of the system. In this scenario, the users chosen to perform the tests will be expected to give the system the kind of usage that it will receive in real life. The best way of performing this testing is to get the users to identify an appropriate set of data for the system test and to enter it into the system themselves. This data is most useful if it is real rather than hypothetical. Whatever kind of processing the system performs can then be instigated (for example, printing reports) and the results scrutinized carefully. Ideally, the development and testing team will have little or no input into this process, other than to answer questions and to confirm the existence of any bugs that crop up. Apart from this careful input of prepared data, the system should also be used "normally" for a while to determine the level of confidence that can be attributed to the system. If this confidence level is satisfactory, the system can be signed off and a system rollout can commence. If possible, a partial rollout would initially be preferable not only for prolonged confidence tests but also to ease the burden on the support team. These people will encounter more queries as to the use of the system during these early days than at any other time during its lifetime, so if the volume of queries can be spread out, so much the better. It also gives them an idea of the most frequently asked questions so that they can organize their knowledge base accordingly.

Regression Testing

Regression testing is the repetition of previously run tests after changes have been made to the source code. The purpose is to verify that things still work to specification in the new build and that no new bugs have been introduced in the intervening coding sessions. Although it is impossible to quantify precisely (some have tried), figures that I have come across from time to time suggest that for every ten bugs that are identified and cleared, perhaps another four will be introduced. This sounds like a realistic figure to me, although I would apply it more to calculation-type code rather than to event handlers, which are more self-contained (which, of course, is a benefit of the object-based model that Visual Basic employs).

Inspections

The inspection process is a major part of the software quality cycle, and it is also one of the most important. It is a recognition that the creation of test scripts or the use of automated testing packages only goes so far in assuring the quality of the code. Computers do not yet possess the levels of reasoning necessary to look at a piece of code and deduce that it is not necessarily producing the result specified by the design document. I guess when that day comes, we'll all be out of a job.

Inspection is the process whereby the human mind reads, analyzes, and evaluates computer code, assessing the code in its own right instead of running it to see what the outcome is. It is, as the name suggests, a thorough examination of two elements:

- The code itself
- The flow of the code

Inspection should also ascertain whether the coding style used by the developer violates whatever in-house standards might have been set (while making allowances for personal programming styles).

The value of the software inspection process should not be taken lightly—it's a very reliable means of eliminating defects in code. As with anything, you should start the process by inspecting your own code and considering what the inspection team is going to be looking for. The sorts of questions that should come up are along these lines:

- Has the design requirement been met?
- Does it conform to in-house development standards?
- Does the code check for invalid or unreasonable parameters (for example, a negative age in a customer record)?
- Are all handles to resources being closed properly?
- If a routine has an early *Exit* subroutine or function call, is everything tidied up before it leaves? For example, an RDO handle could still be open. (The current versions of Windows are much better than their predecessors at tidying up resources, but it's still sloppy programming not to close a resource when you are done with it.)

- Are all function return codes being checked? If not, what is the point of the function being a function instead of a subroutine?

- Is the code commented sufficiently?

- Are *Debug.Assert* statements used to their best advantage? We've been waiting a long time for this, so let's use it now that we have it.

- Are there any visible suggestions that infinite loops can occur? (Look for such dangerous constructs as *Do While True*.)

- Is one variable used for different tasks within the same procedure?

- Are algorithms as efficient as possible?

TESTING VISUAL BASIC CODE

When you're writing a piece of code in any language, it is important to continually ask yourself, "How am I going to test this?" There are several general approaches that you can take.

Partner with Another Developer

One good approach to testing is to partner with another developer with the understanding that you will test each other's code. Then, as you type, you will be asking yourself, "How is Beth going to test this? Does she have all she needs here, or will she have to ask me a load of questions about it?" Some questions are inevitable, but I have found that if you know from the outset that somebody else is going to perform a unit-level test on your code without the same assumptions or shortcuts that you have made, that is excellent news! How many times have you spent ages looking through your own code to track down a bug only to spot it as soon as you start to walk through it with another developer? This is because we often read what we *think* we have written rather that what we actually have written. It is only in the process of single-stepping through the code for the benefit of another person that our brains finally raise those page faults and read the information from the screen rather than using the cached copy in our heads. If you're looking at somebody else's code, you don't have a cached copy in the first place, so you'll be reading what is actually there. One further benefit of this approach is that it will prompt you to comment your code more conscientiously, which is, of course, highly desirable.

Test As You Go

Testing as you go has been written about elsewhere, but it is something that I agree with so strongly that I'm repeating it here. As you produce new code, you should put yourself in a position where you can be as certain as possible of its performance before you write more code that relies on it. Most developers know from experience that the basic architecture needs to be in place and stable before they add new code. For example, when writing a remote ActiveX server that is responsible for handling the flow of data to and from Microsoft SQL Server, you will need a certain amount of code to support the actual functionality of the server. The server will need some form of centralized error handler and perhaps some common code to handle database connections and disconnections. If these elements are coded, but development continues on the actual data interfaces before these common routines are tested, the first time you try to run the code, there will be many more things that can go wrong. It's common sense, I know, but I've seen this sort of thing happen time and again.

The first and most obvious way to test a new piece of code is to run it. By that, I don't mean just calling it to see whether the screen draws itself properly or whether the expected value is returned. I mean single-stepping through the code line by line. If this seems too daunting a task, you've already written more code than you should have without testing it. The benefit of this sort of approach is that you can see, while it's still fresh in your mind, whether the code is actually doing what you think it's doing. This single concept is so important that Steve Maguire devotes an entire chapter to the concept in his book *Writing Solid Code* (Microsoft Press, 1995).

Create Regular Builds

I have always been a fan of regular system builds. They force the development team to keep things tidy. If everybody knows that whatever they are doing is going to have to cooperate with other parts of the system every Friday (for example), it is less likely that horrendously buggy bits of half-completed code will be left in limbo for so long that the developer who wrote it cannot remember why he or she was doing it the way that it was done. See?

If I'm writing a set of remote ActiveX servers, I will generally try to have a new build ready each Monday morning for the other developers to use. If I'm working on a large GUI-based system, I would probably look more toward a build every other week. If you are in a team development, all team members should discuss the timing of new builds at the beginning of the coding cycle so that you can obtain a group consensus as to what would be the best policy for your particular project. You will inevitably get slippages, and you might well decide to skip the occasional build while certain issues are resolved, but overall it will allow everybody to get a feel for how the project is shaping up.

Write Test Scripts at the Same Time You Code

Having stepped through your code, you need to create a more formal test program, which will confirm that things do indeed work. Using a test script allows for the same test to be run again in the future, perhaps after some changes have been made. The amount of test code that you write is really a matter of judgment, but what you're really trying to prove is that a path of execution works correctly and that any error conditions that you would expect to be raised are raised. For critical pieces of code—for example, the mortgage calculation algorithm for a bank—it might be worthwhile to actually write the specific code a second time (preferably by someone else) and then compare results from the two. Of course, there is a 50 percent chance that if there is a discrepancy, it is in the test version of the algorithm rather than the "real" version, but this approach does provide a major confidence test. I know of a case within a company where they were so sensitive about getting the accuracy of an algorithm correct that they assigned three different developers to each code the same routine. As it happened, each piece of code that was written produced a slightly different answer. This was beneficial because it made the analyst behind this realize that he had not nailed down the specification tight enough. This is a good example of the prototype/test scenario.

Decide Where to Put Test Code

This might seem a strange heading, but what we need to consider is whether the nature of the development warrants a dedicated test harness program or whether a bolt-on module to the application itself would be suitable. Let's examine this further.

A major component—for example, a remote ActiveX server—has clearly defined public interfaces. We want to test that these interfaces all work correctly and that the expected results are obtained, and we also need to be sure that the appropriate error conditions are raised. Under these circumstances, it would be most suitable to write an application that links up to the remote server and systematically tests each interface. However, if a small GUI-based application were being created that was entirely self-contained (no other components were being developed and used at the same time for the same deliverable), it might be more appropriate to write the test code as part of the application but to have visible interfaces (for example, a menu item) only visible if a specific build flag is declared.

Understand the Test Data

This is an obvious point, but I mention it for completeness. If you are responsible for testing a system, it is vital that you understand the nature and meaning of whatever test data you are feeding to it. This is one area in which I have noticed that extra effort is required to coax the users into providing the necessary information. They are normally busy people, and once they know that their urgently needed new system is actually being developed, their priorities tend to revert to their everyday duties. Therefore, when you ask for suitable test data for the system, it should be given to you in a documented form that is a clearly defined set of data to feed in. This pack of test data should also include an expected set of results to be achieved. This data should be enough to cover the various stages of testing (unit, integration, and system) for which the development team is responsible. You can bet that when the users start user acceptance testing, they will have a set of test data ready for themselves, so why shouldn't they have a set ready for you? Coax them, cajole them, threaten them, raise it in meetings, and get it documented, but make sure you get that data. I realize that if you are also the developer (or one of them), you might know enough about the system to be able to create your own test data on their behalf, but the testing process should not make allowances for any assumptions. Testing is a checking process, and it is there to verify that you have understood the finer points of the design document. If you provide your own test data, the meaning of the test might be lost.

Get the Users Involved

The intended users of a system invariably have opinions while the system is under development and, if given the opportunity to express them, can provide valuable feedback. Once a logical set of requirements starts to become a real-life set of windows, dialog boxes, and charts that the user can manipulate, ideas often start to flow. This effect is the true benefit of prototyping an application because it facilitates early feedback. It is inevitable that further observations will be forthcoming that could benefit the overall usability or efficiency of the finished result. Unless you are working to very tight deadlines, this feedback should be encouraged throughout the first half of the development phase (as long as the recommendations that users make are not so fundamental that the design specification needs to be changed). A good way of providing this allowance for feedback is to make a machine available with the latest system build that is accessible to anybody. This will allow people to come along at any time and play. This is a very unstructured approach, but it can lead to a lot of useful feedback. Not only can design flaws be spotted as the system progresses, but other pairs of eyes become involved in the debugging cycle.

To make this informal approach work, it is necessary to provide a pile of blank user feedback forms that anybody can fill out and leave in some prearranged in-tray for the attention of the development team. A nominated individual should be responsible for maintaining a log of these feedback reports and should coordinate among the development team any actions that arise out of them. I've included a sample feedback form on the accompanying CD. (See the beginning of this chapter.)

Having extolled the virtues of allowing the users to give you continual feedback, I must point out one disadvantage with this approach. If the currently available build is particularly buggy or slow (or both), this could quite possibly cause some anxiety among the users and thus could earn the system a bit of bad publicity before it gets anywhere near to going live. Again, common sense is the order of the day. Some users are familiar with the development cycle and will take early-build system instabilities in their stride, but others won't. Make the most of the users and the knowledge that they can offer, but don't give them a reason to think that the final system will be a dog!

TEST PLANS

A test plan is analogous to the main design document for a system. Though focused entirely on how the system will be tested rather than on what should be in it, the test plan should be written with the same degree of seriousness, consideration, and checking as the main design document because it determines the quality of the system. As Tamara Thomas states in her MSDN article, "The Benefits of Writing a Good Test Plan," a good plan should allow any team member to continue in your absence. One day in the future, you will have moved on, but the system will still be there. Companies very rarely stand still these days, and changes to their working practices, and therefore to the system, will follow. Whatever changes need to be made, it will be a tremendous boost to the new development team if they have test scripts that are documented and are known to work from the start.

Test plans have other purposes than the scenario I have just described. They provide a formal basis from which to develop repeatable (that is, regression) tests. As systems evolve or as new builds are created during the debug cycle, it is essential to know that the existing stability of the system has not been broken. This can best be achieved by being able to run the same tests over and over as each new build is produced. Also, test plans provide a basis from which the test strategy can be inspected and discussed by all interested parties.

A good test plan will start with a description of the system to be tested, followed by a brief discussion of the objectives of the test. The following elements should be included in the plan:

- The objectives of the test exercise.

- A description of how the tests are going to be performed. This will explain the various degrees of reliance that will be made on key testing components, such as rerunnable test scripts, manual checklists, end-user involvement, and so on.

- A description of the environment in which the test will occur. For example, if your organization supports several base environment configurations, you should clearly state which of them you will be testing against.

- A listing of the test data that will need to be made available for the tests to be valid.

- A discussion of any restrictions that might be placed on the test team that might have an impact on the reliability of the test results. For example, if you are testing a system that is likely to be used by a very large number of people and that accesses a central database, it might be difficult for you to simulate this level of volume usage.

- A declaration of the relative orders of importance that you are placing on different criteria—for example, your concern for robustness compared to that of performance.

- Any features that you will not be testing, with a commentary explaining why not (to enlighten those who come after you).

- An intended test schedule showing milestones. This should tie into the overall project plan.

Then, using the same breakdown of functionality as was presented in the design specification, start to list each test scenario. Each scenario should include:

- A reference to the item to be tested
- The expected results
- Any useful comments that describe how these test results can definitely confirm that the item being tested actually works properly (success criteria)

Test Scripts

A test script can be either a set of instructions to a user or to another piece of code. Generally speaking, I am referring to code-based test scripts in this section. So a good test script should be approached in the same way as the code that it is supposed to be testing. Therefore, it should be designed, documented, commented, and tested. Tested? No, that doesn't necessarily mean writing a test script for it, but it does mean single-stepping through your test code while it runs to ensure that it is doing what you expect it to. If the code that you are testing is a particularly important piece, the test code should be inspected and walked through as would any normal code. The following rules apply to test scripts:

- Test script functionality should be kept in sync with the application code.
- The version/revision number of the test script must be the same as the application.
- Test scripts should be version controlled, just like the application code. Use Microsoft Visual Source Safe (or an equivalent) to keep track of any changes that you make. That way, if you need to roll back to an earlier version of the code for any reason, you will have a valid set of test scripts to go with it.

Stubs and Drivers

An application is basically a collection of software units connected by flow-control statements. The best time to test each individual unit is immediately after it has been written, if for no other reason than it is fresh in your mind (and because if you don't do it now, you'll never have the time later). Of course, having a software unit that relies on a call to another unit is only testable if you either comment out the call or substitute a dummy implementation. This dummy is known as a *stub*. Conversely, if you are testing a unit that would normally be called by a higher-level unit, you can create a temporary calling routine, called a *driver*. Let's take a closer look at these concepts.

Stubs

A stub is a temporary replacement piece of code that takes the place of a unit that has yet to be written (or made available by another developer). The implementation of the stub can be simple or somewhat complex, as conditions require. For instance, either it can be hard-coded to return a set value, or it can perform any of the following:

- Provide a validation of the input parameters.
- Provide a realistic delay so as not to convey a false impression that your new application is lightning-fast.
- Provide a quick-and-dirty implementation of the intended functionality of the unit that you are substituting. Be careful not to be too quick-and-dirty; otherwise, you'll waste valuable time debugging throwaway code.

A useful task that you can perform with a stub is to pass the input parameters into the debug window. In most cases, this will merely show you what you expect to see, but it will occasionally throw up a parameter value that you never expected. Although you would have (probably) found this out anyway, you will have immediately been given a visible sign that there is something wrong. While formalized testing is a good method of identifying bugs, so is the commonsense observation process ("that can't be right...").

Drivers

These either contain or call the unit that you are testing, depending on the nature of the code. For a simple unit of code such as a calculation routine, a dedicated piece of test code in another module is sufficient to call the piece of code being tested and to check the result. The idea of using a driver is to provide a basic emulation of the calling environment to test the unit.

The advent of the ActiveX interface now means that it is possible to invoke a test container simply by starting up a new instance of Visual Basic and creating a reference to your piece of code. This does, of course, mean that your code must be given a public declaration and so on, but this client/server-based approach truly leads to flexibility in your systems. And, of course, if you are creating ActiveX documents, you can test your development only in a driver-style environment—for example, Microsoft Internet Explorer.

A Visual Basic Test Script

Let's have a look at a simple piece of code and a test script for it. First we'll specify what we want, and then we'll write the test script.

Function Specification

Produce a public function named *GetPaddedStringFromLong* (using company naming standards). It should accept a long integer value only and return a string value. The long integer value should be converted to a string equivalent, but the length of this string should always be 10 characters. The left side of the string should be padded with as many zeros as required to make the length exactly 10. The value 0 should be returned as 10 zeros. The uppermost value of a long integer (2,147,483,648) will have no leading zeros. Negative values will be treated as a value 0. In the event of any internal errors occurring, a string value of 10 zeros will be returned, but the error will be written to the central error repository.

```
Public Function sPuFooGetPaddedStringFromLong(lNumber As Long)
' ============================================================
On Error GoTo Error_GetPaddedStringFromLong

    Dim sReply As String

    ' Cater for zero or negative value condition.
    If lNumber <= 0 Then
        sPuFooGetPaddedStringFromLong = "0000000000"
        GoTo Exit_GetPaddedStringFromLong
    End If

    ' Get string version of long number.
    sReply = Trim$(CStr(lNumber))

    ' Add a leading zero while length is less than 10.
    Do While Len(sReply) < 10
        sReply = "0" & sReply
    Loop

    ' Assign function reply.
    sPuFooGetPaddedStringFromLong = sReply

    GoTo Ezxit_GetPaddedStringFromLong
```

```
                    Error_GetPaddedStringFromLong:
   >>                   SomeDiagnosticCall Err.Number, Err.String, _
                            "sPuGetPaddedStringFromLong"
                        Err.Clear
                        sPuFooGetPaddedStringFromLong = "0000000000"

                    Exit_GetPaddedStringFromLong:
                        ' Common function exit point

                    End Function
```

Test Script Specification

Write a program to ensure the correct operation of *GetPaddedStringFromLong*. Test the following conditions:

- Normal operation using a range of typical long integer values that vary in length from 1 to 10 numeric characters. All result strings should always be confirmed to be 10 characters long.

- Operation with a parameter 0.

- Operation with a negative parameter.

```
Public Sub Test_GetPaddedStringFromLong()

    Dim iLoopCount As Integer   ' Loop count variable
    Dim lTestValue As Long      ' Parameter to be sent
    Dim sReply As String        ' Reply from function

    On Error GoTo Error_Test_GetPaddedStringFromLong

    ' Initialize variables.
    lTestValue = 1&

    ' Send initial debug message.
    Debug.Print "Starting test series for " & _
        "sPuFooGetPaddedStringFromLong at " & Now

    ' Test the length of each reply from an initial
    ' single numeric value (i.e., < 10), increasing in
    ' magnitude by a factor of 10 up to the billion
    ' range (i.e., 1 significant number and 9 zeros).
    ' ==================================================
```

```
For iLoopCount = 1 To 10

    ' Make a call to the function being tested.
    sReply = sPuFooGetPaddedStringFromLong(lTestValue)

    ' Check that the length is 10.
    If Len(sReply) <> 10 Then
        Debug.Print "Reply was wrong size on iteration " _
            & iLoopCount & "(" & sReply & ")"
    Else
        Debug.Print "Iteration." & iLoopCount & ": " _
            & sReply
    End If

    ' Increase of test parm by factor of 10
    If iLoopCount < 10 Then lTestValue = lTestValue * 10&

Next

' Test for a zero value parameter.
' =================================================

' Make a call to the function being tested.
sReply = sPuFooGetPaddedStringFromLong(0&)

' Check that the reply is what we expect.
If sReply <> "0000000000" Then
    Debug.Print "Zero check test failed (value:" & sReply & ")"
Else
    Debug.Print "Zero check test succeeded"
End If

' Test for negative value.
' =================================================

' Make a call to the function being tested.
sReply = sPuFooGetPaddedStringFromLong(-1&)

If sReply <> "0000000000" Then
    Debug.Print "Negative value test failed (" _
        & sReply & ")"
Else
    Debug.Print "Negative value test succeeded"
End If
```

```
      ' Print end of sequence message.
      Debug.Print "Test_GetPaddedStringFromLong complete"

      GoTo Exit_Test_GetPaddedStringFromLong

Error_Test_GetPaddedStringFromLong:

      Debug.Print "Test_GetPaddedStringFromLong error: " _
          & Err.Description
      Err.Clear
      GoTo Exit_Test_GetPaddedStringFromLong

Exit_Test_GetPaddedStringFromLong:
      ' Common function exit point

End Sub
```

In the output from the test script, I have deliberately chosen two different styles of reporting the results of the run. The iteration test actually prints the results of each function call in the debug window to allow for a visual inspection of the returned data. However, for the two subsequent tests a more simple *failed/succeeded* message is displayed. Use either approach as necessary.

As an aside, you might notice that the test script is actually longer than the code that is being tested. Welcome to the world of professional software development! Now when you use your time-honored method of estimating how long a programming task will last and then doubling it, you won't feel so guilty.

PERFORMANCE TESTING

Performance testing is somewhat less rigid in its documentation requirements than the other types of testing. It is concerned with the responsiveness of the system, which in turn depends on the efficiency of either the underlying code or the environment in which the system is running. For example, a database system might work fine with a single tester connected, but what is the performance when 20 users are connected? For many systems, performance is just a matter of not keeping the user waiting too long, but in other cases, it can be more crucial. For example, if you are developing a real-time data processing system that constantly has to deal with a flow of incoming data, a certain level of performance expectation should be included in the design specification.

Performance is partly up to the efficiency of the network subsystem component within Windows, but it is also up to you. For example, if you are accessing a database table, what kind of locks have you put on it? The only way to find out how it will run is through volume testing. But performance is also a matter of perception. How many times have you started a Windows operation and then spent so long looking at the hourglass that you think it has crashed, only to find two minutes later that you have control again? *The Windows Interface Guidelines for Software Design* (Microsoft Press, 1995) offers very good advice on how to show the user that things are still running fine (using progress bars, for instance).

Profiling your code is an obvious step to take where performance is an issue, particularly for processor-intensive operations. It can point out where the most time is being consumed in a piece of code, which in turn will show you the most crucial piece of code to try to optimize.

PREPARING A SUITABLE TEST ENVIRONMENT

If you are testing a system for a corporate environment, it's a good idea to have a dedicated suite of test machines. As a result, machines are available for end users to try out the new system without being an inconvenience to you, and they can also focus on the task at hand by being away from their own work environment. More important, it means that you are not running the software on a machine that might contain other versions of the system (or at least some of its components) that you are developing.

The nature, size, and variety of the test environment will inevitably depend on the size of your organization. A large corporation will conceivably have dedicated test rooms containing a dozen or so test machines, which will not only offer the scope to test the software under different conditions but will also allow for a degree of volume testing (several different users using the same network resources at the same time, particularly if you have developed a product that accesses a shared database). If you work for a small software house or you are an independent developer, chances are you will not be able to provide yourself with many testing resources.

Most software these days will have one of two target markets. The software will either be intended for some form of corporate environment or for commercial sale. Corporate environments can normally provide test environments, and if you work for a small software house or you are an independent developer, you will probably be expected to perform system testing on site anyway. (Obviously your user-acceptance tests must be on site.) If, however, there is no mention of this during your early contract negotiations or project planning, it is worth asking what sort of test facilities your employer or client will be able to provide for you. It's better to arrange this at the outset rather than muddle your way through a limited test.

Test Machine Configurations

If you are testing a system for a corporate environment, it is worthwhile having two different types of test machine configurations. A "vanilla," or basic, configuration gives you a benchmark with which to work. A second configuration that contains a typical corporate build will highlight any problems you might encounter. Let's examine them in more detail.

The plain-vanilla configuration

In this configuration, a plain-vanilla machine is configured solely for the purpose of testing your new system. Preferably, the hard disk will have been formatted to remove everything relating to previous configurations. The machine should then be loaded with the following:

- The version of Windows you are testing against.
- The minimum network drivers that you need to get your configuration to work. By this, I mean that if your corporate environment runs on a TCP/IP-based protocol, check that the machine is not also running NetBEUI or IPX/SPX.
- The build (and only that build) of the system that you are testing.

This test will allow you to assess the performance in a pure environment. Whatever problems arise during this test are either straightforward bugs in your system or are fundamental problems in the way that you are trying to work with the Windows environment. By testing in such an uncontaminated environment, you can be sure that the problems are between you and Windows and that nothing else is causing any problems that arise at this stage.

I have a personal reason for being so particular about this point. A few years back, I was writing a client/server system using a non-Microsoft development tool. The product itself was buggy, and it was difficult to get any form of stable build from it at all. Eventually, everything that went wrong was blamed on the development tool. Because we concentrated on trying to get some common routines built first, my codeveloper and I did not attempt to hook up to the Microsoft SQL Server service for a couple of weeks. When we did try, it wouldn't work. We both blamed the tool again. Because we had seen it done in a training course, we knew that it should work. Therefore, we reasoned, if we tried doing the same thing in different ways, we eventually would find success. We didn't. Only when we came to try something else that involved a connection to SQL Server did we find that it was the current Windows configuration that was at fault. We decided to reload Windows to get a plain-vanilla environment, and, sure enough, we got our database connection. As we reloaded each additional component one by one, we found out that the antivirus TSR program that we were both using was interfering with the SQL Server database-library driver! When we swapped to a different antivirus tool, the problem went away.

The corporate configuration

Having gained a benchmark against what works and what doesn't, you can then repeat the tests against a typical corporate environment. For example, your company might have several standard configurations. The base environment might consist of Windows 95, Microsoft Office (a mixture of standard and professional editions), a couple of in-house products (an internal telephone directory application that hooks up to a Microsoft SQL Server service somewhere on the network), and a 16-bit third-party communication package that allows connectivity to the corporate mainframe. Typically, additional install packs are created that add department-specific software to the base environment. For example, the car fleet department will probably have an off-the-shelf car pool tracking system. Allowances need to be made in your testing platforms to take into account more diverse variations of the corporate base environment, but only if the software that you have developed is likely to run in this environment, of course.

In a perfect world, there would be no problem running your new system in these environments. However, inconsistencies do occur. Products produced by such large companies as Microsoft are tested so widely before they are commercially released for sale that issues such as machine/product incompatibility are addressed either internally or during the beta test cycle. (Indeed, the various flavors of Windows currently available do contain the occasional piece of code that detects that it is running on a specific piece of hardware or with a specific piece of software and that makes allowances accordingly.) One of these inconsistencies can be attributed to executable file versions. For example, different versions of the winsock.dll file are available from different manufacturers. Only one of them can be in the Windows System or System32 directory at any time, and if it's not the one you're expecting, problems *will* occur.

Another problem that can arise in some companies—as incredible as it seems—is that key Windows components can be removed from the corporate installation to recover disk space. Many large corporations made a massive investment in PC hardware back when a 486/25 with 4 MB of RAM and a 340-MB hard disk was a good specification. These machines, now upgraded to 16 MB of RAM, might still have the original hard disks installed, so disk space will be at a premium. If your organization doesn't suffer from this situation, all is well. But it is a common problem out there. I am aware of one organization, for example, that issued a list of files that could be "safely" deleted to recover a bit of disk space. Apart from the games, help files for programs such as Terminal and the object packager (ever use that? me neither), there was also the file mmsystem.dll. This file is a key component of the multimedia system. In those days (Windows 3.1), very few of the users had any multimedia requirements, so the problem went unnoticed for a while. The fix was obviously quite straightforward, but it still would have caused problems. If your attitude is "Well, that's not my problem," you are wrong. You need to be aware of *anything* that is going to prevent your system from running properly at your company, and if a show-stopping bug is not discovered until after the rollout, it will be you who look bad, whoever else you try to blame.

A good indication of the amount of effort that went into producing a build of the first version of Windows NT can be found in the book *Show-Stopper: The Breakneck Race to Create Windows NT and the Next Generation at Microsoft,* by G. Pascal Zachary (Free Press, 1994). Not only is it an interesting read, it describes well the role of the testing teams within a large development environment—larger than most of us will be exposed to during our careers, I dare say. But the book conveys very well the necessity of structure and discipline that must be maintained in large developments.

A Final Word of Caution

And now for the bad news; once you have completed the testing, your application or component will still probably have bugs in it. This is the nature of software development, and the true nature of testing is unfortunately to reduce the number of bugs to a small enough number that they do not detract from the usefulness and feel-good factor of the product. This includes the absence of "show-stopper" bugs—there is still no excuse for shipping something that has this degree of imperfection. In running through the testing cycles, you will have reduced the number of apparent bugs to zero. At least everything should work OK. However, users are going to do things to your system that you would never have imagined, and this will give rise to problems from time to time. In all likelihood, they might trigger the occasional feature that cannot apparently be repeated. It does happen from time to time, and the cause is most typically that the pressures (commercial or otherwise) on the project management team to deliver become so strong that they succumb to the pressure and rush it out before it's ready. They then find that the users come back to them with complaints about the stability of the product. Sometimes you just can't win.

Multimedia and the User Interface in Business Applications

Steve is a TMS Associate who has been working in IT for more years than he cares to admit and with Visual Basic since version 2. He has written several books, including *The Instant Guide to VB3* and *Complete VB4 Development,* as well as helping out on a few others. His areas of specialty are multimedia, database design, large client/server application development, and book and article writing. He works mainly in the financial and insurance markets but occasionally manages to do some really interesting stuff too. Steve is a Microsoft Visual Basic Certified Professional.

STEVE DOLAN

In this chapter, we'll take a look at multimedia and user interface elements to see how they can help you as a developer in a commercial environment and how they can enhance the user's experience with your applications.

In this chapter, I'll show you ways in which multimedia and attention to user interface issues can enhance your applications in Visual Basic 5 without reams of difficult code. Along the way, you might need to set aside any preconceived notions that multimedia is just a set of bells and whistles for the latest home market product and that it is not for business applications.

It's time to put away those ideas about multimedia and look at how you can produce good-looking systems that not only run well but are easy and intuitive to use and also help reduce the time it takes to get your users up to speed with your applications.

WHAT'S IN THIS CHAPTER?

The initial section of this chapter looks at ways you can help users get up to speed with your applications by using context-sensitive help as well as ways to support your applications.

The next section will consider how you can create interfaces other than the multiple-document interface (MDI) that most business systems use today. Although in most cases the MDI is satisfactory, there may well be cases in which an alternative interface would better suit the application. We'll look at one such alternative, the single-document interface (SDI).

Building on the material presented in the first two sections, we'll consider how multimedia and the user interface can assist with often expensive training requirements when a new system is deployed. We'll look at how you can create a computer-based training (CBT) system for your application by taking each of the elements that make up a CBT system and seeing how they can be implemented using the features of Visual Basic 5.

We'll round off the chapter by considering other issues related to multimedia and the user interface in a commercial environment. As an example, we'll look at how to create a document-management system and how this system can be extended to include workflow.

THE MULTIMEDIA CONTROL

Before we leap into the chapter, let's look briefly at the multimedia control that ships with Visual Basic 5 as one of the custom controls. I must confess that in the last two releases of Visual Basic, I've tended to ignore the control and go with using the media control interface (MCI) directly, especially because the MCI is so easy to use. Visual Basic 5 looks more functional than its predecessors, but it still has a few limitations. If you require only simple multimedia tasks, you might find that the control is adequate, but for more control over multimedia files you'll still need to resort to the MCI. In this chapter, we'll be looking at how to use the MCI rather than how to use the MCI control.

Multimedia in Help Systems

One of the areas that suffers most in the development life cycle and is seldom fully accounted for in project estimates and schedules is the production of a help system for an application. There are many reasons for this: development time frames, indecision over the audience level for the help file, changing requirements throughout the build, and just plain forgetfulness until the users start asking for some help. Although there are many add-ins for producing Windows help files, whatever way you cut it, it's still a lot of work.

For commercial products, the type, style, and audience level of the help system is essential because you won't get a second chance. A useful and comprehensive help system is essential if you don't want to be tied down with taking support calls for your products.

Can you use multimedia to address some of these issues? Of course. There is as yet no replacement for a well-written Windows help file, but how do you best focus the work and determine the audience level? When the users start using the system, they need a basic level of help to get up and running with the application. As they become more familiar with it, they might need some how-to help. When they become expert users, they expect help to act as a reference and a memory jogger. Producing a help system that covers all these scenarios, although not impossible, is difficult and costly. So how can multimedia help address some of these problems?

Let's look at each of these cases in turn and see how we can use Visual Basic 5 and the Windows multimedia facilities to address some of these issues. To keep the example simple, we'll use only a limited amount of multimedia.

Help for the Early Stage After Release: Context-Sensitive Spoken Help

The first stage is getting the users up and running with your application. This can be a very costly exercise, especially on a large rollout, because it will tie up your expensive IT staff and require large-scale training—and it's almost impossible to get "just-in-time" training. The training will occur too early, too late, or not at all, and retention of information on such courses, no matter how well presented, is fairly low. Even if you manage to get the timing right and you have enough staff to achieve the required training, those first few weeks will still be traumatic and will have a large impact on the perceived success of the project. So what do you do?

Providing the right level of help at the right time is a bit of a juggling act. Some users will come up to speed very quickly, and others will require more help to become familiar with the application. This is where a context-sensitive spoken help system, in association with a good midlevel Windows help system, can support all users through these early phases. For a commercial application, this may well be the level that's required, and it should be aimed for. You need to get new users of the system up and running, but you need to support the more experienced ones too.

This might sound like a difficult goal to achieve, but it's really very simple. By using a resource file for the links to the sound clip, you can create several levels of help (such as beginner, intermediate, and advanced) and upgrade the help system without having to change a single line of code. This could prove useful as the user's knowledge increases. It's also easy to accommodate another set of new users who start using your application later. For commercial or shareware products, you can ship an initial resource file and then upgrade it when the user requests the next level. This may cost a little more, but your user base will be suitably impressed by your level of service, and providing this service should also cut down on technical support inquiries.

The main disadvantage of this type of system is that sound files take up a lot of space, which means that they are really only suited to supporting other types of help. What does it take to produce a spoken help system as part of a comprehensive application help system? Read on.

Where to use a spoken help system

You'll find that incorporating a spoken help system is easy and useful when applied correctly. Probably the area in which spoken help can be most useful is in helping the user become familiar with the user interface. How many times have you loaded a new application only to be overwhelmed by a huge array of tools, menus, and buttons? (Even Visual Basic 5 is guilty of this.) To make matters worse, you might be familiar with some of these elements, but you now find that they don't do what you expected. The ToolTips help, and some applications also have help text displayed in the status bar. Furthermore, the first thing that many users do when they get new software is rip off the wrapper, load it, and start to play with it. All the wonderful manuals and the superb user guides that you've painstakingly written remain in the box unopened and are later filed on the shelves to gather dust. Wouldn't it be great if someone could briefly explain what that new widget you're dying to try is actually supposed to do?

As you might have guessed, this is where spoken help not only will get your users over the usual teething troubles they experience when using new software, but it'll also impress them with your attention to detail.

Elements of a spoken help system

To make the help system reusable, you need to make it application-independent. The details of the WAV files that need to be played can be in a Microsoft Access database or in a resource file. If you use a database, you should set up the location details in the Registry so that you avoid hard coding the paths in your applications. This will also provide you with the ability to upgrade or alter the help system for your application by updating the Registry to use another database or by recompiling with a new resource file if that's the route you've chosen. As the users' expertise grows, you can produce more complex spoken help that replaces the previous help files, while retaining the ability to return to a previous help system if required. You also need a set of functions that will play the requested help file, and you need a way of linking these files into the user interface. Let's look at several ways that this linking can be achieved in a sample application.

Creating the spoken help system

For the sample application, we'll hold the WAV file details in a resource file, which will be compiled using the resource compiler that ships with Visual Basic 5. Because we're interested only in how the spoken help system works, we'll use a skeleton MDI system to illustrate its uses, as shown in Figure 11-1.

FIGURE 11-1

A spoken help application

Let's take a look at the project itself. We won't be going through all the code—you'll find that on the companion CD to this book as SpkHelp.vbp. Code that we aren't interested in for the purposes of the discussion here, such as error handling and validation, is not included in this book but is on the CD.

As you can see in Figure 11-1, the application is a software catalog viewer. This type of application likely will be shipped to the general public, so you need to make it very user-friendly and minimize the amount of work required to support it. Because this type of catalog is usually shipped free, it probably won't be accompanied by any written help beyond how to load the application. This is an ideal application for a spoken help system.

After the application is written, you need to record the WAV files and then produce the resource file. At this time, you might want to consider how best to structure your files. For a large multimedia project, it is not really sensible to store all the files in the root directory, so some form of organization is required. This is the approach taken throughout the chapter—all of the multimedia files are stored below the application path. If you move the files when copying them from the CD, please be aware that you might have to alter the paths either in the code or in the following resource file.

Creating the application resource file

A resource file consists of string and binary data. These entries are identified by an ID, which we use within Visual Basic to load the resource. The string details can be anything textual, such as filenames or messages that are to be used in the application.

The following is the resource file that is used with the spoken help application:

```
// This is the Resource file for the spoken help project.
// It contains the path and name of all of the
// multimedia clips used in the application.

STRINGTABLE

BEGIN
//Spoken Help Path and File details
    1001 "\wav\mdifile.wav"
    1002 "\wav\mdiform.wav"
    1003 "\wav\index.wav"
    1004 "\wav\packview.wav"
    1005 "\wav\packexit.wav"
    1006 "\wav\narrdesc.wav"
    1007 "\wav\narrexit.wav"
```

```
1008  "\wav\mditools.wav"
1009  "\wav\mdihelp.wav"
1010  "\wav\mdiform.wav"

//Product text
5001 "This is the Microsoft Art Gallery Product. It has details of " &
     "pictures from the Art Galleries in London"

END

// The non-string data follows...

    Art1 BITMAP   atopen.bmp
```

Resource files are an efficient means of using string and picture data because they are compiled and usually loaded only on request. If you're writing a heavyweight application that is very resource hungry, this might be one method to make it slightly more Windows-friendly and economical in its use of resources.

For the sample application, we'll use the string section to hold the details of software products and the partial path and filename of the WAV files. The application path will be appended to these paths to produce the full path for the file. (This will enforce a sensible directory structure on the application and—more important—will ensure that absolute paths are not coded into the application.) To demonstrate its other textual function, it also shows a description of the product. For demonstration purposes, there's only one product, so there's only one entry (5001).

For the pictures of the products, it uses the bitmap data type. This holds a pointer to the bitmap details when the file is compiled rather than holding the actual bitmap image.

As you can see by these details, the string details are held in an area called the STRINGTABLE. These string resources start with a numeric ID, followed by the actual string. For data resources, you can create nonnumeric IDs, although there are some documented limitations. The only entry for this sample application is the bitmap that will be displayed when you load the Fine Art details.

Linking the resource file details to the application

As with most programming for Windows, there are several ways of linking the IDs in the resource file to the user interface. The most obvious and the easiest to use is the *Tag* property of the controls, but it does have a few drawbacks. One drawback is that this property might be required for other purposes.

Another drawback is that there are no tag properties for the menus. You could set up some custom controls of your own, based on the controls that you are going to use, and add a custom property and a custom event to handle the spoken help details, but that's a bit like using a sledgehammer to crack a peanut. In this application, I've created a constants module that holds the ID details, which can be easily kept up-to-date as the application changes.

The following code shows the beginning of the MDI parent form, *MDIShow*:

```
Public bPuSpoken As Boolean ' Used to determine whether spoken help required

Private Sub MDIForm_Click()
    If bPuSpoken Then ' The Help system is active.
        Call PlayWav(MDI_FORM)
    End If
End Sub

Private Sub MDIForm_Load()
' Initialize the spoken help flag.
    bPuSpoken = False

    ' Load the Pack shot form.
    frmPack.Show

End Sub
```

The public Boolean variable *bPuSpoken* is used to determine whether the main Click event code of the object is to be called or whether the spoken help system is activated. You can see this code in action in the *MDIForm_Click* event, where the variable is checked and *puPlayWav* is called if it's true.

The code that handles the playing of the WAV file is in the *modPlayWav* code module:

```
Public Sub PlayWav(ByVal niWavID As Integer)
' This subroutine plays the help file and resets the
' spoken Boolean on the MDI form.

    Dim lResult  As Long ' Return parameter from sndplaysnd.
    Dim lReturn  As Long
    Dim sWaveFile As String ' Name of the WAV file

    Static bPlayWav As Boolean ' Determines whether a WAV is playing

    ' Get the WAV filename from the resource file using the
    ' WAV ID passed in.

    sWaveFile = LoadResString(niWavID)
```

```
' If WAV file currently open, stop it and close it.
If bPlayWav Then lReturn = WinsndPlaySound("", SND_NODEFAULT)

' Set the WAV file open flag to True.
bPlayWav = True

' Play it
lReturn = WinsndPlaySound(sWaveFile, SND_NODEFAULT + SND_ASYNC)

mdiShow.bPuSpoken = False ' Turn help off.
mdiShow.MousePointer = 0 ' Reset the mouse pointer.
```

End Sub

The procedure is really very simple. First, the required path and filename for the WAV file is retrieved from the resource file using *LoadResString*. Then, if a WAV file is currently playing, it's stopped, and the new WAV file is played. Finally, *bpuspoken* is reset so that the user interface is once again active.

The function used to play the WAV file is the *sndPlaySnd* function, which is in the WinMM DLL. Its declaration is as follows:

```
Declare Function WinsndPlaySound Lib "winmm.dll" _
    Alias "sndPlaySoundA" (ByVal lpszSoundName As String, _
    ByVal uFlags As Long) As Long
```

The *sndPlaySound* function This function is used to play WAV files. The first parameter is the name of a sound file, and the second parameter is a flag that tells the function how to play the sound, as defined in the following table:

Flag	Value	Function
SND_SYNC	0	Plays a sound synchronously. Does not return until the sound has finished playing.
SND_ASYNC	1	Plays a sound asynchronously. Returns as soon as the sound file starts.
SND_NODEFAULT	2	If the file cannot be found, returns silence.
SND_LOOP	8	Loops the WAV file. You must also use SND_ASYNC with this flag. Call *sndPlaySound* with the file parameter "" and the flag SND_NODEFAULT to stop.
SND_NOSTOP	16	If a sound is playing, returns false without playing the specified WAV file.

This function does nothing except play WAV files, so it's fairly restricted but very easy to use and understand. If you're going to use other types of multimedia files, you'll need to use the MCI, which we'll look at in the next section.

Expanding spoken help to a fully multimedia help system

Now that you've seen how easy it is to play a WAV file, why not extend the system to include AVI files? This means that you'll need to use a different function—*MCISendString* instead of *SndPlaySnd*—but little else changes. The following procedure will play either a WAV file or an AVI file by checking its extension. This means that we can now use sound or video for our multimedia help system without having to make any changes to the infrastructure. By using the MCI, it's fairly simple to extend the code to play any type of multimedia file that is supported by the MCI.

```
Public Sub PlayHelp(ByVal niMMID As String)
' This subroutine plays a multimedia help file. It will select
' the type of call to the MCI depending on the file retrieved.

    Dim sMMFile  As String ' File returned from the resource file

    Dim nIndex   As Integer ' Saves the period location
    Dim sExtension As String ' The file extension
    Dim lReturn  As Long ' The return details from the MCI

    Static bAviOpen As Boolean ' Is AVI playing?
    Static bWavOpen As Boolean ' Is WAV playing?

    ' Get the multimedia filename from the resource file using
    ' the multimedia ID passed in.

    sMMFile = App.Path & LoadResString(niMMID)

    ' Now we can check for the file type--WAV or AVI--and
    ' play the help file indicated from the resource file.
    ' Check the extension.

    nIndex = InStr(sMMFile, ".")
    sExtension = Mid$(sMMFile, nIndex + 1)

    ' Play the multimedia file, depending on its extension.

    Select Case LCase$(sExtension)

    ' WAV files.
    Case "wav"
```

```vb
        ' If a WAV file is open, then...
        If bWavOpen Then
            ' Stop it, and close it.
            lReturn = WinmciSendString("Stop WaveFile", "", 0, 0)
            lReturn = WinmciSendString("Close WaveFile", "", 0, 0)
        End If

        ' Set the WAV file open flag to true.
        bWavOpen = True

        ' Open it.
        lReturn = WinmciSendString("Open " & sMMFile & _
            " alias WaveFile type WaveAudio", "", 0, 0)

        ' Play it (NoWAIT).
        lReturn = WinmciSendString("Play WaveFile", "", 0, 0)

    ' AVI files.
    Case "avi"

    ' If an AVI file is open, then...
        If bAviOpen Then
            ' Stop it, and close it.
            lReturn = WinmciSendString("Stop AviFile", "", 0, 0)

            lReturn = WinmciSendString("Close AviFile", "", 0, 0)

        End If

        ' Set the AVI file open flag to True.
        bAviOpen = True

        ' Open it.
        lReturn = WinmciSendString("Open " & sMMFile & _
            " alias AviFile type AviVideo", "", 0, 0)

        ' Play it (NoWAIT) in full screen mode.
            lReturn = WinmciSendString(_
                "Play AviFile fullscreen ", "", 0, 0)

    End Select

    mdiShow.bPuSpoken = False ' Turn help off.
    mdiShow.MousePointer = vbDefault 'Reset the mouse pointer.

End Sub
```

As with the previous procedure, the path and file details are first retrieved from the resource file. To determine what type of multimedia file to play by means of the MCI, the file extension is extracted. If a file of the type indicated by the extension is currently playing, the file is stopped, and the selected file is then played using *MCISendString*.

The MCI

Describing the MCI could take a whole book in itself, and the details are fully documented on MSDN in the Win32 SDK book in the multimedia section. (A slimmed-down version ships on the Visual Basic CD.) It's beyond the scope of this chapter to explain the MCI fully, but we will use it throughout the chapter, so we'll look at the basics. You can also use the MCI through the custom ActiveX multimedia control, but it is more restrictive.

A brief look at *MCISendString* Basically, the MCI is a programmable interface that is accessed by using the *MCISendString* Windows API call. The declaration for the call is as follows:

```
Declare Function WinmciSendString Lib "winmm.dll" _
    Alias "mciSendStringA" (ByVal lpstrCommand As String, _
    ByVal lpstrReturnString As String, ByVal uReturnLength As Long, _
    ByVal hwndCallback As Long) As Long
```

The return variable is a long that contains 0 if the call succeeded; otherwise, it contains an error value, which can be deciphered. For the vast majority of calls, the only parameter that is set is the first one. This is the command string that is passed to the MCI, and it has a structure itself. It generally takes the format *Command - File - Arguments*. The commands that we are interested in as part of this chapter are Open, Close, Play, Window, and Where. In most cases, the file will be an alias name that we'll set when we open the file. This has a couple of advantages in that we can change the alias to a shorter and more meaningful name to save typing, and we can make subsequent calls to the MCI file independent. The arguments that you can use will usually depend on the command type, but the main ones that we will be using are alias, type, handle, and destination. Some examples of passing parameters to the MCI are as follows:

```
lReturn = mciSendString("Stop WaveFile", "", 0, 0)
lReturn = mciSendString("Play WaveFile", "", 0, 0)
lReturn = mciSendString("Window AviFile handle " & _
    Str$( picVideo.hwnd), "", 0, 0)
mciSendString("Where AviFile destination", ByVal sReturn, _
    Len(sReturn) - 1, 0)
```

Don't worry if it doesn't make much sense yet—we'll see all of these in action as we go through the chapter.

Help for the Second Stage After Release: Wizards

As users become more familiar with your application and how to navigate the user interface, they tend to move away from the "What is this?" type of question (previously answered with our multimedia help system) to the "How can I do this?" type of question. You could replace the multimedia clips in the multimedia help system to give intermediate users more detailed information about your application. However, more and more applications are using an invaluable new part of the Windows ethos, the wizard. Just look at how many wizards now appear in Visual Basic 5 and Access. Midlevel Windows help files may well take the user through the how-to for a particular task, but there's no substitute for doing it, especially with help from a friendly wizard. So, what does it take to create one?

Wizards are surprisingly easy to produce, and they can be of further use by also including the multimedia-style help as part of the interface. With a little thought, you might even be able to show how they can be filled in to further help the user by extending the spoken help concept. Instead of playing a help file indicated by the resource file, you can load text into the text boxes in the wizard from your resource file and demonstrate the values to be entered into the wizard.

Wizards in Visual Basic 5

Microsoft has recognized the need for wizards to simplify complex tasks and has included an add-in wizard that ships with Visual Basic 5. This wizard is designed to allow you to create your own add-in wizard to create an add-in. When you start a new project, select VBWizard Manager in the Add-In Manager to make the wizard-creation add-in available. The best way to come to grips with this is to try it out, so let's look at a sample.

The wizard skeleton   The wizard produced by the add-in is pretty sophisticated, but it is geared to producing an add-in for the Visual Basic development environment. By looking through the code, you should be able to remove the Visual Basic IDE–related code and use the remaining code as a template for your own application wizards. If your site is likely to need a lot of wizards, it might be a good idea to use the Wizard wizard to produce an add-in wizard that produces wizards for your application. (You might need to reread that last sentence, but it does make sense!) To demonstrate how to do this is beyond the scope of this chapter, but I'd rather not leave you out on a limb, so I've created a skeleton wizard application, as shown in Figure 11-2, that you can use as the basis for your wizards, or you can crib the details to produce your own. You'll find it on the CD as WizSkel.vbp.

FIGURE 11-2

The skeleton wizard application

```vb
Private Sub cmdWiz_Click(Index As Integer)
' This is the click event for the command button array.
' Most of your code will be called from here.

    On Error GoTo ErrDetected ' Set an error trap.

    Select Case Index
    Case Wiz_Next_Step ' The Next button was clicked.

        ' Set the step details.
        nPiStepPrev = nPiStep
        nPiStep = nPiStep + 1

        ' Hide/show the last/current step.
        fraWiz(nPiStepPrev).Visible = False
        fraWiz(nPiStep).Visible = True

        cmdWiz(1).Enabled = True
        ' Alter to the number of steps to handle the
        ' command button enable/disable.
        If nPiStep = 1 Then
            cmdWiz(2).Enabled = True
            cmdWiz(0).Enabled = False
        End If

    Case Wiz_Previous_Step ' The Prev button was clicked.

        nPiStepPrev = nPiStep
        nPiStep = nPiStep - 1
```

```
        If nPiStep = 0 Then cmdWiz(1).Enabled = False
        fraWiz(nPiStepPrev).Visible = False
        fraWiz(nPiStep).Visible = True

        ' Show the previous tab.

        cmdWiz(0).Enabled = True
        If nPiStepPrev = 1 Then
            cmdWiz(0).Enabled = True
            cmdWiz(2).Enabled = False
        End If

    Case Wiz_Finish ' The Finish button was clicked.
        ' Time to do all of the work. Enter your wizard finish
        ' code here. It's here that you will trigger your wizard
        ' functions.
        MsgBox "You have completed the wizard. Because this " & _
            "is only a template, there is no functionality " & _
            "behind it.", vbInformation, "Wizard Template"
        Unload Me


    Case Wiz_Cancel ' Cancel the wizard.
        MsgBox "The ??? wizard template was canceled"
        Unload Me
        Exit Sub

    End Select

' You can enter a Select Case statement for the step-specific
' code here.

    ' Select Case pinstep ' Selects the current step details.

        ' Place any step-specific code (such as validation) here.

    ' End Select
    Exit Sub

ErrDetected:
' This is the error handler.
End Sub
```

The navigation through the wizard is handled by buttons 0 and 1 in the array, where 0 is the Next button and 1 the Prev button. First, you need to set the current and previous step variables. (These can be used to "warp" to different steps if you want smart navigation.) Next, hide the currently displayed frame, and show the frame of the new step. The form has a frame control array, in which the step matches the frame displayed. Finally, determine which command buttons should be enabled and disabled for each step.

When the wizard is finished, the command button 3 code is run. It's at this stage that you'll want to call the majority of your code. If you have step-specific code to run, you can create another Select Case statement that checks the current or previous step variables to determine what code should be run. Between this application and the details generated by the Wizard wizard, I'm sure that you'll be conjuring up your own wizards in no time at all.

The other method of creating wizards is to use a custom tabbed dialog control. Basically, create a tab for each step, and set the tab height to 0. Now all you need to do is step back and forth through the tabs collection to alter your wizard steps. The actual method you use will depend on the size of the wizard, the resource usage, and the stability of the Tab control that you use.

Help for Advanced Users

The final scenario is a help system for the advanced user who is familiar with the application and its workings. To be honest, apart from having a detailed reference to hand over by means of Windows help files, there's not a lot more support that you can give. However, experienced users tend to use an application in habitual ways. Not only are they not using all of the functions and facilities available, but they are not using the system in the best and most efficient manner. Are you a competent Word user who has found one way to do something and always does it that way? You might someday find that there is a better way of doing that task that could have saved ages if only you'd known about it. This illustrates the value of good training at the outset—good habits can be learned early and used throughout the lifetime of the application. For example, 80 percent of the calls to Microsoft's Wish Line are for features that already exist in the product!

Another interesting phenomenon of experienced users is that they tend to find it more difficult to break those ingrained habits and learn new functions as the application is upgraded. Using Word as an example again, I use Word 97 in the same manner as I used Word 2. I haven't a clue as to what all of the extra functions do (unless they are obvious). This means that over time, you'll have users who are expert at some things and novices at others. Another excellent illustration of this is Visual Basic 5. As the functionality expands, it becomes more and more difficult to keep up-to-date with Visual Basic, let alone be an expert in all the areas that it now covers.

Interfaces Beyond MDI

Making the systems easier to use and more friendly should be the aim of all software developers. So beyond the help system and training, what else can we do? The one area of the market where the user-friendly interface abounds is the edutainment market. Buy one of the reference CDs, and you'll almost certainly be able to use it out of the box, without resorting to any documentation. Why should this friendly style of interface be exclusively in the realm of the home market?

There are a couple of good reasons to stick to the traditional MDI business interface. The first, and perhaps most significant, is that this interface is now so common that, provided you follow convention, the look and feel of your system will be familiar to your users even though your users have never seen it before. The second, and less significant, is that the MDI interface is well supported by Visual Basic 5. So it's not too much work to produce an application that has a standard Windows look and feel, especially if you use the MDI application–generating wizard to produce a skeleton MDI application. There are a few drawbacks, though. Once you get past the look, your users will find that your system is unique and behaves in a manner different from other applications that have the same look and feel. After all, isn't that why you wrote it? For instance, Visual Basic 5, Excel, Word, and Paint Shop Pro all share a similar-looking standard MDI interface, but once you get beyond the look and feel, they are entirely different animals. So perhaps this standard look is not as advantageous as it first appears because it can lull your users into a false sense of security, and there's even less chance that the manuals will see the light of day.

I'm not advocating a departure from tried and trusted standards. (The majority of systems that I write are still based on the MDI standard.) However, there are definite cases in which a custom interface would be more suitable. So why aren't custom interfaces more common? Developers give a couple of reasons for this.

First, to produce a nonstandard-looking interface requires the use of a lower-level language such as C++—Visual Basic 5 cannot hack it. Believe me, this just isn't true, although you do have to write slightly more code than for a standard MDI application and you will have to resort to the Windows API. But this should not prove to be an obstacle. Trust me, it's really not as difficult as it might seem at first.

Second, to produce a good-looking interface requires some level of artistic skill and know-how. Well, I'm afraid that this is true, but most developers nowadays can put something together that's pretty good. If you're producing commercial titles, you'll probably be using an artist anyway. On the positive side, because you will be designing or drawing the interface, the look and feel are constrained only by your own imagination (or perhaps by some corporate standard).

Assuming you're able to create a good-looking interface, how do you build the functionality behind it?

From MDI to SDI

We'll take it one step at a time and first look at how to link windows together without having to use the MDI. To do this, we will use the software catalog application that we developed earlier in this chapter. Well, we'll develop the forms anyway—there's no functionality within them for this project. You will find this project, shown in Figure 11-3, on the CD as SDIdemo.vbp.

FIGURE 11-3

The software viewer as an SDI application

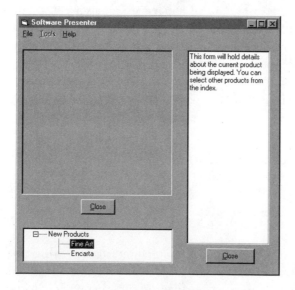

The Windows API call that we'll be using to create the interface is *SetParent.* Its declaration is as follows:

```
Declare Function WinSetParent Lib "user32" _
    Alias "SetParent" (ByVal hWndChild As Long, _
    ByVal hWndNewParent As Long) As Long
```

As you might be able to determine from Figure 11-3, a few changes have been made. Instead of all of the forms being child forms, we are now manipulating frames rather than forms. This is because the usual use of *SetParent* is to manipulate container controls, such as frames, picture boxes, and panels.

The SDI application

Indeed, this Windows API call can help in wizard applications if there are a lot of steps. This is because it's difficult to manipulate many frames from a single screen at design time. You might find it easier to create a form for each of the frames and then use *SetParent* for the required frame when the Prev or Next button is clicked. Another advantage of this approach is that the resources are loaded on demand rather than all of the required resources being loaded within a single form having a tabbed dialog box.

To call a new form from the menu on the parent form, we now actually call a public method of the child form that we've created rather than call the *Form_Load* method:

```
Private Sub mnuFileDesc_Click()
    frmText.SetChild
End Sub
```

The *SetChild* procedure is similar in all of the forms, so here's the one from the pack form:

```
Public Sub SetChild()
Dim lResult As Integer
' Lock the display panel onto the parent form.

    If Not bLocked Then
        fraPack.Top = frmParentLFont.fraPack.Top
        fraPack.Left = frmParentLFont.fraPack.Left

        lResult = WinSetParent(fraPack.hWnd, frmParentLFont.hWnd)

        DoEvents
        bLocked = True
    Else
        fraPack.Visible = True

    End If
End Sub
```

At the start, we're checking to see whether the form is loaded. If it is, the frame is brought into view. In the case of a wizard, you may well leave the forms loaded and then just change the z-order of the frames to display the data. This will be more efficient than unloading and reloading, but it will take more resources.

If the form is being loaded, the top and left of the form frame are set to match those on the parent form, and the *SetParent* Windows API call is used to set the parent of the frame to the parent form from the pack form. The *DoEvents* call ensures that *SetParent* is acted on. Finally, the *bLocked* variable is set.

NOTE

Using the Windows API can be unpredictable, so you should always save your work before you run your code. Also, you need to test extensively when using the API, and compile and test your application for every version of the Windows operating system that you intend to run under.

You'll need to code the *QueryUnload* event of the parent form to unload the other forms:

```
Private Sub Form_QueryUnload(Cancel As Integer, UnloadMode As Integer)
    Unload frmIndex
    Unload frmPack
    Unload frmText
End Sub
```

If you forget to do this, the application will not end because the other forms will remain in memory.

The SDI interface

This is just one means of linking forms (or parts of forms). If you want to handle your SDI application at the form level or you need your own form handling, there are several ways of achieving this. First, you'll need to design the window navigation to determine how your application hangs together, and you'll need to draw up a window hierarchy chart. This will show you which screens call which others and their interdependence. With this type of diagram, you will also be able to determine which screens can be closed and which need to remain open. From here, you can decide the best way to handle the interface and make decisions such as, "Will there be a single parent window?" "Are some branches of the hierarchy modal?" and "How will the application work?"

From a nonmultimedia perspective, drawing up a window hierarchy allows you to design and map your transaction scope if you're using a database. This might also affect your locking strategy, so it's a useful step to perform, no matter what type of application you're building.

Let's consider an interface that is driven from a single parent screen. An example of this could form part of a workflow application. One method of controlling the interface is to create a status property for each form created on the parent form. You can now write to this property from the child forms, holding details such as moves, minimizes, and maximizes.

You can also test for the status of a window by using the Windows API. Several calls return 0 on failure and nonzero on success. Two that you might find useful are *IsChild*, which determines whether the window is a child of another window, and *IsIconic*, which tells you whether the window has been minimized. To restore a window from a minimized state, use the *OpenIcon* call, or change the *WindowsState* property. I'm sure that with a little thought and planning, you'll find that you are no longer restricted to the MDI-style interface.

Producing a Nonstandard Interface

Now that we have looked at multimedia, at MDI, and at how to create the same effect in SDI, there's no real reason why we should not also step away from the traditional-looking Windows interface to something that is a little more intuitive to use and more user-friendly. To help out the user, we can still create context-sensitive multimedia help and have a fallback position of the Windows help system, but now we can be more creative in our approach to the user interface. The basis for building and activating this user interface is the concept of the hot spot, which is a region on the screen that detects mouse operations and then acts accordingly. The elements that we require are the user interface design, the hot spots, and the actions associated with the hot spots.

The interface

Because we are no longer relying on the Windows controls to produce and activate the interface, we really can have a free hand in designing the look and feel of the application. After you have drawn the interface, I recommend that you save it as a bitmap in the resolution in which the application will be running.

The bitmap can then be used as the background picture for a form (with *Borderstyle* set to none and, if required, *maximized* set to true) so that it fills the screen, and it no longer looks like a Windows application at all. This will, of course, depend on the screen resolution in which the end user will be running, and ideally the bitmap that you create should match that resolution.

It is against this bitmap that we will be creating the hot spots so that the screen can respond to the actions of the user. This also ensures that the hot spot covers the correct area on the bitmap, as specified at build time. If you let the user resize the interface, you will have all sorts of problems with the hot spots not matching the background image. (That's one reason you'll find that the interfaces used on multimedia products are generally fixed and you are not able to resize them.)

NOTE

> At first glance, this may seem like a small problem, and with a bit of math, you could resize the hot spots. I've made several attempts and managed to get reasonably close with rectangular hot spots, by using ratios and offsets to resize and relocate them as the form is expanded and contracted. I've never managed to get anywhere near with irregular hot spots. The math for this is beyond my mathematical skills. If you manage to solve this, I'll be interested to see your solution.

There is, of course, nothing to stop you from also using Visual Basic and other Windows controls, along with your own graphics and hot spots. Indeed, this can often cut down on the amount of work that you have to do.

Methods of hot-spotting graphics

The easiest hot spot shape to produce is the rectangle. This is because you can use the Visual Basic Image control with the background set to transparent, and it will trap all of the mouse events for you. In fact, in many cases, even with slightly irregular shapes, you can map a rectangle, or you can use two rectangles to be accurate enough that it makes no difference. The user cannot see your Image control and will generally click as near to the middle of the designated area as possible.

For producing irregularly shaped hot spots—for example, to map a hot spot to an irregularly shaped polygon—we need to produce a bit more code because of the need to log all of the points of the irregular polygon that represents the hot spot. We also need to write the event handling code, such as mouse moves, clicks, and so on. Don't worry—all of this is achievable using the Windows API and is really pretty simple. First, we'll look at producing an interface that uses the rectangular hot spots before taking on the challenge of irregular hot spots.

Using the Image control as a hot spot

In this application, we will alter the SDI interface slightly by introducing a custom-drawn toolbar. The forms will be loaded by clicking on one of the buttons. The click event is handled by placing a transparent Image control over the button area. To give the illusion of the button being pressed, I've gone for the option with the least code, at the expense of resources. There are many techniques for giving the impression of a button click on a graphic, and I'll cover a few at the end of this section. You'll see others as we go through the chapter. You will find this application on the CD as HotRec. The application, as it appears at design time, is shown in Figure 11-4.

FIGURE 11-4

The image hot spot application in development mode

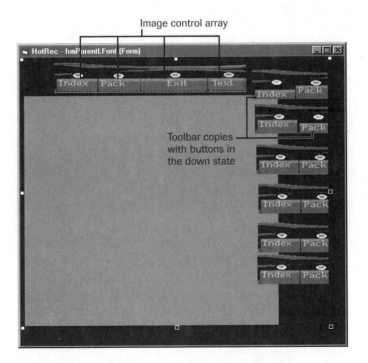

As you can see, I've created a copy of the toolbar for each instance of a button depression, which will be off the screen at run time. When a particular Image control is clicked, the relevant bitmap is copied to the display area.

When you are using the Image control or any other Visual Basic control in a fixed position interface, the resolution in which you design and the font size can be significant. To avoid problems and to provide an interface that is resolution independent, you need to use the *twipsperpixel* properties of the Image control to work in pixels. As we will see later, this is not a problem for the irregular hot spot applications because all Windows API calls are in pixels.

The buttons bitmap is covered with a transparent Image control, with its mouse events coded to simulate a mouse click. The business end of the MouseDown event is as follows:

```
' Work out where we are in terms of pixels.
nXOffset = X \ Screen.TwipsPerPixelX
nYOffset = Y \ Screen.TwipsPerPixelY

' Determine whether we hit a button. (We must have if Y is in
' range.)
If nYOffset > START_Y And nYOffset < END_Y Then
    ' We hit one! Determine which button.
    Select Case nXOffset

        Case START_INDEX To END_INDEX
            picTools(0).Picture = picTools(1).Picture
            frmIndex.SetChild
            frmIndex.fraIndex.BackColor = 0
        Case START_PACK To END_PACK
            picTools(0).Picture = picTools(2).Picture
            frmPack.SetChild
            frmPack.fraPack.BackColor = 0
        Case START_EXIT To END_EXIT
            picTools(0).Picture = picTools(3).Picture
            Unload Me
        Case START_TEXT To END_TEXT
            picTools(0).Picture = picTools(4).Picture
            frmText.SetChild
            frmText.fraText.BackColor = 0
        Case START_HELP To END_HELP
            picTools(0).Picture = picTools(5).Picture
            MsgBox "Spoken help has not been activated"

            ' Have to reset in line because the MouseUp event
            ' will not trigger because of the OK click in the
            ' message box.
```

```
        picTools(0).Picture = picTools(6).Picture
    End Select

  End If
End Sub

Private Sub imgHot_MouseUp(Button As Integer, Shift As Integer, _
    X As Single, Y As Single)
' Set the toolbar back to a neutral state.
    picTools(0).Picture = picTools(6).Picture
End Sub
```

The *MouseDown* event loads the toolbar that has the relevant button in a down state. It determines the correct toolbar by the position of the mouse pointer (in *x,y* coordinates) on the image. A set of constants is used as the bounds of each section and is declared at the beginning of the event.

The *MouseUp* event reloads the neutral toolbar. That's really all there is to it. As I said, I used the method with the least code, but it does serve to illustrate the technique and show how easy it is to use.

Other methods for consideration

As I mentioned earlier, there are many other ways of achieving the same effect. Over time, you might use them all, and you might discover a few of your own.

The first improvement you could make is to produce a bitmap of all the states that you require and then use the PictureClip control for the button states. This is a short step forward from the project as it is presented here.

If you are using the Image control, you can create individual images for each button and then load each icon into an Image control. You can then use the *Move* method in the MouseDown and MouseUp events to move the Image control down and then up. This is efficient because it uses only one set of bitmaps and controls, but it might not work if you've created a fully rendered interface.

If for some reason you want to use nonbitmap pictures and you cannot therefore use the PictureClip control, you can still create a bitmap of all of your controls in a down state and then use the *PaintPicture* method. This does take a little more work because you'll need to determine the exact areas that need to be copied, and you have to use PictureBox controls. The *PaintPicture* method was introduced in Visual Basic 4 as a replacement method for the *BitBlt* Windows API call, but it does not have as much flexibility, it's not as resource friendly, and it's not as quick, especially for animation. For these reasons, I recommend that you use *BitBlt* if you're familiar with it.

CAUTION

> As mentioned earlier, you should use some care and consideration when mixing your own interface details with Visual Basic and Windows controls. All of the irregular hot spot details work in any resolution or font size, so we'll look at these next.

More complex hot spots

Using rectangular hot spots is fine for many uses, such as toolbars, but there may well be cases for which you need to be able to produce hot spots around complex objects. A good example of this is the *Living Book* series of children's edutainment, in which the cartoon pages have many hot spots of different shapes that enable the user to interact with the images on the page.

There are two stages to building irregular hot spots, as you'll see in the following sample application. (*Note:* This program is intended for Windows 95 only.) The first is defining the hot spot area by using the Windows API to produce a polygon object in memory. After you've created the hot spots, you should save them so that you can use them in the second stage. Using this area against a background image, we can activate the hot spot and undertake the action required. The actual method used to save the details will depend on your requirements, but with the improvements to the Jet database engine, this has become a viable option, so we'll create a hot spot editor using Jet as our storage medium. You will find this application on the CD as Irreg.vbp.

An irregular hot spot   A BAS file (DEFINE.BAS) in the application holds the public variable declarations, but more important, it holds the Windows API declarations that make this application work:

```
' Public definitions for the project
Public bPuStart As Boolean ' Tells system that polygon is
                             ' started.
Public bPuDraw As Boolean ' Put application into draw mode.
Public bPuOpendb As Boolean ' Check for open database.
Public sPuHotdb As String ' Name of the hot spot database
Public dbPuHot As Database ' The database object
Public sPuImageFile As String ' Name and path for the image

' Type definition for the polygon region points
Type POINT32
    x As Long
    y As Long
End Type
```

```
' 32-bit Windows API declarations
Declare Function WinCreatePolygonRgn Lib "gdi32" _
    Alias "CreatePolygonRgn" (lpPoint As POINT32, _
    ByVal nCount As Long, ByVal nPolyFillMode As Long) _
    As Long
Declare Function WinPtInRegion Lib "gdi32" _
    Alias "PtInRegion" (ByVal hRgn As Long, _
    ByVal x As Long, ByVal y As Long) As Long
Declare Function WinDeleteObject Lib "gdi32" _
    Alias "DeleteObject" (ByVal hObject As Long) As Long
```

The first two Windows API functions are the ones that create and activate the hot spot. The first, *CreatePolygonRgn*, takes an array of *x,y* coordinates to produce a closed polygon object in memory. It uses a structure named POINT32, which is an array of *x,y* coordinates that make up the polygon. If you do not close the polygon, Windows will close it for you. With the creation program, I'm allowing a 10-pixel error margin in the creation of a hot spot. Feel free to change this if you're an excellent mouse driver or you have a big monitor and accuracy is not a problem. You might also need to change this if the object you want to make a hot spot is very small.

PtInRegion determines whether you have the mouse pointer within the region specified by a handle, which is the return value of *CreatePolygonRgn*. At the end of the application, you should destroy all objects that you create by using *DeleteObject*. If you don't do this, at best you will get "memory leak," which means that even after your application has ended, it will still be reserving GDI resource and memory because it was never released. This principle applies for all Windows API objects. It's excellent practice to tidy up when you've finished.

The hot spot editor   The next task is to create the database, the structure of which is shown in Figure 11-5, and table structures. This application contains two tables—the first is essentially a hot spot header table that holds the image details, and the second is the hot spot ID. The hot spot ID table is the parent of a table that holds the *x,y* coordinates that make up the hot spot.

Figure 11-5

The hot spot database

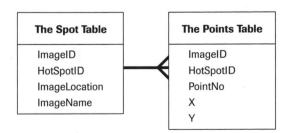

The Spot Table	The Points Table
ImageID	ImageID
HotSpotID	HotSpotID
ImageLocation	PointNo
ImageName	X
	Y

You will find a blank database on the CD named HotBlank.MDB. This is the template from which you can set up hot spot databases. To use the application, copy the project and directory structure to your hard disk. Be sure that HotBlank.MDB is in the database directory and that the bitmaps directory also exists under the application (or alter the code in the menu events).

The application will allow you to load an image into the picture box and then set up and test the hot spots for the image. When you complete a hot spot, write its details to the database by choosing Save Hot Spot from the Hot Spot menu. When you add a new image, the filename will be loaded into the Spot table, and the image will be copied into the bitmaps directory below the application directory. This approach ensures that no absolute paths are used and produces a tidy directory structure.

For simplicity, I didn't include the ability to edit the data on the database or the ability to edit hot spot details, although you can add hot spots to a saved image. Try writing these yourself. This will help you become familiar with the techniques involved, and you'll find that you learn more by actually coding than reading about it.

The hot spot editor at run time is shown in Figure 11-6.

FIGURE 11-6

The hot spot editor at run time

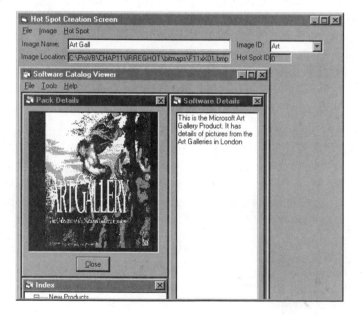

FIGURE 11-7

The hot spot editor menu structure

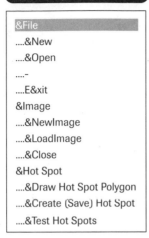

The Hot Spot Editor Menu

&File
....&New
....&Open
....-
....E&xit
&Image
....&NewImage
....&LoadImage
....&Close
&Hot Spot
....&Draw Hot Spot Polygon
....&Create (Save) Hot Spot
....&Test Hot Spots

To open a saved database, select the details that you want to load from the Image ID combo box. The editor will load the image and set up the hot spot details saved in the database. When you select a new database, the database is created from the blank database and then is ready for you to create image and hot spot details. The menu structure for the hot spot editor is shown in Figure 11-7.

Taking it from the top, let's see what each of the menu items does, and review some of the more interesting code.

The File New menu item This menu item uses the CommonDialog control to get the path and filename for your new hot spot database and then copies the blank hot spot database to the specified location. Finally, the database is opened, along with the recordsets for the two tables.

NOTE

I'm using dynaset recordsets so that the application can run against other backend databases. If you're certain that you will be using only Jet, you can use table types to be more efficient.

At the end of the event, the indexes and the hot spot array are reset, ready for you to enter the new details.

The File Open and Menu Exit items The File Open menu item is similar to File New, with a few notable exceptions. The initial code at the start (not shown here) gets the name and path of an existing database. If a database is open, the *HotSpotDBClose* procedure is run. *HotSpotDBClose* closes the database and resets the hot spots. (We'll look at these a little later.) Then the recordsets are opened, and a combo box is populated with the Image IDs from the hot spot table. These are used to load the associated image at a later date. The error trap is used to determine whether any images are set up. In this instance, the error 3021 means that there are no records in the recordset.

The Menu Exit menu item calls the *HotSpotDBClose* procedure and then unloads the form.

```
        If bPuOpendb Then Call HotSpotDBClose ' Close the current
                                              ' database.
        ' Open the database in the default workspace.
        Set dbPuHot = DBEngine.Workspaces(0).OpenDatabase(sPuHotdb)
        bPuOpendb = True

        ' Open the recordsets.
        Set rsPiSpot = dbPuHot.OpenRecordset("Spot", dbOpenDynaset)
        Set rsPiPoint = dbPuHot.OpenRecordset("Points", _
            dbOpenDynaset)
        mnuHotSpot.Enabled = True

        ' Load the image IDs into the combo box.
        rsPiSpot.MoveFirst
        sID = rsPiSpot!ImageID

        Do
            cboImageID.AddItem sID
            rsPiSpot.FindLast "imageid = '" & sID & "'" ' Find the
                                                        ' last record
                                                        ' with the ID.
            ' Move to the next record. (This should be the first of
            ' a new image.)

            rsPiSpot.MoveNext
            If rsPiSpot.EOF = False Then sID = rsPiSpot!ImageID
        Loop Until rsPiSpot.EOF

    Exit Sub
ErrDetect:
' Handle the blank database error.
    If Err.Number = 3021 Then ' No current record
        MsgBox "The database is blank; please set up a " & _
            "new set of details", vbInformation
        Exit Sub
    End If

    MsgBox "The error " & Err.Description & " has occurred"

End Sub
```

The New Image menu item   The initial section of code calls the common dialog box to get the name of the image to be loaded. The filename is extracted from the file details with a small function named *FileNameGet*. The *ResetHotSpots* procedure is called to clear all of the currently specified hot spots. The image is copied and loaded, and the user is reminded to enter a unique Image ID and a name for the image. If you don't select an image, a message box is displayed, and the procedure exits.

The Load Image menu item   This is a little more complex than the New Image menu item because we need to get the details from the database and then load the image and set up the currently defined hot spots. Because this is the key to the editor, here is the full event code:

```
Private Sub mnuImageLoad_Click()
' Load an image from the database, and set the indexes
' and the hot spots.
Dim nSpot   As Integer ' Current hot spot
Dim nPoints As Integer ' Number of points for the hot spot

    If cboImageID.Text = "" Then
        MsgBox "Please select an image ID to load!", _
            vbCritical, "Image Load Error"
        cboImageID.SetFocus
        Exit Sub
    End If
    ResetHotSpots ' Reset the indexes.

    ' Get the Image details.
    rsPiSpot.FindFirst "ImageID = '" & cboImageID.Text & "'"
    If rsPiSpot.NoMatch Then
        MsgBox "The ID you have selected does not exist. " & _
            "Please select from the combo box", vbCritical, _
            "Image Load Error"
        cboImageID.SetFocus
        Exit Sub
    End If

    txtName.Text = rsPiSpot!imagename
    txtName.Enabled = False
    sPuImageFile = App.Path & "\bitmaps\" & _
        rsPiSpot!ImageLocation
    lblLocation = sPuImageFile

    picHot.Picture = LoadPicture(sPuImageFile)

    ' Set up the current hot spots from the points table.
    rsPiPoint.FindFirst "ImageID = '" & cboImageID.Text & "'"
```

>>

```
                nSpot = rsPiPoint!HotSpotID
   >>           nPoints = 0

                Do
                    If nSpot = rsPiPoint!HotSpotID Then ' Same hot spot
                        PolyPoints(rsPiPoint!PointNo).x = rsPiPoint!x
                        PolyPoints(rsPiPoint!PointNo).y = rsPiPoint!y
                        nPoints = nPoints + 1
                    Else ' Create the hot spot region and save it.
                        ReDim Preserve lPiHotSpots(nSpot)
                        lPiHotSpots(nSpot) = WinCreatePolygonRgn( _
                            PolyPoints(0), nPoints, 0)

                        nSpot = rsPiPoint!HotSpotID
                        PolyPoints(rsPiPoint!PointNo).x = rsPiPoint!x
                        PolyPoints(rsPiPoint!PointNo).y = rsPiPoint!y
                        nPoints = 1

                    End If
                    rsPiPoint.FindNext "ImageID = '" & _
                        cboImageID.Text & "'"
                    If rsPiPoint.NoMatch Then ' Save the last hot spot.
                        ReDim Preserve lPiHotSpots(nSpot)
                        rsPiPoint.FindLast "ImageID = '" & _
                            cboImageID.Text & "'"
                        lPiHotSpots(nSpot) = WinCreatePolygonRgn( _
                            PolyPoints(0), rsPiPoint!PointNo + 1, 0)
                        nPiHotIndex = rsPiPoint!HotSpotID
                        lblHotSpotID = nPiHotIndex
                        rsPiPoint.FindNext "ImageID = '" & _
                            cboImageID.Text & "'"
                    End If

                Loop Until rsPiPoint.NoMatch

            End Sub
```

The image details are loaded from the selection in the combo box, and the hot
spots are cleared. Because we have all of the reference details, these are displayed and then the text boxes are disabled. Now we need to set up the hot
spots for the selected image. This involves looping through the spot recordset
for the selected image, using *FindNext*, and picking up the associated *x,y* coordinates from the points table. These are then loaded into the *Polypoints* array.

When the hot spot ID changes, the hot spot is created using *CreatePolygonRgn*. Creating the hot spot requires only a call to *CreatePolygonRgn* with all of the *x,y* points declared.

To pass an array structure (in this case, an array of POINT32 structures) to a Windows API function, pass the first element of the array. This has the effect of passing a pointer to the array in memory because all of the array elements are contiguous in memory. The second parameter is the number of elements in the array, which is one more than the index. (Remember that arrays are zero-based unless you use the *Option Base* statement.) The final parameter is the polygon fill mode. We do not use the polygon fill mode in this application, so set the parameter to 0. You will now be able to add to the hot spots for the loaded image.

The Close Image menu item   The Close Image menu item resets the hot spots, removes the image from the picture box, and clears the data from the text boxes.

The Draw and Test Hot Spot menu items   The Draw Hot Spot Polygon menu item sets the editor to draw mode by setting the draw flag *bpuDraw* to true and the *Polypoints* index to –1 so that when 1 is added to the index, it is at the starting point 0. *bPiDirty* is used to determine whether a polygon has not been saved.

The Test Hot Spot menu item sets the *bpuDraw* variable to False, which, in effect, switches the drawing off so that the system can respond to mouse events.

```
' Define a new hot spot for the image.
   ' Check that the last polygon has been completed first.
   If bPiDirty Then
       MsgBox "You have a polygon defined. Save the " & _
           "hot spot and try again."
       Exit Sub
   End If

   ' Reset the flags to start a new polygon.
   bPuDraw = True
   nPiPointIndex = -1
```

The Save Hot Spot menu item   The Save Hot Spot menu item is used to save all of the hot spot details to the database. If this is the first hot spot that has been defined, the image details are also saved because they are not saved anywhere else.

```
Private Sub mnuHotSpotCreate_Click()
' Create the polygon region so that the hot spot area can be
' tested, and then save the details to the hot spot database.
Dim nCount As Integer

    If bPiDirty = False Then ' Nothing to save
        MsgBox "You do not have anything unsaved", _
            vbInformation, "Save not required"
        Exit Sub
    End If

    If txtName = "" Or cboImageID = "" Then ' Missing details
        MsgBox "You must supply the name and ID for the image", _
            vbCritical, "Image Detail Error"
        txtName.SetFocus
        Exit Sub
    End If
    txtName.Enabled = False
    ' cboImageID.Enabled = False
    nPiHotIndex = nPiHotIndex + 1
    ReDim Preserve lPiHotSpots(nPiHotIndex)

    lblHotSpotID.Caption = nPiHotIndex

    ' The return variable is the handle to the polygon region.
    lPiHotSpots(nPiHotIndex) = WinCreatePolygonRgn(PolyPoints(0), _
        nPiPointIndex + 1, 0)
    bPiDirty = False

    ' Save the data to the database.
    rsPiSpot.AddNew
    rsPiSpot!ImageID = cboImageID.Text
    rsPiSpot!ImageName = txtName.Text
    rsPiSpot!HotSpotID = nPiHotIndex
    rsPiSpot!ImageLocation = FileNameGet(sPuImageFile)
    rsPiSpot.Update

    ' It's a new image; add its ID to the combo box.
    If nPiHotIndex = 1 Then cboImageID.AddItem cboImageID.Text

    ' Now save the points.
    For nCount = 0 To nPiPointIndex
        rsPiPoint.AddNew
        rsPiPoint!ImageID = cboImageID.Text
        rsPiPoint!HotSpotID = nPiHotIndex
```

```
        rsPiPoint!PointNo = nCount
        rsPiPoint!x = PolyPoints(nCount).x
        rsPiPoint!y = PolyPoints(nCount).y
        rsPiPoint.Update
    Next nCount

End Sub
```

The multiple hot spots are handled by creating an array of polygon handles, which are already defined in memory. The checks at the start of the procedure ensure that there is something to be saved and that the key information is entered into the text boxes to save the details to the database. After the checks, the hot spot ID is generated and displayed in a label. The polygon is then created in memory, and the handle is saved in the array. At the end, the new hot spot details are saved to the database. If it's the first hot spot of a new image, the image ID is added to the combo box so that you can work on it later without having to restart the application.

The mouse events   The mouse events have two modes. In draw mode, the hot spot details are being drawn, and in normal mode, the hot spot details can be checked and tested.

The MouseDown event code is used to save the current hot spot details when the application is in draw mode:

```
Private Sub picHot_MouseDown(Button As Integer, _
    Shift As Integer, x As Single, y As Single)

' Check the draw mode. If we're in drawing mode, save the
' coordinates to start a new line.

    If bPuDraw Then ' We are in drawing mode.
        nPiPrevX = x
        nPiPrevY = y

        ' Add 1 to the index, and save the points.
        nPiPointIndex = nPiPointIndex + 1
        PolyPoints(nPiPointIndex).x = x
        PolyPoints(nPiPointIndex).y = y
        bPiDirty = True
    End If

End Sub
```

In the MouseMove event for draw mode, a line is drawn to indicate the hot spot details. In normal mode, the hot spot can be tested by calling a function *nHotSpot*, which is passed the *x,y* mouse coordinates and checks to see whether it's over a hot spot:

```
Private Sub picHot_MouseMove(Button As Integer, _
    Shift As Integer, x As Single, y As Single)
' Draw the line as the mouse is dragged.

    If bPuDraw And nPiPointIndex > -1 Then ' We are in drawing
                                           ' mode.
        picHot.Line (PolyPoints(nPiPointIndex).x, _
            PolyPoints(nPiPointIndex).y)-(nPiPrevX, nPiPrevY)
        nPiPrevX = x
        nPiPrevY = y
        picHot.Line (PolyPoints(nPiPointIndex).x, _
            PolyPoints(nPiPointIndex).y)-(nPiPrevX, nPiPrevY)

    Else ' We are in hot spot mode, so check the mouse pointer
        ' location.
        Call nHotSpot(x, y)
    End If ' End of draw mode check
End Sub
```

The MouseMove event has a couple of functions. The first is used when you are in drawing mode and you want to draw a line on the screen that shows the bounds of the hot spot. This is done using the *Line* method. The PictureBox control draw mode is set to 6 - Invert so that the previous line can be easily erased by drawing over it.

NOTE

There are, in fact, 16 draw modes available. The draw modes determine the pen style used to produce the graphic image. You'll find out more about graphic objects and draw modes in the Visual Basic help files or on MSDN. If you plan to use graphic objects or you want to produce special effects, you might find some of the draw modes useful.

The first line drawn erases the previous one. Then the *x,y* coordinates are saved before the second line is drawn. If the hot spot has been drawn, the MouseMove event is used to check whether the mouse pointer is over a hot spot by calling *nHotSpot*:

```
Private Function nHotSpot(ByVal inX As Single, _
    ByVal inY As Single) As Integer
' Check whether the mouse is in the hot spot, and pass back the ID.
    Dim nCount As Integer

    For nCount = 0 To nPiHotIndex
        If WinPtInRegion(lPiHotSpots(nCount), inX, inY) Then
            picHot.MousePointer = vbCrosshair
            nHotSpot = nCount
            Exit Function
        Else
            picHot.MousePointer = vbDefault
            nHotSpot = -1
        End If ' End of region check
    Next nCount

End Function
```

As you can see, the function loops through the hot spot index, checking to see whether the mouse pointer is over a hot spot. If it is, the mouse pointer is altered, and the index of the hot spot is returned. By convention, the pointer shape used is that of a hand, but Visual Basic 5 still does not ship with this cursor as one of its choices, so you'll need to create one yourself and load it as a custom cursor.

We'll see this in use next in the MouseUp event:

```
Private Sub picHot_MouseUp(Button As Integer, _
    Shift As Integer, x As Single, y As Single)

    Dim nDiffX As Integer, nDiffY As Integer

    ' Check whether draw mode is off and hot spot clicked.
    If Not bPuDraw Then ' Hot spot clicked

        ' Put function here to decide what to do for each image.
        If nHotSpot(x, y) > -1 Then ' On a hot spot
            MsgBox "You have clicked hot spot " & _
                Str(nHotSpot(x, y))
        End If

        Exit Sub
    End If
```

```
If bPuDraw And nPiPointIndex > 0 Then ' We are in drawing mode.

    ' Determine the distance from the the start of
    ' the polygon.
    nDiffX = Abs(PolyPoints(0).x - x)
    nDiffY = Abs(PolyPoints(0).y - y)

    ' Check to see whether we're within 10 pixels of the start
    ' of the polygon; if so, close the polygon.
    If nDiffX < 11 And nDiffY < 11 Then bPuDraw = False
End If ' End of first draw check

End Sub
```

The checking of the return value of *nHotSpot* determines the hot spot that has been clicked. The test here is pretty basic, but it does illustrate how to test each of the hot spot regions.

In a full application, to take some action depending on the hot spot clicked will mean checking the image details in the database to find out which image is loaded and which action is required. We'll see how this works in a bit.

When the application is in draw mode, there is a check to see whether the mouse pointer is within 10 pixels so that the draw mode can be switched off. (The Windows API call to create the polygon will close it for you.) If you need better accuracy for smaller hot spots, alter the check to the accuracy required. I must confess that I really hate drawing packages that insist on a pixel accuracy to close a polygon, especially if I'm working on a small monitor.

That's pretty much all of the code covered except for the two tidy-up routines mentioned earlier:

```
Private Sub ResetHotSpots()
' This procedure clears the hot spots and resets the ID
' and the index.
    Dim nCount As Integer
    Dim lResult As Long

' Loop through the hot spots.
    For nCount = 0 To nPiHotIndex
        lResult = WinDeleteObject(lPiHotSpots(nCount))
    Next nCount

    nPiHotIndex = 0
    lblHotSpotID = nPiHotIndex
    lblLocation = ""

End Sub
```

The *ResetHotSpots* routine clears any currently defined hot spots from memory by looping through the hot spot array and deleting all of the objects. This is called by the following:

```
Private Sub HotSpotDBClose()
' This routine will destroy all of the current hot spots
' and close the database that's open.

    ResetHot spots

    rsPiSpot.Close ' Close the recordsets.
    rsPiPoint.Close
    dbPuHot.Close ' Close the open database.

End Sub
```

After deleting the hot spots, this code closes the currently open database and then closes the recordsets. And that's all there is to it! If you look closely, you'll see that we've managed to build a reasonable set of functionality for an irregular hot spot editor with very little code. OK, it's not completely bullet-proof, but it does demonstrate the techniques and methods required to be able to produce fully customizable user interfaces. It also demonstrates that what appears at first to be a very difficult and complex task is relatively simple once you understand the techniques.

UP AND RUNNING

Now that we've looked at how to incorporate sound and video into our applications and at methods of producing custom interfaces, we can put it all together and address one of the problem areas highlighted in the first section: computer-based training. We will look at how to use multimedia techniques to produce custom titles that can be mastered to CD and given to the users. With the cost of mastering CDs dropping so radically, this has become a cheap and efficient means of training because it saves valuable IT resources, allows users to learn at their own pace (and possibly on their own time), and is reusable.

The Computer-Based Training System

What does it take to produce a CBT system? Well, it is, in effect, two applications: the builder, which is used to produce the CBT details, and the presenter, which is the user interface for the system. For the user interface, you can produce something that does not resemble a Windows application by using the techniques in the previous section, produce a standard MDI application, or produce something in between. Because of the limitations of space for this chapter, the demonstration application will have a nonstandard toolbar, but it will still look like a Windows form. I'm sure that with a bit of thought you'll be able to take this a step further and produce the look and feel that you require. This is an ideal application for producing your own fully customized interface, using hot spots to activate areas of the interface.

To be able to make the most of presenter and builder, you need to produce generic functions and facilities so that they can be used by non-IT developers to produce the required CBT titles. This has some advantages and disadvantages that you need to consider before you jump into development. Some aspects can be both advantages and disadvantages, depending on the requirements and how they are viewed.

Some advantages

By producing a generic CBT system, you can use resources other than your IT developers, who may well be among your most expensive resources. This may be especially useful for large rollouts, where more formal training will occur. By using the trainers who will undertake the formal user training, you can kill two birds with one stone. The trainers will become familiar with the application as they build the CBT course, and they will then be able to tailor the formal training to fit in with the course that they have designed. The other main advantage is that a generic system can be reused for other application rollouts. Of course, some tweaking may well be required to provide extra functionality, but in essence you will not need to undertake any further development.

Some disadvantages

Not all is rosy with this approach. There are one or two drawbacks that you may well need to consider. The first is that you might find that the tweaking could snowball and reach a point where it would have been simpler and more economical to start over than amend the generic application. Another drawback is that by using a generic system, no matter what the application, the interface will of necessity be the same. Depending on the requirement, this might be an advantage, especially if the users will be learning more than one system. But by producing a custom user interface, you can create a more focused front end that helps with the training system. Above all, whatever interface you finally adopt, it must be intuitive and easy to use because you should not add to the user burden with a large learning curve for the CBT system. You might also find that the functionality of a generic system does not get the job done because you'll need to code to the lowest common denominator and try to outguess future requirements. The final consideration is that if you decide to produce custom CBT systems for your applications (or at least the large ones), you shouldn't need to write a builder application. You will be producing all the details required as you write the system. As with most things in the IT industry, it's a trade-off.

The CBT System

In this section, we will build a working CBT system, but without a lot of the bells and whistles that you'd associate with a commercial product. The intention here is to look at each of the components and see how it works, in effect concentrating on the methods and techniques.

We'll also look at the areas you need to extend to produce a commercial-quality system. The system on the CD is functional in that you can build and view project details, create and use hot spots on the project forms, and add some text for each form. These are the basic elements that would make up any comprehensive CBT system. You will find the code and all the supporting files on the CD in the CBT directory structure. If you want to play with this application, copy the files to your hard disk so that you can edit them. As with all the other applications in this chapter, the directory structure is significant and is used to avoid coding absolute paths into the application. For a commercial application, you'd probably create an install routine and allow the user to determine the path, although it would be sensible to keep the directory structure.

The CBT database

The first enhancement that you might want to make is in the area of screen navigation. To keep the model simple, I've allowed for a form to have only a single entry and exit. In a real-world application, this would be a many-to-many relationship to allow the presenter to show the end user the navigation routes through the system. To do this here would have added substantially to the complexity and the amount of code without showing any useful multimedia techniques. I'm sure that you'll have no trouble extending the system in this area.

As with the irregular hot spot project, there is a blank database called CbtBlank.mdb, which you can use to create new databases. The details are set up on the database using the builder application that you will find on the CD as CbtBuilder.vbp. The CBT database is shown in Figure 11-8.

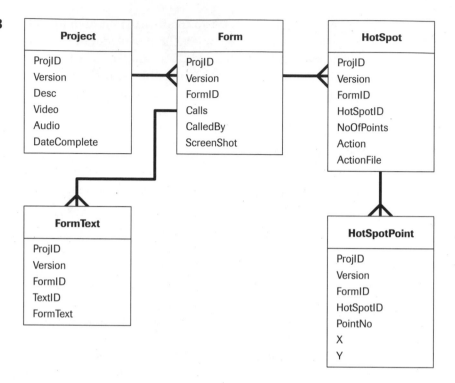

FIGURE 11-8

The CBT database

The CBT builder application

To get a flying start with the application, I have used the Visual Basic Application wizard to produce a skeleton MDI application. (*Note:* This program is intended for Windows 95 only.) I won't cover any of the generated code or forms here. You should be able to review that at your leisure, either by using what's on the CD or by generating a skeleton application yourself.

A substantial amount of the code that we will be creating in the builder application will also be used in the presenter application, albeit with some minor changes. You will also see striking similarities between a lot of the builder code and the code that we have developed for the previous applications. We will be building on the knowledge gained so far.

The builder will allow you to create a project and then add images for each of the forms that make up the application. The main limitation here is that you can create only one calling link and one called link for each form. You can create hot spot regions on these images and link hot spot actions for these regions. You can also create help text for each of the forms.

At the start of the application, a splash screen is displayed. There has been no alteration to this form from generation except for a few changes to labels, so I'll ignore this form. We'll look at the other areas of functionality in the order that they appear in the menu on the MDI parent form. The builder MDI at run time is shown in Figure 11-9.

Figure 11-9

The CBT builder MDI at run time

The File menu   The first set of menu items consists of the File menu functions. These are functionally identical to the File menu functions for the hot spot editor project. The New menu item creates a new CBT database from a blank template database and then allows you to set up all the details. The Open menu item opens a CBT database that has been previously created so that you can continue work on it, and Close closes the database that's currently open. The Exit menu item shuts down the application by deleting any objects in memory (using the *ResetHotSpots* function developed in the hot spot editor project), closing the database and unloading the form.

The Edit menu   No code has been written for the Edit menu items, but the items have been left in the application. In a commercial application, there would be at a minimum Cut, Copy, and Paste items. You will also notice that there are icons on the toolbar for formatting text. These have also been left in so that you can code them for formatting the text you'll create to describe the forms. In a commercial application, you'd add a flag to the database that indicates whether the text is in an external file or held within the database. After all, it's easier to use another editor than code one yourself.

The View menu   The last item on the View menu (Project Detail) has been added from the details generated. This item calls a form that allows the user to view the project details that have been set up. This form has been generated using the Data Form Wizard and has not been altered in any way. The form allows the user to view the project details and the forms that have been set up for the project so far.

The Project menu   When you have created or opened a database, you first create or open a project. The CBT system has been designed to be a multiproject database, so you can hold details about more than one application in a single place. The New and Amend menu items each load forms that allow the user to set up a new project or amend an existing project. These forms were generated with the Data Form wizard, so I'll leave you to review the code at your leisure.

To let the user open a project and make it the current project, a small dialog box, *frmProjSel*, is displayed that lets the user select from a list of projects previously set up on the database:

```
Dim strSQL As String

    On Error GoTo ErrDetect

    ' Get the project details.
    strSQL = ""
    strSQL = strSQL & "SELECT    ProjID"
    strSQL = strSQL & "          ,Version "
    strSQL = strSQL & "FROM Project"
    Set rsPiProject = dbPuProj.OpenRecordset(strSQL, _
        dbOpenSnapshot)

    ' Load them into a combo box.
    rsPiProject.MoveFirst

    Do
       cboProj.AddItem rsPiProject!ProjID & "-" & _
           rsPiProject!Version
       rsPiProject.MoveNext
    Loop Until rsPiProject.EOF

    Exit Sub
```

For the demonstration application, I'm using SQL directly from within the code. Although this is more efficient than using DAO, there are a few things that you might like to consider. In a commercial application, for added efficiency you may find stored procedures or stored queries in a Jet database more effective. If you don't want to create stored procedures but you want to maintain a reasonable amount of decoupling from the database for security or maintenance reasons, you can create the SQL in a resource file and load it as required. The actual method will, as usual, depend on your requirements.

The Form_Load event reads all of the projects on the Project table and populates a combo box with the details.

The cancel Button_Click event closes the recordset and unloads the form but does not reset the current project.

The SelectClick event sets the two public variables that reset the current project and version. These are used throughout the rest of the application to access and set up the project-specific and version-specific details.

If you neither set up a new project nor select a current project, you will not be able to use the form functions. In a commercial system, a useful feature would be to save the application settings in the registry so that when the CBT system is reloaded you can resume where you left off.

The Form menu   Because most projects are based on forms, the majority of the functionality is focused on the Form menu items. To create a new form for your project, you choose Set Up New Form Image. This displays a common dialog box to get the path and name of the image that represents the form and then sets up the image form in N (new) mode.

If you want to test or edit form hot spot details, select Add To Saved Image. This loads a dialog box (named frmFormGet) modally, which allows the user to select a previously set up form.

```
frmFormGet.Show vbModal
    If frmFormGet.FormToLoad = "" Then Exit Sub ' Cancel selected

    frmImage.FormImage = frmFormGet.FormToLoad
    frmImage.FormStyle = "A"

    Load frmImage
    frmImage.Show
```

After a selection is made, the image form is loaded in A (amend) mode. The code for frmFormGet selects all of the forms for the project from the database and sets a set of properties, depending on the selection. These are used in frmImage, which we'll look at next.

The Image form   This form has functionality similar to that of the irregular hot spot editor of the previous project. You set up the form details, define hot spot regions, and save the hot spot regions to the database. The functionality is extended in that you can define actions for each hot spot and each is saved in the database and can be tested there. For this demonstration application, the actions available are showing a BMP, playing a WAV file, or playing an AVI file. In a commercial system, these actions could be extended to allow for the playing of other multimedia files or animating the hot spot that was clicked. When the hot spots are loaded from the database, a visual representation is added by creating a brush icon and filling in the defined polygon. You can then test the hot spot actions, alter the action details, or add new hot spots. The Image form at run time is shown in Figure 11-10.

FIGURE 11-10

The Image form with hot spots defined at run time

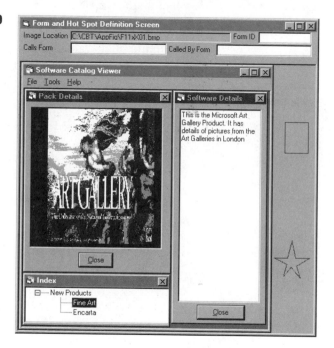

As you can see in Figure 11-10, two hot spots are defined for the image. To clearly show the hot spot definitions, the two defined are not actually on the image itself. Once again, in a commercial application, you should ensure that the hot spot definitions fit the image. Before the form is called from the MDI parent form (or the form get dialog box), the *FormStyle* and *FormImage* custom properties are set. These are used in the FormLoad event, which loads the form with all of its hot spots:

```
Private Sub Form_Load()
Dim nSpot As Integer ' Current hot spot
Dim nPoints As Integer ' Number of points for the hot spot
Dim sSQL As String ' SQL
Dim lReturn As Long ' Return from API calls
```

```
' Open the recordsets, restricting them to the current
' project and version.

Me.Width = 7480 ' Set the initial form size.
Me.Height = 6200
sSQL = ""
sSQL = sSQL & " SELECT * "
sSQL = sSQL & " FROM"
sSQL = sSQL & " HotSpot"
sSQL = sSQL & " WHERE"
sSQL = sSQL & "      HotSpot.ProjID = '" & _
    sPuCurrProject & "'"
sSQL = sSQL & " AND HotSpot.Version = '" & _
    sPuCurrVers & "'"

Set rsPiSpot = dbPuProj.OpenRecordset(sSQL, _
    dbOpenDynaset)

sSQL = ""
sSQL = sSQL & " SELECT * "
sSQL = sSQL & " FROM"
sSQL = sSQL & " HotSpotPoint"
sSQL = sSQL & " WHERE"
sSQL = sSQL & "      HotSpotPoint.ProjID = '" & _
    sPuCurrProject & "'"
sSQL = sSQL & " AND HotSpotPoint.Version = '" & _
    sPuCurrVers & "'"

Set rsPiPoint = dbPuProj.OpenRecordset(sSQL, _
    dbOpenDynaset)

sSQL = ""
sSQL = sSQL & " SELECT * "
sSQL = sSQL & " FROM"
sSQL = sSQL & " Form"
sSQL = sSQL & " WHERE"
sSQL = sSQL & "      Form.ProjID = '" & _
    sPuCurrProject & "'"
sSQL = sSQL & " AND Form.Version = '" & _
    sPuCurrVers & "'"

Set rsPiForm = dbPuProj.OpenRecordset(sSQL, dbOpenDynaset)

bPuStart = False
```

>>

```
nPuPointIndex = -1
bPiDirty = False
bPiAction = False
nPuHotIndex = 0
ReDim lPuHotSpots(0)

Select Case sPiStyle

Case "N" ' It's a new image.
    ' Set the picture property of the image.
    lblLocation.Caption = App.Path & "\AppFig\" & sPiImage
    picImage.Picture = LoadPicture(lblLocation.Caption)
    sPuImageFile = sPiImage

Case "A" ' Load a previously saved image and hot spots.

    Call ResetHotSpots

    ' Set a hatch brush.
    hPiBrush = WinCreateHatchBrush(1, vbButtonFace)

    ' Get the image details.

    txtImageID.Text = sPiImage
    txtImageID.Enabled = False
    lblLocation.Caption = App.Path & _
        "\AppFig\" & sPuImageFile
    txtCalls.Text = frmFormGet.FormCalls
    txtCalledBy.Text = frmFormGet.FormCalledBy
    picImage.Picture = LoadPicture(lblLocation.Caption)

    ' Check to see whether any hot spots are declared.
    rsPiSpot.FindFirst "FormID = '" & sPiImage & "'"
        If rsPiSpot.NoMatch Then
        MsgBox " There are no hot spots declared yet " & _
            "for this image", vbInformation, "Image Load"
        Exit Sub
    End If

    ' Set up the current hot spots from the points table.
    rsPiPoint.FindFirst "FormID = '" & sPiImage & "'"

    nSpot = rsPiPoint!HotSpotID
    nPoints = 0
```

```
        Do
            If nSpot = rsPiPoint!HotSpotID Then ' Same hot spot
                PolyPoints(rsPiPoint!PointNo).x = rsPiPoint!x
                PolyPoints(rsPiPoint!PointNo).y = rsPiPoint!y
                nPoints = nPoints + 1
            Else ' Create the hot spot region and save it.
                ReDim Preserve lPuHotSpots(nSpot)
                lPuHotSpots(nSpot) = WinCreatePolygonRgn( _
                    PolyPoints(0), nPoints, 0)

                lReturn = WinFillRgn(picImage.hdc, _
                    lPuHotSpots(nSpot), hPiBrush)

                nSpot = rsPiPoint!HotSpotID

                PolyPoints(rsPiPoint!PointNo).x = rsPiPoint!x
                PolyPoints(rsPiPoint!PointNo).y = rsPiPoint!y
                nPoints = 1

            End If
            rsPiPoint.FindNext "FormID = '" & sPiImage & "'"
            If rsPiPoint.NoMatch Then ' Save the last hot spot.
                ReDim Preserve lPuHotSpots(nSpot)
                rsPiPoint.FindLast "FormID = '" & _
                    sPiImage & "'"
                lPuHotSpots(nSpot) = WinCreatePolygonRgn( _
                    PolyPoints(0), rsPiPoint!PointNo + 1, 0)
                lReturn = WinFillRgn(picImage.hdc, _
                    lPuHotSpots(nSpot), hPiBrush)

                nPuHotIndex = rsPiPoint!HotSpotID

                rsPiPoint.FindNext "FormID = '" & _
                    sPiImage & "'"
            End If

        Loop Until rsPiPoint.NoMatch

        txtImageID.Text = sPiImage
        txtImageID.Enabled = False

    End Select
    WinDeleteObject (hPiBrush)

End Sub
```

The initial SQL sets up and loads the recordsets for the form, hot spots, and hot spot points, which are restricted to the current project and version. This code is fairly mundane and can be reviewed on the CD.

Next, the flags and indexes are initialized. You will notice a new flag called *bPiAction*, which didn't appear in the hot spot editor project. This will be used to determine whether the user wants to set up or amend hot spot action details.

The select case determines the mode of the form, which will be N (new) or A (amended). For a new image, the image is loaded, and the user can then create a form ID and set up hot spots. For an amended image, a brush icon is first created, and then the image details are retrieved from the database as in the hot spot editor project. The only addition to this section of code is that the Windows API call *fillrgn* is used to give a visual indication as to where the hot spots are defined on the image. The hot spot image is inverted because the pen type is set to 6-invert. After all of the hot spots are declared and painted, the brush is destroyed.

The Form menu   The items on the Form menu reset the form details and exit the form. The majority of the work is undertaken by the Hot Spot menu items. The New Hot Spot menu item is the same as in the irregular hot spot editor project except that it sets the flags to indicate that a new hot spot is to be drawn. The Save Hot Spot item is identical to its counterpart in the hot spot editor project. It saves the hot spot details and all of the hot spot points to the database. The Set Hot Spot Action item sets the *bAction* flag to True so that it can be picked up in the mouse events and calls the Action Set Up dialog box. The final item, Test Hot Spot, sets the flags so that the hot spot action can be tested. This is detected in the MouseUp event for the picture:

```
Private Sub picImage_MouseUp(Button As Integer, _
    Shift As Integer, x As Single, y As Single)

Dim nDiffX As Integer
Dim nDiffY As Integer ' X and Y differences used to
                      ' close polygon
Dim nIndex As Integer ' Index of current hot spot
Dim nReply As Integer ' Reply to message box

    ' Check whether draw mode off and hot spot clicked.
    If bPuDraw = False And bPiAction = False Then
        ' Hot spot clicked and test required
```

```
        nIndex = nHotSpot(x, y) ' Decide which hot spot clicked.
        ' Run the action required.
        Call ActionRun(nIndex)

    End If

    ' Check whether it's an action setup.
    If bPuDraw = False And bPiAction Then ' Set up an action
                                          ' for the current
                                          ' hot spot.
        nIndex = nHotSpot(x, y) ' Decide which hot spot clicked.
        If nIndex <> -1 Then
            nReply = MsgBox("Do you want to set up an " & _
                "action for this hot spot", _
                vbQuestion + vbYesNo, "Hot Spot Action")
        Else
            Exit Sub ' Not on a hot spot, so no action set up.
        End If
        If nReply = vbNo Then Exit Sub

        ' Set up an action for this hot spot.
        With frmAction
            .HotSpotID = nIndex
            .FormID = txtImageID.Text
        End With
        Load frmAction
        frmAction.Show vbModal
        bPiAction = False
        Exit Sub
    End If ' End of Action setup check

    If bPuDraw And nPuPointIndex > 0 Then ' We are in
                                          ' drawing mode.

        ' Check whether we're close to the start to close the polygon.
        nDiffX = Abs(PolyPoints(0).x - x)
        nDiffY = Abs(PolyPoints(0).y - y)

        ' Check to see whether we're within 10 pixels, and
        ' close the polygon.
        If nDiffX < 11 And nDiffY < 11 Then bPuDraw = False
    End If ' End of first draw check.
End Sub
```

The main addition to this event is the test to see whether a test of the hot spot is required. Instead of the Select Case that we saw in the hot spot editor project, we now have a call to the *ActionRun* procedure, passing it the index of the hot spot that is clicked. This is used to test the action that's set up for the hot spot:

```
Private Sub ActionRun(ByVal inHotSpotID As Integer)
' This procedure runs the action associated with the hot spot
' if one has been set up.
Dim lReturn     As Long ' The return details from the MCI
Dim sMCIReturn  As String * 128 ' MCI return string
Dim sSQL        As String ' SQL for the find clause
Dim nFileNo     As Integer ' File number
Dim sLine       As String ' Text line

Static bAviOpen As Boolean ' Is AVI playing?
Static bWavOpen As Boolean ' Is WAV playing?

    On Error GoTo ErrDetect

    If inHotSpotID = -1 Then Exit Sub ' Not on a hot spot

    sSQL = "HotSpotID = " & inHotSpotID
    sSQL = sSQL & " AND FormID = '" & sPiImage & "'"
    ' Now find the hot spot record.
    rsPiSpot.FindFirst sSQL

    ' Now undertake the required multimedia action. It will
    ' select the type of call to the MCI, depending on the
    ' action retrieved.

    ' Play the multimedia file, depending on its extension.

    Select Case rsPiSpot!Action

    ' WAV files
    Case "P"
        ' If a WAV file is open, then...
        If bWavOpen Then
            ' Stop it, and close it.
            lReturn = WinmciSendString("Stop WaveFile", _
                "", 0, 0)
            lReturn = WinmciSendString("Close WaveFile", _
                "", 0, 0)
        End If
```

```
        ' Set the WAV file open flag to True.
        bWavOpen = True

        ' Open it.
        lReturn = WinmciSendString("Open " & App.Path & _
            "\AppWav\" & rsPiSpot!ActionFile & _
            " alias WaveFile type WaveAudio", "", 0, 0)

        ' Play it (NoWAIT).
        lReturn = WinmciSendString("Play WaveFile", "", 0, 0)

' AVI files
Case "R"

' If an AVI file is open, then...
    If bAviOpen Then
        ' Stop it, and close it.
        lReturn = WinmciSendString("Stop AviFile", _
            "", 0, 0)
        lReturn = WinmciSendString("Close AviFile", _
            "", 0, 0)
    End If

    ' Set the AVI file open flag.
    bAviOpen = True

    ' Open it.
    lReturn = WinmciSendString("Open " & App.Path & _
        "\AppAvi\" & rsPiSpot!ActionFile & _
        " alias AviFile type AviVideo", "", 0, 0)
    ' Play it, wait for it to finish, and then close.
        lReturn = WinmciSendString( _
            "Play AviFile wait ", "", 0, 0)
        lReturn = WinmciSendString( _
            "Close AviFile", "", 0, 0)

Case "S" ' BMP
    imgAction.Picture = LoadPicture(App.Path & _
        "\AppFig\" & rsPiSpot!ActionFile)
    picImage.Visible = False
    imgAction.Visible = True

Case "T" ' Text
    ' Open the file.
    nFileNo = FreeFile
```

>>

```
        Open App.Path & "\AppFig\" & _
            rsPiSpot!ActionFile For Input As #nFileNo
        ' Read the records and load into RTF text box.
        Do While Not EOF(nFileNo)
            Line Input #nFileNo, sLine
            txtText.Text = txtText.Text & sLine & vbCrLf
        Loop
        Close #nFileNo
        txtText.Visible = True

    Case Else ' No action set up
        MsgBox "You have not set an action up " & _
            "for hot spot number " & Val(inHotSpotID)

    End Select
    Exit Sub

ErrDetect:
' Error trap
    If Err.Number = 53 Then ' Missing action file
        MsgBox "The path of the file for the hot spot " & _
            "action is incorrect. Please reset the action", _
            vbCritical, "Action Path Error"
        Exit Sub
    End If

    MsgBox "The error '" & Err.Description & _
        "' has occurred.", vbCritical

End Sub
```

The initial section of code builds an SQL statement that gets the hot spot record from the database. This will contain the action that has been set up, which is then used in the following Select Case statement to determine the multimedia action required. This code should look familiar to you—it's similar to the code used in the spoken help application we developed earlier. The main difference is that the AVI file is now played in wait mode, which means that the system will wait until it's finished before resuming. The file is played in the default window.

In the presenter, we will look at how we can create our own window and use this to play the AVI clips. This is a useful technique for multimedia developments because you can play video clips wherever you want them and build this feature into your custom user interface.

The Case Else statement is triggered when no actions are set up for the current hot spot, and a message is displayed to the user. This, in effect, tests the hot spot region, even though no actions have been set up.

Additional details Most of the general functions in the CBT builder application have been generated at this point, and the specific functionality has been built on the projects that we created earlier (with some small alterations). What we now have is an application that will allow you to create projects and, within projects, form details that can be used as a basis for end user training. We've managed to link graphics, text, sound, and video to these forms, and there is no limit (within reason) to the amount of information that we can log for each form in a project. Now that we have these details logged, we need to be able to present them to the user.

As with the builder, the demonstration presenter will concentrate on techniques rather than bells and whistles, but we will look at ways to enhance the application as we go.

The presenter application

We'll employ most of the techniques we've learned so far to produce the presenter application, which uses the spoken help system (a semi-Windows-style interface), and we'll use a fair amount of code from the builder application to activate the hot spots. (*Note:* This program is intended for Windows 95 only.)

The presenter is an SDI-style system. The interface has a non-Windows standard look and feel, and if you knew the target screen resolution, you could ensure that your interface fills the screen, fully immersing the user in your application.

Start up When the application starts, it displays a splash screen, which contains a common dialog box so that the user can select a database to work with.

(If this were a commercial application, I'd expect some sort of logon screen that would allow the user to connect to and log onto the database.)

If a database is not selected, the application terminates. This is controlled from a *startup Sub_Main* procedure in PresCode.Bas. This BAS file contains all of the functions and procedures that handle hot spots, as well as the public variables and Windows API declarations for the application. If the user selects a database, the form frmInterface is loaded. The presenter application at run time is shown in Figure 11-11.

FIGURE 11-11

The presenter application at run time

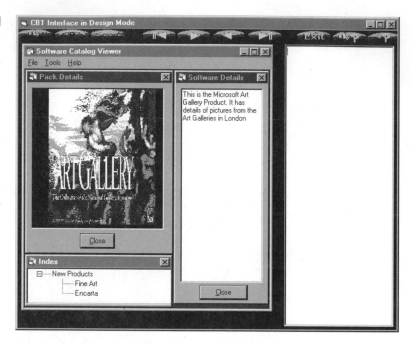

The presentation form   The FormLoad event for the presenter is pretty simple. It initializes the environment and opens the selected database. The user can then select the project to open from the current database.

Even though the buttons are totally nonstandard, if you hold the cursor over one, the standard ToolTip will pop up, and to help further, a spoken help system is built in. The ToolTips and all of the mouse handling for the toolbar are achieved through the use of an image array, even though the buttons are not rectangular.

I'm using the MouseDown event for this control array to play a click sound and then move the image down by two pixels. This gives the illusion of the button being depressed and is a very resource-friendly method because only one set of bitmaps is loaded for the toolbar.

```
Private Sub imgTools_MouseDown(Index As Integer, _
    Button As Integer, Shift As Integer, _
    X As Single, Y As Single)
' Play the button click sound...
    Call ActionRun(-1, "X")
' ...and move the button down to indicate a click.

    imgTools(Index).Top = imgTools(Index).Top + 2

End Sub
```

This event plays a click sound by calling a procedure named *ActionRun*. This is the multimedia player for this application. We'll look at it in more detail later. For now, we'll look at the functionality behind each of the buttons. This code resides in a Select Case statement in the *imgTools* Click event:

```
Select Case Index
    ⋮
```

Case 0: The current sound clip   This is the code to play the current sound clip. This is achieved by calling *ActionRun* with a hot spot ID of –1 to indicate that no hot spot action is required, and a multimedia action of W to play the current WAV file.

```
    ⋮
If bPuSpeak Then ' The spoken help system is active.
    Call ActionRun(PLAY_SOUND, "K")
    Exit Sub
End If
' Play the current sound.
Call ActionRun(-1, "W")
```

The initial *If* statement in this section of code is repeated in all the case sections. It handles the playing of a spoken help clip by passing the ID set up in the resource file as the hot spot ID and setting the action to K to play the associated spoken help clip. The IDs are set up as constants in the same way as those in the spoken help application and are held in SpeakConst.bas.

Case 1: The current video clip   The principle for the current video clip is identical to the one for the current sound clip. As promised earlier, the video is played in its own window, positioned in the center of the screen. The application can be extended to differentiate between video clips, and you can position the viewports for the video clips and then build the rest of the interface around these windows. This technique integrates the video into your interface and is used in quite a few multimedia titles.

```
    ⋮
ActionRun -1, "V"
    ⋮
```

Case 2: Toggle the text view   This button code toggles the text view on and off by expanding and contracting the interface form. Once again, when you know the target resolution, you should be better able to integrate the text into your interface than by using view/hide, load/unload, or toggle on/off, depending on the style that you prefer. With larger screens and higher resolution capabilities, screen real estate is not such an issue, but it can still be a problem that needs considering.

Case 3: Load a project   This is the code that loads a project from the currently open database by displaying a Project Open dialog box. In fact, it's the same Project Open dialog box we used in the builder application. When the user has selected a project from the dialog box, the rest of the interface is initialized. The first section of SQL gets the project details and sets the current sound and video clips to those set up for the project.

At the moment, this is the only way to play the sound and video clips associated with the project. What I'd do in a commercial application is to play either the sound or the video clip at startup, depending on a flag setting in the database. This could then be used as an introduction to your system. The toolbar could then be extended to allow the user to replay the clips at any time. The last thing that this section of code does is to call a procedure named *FirstForm*, which basically loads the first form in the project. We'll look at this procedure later on.

Case 4: Next screen   This code goes to the next screen in the project, based on the form ID set up in the *Calls* field for the form. It calls a procedure named *NextForm*, which is similar to *FirstForm*.

Case 5: Previous form   This code takes us to the previous form in the project, based on the form ID set up in the *Called By* field. In a manner similar to those already described, it calls a procedure named *PrevForm* to load the previous form details.

Case 6: Last form   This code jumps to the last form in the forms recordset. Provided that you've set up all of the calls and Called By fields in the recordset, you'll find that you can still go to the next and previous forms because the jumps are dependent on the data in the database, rather than on the position of the records in the recordset. This can prove to be a useful technique when you want to process records in an order other than one based on a records position in a recordset or cursor.

Case 7: Exit   There's not really a lot to this one. It exits the application by unloading the form.

Case 8: Spoken help   This code activates the spoken help system. This works in exactly the same manner as the spoken help system we saw at the start of this chapter. Again, for a commercial system, I'd probably create a special video window and use a mix of spoken and video help for the user.

Case 9: Windows help   This is the area where you'd code the links to your Windows help system, although none has been coded for the demonstration application. In a commercial version of the application, you may face a bit of a dilemma here: Do you load help for the application that you are demonstrating or help for the CBT system? I'll leave you to decide for yourself.

The other events   If you look at the code for the application on the CD, you'll see that the Click events for all of the controls on the interface have been coded. This handles the playing of the spoken help system except for *picVideo*, which hides *picVideo* and shows *picImage*. This is done to hide the bitmap that's loaded in a hot spot action.

The form handling procedures   All of the procedures for loading the forms are similar, so we'll look at the most complex, *FirstForm*:

```
Private Sub FirstForm()
' Loads the first form in a project, and sets up the form details.
Dim sSQL As String

    ' Set up the Form recordset.
    ' All forms in the project.
    sSQL = ""
    sSQL = sSQL & " SELECT * "
    sSQL = sSQL & " FROM"
    sSQL = sSQL & " Form"
    sSQL = sSQL & " WHERE"
    sSQL = sSQL & "     Form.ProjID = '" & sPuCurrProject & "'"
    sSQL = sSQL & " AND Form.Version = '" & sPuCurrVers & "'"

    Set rsPuCurrForm = dbPuProj.OpenRecordset(sSQL, _
        dbOpenSnapshot)
    ' Set to the first form.
    rsPuCurrForm.MoveFirst

    ' Get the image details and load into the picture box.
    sPuImageFile = App.Path & "\AppFig\" & _
        rsPuCurrForm!Screenshot
    picImage.Picture = LoadPicture(sPuImageFile)

    ' Now load all of the hot spots for the current form.
    Call ImageSetUp

    ' Load the default text.
    Call TextLoad

End Sub
```

The initial section creates a recordset of all of the forms in the project. This is the recordset that's used by the other form procedures to determine the next, previous, and last forms to get the requested form in the link. Having found the required record (in this case, the first in the recordset), the image is loaded into *picImage*, the hot spots are set up by calling *ImageSetUp*, and the associated text is loaded by calling *TextLoad*.

ImageSetUp This procedure is similar to the Form_Load event code for *frmImage* in the builder application, so we won't go through the code here. It builds a hot spot recordset to get the hot spots for the form and then goes through the hot spot points building the polygons in memory. Because this is the presenter application, the brush icon that we saw in the builder is not used to show where the hot spots are. Instead, when the user is over a hot spot, the mouse pointer changes to the pointing finger shape we first saw in the irregular hot spot project.

TextLoad This procedure sets up the form text recordset and loads the text from the first record into the Rich Text Format (RTF) text box.

```
Private Sub TextLoad()
' Load the text from the newly loaded form.
Dim rsText As Recordset ' FormText recordset
Dim sSQL As String
    ⋮
    'SQL to load the text
    ⋮
    Set rsText = dbPuProj.OpenRecordset(sSQL, dbOpenSnapshot)
    ' Set to the first form.
    rsText.MoveFirst

    rtfDesc.Text = rsText!formtext

End Sub
```

As previously mentioned, there is no means of loading any but the text from the first record from within the demonstration application. In a commercial application, there would be facilities to load the different sections of text either by clicking a hot spot or perhaps by using a TreeView control built into the interface. Once again, how this is handled will depend on the target environment and the type of user interface that you opt for.

PresCode.Bas The rest of the code for the presenter resides in PresCode.Bas. The majority of the procedures are copied from the projects that we've developed so far, so we'll look only at new or significant code here. In fact, the only procedure that bears close scrutiny is *ActionRun*. This is used to handle all of the multimedia clips and all of the hot spot actions. (Apologies for the long listing, but this is the core of the presenter.)

```
Public Sub ActionRun(ByVal HotSpotID As Integer, _
    Optional ByVal Action As Variant)
' This procedure runs the multimedia details requested. If
' Action is specified, the action is on the current
' details or a request for spoken help; otherwise, the action
' associated with the hot spot is run.
' Valid Actions are:-
    ' W - Play current sound clip.
    ' V - Play current video.
    ' K - Spoken help clip.
    ' H - Hot spot action.
    ' X - Play click sound for button press.

Dim lReturn      As Long ' The return details from the MCI
Dim sMCIReturn   As String * 128 ' MCI return string
Dim sPlayAction  As String * 1 ' Actual action required
Dim nPos         As Integer ' Index position of string
Dim nStart       As Integer ' Start position for the string
Dim sReturn      As String * 128 ' Return string from MCI
Dim nWidth       As Integer ' Width of video clip
Dim nHeight      As Integer ' Height of video clip
Dim nFileNo      As Integer ' File number
Dim sLine        As String ' Text line

Static bAviOpen As Boolean ' Is AVI playing?
Static bWavOpen As Boolean ' Is WAV playing?

    If HotSpotID = -1 Then Exit Sub ' Not on a hot spot

    If IsEmpty(Action) Or Action = "H" Then
        ' Now find the hot spot record.
        rsPuCurrHotSpot.FindFirst "HotSpotID = " & HotSpotID

        If IsNull(rsPuCurrHotSpot!Action) Then
            MsgBox "No details are set up for " & _
                "this object", vbInformation
            Exit Sub
        End If
        sPlayAction = rsPuCurrHotSpot!Action
    Else
        sPlayAction = Action
    End If
```

>>

>>

```vb
' Now undertake the required multimedia action. The following code
' selects the type of call to the MCI depending on the action
' retrieved or the action specified.

Select Case sPlayAction

' WAV files
Case "P", "W", "K", "X"
    ' If a WAV file is open...
    If bWavOpen Then
        ' Stop it, and close it.
        lReturn = WinmciSendString("Stop WaveFile", _
            "", 0, 0)
        lReturn = WinmciSendString("Close WaveFile", _
            "", 0, 0)
    End If

    ' Set the WAV file open flag to True.
    bWavOpen = True

    ' Open it.
    If sPlayAction = "X" Then ' Play click.
        lReturn = WinmciSendString("Open " & App.Path & _
            CLICK_SOUND & " alias WaveFile type WaveAudio", _
            "", 0, 0)
    ElseIf sPlayAction = "P" Then ' Hot spot play.
        lReturn = WinmciSendString("Open " & App.Path & _
            "\AppWav\" & rsPuCurrHotSpot!ActionFile & _
            " alias WaveFile type WaveAudio", "", 0, 0)
        ' Set it to the current clip.
        sPuCurrSound = App.Path & "\AppWav\" & _
            rsPuCurrHotSpot!ActionFile
    ElseIf sPlayAction = "W" Then ' Play current sound clip.
        lReturn = WinmciSendString("Open " & sPuCurrSound & _
            " alias WaveFile type WaveAudio", "", 0, 0)
    ElseIf sPlayAction = "K" Then ' Spoken help clip
        lReturn = WinmciSendString("Open " & App.Path & _
            LoadResString(HotSpotID) & _
            " alias WaveFile type WaveAudio", "", 0, 0)
        bPuSpeak = False ' Turn spoken help off.
        Screen.MousePointer = 0 ' Reset the mouse pointer.

    End If
    ' Play it (NoWAIT).
    lReturn = WinmciSendString("Play WaveFile", "", 0, 0)
```

```
' AVI files
Case "R", "V"

' If an AVI file is open...
    If bAviOpen Then
        ' Stop it, and close it.
        lReturn = WinmciSendString("Stop AviFile", "", 0, 0)
        lReturn = WinmciSendString("Close AviFile", "", 0, 0)
    End If

    ' Set the AVI file open flag.
    bAviOpen = True

    ' Open it.
    If sPlayAction = "R" Then ' Hot spot play video.
        lReturn = WinmciSendString("Open " & App.Path & _
            "\AppAvi\" & rsPuCurrHotspot!ActionFile & _
            " alias AviFile type AviVideo", "", 0, 0)
        ' Set it to the current clip.
        sPuCurrVideo = App.Path & "\AppAvi\" & _
            rsPuCurrHotSpot!ActionFile
    Else
        lReturn = WinmciSendString("Open " & sPuCurrVideo & _
            " alias AviFile type AviVideo", "", 0, 0)
    End If

    ' Set the picture box as the output window for the
    ' video clip.
    lReturn = WinmciSendString("Window AviFile handle " & _
            Str$(frmInterface.picVideo.hWnd), "", 0, 0)

    ' Now get the dimensions for the video clip. It returns
    ' a space-separated string of Left Top Width Height for
    ' the video clip.
    lReturn = WinmciSendString("Where AviFile destination", _
        ByVal sReturn, Len(sReturn) - 1, 0)

    nStart = InStr(sReturn, " ")  ' Left Position
    nPos = InStr(nStart + 1, sReturn, " ")  ' Top position
    nStart = InStr(nPos + 1, sReturn, " ") ' Start of width

    ' Now set up the two integers...
    nWidth = Val(Mid(sReturn, nPos, nStart - nPos))
    nHeight = Val(Mid(sReturn, nStart + 1))
```

>>

>>

```
        ' ...and alter the size of the picture box.
        frmInterface.picVideo.Width = nWidth
        frmInterface.picVideo.Height = nHeight
        frmInterface.picImage.Visible = False
        frmInterface.picVideo.Visible = True

        ' Finally play it, wait for it to finish, and then close.
        lReturn = WinmciSendString("Play AviFile wait ", "", 0, 0)
        lReturn = WinmciSendString("Close AviFile", "", 0, 0)

        ' Then reshow the image.
        frmInterface.picImage.Visible = True
        frmInterface.picVideo.Visible = False

    Case "S" ' BMP
        frmInterface.picVideo.Picture = LoadPicture(App.Path & _
            "\AppFig\" & rsPuCurrHotSpot!ActionFile)

        frmInterface.picImage.Visible = False
        frmInterface.picVideo.Visible = True

    Case "T" ' Text
        ' Open the file.
        nFileNo = FreeFile
        Open App.Path & "\Apptxt\" & _
            rsPuCurrHotSpot!ActionFile For Input As #nFileNo
        frmInterface.rtfDesc.Text = ""
        ' Read the records and load into RTF text box.
        Do While Not EOF(nFileNo)
            Line Input #nFileNo, sLine
            frmInterface.rtfDesc.Text = _
                frmInterface.rtfDesc.Text & sLine & vbCrLf
        Loop
        Close #nFileNo

    Case Else ' No action set up
        MsgBox "There is no associated action for " & _
            "hot spot number " & Val(HotspotID)

    End Select

End Sub
```

The valid actions that can be passed are W to play the current WAV file, V to play the current video clip, K to play the spoken help WAV file, H to trigger the hot spot action, and X to play a click sound for a button depression.

The first piece of code checks to see which action parameter was passed. In a commercial application, you could check to see that the parameter is valid. If the action is H, the hot spot record is accessed, and the hot spot action is determined. If an action has not been set up, a message is displayed to the user.

The select case to determine the type of file to play has been extended to handle the different types of file, but at the core we are still using the MCI command strings that we've seen in previous projects.

Case P, W, K, X: Playing WAV files Each of the four different actions results in a different way of opening a WAV file.

- X uses the constant CLICK_SOUND, which is the path and filename of the click sound for a button click.

- P is the hot spot action, so the location of the WAV file is read from the hot spot record.

- W is the action for playing the current sound, so it picks up the location of the file from the *sCurrSound* variable.

- K is passed when the spoken help system has been activated and gets the location of the file from the resource file, as we saw in the spoken help application.

This demonstrates four different methods that can be used to link multimedia files to your applications. The alias for the filename now proves to be very useful because no matter which method is employed to open the WAV file, its name is aliased as *WaveFile* for all subsequent MCI actions. The last line in this section plays the open WAV file with a *nowait* setting so that the application does not wait for the WAV file to finish playing before resuming.

Case R, V: Playing AVI files Two actions are associated with playing an AVI file: R is the hot spot action and uses the details from the hot spot record, and V plays the current video clip using *sCurrVideo*. As promised, we are going to play the video in our own custom window, which is the *picVideo* picture box. The MCI command that we use is Window, followed by the filename, followed by an argument of the Windows handle for the window that we want to use. Having set the destination window, we need to set its dimensions because not all AVI clips are the same size. The MCI call to get the dimensions is a little different. We'll need to use a return string for the second parameter and determine its size for the third. The actual MCI command string is Where, followed by the filename (or the alias), followed by an argument of destination. The return string will contain the left, top, width, and height details, each separated from the others by a space. The width and height details are extracted, and *picVideo* is set to the new dimensions before *picVideo* is brought into view and the video clip is played.

Case B: Showing bitmaps   In some cases, an illustration may need to be displayed. This is a hot spot action only, and in the demo application, it also uses *picVideo* to display the image. This is the reason why the Click event of *picVideo* is coded to hide it and to show *picImage*. Once again, if you know the target environment, you can build a separate window into the interface to show illustrations and handle the displaying and hiding on the toolbar.

The Completed CBT System

In a remarkably short time and with the application of only a few techniques, we've managed to create a working generic CBT system. Once you understand the principles, you can apply the same techniques to the builder and the presenter so that the actual development requirement is kept to a minimum. In reality, this can be considered only as a prototype system, but the majority of the work required to make it a fully commercial application will revolve around how the interfaces for the builder and, more important, the presenter will work. There have been a few pointers as we looked at the code for the project, and I'm sure that you can now take the project and turn it into a useful application for your company.

OTHER METHODS OF PRODUCING MULTIMEDIA INTERFACES

Before we end our discussion of multimedia interfaces, we should touch on a whole new area of multimedia opening up within Windows and Visual Basic 5. Microsoft is spending a large part of its research budget on the Internet, intranets, and associated development tools and browsers in the form of ActiveX documents, DOC objects and the COM model, and the ability to host applications in Microsoft Explorer. This is a very large topic. To cover it fully would require a book in itself. In fact, don't be surprised to see books appearing on the shelves dedicated to Visual Basic and the Internet. What we'll do here is take a quick time-out and look at the potential of the new set of emerging standards. Consider what we have done in the previous sections: We have managed to include sound and video in our applications, looked at ways and means of stepping beyond the MDI interface, and activated sound and video by adding hot spots.

This is in essence what the new standards and methods are offering us as developers. Currently the scene is changing very rapidly, so it's difficult to determine exactly what's possible or what will be possible, but ActiveX documents and the ability to host them in Microsoft Explorer should be watched closely. Take the CBT application, for example. The way that it stands at the moment, you'll need to produce CDs for your users to use the system. By creating the text in HTML, you get the text-linking that is lacking in the sample application. By setting up the application as an ActiveX document, you can host the application on a Web server and allow your users to access it from many locations, without going into the multimedia facilities available to Web documents.

For commercial software companies, a version of the CBT system can be used as a marketing technique to show off the functions and capabilities of new software if it is loaded on a publicly available Web site. These facilities are now integrated into the Visual Basic 5 language set, and I'm sure that you will find many applications for the new technology. In fact, Microsoft is looking to move away from the current MDI standard toward the more flexible ActiveX document standard hosted in the Explorer shell.

DOCUMENT IMAGE PROCESSING

Now that you have a good understanding of how to create nonstandard Windows applications and how to add multimedia capabilities to your applications, there's really nothing stopping you from producing your own Document Image Processing (DIP) system. There has been widespread interest in these systems since the mid-80s, when the concept of the paperless office was in vogue, but they were expensive to buy a decade ago and required large amounts of storage and powerful machines. Now, in the mid-90s, we have all of those capabilities sitting on almost every desktop. CDs are now the norm rather than the exception, and with CD mastering equipment dropping rapidly in price, it's now possible to master your own CDs.

The basis of a DIP system is the ability to view form and document images in a structured and sensible manner. This usually means using a backend database to log the details. We have already seen how to link form images to details in a database in the CBT application, and these techniques can be successfully applied here. If you require image manipulation, there are a vast array of add-ons to provide the functionality that you require. You can (if you're feeling adventurous) also use the Windows API to provide image manipulation functionality, such as *StretchBlt* for zooming.

Scanning

At the heart of these systems is the scanning and cataloging of the scanned documents. Visual Basic 5 supports the control of serial devices by using the MSComm custom control. How the scanner actually works will depend on the device you use, but I'm sure that it'll be well documented. You can then use Jet or a backend database to catalog the image details, allowing users subsequent access to the images through a controlled interface.

Workflow

Having managed to scan and store your documents and catalog them on a backend database, the next logical step is to expand the functionality of the database to produce a workflow and job-tracking system. This can be achieved by creating jobs, which are made up of a series of steps, and then associating them with form types.

A form can then be tracked and the current status determined by looking at the job step for the form. By linking users with the individual job steps, you can schedule and control the workflow. If you are also running Microsoft Exchange, you can use the MAPI controls that ship with Visual Basic 5 to notify the user that some action is required, directly out of the system.

The diagram in Figure 11-12 illustrates this concept. Doc X arrives and is logged into the DPI/Workflow database. Job X is associated with this document, so a new instance of the job is created. SLD is the first person to take some action in this workflow, so an e-mail notification is sent. After some action, the step completion details are logged, and the system e-mails the next person in the workflow that step 2 is required. This continues until Job X for Doc X is complete. By time-stamping the entries in the job record, you can gather service level metrics (and much more).

These are just a few ideas for using multimedia in a commercial environment. As with many emerging technologies, the takeup is slow at first, but as people become more familiar with its uses, they find new ways to use it.

Figure 11-12

The workflow in a DPI system

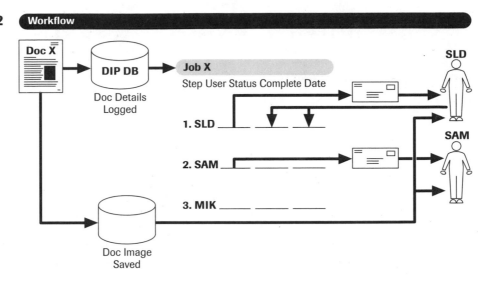

Summary

This was a real roller-coaster ride through multimedia. It's a bit like a stone bouncing on the water. We've touched down in a few places, mostly skimming the surface, but there's still a whole ocean to explore. We've managed to cover enough material for a complete book, so by necessity we've concentrated on the techniques, rather than on production of reams of code. I hope that it's given you some ideas and that you no longer look on multimedia as just bells and whistles that are difficult to implement in an application. I also hope that before you leap into your next application, you at least consider the style of interface that should be used (although I do appreciate that at many sites, rigorous standards are applied). Just maybe you have enough information to question some of these now and show how a little customization of the interface can produce real benefits to your organization.

I would have loved to have covered many of the topics in more depth, but it just wasn't possible. You do have a starting point for finding out more and extending the work that we've done in this chapter. As with most things, the best way to learn is to do, so have at it.

So You Want to Add Another User!

A Guide to Manipulating SQL Server Security

Simon is a TMS Associate who specializes in Visual Basic, SQL Server, and Microsoft Office Integration. He has worked in information technology since graduating with a computing degree in 1984. He has worked on healthcare, financial, personnel, administration, and project planning systems for a variety of companies, large and small. He lives in Gloucestershire with a Gordon Setter named Hamish and a large motorbike. Simon is also a Microsoft Visual Basic Certified Professional.

SIMON JONES

I've always wished there were a clear and concise guide for manipulating SQL Server security. So many people leave security measures out of their applications and hope that the database administrator will do it all for them. The database administrator then gets bogged down with the mundane work of maintaining users and permissions. So here I'm going to provide you with some procedures for manipulating SQL Server security using RDO and Visual Basic. With a little know-how, you can provide security for your applications and enable users to maintain database security themselves.

RDO Basics

Microsoft Visual Basic version 5 has two primary methods of accessing data on SQL Server. One of these is using Data Access Objects (DAO), a method already familiar to many people. It's the same method we've become accustomed to using for manipulating data in Microsoft Access MDB files over the years. Using DAO has always inflicted a big penalty in the form of involving the Microsoft Jet database engine, even when Jet wasn't needed because the data was held in an intelligent server, such as SQL Server. With Microsoft Visual Basic version 4 came a smaller, faster alternative to DAO—Remote Data Objects (RDO). RDO is a very thin wrapper around ODBC functions, and it's optimized for speed and flexibility. It comes with a corresponding Remote Data control (RDC), which binds to other controls just like the ordinary data control. Both RDO and RDC can perform asynchronous queries, which allows the Visual Basic program to get on with other tasks while the server prepares the resultset. For those who aren't familiar with RDO, Figure 12-1 provides a quick tour.

FIGURE 12-1

Collections in the Remote Data Objects library

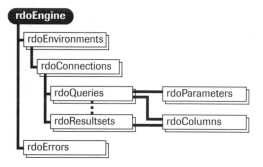

rdoEngine

rdoEngine is a system object that functions as the gateway to SQL Server. It has a few properties and methods and maintains two collections: rdoErrors and rdoEnvironments.

```
rdoEngine.rdoDefaultCursorDriver = rdUseIfNeeded
```

rdoEnvironments

rdoEnvironments objects are used to control transactions. All the data manipulated in one rdoEnvironment can be committed or rolled back with one command—providing, that is, that the back-end database supports transactions, including transactions across multiple servers, if that is what you are doing.

An rdoEnvironment object contains a collection of rdoConnections. Each environment can hold a set of connections to different ODBC data sources, or it can hold a set of connections all to the same data source. The one thing common to all rdoConnections in one rdoEnvironment is that they share the same user name and password.

The following code is an example of connecting to a SQL Server database:

```
Dim en As rdoEnvironment
Dim cn As rdoConnection
Set en = rdoEngine.rdoEnvironments(0)
en.CursorDriver = rdUseOdbc
en.LoginTimeout = 5
en.Name = "TransOp1"
Set cn = en.OpenConnection(dsname:="", _
    prompt:=rdDriverNoPrompt, _
    Connect:="UID=;PWD=;" & _
    "Driver={SQL Server};Server=Bristol2;", _
    Options:=rdAsyncEnable)
sbrStatus.Panels(1) = "Connecting"
While cn.StillConnecting
    sbrStatus.Panels(1) = sbrStatus.Panels(1) & "."
    DoEvents
Wend
sbrStatus.Panels(1) = "Connected"
```

NOTE

In the connect string for the *OpenConnection* method, we have specified a driver and a server rather than a Data Source Name (DSN). You can do it either way—both are valid.

Using a sophisticated back-end database such as SQL Server allows you to make many changes to data in many tables and then commit this data to disk in one go. This is a *transaction*. A classic example of a transaction is a banking transaction. If I give you $10, my account is debited $10 and your account credited $10. A change to one account can't be allowed without a corresponding change to the other account. If, during the transaction, it were discovered that I didn't have enough money or that your account number had been specified incorrectly, neither change would be made and the transaction would be canceled (rolled back); that is, the data would be restored to its original state.

The RDO methods we use to control transactions are *BeginTrans*, *CommitTrans*, and *RollBackTrans*; they can be applied to individual rdoConnections or to rdoEnvironments.

NOTE

Using transactions can speed up your individual queries; typical benchmarks show that queries run up to 17 percent faster inside transactions.

rdoConnections

An rdoConnection is a connection to one ODBC data source that uses the user name and password of the rdoEnvironment in which the rdoConnection resides. You can set properties on an rdoConnection to specify what kind of cursor it uses (server-side, client-side, or none) and also the Login and Query time-outs.

The cursor type specifies where rows of data should be buffered to allow the user to scroll forward and backward through the resultset. A server-side cursor puts more of the burden on the server and the network. Only the data the client requires at any one time is transferred across the network; generally, this means just enough data to present on one screen. Using a server-side cursor usually will reduce network traffic, but it can also increase network traffic under certain circumstances, such as when data is passed from the server to the client many times as the user scrolls up and down the resultset.

Using a client-side cursor means that the complete resultset is transferred to the client at one time and then is held in memory or on disk. A client-side cursor provides a more predictable load on the whole system, but it can slow everything down as large amounts of data are transferred across the network to be stored temporarily on the client PC. This time is wasted if all the user then does is pick the first record.

Using no cursor is a very quick method of fetching rows, but it means the client program can read the resultset only once and can't move backward through the data. It's therefore a useful method when populating static list boxes and combo boxes and when generating reports. It's also useful in three-tier applications when the middle tier makes a quick connection to the back-end data server to retrieve information in one large chunk, which it then passes on to the front-end presentation application in smaller chunks.

rdoQueries

rdoQueries are the equivalent of DAO's QueryDefs, and many of their properties and methods are similar. But rdoQueries are much better suited to working with remote data stores. rdoQuery objects will work with SQL statements that you construct on the fly, bolting clauses together with the contents of variables, as shown in this example:

```
StrSQL = "SELECT * FROM " & strTableName & " WHERE " & _
    strColumnName & " LIKE '" & strRestriction & "*'"
```

But rdoQuery objects work even better when you construct the SQL statement with placeholders for parameters, as shown here:

```
StrSQL = "SELECT * FROM ? WHERE ? LIKE ?"
```

The question marks are replaced when you set the parameters for the query, as you can see in this example:

```
Set qryOne = conConnection.CreateQuery("One", strSQL)
qryOne.rdoParameters(0) = strTableName
qryOne.rdoParameters(1) = strColumnName
qryOne.rdoParameters(2) = strRestriction & "*"
```

If you want to use stored procedures on the back-end database, these procedures often take parameters and return values. rdoQueries can be used too, as demonstrated here:

```
strSQL = "{? = call ParameterTest(?, ?, ?)}"
Set qryTwo = conConnection.CreateQuery("One", strSQL)
qryTwo.rdoParameters(0).Direction = rdParamReturnValue
qryTwo.rdoParameters(2).Direction = rdParamInputOutput
qryTwo.rdoParameters(1) = strType
qryTwo.rdoParameters(2) = intApples
qryTwo.rdoParameters(3) = dteSellBy
```

After you have constructed your query, you can do two things with it. If it's going to return a resultset, you use the query's *OpenResultset* method. If it's not going to return a resultset, you call its *Execute* method.

Only two other methods are available with rdoQueries: the *Cancel* method, which is used to stop a query that's executing asynchronously; and the *Close* method, which is used to discard a query that's no longer needed.

Interestingly, rdoQuery objects have events that fire at various times. The WillExecute event is fired before the query is executed, which permits you to make last-minute changes to the SQL or to prevent the query from executing. The QueryComplete event fires when a query has finished executing. The QueryTimeout event fires when the *QueryTimeout* period (a property of the query) has elapsed and the query hasn't yet begun to return rows.

rdoResultsets

rdoResultsets are rows of data contained in columns. They are like DAO recordsets, but with some significant differences. rdoResultsets can contain more than one set of records with different columns in each set. There are no

FindFirst, *FindNext*, or *FindPrevious* methods. Updates to the resultset can be batched together and sent back to the server in one operation. rdoResultsets can be opened asynchronously, which allows the client application to get on with something else while the server is busy. And there are several events that fire when data is ready or when a resultset is associated with (or dissociated from) an rdoConnection.

You can open an rdoResultset from either an rdoConnection or an rdoQuery. If you use an rdoConnection as the basis for the resultset, you then, of course, have to supply an SQL command. An rdoQuery, on the other hand, contains the SQL command that is to be executed, as you see here:

```
Set rsLogins = conPiConnection.OpenResultset(strSQL, _
    rdOpenForwardOnly, rdConcurReadOnly, rdExecDirect)
Set rsUsers = qryUsers.OpenResultset(rdOpenKeyset, _
    rdConcurLock, rdAsyncEnable)
```

The parameters on the *OpenResultset* method are the SQL command (for opening from a connection), the type of cursor, the type of locking (also known as concurrency—hence, the values all start with rdConcur), and the options for asynchronous or direct execution. Not all of the possible parameter combinations make sense or are supported. For example, it doesn't make sense to use rdOpenKeyset with rdConcurReadOnly. One of the points about a KeySet cursor is that it is updatable. If you wanted a read-only, scrollable cursor, you would use rdOpenStatic instead of rdOpenKeyset. Some options might not be available because of the limitations of the back-end database or the ODBC driver. The cursor type and locking parameters must be chosen very carefully for every query and resultset you create.

SQL SERVER SECURITY MODEL

Because of the way it grew up, SQL Server uses terminology and concepts for managing users and groups of users that differ from those used in Microsoft Windows NT (Figure 12-2). This can cause confusion. I hope you will be less confused after reading this section.

Logins

For a person to connect to SQL Server, he or she must have a login record in one of the system tables that specifies his or her login name and password. Only the SQL Server system administrator can add or remove login records.

FIGURE 12-2

The SQL Server security model (slightly simplified)

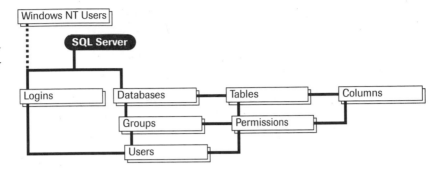

If you're using integrated security, you don't specify either the login name or the password when connecting to SQL Server. SQL Server asks Windows NT to vouch for who you are. (See "Domain managed security" on page 531.)

Users

For each database on the SQL Server, there is a list of people who are allowed to use the database—the database users. Each login record maps to a user name in databases to which they are allowed access. The simplest scenario is that a login record for User B is matched by a user record for User B in the accounts database. Thus, User B can log into SQL Server and have access to the accounts database. Although the user name doesn't have to be the same as the login name, it greatly simplifies things if they are the same.

Aliases

When you want two or more people to have identical privileges in a database, you can use an alias to make one user look like another to the server. For one login, you set up a user name and assign the appropriate privileges; for the other login, you set up an alias of the first user name. The result? Two people and two logins, but one user name and one set of privileges.

Setting up an alias can be useful when you want more than one person to have special privileges, such as the privileges of the database owner. The database owner can grant and revoke privileges from other users and can create new tables and views, but he or she can't transfer the ability to grant these permissions to other users. Setting up an alias for special users to the database owner is the only way for the users to obtain this privilege.

Groups

Groups of users are managed at the database level rather than at the server level. Each database has a list of groups. Every user is a member of the group named public and, optionally, just one other group. It's often useful to create groups for different user roles in a database. You might, for example, create a group for administrators who are allowed to maintain (INSERT, UPDATE, and DELETE) the contents of some tables in the database; other users then would be allowed only to see (SELECT) data from the tables. If you have a table of personnel data, you might create another group for personnel managers who would have complete rights to that table, that is, with the ability to see and change all of the data in the table. Other users, not in that group, might be allowed read-only access to the table but would be prevented from seeing the salary information contained in some of the columns.

Privileges

Permission to use tables, columns, and commands can be assigned to and revoked from a user or a group. The order in which privileges are granted and revoked is important. You should grant and revoke privileges for the public group first, then for other groups, and finally for individual users. Only grant or revoke privileges to individual users where it's really necessary. It's much easier to maintain privileges for groups of users rather than for individual users because there's less work involved for the administrator.

Remember, everyone belongs to the public group, so assign privileges to that group carefully. Also think about the guest user. Should you revoke all privileges for guests or allow them limited access to the database?

NOTE

> The terms *privilege* and *permission* are used interchangeably in SQL Server documentation and mean the same thing.

Table privileges

The database owner can grant or revoke SELECT, INSERT, DELETE, UPDATE, and REFERENCES privileges on a table or view. (REFERENCES allows the user to create foreign key constraints on other tables without having SELECT permission on that table.) Consider carefully what each user or group of users should be allowed to do. General users should be granted only SELECT permission on lookup tables. Another group of users would be given permission to INSERT,

DELETE, and UPDATE the data in those tables. You might revoke UPDATE and DELETE permissions from all users on tables that form a transaction log. You wouldn't want the data in invoice or sales order tables, for example, to be altered once it was written.

Column privileges

The database owner can grant or revoke SELECT and UPDATE privileges on individual columns in a table or view. Thus, a group of users might be able to see a column but not change it. (There might be an application out there that requires users to be able to change the data in a column but never see the values they have changed, but I can't think of one.)

Stored procedure privileges

Stored procedures have the privileges of the user who created them at the time the procedures were created. The database owner grants users and groups the permission to EXECUTE stored procedures. Thus, you can keep a really tight hold on what your users can do. You could revoke *all* privileges from the users and then grant them EXECUTE permission to some stored procedures. These stored procedures then control access to the data, and users can't use ad hoc query tools to carry out unauthorized operations.

Command privileges

Permission to use the CREATE DATABASE, CREATE DEFAULT, CREATE PROCEDURE, CREATE RULE, CREATE TABLE, CREATE VIEW, DUMP DATABASE, and DUMP TRANSACTION commands can be granted to users other than administrators. The commands are of limited use to most people. It's better to restrict these privileges to system administrators and database owners.

Domain managed security

If you are working with a Windows NT network (one with Windows NT servers but not necessarily Windows NT workstations), you already have a sophisticated security system for users and for groups of users. SQL Server can make use of this information by asking the Windows NT domain controller to authenticate a user who tries to log onto SQL Server. This does away with the need to supply a separate login name and password to connect to SQL Server. This login validation procedure is a powerful feature and can greatly simplify the management of security on a network. Unless you can find a good reason for *not* using integrated security, use it.

To pass Windows NT logon information to SQL Server, the SQL Server system administrator (SA) must set SQL Server to accept either integrated or mixed security. If all users are going to use these so-called "trusted connections," you can use integrated security. If some users will be using standard security (supplying login names and passwords), you should specify mixed security. If you don't have a Windows NT network or your network protocol doesn't allow trusted connections, you'll have to use standard security and supply login names and passwords every time you connect to SQL Server.

Trusted connections are supported on named pipes and multiprotocol networks. According to the SQL Server Setup Help file, the Multi-Protocol Net-Library does the following:

- Communicates over most IPC mechanisms supported by Windows NT (Note that for SQL Server version 6.5, only TCP/IP, Windows Sockets, NWLink, IPX/SPX, and named pipes are tested and supported.)
- Allows the use of integrated security over all protocols that RPC supports (including Novell Windows-based clients using SPX or IPXODI)
- Supports encryption for both user password authentication and data
- Offers performance comparable to native IPC Net-Libraries for most applications

All of this, however, is quite transparent to the programmers who are actually using RDO. All they see is that they either do or don't have to supply a user name and password when logging onto SQL Server.

Only the systems administrator can change the security model for SQL Server. To do this, use SQL Enterprise Manager (Figure 12-3); you'll have to restart SQL Server for this change to take effect.

The SQL Security Manager application is used to map Windows NT user names to SQL Server logins. It will map whole groups of Windows NT user names in one go. You can map Windows NT user names to the SQL Server guest login, to SA, or to individual login IDs. The guest login should be used for occasional visitors or for groups from other domains. Most users should be given their own individual login IDs. Users who need administrator privileges are mapped to SA. SQL Server has only one administrator account, and that is SA. All users who are mapped to SA are equal as far as SQL Server is concerned, and they are all-powerful. You should use this mapping carefully because a member of the SA group can do anything, including deleting data and dropping tables, views, indexes, and stored procedures.

FIGURE 12-3

Using SQL Enterprise Manager to set the security mode to Mixed

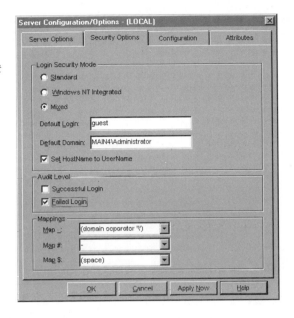

One consequence of using integrated security is that a user or an application can't log onto SQL Server under anything other than its assigned login name. It doesn't matter whether the user or application supplies another login name and password combination, such as one created for a specific application. They will be ignored, which can have unexpected consequences if your applications are written to sign into SQL Server with a defined login. Such applications can fail because the user doesn't have the correct privileges.

Useful Stored Procedures

Several stored procedures are available for you to use in maintaining user groups and permissions. Some of them will return useful information, for example, sp_helpgroup, which lists all of the groups in your database or all of the users in a particular group. Sometimes, however, no stored procedure is available that will return the specific information you require. There's no stored procedure, for example, for listing logins that don't have user names in your database. For these cases, I've provided an SQL SELECT statement that should do the job. My goal was to build a simple form (see Figure 12-4) that you could incorporate into your application to manage the database security. Assuming you've analyzed the user roles for the database, created the appropriate groups for these roles, and assigned permissions to the groups, the only day-to-day maintenance you'll have to do is add and delete users and assign users to groups.

FIGURE 12-4

*Simple admin-
istration using
drag and drop*

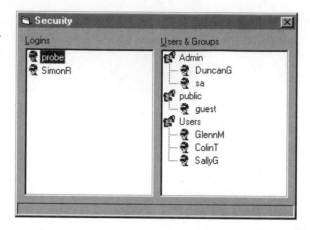

The form you incorporated into your application will have a ListView control that shows all logins in the database that don't have a user name. These logins can be dragged and dropped into a TreeView control that shows all of the groups and the users in the groups. Users can also be dragged and dropped between the groups in the TreeView control or dragged back to the ListView control to revoke their access to the database.

Listing the logins

The stored procedure sp_helplogins will list all logins, but only the system administrator can use it. However, here's a SELECT statement, which anyone can execute, that does the same job.

```
SELECT name, suid FROM master.dbo.syslogins
```

name	suid
sa	1
probe	10
DuncanG	11
SallyG	12
SimonR	13
ColinT	14
GlennM	15
repl_publisher	16382
repl_subscriber	16383

You can see the special logins for the replication processes and for the probe account, which is used for a two-phase commit between servers.

Listing the users in the database

The stored procedure sp_helpuser takes an optional parameter—a user name. It returns details about the user and the group to which the user belongs. It also shows the user's login name (in case it's different from the user name) and identifies the user's default database, as shown in this example:

```
sp_helpuser

UserName GroupName LoginName DefDBName UserID SUserID
-------- --------- --------- --------- ------ -------
ColinT   Users     ColinT    Accounts  3      14
dbo      Admin     sa        master    1      1
DuncanG  Admin     DuncanG   Accounts  4      11
GlennM   Users     GlennM    Accounts  5      15
guest    (null)    (null)    (null)    2      -1
SallyG   Users     SallyG    Accounts  6      12


sp_helpuser ColinT

UserName GroupName LoginName DefDBName UserID SUserID
-------- --------- --------- --------- ------ -------
ColinT   Users     ColinT    Accounts  3      14
```

Listing logins not in the database

If you want to know what users don't have access to the database, you have to run an SQL SELECT statement like the one shown here that compares all of the logins to the users in the database. This comparison does not account for users who are aliased.

```
SELECT name, suid FROM master.dbo.syslogins
WHERE suid NOT IN (SELECT suid FROM sysusers)

name                             suid
-------------------------------- ------
probe                            10
SimonR                           13
repl_publisher                   16382
repl_subscriber                  16383
```

This provides the data you can use to populate the ListView control on your security form.

```
Private envPiEnvironment As rdoEnvironment
Private conPiConnection  As rdoConnection

Private Sub Form_Load()
    Dim rsLogins As rdoResultset
    Dim strSQL    As String

    Set envPiEnvironment = rdoEngine.rdoEnvironments(0)
    Set conPiConnection = envPiEnvironment.OpenConnection( _
        "DSName", rdDriverNoPrompt, False, "uid=;pwd=;")

    ' Retrieve the logins not in the database.
    strSQL = "SELECT name, suid FROM master.dbo.syslogins " & _
        " WHERE suid NOT IN (SELECT suid FROM sysusers)"
    Set rsLogins = conPiConnection.OpenResultset(strSQL, _
        rdOpenForwardOnly, rdConcurReadOnly, rdExecDirect)

    Do Until rsLogins.EOF
        Call lsvLogins.ListItems.Add(, rsLogins!Name, _
            rsLogins!Name, , "Person")
        rsLogins.MoveNext
    Loop

    ' ... More code follows

    rsLogins.Close
End Sub
```

You can see from the code how easy it is to open a connection to the ODBC data source, passing no user ID and no password, which invokes integrated security.

When you open the resultset, specify settings for a forward-only (rdOpen-ForwardOnly), read-only (rdConcurReadOnly) resultset that is to be created without making a temporary stored procedure (rdExecDirect). These settings are chosen because you're going to copy the data out of the resultset into the ListView control and then close the resultset. This routine is executed only once, in the Form_Load procedure, so you don't have to be able to run the statement again (hence the use of rdExecDirect).

Creating a new user

The sp_adduser stored procedure shown below can be run by the database owner or anyone else who has been given an alias as the database owner. The syntax allows you to specify a user name other than the login name, but I can't find anything to recommend your doing so. You also get to specify a group to which this user will belong. If you don't specify a group, the user will belong only to public. Remember, all users are members of public, although each user can also be a member of one other group.

```
sp_adduser login_id [, username [, groupname]]
```

This stored procedure doesn't return any results, so you will execute it differently, as shown here:

```
Private Sub AddUser(ByVal strLogin As String, _
    ByVal strGroup As String)
    Static qryAddUser As rdoQuery

    If qryAddUser Is Nothing Then
        Set qryAddUser = conPiConnection.CreateQuery("AddUser", _
            "sp_adduser ?, ?, ?")
    End If

    qryAddUser.rdoParameters(0) = strLogin ' Login ID
    qryAddUser.rdoParameters(1) = strLogin ' User name
    qryAddUser.rdoParameters(2) = strGroup ' Groupname

    qryAddUser.Execute
End Sub
```

Here we are creating a parameter query, setting the parameters, and executing the query. Parameters can be input or output parameters (or both). But the default direction is input, so we don't have to explicitly specify the direction. The next time we need to execute the query, we will already have it and will only have to set the parameters and execute it. This shortens the execution time considerably.

Deleting a user

The stored procedure sp_dropuser is invoked in the same way as sp_adduser. It takes one mandatory parameter—the name of the user that is to be removed from the database:

```
sp_dropuser username
```

There is a side effect. If any logins were provided with an alias to this user name, they, of course, will also be excluded from the database.

Listing the users in a group

Here's a stored procedure that has two uses. When sp_helpgroup doesn't have a parameter, it will return a list of the groups in the database, as shown on the following page.

```
sp_helpgroup
```

Group_name	Group_id
Admin	16385
public	0
Users	16384

When it's called with a parameter that is a group name, sp_helpgroup will list the users in that group, as shown in this example:

```
sp_helpgroup Users
```

Group_name	Group_id	Users_in_group	Userid
Users	16384	ColinT	3
Users	16384	GlennM	5
Users	16384	SallyG	6

You can use the sp_helpgroup procedure in your Form_Load event to populate the TreeView control:

```
' Retrieve the groups in the database...
strSQL = "sp_helpgroup"
Set rsGroups = conPiConnection.OpenResultset(strSQL, _
    rdOpenForwardOnly, rdConcurReadOnly, rdExecDirect)

' And the users in those groups...
strSQL = "sp_helpgroup ?"
Set qryUsers = conPiConnection.CreateQuery("UsersInGroup", _
    strSQL)

Do Until rsGroups.EOF
    Set objNode = trvUsers.Nodes.Add(, , _
        rsGroups!group_name, rsGroups!group_name, "Group")

    qryUsers.rdoParameters(0) = rsGroups!group_name

    If rsUsers Is Nothing Then
        Set rsUsers = qryUsers.OpenResultset( _
            rdOpenForwardOnly, rdConcurReadOnly)
    Else
        rsUsers.Requery
    End If
```

```
Do Until rsUsers.EOF
    Call trvUsers.Nodes.Add(objNode, tvwChild, _
        rsUsers!users_in_group, rsUsers!users_in_group, "Person")
    rsUsers.MoveNext
Loop

    rsGroups.MoveNext
Loop

rsUsers.Close
qryUsers.Close
rsGroups.Close
```

First retrieve the list of groups; then, as you add each one to the TreeView control, retrieve all the users in that group and add them as children of the group. Because you are going to run the inner query many times, set it up as an rdoQuery and merely change its parameter each time around the loop. For this reason, you call the *OpenResultset* method only once. For all subsequent calls, call the *Requery* method instead.

Adding a user to a group

To move a user from one group to another, use the sp_changegroup stored procedure. No results are returned, and you don't even have to specify what group the user was in originally. You are merely assigning a user to a group.

```
sp_changegroup groupname, username
```

Removing a user from a group

If you want to remove a user from a group but not assign that user to another group, you have to explicitly assign him or her to the public group. This causes problems because "public" is a reserved word in SQL Server's language. So to get around the problem, enclose the word "public" in quotes.

```
sp_changegroup "public", username
```

This is one of SQL Server's many fudges. You have to keep reminding yourself that *all* users are members of the public group anyway. Using this form of the sp_changegroup procedure just cancels the user's membership in another group.

More Information

If you want to find out more about maintaining security in SQL Server, look up the following stored procedures in the SQL Server online documentation or in the Transact-SQL Help files.

sp_addalias	sp_addgroup	sp_addlogin
sp_changedbowner	sp_defaultdb	sp_defaultlanguage
sp_dropalias	sp_dropgroup	sp_droplogin
sp_helpgroup	xp_grantlogin	xp_logininfo
xp_revokelogin		

PERMISSION ERRORS

After you've set up your security permissions in the database, you'll want your application to conform to them and to handle any errors that arise when a user doesn't have permission to do something he or she is trying to do.

There are a couple of ways to reduce the incidence of errors when your application is running. One easy way is to use the sp_helpuser stored procedure to determine the group to which a user belongs at the beginning of the program. Then you can disable menu options that you know he or she may not use. Although this gets around a lot of errors, it also means that you'll have to alter, recompile, and reissue your program if the security settings for that group are revised later on. If you are really set on using the sp_helpuser procedure, you can encapsulate the rules into a Remote Automation server and then call this server from your application. All of these layers, however, do end up slowing down the application.

You can also call the sp_helprotect [sic] stored procedure to determine what permissions a user or group has been assigned for a table, view, or procedure that a user is about to use. But this can be time-consuming; you'll have to check all of the permissions that have been granted to and revoked from the public group, the user's group, and finally the individual in question. If you are dealing with column permissions, the results of the sp_helprotect procedure can be quite long.

Even if you try to code to avoid errors, you'll still get errors cropping up from time to time. It's vital, therefore, for you to understand a little about the rdoErrors collection and how to find out what's gone wrong with your SQL statements.

A common cry from the Usenet newgroups is, "I've got an 'ODBC Call Failed' error. What went wrong?" The answer is to look at the *other* error messages in the rdoErrors collection. The ODBC Call Failed message is just one in a series of messages; you have to read all of them to find out what went wrong.

```
Public Function ErrorHandler(ByVal lngErrorNum As Long, _
    ByVal strDescription As String, _
    ByVal strProcName As String, _
    ByVal intIcon As Integer, _
    ByVal intButtons As Integer)

    Dim strMessage As String
    Dim errError   As rdoError

    strMessage = "Error " & lngErrorNum & vbCrLf & _
        strDescription & vbCrLf & _
        "Occurred in " & strProcName

    For Each errError In rdoEngine.rdoErrors
        strMessage = strMessage & vbCrLf & vbCrLf & _
            "rdoError " & errError.Number & vbCrLf & _
            errError.Description & vbCrLf & _
            "Source " & errError.Source & vbCrLf & _
            "SQL State " & errError.SQLState & vbCrLf & _
            "SQL RetCode " & errError.SQLRetcode
    Next errError

    rdoErrors.Clear

    ErrorHandler = MsgBox(strMessage, _
        intButtons + intIcon, App.Title & " - Error")
End Function
```

Here's a function that you can call from all of your error handlers; it will list all the rdoErrors in complete detail. If you use it to test your application, you'll find out quickly what's going wrong, and you'll be able to code more helpful messages at appropriate points in the application.

Database Access Options

Vaughan is a TMS Associate who has been working with computers since university. He has been working with PCs and Microsoft Windows since 1987. Vaughan lives in the west of England with his wife and two children. Despite a dislike of cities, he finds himself working mainly at international banks in the heart of London, where he is focused on financial derivatives.

When I first received Visual Basic 1, I had distinctly mixed emotions. I had just written my first Windows application using C, and the learning curve had been painful. I can't tell you how satisfying it was the first time I got a program to compile, run, and display a basic window. It had taken me a week to grasp the idea of a message loop, so just to see a window appear on the screen was bliss. I expanded this program and eventually worked out how to add text boxes, lists, and buttons. However, it was hard work; I just couldn't see how I was ever going to be as productive under Windows as I had been working in proprietary languages on minicomputers. All this work and I still hadn't read a single character from a database!

So as you might imagine, when I first installed Visual Basic 1 and worked through the calculator sample program, I couldn't believe my luck. Here was an ideal tool for building Windows applications. I could forget about all that message-loop stuff and concentrate on writing the application. The user interface became a trivial problem. (Actually it didn't, but that's another story.) I could stop worrying about things like what to do with a WM_PAINT message—and get back to building commercial systems, which is what I'm paid to do.

However, there was one problem with this initial version of Visual Basic—it had no database support. And at that time there were few independent Application Programming Interfaces (APIs) available, certainly none for the proprietary database management systems I was using.

Visual Basic 2 was a little more helpful. It shipped with a new specification called Open Database Connectivity (ODBC) and sample programs that showed how to use it. However, the ODBC API was quite complex to use, and it meant I had to find a driver for my data source. There wasn't one. So I still had the problem of finding a way to get at my data.

Then came what I can only describe as a revolution. Microsoft released version 1 of Access, which included not only built-in support for desktop databases such as dBASE and Microsoft FoxPro but also support for ODBC data sources. This feature made Microsoft Access an instant winner. Its popularity had a dramatic effect on database management system (DBMS) suppliers. DBMS vendors and third-party vendors began rapidly producing database drivers. The vendors were helped in this effort by their not having to build an ODBC driver that could support the full range of the ODBC API in order to be compatible with Access. No major DBMS vendor wanted to be the only one whose product was not accessible via Access. Client/server access became something that anyone could achieve with a few clicks of a mouse button.

Microsoft Access also included two features that were even more important to Visual Basic 3 users—Data Access Objects (DAO) and Microsoft Jet. The Jet engine, the driving force behind Access, had the ability to give even quite weak ODBC drivers the appearance of a richly functional data source. And Jet was easy to use too. The advent of bound data controls gave Visual Basic a functionality that was similar to Access and also made database access much easier.

NOTE

Some people believe that Jet is an acronym for "joint engine technology." The truth is that it doesn't actually stand for anything; it's just a play on the words "jet engine."

As time went by, however, corporate developers found that Jet, although flexible, got in the way sometimes, and then performance wasn't as good as it might have been. With Visual Basic 4, we saw the release of remote data objects

(RDO), which provided a much tighter link to the underlying ODBC API than Jet and DAO. Consequently, it was possible to get performance improvements that were previously possible only when using the ODBC API directly.

Now, with Microsoft Visual Basic 5, we are seeing yet more data access options. OLE DB provides access to unstructured data such as e-mail messages and word processing documents. ActiveX (formerly OCX, the OLE version of VBX—the Visual Basic Extension technology) and Distributed Component Object Model (DCOM) can provide Internet access to corporate data. A new version of ODBC (version 3) provides even more functionality than earlier versions; exploiting this expanded functionality can provide more of those all-important commodities, performance and flexibility. Remember, as well, that proprietary APIs are still available for many data sources. The Bulk Copy Program (BCP), for example, is a utility supplied with Microsoft SQL Server that can still be the quickest way to get data into or out of a SQL Server database.

CHOOSING YOUR DATABASE ACCESS METHOD

Once the world was simple. If you could find a method of accessing your database, you'd use it because it was most likely the only option available. Now the world is much more complex. There are more options from which to choose. How can you make the most appropriate choice, and what are the trade-offs? In this chapter, I hope to provide you insight on how to make this decision.

Just about any application or system you build is going to store and manipulate data in a persistent manner. (In other words, the data doesn't just disappear when the application terminates.) The data can be as simple as a text file or as complex as a corporate database with many thousands of tables and millions of records. When you design such an application (I hope you design it), you have three major choices to make:

- What back-end relational database to use
- What data access method to use—the Visual Basic DAO layer, ODBC, or a proprietary back-end interface or interfaces
- What database design to use (There is never just one way to model a system.)

For the purpose of this discussion, I'm going to focus on the second item in the list, what data access method you will need to use.

When to Use the DAO Layer

DAO provides a generic layer of functionality. It's designed to insulate the programmer from the proprietary details of the back-end data source. For example, the following code excerpt will work with any data source, provided this data source has a table named Depts, which has a field named DeptName.

```
⋮
lstDepts.Clear
Set rsDepts = dbEmployees.OpenRecordset("Depts")
Do While Not rsDepts.EOF
    lstDepts.AddItem rsDepts.Fields("DeptName").Value
    rsDepts.MoveNext
Loop
rsDepts.Close
⋮
```

In the case of ODBC databases, the DAO layer provides the interface to the ODBC API. If the databases are local or client-based, such as Microsoft Access or FoxPro, the DAO layer provides a single interface, via Jet, to the diverse database formats.

When to Go Directly to the ODBC Layer

As I mentioned earlier, although ODBC first shipped with version 2 of Visual Basic, it wasn't until Visual Basic 3 and Access 1 that there were drivers for database systems such as Sybase and Oracle. This meant that until Visual Basic 3, not many people were using ODBC through its native API. Most users' first taste of ODBC came through using it via DAO, and these first impressions were frequently poor because performance generally wasn't good. Poor performance was a direct consequence of adding the Jet database engine, which was designed for high generality and for providing a generic library of data access functions that would make Visual Basic code written to the DAO independent of the data source. To achieve this independence, some flexibility and optimization for specific functions were sacrificed.

In bench tests against Microsoft SQL Server, when direct ODBC API rather than DAO calls were compared with calls made using the Microsoft Visual Basic Library for SQL Server (VBSQL) API (which is built on the proprietary DB-Library API—the native API for SQL Server), the average performance numbers were comparable. Some ODBC functions were faster than some DB-Library calls, and vice versa. Getting a connection through the ODBC API, for example, took longer than getting a connection through VBSQL calls, although not by an order of magnitude.

With DAO and RDO programming models, you can build applications that are not only easier to write but also seamlessly compatible with a wide variety of Indexed Sequential Access Method (ISAM) databases, such as Btrieve, or remote engine databases, such as SQL Server or Oracle. Where the target database engine is likely to change or be upgraded over time, DAO and RDO programming models can significantly reduce the time needed to adapt to a new server database.

The ODBC API programming approach is somewhat more difficult to implement, but it also affords much of the same portability as the DAO and RDO models. The ODBC API is more difficult to use primarily because there is more code to write and the functions are more complex. Although you don't write to any data objects with this approach, the ODBC API supports access to any back-end database for which an ODBC driver exists. By querying the driver for server-specific features, you can automatically adapt your data access method to the remote database's functionality.

When to Go Somewhere in Between DAO and ODBC (RDO)

Using the ODBC API directly requires an up-front investment in designing and building a wrapper to use within your own applications. Microsoft found that building wrappers to use with ODBC API was such a common approach they decided to help by building their own wrapper to use with it and shipped it with Visual Basic 4 as RDO.

RDO is similar to DAO except that it uses only ODBC and has no access to the desktop installable ISAM drivers that are built into Jet. RDO has been designed to use some of the optimizations available within ODBC; consequently, performance is frequently better than with the combination of DAO and Jet. However, the increase in performance meant a compromise elsewhere in the functionality. For example, you can use the *Index* object and the *Seek* method to manage ISAM indexes and locate rows based on those indexes. However, because RDO and relational databases manage indexes in entirely different ways, these objects and methods aren't supported in RDO.

Another difference is that Jet supports the creation and modification of the database schema through DAO methods and properties. RDO doesn't support any type of schema modification. But you can still run make-table queries or execute action queries that create, modify, or delete databases and tables using native Structured Query Language (SQL) statements.

When to Use a Proprietary Protocol

Sometimes all you want is pure speed—for example, when you want to upload large quantities of data into a database. There isn't any real functionality involved here, just raw processing speed. In these circumstances, the most appropriate access method can be a proprietary method that has been optimized for just one DBMS. Sometimes you'll have little choice. When there isn't an ODBC driver for your database, you have only two options: change the DBMS or use a proprietary access method.

DAO

In this section, we'll investigate DAO. We'll see how DAO is intimately linked to Jet, Microsoft's desktop database engine, and how Jet's architecture can affect the performance of DAO. We'll look at some ways that this performance can be improved.

First of all, let's take a look at the relationship among the components we are going to cover to help you better understand the discussion that follows. If you look at Figure 13-1, you can see that the architecture is a layered one, with each component linked to the components above and below it. If you were to draw a vertical line through the diagram at any point, you'd be able to see the layers that the particular database access method uses. So for example, an application written using Visual Basic 5 can use DAO, which in turn relies on Jet, which in turn uses either ODBC or built-in ISAM to manipulate a database. What this means is that if you use DAO, it's possible for you to use exactly the same code to build a database application that uses a local Access database or that uses a remote SQL Server database.

FIGURE 13-1

Visual Basic 5 data access architecture

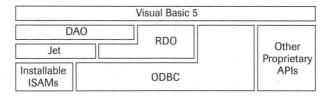

Local vs. Remote Data

I should perhaps explain here what I mean by a *local database* and a *remote database.* Just exactly what do "local" and "remote" mean? When I refer to a local database, I am referring to a database that's accessible via the file system, which could actually mean it's located on a remote file server, not necessarily on a disk drive local to the PC. A local database is manipulated directly by the application. There might be a layered architecture, but there is only one running process—your application. A remote database isn't just something that's physically separate from the PC running the application. (After all, as I've just described, a local database can be physically remote.) A remote database is one that can be accessed only via another process that is separate from your application, a process normally known as a DBMS. The DBMS could be running on the local PC, or it could be running on a distant mainframe.

The distinction between local and remote databases becomes important as soon as the phrase "client/server computing" is mentioned. When the difference between local and remote databases isn't precisely defined, almost any architecture can be described as client/server architecture. So for the purposes of the discussion in this chapter, "client/server" means the use of a remote database that is also physically remote.

DAO and Jet

In Figure 13-1, you can see that Jet and DAO are intimately linked. They are not the same thing, however. Jet is a distinct component, even though only DAO and Microsoft Access know how to use it directly. Therefore, it's not possible to use Jet directly. DAO exists primarily as an access method to Jet. However, as you will see, DAO is able to turn off some of Jet's functionality when using an ODBC data source. This can sometimes have a significant effect on performance. Once again there is a trade-off, however, in performance vs. functionality.

Jet is driven by SQL, and the dialect of SQL that Jet speaks is different from the dialect used by other implementations. This fact has both benefits and drawbacks. When using DAO (and hence, Jet), it's worth learning these differences because they can have a dramatic impact on performance. For example, in many database management systems (such as SQL Server), a join between two tables doesn't have to be explicitly declared. SQL Server will interpret the following SQL statement as an inner join and optimize database access accordingly:

```
SELECT *
FROM Employee, Dept
WHERE Employee.Dept_Id = Dept.Dept_Id
```

This same statement, when used via DAO and Jet, can have a completely different outcome. Rather than use the Dept_Id field to read the unique index in the Dept table, Jet will simply perform a cartesian join (that is, match each Employee record with all Dept records) and then throw away those that fail the criteria specified in the WHERE clause. This means that the number of records read is Count(Employee) * Count(Dept) (read every Dept record for each Employee record) rather than Count(Employee) * 2 (read one Dept record for each Employee record). If these were large tables, the difference in the elapsed time to execute the query could be dramatic.

But it's not all bad news. Jet SQL also has some useful features. Perhaps the feature most widely used is its ability to perform cross-tab queries. For example, suppose you have a query that produces a list of sales by product and month. The output of such a query might look like this:

Product	Period	Sum of Sales
Tea	Jan	100
Coffee	Jan	1200
Orange juice	Feb	550
Tea	Feb	90
Coffee	Feb	1300
Orange juice	Mar	475
Tea	Mar	75
Coffee	Mar	1150
Orange juice	Jan	500

Although this is fine as far as it goes, it would be much nicer to see the query output in this format:

Product	Jan	Feb	Mar
Coffee	1200	1300	1150
Orange juice	500	550	475
Tea	100	90	75

A cross-tab query is able to do exactly this kind of transposition, turning the values of a column in an ordinary select query into column headings in a cross-tab query.

DAO Object Models

DAO offers two different object models. One model is available for data access via Jet. Workspaces in this model are used to access data in Jet databases, Jet-connected ODBC databases, and installable ISAM data sources in other formats, such as Paradox and Lotus 1-2-3. The other model is available for data access via ODBC. Workspaces in the second model are used to access database servers through ODBC without going through the Jet database engine. This access method (ODBCDirect) is new to Microsoft Access 97 and to Visual Basic 5. ODBCDirect isn't an architectural component; rather, it's a mode of operation available to DAO. It's within the realm of possibility that in the future, DAO will become open in the same way that ODBC is now open and will allow other database access methods (OLE DB, for example) to be plugged into the DBEngine-Workspaces paradigm.

The Jet workspace is useful when you need to take advantage of Jet's unique features, such as the ability to join data from different database formats. ODBC-Direct provides an alternative when you need only to execute queries or stored procedures against a back-end server, such as SQL Server, and you do not need the features of Jet. ODBC-Direct itself uses RDO to provide a subset of DAO functionality.

FIGURE 13-2

The primary DAO objects and collections for a Jet database

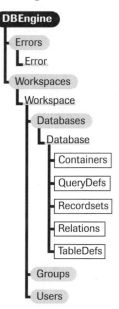

The DAO object model, shown in Figure 13-2, has the *DBEngine* object as its basis, which maintains a Workspaces collection. The type of workspace determines whether the remainder of the object model hierarchy will be Jet or ODBCDirect. In the case of Jet workspaces, there are a number of object collections that provide the ability to manipulate security for Microsoft Access workspaces. Each *Workspace* object also has a Databases collection. Each *Database* object represents all of the objects that might be present within an individual database. Some of these objects are specific to Access databases (*Container*, *QueryDef*, *Relation*); others are generic to all databases (*Recordset*, *TableDef*).

Of these, Recordsets are certainly the most heavily used and are the objects on which this discussion will focus. TableDefs are also useful abstractions that provide simple access to tables and their fields and indexes; they're useful for database management applications. However, they're used only infrequently. In the case of a DBMS such as Oracle or SQL Server, these objects are probably rarely used because table management functions are provided by separate tools that also have functionality not present in the *TableDef* object, such as controlling the physical partitioning of the database and performance tuning. The *Recordset* object provides the means to execute SQL statements and manipulate the resultset (if there is one). This functionality is provided by Jet.

Client/Server Performance

In any client/server application, many factors can affect performance. With most applications, the component that causes the most variability in application behavior is the network. Large corporate networks are complex, and there can be many reasons for differing performance. Network segments might not be the same—some might be fast fiber-optic, other segments might be slower thin-Ethernet. When network traffic through one route is high, messages might be rerouted. At certain times of the day, there might be high levels of network traffic. Networks are complex, so behavior is frequently hard to predict.

For this reason, the answer to improving client/server performance is to cut out the network. That's clearly not a possible solution, so the next best thing is to reduce network traffic to a minimum.

Perhaps this can be better illustrated in an example. One of the more useful GUI design widgets is the list box and its close relation, the drop-down list box, both of which are frequently used to display options for the user to select. A list could contain product numbers with their descriptions, for example, which would make purchase order entry easier. This is fine when the number of products is limited or the data is stored in a local desktop database such as Microsoft Access. Here the time to fill the list when the application starts is small, even with many hundreds of entries to be added to the list.

In a client/server architecture, where the data to be added to the list is transferred across the network and the number of products can easily reach tens of thousands (as in a purchasing system for a supermarket chain), the time required to fill the list soon will become prohibitive and also will hog valuable network capacity. The answer is to change your application design to provide a filtering form, which can be used to limit the number of records retrieved, instead of a list box. For example, you can filter to allow only products with codes within a small range to be retrieved at a time. Such a form could in fact be more useful than the original list box because it could also provide extra detail about the entry and dynamic sorting.

So in short, one of the best performance boosters for client/server systems is to cut down on network traffic. Don't allow your application to request data it doesn't need.

ODBC API Usage

One of the features that make DAO with Jet so flexible is the way it can be used with both built-in ISAM databases and client/server databases through ODBC. For an ODBC driver to be usable with Jet, the following ODBC APIs must be supported:

SQLAllocConnect	SQLExecute	SQLPrepare
SQLAllocEnv	SQLFetch	SQLPutData
SQLAllocStmt	SQLFreeConnect	SQLRowCount
SQLCancel	SQLFreeEnv	SQLSetConnectOption
SQLColumns	SQLFreeStmt	SQLSetParam
SQLDescribeCol	SQLGetData	SQLSetStmtOption
SQLDisconnect	SQLGetInfo	SQLSpecialColumns
SQLDriverConnect	SQLGetTypeInfo	SQLStatistics
SQLError	SQLNumResultCols	SQLTables
SQLExecDirect	SQLParamData	SQLTransact

All the ODBC API functions used by Jet are defined by ODBC to be at either core or level 1 API conformance. (See the sidebar, "ODBC Conformance Levels," on the next page.) This has meant that it's been quite easy to create drivers for a wide diversity of databases. This is also why DBMS vendors were keen to provide access to their data sources. They knew their rivals could easily provide such access, so they had to build drivers themselves or risk being locked out of the growing number of sites using Visual Basic and, of course, Access.

ODBC CONFORMANCE LEVELS

ODBC defines conformance levels for drivers in two areas: the ODBC API and the ODBC SQL grammar (which includes the ODBC SQL data types). Conformance levels help both application and driver developers because the levels establish standard sets of functionality. An application can easily determine whether a driver provides the functionality it needs. Drivers can be developed to support a broad selection of applications without being concerned about the specific requirements of each application.

To conform to a given API or SQL conformance level, a driver must support all of the functionality at that conformance level, whether or not that functionality is supported by the DBMS associated with the driver. However, conformance levels don't restrict drivers to the functionality at the levels to which they conform. Driver developers are encouraged to support as much functionality as they can; applications can determine the functionality supported by a driver by calling *SQLGetInfo*, *SQLGetFunctions*, and *SQLGetTypeInfo*.

API Conformance Levels

The ODBC API defines a set of core functions that correspond to the functions in the X/Open and SQL Access Group Call Level Interface specification. ODBC also defines two extended sets of functionality, level 1 and level 2. The following list summarizes the functionality included at each conformance level.

Note that many ODBC applications require that drivers support all of the functions at the level 1 API conformance level. To ensure that their driver works with most ODBC applications, driver developers should implement all level 1 functions.

Core API

- Allocate and free environment, connection, and statement handles.
- Connect to data sources and use multiple statements on a connection.
- Prepare and execute SQL statements; execute SQL statements immediately.
- Assign storage for parameters in an SQL statement and in result columns.
- Retrieve data from a resultset. Retrieve information about a resultset.
- Commit or roll back transactions.
- Retrieve error information.

Level 1 API

- Include all core API functionality.
- Use driver-specific dialog boxes to connect to data sources.
- Set and query values of statement and connection options.
- Send part (useful for long data) or all of a parameter value.
- Retrieve part (useful for long data) or all of a result column value.
- Retrieve catalog information (columns, special columns, statistics, and tables).
- Retrieve scalar information about driver and data source capabilities, such as supported data types.

Level 2 API

- Include all core and level 1 API functionality.
- Browse connection information, and list available data sources.
- Send arrays of parameter values; retrieve arrays of result column values.
- Retrieve the number of parameters, and describe individual parameters.
- Use a scrollable cursor.
- Retrieve the native form of an SQL statement.
- Retrieve catalog information (privileges, keys, and procedures).
- Call a translation DLL.

SQL Conformance Levels

ODBC defines a core grammar that roughly corresponds to the X/Open and SQL Access Group SQL Common Applications Environment (CAE) specification (1992). ODBC also defines a minimum grammar, to meet a basic level of ODBC conformance, and an extended grammar, to provide for common DBMS extensions to SQL. The following list summarizes the grammar included at each conformance level.

Minimum SQL Grammar

- Data Definition Language (DDL): CREATE TABLE and DROP TABLE
- Data Manipulation Language (DML): simple SELECT, INSERT, UPDATE SEARCHED, and DELETE SEARCHED

>>

- Expressions: simple (such as A > B + C)
- Data types: CHAR, VARCHAR, or LONG VARCHAR

Core SQL Grammar
- Minimum SQL grammar and data types
- DDL: ALTER TABLE, CREATE INDEX, DROP INDEX, CREATE VIEW, DROP VIEW, GRANT, and REVOKE
- DML: full SELECT
- Expressions: subquery, set functions such as *SUM* and *MIN*
- Data types: DECIMAL, NUMERIC, SMALLINT, INTEGER, REAL, FLOAT, DOUBLE PRECISION

Extended SQL Grammar
- Minimum and Core SQL grammar and data types
- DML: outer joins, positioned UPDATE, positioned DELETE, SELECT FOR UPDATE, and unions

Note that ODBC 1, positioned UPDATE, positioned DELETE, and SELECT FOR UPDATE statements and the UNION clause were part of the core SQL grammar; since ODBC 2, they have been part of the extended grammar. Applications that use the SQL conformance level to determine whether these statements are supported also need to check the version number of the driver to correctly interpret the information. In particular, applications that use these features with ODBC 1 drivers need to check explicitly for these capabilities in ODBC 2 or ODBC 3 drivers.

- Expressions: scalar functions such as SUBSTRING and ABS, date, time, and TimeStamp literals
- Data types: bit, tinyint, bigint, binary, varbinary, long varbinary, date, time, timestamp
- Batch SQL statements
- Procedure calls

DAO and Jet Performance
in a Client/Server Environment

Jet can be a limiting factor when you're building applications in a client/server environment. The same features that provide heterogeneous capabilities and comprehensive keyset-driven updatable recordsets will slow client/server performance if these features aren't needed. (A keyset is simply a set of keys that uniquely identify all records in a resultset.) The DAO and Jet model Recordset objects do, however, have features that can improve performance, although there is a consequent loss of functionality.

One of the keys to understanding how to improve DAO performance is understanding the difference between the way dynaset and snapshot recordsets are handled by Jet. You can improve performance generally by buffering data in local memory (or on disk) so that when the data is requested by an application it's retrieved from local memory rather than via a network request. Jet automatically buffers data in different ways according to the type of recordset that has been created.

Dynasets are keyset-driven, which means that when a recordset is created, only the primary key for each record is retrieved and cached locally. The result is that dynaset recordsets can be created quickly since the primary key of a row in a recordset is usually much smaller than the size of the entire row. When a row is retrieved with the *MoveNext Recordset* method, for example, the key that is buffered locally is used to retrieve the rest of the data for the row. This is, of course, the way in which a recordset is dynamic and responds to changes in the underlying data. If another application changes the data in the row the primary key relies upon, the change will be reflected in the data that is retrieved because the data is refreshed each time the row is visited. However, this also means that dynaset-style recordsets produce network traffic every time a row is retrieved.

Snapshots, on the other hand, retrieve the entire row and store it locally. This means that it takes longer to create snapshot-style recordsets than to create the equivalent dynaset-style recordsets. This also explains why snapshots are static with respect to changes made to underlying data rows that have already been retrieved. (Rows that haven't yet been retrieved might show changes made to the data in these rows, but this is DBMS-dependent.) Once a row is retrieved, however, each subsequent request for data in that row produces no network traffic at all because the request is handled entirely from the local memory buffer. So, it's a good idea to use snapshots where recordset data is static but used frequently, for example, in reference or lookup tables.

Recordset Optional Parameters

The *OpenRecordset* method (which is used primarily in conjunction with a *Database* object but is also available to other objects such as a *QueryDef* object) has a number of optional parameters that can take values that will affect client/server performance. The syntax of the *OpenRecordset* method is:

```
Set recordset = object.OpenRecordset(source, type, options, lockedits)
```

We'll look at each of the four parameters in turn.

Source

The *source* parameter (which is not available when the method is applied to *QueryDef Recordset* and *TableDef* objects) is the only one that is required. The subsequent parameters (*type*, *options*, *lockedits*) have options that can affect performance.

Type

As I discussed above, the way data is buffered for the dbOpenDynaset and dbOpenSnapshot recordset types will have an impact on performance.

Reading through rows sequentially only (the dbOpenForwardOnly recordset type) can mean that the DBMS doesn't have to maintain a cursor, which can mean substantial benefits with some systems. (See the sidebar, "Cursors.")

Options

The dbSQLPassThrough option passes an SQL statement to a Jet-connected ODBC data source for processing. This is perhaps the option that boosts performance the most. Virtually all Jet functionality is bypassed, and Jet simply retrieves data and buffers it. However, because no keyset is created, the recordset can't be dynamic, and using this option will always result in a snapshot-style recordset. Also, since Jet is bypassed, there is no syntax checking stage, which means that any command string the DBMS can understand will be sent directly without interpretation.

LockEdits

The dbReadOnly option, like the dbOpenForwardOnly *type* parameter option, can enable the DBMS to handle the recordset in a simpler way because no cursor is required and locks don't need to be maintained. The actual benefit does, however, depend on the server DBMS.

CURSORS

SQL operates on sets of data, whereas an application generally operates on individual records. To resolve this difference, a mechanism is required that can fetch records from the set one by one. Such a mechanism is a cursor. The concept comes from video displays, in which a cursor indicates where the next character that is typed will appear or what character is to be deleted or changed. In other words, it indicates what part of the screen is active. A cursor in SQL has a corresponding purpose, namely to indicate what record in a data set is active. Its placement specifies a current record (often called, awkwardly, "current of cursor") that the program can access. Cursors can be implemented either by the server or by application logic. (DAO achieves this implementation with keysets.)

Server cursors allow individual row operations to be performed on a given resultset or on the entire data set. In SQL Server versions 6 and later, ANSI SQL cursors are server-based. In earlier releases, cursors were provided only through the DB-Library and ODBC cursor APIs.

SQL Server provides two interfaces for cursor functions. When using cursors in Transact-SQL batches or stored procedures, ANSI-standard SQL syntax has been added for declaring, opening, and fetching from cursors as well as for performing positioned updates and deletes. When using cursors from a DB-Library or ODBC program, the SQL Server 6 client libraries transparently call built-in server functions to handle cursors more efficiently.

Upsizing

Because the code associated with the DAO and Jet object models can access many different types of desktop databases and, without any changes, be repointed at a client/server database, it's frequently used as a Rapid Application Development (RAD) tool to quickly build applications in a desktop environment and then deploy them against corporate data. Sometimes this approach works and sometimes it doesn't. In this section, I'll point out some of the problems involved with such a strategy and how these problems can be overcome if you remember that the development and target environments are different.

One of the best reasons to use prototyping and RAD-style development in a desktop environment is that it's quick and easy. The PC doesn't even have to be connected to a network. This means development can be carried out by developers who are off-site or by third parties, confident in the knowledge that their solutions will work no matter what the ultimate data source. But this is true only if the goal is interoperability and not performance.

Performance tips

All programmers have their favorite tricks for improving performance and functionality. Indeed, computer magazines run regular articles describing these tricks. Here are some of the best performance boosters for desktop database programming using the DAO and Jet model—and why you shouldn't use them!

Using table-type recordsets instead of dynaset or snapshot-types   Of all performance boosters, table-type recordsets are probably the best. DAO provides three recordset types: dynaset, snapshot, and table. Of these three types, the table recordset type is the fastest when using desktop databases and one of the easiest to employ when coding. However, using it immediately renders the application incapable of accessing an ODBC data source.

Using the *Seek* method instead of the Find methods   Sometimes it's necessary to search for information within an open recordset. This involves the use of the Find methods (*FindFirst*, *FindNext*, *FindLast*, *FindPrevious*), which can be quite slow. If you select a table-type recordset with an index, you can use the *Seek* method to position the cursor against any criteria that are stored in that index. This will always be the fastest possible way to find a particular piece of data. Even though the Find methods will use indexes whenever possible, the overhead of that mechanism will always be somewhat greater than for the *Seek* method because the Find methods are based on a dynaset or a snapshot. The results of using the *Seek* method as a performance booster can be quite dramatic. Consequently, it can be tempting for a developer using a desktop environment to use this method. However, the technique requires the use of Table-based recordsets, which, as we have already seen, are incompatible with an application that is to be deployed in a client/server environment.

Specifying an index (or a query) instead of using *.Sort*   You might want to just search through a recordset, but you might also want to place the data in a specific order. The *.Sort* property of a recordset object is the usual way of sorting data, but this can be slow. A faster way to sort data is to open the table directly and then specify an index that has the data sorted in the same order in which you want to move through the table. Once again, you have to use nontransportable code.

Dealing with large volumes of data

The pursuit of speed isn't the only place where an upsizing strategy can be upset. Another common problem resides in the user interface. It's only too easy to create an application that works well with a small volume of test data but then fails to perform when repointed at a remote database with large volumes of information.

One example, as mentioned earlier, is that very useful user interface widget, the list box. It can be tempting to provide list boxes and drop-down lists whenever a selection is required that is supported by a lookup table in the database. The problem with this approach is that in a test system you might have only a few entries that need to be added to the list. In a production environment, there can easily be thousands (even tens of thousands) of entries. Where a form appears quickly on the user interface in the desktop environment, there could be a wait of several minutes when it's repointed to a production environment, simply because of the time required to populate the list. Even if this wait is acceptable, having to scroll through an enormous list certainly won't be.

Therefore, a good deal of thought has to be applied to the user interface to ensure that the interface will continue to be useful when the application is finally deployed. It might be necessary to replace some of the user interface widgets with more complex QBE-style (query by example) lookup forms. Or, alternatively, the drop-down lists might have to be eliminated altogether and replaced with a simpler text box with a validation routine.

Work placement

In general, it should be true to say that database management systems are very good at processing SQL statements. Ensuring that a server executes a statement reduces the network traffic that is one of the major bottlenecks in any client/ server system. But making sure that a server executes a statement can be a problem when you are upsizing an application.

One problem that arises is the use of local functions in SQL queries. If a DBMS doesn't support a function that, for example, an Access database does support, Jet will detect this circumstance and, rather than generate an error, will attempt to handle the problem itself. This generally means retrieving all the data from the tables involved and effectively executing the query locally. As an example, take the following SQL statement:

```
SELECT * FROM Employees WHERE Name Like "A*"
```

Suppose the DBMS doesn't support the Like keyword; Jet will detect this and fulfill the query by sending a simpler statement to the server, one which the server can execute:

```
SELECT * FROM Employees
```

Jet will then retrieve all of the data from the server and apply the WHERE clause itself to filter the data. Consequently, the server, which is the correct place to perform the query execution, doesn't get the opportunity to work at its best.

It's well worth taking the time to determine the capabilities of the target DBMS when you are building an application in a desktop environment and to keep these capabilities in mind when coding.

One way to help avoid such problems is to specify that code can't contain explicit SQL statements. Defined queries should be used instead. These can then be converted to DBMS views or stored procedures. If the example above were changed to the code shown here, the defined query could have been upsized by rewriting it as a view that was able to simulate the Like keyword, perhaps by making use of stored procedures.

```
SELECT * FROM qryEmployeesLikeA
```

Thus the code wouldn't have to be changed, and the probability of being able to upsize the application to a number of different database management systems would be improved.

RDO

RDO implements a set of objects to deal with the special requirements of remote data access. It implements a thin code layer over the ODBC API and driver manager that establishes connections, creates resultsets and cursors, and executes complex procedures using minimal workstation resources.

How RDO Works

Using RDO cuts out the Jet layer from the architecture. This can mean significantly higher performance and more flexibility when accessing remote database engines. It's possible to use any ODBC data source with RDO and the RemoteData control; therefore, it's still possible to use desktop databases that have ODBC drivers (for example, Access databases). However, these features are really designed to take advantage of database servers such as SQL Server and Oracle, which use sophisticated query engines. Using RDO with desktop databases that have ODBC drivers, such as Access, can actually *decrease* performance dramatically.

If you use RDO, you can create either simple cursorless resultsets or more complex cursors. You can also run queries that will return any number of resultsets or will execute stored procedures that return resultsets with or without output parameters and return values. You can limit the number of rows returned and monitor all of the messages and errors generated by the remote data source without compromising the executing query. RDO also permits either synchronous or asynchronous operation, so your application doesn't need to be blocked while lengthy queries are executed.

Be aware that RDO and the RemoteData control are features of Visual Basic 5, Enterprise and Professional Editions. You can't develop code using the RDO object library or RemoteData control in the Standard Edition of Visual Basic 5.

RDO vs. DAO

Basically, you can use the RDO in a way that is similar to the way you use the Jet database engine DAO. With RDO, you can submit queries, create a resultset or a cursor, and process the results from the query using database-independent, object-oriented code.

Some of the objects have different names that reflect the underlying ODBC API. For example, the DAO *Workspace* object provides capabilities that are similar to the *rdoEnvironment* object, and the DAO *Database* object is replaced by the *rdoConnection* object. In many ways, the RDO and DAO object models are similar in function and operation. However, there are significant differences that are a result of RDO being more tightly coupled to ODBC and of RDO being oriented to client/server databases rather than to desktop databases.

Jet's table-type *Recordset* object permits direct access to an entire table using a selected ISAM index. Although you can simulate this with RDO, it requires the creation of a cursor that spans the entire table, which is generally impractical. The DAO and Jet model also provides the ability to create a forward-only–scrolling, snapshot-type recordset. This option is similar to an RDO forward-only resultset except that the forward-only *rdoResultset* can be updatable.

RDO refers to rows instead of records and to columns instead of fields (rows and columns are the generally accepted terms used for relational databases). The data returned from an RDO query is in the form of resultsets, which can contain zero or more data rows composed of one or more columns.

Some DAO objects, methods, and properties are designed to implement and support the ISAM structure of Jet and installable ISAM databases. For example, you can use the *Index* object and the *Seek* method to manage ISAM indexes and locate rows based on these indexes. But because the RDO and relational databases manage indexes in an entirely different manner, it isn't possible to implement these ISAM structure DAO objects in RDO.

Jet also supports the creation and modification of the database schema through DAO methods and properties. RDO doesn't support any type of schema modification because such modification is fully supported in the tools and utilities provided with the server systems. But in RDO you can still run make-table queries or execute action queries that create, modify, or delete databases and tables using native SQL statements. You can also execute complex stored procedures that manage the database schema or perform maintenance operations that aren't possible to perform with DAO.

ODBCDIRECT

ODBCDirect is a new feature that was introduced in version 5 of Visual Basic. If you refer back to Figure 13-1, you can see that DAO can use RDO as an optional mode of operation instead of Jet. ODBCDirect provides a simple mechanism for switching from Jet-based to RDO-based data access.

At the time Jet first became available, it made it possible for corporate developers to gain access easily to ODBC and hence to remote databases. However, this had a drawback—the performance of the DAO-Jet-ODBC combination wasn't always as good as the performance available through other APIs, such as DB-Library. A number of pundits placed the blame for this lower performance squarely at the feet of ODBC. However, this was incorrect. The problem stemmed from what is in fact one of Jet's strengths, namely, that it provides a feature-rich environment and at the same time requires little from the ODBC driver that is providing the next layer in the architecture. To overcome some of the performance problems, a pass-through mechanism was provided that made it possible to pass through SQL statements directly to the ODBC driver without Jet being much involved. The advantage of using this mechanism was that many SQL statements executed much more quickly. The disadvantage lay in the fact that because Jet was so little involved in the process, the keyset-driven, dynamic recordsets weren't available, and hence, all returned recordsets were read-only.

RDO was designed specifically to provide an object model that was much closer to the ODBC API. One of the effects of this proximity is that RDO provides keyset-driven, dynamic, updatable recordsets for ODBC data sources in much the same way that Jet provides them. Visual Basic 5 takes advantage of this facility to provide a method of easily converting existing DAO-based applications to use ODBCDirect, which makes the task of upsizing an application easier. This should help those corporations with applications that have outgrown their desktop environments but are too large to be quickly and easily redeveloped.

To use ODBCDirect to switch from Jet to RDO, just add the following line of code somewhere near the beginning of the application before any DAO objects are referenced, and the switch is made:

```
DBEngine.DefaultType = dbUseODBC
```

The main requirement for this simple approach is that the application use only Recordset objects. Although this might seem like a heavy restriction, a Recordset object is the only object type that most applications use anyway. DAO objects are rarely involved in the creation and manipulation of tables, indexes, relationships, and security in most applications.

A feature that is not available with ODBCDirect is the ability to perform heterogeneous joins across tables from multiple data sources—which is one of Jet's major strengths. But although ODBCDirect isn't a replacement for RDO, it can be easily deployed and thus breathe new life into an old application.

The DAO and ODBCDirect object model, shown in Figure 13-3, is quite similar to the DAO and Jet object model (Figure 13-2); however, it contains none of the Microsoft Access database–specific objects, and it's also missing the database definition objects (TableDefs, Relations). The Databases collection of the ODBCDirect Workspace object is present for exactly the purpose that has been described above—to enable easy switching between Jet and ODBCDirect for applications that use only recordsets.

FIGURE 13-3

The ODBC-Direct object model

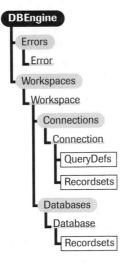

The *Connection* object is the exposed interface to the underlying RDO *Connection* object that DAO uses to provide the ODBCDirect interface. Whenever a database is opened within an ODBCDirect workspace, an equivalent *Connection* object is created automatically. Should you want to use features in your application that are exposed by the *Connection* object, a reference to the *Connection* object is available as a property of the *Database* object. Similarly, each *Connection* object that's created also automatically prompts the creation of a linked *Database* object that can be referenced through a property of the *Connection* object.

Through these processes, an application first can be switched to use ODBC-Direct rather than Jet and then later can be modified to take advantage of some of the *Connection* object facilities. At this point, it would then be possible to modify the application to use *Connection* objects instead of *Database* objects. Once you did this, it would be possible to switch from using DAO to using RDO by changing the references to DBEngine to be *rdoEngine*. Thus, ODBCDirect can be seen as a vehicle for converting a desktop application to a client/server application that uses RDO.

ODBC

ODBC is a core component of Microsoft Windows Open Services Architecture (WOSA). It's Microsoft's strategic interface for accessing data in a heterogeneous environment of relational and nonrelational database management systems. It's based on the Call Level Interface specification of the SQL Access Group and provides an open, vendor-neutral way of accessing data stored in a variety of proprietary personal computer, minicomputer, and mainframe databases. This means independent software vendors and corporate developers don't have to learn multiple APIs because ODBC provides a universal data access interface. With ODBC, application developers can allow an application to concurrently access, view, and modify data from multiple, diverse databases.

ODBC vs. DAO and RDO

If you are accessing a client/server data source, ultimately you will be using ODBC. DAO uses ODBC and enhances it by providing a rich functionality that makes all ODBC drivers appear to have more capabilities than they might actually have. RDO is a thin object model that exposes the most important ODBC features. Since ODBC is the industry standard for accessing SQL data sources, it's worth knowing what it can do for you.

Why ODBC?

Yes indeed, why use the ODBC API directly at all? The simple answer is that you should use the ODBC API directly when you can do something with it that you can't do any other way. So the question should be rephrased: What can I do with ODBC that I can't do with something else? This question isn't quite so easy to answer because other data access methods use the main parts of ODBC functionality; they even add value by using techniques such as caching to improve performance so that you don't have to add performance code yourself. I will show you just a few things here that you can do using the ODBC API directly. I hope this will provide you with enough incentive to get hold of the ODBC SDK and see for yourself just how good ODBC is.

Data Source List

OK, let's start with an easy one. If you use an empty connection string to connect to an ODBC data source, you'll see a dialog box pop up that presents a list of data sources to which you can connect. This is fine as far as it goes. But wouldn't it be nice to be able to get that list of data sources from within your Visual Basic application? Perhaps you don't want to show a dialog box; perhaps you want to list all of the data sources under the File menu; or perhaps you'd like to show a Microsoft Windows Explorer style list with icons that represent the data sources. Maybe you have complex data source names, and you'd prefer to show just part of the name rather than the entire name. Whatever your requirement, if you use the ODBC API, all this can be done easily. Here's how. Add a list box to a form, and call it lstDataSources. Now create a command button, and add the following code to the Click event:

```
Dim nRetcode            As Integer
Dim lHenv               As Long
Dim sServerName         As String * 32
Dim sDescription        As String * 128
Dim nServerNameLength   As Integer
Dim nDescriptionLength As Integer

lstDataSources.Clear

nRetcode = SQLAllocHandle(SQL_HANDLE_ENV, SQL_NULL_HANDLE, _
    lHenv)
nRetcode = SQLSetEnvAttr(lHenv, SQL_ATTR_ODBC_VERSION, _
    SQL_OV_ODBC3, SQL_IS_INTEGER)
nRetcode = SQLDataSources(lHenv, SQL_FETCH_FIRST, sServerName, _
    Len(sServerName), nServerNameLength, sDescription, _
    Len(sDescription), nDescriptionLength)

Do While nRetcode = SQL_SUCCESS
    lstDataSources.AddItem Left$(sServerName, _
        nServerNameLength)
    nRetcode = SQLDataSources(lHenv, SQL_FETCH_NEXT, _
        sServerName, Len(sServerName), nServerNameLength, _
        sDescription, Len(sDescription), nDescriptionLength)
Loop

nRetcode = SQLFreeHandle(SQL_HANDLE_ENV, lHenv)
```

Now add the following constants and function declarations to a module:

```
Global Const SQL_NULL_HANDLE = 0
Global Const SQL_HANDLE_ENV = 1
Global Const SQL_HANDLE_DBC = 2
Global Const SQL_HANDLE_STMT = 3
Global Const SQL_HANDLE_DESC = 4

Global Const SQL_FETCH_NEXT = 1
Global Const SQL_FETCH_FIRST = 2

Global Const SQL_SUCCESS = 0
Global Const SQL_SUCCESS_WITH_INFO = 1
Global Const SQL_NO_DATA = 100
Global Const SQL_ERROR = (-1)
Global Const SQL_INVALID_HANDLE = (-2)
Global Const SQL_STILL_EXECUTING = 2
Global Const SQL_NEED_DATA = 99

Global Const SQL_ATTR_ODBC_VERSION = 200
Global Const SQL_OV_ODBC3 = 3
Global Const SQL_IS_INTEGER = -6
Global Const SQL_C_SLONG = -16

Declare Function SQLAllocHandle Lib "odbc32.dll" (ByVal _
    HandleType As Integer, ByVal InputHandle As Long, _
    OutputHandlePtr As Long) As Integer
Declare Function SQLSetEnvAttr Lib "odbc32.dll" (ByVal _
    EnvironmentHandle As Long, ByVal EnvAttribute As Long, _
    ByVal ValuePtr As Long, ByVal StringLength As Long) _
    As Integer
Declare Function SQLDataSources Lib "odbc32.dll" (ByVal _
    EnvironmentHandle As Long, ByVal Direction As Integer, _
    ByVal ServerName As String, ByVal BufferLength1 As Integer, _
    NameLength1Ptr As Integer, ByVal Description As String, _
    ByVal BufferLength2 As Integer, NameLength2Ptr As Integer) _
    As Integer
Declare Function SQLFreeHandle Lib "odbc32.dll" (ByVal _
    HandleType As Integer, ByVal Handle As Long) As Integer
```

When you run the program and then click the command button, the list box will show all of the available data sources. You can easily change this code to list only user data sources or system data sources. You can also extend it to include file data sources. In addition, you can modify the data source name that is retrieved to strip unwanted information. Keep in mind that the description of the data source is retrieved but not used in the example. Note also that the *iRetcode* variable contains only an error indicator and that for proper error checking, calls should be made to the *SQLError* function (or, perhaps, for more sophisticated requirements, to *SQLGetDiagRec* and *SQLGetDiagField*).

API Details

The previous example is very simple; it requires no connections and only a minimum number of API calls. A more complex example would have included connections, connection options, statements, statement options, comprehensive error handling, transaction control, recordset manipulation, bulk operations, and so forth—in fact, many more things than I could hope to cover in one short chapter. In most cases, you will be most productive when you use one of the object models provided by Visual Basic for standard database access, such as executing SQL statements and retrieving the results—it's much easier. However, when you need fine-grained control or you need to reach functionality that isn't exposed by DAO or RDO, the ODBC API is the tool for the job.

Because the ODBC API is designed for C programmers, the best approach can be to use Microsoft Visual C++ to write the actual code and then expose functions to Visual Basic in the form of a DLL. This enables you to take advantage of some features that are really usable only when you're manipulating memory pointers. For example, when you're retrieving variable length string data, it's not possible to know how much memory will be required to store the data until it's all been retrieved. This leads to the problem of overspecification— allocating much more memory than will actually be required. As an example, imagine you're retrieving variable length strings from a table that contains descriptive memos for accounting transactions and that these strings can be anywhere from 0 to 4096 characters long. Most of the time, they'll only be a few characters long; however, the application will have to allocate buffers that are at least 4096 bytes long (Figure 13-4) to accommodate the records that are longer than a few characters.

FIGURE 13-4

*Memory used
vs. memory
allocated to
buffers*

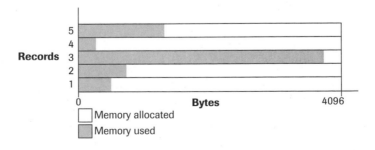

Version 3 of ODBC introduces the capability of assigning a single large buffer, with strings stored sequentially within the buffer as they are retrieved. A pointer must be maintained for each record that points to the beginning of the field in the buffer (Figure 13-5). This kind of pointer manipulation is easy in C but much harder in Visual Basic.

FIGURE 13-5

Pointers to records in a buffer

DB-LIBRARY

DB-Library for C is an API that consists of C functions and macros that allow an application to interact with SQL Server. Included in this API are functions that send Transact-SQL statements to SQL Server and functions that process the results of those statements. Other functions handle errors and convert data.

Features

DB-Library provides a complete programming interface for executing and retrieving SQL statements. The main difference between the DB-Library API and the ODBC API is that DB-Library is designed to work with just one data source, Microsoft SQL Server, whereas ODBC is an open interface that is designed to provide generic access to a wide range of data sources.

Much of the functionality in DB-Library is similar to ODBC; however, because this API is much more tightly coupled to the data source, it also includes some unique features. Like ODBC, DB-Library for C offers a rich set of functions for these tasks:

- Opening connections
- Formatting queries
- Sending query batches to the server and retrieving the resulting data
- Executing stored procedures or remote stored procedures
- Using scrollable cursors

But unlike ODBC, DB-Library also provides functions for these additional tasks:

- Bulk copying data from files or program variables to and from the server (BCP)
- Controlling two-phase commit operations between several participating SQL servers
- Obtaining the names of SQL servers either locally or over the network

These functions allow the application developer to control features that are not available through any other interface. Let's look at two of these features in more detail.

BCP: The Fastest Thing Since Speedy Gonzales

BCP is a DB-Library utility for copying large amounts of data into or out of SQL Server. BCP is used primarily for copying data from a SQL server for use with other programs (or spreadsheets), to upload data files from different databases, and to copy information from one SQL server to another SQL server. It provides a bulk-copy API that is guaranteed to be quicker than any other method for inserting records into SQL Server database tables.

The normal method of inserting a row into a table in a data source is to execute an INSERT SQL query. This is fine for the normal day-to-day activities that are part of any database application. The DBMS will ensure that the data that is inserted is of the correct types for the fields and will update indexes and enforce referential integrity constraints as well as run triggers that might be attached to the table or fields. Unfortunately, this can make the process of inserting a record slow. I should say here that this "slowness" is relative; most Insert queries will execute in a fraction of a second. The difference between executing 10 inserts per second and 100 inserts per second isn't something that would usually affect most applications; however, when you're importing a large number of records, this difference could grow from minutes to hours.

Two-Phase Commit

A two-phase commit service allows an application to coordinate updates among multiple SQL servers. This implementation of distributed transactions treats transactions on separate SQL servers as a single transaction. The service uses one SQL server as the commit server, the record keeper that helps the application determine whether to commit or to roll back transactions, which means that either all databases on the participating servers are updated or that none are.

A distributed transaction submits Transact-SQL statements to SQL servers through DB-Library functions. An application opens a session with each server, executes the update commands, and then prepares to commit the transaction. Through DB-Library, the application sends the following statements to each participating server:

- A *BEGIN TRANSACTION* statement that includes identifying information about the application, the transaction, and the commit server
- Transact-SQL update statements
- A *PREPARE TRANSACTION* statement, which indicates the updates have been performed and the server is prepared to commit (This statement can't be used outside the context of DB-Library.)

After all servers participating in the distributed transaction have been updated, the two-phase commit begins:

1. All servers agree that they are ready to commit.
2. All servers commit—that is, a *COMMIT TRANSACTION* statement is sent to all servers.

The application then tells the commit server that the transaction is complete, and the connections are closed. If an error occurs between phase one and phase two, all servers coordinate with the commit server to determine whether the transaction should be committed or canceled.

OLE DB

OLE DB is the latest data access technology and, as such, deserves some attention when you're deciding on a data access method for your application. In fact, the technology is so new that few people have, at the time of this writing, used it. The basic philosophy that underpins OLE DB is Microsoft's quest for the holy grail: "information at your fingertips." So far, this quest has led to integrated applications suites (such as Microsoft Office) that are able to share data in a way that improves much on previous generations of software. It has also led to the development of standard APIs, such as ODBC, that provide transparent access to a multiplicity of databases. However, there are more data stores that contain unstructured (or non-DBMS) data than there are those that contain structured data. By data store it would be fair to say that I mean *any* file stored on your computer hard disk or network, such as project plans, e-mail, and bulletin boards. Until now, there has been no single way to integrate this data. OLE DB provides the way to access these diverse data sources.

OLE DB is a set of OLE interfaces that provides applications with uniform access to data stored in diverse information sources. These interfaces support the specific amount of DBMS functionality appropriate to the data source, enabling the data source to share its data.

What Is OLE DB?

OLE DB is to diverse unstructured data what ODBC is to structured SQL-based databases. It is a unifying access method that provides a single route to accessing any data. So in a way similar to that used by ODBC, OLE DB employs a layered model. Thus diagrams of the two architectures might at first seem similar, as you can see in Figure 13-6 and Figure 13-7.

FIGURE 13-6

*ODBC archi-
tecture*

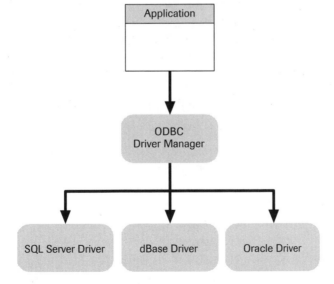

FIGURE 13-7

*OLE DB
architecture*

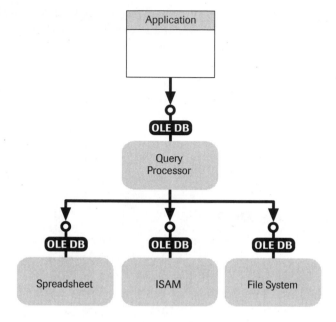

OLE DB is different in two important aspects, however. First, unlike ODBC, OLE DB is based on OLE technology rather than on a simple API approach. Second, also unlike ODBC, OLE DB is not constrained by requiring all data access and manipulation to be performed via SQL. The only criterion that OLE DB imposes is that the data returned by a command be in the form of a table. So provided that the result of a file system query can be represented by a table (which ultimately all data can be—that is, a table of just one row and one column), an application using OLE DB should be able to retrieve and display the data.

Actually, I have cheated. There is a third major distinction between OLE DB and ODBC. OLE DB is heterogeneous in the same way that DAO builds added value onto ODBC by enabling the user to execute table joins between different data sources. For example, consider the following SQL code:

```
SELECT  *
FROM  employees, deptsales
WHERE employees.deptid = deptsales.deptid
```

In this example, the employees table could be in a SQL Server database containing information for a corporate human resources system, and the deptsales table could be a Microsoft FoxPro table maintained by the sales department.

In a similar way, OLE DB enables data to be joined from vastly different types of data sources, as shown here:

```
REPORT email_address
TO system_supervisor
USING email_sent, stored_attachments
WHERE email_sent.owner = stored_attachments.owner
    AND stored_attachments.size > 10k
```

In this example, the email_sent table is exposed by an OLE DB object that can read an e-mail system, and the stored_attachments table is a table that represents a particular set of disk files. I have altered some of the keywords from their SQL equivalent to emphasize the fact that OLE DB is not SQL-based and commands can be syntactically quite different.

One last point to remember is that because OLE DB uses the OLE Component Object Model (COM) infrastructure, OLE DB is perhaps the best choice for access to data in a COM environment.

ADO

Despite its obvious benefits, the OLE DB programming interface is designed primarily for the C++ developer who is familiar with the details of the OLE programming model. This means that OLE DB is not particularly accessible to the Visual Basic developer. One way to overcome this is by utilizing ActiveX data objects (ADO). ADO provides an interface to the OLE DB world in a way that is readily understood by Visual Basic developers. Without going into too much depth, I'll present the basic details of ADO here.

FIGURE 13-8

The ADO object model

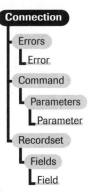

The ADO object model, shown in Figure 13-8, will be immediately familiar to anyone who has used any of the other data access object models discussed here. The names of the objects themselves are perhaps most similar to the object names in the RDO object model. This should come as no surprise since the design of OLE DB (on which ADO is based) was influenced by the considerable input from the designers of ODBC (on which RDO is based). This familiar object model will enable the Visual Basic 5 developer to easily convert applications to using ADO.

The main difference in using ADO is in the method of connecting and creating recordsets. Once they are created, recordsets can be handled in much the same way that DAO and RDO recordsets are handled. For example, the following code fragment shows the creation and navigation of an ADO recordset:

```
Dim oConn As Object
Dim oRS As Object

Set oConn = CreateObject("ADO.Connection")
oConn.Connect "pubs", "sa", ""
Set oRS = oConn.Execute("select * from authors")
Do While Not oRS.EOF
    Debug.Print oRS.Fields("au_lname").Value
    oRS.MoveNext
Loop
```

The first thing to note is that because ADO provides an Automation interface, instances can be easily created and manipulated with code that is already familiar. This example shows fetching data from an SQL database (actually, a sample database supplied with SQL Server); the thing to remember is that OLE DB supports a command interface that doesn't have to be the SQL command language. The commands that a particular OLE DB data provider could accept for a project management database might be something like this:

```
List tasks(outstanding) for project("implement oledb")
```

Because ADO is an ActiveX object, it's also available, of course, to creators of Internet Web pages through Microsoft Visual Basic, Scripting Edition, and Visual Basic 5. This is one of the reasons I believe ADO might in the future become the data access method of choice. If data can be represented in a tabular format, an OLE DB provider can be built for it. Once a provider has been created, any ADO-enabled application will be able to manipulate it. This is perhaps the first time that Microsoft's goal of "information at your fingertips" can be seen as a viable reality. Although it's too early to say much more about ADO, I think it's an option worth considering and a technology worth watching because it provides wider interoperability between data sources than even ODBC.

POSTSCRIPT

I hope that this chapter has provided you with sufficient information regarding the data access options available to a Visual Basic developer for you to be able to make an informed decision about which method is best for your application. Figure 13-9 is a summary diagram that you might find useful. However, no two applications are ever quite the same, so please do your own research and test all the appropriate options before making your final design decision.

FIGURE 13-9

Data access method selection

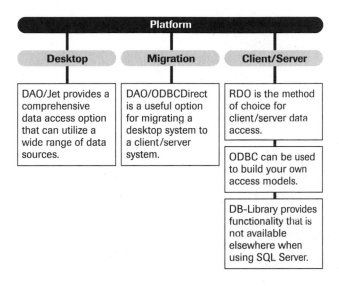

Programming on Purpose

A Window on Detailed Design

MARK HURST

Mark is a TMS Associate who is also a writer, painter, pilot, filmmaker, and enthusiastic, if only mildly talented, ragtime guitarist. He risks life and limb daily by charging through London traffic on a gigantic Yamaha trail bike, and he almost never wears a tie. Since graduating with a computer science degree in 1985, Mark has made a living out of software. Mark is an accomplished C, C++, and Pascal programmer, and he has also worked as a designer, analyst, system tester, configuration manager, and trainer. He has worked with Visual Basic since the 2.0 beta program and is a Microsoft Certified Professional. Mark has presented at VBITS and the Visual Tools Developers' Academy and has published many articles in industry journals and beyond.

It's a popular myth that Microsoft Visual Basic has changed programming. I disagree. Programming is as hard as it always was—most people who say that Visual Basic projects are easy just aren't doing them right. Perhaps Visual Basic has advanced the state of the art of Microsoft Windows programming a notch or two; but behind the form designers and the wizards lies procedural code, with all the traditional problems developers have come to expect. A dangerous side effect of making a programming tool as easy to use as Visual Basic is the illusion that this somehow dispenses with the need for detailed design—that the code somehow writes itself. The truth, scribbled in the margin of many a project postmortem report, is that programming in Visual Basic is *programming* first and Visual Basic second.

This chapter is about detailed design. To illustrate the kinds of things you need to think about when designing an application, we'll be looking at the design and construction of a window-management scheme, perhaps the most fundamental part of any Windows program. You'll be reading a lot about the graphical user interface (GUI), but you won't be seeing anything about button sizes, mouse-pointer psychology, or the choice of fonts and colors—the approach in this chapter is from a different angle, addressing the kinds of problems that will sink a GUI no matter how nice the screens look. You'll be seeing the choices Visual Basic offers for designing window-management schemes, some of the obstacles Visual Basic puts in your way, and how you can use some of the more advanced features of Visual Basic to get what you want. In all of this, you'll be focusing on two particular areas: how to use classes to build value-added forms and how to manage complexity with finite state machines.

Managing Windows

The most striking feature of the majority of commercial Visual Basic applications is the set of windows they create and manipulate, including the way the user gets around these windows and the ways in which the windows interact with one another. Often a window-management scheme is something that simply evolves during implementation: the developer might not have a clear idea about how each window will behave with respect to other windows, and the window-management features built into Visual Basic might be the factor that most influences how the design turns out. This isn't so much a poor design strategy as the lack of a strategy, and the resulting problems can be anything from poor usability to insidious bugs.

Visual Basic has a mixed bag of window-management tricks, the simplest of which are *MsgBox* and *InputBox*. These are modal dialog boxes, so you must deal with them before the program will remove them and continue its processing. There isn't much to say about *MsgBox* and *InputBox* except that they are inflexible. In particular, you can't change the button captions, and you can't control where on the screen the dialog boxes are displayed. For added flexibility, you can, of course, write your own Visual Basic functions named *MsgBox* and *InputBox* to override the Visual Basic ones. Interestingly, doing this allows you to make nonmodal message boxes, the consequences of which will become clear later.

Visual Basic also has features to support multiple-document interface (MDI) applications, and the decision to build with MDI will have a major influence on the way your application works. MDI has some advantages—chiefly that it is well defined and that Visual Basic will implement some of the features for you (menu management, window arrangements, and so on). On the other hand, adopting MDI for these reasons alone is futile if the application you want to build doesn't fit the rigid MDI model. MDI supports a document model and usually makes sense only if your application is going to work with multiple instances of things that are somehow document-like. Document-like qualities include serialization (binding to permanent storage) and size independence, which gives meaning to the familiar MDI window-arrangement functions Tile and Cascade.

On the other side of the fence from MDI is single-document interface (SDI). Because Visual Basic has no specific functions to support SDI, however, a more accurate description would be "not MDI." You have much more flexibility when building non-MDI applications, but you lose out on some of the free functionality such as window arrangement, child window menu handling, and Ctrl+Tab to switch between child windows. On the other hand, you have more control over your application's appearance, and you can choose whether to make your child forms modal or modeless.

Finally, you can build hybrid applications that borrow some features from MDI without using built-in functionality. You can, for example, create multiple instances of an ordinary form (forms behave just like classes in many ways), and you can even create MDI parent forms dynamically within a non-MDI application. It's important to consider these issues in advance and to plan a window-management scheme appropriate to the application you want to build.

Modal or Modeless?

Whether you choose MDI, SDI, or your own brand of DIY-DI (do-it-yourself document interface), you'll need to think about modality. Modality is one of the most critical issues in the design of your window-management scheme, since it can significantly affect program complexity. Using modal forms wherever possible helps to control complexity, but it can also get in the way by imposing artificial restrictions on users. Although modality is one of the more contentious issues of user interface design, the evidence in favor of radical modeless design is far from conclusive. Suffice it to say that in this chapter the concern is with the implications of modality on implementation rather than with the psychology of interface design.

When you show a form, Visual Basic lets you specify whether you want to show it modally or nonmodally, using the constants vbModal and vbModeless. This isn't a very flexible way of implementing modes, however; a vbModal form is task-modal, which means it locks out all user input from the rest of the application. This type of modality is really suitable only for pop-up dialog boxes. When you specify vbModal when you show a form, the only way you can show two forms together is if they have a parent-child relationship. This restriction imposes a particular set of design restrictions on your application, and it might prevent you from doing what you want. It's also impossible to display a nonmodal form from a modal form, another potentially intolerable situation.

Consider the example shown in Figure 14-1, which is a non-MDI application with several distinct functions invoked from a main menu. Perhaps it's a database maintenance program, and you would like to be able to refer to display functions while using update functions. In Figure 14-1, I've shown two functions executing at the same time; forms A and C can be considered parent forms for Function 1 and Function 2, respectively. Parent form A is also displaying a child form, form B.

FIGURE 14-1

An example of function modality: form A is not accessible here.

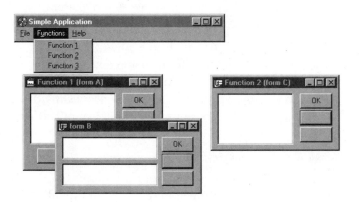

Although the forms shown in Figure 14-1 are relatively simple, it's likely that you'll want form A to display form B modally, or more specifically, for form A to be inaccessible for as long as form B is on the screen. The conventional way to code this is for form A to do *FormB.Show vbModal*, but this locks all user input from any form except form B—including the main menu. Hence, it wouldn't be possible to reach the situation shown in Figure 14-1. The alternative, *FormB.Show vbModeless*, doesn't prevent you from accessing multiple functions at the same time, but it interferes with the design of each function and greatly increases the complexity of the program. Clearly, you need to find something in between.

Visual Basic's built-in support for modal forms is geared toward simple pop-up dialog boxes, but that doesn't stop you from building modes by other means. Forms have an *Enabled* property that, when set to False, effectively mimics what happens to a parent form when it shows a vbModal child. Now that you're in control, however, you're free to enable and disable forms at will, without the restrictions imposed by vbModal.

Returning to the example in Figure 14-1, all you need to do is to disable form A when form B loads and reenable it when form B unloads (or possibly on *Show* and *Hide* instead of Load and Unload). This implements a new kind of mode that's more appropriate to your requirements; you might call it "function modality," since you're creating an architecture in which it's permissible to hop back and forth between functions yet each function is effectively a modal cascade of forms. This architecture is only one possibility; a less orthodox architecture is shown in Figure 14-2.

FIGURE 14-2

The Create New Publication and Review Publication forms swap with each other.

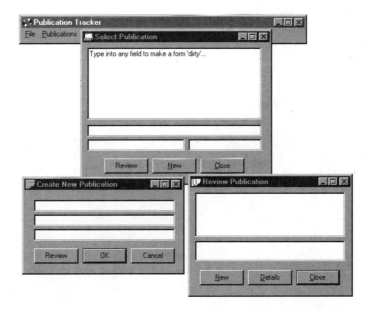

Figure 14-2 shows a database application that's used to keep records of technical publications. Users can choose an existing entry from the list and edit it using the Review Publication form, or they can enter a new publication by calling Create New Publication. Notice that the Create New Publication window has a Review button, and the Review Publication window has a New button. This arrangement could imply multiple instances of each screen, but let's say that the design calls for screens to be *swapped* when these buttons are used. For example, the user could call up the Create New Publication window to enter the details for a new publication and then press the Review button to

FORMS ARE CLASSES TOO

Forms are really classes in disguise. Once you realize this fact, you can start using it to your advantage. The similarity isn't obvious because you don't have to define instances of forms before you can use them. However, you can use a form's *Name* property to create new instances of the form at run time, just as if it were a class. What's a little confusing is that if you don't create any instances at run time, you always get one for free—and it has the same name as the class. Thus, referring to Form1 at run time means different things in different contexts:

```
Form1.Caption = "My Form"            ' Form1 is an object name.
Dim frmAnotherForm As New Form1      ' Form1 is a class name.
```

The fact that forms are really classes is why defining public variables at the module level in a form appears not to work—trying to assign to these variables causes "Variable not defined" errors. In fact, you're defining *properties* of the form, and these work in exactly the same way as class properties do. To refer to such properties in code, you need to qualify them with the object name, which, you'll recall, is usually the same as the class name. (This is confusing if you do actually create multiple instances.) Even more interesting is that you can also define *Property Let* and *Property Get* procedures, Public methods, and even Friend functions in forms, just as you can in classes.

Because Visual Basic doesn't support inheritance at the source code level, you can't build value-added form classes; the best you can do is to build value-added form *instances* by adding custom properties and methods to your forms. You can do this by exploiting the classlike nature of forms and writing a form *base class* that contains extra properties and methods you'd like to see on every form. This works very well in practice, although it relies on you adding some standard code to every form you create. To see how this works, let's build some methods to save and restore a form's position when it loads and unloads.

The first thing you need to do is define a class, named CFormAttributes. You'll create a Public instance of this class in every form you create, and this instance will appear as a property of the form. When you store the form positions with *SaveSetting*, it would be nice to use the form name as a key; unfortunately, there isn't any way for an instance of a Visual Basic class to refer to the object that owns it. This means you'll need to define the owner as a property in your CFormAttributes class and arrange to set it when you create the instance. Here's the class:

>>

```
Private frmPiSelf As Form

Public Sub SavePosition()
    SaveSetting App.Title, "Form Positions", _
                    frmPiSelf.Name & "-top", frmPiSelf.Top
    ⋮
End Sub

Public Sub RestorePosition()
    ⋮
End Sub

Public Sub LoadActions(ByVal frmiMe As Form)
    Set frmPiSelf = frmiMe
    RestorePosition frmPiSelf
End Sub

Public Sub UnloadActions()
    SavePosition frmPiSelf
End Sub
```

Notice that the *LoadActions* and *UnloadActions* methods are also defined. These make the class more general for when you add to it later. To add new properties to a form, you need to adopt certain conventions. First you need to define an instance of the class as a form-level variable:

```
Public My As New CFormAttributes
```

The variable is named *My* because it's pretty close to *Me*, and semantically the two are similar. For example, you can now refer to *My.UnloadActions*. The only other thing you need to do is to make sure the *LoadActions* and *UnloadActions* routines are called:

```
Private Sub Form_Load()
    My.LoadActions Me
End Sub

Private Sub Form_Unload()
    My.UnloadActions
End Sub
```

You do have to pass the owner form reference to *LoadActions* to initialize the class's *Self* property. You can find the complete class on the companion CD in CHAP14\atribcls\pubatrib.cls, and CHAP14\atribs\atr.vbp is an implementation of the program shown in Figure 14-2 on page 583.

move immediately to the Review Publication window to enter a review of it. As the Review Publication window loads, it *replaces* the Create New Publication window, which is unloaded. The Select Publication window is disabled when either the Review Publication window or the Create New Publication window is displayed.

There is no elegant way to implement this architecture using Visual Basic's standard modality features. You would somehow have to defer your request for the review form to be displayed until the Create New Publication form was unloaded. You could make it work, but it would be tricky and it would be ugly. You'd be much better off devising a general mechanism to support the kinds of modes you want to enforce.

Toward a General Modality Class

You can both create and manipulate value-added forms by building a CFormAttributes class (see the "Forms Are Classes Too" sidebar on page 584) and adding the function modality mechanism to it. The central requirement for such a mechanism is to associate a parent with each form you create. You can do this by adding a *Parent* property to the CFormAttributes class:

```
Public Parent As Form
```

Now you have somewhere to store a reference to the parent form, so you need to arrange for this reference to be set when the form is loaded. Since you can't pass parameters to a form's *Show* method (or to the CFormAttributes instance), you need to do this manually from outside the CFormAttributes class. You want to be able to do something like this:

```
Public Sub ShowChild Child:=frmReview, Parent:=Me
```

You could make this a global procedure and give it its own BAS file, but it's better to keep all the code in one place by making *ShowChild* a method of the CFormAttributes class. Obviously, this means you can't invoke *ShowChild* to display the first form in a hierarchy, but the only implication of this is that you need to make sure that the CFormAttributes class recognizes that it has no parent when it is destroyed. You can also dispense with the *Parent* parameter since you already have a *Self* reference in the CFormAttributes class. Here's the method in the CFormAttributes class, which is named *NewChild*:

```
Public Sub NewChild(ByVal frmiChild As Form)
    frmiChild.Show
    Set frmiChild.My.Parent = frmPiSelf
    frmPiSelf.Enabled = False
End Sub
```

The last statement is the significant one because it's the one that disables the parent form and creates a new mode. You need a reciprocal action to reenable the parent when the form unloads, so you need to define another method:

```
Public Sub EnableParent()
    If Not Me.Parent Is Nothing Then Me.Parent.Enabled = True
End Sub
```

Unfortunately, there's no elegant way to bind this to a form unload; you must ensure that you call this method from each *Form_Unload* event:

```
Private Sub Form_Unload()
    My.EnableParent
End Sub
```

In fact, the sample code in CHAP14\atribcls\pubatrib.cls has a generic *UnloadActions* method, which takes the place of *EnableParent*, but this discussion is clearer if I continue to refer to an *EnableParent* method.

That takes care of modal child forms, as long as you invoke them with *My.NewChild* and include the appropriate reciprocal call in the *Form_Unload* event. You can now build on this to extend the mechanism. To cope with the swapping in the sample program, for example, you need to do a couple of extra things: pass on the outgoing form's parent reference to the new form and then prevent the parent from being reenabled when the old form unloads. You can do this by adding a new method and modifying the *EnableParent* method slightly so that the two communicate through a module-level flag:

```
Private bPiKeepParentDisabled As Boolean

Public Sub SwapMe(ByVal frmiNewChild As Form)
    frmiNewChild.Show vbModeless
    If frmiNewChild.Enabled Then
        Set frmiNewChild.My.Parent = Parent
        bPiKeepParentDisabled = True
    End If
    Unload frmPiSelf
End Sub

Public Sub EnableParent()
    If Not bPiKeepParentDisabled Then
        If Not Parent Is Nothing Then Parent.Enabled = True
    End If
End Sub
```

Notice the check to find out whether the form you're trying to swap to is enabled. If it isn't, it must already have been loaded, in which case you'll just leave the *Parent* property alone. This is an ad hoc test that works in the simple examples shown here, but it might not be general, and so you'll need to extend the mechanism to cope with other situations. For example, the mechanism as it stands won't prevent you from trying to swap to a form that's in the *middle* of a modal cascade—in fact, this would orphan any child forms in the cascade. With a little thought, you should be able to extend the mechanism to allow swapping to remove child forms of the form you're trying to swap to, to prevent swapping between forms belonging to other functions in a function modal situation, or to support any other flavors of modality you care to invent.

Extending the CFormAttributes Class

The beauty of a value-added form class is that it's a simple matter to add new features retrospectively. As an example, let's look at how you can add support for pseudo-MDI minimize and restore behavior. Because all document windows in an MDI application are contained within the client area of the parent window, minimizing that window naturally takes away all of the children too. This is convenient since it instantly clears the application off the desktop (without closing it, of course).

The MDI window feature in Visual Basic gives you this minimize behavior for free. With an SDI or a DIY-DI application, however, you have no such luxury. Because a Visual Basic form has no Minimize event, you must write code that plugs into the Resize event and decide for yourself when a form is minimized or restored by investigating the *WindowState* property. The behavior we're going to construct will watch for transitions from normal to minimized and from minimized back to normal. (This second operation is usually called "restore.") We'll write the code as a new method of the CFormAttributes class and then simply add a call to it from appropriate Resize event handlers.

Trapping the event, of course, is only half the story—you also need to do something to take away the rest of the forms. One possibility is to set the *WindowState* to follow the window containing the trap, but in practice that looks messy because Windows animates zoom boxes all over the place and you end up with lots of task bar buttons (or icons for earlier versions of Microsoft Windows NT). It's quicker and visually more effective to hide all the other forms when you trap a minimize event and to restore them when you trap a restore event. The only tricky part is to remember the prevailing state of each form before hiding it, just in case any were hidden already. Here's the code you'll need:

```
Public PreviouslyVisible As Boolean
Private nPiPrevWindowState As Integer

Public Sub PropagateMinMaxEvents ()
    If frmPiSelf.WindowState = vbMinimized _
            And nPiPrevWindowState = vbNormal Then
        Call HideAllForms
    ElseIf frmPiSelf.WindowState = vbNormal _
            And nPiPrevWindowState = vbMinimized Then
        Call UnhideAllForms
    End If
    nPiPrevWindowState = frmPiSelf.WindowState
End Sub

Private Sub HideAllForms()
    Dim frmForm As Form
    For Each frmForm In Forms
        If Not frmForm Is frmPiSelf Then
            frmForm.My.PreviouslyVisible = frmForm.Visible
            frmForm.Visible = False
        End If
    Next frmForm
End Sub

Private Sub UnhideAllForms()
    ' This is just the opposite of HideAllForms.
End Sub
```

To activate the new behavior, you need to choose which forms will trigger it and call *PropagateMinMaxEvents* from their Resize event handlers. The publication editing program referred to in Figure 14-2 on page 583 has this call coded in the Resize events of all the forms, so minimizing any form hides all the others and shows a single button on the task bar. Restoring from that button restores each form to its previous state. To add minimize behavior to the example application shown in Figure 14-1 on page 582, you would code a single call to *PropagateMinMaxEvents* in the Resize event of the main form (the one carrying the menu bar). This mimics the MDI paradigm more closely because of the definite parent form.

Visual Basic 5 has another trick that you could use here, which is to add custom Minimize and Restore events to your forms through the CFormAttributes class. You can do this very simply by making a small modification to the *PropagateMinMaxEvents* method on the following page.

```
Event Minimize()
Event Restore()

Public Sub PropagateMinMaxEvents ()
    If frmPiSelf.WindowState = vbMinimized _
            And nPiPrevWindowState = vbNormal Then
        RaiseEvent Minimize
    ElseIf frmPiSelf.WindowState = vbNormal _
            And nPiPrevWindowState = vbMinimized Then
        RaiseEvent Restore
    End If
    nPiPrevWindowState = frmPiSelf.WindowState
End Sub
```

In case you didn't spot it, calls to *HideAllForms* and *UnhideAllForms* have been replaced with calls to a new Visual Basic procedure, *RaiseEvent*. This diminutive keyword is very powerful, and you'll see other examples of it later. When you define the CFormAttributes instance on a form, a new object, *My*, appears in the code window's Object drop-down list box, and when you choose it, you'll see Minimize and Restore events in the Procedure drop-down list box. These events work in exactly the same way as normal events do, so selecting Minimize inserts an empty procedure named *My_Minimize* into the code. One caveat is that the syntax for defining the CFormAttributes instance is slightly different if you want to see the events:

```
Public WithEvents My As CFormAttributes
```

Unfortunately, the New keyword is not allowed in combination with the WithEvents keyword, so you'll also need to add a line to the *Form_Load* event:

```
Private Sub Form_Load()
    Set My = New CFormAttributes
    My.LoadActions Me
End Sub
```

DEALING WITH COMPLEXITY

Building a mechanism like the one above is a good way to get a feel for the architectural design of your GUI, but it's tempting to channel design resources into such details as how many forms you're going to use and what fields you need on each form and to let seemingly peripheral issues such as navigation and modality take a back seat. You can get away with this for smaller projects because it's possible to have an intuitive grasp of the interactions among a small number of forms. In general, however, ignoring questions such as how each form is invoked and which forms can be on the screen at the same time can lead to disaster.

By allowing multiple forms to be active at the same time, you dramatically increase the complexity of the underlying code because manipulating data on one form can affect other forms that are also being displayed. For even a modest-size application, the view ahead is daunting, since you have to examine every possible combination of forms that can be active at the same time and then consider the effects of all possible inputs for each combination. Any modes you've designed will help to limit form interactions, but doing the analysis ad hoc invites unplanned side effects—inevitably, you'll fail to plan for some situations.

Figure 14-3 shows an application that manages a cascade of forms that lead the user down through successive layers of data. If you use modeless forms, editing the data on form A invalidates the data on forms B and C. You also need to consider what happens if the user closes form A before closing forms B and C. Clearly, you need to decide whether these actions have any useful meaning in the application; if they don't, you can simply prevent them; but if they do, you want to know up front because they can affect the implementation. (You don't want the forms to share data, for example.)

FIGURE 14-3

A cascade of forms—but modal or modeless?

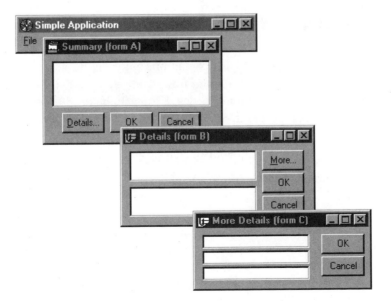

You might be feeling skeptical about the complexities of a three-form application. Some simple arithmetic can be illuminating. There are seven possible ways in which combinations of the modeless forms A, B, and C can be active. (Let's call these combinations "states.") Now let's say the user presses the Cancel button on form A. Let's also assume you've decided never to leave forms B and C up when the user closes form A. It's clear that the event handler for form A's Cancel Click can't simply unload the form—it must look around to see what other forms are up and maybe close those forms too.

If you add another form to the application, the number of states goes up to 15. Even discarding the states that don't contain form A, you are left with 8 different situations to consider in each Cancel Click event handler. In fact, the number of states (combinations of forms) is $2^n - 1$, where n is the number of forms. This number increases *geometrically* as you add forms, which means the number of states gets out of hand very quickly. There is a set of events for which you must consider all of these states, and the handlers for such events need to be aware of the environment and adjust their behavior accordingly.

It should be clear by now that you need a formal way to define the interactions between forms. The model we'll use to track form interactions is the *finite state machine* (FSM). The principles of an FSM, which is essentially an abstract representation of a set of states and events, are described in the following section.

The Art of the State

An FSM is a virtual machine characterized by a set of internal states, a set of external events, and a set of transitions between the states. You might also hear FSMs referred to by the name finite state automata, deterministic finite automata, or simply state machines. FSMs can be used to model an entire application, a small part of it, or both, and they are extremely common in the design of real-time systems, compilers, and communications protocols. FSMs are ideal tools for representing event-driven programs such as GUIs.

States are labels assigned to particular sets of circumstances within the application. Although FSMs are often used to model the GUI part of applications, states are not forms, and events are not necessarily Visual Basic events. You generate a set of predefined events from real-world stimuli and apply them as inputs to the FSM to drive it through transitions into different states. Transitions can have arbitrary lists of actions associated with them, and these actions are executed as you drive the FSM from state to state by repeatedly applying events. An FSM is deterministic because each combination of state and event unambiguously defines the next state to move into.

An FSM can be represented as a state transition diagram or as a pair of tables, one table defining the next state to move into when a particular state/event combination is detected and the other a list of actions to be performed along the way.

Figure 14-4 shows an FSM for a program to strip C comments out of a text stream. (Comments in C are delimited by /* and */.)

FIGURE 14-4

Comment stripper FSM

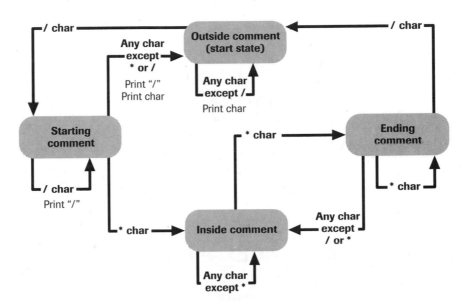

The bubbles in Figure 14-4 represent states, and the arrows represent transitions between states. Each transition is labeled with the event that stimulates it and the list of associated actions. One state is designated the start state, which is the initial state when the FSM starts to operate. Here is the FSM in tabular form:

STATE TABLE

Event	State			
	Outside	Starting	Inside	Ending
/	Starting	Starting	Inside	Outside
*	Outside	Inside	Ending	Ending
Any other char	Outside	Outside	Inside	Inside

ACTION TABLE

Event	State Outside	Starting	Inside	Ending
/	N/A	Print "/"	N/A	N/A
*	Print char	N/A	N/A	N/A
Any other char	Print char	Print "/" Print char	N/A	N/A

These tables provide the basis for implementing an FSM as a program. An FSM program has the following elements:

- A static variable to track the current state and a set of constants to represent all available states

- A table or equivalent program network to look up a state/event pair and decide which state to move into

- A set of constants to represent FSM events

- A driver loop that captures real-world events and decodes the state/event pair

Modeling a GUI with an FSM

Figure 14-5 shows a GUI fragment modeled on a real application. This application provides a summary and two different detailed views of a database. The forms are modeless, so the user can edit any form on the screen, potentially invalidating data on either of the other forms. Although the maximum possible number of states is seven, the design of this application permits access to only four combinations of forms: A, A + B, A + C, and A + B + C. The only events we'll consider are the button clicks; there are 11 buttons, so this is the number of events that must be accounted for in every state.

The application has been designed so that only form A's OK or Apply button commits data to the database. Each form has a buffer in which it holds edits to its own subset of the data, and the contents of these buffers are shuffled around as the OK, Apply, and Cancel buttons are manipulated on forms B and C. Figure 14-6 shows the state transitions for this GUI, and Figure 14-7 on page 596 is a close-up view of two states, showing the actions the application will take on each transition.

FIGURE 14-5

A deceptively simple-looking application

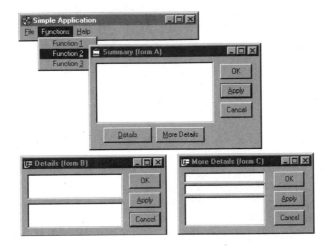

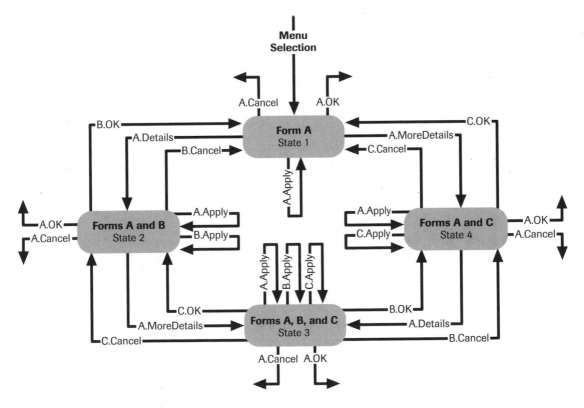

FIGURE 14-6   *FSM for the application shown in Figure 14-5*

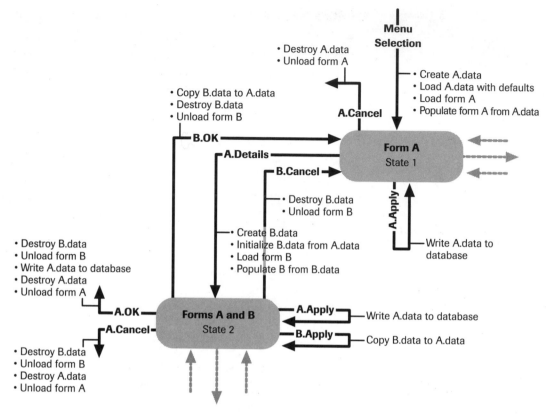

FIGURE 14-7   *Close-up view of a fragment of Figure 14-6*

Close examination of Figures 14-6 and 14-7 reveals some omissions. There are 11 events, but not all states have 11 arrows leaving them. This is partly because not all events can occur in all states. For example, it isn't possible to click form C's Apply button in state 1. But some events, such as the Detail button events in states 2 and 3, are omitted because there just isn't enough space for them. Leaving out events like this undermines a basic reason for using an FSM, which is to verify that you've considered all state/event combinations. This is where the tabular form is a much better representation—it's easier to draw, and it clearly shows all state/event combinations. The two notations complement each other, and in practice the state diagram is a useful sketch that conveys the feel of the GUI, while the tables provide a basis for implementation.

The End of the Elegance

The finite state machine (FSM) notation is simple and elegant, but you'll run into problems when you try to apply it to real programs. One class of problem, the conditional state transition, is exemplified by the need for validation when you're unloading forms. For example, if you consider form B's OK Click event, you can see that the FSM changes state and does the associated actions *unconditionally*. If you want to do a form-level validation before committing changes, you'll have a problem. In practice, the solution depends on how far you're prepared to go in carrying the FSM through into the implementation of your program. For smaller applications, it's wise to stop at the design stage and just use the state diagram and tables for guidance when writing the program. For more complex programs, you can carry the FSM right through to the implementation, as you'll see below.

For a pure FSM implementation, you can get around the validation issue by introducing extra states into the machine. Figure 14-8 shows a new state between states 2 and 1 for form B's OK event. The only difference is that this state is *transient* because the FSM immediately flips out of it into state 1 or state 2. This happens because you queue an event for the new state before you even get there. Validation states are also required for confirmation, such as when a user tries to abandon an edited form without saving changes.

FIGURE 14-8

*Introducing
transient
states to avoid
conditional
transitions*

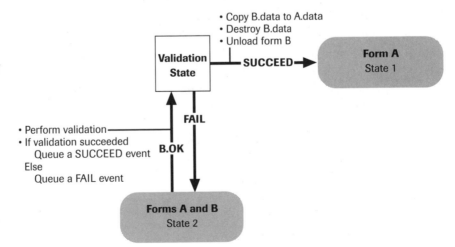

Implementing FSMs

If you want to carry an FSM through to the bitter end, you can implement it directly as program code. This requires a leap of faith because the code can often appear long-winded. In spite of this, if you're taking the trouble to implement the FSM, you'll gain much more by sticking rigorously to the mechanism without being tempted to introduce shortcuts, particularly in trying to avoid repetition of code. Recall that we're using an FSM to *formalize* the design of the GUI, and for a complex GUI the direct translation to code pays dividends by virtually eliminating the need for debugging. By introducing shortcuts, not only do you lose this integrity, but you also make the code harder to read.

Building an FSM with code is a straightforward affair that can be abstracted in a simple conditional statement:

```
If we're HERE and THIS happens Then
    do THAT and GoTo THERE
```

The only thing you have to keep track of is the current state, and most of your effort will be concerned with the mechanics of processing events and invoking the action procedures. You can build an FSM in any language that supports conditional statements, so let's start by looking at an implementation that can be adapted to any version of Visual Basic.

For this example, you will implement the C comment stripper described earlier and build it into a simple application using the form shown in Figure 14-9. The application displays the text as you type, minus any C-style comments. You will drive the FSM in real time—that is, the events will be caused directly by your keypresses, and the states and events will be displayed in the other boxes on the form.

FIGURE 14-9

The comment stripper FSM program

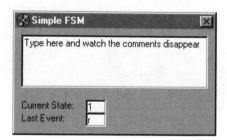

The first thing you need is a state, which can be represented as a simple integer. It doesn't matter what data type you choose for the state, since there is no concept of ordering. The only requirement is that the states be unique. In real life, you'll usually want to define constants for the states and events. In this example, however, you're not going to use event constants because it's convenient to represent events with the ASCII codes generated by the keypresses. Here's how to define the states:

```
Private Const S_OUTSIDE = 1
Private Const S_STARTING = 2
Private Const S_INSIDE = 3
Private Const S_ENDING = 4

Public nPuState As Integer
```

TIP

If you're defining a group of constants to use as an enumerated type (you're effectively defining a State type here), always start the numbering at 1, not 0. This will help you spot uninitialized variables, since Visual Basic initializes integer variables to 0. Visual Basic 5 allows you to define enumerated types explicitly, but since they are freely interchangeable with longs, the same rule applies. (Unfortunately, none of this applies if you want to use your constants to index control arrays since the designers of Visual Basic chose to base them at 0.)

If you refer to the FSM tables (pages 593 and 594) for the comment stripper, you'll see that there are 12 different combinations of state and event, so your conditional logic needs to guide you along 12 different paths through the code. To implement this with simple conditional statements, you have the choice of using *If-Then-ElseIf* or *Select Case* statements; for this example, we'll arbitrarily choose the latter. To decode one particular path, the code will contain a fragment such as this:

```
Select Case nState

    Case S_OUTSIDE:
        Select Case nEvent
            Case Asc("/")
                nState = S_STARTING
            Case Asc("*")
                txtOutBox.Text = txtOutBox.Text & Chr$(nEvent)
                nState = S_OUTSIDE
            Case Else
```

>>

>>

```
                    txtOutBox.Text = txtOutBox.Text & Chr$(nEvent)
                    nState = S_OUTSIDE
            End Select

        Case S_STARTING:
            ⋮
End Select
```

You can see that each of the 12 cells in the FSM tables has a piece of code inside a pair of nested *Select Case* statements. The State and Event tables are combined here, so the last statement in each case assigns a new value to *nState* (which we'll assume is a reference parameter). The rest of the code for each decoded state/event pair depends on what you want this particular implementation of the comment stripper to do—in fact, we're just going to add the text to the text box or not, so the actions here are simple. In practice, the code will usually be more manageable if you divide it up so that each state has its own function. Thus, the example above becomes something like this:

```
Select Case nState
    Case S_OUTSIDE DoStateOUTSIDE(nState, nEvent)
    Case S_STARTING DoStateSTARTING(nState, nEvent)
    ⋮
End Select

Sub DoStateOUTSIDE(ByVal niEvent As Integer, _
                   ByRef noState As Integer)
    Select Case niEvent
        Case Asc("/")
            noState = S_STARTING
        Case Asc("*"):
            txtOutBox.Text = txtOutBox.Text & Chr$(nEvent)
            noState = S_OUTSIDE
        Case Else
            txtOutBox.Text = txtOutBox.Text & Chr$(nEvent)
            noState = S_OUTSIDE
    End Select
End Sub
```

Now you have the state variable and the logic for decoding the state/event pairs, and all you need is a source of events. In this example, you'll trap keypresses by setting the *KeyPreview* property of the form and generating an event for each keypress. All you need to do now is feed the events to the FSM by calling a function that contains the decoding logic (let's call it *DoFSM*). The keypress event handler looks something like this:

```
Private Sub Form_KeyPress(KeyAscii As Integer)
    Call DoFSM(nPuState, KeyAscii)
    KeyAscii = 0 ' Throw away the keypress
End Sub
```

In this example, the event codes and the real-world events that map onto them are one and the same—hence, the "action" code in each DoState routine can get the ASCII codes directly from the *nEvent* parameter. Most applications don't have such coupling, and you would need to arrange for any such real-world data to be buffered somewhere if you wanted the action routines to have access to it. Consider, for example, the Unix tool yacc (yet another compiler-compiler), which builds table-driven parsers that process sequences of tokens read from an input stream. A parser generated by yacc gets its tokens by successive calls to a C function named *yylex()*, which is the direct equivalent of the KeyPress event handler. The *yylex()* function returns a numeric token, equivalent to the *nEvent* parameter, but it also copies the full text of the actual word it recognized into a global variable named *yytext*. This variable is available to any code in the yacc-generated program.

The only element missing from the FSM program is something to initialize the state variable. Recall that one state of the FSM is always designated the start state, so you need a line of code to assign that to the state variable before you start generating events:

```
nPuState = S_OUTSIDE
```

This can go in the *Form_Load* event of the comment stripper program. You'll find the source code for this program in CHAP14\fsm\simple\sim.vbp.

Recursion: See recursion

The comment stripper FSM works OK, but it has a dangerous flaw. It's a flaw that is inherent in event-driven systems, and one that also crops up in regular Visual Basic programs. The problem is reentrant code, and you might have come across it when working with data controls, *Form_Resize* events, or code that uses *DoEvents*.

Let's have a look at a simple example of reentrancy using a data control. The program shown in Figure 14-10 on the following page (which is in CHAP14\recurse\broken\rcb.vbp) is about as simple as it gets, with a single data-bound list wired up through a data control to the Visual Basic sample database BIBLIO.MDB. Assume that the list contains a set of records you need

FIGURE 14-10

Recursion in the data control's Reposition event

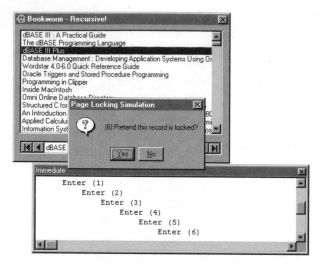

to process somehow and that it doesn't matter in which order the records are processed. Clicking in the list causes a Reposition event, and the program puts up a message box that lets you simulate the kind of Jet page-locking error you might encounter in a multiuser application. You can think of the Reposition event handler as the equivalent of the *DoFSM* function in the comment stripper program.

Clicking No when the message box pops up simply continues, and this is where you'd process the new record. Clicking Yes simulates a locking error and simply skips to the next record by calling the *MoveNext* method of the data control's recordset. The idea is that you'll reach the end of the locked page after skipping a few records and so find a record you can process. The problem here is that you're calling *MoveNext* from within the Reposition event handler, which causes *another* reposition event before the first one has finished—this is recursion. The example program maintains a static variable to count the number of recursions; the count is displayed on the message box, and the program also prints the entry and exit traces for the reposition event to the Immediate window when you run the program in the IDE. You can also see the effects of the recursion by pressing Ctrl+Break and selecting Call Stack from the View menu.

This example, which comes from a real program, might not have particularly serious consequences because it's a pure recursion that doesn't nest too deeply, and it involves no static data (except for the counter, of course). Generally, however, and particularly when you're devising code such as FSMs to control the loading and unloading of forms, the code will break as soon as you try to invoke it recursively. You might, for example, end up in a situation in which you're trying to load a form from its own *Form_Load* event.

Coming back to the recursive Visual Basic program, it's not immediately obvious how to fix the problem. It turns out that this is quite a common class of problem, and one that conveys the true flavor of event-driven code. What you *want* to do when you find a lock is to exit the event handler and then immediately issue a *MoveNext* on the recordset. Unfortunately, Visual Basic can't do this because as soon as you exit the event handler, control passes back to the run-time system (the <Non-Basic Code> you see when you select View/ Call Stack in break mode). What you need to be able to do is to post some kind of request for a *MoveNext* and have it execute after you've left the Reposition event handler.

Just because Visual Basic won't do this kind of thing for you doesn't mean that you can't implement it yourself. CHAP14\recurse\fixed\rcf.vbp is a modified version of the pathological data control program that uses a simple event queue to achieve what you need. You use an unsorted list box as a convenient event queue and a timer control that continually polls the queue looking for events. There's only one kind of event in the program, so you don't even need to look at its value when you find it on the queue—always consider it a request for a *MoveNext*.

The program works like this: inside the Reposition event, instead of directly calling *MoveNext* when a locked record is encountered, we post an event onto the queue and then exit the event handler. The queue manager (the timer control) then comes along and, finding an event on the queue, kindly calls *MoveNext* for us. Now, however, the *MoveNext* is called from the timer's event handler, and there's no recursion. Notice that it doesn't matter how fast you push event requests into the queue; you never get recursion because the events are processed one by one in sequence.

Adding an event queue to an FSM

To prevent reentrant code, you need to add a queue to the FSM model. Strictly speaking, the comment stripper program doesn't need a queue because it doesn't do anything that will cause recursion. Because it's an example program, however, we'll add the queuing now so that you can build on it when you design real-world FSM programs later.

The queue built in the previous example worked adequately, but it needed a form to carry the list box and the timer control. This awkwardness over essentially nonvisual code has dogged Visual Basic from the start, and it means, for example, that you can't define a queue inside a class or a startup module without creating a dummy form. You could dump the controls onto an existing form, of course, but that's anathema to modular design, and it means you must contrive to load the form before starting the event queue. Getting rid of the list box isn't too hard, but until now there's been no getting around that timer control without doing something horrific like this:

```
Sub Main()
    Dim nEvent As Integer
    frmMain.Show vbModeless      ' Main program is in here.
    Do
        If bGetEventFromQueue(nEvent) Then
            DoFSM nPuState, nEvent
        End If
        DoEvents
    Loop
End Sub
```

With Visual Basic 5, however, you can at last devise acceptable code-only solutions to this kind of problem—in this case, to build an event queue. By using the *AddressOf* operator, you can call the *SetTimer* API function and pass a Visual Basic routine as the timer's callback procedure. This means you can create a timer from pure code, and just like a Visual Basic Timer control, it will invoke the Visual Basic procedure asynchronously at the requested interval. Creating a timer is simple:

```
lTimerId = SetTimer(0&, 0&, 500&, AddressOf MyFunc)
```

The first two parameters are NULL values, which simply signify that the timer isn't associated with any window, and the third is the timer interval, in milliseconds. The last parameter is the interesting one; it passes a pointer to a Visual Basic function that will be invoked by Windows whenever the timer fires. Windows expects this function to have the following interface and will pass the appropriate parameters:

```
Sub MyFunc(ByVal lHwnd As Long, _
           ByVal nMsg As Long, _
           ByVal lEventId As Long, _
           ByVal lTime As Long)
```

When working with callback functions, be careful to include the *ByVal* keywords. If you miss a *ByVal*, simply moving your mouse pointer over the parameter name in the Visual Basic debugger is enough to crash Visual Basic. This happens because of Visual Basic 5's instant quick watch feature, which displays a variable's value as a ToolTip. Because Visual Basic thinks you passed a reference parameter (*ByRef* is the default), it tries to dereference an illegal pointer value, which almost always causes an access violation. You can turn off this feature with the Auto Data Tips check box under Tools/Options/Editor.

For now, just ignore the parameters. Make sure to destroy the timer when you're finished with it:

```
Call KillTimer (0&, lTimerId)
```

That takes care of the queue manager, so now all you need to do is provide a queue for it to manage. A simple way to do this is to use a Visual Basic collection:

```
Dim colPuEventQueue As Collection
```

You'll see a more sophisticated use of collections later, but for now you can use one as a simple queue by defining a couple of routines:

```
Sub AddEventToQueue(ByVal niEvent As Integer)
    colPuEventQueue.Add niEvent
End Sub

Function bGetEventFromQueue(ByRef noEvent As Integer) As Boolean
    If colPuEventQueue.Count = 0 Then
        bGetEventFromQueue = False
    Else
        noEvent = colPuEventQueue.Item(1)
        colPuEventQueue.Remove 1
        bGetEventFromQueue = True
    End If
End Function
```

And that's it—a code-only asynchronous queue manager that you can build into a class or a normal module. The program CHAP14\fsm\qman\qman.vbp on the companion CD is the comment stripper FSM program amended to use the new event queue.

Data-Driven Code

In an ideal implementation of a table-based design such as a finite state machine (FSM), the program is built from the tables themselves. In this kind of program, the tables are embedded in the code and somehow direct the flow of execution. The wisdom of this is clear: the tables are a product of your design process, and using them directly unifies the design—or at least some elements of it—with

BUILDING A BETTER EVENT QUEUE

Remember Message Blaster? Message Blaster is a custom control that lets you intercept Windows messages sent to any Visual Basic control. Windows messages are the raw material of Visual Basic events, but the Visual Basic designers filtered out most of the messages when they decided which events Visual Basic programmers were likely to need. A form's Resize event, for example, occurs *after* the resize has happened, which makes implementing size limits for a resizeable form ugly because you have to snap the size back in the Resize event handler. With Message Blaster, you can intercept the WM_SIZE message and change the form's size with a suitable API call before Windows repaints it.

Now that you know what Message Blaster is, forget it. Visual Basic 5 lets you do all the things that Message Blaster did, directly from Visual Basic code. Message Blaster is an example of a *subclassing* control; subclassing is what Windows programmers do to hook a custom message handler (usually called a window procedure) onto a window, and subclassing controls were an inelegant hack to make this possible in earlier versions of Visual Basic. By allowing Windows callback functions to be coded in Visual Basic, Visual Basic 5's new *AddressOf* operator opens up subclassing directly to Visual Basic programmers.

The theory goes like this: You nominate any object that you have (or can get) a window handle for and tell Windows the address of a Visual Basic procedure to call whenever it receives a message for that object. For messages you don't want to handle, you simply call the original message handler. To fix the resizing problem outlined above, you'd write something like this:

```
pcbOldWindowProc = SetWindowLong(Me.hWnd, GWL_WNDPROC, _
                             AddressOf lMyWindowProc)
⋮

Function lMyWindowProc(ByVal hWnd As Long, _
                  ByVal lMsg As Long, _
                  ByVal wparam As Long, _
                  ByVal lparam As Long) As Long
```

>>

the code. It's also easier to make design changes because you don't have to translate between logical and physical models.

When it comes to building data-driven programs, working with more traditional Windows programming languages such as C and C++ offers two definite advantages over Visual Basic. First, you can maintain tables of pointers to functions and invoke those functions directly through indexes into the tables.

>>

```
    If lMsg = WM_SIZE Then
        ' Play with the size here.
    End If

    lMyWindowProc = CallWindowProc(pcbOldWindowProc, hWnd, _
                                   lMsg, wParam, lParam)
End Function
```

Any messages that Windows receives for a window are queued so that they arrive in sequence, and you can use this behavior to make a queue for FSMs. The simplest way is to hang a window procedure off an arbitrary control and start sending messages to the queue with *PostMessage*, but this is a bit ugly and can't be done unless you have a form loaded. A better way is to create a window for your own exclusive use behind the scenes. The code is straightforward:

```
lHwnd = CreateWindowEx(WS_EX_TRANSPARENT, "static", _
                       "My Window", WS_OVERLAPPED, _
                       0&, 0&, 0&, 0&, 0&, 0&, _
                       CLng(App.hInstance), 0&)

lEventMsg = RegisterWindowMessage("FSM Event")
```

The choice of *style* and *extended style* parameters is arbitrary and doesn't really matter since you're never going to display the window. Now all you have to do is hook up an event handler to the window and start sending messages. It's a good idea to register a private message as done here, but you could just use any message number greater than WM_USER. It's best to encapsulate the code in Visual Basic functions or a class (CHAP14\fsm\fsmcls\pubfsm.cls shows one possible way), but be aware that the window procedure must be in a standard module. All the constants and Visual Basic declarations for all the functions can be pasted from the API Viewer tool supplied with Visual Basic. This tool is run from the file Apiload.exe, which is located in the VB=Winapi folder on the Visual Basic 5 CD.

This removes the need for the unwieldy jumble of conditional statements needed in our first stab at an FSM in Visual Basic, reducing the *DoFSM* function to just two statements:

```
void fvDoFSM(int nState, int *nEvent)
{
    (aapvActionTable[nState][*nEvent])();
    nEvent = aanStateTable[nState][*nEvent];
}
```

Second, you can lay out the tables in compile-time initialization statements. This is where the design and implementation intersect since you can lay out the table in a readable fashion and any changes you make to it are *directly* changing the code. Here's what the comment stripper FSM tables might look like in a C program:

```
void (*aapvActionTable[NUM_STATES][NUM_EVENTS])() =
{
//                  E_SLASH     E_STAR      E_OTHER

/* S_OUTSIDE  */ {fvOutSlash, fvOutStar, fvOutOther},
/* S_STARTING */ {fvStaSlash, fvStaStar, fvStaOther},
/* S_INSIDE   */ {fvInsSlash, fvInsStar, fvInsOther},
/* S_ENDING   */ {fvEndSlash, fvEndStar, fvEndOther}
};

int aanStateTable[NUM_STATES][NUM_EVENTS] =
{
//                  E_SLASH     E_STAR      E_OTHER

/* S_OUTSIDE  */ {S_STARTING, S_OUTSIDE, S_OUTSIDE},
/* S_STARTING */ {S_STARTING, S_INSIDE,  S_OUTSIDE},
/* S_INSIDE   */ {S_INSIDE,   S_ENDING,  S_INSIDE},
/* S_ENDING   */ {S_OUTSIDE,  S_ENDING,  S_INSIDE}
};
```

Unfortunately, although Visual Basic has an *AddressOf* operator, the only useful thing you can do with it is pass the address of a function or procedure in a parameter list. (C programmers will be disappointed to find that *AddressOf* isn't really like C's unary & operator.) Although you *can* use *AddressOf* in calls to Visual Basic functions, ultimately you can't do much inside those functions except pass the address on to a Windows API function. This capability is a major leap forward from all previous versions of Visual Basic, but the fact that you can't invoke a Visual Basic function from an address means that you can't implement an action table like the C one shown above.

Or can you? You can certainly store Visual Basic function addresses in a table by passing them to a suitable procedure. Visual Basic permits you to store function addresses in long variables:

```
Sub AddAddressToTable(ByVal niState As Integer, _
                      ByVal niEvent As Integer, _
                      ByVal pcbVbCodeAddr As Long)
    ActionTable(niState, niEvent) = pcbVbCodeAddr
End Sub
```

Unfortunately, that's as far as you can go with pure Visual Basic. Perhaps a future version of Visual Basic will have a dereferencing operator or maybe a *CallMe* function that accepts an address and calls the function at that address; for now, however, you're on your own.

But don't despair, because you're not sunk yet. Visual Basic doesn't have a *CallMe* function, but there's nothing to stop you from writing your own. You'll need to write it in another language, of course, but if you're one of those Visual Basic programmers who breaks out in a cold sweat at the thought of firing up a C compiler, take heart—this is likely to be the shortest C program you'll ever see. Here's the program in its entirety:

```
#include "windows.h"

__declspec(dllexport) int LibMain(
                          HANDLE hModule,
                          WORD wDataSeg,
                          WORD cbHeapSize, LPSTR pszCmdLine)
{
    return 1;
}

__declspec(dllexport) int _WEP(int bSystemExit)
{
    return 1;
}

void __stdcall CallMe(void (*pfvVbCode)(void))
{
    pfvVbCode();
}
```

The business end of this code is a single statement; the rest is scaffolding to make a DLL. (You also need to use a DEF file to make the linker export the *CallMe* symbol.) Now all you need to do is include a suitable *Declare* statement in your Visual Basic code, and you can call Visual Basic functions from a table!

```
Declare Sub CallMe Lib "callme.dll" (ByVal lAddress As Any)
  ⋮
CallMe ActionTable(nState, nEvent)
```

The source code for the DLL and a Visual Basic program that calls it can be found in CHAP14\callme.

CallMe old-fashioned

The *CallMe* DLL is pretty simple, but it's still a DLL. It turns a programming project into a mixed-language development, it means you have to buy a compiler, and it adds an extra component to the distribution package you're going to have to build when you ship the product. Finding a way to do without a DLL would certainly be an attractive option.

Figuring out the answer simply requires a bit of lateral thinking. You've already seen how API functions that take a callback parameter can invoke Visual Basic functions, so it takes a simple shift of perspective to see such API functions as obliging *CallMe* servers. All you have to do is find an API function that takes a callback function, calls it once, and preferably doesn't do much else.

A quick trawl through the Win32 API documentation (unfortunately not supplied with Visual Basic) reveals *SetTimer* as a possibility since its sole purpose is to invoke an event handler that you register with it. The only problem with this is that *SetTimer* keeps calling the function until you kill the timer, so you must find a way to kill the timer after a single invocation. You could do this by including a call to *KillTimer* in the callback procedure itself, but this is ugly because the mechanism is inextricably bound up with the functions you want to call—if you're building an FSM, for example, all your action functions must look like this:

```
Sub Action1()
    Call KillTimer lTimerId
    ' Real action code goes here
End Sub
```

The consequence of leaving out a call to *KillTimer* is a ceaseless barrage of calls to the offending function, with who knows what consequences—yuck!

There are other candidates, but one that works nicely is *CallWindowProc*. This function is normally used to attach a custom message handler (a.k.a. a window procedure) to a window; the custom message handler passes on unwanted messages using *CallWindowProc*, which tells Windows to invoke the default window procedure. You're not chaining any message handlers here, and you don't even have a window; but you can still invoke *CallWindowProc* to call a Visual Basic function. The only restriction is that your Visual Basic function must have the following interface:

```
Function Action1(ByVal hWnd As Long, _
                 ByVal lMsg As Long, _
                 ByVal wParam As Long, _
                 ByVal lParam As Long) As Long
```

Windows 95 lets you call a parameterless procedure as long as you trap the "Bad DLL calling convention" error (error 49*), but for reasons of portability—and good programming practice—you shouldn't rely on this.

All you need to do now is to wrap the *CallWindowProc* call up in a Visual Basic function, and you have a *CallMe*, effectively written in Visual Basic:

```
Sub CallMe(ByVal pcbAddress As Long)

    Call CallWindowProc(pcbAddress, 0&, 0&, 0&, 0&)

End Sub
```

Return of the comment stripper

It's time to return to the comment stripper. This time you're going to build a reusable FSM class using everything you've learned up to now—maybe you'll

---

* The error 49 is generated when Visual Basic detects a stack frame anomaly on return from *CallWindowProc*, although there's nothing wrong with the API call itself. In fact, the error happens earlier, when the *Action1* routine returns to *CallWindowProc*. *CallWindowProc* pushes four parameters onto the stack and expects the action function to remove them before it returns. (This is the Pascal, or *stdcall*, calling convention.) Our function doesn't oblige since it thinks there were no parameters, but because Windows 95 doesn't do stack checking at run time, the error goes undetected. Visual Basic *does* do stack checking, so it detects the error when the API call returns.

Windows NT is less forgiving here—it immediately detects the stack error and raises an exception inside *CallWindowProc*. You can't trap operating system exceptions in Visual Basic, so this kills the program (or kills Visual Basic if you're in the IDE). This, of course, is exactly what should happen, and it's a useful reminder that you shouldn't be taking such liberties! The sample program in CHAP14\fsm\tabldriv on the companion CD uses conditional compilation to demonstrate the use of parameterless action procedures.

even pick up a few more tricks along the way. To see how the same FSM can be used to drive different external behaviors, you'll also make a slight modification to the program by displaying the text of the comments in a second text box. Figure 14-11 shows the new-look comment stripper. You can find the code in CHAP14\fsm\tabldriv on the companion CD.

FIGURE 14-11

Return of the comment stripper

First the bad news: you won't be able to match C's trick of laying out the FSM table readably in code. Visual Basic fights this on every front: you can't write free-format text, you run out of line continuations, there's no compile-time initialization, and even Visual Basic's comments aren't up to the job. However, this is the only bad news because using what you've learned about Visual Basic 5, you can do everything else the C program can do.

Let's start by looking at the interface to the FSM class. Since the class is to be general and you don't want to code the details of a particular FSM into it, you need to define methods that can be used to describe the FSM at run time. An FSM description will have four components: a list of states, a list of events, a table that defines state transitions, and a table that associates actions with the state transitions. In principle, the only other interface you need to the FSM class is a method you can call to feed events to the FSM. In practice, the restriction that demands that you put callback functions in a regular BAS file means you also need a method to register the event queue handler function with the FSM.

Here's what the run-time definition of the comment stripper FSM looks like:

```
Set oPiFSM = New CFSMClass

oPiFSM.RegisterStates "OUTSIDE", "STARTING", "INSIDE", "ENDING"
oPiFSM.RegisterEvents "SLASH", "STAR", "OTHER"
oPiFSM.RegisterEventHandler cblEventQueueMessageHandler

oPiFSM.TableEntry viState:="OUTSIDE", viEvent:="STAR", _
                  viNewState:="OUTSIDE", _
                  pcbiFunc:=AddressOf OutsideStar
oPiFSM.TableEntry viState:="OUTSIDE", viEvent:="STAR", _
                  viNewState:="OUTSIDE", _
                  pcbiFunc:=AddressOf OutsideStar
' ...etc.
```

This code shows how the states and events are defined and also includes a couple of the table-definition statements. *RegisterEventHandler* creates a hidden window to act as the event queue and installs the *cblEventQueueMessage-Handler* function as its window procedure. We'll look at the table definitions in a moment, but first let's examine the *RegisterStates* and *RegisterEvents* methods. These work identically, so we'll take *RegisterStates* as an example.

To make the class general, you need to be able to supply this method with a variable number of arguments. There are two ways to do this, but *ParamArray* is the best. The definition of *RegisterStates* looks like this:

```
Public Sub RegisterStates(ParamArray aviStates() As Variant)
    ' Some code here
End Sub
```

ParamArray members are Variants, which is convenient in this situation because the FSM class will allow you to choose any data type to represent states and events. The example program uses strings, mostly because they're self-documenting and can be displayed on the form. In real applications, you might prefer to use enumerated types or integer constants. Without making any changes to the class definition, you could define your states like this:

```
Const S_OUTSIDE = 1
Const S_STARTING = 2
Const S_INSIDE = 3
Const S_ENDING = 4
  ⋮
oPiFSM.RegisterStates S_OUTSIDE, S_STARTING, S_INSIDE, S_ENDING
```

Or like this:

```
Enum tStates
    Outside = 1
    Starting
    Inside
    Ending
End Enum
⋮
oPiFSM.RegisterStates Outside, Starting, Inside, Ending
```

Enumerated types are new in Visual Basic 5, and in use they are equivalent to long constants defined with *Const*. Enumerations are better because they associate a type name with a group of constants, so in this example you can define variables of type *tStates* (although there is no run-time range checking). A more important difference is that you can define public enumerated types inside classes, which means you can now associate groups of constants directly with classes. If you were coding a comment stripper FSM class (instead of a *general* class that we'll use to implement the comment stripper), for example, you could define public *tStates* and *tEvents* as enumerated types in the class itself.

The FSM class can cope with any data type for its states and events because internally they are stored as integers and use collections to associate the external values with internal ones.

Here's the code behind *RegisterStates*:

```
Private Type tObjectList
    colInternalNames As New Collection
    colExternalNames As New Collection
End Type

Private tPiList As tObjectList
⋮
tPiList.colInternalNames.Add nInternId, key:=CStr(vExternId)
tPiList.colExternalNames.Add vExternId, key:=CStr(nInternId)
```

This code creates two reciprocal collections: one storing integers keyed on external state names and the other storing the names keyed on the integers. You can now convert freely between internal (integer) and external (any type) states. Since you can store any data type in a collection, you are free to choose whichever data type is most convenient.

TIP

> Using pairs of collections is a powerful way to associate two sets of values. Usually, one set is how the values are represented on a database and the other set is how you want to display them to the user.

The FSM table itself is created dynamically inside the *RegisterStates* or *RegisterEvents* routine (whichever is called last), using the *Count* properties of the state and event collections for its dimensions:

```
Private Type tTableEntry
    nNextState As Integer
    pcbAction As Long
End Type
!
ReDim aatPiFSMTable(1 To nStates, 1 To nEvents) As tTableEntry
```

Now you need to fill in the empty FSM table with details of the state transitions and actions. To do this, you make repeated calls to the *TableEntry* method, with one call for each cell in the table. The values you want to insert into the table are successor states, which have one of the values defined earlier in the state list, and subroutine addresses, which you obtain with the *AddressOf* operator. The action routines are all parameterless subroutines, defined together in a single BAS file. Here's what the *TableEntry* function does:

```
aatPiFSMTable(nState, nEvent).nNextState = niNewState
aatPiFSMTable(nState, nEvent).pcbAction = pcbiFunc
```

The *nState* and *nEvent* integers are first obtained by looking up the external names passed as parameters.

Once the table is in place, the FSM is ready to go. In fact, the FSM is running as soon as you define it since *RegisterEventHandler* creates an event queue and registers a callback function to service it. *RegisterStates* puts the FSM into its start state, but it won't actually do anything until you start feeding events to it.

The event queue is implemented as an invisible window created with Windows API functions as described earlier. The only minor problem here is that Visual Basic insists that you define callback functions in normal BAS files, so you can't include the queue event handler in the class definition. You can *almost* do it because you can define the event handler in the class as a *Friend* function; the function you register is a simple shell that calls the *Friend* function, although it still has to be in a normal BAS file. Turn the page to find out what the class must contain.

```
Friend Function cblEvHandler
(
    ByVal hwnd As Long, _
    ByVal lMsg As Long, _
    ByVal wparam As Long, _
    ByVal lparam As Long
) As Long
```

This is a standard window procedure (don't forget the *ByVal*s!), and you send events to it using the *PostMessage* API function. A *Friend* function is essentially a public method of the class, but the scope is limited to the current project even if the class is defined as *Public*. A call to *PostMessage* is the essence of the *PostEvent* method, and Windows arranges for the messages to be delivered asynchronously, via calls to the *cblEvHandler* function, in the sequence they were posted.

Calls to *PostEvent* are made in response to external stimuli, and in this case these are all Visual Basic keypress events. The calls are made from the KeyPress events, where the translation from ASCII code to an appropriate event value ("STAR", for example) is made. After the FSM is initialized, the KeyPress events are the *only* interface between the FSM and the outside world.

The queue event handler is the focus of the FSM since here is where the table lookup is done and the appropriate action procedure is called:

```
CallMe aatPiFSMTable(nPiCurrentState, wparam).pcbAction
nPiCurrentState = aatPiFSMTable(nPiCurrentState, wparam).nNextState
```

The only other noteworthy feature of the queue event handler is that it contains calls to *RaiseEvent*. The FSM class defines four different events that can be used in the outside world (the comment stripper program in this case) to keep track of what the FSM is doing. These are the events:

```
Event BeforeStateChange(ByVal viOldState As Variant, _
                        ByVal viNewState As Variant)
Event AfterStateChange(ByVal viOldState As Variant, _
                        ByVal viNewState As Variant)
Event BeforeEvent(ByVal viEvent As Variant)
Event AfterEvent(ByVal viEvent As Variant)
```

You saw an example of *RaiseEvent* earlier on page 590; this time, you're defining events with parameters. You define two sets of events so that you can choose whether to trap state changes and events before or after the fact. For the comment stripper, use the *AfterEvent* and *AfterStateChange* events to update the state and event fields on the form.

Doing it for real

The comment stripper is a simple example, and the FSM it demonstrates doesn't deal with window management. As a slightly more realistic example, let's look at an implementation of the GUI from Figure 14-5 (shown on page 595). You'll find the source for this program in CHAP14\fsm\realwrld\rlw.vbp. The FSM controls the hypothetical Function 1, and the FSM starts when that function is chosen from the Function menu. Other functions would be implemented with their own FSMs, which is straightforward because the FSM was built as a class. You're not really implementing the whole program here, just the window-management parts; all the event routines are there, so adding the code to do the database actions would be painless.

The second thing you'll notice, right after you notice those bizarre event names, is that the nice, friendly action routine names have gone, replaced by the anonymous subroutines *a01* through *a44*. With 44 subroutines to code, the only sensible names are systematic ones—using the state and event names as before is just too unwieldy. In fact, the action names are irrelevant because their corresponding state/event combinations are much more useful identifiers. Here's a portion of the FSM table definition:

```
oPuFSM.TableEntry A__, A_Ok_____, EXI, AddressOf a01
oPuFSM.TableEntry A__, A_Cancel_, EXI, AddressOf a02
oPuFSM.TableEntry A__, A_Apply__, A__, AddressOf a03
oPuFSM.TableEntry A__, A_Details, AB_, AddressOf a04
oPuFSM.TableEntry A__, A_More___, AC_, AddressOf a05
oPuFSM.TableEntry A__, B_Ok_____, ERO
oPuFSM.TableEntry A__, B_Cancel_, ERO
```

The key description of this code is "systematic," which is also why we've adopted such a strange convention for the state and event names. We're fighting Visual Basic's unreasonable layout restrictions by making the names the same length so that the list of *TableEntry* calls is readable. You can't quite make a table layout as in the C code example earlier, but the result is an acceptable facsimile that is reasonably self-documenting.

Notice that two pseudostates have been introduced for this example: EXI, which represents termination of the FSM, and ERO, which denotes an error condition. Neither of these conditions should be encountered by the FSM: EXI successor states are never reached because the action routines associated with their transitions halt the FSM, and ERO successor states can be derived only from illegal inputs. The FSM driver function (*oPuFSM.EvHandler*) traps these pseudostates and raises an *FSM_Error* event. This is the FSM equivalent of a *Debug.Assert* statement.

The use of ERO states also permits you to omit coding for state transitions that will never happen. As well as modifying the driver to raise an error on illegal transitions, we've also modified the *TableEntry* method to make the action function optional. In this case, it saves 12 action functions and nicely distinguishes error conditions in the matrix. It's tempting to omit these lines from the list, but you should avoid the temptation vigorously, because if you do so you can no longer tell whether you've covered all possible situations by simply counting the table entries.

Another temptation is to factor code by reusing action routines—for example, *a01* and *a02* appear to be the same, as do *a12* and *a13*. However, discarding *a02* and wiring up *a01* in its place can be disastrous because it introduces a dependency that will cause problems if you later want to change the actions for either transition independently of the other. You could, of course, define a helper subroutine that's called by both action routines. (*ConfirmDiscardEdits* is such a function.) Remember that a *system* is useful because it takes some of the intellectual load off managing complexity, and it goes without saying that circumventing the system—for whatever reason—stops it from being systematic.

One final comment about this example is that it doesn't include validation or confirmation states. Such states would amplify the complexity by adding a new state for each OK and Cancel event, along with 11 corresponding table entries (in this case). In real life, validation and confirmation are best handled by building a conditional mechanism into the FSM. This does *not* mean you should do such processing ad hoc, and control over the successor state should remain with the FSM driver function (*FSM.EvHandler*). This means you can't use Visual Basic's *Form_QueryUnload* or *Form_Unload* event to trigger validation or confirmation since a form unload must always succeed. (Canceling an unload from QueryUnload will cause havoc because the FSM thinks the form has been unloaded and now its state information is incorrect.)

An acceptable way to implement both types of condition is to add an *abort transition* method to the FSM class:

```
Public Sub AbortTransition()
    bPuTransitionAborted = True
End Sub
```

Now you can modify the FSM driver to check the bPuTransitionAborted flag before setting the successor state:

```
Public Sub EvHandler
    ⋮
    CallMe aatPiFSMTable(M_nCurrentState, wparam).pcbAction
    If Not bPuTransitionAborted Then
        nPiCurrentState = aatPiFSMTable(nPiCurrentState, _
                                        wparam).nNextState
    End If
    ⋮
End Sub
```

This might be simple, but it adds considerable complexity to the action routines because you must be very careful about which forms you unload. More specifically, if you cancel a transition, you need to be sure that you don't change anything that characterizes the current state. In this case, the states are defined entirely in terms of forms, so you need to ensure that the action routine has the same forms loaded when you leave that were loaded when you entered. For example, assuming you're in state AB_ (forms A and B loaded), you need either to unload both forms or to leave them both loaded. The following code correctly describes the validation logic for an A_Ok event in this state:

```
Public Sub a12()

    Dim bUnload As Boolean

    bUnload = True

    If frmDetails.My.Dirty Or frmSummary.My.Dirty Then
        If Not bConfirmDiscardEdits Then
            bUnload = False
        End If
    End If

    If bUnload Then
        Unload frmDetails
        Unload frmSummary
    Else
        oPuFSM.CancelTransition
    End If

End Sub
```

AFTER THE DUST HAS SETTLED

Visual Basic was an innovation. Five years ago, the Windows programming club was an exclusive one, and coding for Windows was intensely technical: virtuosity in C was the entrance requirement, and becoming productive relied on mastery of the arcane Windows API. Visual Basic changed all that, opening up Windows programming to all comers and pioneering whole new development cycles by making rapid GUI prototyping a reality.

But there is a darker side. By eliminating the obscure programmatic hoops we must jump through even to display anything on the screen, Visual Basic has taken the technical edge off Windows development, and from the wrong perspective this can have dangerous consequences. Behind the GUI facade, developers face the same problems of design, verification, construction, redesign, testing, and change management that they always have, and without conscientious technical management, these fundamentals can take a back seat while the product is "prototyped" to market.

To ensure success in a Visual Basic project, you need to concentrate on development fundamentals as much as on the database design and graphical veneer, and you must quash unreasonable productivity expectations. Visual Basic is a tinkerer's delight, but the delusion of Visual Basic programming as child's play is short-lived and a recipe for disaster. A Visual Basic project can seem like a whirlwind of fantastic productivity—for the first few months. Only after the dust has settled is the truth apparent: excellent applications happen by design, not by accident.

Didn't I Write That Function Last Week?

Effective Code Reuse

Chris, a TMS Developer, has worked on several large client/server developments, in particular a leading-edge three-tier application for a major organization. He is especially interested in the design of user interface code from a coding point of view rather than for aesthetic appearance and the use of structured reusable code, at both a programmer and a business level. Chris is a Microsoft Visual Basic Certified Professional.

CHRIS DEBELLOT

STEVE OVERALL

Steve is a TMS Developer who has been programming with Visual Basic since Version 3 and with various other languages prior to that. His main areas of interest are standards, training, and user interface design. In the analog world, Steve is a keen cricketer, a lover of loud rock music, an avid reader of science fiction, and a bit of an American football fan. He lives in Surrey with his plants and his beloved hi-fi.

Reusability, as its name suggests, is the ability of something that is designed for a specific purpose to be used in more than just that one situation. A good example of reuse can be found in the motor vehicle industry. Low-specification vehicles are usually fitted with blanking plates where more expensive options (such as air conditioning) would normally be located. Vehicle manufacturers do this for a purpose: to save money. If manufacturers use a generic dashboard and plug the holes in vehicles in which certain items are not selected, they save money because they don't have to create a separate dashboard for every option package. Obviously, it's cheaper to manufacture blanking plates than dashboards! Another advantage is that the manufacturer doesn't have to rebuild the vehicle whenever a customer wants an item installed as an optional extra—because although the component isn't in place, the wiring and connections usually are. The electronics industry also makes use of reusability. If you've ever taken apart your computer, you've probably noticed that the expansion cards plug into the motherboard. The advantage here is that if a complex component fails, you just need to replace a board, not the entire system.

ISSUES AFFECTING CODE REUSABILITY

So if reuse is such a good thing, why not apply it to computer programs? Well, the good news is that you can. Reuse has been around for years. The bad news is that not many companies take advantage of it. Reasons such as tight schedules, the changing nature of technology, and the difficulty of putting together a top-notch development team all account for the lack of reuse.

Deadline Pressures

Many projects come under pressure when schedules start to slip. When the pressure reaches a certain point, good design, coding practices, and coding standards are often forgotten in a mad panic to deliver. Designing and writing reusable modules and applications takes discipline and the enforcement of consistent standards; unfortunately, these practices are usually the first casualties when a project threatens to overshoot deadlines. (See Chapter 16 for more about how to manage projects successfully in today's competitive and hectic development environment.)

Knowledge of Current Technologies

To develop good reusable code, you must know first what you're trying to achieve through reuse and second how to achieve your goal with the tools you're using. Computer programming languages have come a long way since the early days, and most now support the creation of reusable components to some degree. Technology—especially object technologies such as ActiveX and COM—has also improved. Keeping up with the ever-increasing number of languages and technologies can be hard work, and many organizations are tempted to stick with what they know. Although this conservative approach doesn't prevent developing reusable solutions, it does mean that opportunities to develop more effectively are missed.

Quality of Development Teams

The quality of the development team plays a big part in the process of developing for reuse. The project manager must understand the technology and the business in order to set priorities and to justify the effort required to build high-level and reusable business components. Many companies employ project managers who are not technical. This practice is based on the business theory that a manager should be able to apply the same management techniques to any type of project to achieve the same results. The Mandelbrot Set (International)

Limited (TMS) has a policy of assigning project managers who are also good coders. The benefit of a technical project manager is that he or she is acutely aware of problems that can occur and is able to counter them. The project manager can also carry out design and code reviews to ensure that the design is realistic and the code follows the design. This ability is extremely important if external contractors whose standards of work are unknown are hired to work on the project.

Analysts and designers also need to be aware of the technology to ensure that the application's design is realistic and achievable in the scheduled time. Often the application design is incomplete when development starts. An incomplete design will almost certainly result in costly redevelopment of certain components. In the worst case, redesign might not be possible because of time or other constraints. If a reusable component is not designed and built correctly, any future development dependent on that component will suffer because of the effort required to rectify the original flaws. A future development team will probably just write its own version of the component.

The programmers have the important job of building the application to specification. Their task will be harder if the specifications and design are not complete or correct. Programmers should also ensure that the infrastructure code is reusable. It is here, in the program's infrastructure, that reusability can have a major impact, not through the reuse of business components but through the reuse of common code—that is, code that can be used by other programmers on the same application or in other development projects. Good communication is needed among programmers so that they all are aware of what code is available. The programmers also need to be sure that any code designed for reuse is well documented so that other team members know exactly how to use a particular unit of code. How many times have you written a particular function, only to discover that it already existed? Or tried to use an existing function but ended up writing your own version because you couldn't figure out the correct parameters for the existing function?

THE BUSINESS CASE FOR REUSE

If you're managing a development project, you should seriously consider reuse—in fact, you should think of reuse as a requirement, not just an option. Whether or not you realize it, reuse is one of the most efficient ways of reducing development time and effort. Unfortunately, many companies develop each application in isolation, viewing each one as a single entity encapsulated within a particular budget. If you intend to implement multiple applications, you'll gain reuse benefits in the form of business components—that is, units of functionality that dictate specific areas of corporate policy. An example of such a policy is, "Account managers may authorize discounts of up to 20 percent for regular customers." If you create a single business object to implement this policy for all customer accounts, you'll be able to enforce the integrity of this rule. You'll also have the advantage of being able to change the rule in a single place, which is an important capability given that business rules will change as company policies change.

Business components are not the only area in which you can benefit from reuse. Think of a company that starts each development from scratch, and imagine the number of times a particular unit of code (for example, an error handler or a *FileExist* function) is written. At TMS, we have a reuse strategy. We have an application template that contains core functionality such as error handling, custom messaging, and general utility functions. When we start developing a system for a customer, we give our client the option of purchasing the application template. This creates extra revenue for TMS but, more important, also cuts off about a month of development time because we start building code from this template, which has already been fully debugged and tested. Some companies have unassigned staff between projects with nothing to do. Using such downtime to develop generic "auxiliary" code—the type of code that gets written in almost every project—would be an ideal way to start gearing everyone toward the goal of writing reusable code.

Just because a component is designed for reuse does not necessarily mean that the component must be reused. One benefit of having encapsulated and loosely coupled components is that maintenance becomes much simpler. (Encapsulation and coupling are key elements of reuse and are explained in more detail in the next section.) Imagine a maintenance programmer fixing a bug in a component. If the component is totally self-contained, the programmer doesn't need to know anything about the application outside that component. This makes it easier to control changes in the maintenance phases and allows greater flexibility when allocating people to do the work. Another important advantage of encapsulation and loose coupling is that it's easier to identify components that need to change if maintenance work becomes necessary.

For those of you still not convinced that reusability has real benefits, think of the interface changes made to Microsoft Windows 95. If you're familiar with both Windows 95 and Windows 3.*x*, one of the prominent interface changes you'll have noticed in Windows 95 is the new look of the controls. Think for a moment of the humble command button. Command buttons previously had a 2-pixel border and bold captions. In Windows 95, the command button changed: the button border is now only 1 pixel wide, and the caption font is no longer bold. You'll also notice that these characteristics change automatically between the versions of Windows. This automatic change in appearance was possible only because the command button, as well as many other controls, does not draw its own borders and captions—a Windows function does it. Imagine the amount of additional development time that would have been required to change the drawing functions if each control had contained its own!

THE KEYS TO REUSE

To achieve effective reuse, you must first understand what makes good reuse. Two key attributes are required in any component that will be reused: encapsulation and generic functionality.

As the name suggests, *encapsulation* means that a unit of functionality is enclosed to such a degree that you are able to extract and use that functionality in a physically different environment. The unit of functionality contains everything it requires, and provided that the correct inputs can be applied, it will function in exactly the same way in any environment. The degree of encapsulation can also be expressed in terms of how the unit couples. A unit of functionality that is dependent on many external conditions is said to be tightly coupled. The converse is true of a loosely coupled unit. As a programmer, you'll no doubt have tried at least once to extract and reuse a block of code that had so many dependencies that it was easier to rewrite the code to fit your needs than to reuse it. This difficulty is a direct consequence of a tightly coupled unit and serves to highlight the importance of coupling when designing or coding a unit. The fact that an experienced programmer will understand the issues involved with coupling is one reason why experienced and disciplined programmers are valuable assets to a company.

The second key attribute of reuse has to do with how *generic* a piece of *functionality* is. If you want to use some functionality elsewhere, it stands to reason that the functionality should be able to apply to a number of different situations. Imagine a function written to take a date input and to check that the date is valid and in the range 3/2/1997 through 5/10/1997. The pseudocode on the next page should help you visualize this.

```
Function IsDateOK(Input DateIn)
    If DateIn is between "3/2/1997" and "5/10/1997" Then
        Return True
    Else
        Return False
    End If
End Function
```

This function is clearly reusable because it has no external dependencies; that is, it doesn't call any other procedures within the application. In terms of actual reuse, however, it's pretty useless unless you specifically want to compare against the same date range in every instance in which you use this function. The function would be far more useful if you were to add inputs for a minimum and a maximum date because the function could then check whether a date is valid and falls between ranges specified by the routine calling the function. Here is an amended version of the same function; this time, it's more useful because it's generic enough to be applied in a number of situations:

```
Function IsDateOK(Input DateIn, Input MinDate, Input MaxDate)
    If DateIn is between MinDate and MaxDate Then
        Return True
    Else
        Return False
    End If
End Function
```

For a piece of functionality to be reusable, it doesn't have to be totally decoupled from other routines in the application; in fact, doing so would make reuse impractical. What you must keep in mind, however, is that a unit of functionality is truly reusable only if all of its dependencies are present. To achieve good reusability, you need to set the boundaries or scope of a unit's functionality. For example, a reusable unit might be a single procedure, a collection of procedures, or an entire application. As long as the unit is not coupled to anything outside its bounds, it will be reusable. In programming terms, this means reducing the number of global (for Visual Basic 3) or public variables. In the days of Visual Basic 3, one of the recommended practices was to place global variables in a BAS module. Programmers should have dropped this practice with Visual Basic 4 because of the ability to encapsulate variables within class or form module properties. However, even in Visual Basic 4, constants still had to be made public because class and form objects couldn't expose constants as part of their interface. One way around this was to write type libraries. But type libraries, being external components, are contrary to encapsulation and can be difficult to maintain across multiple projects or components. To avoid public constants, Visual Basic 5 has introduced a feature named enumerated constants, which allow constants to be exposed as part of the interface of the component to which they belong. This new addition enables you to completely encapsulate a component. (We'll explain enumerated constants in more detail later in this chapter.)

One of the most widely used bad programming practices is to link areas of functionality with variables of global scope. Imagine an application with a modest 30 public variables. Any unit that couples to those variables is guaranteed to be difficult to reuse in another application because you'll have to re-create these variables and their values. Even in the same application, the state of global variables will change and might depend on certain event sequences, sometimes complex, being executed. Chapter 2 indicates some circumstances in which you can get components to share the same global data, with unfortunate results. And Chapter 5 includes even more on why you shouldn't use global variables.

MEETING REUSE REQUIREMENTS EFFECTIVELY

Visual Basic offers a rich selection of methods to achieve effective reusability. As with many things that involve a choice, you can choose either correctly or incorrectly. In a large computer application, an incorrect choice can mean weeks or months of extra effort. Mistakes will also inevitably occur because of the wide range of options available. For example, you can be sure that many Visual Basic programmers will be eager to create custom controls simply because they now can thanks to Visual Basic 5. A particular problem to watch for is the "gold-plating" syndrome, which occurs when a programmer spends too much time adding unnecessary features. Although such features work, they serve only as superfluous gloss on the application—and, worse yet, the time spent fiddling with them can put your schedule in jeopardy.

The following sections provide an overview of the different methods you can use to achieve effective reuse.

Code Reuse Using Objects

Creating and distributing objects is one of the most powerful means of achieving reusability. An object is a discrete unit of functionality. Object components within Visual Basic can be either internal or external to an application, and they can be shared between applications, as shown in Figure 15-1. External object components have an advantage in that they can be physically deployed anywhere on a network. By strategically deploying object components to maximize resources, you can save possibly thousands of dollars when you consider that a typical development's cost comprises both development and deployment overheads.

FIGURE 15-1

Applications sharing object components

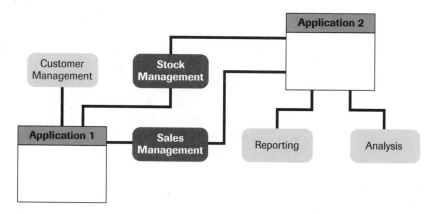

Inherently, object components are loosely coupled and generic. Each object component in Figure 15-1 is totally self-contained and can be used by any number of applications or components. An object component should have no "knowledge" of the outside world. For example, if you have an object component that contains a method to retrieve a list of customers for a given criterion, that method should accept the criterion as input and return the list of customers. It is up to the caller, or client, using the object's, or server's, method to display or process the results. You could code the object's method to fill a list of customers on the form, but that object would be tied to the particular interface component on the form. If you wanted to reuse the object's method in another application, you would need to have an interface component of the same type and name on that application's form. The object would therefore be tightly coupled because it "knew about" the interface.

From a business perspective, object components provide a way of controlling and managing business logic. Business logic consists of rules that can change to meet the needs of the business. By placing such logic in object components and locating these on a server, you can make changes instantly available with low installation overhead, especially since polymorphic (multiple) interfaces in Visual Basic 5 allow you different interfaces within the same component. For example, if a bank were offering an additional 2 percent interest to any customers with over $10,000 in their savings accounts, the functionality could be specified in an account calculations object as shown in the following pseudocode:

```
Procedure Calculate Monthly Interest For Customer Cust_No
    High_Interest_Threshold = 10000
    Get Customer_Balance for Customer Cust_No
    Get Interest_Rate_Percent

    If Customer_Balance < High_Interest_Threshold Then
        Add Interest_Rate_Percent to Customer_Balance
    Else
        Add Interest_Rate_Percent + 2% to Customer_Balance
    End If

End Procedure
```

In this example, the special offer might have been an incentive that was not anticipated when the application was originally designed. Thus, implementing the functionality in a non-object-component environment would probably involve quite a few additional steps:

- Adding a high interest threshold field to the database
- Adding to the maintenance functionality to amend the high interest threshold
- Amending the monthly balance calculation formula to include an additional calculation
- Shutting down the database to make changes
- Rebuilding the application EXE file
- Testing and debugging
- Reinstalling the application on the client PCs

As you can see, a relatively simple change request can involve a lot of time and money. Using an object component design, you can drastically reduce the amount of effort required to implement such a change. To make the same change in an object component system requires slightly less effort. The differences are explained here:

- The account calculations object calculates interest payments, so locating the code module to change will be fairly simple.

- Because only the account calculations object requires a change, only this component needs to be rebuilt. With this type of design, the object components are most likely to be installed on a server so that only one copy of the object needs to be reinstalled. The object can also be made to work in the new way for some applications and in the old way for other applications without any of the applications changing at all.

- Testing will be limited to the object that has changed because its functionality is completely encapsulated.

This very simple example shows how objects—in this case, distributed objects—offer a major advantage in terms of maintenance. A good example of how shrewd object distribution can save money is one that Peet Morris (author of Chapters 1 and 8) often uses in his seminars:

> If you imagine an application that utilizes a word processor to print output, by installing the print object and a copy of the word processor on the server, each user can access the single installation for printing. Whether you have 5 or 500 users, you still need only one copy of the word processor.

Another advantage of distributed objects is that you can install object components on the most suitable hardware. Imagine that you have several object components, some that perform critical batch processing and some that perform noncritical processes. You can put the critical tasks on a dedicated fault-tolerant server with restricted access and locate the noncritical processes on a general-purpose server. The idea here is that you don't necessarily need all your hardware to be high specification: you can mix and match. The capability to move object components away from the desktop PC means that the client or user interface code can be much smaller and won't require high-end PCs to run. With distributed objects, it's a simple enough task to relocate object components so that you can experiment almost on the fly to determine the best resource utilization.

Cost benefits of object reuse

So far, we've discussed how object components can be reused by many applications and how maintaining applications using this design can be simplified. The reuse advantage should not be underestimated, especially by business managers. Examine Table 15-1, which shows the budget estimate for a warehouse stock inventory and ordering system. The development is estimated to be completed within 12 months from start to finish, which includes the time required for the project manager and the technical lead to prepare the functional and technical specifications.

Table 15-1

Budget Estimate for a Warehouse Stock Inventory and Ordering Application

Resource	Cost per Day ($)	Duration (Months)	Cost ($)*
1 Project manager	750	12	180,000
1 Technical lead	600	12	144,000
3 Programmer	450 × 3 = 1,350	10	270,000
1 Tester	300	5	30,000
TOTAL	**3000**		**624,000**

* Based on working 20 days a month.

Some simple arithmetic shows that if all goes as planned, based on a 5-day week, the total cost of the project will be $624,000. The company has decided that this will be the first of three development projects. The second will be a system to allow the purchasing department to do sales-trend analysis and sales predictions. The budget estimate for the second project is shown in Table 15-2.

Table 15-2

Budget Estimate for a Sales-Trend Analysis Application

Resource	Cost per Day ($)	Duration (Months)	Cost ($)*
1 Project manager	750	10	150,000
1 Technical lead	600	10	120,000
2 Programmer	450 × 2 = 900	8	144,000
1 Tester	300	3	18,000
TOTAL	**2550**		**432,000**

* Based on working 20 days a month.

The third project will be an Internet browser that allows customers to query availability and price information 24 hours a day. The budget estimate for this project is shown in Table 15-3.

Table 15-3

Budget Estimate for an Internet Browser

Resource	Cost per Day ($)	Duration (Months)	Cost ($)*
1 Project manager	750	9	135,000
1 Technical lead	600	9	108,000
1 Programmer	450	8	72,000
1 Tester	300	4	24,000
TOTAL	**2100**		**339,000**

* Based on working 20 days a month.

If we examine all three applications as a single system and then build the applications in sequence, it becomes apparent that the second and third applications will require far less development time than the first because they build on existing functionality. One advantage here is that building the second and third systems need not affect the first system. This situation is ideal for phased implementations. The success of this strategy depends largely on how well the design and analysis stages were completed. Figure 15-2 shows the design of all three applications. The three applications are treated as a single development for the purpose of planning. Reusable functionality is clearly

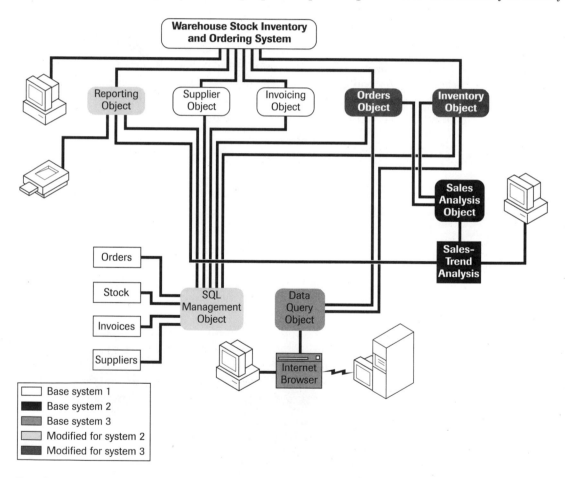

FIGURE 15-2   *Single development comprised of three application systems*

visible, and although the developments will be written in phases, the reusable components can be designed to accommodate all the applications.

In the development of a multiple application system, design is of the utmost importance. It is the responsibility of the "business" to clearly define system requirements, which must also include future requirements. Defining future requirements as well as current ones helps designers to design applications that will be able to expand and change easily as the business grows. All successful businesses plan ahead. Microsoft plans its development and strategies over a 10-year period. Without knowledge of future plans, your business cannot make the most of object component reusability.

Looking back at the application design in Figure 15-2, you can see that all three systems have been included in the design. You can clearly see which components can be reused and where alterations will be required. Because the design uses object components, which as you'll recall are loosely coupled inherently, it would be possible to build this system in stages—base system 1, then 2, then 3.

Let's consider the estimates we did earlier. The main application was scheduled to be completed in 12 months and will have 12 major components. So ignoring code complexity, we can do a rough estimate, shown in Figure 15-3 on the following page, of how much effort will be required to implement the other two applications. Take the figures with a grain of salt; they're just intended to provide a consistent comparison. In reality, any computer application development is influenced by all kinds of problems. It's especially important to keep in mind that new technologies will always slow down a development by an immeasurable factor.*

The estimates for the three applications when viewed as stand-alone developments could well be feasible. When viewed as a whole, they give a clear picture of which components can be shared and therefore need to be written only once. The reusable components can be designed from the start to meet the

---

* For those of you interested in estimating and development time issues, we recommend the book *Rapid Development,* by Steve McConnell (Microsoft Press, 1996). He does for project managers what he did for developers with *Code Complete* (Microsoft Press, 1995). See how many of the 36 Classic Mistakes of Software Development you've encountered!

FIGURE 15-3

Rough time estimate for coding and testing three applications

Assumptions (*Time*)

Person-months to code one new unit	1.5
Person-months to modify one new unit for reuse	0.75
Person-months to test one new unit	0.5
Person-months to code one modified unit	0.25

Development Estimate (*Coding and Testing Only*)

Application	Number of Code Units Required for Application		Development Time in Months (Based on Assumptions Above)				Total Time (Months)
			Coding		Testing		
	New	Reused	New	Reused	New	Reused	
Stock Inventory	12	0	18	0	6	0	24
Sales-Trend Analysis	2	4	3	3	1	1	8
Internet Browser	2	2	3	1.5	1	0.5	6

needs of the second and third applications. Although this might add effort to the first project, the subsequent projects will in theory be shortened. Here are the three major benefits:

1. The design anticipates and allows for future expansion.

2. The overall development effort is reduced.

3. Functionality can be allocated to the most appropriate resource. For example, a print specialist can code the print engine without affecting the interface coder.

As you can see, object components provide a number of advantages. Object components are vital to high-level code reuse because of their encapsulation, which allows functionality to be allocated to the most suitable resource. As Fred Brooks points out in *The Mythical Man-Month: Essays on Software Engineering* (Addison-Wesley, 1995), "Only through high-level reuse can ever more complex systems be built."

Object component practicalities

Object components are built using a special Visual Basic module type called a class module. The class module can contain properties, methods, and events and can consume properties, methods, and events from other classes (described later). Our example diagrams so far have been high level; that is, only the overall functionality of the object has been shown. In reality, an object component will usually consist of contained classes—each with properties, methods, and events. Figure 15-4 shows a more detailed example of how applications might interact with object components.

FIGURE 15-4

Classes within object components

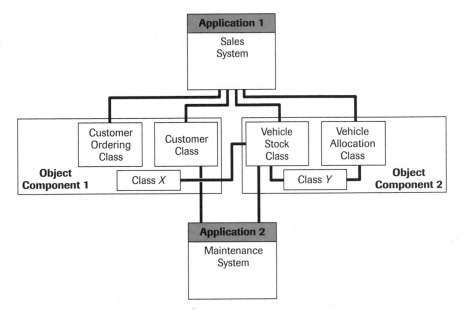

For the programmer, using object components couldn't be simpler. An object component is written in ordinary Visual Basic code. To use an object, the programmer simply has to declare the object, instantiate it, and then call its methods and properties. Two additional and powerful features have been added to Visual Basic 5 that greatly increase the power of object components: the *Implements* statement and the Events capability.

The *Implements* statement allows you to build objects (class objects) and implement features from another class (base class). You can then handle a particular procedure in the new derived class or let the base class handle the procedure. Figure 15-5 on the following page shows an imaginary example of how *Implements* works in principle. The exact coding methods are not shown here because they are covered fully in the online documentation that comes with Visual Basic 5. The example in Figure 15-5 is of an airplane autopilot system.

Figure 15-5 shows a base Autopilot class that has *TakeOff* and *BankLeft* methods. Because different airplanes require different procedures to take off, the base Autopilot class cannot cater to individual take-off procedures, so instead it contains only a procedure declaration for this function. The *BankLeft* actions, however, are pretty much the same for all airplanes, so the Autopilot base class can perform the required procedures.

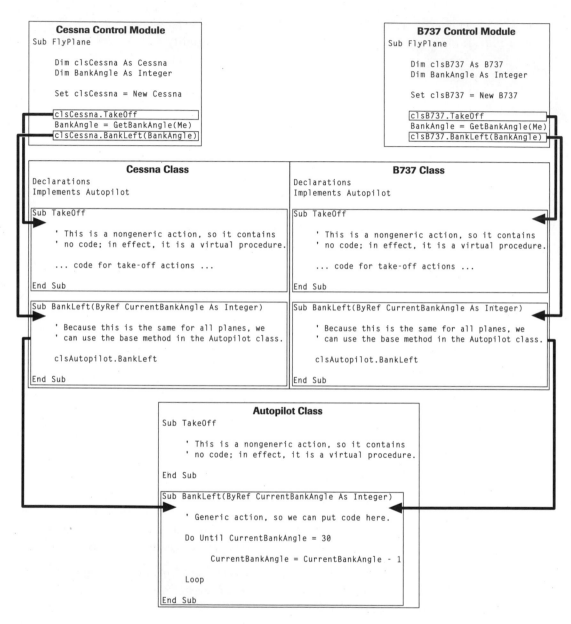

FIGURE 15-5   *Example using the* Implements *statement*

There are two types or classes of airplane in this example: a B737 and a Cessna. Both classes implement the autopilot functionality and therefore must also include procedures for the functions that are provided in the Autopilot base class. In the *TakeOff* procedure, both the Cessna and B737 classes have their own specific implementations. The *BankLeft* procedures, however, simply pass straight through to the *BankLeft* procedure in the Autopilot base class. Now let's say that the *BankLeft* procedure on the B737 changes so that B737 planes are limited to a bank angle of 25 degrees; in this case, you would simply replace the code in the B737 class *BankLeft* procedure so that it performs the required action.

Visual Basic 4 users might have noticed something interesting here: the Cessna and B737 classes have not instantiated the Autopilot class. This is because the instancing options for classes have changed in Visual Basic 5. It is now possible to create a class that is global within the application without having to declare or instantiate it. Here are the new instancing settings:

- **PublicNotCreatable** Other applications cannot create this class unless the application in which the class is contained has already created an instance.

- **GlobalSingleUse** Any application using the class will get its own instance of the class. You don't need to *Dim* or *Set* a variable of the class to use it.

- **GlobalMultiUse** An application using the class will have to "queue" to use the class because it has only a single instance, which is shared with any other applications using the class. You don't need to *Dim* or *Set* a variable of the class to use it.

To set the *Instancing* property, you must first set the Project Type to ActiveX EXE. The ActiveX DLL option doesn't allow any of the SingleUse options, and the ActiveX Control option allows only Private or PublicNotCreatable. For more information on the use of the *Instancing* property, see Chapter 2.

The new Events capability in Visual Basic 5 is the second useful and powerful new feature that is available to object classes. Essentially, it allows your object class to trigger an event that can be detected by clients of the object class. The "Introducing the progress form" section on page 641 gives an example of how events are used.

Forms as Reusable Components

Many developers overlook the fact that forms can make very good reusable components. In addition to the traditional code reuse benefit of reduced development time through the use of previously debugged and tested code, a second, possibly less tangible, benefit is one of user interface consistency across applications. This need for a consistent user interface has become far more apparent over the last two to three years, with the exploding office suite market. A major selling point of all the competing suites is consistency of user interface across the separate suite applications. Consistency reduces wasted time: the user doesn't have to pore over many different manuals learning how things work. Once the user has mastered something in one application, he or she can apply the same skill to the other members of the suite. Reusing forms can be a real win-win tactic. In the long run, you save development time, and the user requires less training.

The types of forms you should be looking to make reusable are what can be considered auxiliary forms. Those that display an application's About information, give spell check functionality, or are logon forms are all likely candidates. More specialized forms that are central to an application's primary function are likely to be too specific to that particular development to make designing them for reuse worthwhile. Alternatively, these specialized forms might still be considered worth making public for use by applications outside those in which they reside.

Writing forms to be reusable

As programmers, we should all be familiar with the idea of reusing forms by now. Windows has had the common File, Print, and Font dialog boxes since its early versions, and these have been available to Visual Basic users through the CommonDialog control right from the first version of Visual Basic. What is new in Visual Basic 5 is the ability to reuse custom-developed forms in a truly safe way. Visual Basic 4 gave us the ability to declare methods and properties as Public to other forms. Prior to this, only code modules could have access to a form's methods and data. This limitation made form-to-form interaction a little convoluted, with the forms having to interface via a module, and generally made creating a reusable form as a completely encapsulated object impractical.

Visual Basic 5 provides another new capability for forms. Like classes and controls, forms can now raise events, extending our ability to make forms discrete objects. Previously, if we wanted forms to have any two-way interaction, the code within each form had to be aware of the interface of the other. Now we have the ability to create a form that "serves" another form or any other type of module, without any knowledge of its interface, simply by raising events that the client code can deal with as needed. The ability to work in this way is really a prerequisite of reusable components. Without it, a form is always in some way bound, or coupled, to any other code that it works with by its need to have knowledge of that code's interface.

In the following progress report example, you'll find out how to design a generic form that can be reused within many applications. You'll also see how to publicly expose this form to other applications by using a class, allowing its use outside the original application. This topic covers two areas of reuse: reuse of the source code, by which the form is compiled into an application; and reuse of an already compiled form from another application as a distributed object.

Introducing the progress form

The form we'll write here, shown in Figure 15-6, is a generic progress form of the type you often see when installing software or performing some other lengthy process. This type of form serves two basic roles. First, by its presence, the form confirms that the requested process is under way, while giving the user the opportunity to abandon the process if necessary. Second, by constantly displaying the progress of a process, the form makes the process appear faster. With Visual Basic often wrongly accused of being slow, this subjective speed is an important consideration.

FIGURE 15-6

A generic progress form in action

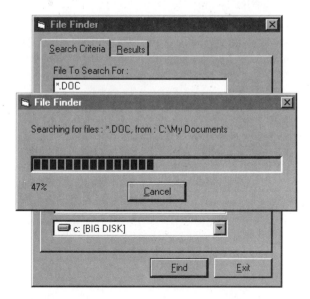

This example gives us a chance to explore all the different ways you can interact with a form as a component. The form will have properties and methods to enable you to modify the form's appearance. Additionally, the form will be able to raise an event, showing that this ability is not limited to classes.

When designing a form's interface, you must make full use of property procedures to wrap your form's properties. Although you can declare a form's data as Public, by doing so you are exposing it to the harsh world outside your component—a world in which you have no control over the values that might be assigned to that component. A much safer approach is to wrap this data within *Property Get* and *Property Let* procedures, giving you a chance both to validate changes prior to processing them and to perform any processing you deem necessary when the property value is changed. If you don't use property procedures, you miss the opportunity to do either of these tasks, and any performance gains you hope for will never appear because Visual Basic creates property procedures for all public data when it compiles your form anyway.

It's also a good policy to wrap the properties of any components or controls that you want to expose in property procedures. This wrapping gives you the same advantages as mentioned previously, plus the ability to change the internal implementation of these properties without affecting your interface. This ability can allow you to change the type of control used. For example, within the example progress form, we use the common Windows 95 progress bar control. By exposing properties of the form as property procedures, we would be able to use another control within the form or even draw the progress bar ourselves while maintaining the same external interface through our property procedures. All this prevents any changes to client code, a prerequisite of reusable components.

The generic progress form uses this technique of wrapping properties in property procedures to expose properties of the controls contained within it. Among the properties exposed are the form caption, the progress caption, the maximum progress bar value, the current progress bar value, and the visibility of the Cancel command button. Although all of these properties can be reached directly, by accessing them through property procedures, we're able to both validate new settings and perform other processing if necessary. This is illustrated by the *AllowCancel* and *ProgressBarValue* properties. The *AllowCancel* property controls not only the Visible state of the Cancel command button but also the height of the form, as shown in this code segment:

```
Public Property Let AllowCancel (ByVal ibNewValue As Boolean)

    If ibNewValue = True Then
            cmdCancel.Visible = True
            Me.Height = 2150
        Else
            cmdCancel.Visible = False
            Me.Height = 1750
    End If

    Me.Refresh
End Property
```

The *ProgressBarValue* property validates a new value, avoiding an unwanted error that might occur if the value is set greater than the current maximum:

```
Public Property Let ProgressBarValue(ByVal ilNewValue As Long)

    ' Ensure that the new progress bar value is not
    ' greater than the maximum value.
    If Abs(ilNewValue) > Abs(gauProgress.Max) Then
        ilNewValue = gauProgress.Max
    End If

    gauProgress.Value = ilNewValue
    Me.Refresh

End Property
```

We need to give the form a *Display* method to show the form modelessly so that the client code continues once the form has been displayed. A modal form would halt execution of this code until the form was dismissed. Progress forms are usually displayed in a modal state because they're needed while the program is busy. If we want our progress form to appear to be modal, we have to imitate this functionality by disabling all other forms in the application while this form is being displayed. The following code, when placed in the form's *Display* method, does just this. After creating this method, all we have to do is put similar code in the form's *Form_Unload* event to reenable those forms that were disabled, and we have an instant modal form.

```
Public Sub Display(ByVal inCmdShow As Integer)
    Dim frmForm As Form

    ' If the form is to be displayed modally,
    ' imitate modal behavior by disabling all other forms.
    If inCmdShow = vbModal Then
```

```
For Each frmForm In Forms
    If frmForm.Name <> Me.Name _
            And frmForm.MDIChild = False Then
        frmForm.Enabled = False
    End If
Next frmForm

End If

' Show the form modelessly.
Me.Show vbModeless
Me.Refresh

End Sub
```

The final example piece of code that we need to look at within our progress form is the one that generates the QueryAbandon event. This event allows the client code to obtain user confirmation before abandoning what it's doing. To have our form generate events, we must declare each event within the general declarations for the form as shown here:

```
Public Event QueryAbandon(ByRef Cancel As Boolean)
```

This event is then triggered when the Cancel command button is pressed. By passing the *Cancel* Boolean value by reference, we give the event handling routine in the client the opportunity to change this value in order to work in the same way as the *Cancel* value within a form's QueryUnload event. When we set *Cancel* to True, the event handling code can prevent the process from completing. When we leave *Cancel* as False, the progress form will continue to unload. The QueryAbandon event is raised as follows:

```
Private Sub cmdCancel_Click()
    Dim bCancel As Boolean
    bCancel = False
    RaiseEvent QueryAbandon(bCancel)
    If bCancel = False Then Unload Me
End Sub
```

From this code, you can see how the argument of the QueryAbandon event controls whether or not the form is unloaded, depending on its value after the event has completed.

Using the progress form

The code that follows illustrates how the progress form can be employed. First we have to create an instance of the form. This must be placed in the client module's Declarations section because it will be raising events within this module, much the same way as controls do. Forms and classes that raise events are declared as WithEvents, in the following way:

```
Private WithEvents frmPiProg As New frmProgress
```

We must declare the form in this way; otherwise, we wouldn't have access to the form's events. By using this code, the form and its events will appear within the Object and Procedure combo boxes in the code window, just as for a control.

Now that the form has been instantiated, we can make use of it during our lengthy process. First we set the form's initial properties and display it. Then we can continue with our process, updating the form's *ProgressBarValue* property as we go, as illustrated here:

```
' Set up the form's initial properties.
frmPiProg.FormCaption = "File Search"
frmPiProg.ProgressBarMax = 100
frmPiProg.ProgressBarValue = 0
frmPiProg.ProgressCaption = _
    "Searching for file. Please wait..."

' Display the progress form.
frmPiProg.Display vbModal

' Find our file.
    ⋮
frmPiProg.ProgressBarValue = nPercentComplete
```

The final piece of code we need to put into our client is the event handler for the QueryAbandon event that the progress form raises when the user clicks the Cancel button. This event gives us the chance to confirm or cancel the abandonment of the current process, generally after seeking confirmation from the user. An example of how this might be done follows:

```
Private Sub frmPiProg_QueryAbandon(Cancel As Boolean)
    If MsgBox("Are you sure you want to cancel?", _
            vbQuestion Or vbYesNo, Me.Caption) = vbNo Then
        Cancel = True
    End If
End Sub
```

From this example, you can see that in order to use the progress form, the parent code simply has to set the form's properties, display it, and deal with any events it raises.

Making a form public

Although forms do not have an *Instancing* property and cannot be made public outside their application, you can achieve this effect using a class module as an intermediary. By mirroring the events, methods, and properties of your form within a class with an *Instancing* property other than Private, making sure that the project type is ActiveX EXE, you can achieve the same results as you can by making a form public.

Using the progress form as an example, we will create a public class named CProgressForm. This class will have all the properties and methods of the progress form created earlier. Where a property of the class is accessed, the class will merely access the property of the underlying form, making that property public. Figure 15-7 shows this relationship, with the client application having access to the CProgressForm class but not frmProgress, but the CProgressForm class having an instance of frmProgress privately. To illustrate these relationships, we will show how the *ProgressBarValue* property is made public.

FIGURE 15-7

Making a form public using a public class as an intermediary

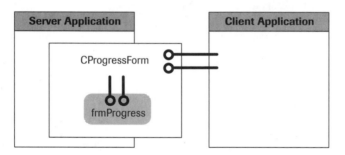

First we need to declare a private instance of the form within the Declarations section of our class:

```
Private WithEvents frmPiProgressForm As New frmProgress
```

Here we see how the *ProgressBarValue* property is made public by using the class as an intermediary:

```
Public Property Let ProgressBarValue(ByVal ilNewValue As Long)
    frmPiProgressForm.ProgressBarValue = ilNewValue
End Property

Public Property Get ProgressBarValue() As Long
    ProgressBarValue = frmPiProgressForm.ProgressBarValue
End Property
```

Similarly, we can subclass the QueryAbandon event, allowing us to make public the full functionality of the progress form. We subclass this event by

Didn't I Write That Function Last Week? Chapter

15

raising a further QueryAbandon event, in reaction to the initial event raised by the form, and passing by reference the initial *Cancel* argument within the new event. This way the client code can still modify the *Cancel* argument of the original form's event.

```
Private Sub frmPiProgressForm_QueryAbandon(Cancel As Boolean)
    RaiseEvent QueryAbandon(Cancel)
End Sub
```

There is a difficulty with exposing the progress form in this way. The form has a *Display* method that is used to make it appear modal to the user by disabling all other forms within the application. Because we're using the form within another separate application, this method won't work. The solution is to change the *Display* method of the CProgressForm class so that it always displays the progress form modelessly.

This example highlights the weakness of using forms in this way. Because the forms are not part of the client application, they cannot be modal to the client. Although classes from a server application can be used seamlessly within a client, the visible aspect of forms makes them a far more thorny prospect.

Creating Your Own Controls

A lot of interest in Visual Basic 5 has been focused on the ability to create custom controls. This ability has greatly extended the capabilities of the product, in a way that some felt should have been possible from the start.

Prior to Visual Basic 4, the custom control was the primary source of reuse. Controls and their capabilities took center stage and appeared to take on a life of their own, becoming software superstars. In some instances, complete projects were designed around a single control and its capabilities! The problem with this was that you couldn't write these wonderful, reusable controls using Visual Basic—you had to resort to a lower-level language such as C++. This situation was hardly ideal, when one of the reasons for using Visual Basic in the first place was to move away from having to get your hands dirty with low-level code.

With Visual Basic 4, the emphasis moved away from controls to classes and objects as a means of reuse. Controls are great as part of the user interface of an application, but they're not really cut out to provide anything else because of their need to be contained in a form. This limitation is significant if you want to write a DLL or a distributed object. This limitation still holds true in Visual Basic 5, even though classes and objects have become even more flexible.

Although the ability to write your own controls is a major boon, it isn't the solution for all your problems. Don't overuse this ability just because you can or because you want to. You can do a great deal much more effectively than by resorting to writing a control. Again, beware of the gold-plating syndrome.

What can (and can't) Visual Basic controls do?

For those of you who have been waiting for the day when Visual Basic could finally create its own controls, pay attention here. Although some might complain that this capability is long overdue, Microsoft appears to have made it worth the wait. The following list is a brief rundown of what you can do with Visual Basic 5 controls:

- You can create controls to be used in one of two ways. You can use the well-known ActiveX implementation and create a separate OCX file and, new to Visual Basic 5, you can create a source code module, with the new CTL extension, and compile it into an application. See the next section for more information on these two methods.

- You'll find built-in support for creating property pages, with the inclusion of the new PAG module. Standard Font and Color property pages are also provided (more on these later).

- You can create a control that combines a number of other existing controls.

- You can create ActiveX control projects that contain more than one control in a single OCX file.

- You can create bound controls with very little effort.

- You can now use Visual Basic to create controls for use in other languages and within World Wide Web pages.

- With the ability to have multiple projects within a single Visual Basic session, debugging your controls is very easy. Other server projects such as ActiveX DLLs are also simple to debug.

That was the good news. Here are the limitations:

- Controls are not multithreaded within a single instance. They are In Process servers and as such run in the same process as their client. Visual Basic 5 only gives you the ability to have multithreaded objects that have no user interface.

- Because they run in the same process as the client, controls created using Visual Basic 5 cannot be used with 16-bit client applications.

ActiveX or in line? That is the question

When creating controls, you need to be aware of how they are to be distributed or used. Visual Basic 5 is the first version to support controls in code (as opposed to separately compiled objects). This opens the question of whether to compile your controls into traditional ActiveX controls for distribution as separate OCX files or to use them as source code objects and compile them into your application.

As with most things in life, there is no definitive answer, but there are some factors to consider when deciding.

The case for ActiveX controls   Here are some advantages of using ActiveX controls, along with a couple of drawbacks with using in-line controls.

- ActiveX controls can be used in languages and development environments other than Visual Basic, and of course they can be used in Web pages.
- ActiveX controls are of benefit if your control is to be used widely, across many applications.
- With ActiveX controls, bug fixes require only the OCX file to be redistributed. If the control is in line, you might have to recompile all applications that use that control.
- Because they are included in the client as source code, in-line controls are susceptible to hacking. They are more difficult to control (no pun intended) when curious programmers are let loose on them.

The case for in-line controls   Consider the following factors when thinking about using in-line controls:

- You might have to look into licensing implications if you're distributing your ActiveX controls with a commercial application. This is obviously not an issue with in-line controls. (Licensing is covered in more detail shortly.)
- The reduction of the number of files that you have to distribute can make ongoing maintenance and updates easier to support with in-line controls.

Your deployment policy will largely be selected by your environment. If you're writing an application for a system that has very little control over the desktop environment, incorporating controls into your application might well be a way of avoiding support nightmares. If the system supports object-based applications and has strong control over the desktop, the benefits of creating controls as separate OCXs are persuasive.

Licensing implications

Because of their dual nature, controls present unique licensing issues in both design-time and run-time environments. Two main issues are associated with creating and distributing ActiveX DLLs. The first involves licensing your own control. Microsoft has made this deliriously easy. Just display the Properties dialog box for your ActiveX Control project, and check the Require License Key check box, at the foot of the General tab. This creates a license key that is placed in the system Registry when your ActiveX control is installed. This key enables the control to be used within the development environment and to be included in a project. When the project is distributed, however, the key is encoded in the executable and not added to the Registry of the target machine. This prevents the control from being used within the design-time environment on that machine. Visual Basic does it all for you!

The second licensing issue surrounds the use of third-party controls embedded within your own control. When you compile your control, the license keys of any constituent third-party controls are not encoded in your control. Additionally, when your control is installed on another machine, the license key for your control will be added to the Registry, but the license keys of any of these contained controls are not. So although your control might have been installed correctly, it won't work unless the controls it contains are separately licensed to work on the target machine.

If you're writing for an in-house development, licensing will be largely irrelevant. For those writing controls for a third-party product or as part of a commercial product, however, licensing is an important issue. You need to be able to protect your copyright, and fortunately you have been given the means to do so.

Storing properties using the *PropertyBag* object

PropertyBag is a new object introduced with Visual Basic 5. This object is of use exclusively for creating controls and ActiveX documents.

The *PropertyBag* object is a mechanism by which any of your control's properties set within the Visual Basic Integrated Development Environment (IDE) can be stored. All controls have to store their properties somewhere. If you open a Visual Basic form file in a text editor such as Notepad, you'll see at the start of the form file a whole raft of text that you wouldn't normally see within the Visual Basic development environment. This text describes the form, its settings, and the controls and their settings contained within it. This is where

PropertyBag stores the property settings of your control, with any binary information being stored in the equivalent FRX file.

This object is passed to your control during the ReadProperties and WriteProperties events. The ReadProperties event occurs immediately after a control's Initialize event, usually when its parent form is loaded within the run-time or the design-time environment. This event is an opportunity for you to retrieve all of your stored property settings and apply them. You can do this by using the *ReadProperty* method of the *PropertyBag* object. This is illustrated in the following ReadProperties event from the DateEdit example control found on the book's companion CD in the CHAP15 folder.

```
Private Sub UserControl_ReadProperties(PropBag As PropertyBag)

    '
    ' Load property values from storage.
    '
    Set m_MouseIcon = PropBag.ReadProperty("MouseIcon", Nothing)
    Set Font = PropBag.ReadProperty("Font", Ambient.Font)
    txtDateEdit.ForeColor = PropBag.ReadProperty("ForeColor", _
        &H80000008)
    txtDateEdit.FontName = PropBag.ReadProperty("FontName", _
        "MS Sans Serif")
    txtDateEdit.FontSize = PropBag.ReadProperty("FontSize", 8.25)
    txtDateEdit.FontBold = PropBag.ReadProperty("FontBold", 0)
    txtDateEdit.FontItalic = PropBag.ReadProperty("FontItalic", 0)
    ⋮
    '
    ' Convert any Null dates to empty strings.
    '
    If IsNull(m_MinDate) Then m_MinDate = ""
    If IsNull(m_MaxDate) Then m_MaxDate = ""

End Sub
```

The *ReadProperty* method has two arguments: the first is the name of the property you want to read; and the second, optional, argument is the default value of that property. The *ReadProperty* method will search the *PropertyBag* object for your property. If it finds it, the value stored will be returned; otherwise, the default value you supplied will be returned. If no default value was supplied and no value was retrieved from *PropertyBag*, nothing will be returned and the variable or the object you were assigning the property to will remain unchanged.

Similarly, you can make your properties persistent by using the WriteProperties event. This event occurs less frequently, usually when the client form is unloaded or after a property has been changed within the IDE. Run-time property changes are obviously not stored in this way. You would not want them to be persistent.

The *WriteProperty* method has three arguments: the first is the name of the property you want to store; the second is the data value to be stored; and the third is optional, the default value for the property. This method will store your data value and the associated name you supply unless your data value matches the default value. If you specified a data value that matches the default value, no value is stored, but when you use *ReadProperty* to find this entry in *PropertyBag*, the default value will be returned. If you don't specify a default value in your call to *WriteProperty*, the data value will always be stored.

The following code is from the WriteProperties event of the DateEdit control. It illustrates the use of *PropertyBag*'s *WriteProperty* method.

```
Private Sub UserControl_WriteProperties(PropBag As PropertyBag)

    '
    ' Write property values to storage.
    '
    Call PropBag.WriteProperty("ForeColor", txtDateEdit.ForeColor, _
        &H80000008)
    Call PropBag.WriteProperty("Enabled", m_Enabled, m_def_Enabled)
    Call PropBag.WriteProperty("FontName", txtDateEdit.FontName, _
        "")
    Call PropBag.WriteProperty("FontSize", txtDateEdit.FontSize, 0)
    Call PropBag.WriteProperty("FontBold", txtDateEdit.FontBold, 0)
    Call PropBag.WriteProperty("FontItalic", _
        txtDateEdit.FontItalic, 0)
    ⋮

End Sub
```

Property pages

Also new to Visual Basic 5, and of exclusive use to controls, are property pages. These are dialog boxes you can call up from within the Visual Basic IDE that display a control's properties in a friendly tabbed dialog box format. Each property page is used as a tab within the tabbed dialog box. Visual Basic controls the tabs and the OK, Cancel, and Apply buttons for you. Additionally, you are provided with ready-made Font, Picture, and Color pages to use if necessary, which you should use whenever possible for a little more code and user interface reuse. Figure 15-8 shows the Property Pages dialog box for the DateEdit control.

Visual Basic 5 allows you to create pages that can be included in the dialog box for your control. It is important to do this. If you have gone to the trouble of writing the control in the first place, you owe it to yourself and others to make the control as easy to use as possible. Designing a property page is no different from designing a form: you can drop controls directly onto it and then write your code behind the events as usual.

When any changes are made to a property using your property page, you need to set the property page's *Changed* property to True. This tells Visual Basic to enable the Apply command button and also tells it to raise a new event, ApplyChanges, in response to the user pressing the OK or the Apply command button. Apply the new property values when the user presses OK or Apply; don't apply any changes as the user makes them because by doing so, you would prevent the user from canceling any changes: the ApplyChanges event is not raised when the Cancel command button is pressed.

Since more than one control can be selected within the IDE, property pages use a collection, SelectedControls, to work with them. You'll have to consider how each of the properties displayed will be updated if multiple controls are selected. You wouldn't want to try to set all of the Indexes in an array of controls

FIGURE 15-8

Property pages in use within the Visual Basic IDE

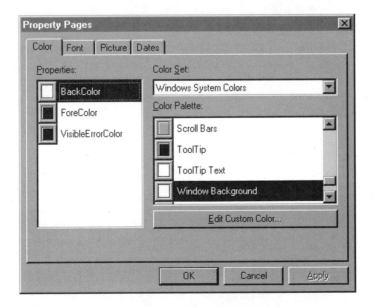

to the same value. You can use another new event, SelectionChanged, which is raised when the property pages are first loaded and if the selection of controls is changed while the property pages are displayed. You should use this event to check the number of members of the SelectedControls collection. If this number is greater than 1, you need to prevent the user from amending those properties that would not benefit from having all controls set to the same value, by disabling their related controls on the property pages.

Binding a control

As mentioned previously, Microsoft has also given us the ability to bind our controls (through a Data control or a RemoteData control) to a data source. This is remarkably easy to do as long as you know where to look for the option. You have to select the Procedure Attributes option from the Tools menu. This will display the Procedure Attributes dialog box shown in Figure 15-9.

This dialog box is useful when you're designing controls. It allows you to select the Default property and the category in which to show each property within the categorized tab of the properties dialog box. It also allows you to specify a property as data bound, which is what we're interested in here. By checking the option Property Is Data Bound in the Data Binding section, you're able to select the other options that will define your control's bound behavior.

Option	Meaning
This Property Binds To DataField	This option is fairly obvious. It allows you to have the current field bound to a data control. Visual Basic will add and look after the *Data-Source* and *DataField* properties of your control.
Show In DataBindings Collection At Design Time	The DataBindings collection is used when a control can be bound to more than one field. An obvious example would be a grid control, which could possibly bind to every field available from a Data control.
Property Will Call CanProperty-Change Before Changing	If you always call *CanProperty-Change* (see below), you should check this box to let Visual Basic know.

By using the first option, you're able to create a standard bound control that you'll be able to attach immediately to a Data control and use. The remaining options are less obvious.

FIGURE 15-9

The Procedure Attributes dialog box showing Advanced options

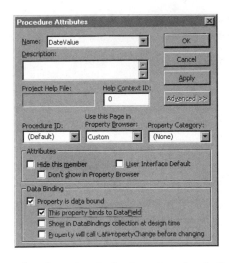

The DataBindings collection is a mechanism for binding a control to more than one field. This obviously has a use where you create a control as a group of existing controls, for example, to display names stored in separate fields. By selecting *Title, Forename,* and *Surname* properties to appear in the DataBindings collection, you're able to bind each of these to the matching field made available by the Data control.

You should call the *CanPropertyChange* function whenever you attempt to change the value of a bound property. This function is designed to check that you are able to update the field that the property is bound to, returning True if this is the case. Visual Basic Help states that currently this function always returns True and if you try to update a field that is read-only no error is raised. You'd certainly be wise to call this function anyway, ready for when Microsoft decides to switch it on.

The wizards

Microsoft supplies two useful wizards with Visual Basic 5 that can make creating controls much easier. The ActiveX Control Interface Wizard, shown in Figure 15-10 on the following page, helps in the creation of a control's interface and can also insert code for common properties such as *Font* and *Back-Color.* The Property Page Wizard does a similar job for the creation of property pages to accompany your control. Once again, standard properties such as *Font* and *Colors* can be selected from the ready-made property pages. Using these wizards can prove invaluable in creating the controls and their property pages and also in learning the finer points in their design.

You should use both these wizards: between them, they promote a consistency of design to both the properties of your controls and the user interface used to modify these properties. The example DateEdit control used throughout this section was created using both of these wizards. Any chapter about code reuse would be churlish if it failed to promote these wizards. Of course, no wizards yet created can control what you do with the user interface of the controls themselves!

FIGURE 15-10

The ActiveX Control Interface Wizard

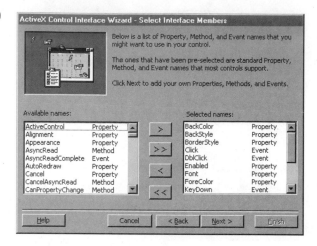

Controls: A conclusion

The ability to create controls is an important addition to Visual Basic's abilities. Microsoft has put a lot of work into this feature. As a means to code reuse, the abilities of controls are obviously limited to projects that contain forms, but the strength of controls has always been in the user interface.

A lot more could be written about controls—far more than we have space for in this chapter. Do take the time to read the Visual Basic manuals, which go into more depth, and experiment with the samples. After all, writing controls in Visual Basic is certainly much easier than writing them in C++!

Using a ROOS

Another aid to reusability, first mentioned in Chapter 1, is the ROOS (Resource Only OLE Server), pronounced "ruse." We've referred to OLE servers as object components for most of this chapter, but they are two different names for the same object. (To be politically correct, they should really be called ActiveX components, but ROAC is not as easy to pronounce!) A ROOS essentially stores string, bitmap, and other resources that are liable to be changed at some time. Another use for a ROOS is to store multilanguage strings. If you wrote an application to be sold in the United States and in France, using the normal Visual Basic method of setting display text in code would mean that you would have to create two versions of the application: one with English display text and captions and one with French. Obviously, this would create a significant maintenance overhead, because if you have to apply a bug fix to one of the versions, you also need to apply the change to the other. The ROOS is exactly the same in principle as a resource-only DLL as used by many C and C++

programmers. The difference between a ROOS and its DLL counterpart is that the ROOS is an object component and as such can be deployed anywhere on a network and used by any client components.

You can store many types of resources in a ROOS:

Accelerator table	Group cursor
Bitmap resource	Group icon
Cursor resource	Icon resource
Dialog box	Menu resource
Font directory resource	String resource
Font resource	User-defined resource

A ROOS has two components. The first is the resource module, a special file created with an application such as Microsoft Visual C++. The resource module contains all the resources you want to store and retrieve. The second element of the ROOS is a method to retrieve a resource from the resource module. At TMS, we prefer to expand the functionality of the ROOS methods so that string values can be parsed with input parameters. The following example illustrates this.

Resource Entries

```
String ID:    400
String value: "The operation completed with % errors"
```

Client Code

```
StringID = 400
MyText = GetStringFromROOS(StringID, "no")
```

ROOS Code

```
Public Function GetStringFromROOS(StringID As String, _
    Param) As String
    Dim sText  As String

    sText = GetString(StringID)
    sText = MergeString(sText, Param)
    GetStringFromROOS = sText

End Function
```

Result

```
MyText: "The operation completed with no errors"
```

Many projects store custom error messages or other display text in a database file. In an error handler, the custom error text is better in a ROOS because the execution speed is much faster, and many organizations restrict access to make database changes to the database administrator—no good if you're a programmer and have to wait two days to change the caption on a button! Another excellent use of a ROOS is to store icons and bitmaps. Imagine you're lucky enough to have an artist to create all your graphics. You can create a ROOS with dummy resources, and then the artist can add the real graphics to the ROOS as they become available without having to access any source code. (No more multiple access problems!)

Creating a resource module is easy if you have the right tools. You simply enter the resources you want. Each resource has an ID value, which is a long integer. To retrieve the resource from the resource module, you simply use the *Load-ResData*, *LoadResPicture*, or *LoadResString* command specifying the resource's ID. Figure 15-11 shows a typical resource file in Microsoft Visual C++ 5. Once the resource module is created (it's actually an RC file), you simply compile it with the RC.EXE program (supplied on the Visual Basic CD-ROM) to create a RES file that you can add to your ROOS project. You can have only one RES file in a single Visual Basic project, but one is plenty! (If you don't have access to Visual C++ or any other tool for creating resource files, you can use an editor such as Notepad. Before attempting this, however, you should study an RC file and a Resource.h file to become familiar with their format.)

Obviously, any client requesting data from the ROOS will need to know the ID value for each resource. In Visual Basic 4, you would need to include your ID constants in each client application, either as hard-coded constants or in a shared type library. With Visual Basic 5, you can declare all your IDs within the ROOS as enumerated constants, which makes them automatically available to client applications.

Listing 15-1 shows a slightly more advanced ROOS that retrieves string and bitmap resources. The ROOS allows you to merge an unlimited number of tokens into a string resource. To create a string resource with tokens, simply insert a % symbol in the string where the supplied parameter(s) will be substituted.

FIGURE 15-11

A resource file created in Microsoft Visual C++ 5

String constant name   Constant value   String text

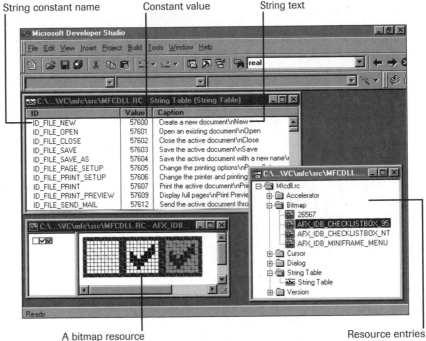

A bitmap resource   Resource entries

LISTING 15-1

ROOS for retrieving string and bitmap resources

```
' The following Enums declare the resource ID of the bitmaps
' in our RES file. The include file "resource.h" generated
' by the resource editor defines the constants to match each
' bitmap. Checking this file shows the first bitmap resource
' ID to be 101; therefore, these Enums are declared to match
' this.
Public Enum BITMAPS

' ***
' *** NOTE: Any new bitmaps added must be inserted between
' *** IDB_TOPVALUE and IDB_LASTVALUE because these constants are
' *** used to validate input parameters.
' ***
    idb_topvalue = 100
    IDB_SELECTSOURCE
    IDB_SELECTDESTIN
    IDB_NUMBERSOURCE
    IDB_COMPLETED
    idb_lastvalue
End Enum
```

>>

LISTING 15-1

```
Public Enum STRINGS

    ' VBP project file key ID words
    IDS_VBP_KEY_FORM = 500
    IDS_VBP_KEY_CLASS
    IDS_VBP_KEY_MODULE
    IDS_VBP_SEP_FORM
    IDS_VBP_SEP_CLASS
    IDS_VBP_SEP_MODULE
    IDS_VBP_SEP_RESFILE
    IDS_VBP_KEY_RESOURCE16
    IDS_VBP_KEY_RESOURCE32

    ' Procedure keywords
    IDS_PROCKEY_SUB1 = 600
    IDS_PROCKEY_SUB2
    IDS_PROCKEY_SUB3
    IDS_PROCKEY_FUNC1
    IDS_PROCKEY_FUNC2
    IDS_PROCKEY_FUNC3
    IDS_PROCKEY_PROP1
    IDS_PROCKEY_PROP2
    IDS_PROCKEY_PROP3
    IDS_PROCKEY_END1
    IDS_PROCKEY_END2
    IDS_PROCKEY_END3
    IDS_PROCKEY_SELECT
    IDS_PROCKEY_CASE
    IDS_PROCKEY_COMMENT

    ' File filter strings
    IDS_FILTER_FRX = 700
    IDS_FILTER_PROJECT
    IDS_FILTER_CLASS
    IDS_FILTER_FORM
    IDS_FILTER_MODULE
    IDS_FILTER_CONFIG
    IDS_FILE_TEMP

    ' Displayed caption strings
    IDS_CAP_STEP1 = 800
    IDS_CAP_STEP2
    IDS_CAP_STEP3
    IDS_CAP_STEP4
    IDS_CAP_NUMBER
```

LISTING 15-1

>>

```
        IDS_CAP_UNNUMBER
        IDS_CAP_CANCEL
        IDS_CAP_FINISH
        IDS_CAP_CANCEL_ALLOWED

        ' Message strings
        IDS_MSG_NOT_TEMPLATE = 900
        IDS_MSG_COMPLETE_STATUS
        IDS_MSG_TEMPL_CORRUPT
        IDS_MSG_INVALID_CONFIG
        IDS_MSG_CREATE_TMPL_ERR
        IDS_MSG_NO_SOURCE
        IDS_MSG_INVALID_DESTIN
        IDS_MSG_SAME_SRC_DESTIN
        IDS_MSG_QUERY_EXIT
        IDS_MSG_ABORTED

        ' Err.Description strings
        IDS_ERR_GDI = 1000
        IDS_ERR_PROCESS_ERROR
End Enum

' Resource ROOS error constants
Public Enum RR_Errors
        RR_INVALID_BITMAP_ID = 2000 ' Invalid bitmap resource ID
        RR_INVALID_STRING_ID        ' Invalid string resource ID
End Enum

Public Sub PuGetBmp(ByVal ilBitmapID As Long, _
        ByVal ictl As Control)

        ' Check that the ID value passed is valid. This is an
        ' Assert type of message, but the class cannot be part
        ' of the design environment, so raise an error instead.

        If ilBitmapID <= idb_topvalue Or _
                ilBitmapID >= idb_lastvalue Then

                Err.Description = "An invalid bitmap ID value '" & _
                        ilBitmapID & "' was passed."
                Err.Number = RR_INVALID_BITMAP_ID
                Err.Raise Err.Number
                Exit Sub
        End If
```

>>

LISTING 15-1

```
            ' Load the bitmap into the picture of the control passed.
            ictl.Picture = LoadResPicture(ilBitmapID, vbResBitmap)
End Sub

Public Function sPuGetStr(ByVal ilStringID As Long, _
    Optional ByVal ivArgs As Variant) As String

        Dim nIndex          As Integer
        Dim nPointer        As Integer
        Dim nTokenCount     As Integer
        Dim sResString      As String
        Dim vTempArg        As Variant

        Const ARG_TOKEN     As String = "%"

        sResString = LoadResString(ilStringID)

        If IsMissing(ivArgs) Then GoTo END_GETRESOURCESTRING

        If (VarType(ivArgs) And vbArray) <> vbArray Then

            ' Single argument passed. Store the value so that we can
            ' convert ivArgs to an array with this single
            ' value.
            vTempArg = ivArgs
            ivArgs = Empty
            ReDim ivArgs(0)

            ivArgs(0) = vTempArg
        End If

    nTokenCount = 0

    Do While nTokenCount < UBound(ivArgs) _
        = LBound(ivArgs) + 1

        nPointer = InStr(sResString, ARG_TOKEN)
        If nPointer = 0 Then

            ' There are more arguments than tokens in the RES
            ' string, so exit the loop.

            Exit Do
        End If
```

LISTING 15-1

>>

```
            Call sPiReplaceToken(sResString, ARG_TOKEN, _
                ivArgs(LBound(ivArgs) + nTokenCount))
            nTokenCount = nTokenCount + 1
    Loop

END_GETRESOURCESTRING:
    sPuGetStr = sResString
End Function

Private Function sPiReplaceToken(ByRef iosTokenStr As String, _
    ByVal isToken As String, ByVal ivArgs As Variant)

    Dim nPointer As Integer

    nPointer = InStr(iosTokenStr, isToken)
    If nPointer <> 0 Then
        iosTokenStr = Left$(iosTokenStr, nPointer - 1) & _
            ivArgs & Mid$(iosTokenStr, nPointer + 1)
    End If
End Function
```

REUSE ISSUES FOR THE PROGRAMMER

Good computer programming relies on a structured methodology that consists of a number of individual disciplines. For example, commenting your code as you write it is a discipline that you must practice until it becomes second nature. It is a well-known fact that many programmers either do not comment their code at all or comment it only after it's been written. One of the reasons you should comment code as you write it is because at that time you know your exact thought processes and the reasons behind the decisions you're making. If you were to comment the code two weeks after writing it, you might still understand how it works, but you will probably have forgotten subtle details about why you coded something a certain way or what effects a line of code might have on other parts of the application. If you ever see lots of totally meaningless comments, you can be sure they were inserted after the code was written!

The discipline of coding for reusability is very important and comes only with practice. You will know when you've mastered this habit because you'll start writing less code. You should view any piece of code you write as a potentially reusable component. The experience gained from adopting this practice will help you not only to identify reusable units but also to anticipate the situations in which those units might be used. It will also enable you to make better decisions about how loosely or tightly the code can be coupled—it's not possible or efficient in all cases to decouple a code section completely from the other parts of the application. You should also remember that in a multiple-programmer project, other programmers will look to reuse code that other team members have written. Imagine you want a function and that function already exists: will you write it again or use the existing one? Obviously, you will reuse the existing function unless one or all of these conditions are true:

- You think the code is of poor quality.

- The code doesn't meet your requirements.

- You don't know the code exists.

- The code is poorly documented or commented.

Experience will also help you make the right choices about the way that a unit couples to other units. A good practice to adopt is to write all your code modularly, encapsulated as much as possible. A typical program consists of a series of calls to functions and subroutines. At the top level—for example, in a text box KeyPress event—a series of calls can be made. The functions that you call from within this event should, wherever possible, be coded as if they were contained in object components; that is, they should have no knowledge of the environment. It is the linking code, or the code in the KeyPress event, that needs to know about the environment. By coding functions and subroutines in a modular way, you can reuse them in a number of situations. You should also avoid embedding application-specific functionality in these top-level events because this prevents the code from being reused effectively. Look at the following sample code, which capitalizes the first letter of each word in the text box Text1:

```
Sub Text1_KeyPress(KeyAscii As Integer)

    If Text1.SelStart = 0 Then
        ' This is the first character, so change to uppercase.
        KeyAscii = Asc(UCase$(Chr$(KeyAscii)))
    Else
        ' If the previous character is a space, capitalize
        ' the current character.
```

```
        If Mid$(Text1, Text1.SelStart, 1) = Space$(1) Then
            KeyAscii = Asc(UCase$(Chr$(KeyAscii)))
        End If
    End If
End Sub
```

The functionality in the KeyPress event is tied explicitly to Text1. To reuse this code, you would have to cut and paste it and then change every reference made to Text1 to the new control. The code would be truly reusable if written like this:

```
Sub Text1_KeyPress(KeyAscii As Integer)
    KeyAscii = nConvertToCaps(Text1, KeyAscii)
End Sub

Function nConvertToCaps(ByVal ctl As Control, _
    ByRef nChar As Integer) As Integer

    If ctl.SelStart - 0 Then
        ' This is the first character, so change to uppercase.
        nChar = Asc(UCase$(Chr$(nChar)))
    Else
        ' If the previous character is a space, capitalize
        ' the current character.
        If Mid$(ctl, ctl.SelStart, 1) = Space$(1) Then
            nChar = Asc(UCase$(Chr$(nChar)))
        End If
    End If

    nConvertToCaps = nChar
End Function
```

The *nConvertToCaps* function has no knowledge of the control it is acting on and therefore can be used by any code that has appropriate input parameters. You will often write procedures that you might not foresee anyone else using. By assuming the opposite, that *all* your code will be reused, you will reduce the time you or others require to later modify functionality for reuse.

The effects of not writing for reuse can be seen in many development projects but might not be obvious at first. At a high level, it is easy to break down an application into distinct components and code those components as discrete modular units using any of the methods described above. However, there is nearly always a large expanse of code that doesn't fit neatly into a distinct modular pattern. This is usually the application's binding code—that is, the logic that controls program flow and links various system components. Processes that are not major components in themselves but simply provide auxiliary functionality are normally assumed rather than specified formally, which is yet another reason why estimating can go wrong when this functionality is not considered. The result of bad design of these elements will usually lead to spaghetti code. The following sections discuss some habits that you should practice until they become automatic.

Make Few Assumptions

In an application, you'll often need to use variables that contain indeterminate formats. For example, an application might have several variables or properties storing directory names. When using these variables, you have to add a filename to get a full file specification. How do you know whether the path stored in the variable contains a backslash? Most applications have an *Append-Slash* routine that adds a backslash to a path if it doesn't have one, so you might be tempted to assume the format just because you've run it once in debug mode to check. You need to keep in mind, especially in large projects, that values of variables are often changed by other programmers, so a path that has the trailing backslash in one instance might not in another. Depending on the application, you might discover these errors immediately or not until some later time. In the case of the backslash, rather than rely on it being there, assume it could be missing and use your *AppendSlash* routine to check for it everywhere. You should apply this thinking whenever a particular format cannot be guaranteed.

Develop a Coupling Strategy

Nonspecified code can often suffer problems caused by tight coupling. Because nonspecified code doesn't form part of a major unit, programmers often pay less attention to its interaction with other parts of the application. Where possible, you should pass parameters into procedures rather than use module-level variables. Input parameters that won't need to be changed should always be declared by value (*ByVal*) rather than the default, by reference (*ByRef*). Many programmers choose the by reference method simply because it saves typing.

Another common excuse for using *ByRef* is the argument of speed: passing by reference is a few milliseconds faster than passing by value because Visual Basic has to create a copy of the variable when it's passed by value. But the consequence of misusing *ByRef* can be severe in terms of debugging time. Imagine a seldom-used application configuration variable that gets inadvertently changed by another procedure. You might not detect the error until someone uses the configuration function several times, maybe even long after you've written the code. Now imagine trying to trace the cause of the problem! As a rule, always pass parameters by value unless you explicitly want changes to be passed back to the caller.

The purposes of passing parameters to a procedure rather than using module-level variables are to make it obvious to anyone not familiar with the code exactly what external dependencies are being used and to allow the procedure to be rewritten or reused more easily. A good practice is to document procedure parameters in a header box. A header box is simply a series of comments at the beginning of a procedure that explain the purpose of the procedure. Any external dependencies should also be documented here. Often programmers do not reuse functionality simply because the parameters or dependencies are unclear or not easy to understand. Imagine a procedure that accepts an array containing 20 data items. If the procedure is dependent on all 20 data items being present, other programmers might find it difficult to use unless it is well documented.

Passing parameters to procedures allows you to create code that is loosely coupled and therefore potentially reusable. The following code fragment shows a would-be reusable procedure that is too tightly coupled to the form it's in to be reused anywhere else in that application, let alone in another application:

```
Sub SearchForFile(ByVal isFile As String)

    ' Disable all buttons.
    cmdClose.Enabled = False
    cmdView.Enabled = False

    ' Process
    ⋮
    labStatus = "File " & isFile
    ⋮
```

The procedure is rewritten here in a more reusable way:

```
Sub cmdProcess_Click()

    Dim ctlDisableArray(0 To 1) As Control
    Dim sFile                   As String

    ' sFile = filename
    ctlDisableArray(0) = cmdClose
    ctlDisableArray(1) = cmdView

    Call SearchForFile(sFile, ctlDisableArray(), labStatus)
    ⋮
End Sub

Sub SearchForFile(ByVal isFile As String, _
    Optional ctlDisable() As Control, _
    Optional labUpdate As Label)

    Dim nIndex    As Integer

    ' Disable all buttons if any are specified.
    If Not IsMissing(ctlDisable) Then
        For nIndex = LBound(ctlDisable) To UBound(ctlDisable)
            ctlDisable(nIndex).Enabled = False
        Next nIndex
    End If

    ' Process
    ⋮
    If Not IsMissing(labUpdate) Then
        labUpdate = "File " & isFile
    End If
    ⋮
```

Now the procedure is totally decoupled and can be called from anywhere in the application.

Another good practice to adopt is using more flexible parameter types for inputs to a procedure. In Chapter 5, Jon Burn says, "Use variants for everything." If you take Jon's advice, you should be careful to validate the parameters and display helpful errors. In a simple application, you can easily locate the cause of an error; but if the error occurs in a compiled ActiveX control, it might be a different story. The sample code here is the procedure declaration for a subroutine that fills a list box from an array:

```
Public Sub FillList(lst As ListBox, anArray() As Integer)
```

The function might work fine, but it's restrictive. Imagine you have another type of list box control that has some added functionality. You won't be able to pass it into this function. It's also possible that someone might want to use this routine with a combo box. The code will be similar, so this is a feasible request. However, you won't be able to use the procedure above with a combo box. If the routine is part of the application, you can rewrite it; more than likely, however, you'll write another routine instead. If the routine is in a DLL file, rewriting it might not be so easy. In the following code, the procedure header is changed to make it more generic and the rest of the code is added as well:

```
Public Sub FillList(ctl As Control, anArray() As Integer)
    Dim nIndex  As Integer

    For nIndex = LBound(anArray) To UBound(anArray)
        ctl.AddItem anArray(nIndex)
    Next nIndex

End Sub
```

Notice the potential problem now in this routine, however. If any control that doesn't have an *AddItem* method is passed to the routine, it will fail. It might be some time later, when another programmer calls the routine, that the error is detected; and if the routine is in a DLL, it might take some time to debug. What we need is some defensive programming. Always try to code as if the procedure is part of an external DLL in which other programmers cannot access the source code. In this example, you can use defensive coding in two ways: by using *Debug.Assert* or by raising an error.

The *Debug.Assert* method, new to Visual Basic 5, evaluates an expression that you supply and, if the expression is false, executes a break. C programmers use these assertions in their code all the time. This method is intended to trap development-type errors that you don't expect to occur once the system is complete. You should never use assertions in a built executable; therefore, the method has been added to the *Debug* object. In a built executable, *Debug.Assert* is ignored, just as with the *Debug.Print* method. You could use an assertion here like this:

```
Public Sub FillList(ctl As Control, anArray() As Integer)

    Dim nIndex  As Integer

    ' Assert - This subroutine handles only ListBox and ComboBox.
    Debug.Assert TypeOf ctl Is ListBox Or _
        TypeOf Ctl Is ComboBox

    For nIndex = LBound(anArray) To UBound(anArray)
        :
```

This will now trap the error if the routine is running in design mode. Because the debugger will break on the assert line, it's always best to put a comment around the assert so that another programmer triggering the assert can easily identify the problem.

With our example, the assert is not a good method to use for defensive programming because we might put this routine into a DLL, in which case the assert would be ignored and the user would get an error. A better way would be to raise an error. When you raise an error, the code that calls this function will have to deal with the problem. Think of the File Open procedure in Visual Basic. If you try to open a file that doesn't exist, the Open procedure raises an error: "File not found." We can do the same with our routine:

```
Public Sub FillList(ctl As Control, anArray() As Integer)

    Dim nIndex  As Integer

    Const ERR_INVALID_CONTROL = 3000

    If Not(TypeOf ctl Is ListBox) And _
        Not(TypeOf ctl Is ComboBox) Then

        Err.Number = ERR_INVALID_CONTROL
        Err.Description = "An invalid control " & ctl.Name & _
            " was passed to sub 'FillList' - "
        Err.Raise Err.Number

    End If

    For nIndex = LBound(anArray) To UBound(anArray)
        :
```

This method will work in any situation, but it has two problems. The first problem is not really a problem in this instance because the caller won't be expecting an error. If the caller were anticipating an error, however, we might want to check the error number and perform a specific action. Visual Basic 4 allowed type libraries in which you could declare constants and declarations to include in a project. The main problem with these was that you couldn't create a type library within Visual Basic. It also meant that any client project would need to include the type library, thus increasing dependencies.

In Visual Basic 5, you can use a new feature, Enum constants. Let's see how the code looks before we explain what's happening:

```
' General declarations

Public Enum CustomErrors
    ERR_INVALID_CONTROL = 3000
    ERR_ANOTHER_ERROR
    ⋮
End Enum

Public Sub FillList(ctl As Control, anArray() As Integer)

    Dim nIndex  As Integer

    If Not(TypeOf ctl Is ListBox) And _
        Not(TypeOf ctl Is ComboBox) Then

        Err.Number = CustomErrors.ERR_INVALID_CONTROL
        Err.Description = "An invalid control " & ctl.Name & _
            " was passed to sub 'FillList' - " &
    ⋮
```

The constants are declared between the Enum...End Enum, just as in a user-defined type. The Enum name can be used to explicitly scope to the correct constant if you have duplicates. Notice that the second constant in the example doesn't have a value assigned. With enumerated constants, if you specify a value, it will be used. If you don't specify a value, one is assigned, starting from 0 or 1 plus the previous constant. Enumerated constants can contain only long integers. The big advantage in using enumerated constants is that they can be public. For example, if you create a class, any client of that class can access the constants. Now you don't have to have constants with global scope, and you don't need to create type libraries. In effect, the module becomes more encapsulated.

The second potential problem with the function on page 670 is that the array might be empty—but not the kind of empty that you can check with the *IsEmpty* function. If our sample code were to be passed an array that didn't contain any elements (for example, it might have been cleared using *Erase*), you would get a "Subscript out of range" error as soon as you used *LBound* on it. A much better way of passing arrays is to use a Variant array. A Variant array is simply a variable declared as type Variant that you ReDim. If the array has no elements, *IsEmpty* will return True. You can also check that an array as opposed to, say, a string has been passed. The code looks something like this:

```
Public Sub FillList(ctl As Control, vArray As Variant)

    Dim nIndex  As Integer

    ' Exit if array is empty.
    If IsEmpty(vArray) Then Exit Sub

    ' Exit if not an Integer array.
    If VarType(vArray) <> (vbArray Or vbInteger) Then
        ' Error
```

The techniques described all help you to achieve the following benefits:

- Create reusable and generic code by creating loosely coupled routines and components
- Help others to reuse your code
- Protect your code from errors caused by client code

Group Functionality

You might be surprised at how many applications contain functions that fall into a particular category but are fragmented across the application. Such fragmentation often occurs when many programmers are working on the same application and the module names don't clearly identify the type of functionality the modules contain. The ownership aspect also comes into play: some programmers don't like to amend another programmer's code. Access conflict might also be an issue. It is good practice to familiarize yourself with other modules in the application so that you can group functionality and also identify functionality that you can use. Grouping reusable functionality has the added benefit that it can be extracted in separate DLLs at a later stage.

Document Your Code

Visual Basic now has an excellent Object Browser. You can include detailed documentation about your functions that will prevent others from constantly having to ask questions about routines you have written. Unfortunately, for many programmers, writing documentation is like going to the dentist. It is also a task that never gets included in project plans, so it almost never gets done. It is vital that you increase your estimates to allow time for these tasks.

Refine Your Habits

We've made only a few suggestions here—there are lots more. If you decide on a set of good habits and constantly practice and refine them, your organization will benefit because of the development time you'll save, and you will benefit because you'll need to do much less debugging. Each time you complete a project, review it and identify areas that you could have improved.

Reusability is an issue that has to be supported by the business, designed by the designers, and coded by the programmers. Unless all sides commit to the goal of reusability, you will be doomed to continually rewrite most of your code.

How to Juggle 30 Balls Blindfolded

Making Enterprise Development a Success

MARK SEWELL

Mark is a Director and a cofounder of TMS. He is TMS's expert on software development processes, project management, and team structures. Mark is a Microsoft Visual Basic Certified Professional; cowrote a Visual Basic programmer's product, "TMS Tools"; teaches Visual Basic; and project managed the development of MicroHelp's Code Complete. Mark has presented at VBITS and other conferences and writes many articles. He previously worked for Price Waterhouse, Logica, Sema Group, and IBM. He likes to spend most of his spare time with his wife and children, avoiding anything to do with computers.

ALAN INGLIS

Alan is a TMS Associate who specializes in client/server design and project management. He started his career writing protocols and building cables to connect early microcomputers to Datapoint minis. Alan moved on to a major IBM MVS shop to write graphics and systems management utilities. Alan has since worked as designer, project manager, and consultant in IBM mainframe, AS/400, UNIX, Unisys, and PC environments.

God gave burdens, also shoulders.
Yiddish proverb

Software development has been going on for more than thirty years, so you'd think that by now successful development projects would be the norm. Yct consider these statistics: More than 80 percent of all software projects fail. The average large project is a year late. The average small project time estimate is off by more than 100 percent. The problems are well known and widely published, but in project after project, in company after company, the same mistakes are made over and over again. Plan, estimate, schedule, manage—and when the going gets tough, throw it all away and code. Postmortem reviews reveal the only universal strategy: start at the beginning, keep going until you reach the end, and then stop.

Visual Basic has become much more complex with each new version. Unless projects—particularly large enterprise ones—are properly managed, embarrassing statistics such as those mentioned above will only worsen. This chapter outlines some of the fundamental issues involved in developing large-scale client/server projects using Visual Basic 5. It is aimed at all Visual Basic 5 developers, but project managers who need to understand how the technical environment affects their planning and management should find it particularly useful. System designers and quality assurance (QA) staff who need to understand how important their roles are in delivering a successful project will also find it helpful.

As software development consultants, we at The Mandelbrot Set (International) Limited (TMS) are often asked to comment on why things aren't going quite right with a client's current development project. To find the problem, we normally carry out a project health check and a technical review. We consistently find that in the haste to deliver, Visual Basic developers have abandoned software engineering disciplines that, though not perfect, have evolved over thirty years and are certainly a lot better than the plain code hacking that replaces them. This slack behavior is exhibited by the full range of developers, from junior programmers through project managers. As a result, we keep seeing low-quality, unmaintainable Visual Basic code being written by developers at a high proportion of our client companies, big and small. Why is this happening?

A VISUAL BASIC QUALITY CRISIS?

Visual Basic is great! It's an easy, economical, and fast application-development tool, it's a good prototyping tool, and developers love using it. It's fun too! Certainly these comments were true about versions 1, 2, and 3. But with versions 4 and 5 (particularly the Enterprise Editions), things have become a lot more complex. It is essential that the Visual Basic development mind-set changes—developers need to become much more professional in their approach to programming projects.

Like any high-level programming language, Visual Basic lets the programmer write really awful programs, and with Visual Basic, you can screw up more easily and faster than ever! As with programs in any language, a bad program in Visual Basic can be very hard to maintain. It can be hard to adapt to meet changing business requirements. But with Visual Basic programs, there is a greater danger than with other languages that developers will focus too much on a pretty front end without designing a solid structure on which to hang it. Important business logic can be attached to GUI widgets rather than placed in reusable objects, making it hard to share and reuse code. And of course, Visual Basic is the perfect tool for maverick code warriors to pump out reams and reams of undocumented and incomprehensible programs. All these factors can lead to severe maintenance and quality problems.

Managers often forget that the Visual Basic coding phase typically takes about 20 to 30 percent of the overall development life cycle. Their expectations of the massive productivity gains to be had from using Visual Basic are totally unrealistic. They have been suckered by the RAD hype. We feel sorry for Visual Basic—unrealistic plans for it are often drawn up and agreed to, and later the true picture becomes apparent. Then we often hear such laments as, "We can't cut functionality—the business won't tolerate it" or "We can't slip the deadline— it's set in stone" or "We can't throw any more bodies at it without blowing the budget!" When the going gets tough, one or more of the following four things tends to happen:

- Functionality is cut.
- Deadlines are slipped.
- Bodies are added.
- Quality is reduced.

So what gives? Invariably, it's the quality that suffers the most. And Visual Basic gets the blame.

The goals of the organization often conflict with the goals of the Visual Basic team. The organization realizes that building reusable components increases its ability to build better solutions more quickly, whereas individual project teams are typically focused on solving specific problems under tight schedules. The Visual Basic team is pushed so hard that it's next to impossible to consider reuse, despite the fact that the team members would love to generalize their code and make it available to other teams. Unfortunately, they don't have the time to consider problems outside their project.

So is Visual Basic a poor tool for serious enterprise development? We don't think so—quite the contrary. Does Visual Basic 5 solve the problems of the past? It certainly helps. But it can't help solve many of the problems highlighted above because most of the problems relate to people—their attitudes toward Visual Basic software development and the processes they use.

How can Visual Basic software quality be maintained in an enterprise environment? Advanced programmers need the answer. In this chapter, we've listed the simple measures that we consider lead to the production of high-quality Visual Basic 5 applications. We don't aim to present detailed and reasoned arguments. Our views have been honed from years of experience observing both good and bad practices in many large organizations developing Visual Basic client/server systems: self-evident truths.

RISK MANAGEMENT

I don't want the cheese, I just want to get out of the trap.
Spanish proverb

Risk is multidimensional, involving business, technical, and people risks that must be managed within the context of the development project's architecture, analysis, design, and implementation phases. (See Figure 16-1.) These risks affect the whole project life cycle. In this section, we'll focus on the technical risks that the introduction of Visual Basic 5 brings.

FIGURE 16-1

Risk management is central to successful system development.

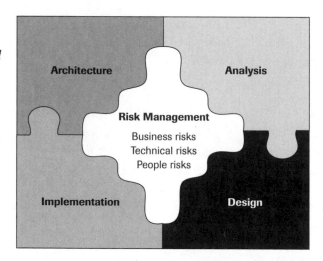

Traditionally, project managers have three major objectives: deliver on time, stick to budget, and create a system that fits its intended purpose. To manage the risks inherent in Visual Basic 5 client/server development, project managers must be aware of business needs, be technically competent and customer focused, and be great team leaders. This kind of development—with its integration of differing, fast-changing components and technologies—has such a high level of risk that some might say only the foolhardy would attempt it! Given such extreme risks, a risk-management strategy is fundamental to successful delivery.

A key factor in heading off problems is moving the technical risks to the beginning of a large project and handling them there. Often, major risks are not addressed until the system test or live running, settings in which the costs of rework or failure are substantially higher. Dealing with the risks early provides a forum for discussing how the project will work and allows broader issues to be addressed. Think of this early technical review as a form of insurance.

Some crucial issues need to be addressed in managing risk: the technical infrastructure, the business environment, and change management.

Technical Infrastructure

Historically, in the mainframe world, we have seen relatively slow evolution of the technical infrastructure and long project-delivery times. This slower pace allowed developers to implement a technical strategy that used a proven technical infrastructure for major system components. The same sort of infrastructure must be established to develop robust systems for Visual Basic 5. Visual Basic 5 Enterprise Edition provides the opportunity for a powerful and flexible development environment, but only if this flexibility is designed into the project. It will be a hefty investment to get it right, and a very expensive mistake to get it wrong.

The technical infrastructure includes the hardware, the network, the operating systems, and the tools. All the elements of the infrastructure interact and are constantly changing. This interaction and change is one of the biggest risks. You must work out a method for developing successful systems in this environment.

Visual Basic has recently gone through two releases (4 and 5), both with order-of-magnitude changes in complexity that require very different approaches to development. We've seen Microsoft Windows 95, Microsoft Windows NT 4, Netware 4, and the Internet change the operating environment. Distributed objects and open host operating systems are becoming a reality. Hardware continues to become faster and less expensive. Utility packages such as word processors and spreadsheets have become development tools. The legacy environment, together with these and other tools, forms an ever-changing development infrastructure.

You must be sure of the robustness and performance of the infrastructure under the stresses of live running. If the infrastructure is not proven, then prove it! And keep on proving it!

Business Environment

The business world that our systems support is generally becoming more volatile and is demanding new systems of greater complexity in shorter time frames. We need to develop systems in the context of a corporate business systems architecture that allows rapidly developed systems to integrate and form a basis for future change and development. Systems such as this will help us manage the problems that occur when rapid development approaches are applied to large projects.

Change Management

The more innocuous the modification appears to be, the further its influence will extend and the more plans will have to be redrawn.

Second Law of Revision

You need to anticipate technical and business changes. Databases grow and need restructuring, and underlying system software changes. You should build applications with an architecture that can accommodate change.

Small, simple applications that deliver benefits quickly are preferable to monolithic applications, but the combination of small and very large applications should also provide the same benefit. You need to anticipate the growth of applications—organic growth is natural in successful applications, and you should allow for it.

CRITICAL FACTORS IN SUCCESSFUL ENTERPRISE DEVELOPMENT

Unfortunately, we can offer no formula you can follow that will guarantee the success of your enterprise development. You can greatly improve your odds of succeeding, however, if you adhere to some guidelines as you proceed through the development process. We've discovered, often the hard way, that certain factors are critical to successful enterprise developments.

Insist on Great Project Management

Misfortunes always come in by a door that has been left open for them.

Anonymous

Effective project management is critical to the success of Visual Basic development projects. Strong project management can lead to success even in difficult circumstances. Weak project management can result in failure when success is there for the taking. In the Visual Basic world, many good project managers seem to have mentally wandered off, neglecting their professional responsibilities. The most basic disciplines such as planning, phasing, tracking, change management, and milestone setting seem to have been forgotten. Project managers seem to be sucked into a way of working that in their heart-of-hearts they know is wrong—but they do it anyway. The best project managers are prepared to put their jobs on the line to do what's right. They realize that their job is at risk anyway. Even the best project managers will be seen to be at fault by someone whatever the outcome of the project, so why not do the job the right way from the start? *It is essential that proper, disciplined project management occur within every Visual Basic 5 team.*

Visual Basic project managers are typically not technical enough. Project managers cannot lead effectively unless they have credibility within the team and are able to discuss critical design issues. Many of the project managers we speak to don't know, for example, what system resources are or what MDI is even though their team is being forced to code a complex finite state machine as a result of this interface style being chosen.

When we ask a project manager why a substandard Visual Basic application has been released, we normally hear something along the lines of, "The business demanded it quickly," "Our competitors have one, so we had to have one," "We'll use it now and fix it later," "The users expect it now," or "The users are already using it, so we can't withdraw it." The poor management of user expectations and requirements is to blame for much of Visual Basic's bad press. All too often, a manager will allow a program to go live because he or she has failed to adequately manage the expectations of the users (or perhaps of the senior managers).

Visual Basic 5 offers the opportunity to produce component-based solutions. Managing a project of clients and servers in which you do parallel development by using a defined interface (building stubs and then filling them with real functionality) works up to a point; the difficulty comes on the human side. Parallel development requires a high degree of flexibility and interaction from all members of the team. Developers, especially inexperienced ones, or people who haven't been on a team before find the personal-contract nature of this type of development difficult and would prefer to be told what to do in what order and by what date rather than to make personal, flexible "contracts" with team members. The only way to pull off a parallel development project is with the following ingredients:

- A great deal of project management effort (micromanaging)
- A highly cooperative, established team
- Long lags and leads

The difficulties compound because of the tendency to fiddle (and think you can) with declared object interfaces after they are defined.

On the technical front, beware of technical customers—they'll continually want to revisit the design without ever recognizing the impact of this dabbling on the project. Also, even with small teams, on a highly technical project in which people take responsibility for certain areas, the project manager will have trouble keeping on top of the day-to-day technical details. The best way for the project manager to keep track of the details is to delegate responsibility and require written notification (e-mail works well) of how things are progressing.

Know Why You're Taking the Risk

New, inexpensive technology provides greater access to and more uses for information. With Visual Basic 5, there is a major challenge to technical departments to deliver the technology benefits quickly. Effective development means delivering swiftly and economically so that the business can gain competitive advantage or make strategic shifts.

New technology provides businesses with new opportunities to one-up their competitors. This advantage will be short-lived because the competition will rapidly equal or better the development. This competitiveness produces even more pressure to achieve results in record time.

The same new technology provides IT departments with the challenge of learning about and using it. The pace of change, the visibility of new technology, and the need to exploit it quickly mean that system development has become very high risk. You can lower this risk by ensuring that you understand the technology.

In this context, it's vital to understand how to balance risk and benefit. Only the business managers can judge whether the benefits are worth the risks, so project managers must be able to communicate with the business managers about these issues.

Visual Basic 5 provides a series of productivity tools and tools to build productivity tools. You can reduce the risks if you invest in learning and developing wizards, add-ins, templates, and other reusable components.

Understand Where You Came From

A traditional development environment (such as the one depicted in Figure 16-2) in a large, well-established organization has typically grown up over a period of thirty years or more. During this time, procedures and practices have been implemented to control and manage the development, operation, support, and maintenance of the IT function. The environment is mature.

FIGURE 16-2

A traditional corporate environment

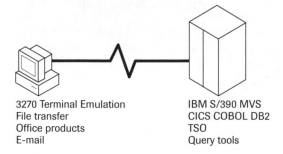

3270 Terminal Emulation
File transfer
Office products
E-mail

IBM S/390 MVS
CICS COBOL DB2
TSO
Query tools

This type of mature technical environment was relatively slow to change, so methods and people were able to adapt easily to the changes. The environment was relatively simple and stable. This slower change and general stability meant that a small number of well-trained staff could investigate change, develop a coherent technical strategy, and adapt the system management practice to take account of this change. The skills required of the majority of development and support staff were relatively low level.

Understand Where You Are

Make it work first before you make it work fast.
Bruce Whiteside

Today large-scale Visual Basic 5 client/server systems, such as the one depicted in Figure 16-3, are normally attempting to achieve high levels of integration within a business. This implies integration among systems that might require links to e-mail, workflow, document image databases, multiple conventional data sources, and the Internet.

Figure 16-3

A modern corporate environment

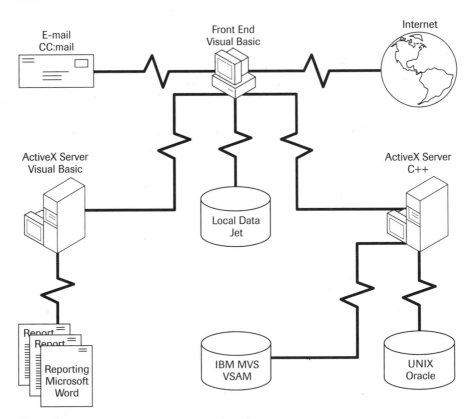

To achieve the necessary integration and performance, you might need to use multiple APIs and protocols. The technical skills required to architect, design, implement, and support such systems are significantly higher level than those called for in traditional mature environments.

With so many technologies and products involved, the development environment and tools are very fluid. The tools are increasingly complex in order to cope with the complexity of the environment. With the move from Visual Basic 3 to Visual Basic 5, we have seen Visual Basic move through two major leaps in functionality and capability. Practice and skills in this environment are immature.

The most significant changes in Visual Basic 5 are in the capability to distribute the application by distributing processing (through ActiveX components) and data (via various flavors of ODBC). Learning how to achieve high performance and stability must be an early objective of the introduction of Visual Basic 5. This issue involves development, deployment, and support.

Build Commitment and Understand Users

Pick battles big enough to matter, small enough to win.

Jonathan Kozol

Project managers and users often have problems with defining project scope and keeping it in line with schedules and budgets. Continual commitment to dialogue is essential to ensure that business domains and technological solutions actually produce benefits in spite of the fact that normally not everyone involved completely understands these domains and solutions. The effect of normal business risks on a project can be greatly magnified to job-threatening and sometimes business-threatening proportions.

Your approach to development must make it possible for you to cope with large projects. Many attempts at rapid development have been based on scaling up small-project development practices. This model of development provides some useful lessons, but it must be placed in a framework designed for large-scale developments.

The development process must allow for managing changes in requirements without excessive bureaucratic burden and large amounts of rework. Often a way to achieve this goal is through prototyping. Visual Basic has always been an excellent prototyping tool that can be used to improve the understanding of requirements. Keep in mind, though, that the techniques for building rapid prototypes are very different from the effective use of Visual Basic 5 for building robust client/server systems. Users must not be misled into thinking that prototypes are anything other than prototypes. This misconception is a classic way of losing your users' confidence and commitment. (For more information about prototyping, see the "Why Are You Prototyping?" section later in this chapter.)

User commitment and involvement are critical factors to all application development. These factors have traditionally involved a contractual, even adversarial, relationship. On this basis, user commitment and involvement have been relatively easy to manage but not necessarily successful. If you are to speed up development, you must make users part of the development team and involve them continually.

The commitment from the business manager must be to assign to work with the development team a user who understands the business in sufficient depth to answer developers' questions, has the authority to make decisions on behalf of the business, and can live with the result of his or her decisions. To find such a user and release him or her to an IT project takes commitment. Major projects typically cross functional boundaries. Giving someone authority to make decisions across those boundaries means commitment from the top.

Understand the Technology

Any sufficiently advanced technology is indistinguishable from magic.
Clarke's Third Law

To manage risk on Visual Basic 5 client/server projects, managers must get closer to the technology. Managers need to be clear about why and how design decisions are made. If you're hanging your career on a technology, you'd better understand that technology.

Managers need to know where tools are weak and understand how different architectures perform. For example, Visual Basic 5 provides data access through bound forms, file access, the repository, DAO, ODBC calls, native API calls, RDO, and OLE DB. Each approach has differing technical performance implications, skill requirements, complexity, and delivery schedules.

Often when there is a decision to be made about what tools to use, what method to take, and so on, there is no clear-cut choice, so the project management approach must take this uncertainty into account so that correct decisions can be made at the appropriate time. It might be necessary to test different approaches prior to making a decision. Time must be figured into the development schedules for research and benchmarking.

ADVANCED MICROSOFT VISUAL BASIC 5

With any major new technology, you should set up a Pathfinder project to investigate the technology. A *Pathfinder project* is a miniature, timeboxed project that identifies the risks within a larger project. Typically, such investigations are not emphasized enough. Users often don't want to pay for something that they see as producing nothing at the end. Instead, you might hear a manager say, "We recognize the need to learn more about the technology, and if our developers need more knowledge, we'll send them to a class." However, with the rapid growth of technology and the complex way in which it applies to existing businesses, there is not often an applicable class, so the Pathfinder approach is a better way to investigate new technology. See the "Creating a Foundation with a Pathfinder Project" section on page 707 for more detailed information about such projects.

One of the objectives of the Pathfinder approach is to provide an initial knowledge base. Providing a knowledge base must be handled carefully, however. Many companies have older, established development environments on which they have spent a great deal of time, effort, and money. They might be reluctant to compromise the status quo by chasing after some new, unproven technology. New skills and methods need to be incorporated alongside existing strengths so that the current knowledge base can be improved rather than undermined or replaced.

At TMS, the approach we have used successfully in setting up Pathfinder projects is to create a small, highly skilled team to develop and prove the infrastructure and the tools. In subsequent project phases (after this Pathfinder project), this team carries out the technical supervision of other teams involved in the project to maintain the technical integrity of the application architecture. This core team, or "SWAT" team, has a role in developing skills in the other teams. It also helps other teams by providing resources to assist in clearing tasks on the critical path.

Some technical decisions have to be made early. For example, the choice of hardware platform or the database management system to be used is often fixed, or at least assumed, before the formal development project is kicked off. Inappropriate decisions at this stage can be very expensive. For example, we know of several cases in which relational approaches were used to address problems that are better suited to Online Analytical Processing (OLAP) solutions, the consequence being that effort was expended writing complex SQL and application code to produce functionality that already existed in the OLAP extensions to the relational database. Hasty decisions such as these can lead to a 30 to 50 percent increase in development costs. The ongoing cost of maintenance is also much higher than necessary. Such costs normally don't come to light because of the general ignorance of the appropriate use of technology or through inertia. However, there are kudos to be gained by stepping out, taking a risk, and delivering a better solution ahead of schedule.

It is vital that you understand Visual Basic 5 if you want to use the technology to its full advantage and to avoid pitfalls. Using a sophisticated technology such as Visual Basic 5 without adequate knowledge could cost you your job.

Create a Sensible Management Structure

It was a relief to know that it was just bad management and not technical problems.

Development manager after firing the head of IS

The rapid development of new tools and operating environments has meant that many information systems development management staff have little understanding of the technical issues and risks involved in these new technologies. As we have said, a key role of a project manager is to manage risk. Rapidly changing technology increases risks dramatically. Technical managers must understand the technology sufficiently to assess risk and act appropriately. The management structure might need to change to ensure that managers are close enough to the technical issues to manage risk. This generally means flattening the structure and devolving responsibility. The implications of this type of change extend to all facets of the information systems development organization, including organizational structures, salary and reward structures, skills planning, and training.

If a project involves prototyping, it might be necessary to give more responsibility at lower levels for managing user relationships and expectations. Prototyping provides an opportunity for developers to work more closely with users and to become more involved with business issues.

Get a Process

Standards were ignored, no method was applied, the system was not designed, staff were not adequately trained, management did not have sufficient technical knowledge to run the project, poor internal support mechanisms, no quality assurance, no test plans, no resources for testing, poor development environment, no risk analysis, 100 percent staff turnover, little documentation, no application architecture.

Project review

Project managers must plan the project and use an appropriate process to deliver the application. The approach they adopt should be based on the business and technical architectures and the project risks. The approach can be pure waterfall, spiral, incremental, or evolutionary. The life-cycle model used should not be dictated by a method but should instead be based on the characteristics of the project. Standards are no substitute for a project manager's experience and judgment.

Given the technical complexity of Visual Basic 5 client/server development, any approach must allow sufficient time for architecture and physical design. Doing these tasks up front can provide significant productivity gains by reducing rework and allowing more tasks to be carried out in parallel.

If Visual Basic 5 client/server development is used for high-profile and high-risk projects, a number of issues need to be addressed. A formal approach to the management, specification, design, and development of applications will be needed. A risk-driven design method that focuses on creating an appropriate application architecture will have to be created.

Visual Basic 5 client/server development lends itself to object-oriented analysis and design and to rapid development. Object techniques can be used to enhance communication between users and development professionals. Version 5 has extended the object-oriented character of Visual Basic. To make best use of Visual Basic, the development process must reflect this character and take advantage of it. This endeavor will bring challenges in developing the skills of staff and managers.

Visual Basic 5 offers a range of productivity features, including templates, new application packaging options, ActiveX documents, improved client/server development, and deployment. These features must be integrated into the development process. The public ActiveX interface of Visual Basic and the extensibility and configurable integrated development environment (IDE) provide the opportunity to integrate Visual Basic and other tools that automate and control the development process. To exploit the power of Visual Basic 5 fully, you need to take its features into account in the development process.

Choose a Method

Off-the-shelf development methods are often static prescriptions for "how-to" development; more fluid guidelines and a toolkit of techniques might be more appropriate. However, switching to new methodology entails high costs of adjustment. A better approach is to combine the best of existing practices and standards with the newer techniques to evolve an adaptable in-house Visual Basic 5 client/server development method. The key to a successful method is to manage risk while allowing development to proceed rapidly.

A desire for quality and technical purity encourages a rigorous approach to development. Methods such as SSADM (Structured Systems Analysis and Design Method) promote rigor and tend to be used with a waterfall life cycle. This approach works in traditional environments with skilled project managers. In unskilled hands, the level of rigor tends to be too high. When unplanned backtracking also occurs, costs soar and schedules slip. To counter this excessive rigor, iterative rapid application development (RAD) approaches are used. These often produce solutions with short lifetimes because they lack the framework more rigorous approaches provide.

Successful users of prototyping and rigorous methods have concluded that no one approach has all the answers. Controlling the development and project management processes is critical to the successful delivery of a system. Design requires high-quality management and good technicians. Controlled RAD applies rigor where necessary, and prototyping for specific goals can accelerate the development process. It allows you to balance the needs of the business, the limitations of a technical infrastructure, and the desire to deliver quickly.

As illustrated in Figure 16-4, a solid component-based architecture and reusable design patterns allow development activities to be carried out in parallel without compromising design quality. Development phases can be decoupled and development speeded up.

FIGURE 16-4

Decoupling the development process

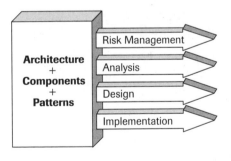

Rapid development is often thought unsuitable for applications in which the design is not visible at the user interface. Using business objects allows design to be taken out of the RAD life cycle. In simple terms, the RAD life cycle then consists of prototyping and gluing together business objects. Business objects, design patterns, and architecture are the key components that capture the design and enable RAD to take place.

ActiveX is Microsoft's component strategy and the core of Visual Basic 5. The new features in Visual Basic for enabling reuse provide a basis for developing a pattern- and component-based architecture.

A critical prerequisite for carrying out controlled RAD is that the main risks are understood and minimized. In taking on the newest version, version 5, of Visual Basic, a new set of risks have been created. Your first Visual Basic 5 project will not be a RAD project, whatever your intention—it will be a learning experience.

For a full discussion of methods, refer to Appendix E. This appendix includes a discussion of both the Microsoft Solutions Framework (MSF) and the Dynamic Systems Development Method (DSDM). These have both overlapping and contrasting approaches to those presented in this chapter.

CASE STUDY

To succeed, Visual Basic teams must work within an appropriate organizational structure, one in which the process of developing Visual Basic code is agreed on, well understood by all, and adhered to. Although the suggestions in the case study that follows are geared toward a particular real-world organization, some of the generalized suggestions are relevant for any Visual Basic 5 enterprise environment.

We were asked to "recommend an optimum Visual Basic 5 client/server development structure and process, irrespective of current process and structure." This request came from a new client who was intending to migrate from mainframe systems. We were asked to consider the following questions:

- How will Visual Basic software quality be maintained?
- How will people multitask across new Visual Basic application development and mainframe application maintenance and support?
- How will Visual Basic applications be installed, implemented, and deployed?
- How will individual projects fit in with an overall client/server architecture?
- How will the optimum culture and attitude be attained?

- How will we make the team dynamic and responsive?
- How will projects be properly planned, tracked, and managed, and who will be responsible for ensuring that this happens?
- How will code reuse be achieved?
- How should the company use prototyping?
- How will external components (for example, ActiveX Servers, DLLs, VBXs, OCXs, and Visual Basic classes) be assessed, procured, and controlled?

The process described below was the result of a series of workshops with in-house staff. A summary of the process is illustrated in Figure 16-5.

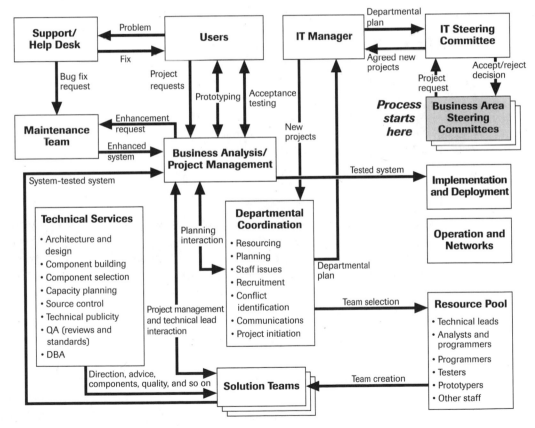

FIGURE 16-5 *A possible Visual Basic 5 development process*

The Process and the Players

The diagram in Figure 16-5 shows *process*, not necessarily *structure*, so the boxes should not be construed as "departments." The approach is very *project-based*. The boxes are essentially people or teams of people, and the arrows are the "things" that pass between them. The following subsections summarize what each person/team does.

Business area steering committees

There is one business area steering committee for each business area. Each committee meets periodically to discuss projects and priorities and to refine its "plan." Business area steering committees look ahead about 12 to 18 months. Any request for a new project they generate has to be submitted to the IT steering committee, where the request is either accepted or rejected.

IT steering committee

The IT steering committee meets quarterly and takes an overall view across the business areas. The IT manager is the IT department's representative on this committee. Considering both business priorities and the department's commitments and constraints, this committee accepts or rejects and prioritizes project requests from the business area steering committees. As do the business area steering committees, the IT steering committee looks ahead about 12 to 18 months.

IT manager

The IT manager needs to have an accurate picture of the activities of the entire department in order to commit (or not) to taking on a new project at the IT steering committee meeting. The departmental coordination team (see the following section) provides the *departmental plan* for this purpose. The IT manager informs the departmental coordination team of any new projects that have been committed to.

Departmental coordination

This "team" is the key to the process. It receives new project requests, maintains a departmental plan, manages resource levels, identifies project/resource conflicts, recruits, manages people issues (such as appraisals), promotes good departmental communications, and so on. When a new project starts, this team identifies a business analyst/project manager (see the next section) and a prototyper from the resource pool (see page 693) for that manager. Also, it creates a team from the resource pool to form a *solution team.* This team always has a *technical lead,* who is the day-to-day project team leader and is the liaison with the business analyst/project manager. The project plan that the business analyst/project manager draws up must be incorporated into the overall high-level departmental plan, and any amendments during the tracking of the project must also be incorporated. Incorporating these changes is an automated process.

Business analysis/Project management

The business analysis/project management team consists of people who are specialists in particular areas of the business. A business analyst/project manager is responsible for a project from start to finish, including both technical and user-related tasks (such as user training). These teams have a lot of user interaction and might receive project and enhancement requests from the users. They manage the requirements specification and prototyping. After the solution team has built the system, they are responsible for performing acceptance testing along with the users before passing the system on for implementation.

Resource pool

The resource pool is a virtual pool of people; that is, it doesn't exist as a team or department and hence requires no management. It's just a pool of people that the coordination team draws from to create solution teams. Its "members" possess a wide range of experience and skills. A person in the resource pool could at any one time be multitasking across projects and wearing different hats on different projects.

Solution teams

Solution teams are formed to actually produce the systems. Solution team members are responsible for the design, code, unit test, and system test of a system. They work closely with the technical services team (see the next section) and have the following responsibilities:

- Ensure that the project design fits with the overall architecture
- Reuse any generally available components
- Have their deliverables reviewed and sent through a quality assurance test

Technical services

The technical services team provides a wide range of technical services, mainly to the solution teams, including those listed at the top of the next page.

- Promote reuse by taking generally useful code from solution teams and turning it into robust components that other solution teams can benefit from
- Dictate the overall architecture that solution teams must fit their systems into
- Provide a QA function to ensure that solution teams are producing high-quality deliverables

Users

To get maximum benefit in the Visual Basic/RAD world, users need to become much more heavily involved with projects than they have traditionally—in fact, to the extent of becoming team members. Their role is particularly important during the early stages (such as helping to develop prototypes) of the process and toward the end, at acceptance test time.

Support/Help desk

The support/help desk serves a reactive function, typically receiving problem reports as its stimulus. These reports are either dealt with within the team or passed on to a maintenance team, who fixes problems.

Maintenance team

The maintenance team is a group of people staffed from the resource pool. Typically, a team member stays in the team for a period of about six months. The primary roles of the team are to deal with any bug fixing in live systems and to add small features requested by users. During slack periods, this team does housekeeping tasks, performs reviews for the solution teams, and the like. A dedicated maintenance team is required so that solution teams are not constantly interrupted by tactical firefighting and therefore have a better chance of sticking to project plans.

Implementation and deployment

This team implements systems in both the test and production environments.

Operations and networks

This team is responsible for the day-to-day operation of the environment, systems, and networks.

The need for consistency, coordination, and design *across* all projects is vital. In this case study, this framework is provided mainly by the coordination team and to a lesser extent by the IT manager and the technical services team.

Getting Started

It's all very well to live in an esoteric consulting world of process and structure, but how does one get started on a real-live project? At TMS, we feel that the best way to begin is to define a target process and structure for the organization and to evolve toward this off the back of a pilot, or Pathfinder, project. On balance, the Pathfinder approach is better than attempting to set up the new process and structure prior to the first project. And of course, it's essential to have the right people with the right skills.

Skill Requirements

Table 16-1 shows the skills that key personnel require to make a first Visual Basic 5 client/server project a success. This information should form the basis of individual training plans.

TABLE 16-1 _____ **Skills Required for a Successful Project** _____

Skill or Knowledge	Business Analysis	Development	Technical Services
Business knowledge and business analysis	High	Medium	Low
Project management	High	Low	Low
Database modeling	High	High	Medium
Help files, user documentation, and the like	High	Medium	Low
Awareness of component availability	Medium	High	High
Systems analysis	Low	High	Low
GUI design skills	Medium	High	Low
Visual Basic prototyping	Medium	High	Low
Client/server design	Medium	High	High
GUI testing	Medium	High	Medium
Visual Basic/VBA programming	Low	High	High
Diagnostics, logging, trace, error handling	Low	High	High
Windows operating system and the PC architecture, memory, and so on	Low	Medium	High
Connectivity, performance	Low	Medium	High
Networking	Low	Medium	High
Server operating system and database, DBA	Low	Medium	High
Security, back-out, recovery	Medium	Medium	High
Implementation, installation	Medium	Medium	High

Infrastructure Requirements

As well as finding people who possess the necessary skills to work on your project, you need to put an appropriate infrastructure in place. These infrastructure requirements should be implemented in parallel with the development of the pilot project. Be sure to allow adequate time in the schedules for these extra tasks.

Infrastructure Requirements

Corporate Visual Basic 5 client/server architecture and strategy

General application design standards

Data design standards

Client/server guidelines (such as connectivity method, use of stored procedures)

GUI style guide

Coding standards

Distribution, installation, implementation, and upgrade guidelines

Development environments (such as development, test, and production servers)

Source control software and associated procedures

Powerful, standardized developers' PCs fully configured with Visual Basic, Microsoft Access, relevant (and tested) custom controls, and a range of supporting utilities and tools

Fully configured and tested server database with associated tools to add test data, stored procedures, and the like

Fully implemented and tested workstation-to-server connectivity (should include network software, ODBC drivers, and so on)

Education and training of those providing any of the above or filling technical roles

THE EARLY STAGES

It is essential that a project get off to the right start. In this section, we detail some of the methods and approaches we use at TMS to make sure this happens.

Vertical Partitioning Means 80 Percent Complete Is 80 Percent Delivered

Who begins too much accomplishes little.

German proverb

Analysis should support the design, implementation, and management processes. If you're using an incremental approach, you should be able to partition the analysis vertically to investigate part of the problem in detail and to defer looking at other areas until later. You should also be able to design and implement each partition without analyzing the other areas in detail. The business architecture will provide the context for any partition. This approach will help you judge the suitability of an application for incremental development and the potential stability of a specific partition.

Partitioning allows you to consider different parts of the problem in isolation. Vertical partitioning allows you to proceed with designing and building the application incrementally with the confidence that rework will be minimal. It also allows the business needs to drive design, build, and roll out. Once the technical foundation is in place, an incremental implementation that meets business priorities can happen. Using an object-oriented approach from analysis to coding allows this incremental implementation to occur.

The careful specification and use of business-oriented ActiveX servers will provide a vertically partitioned design. Late binding and generally decoupling increments will reduce the need for recompilation and rework. From this point of view, out-of-process servers are better than in-process ones. Maintainability should normally rank above performance, a priority you need to make clear early on. (One of the biggest criticisms about a system is often its performance because it's an aspect that is all too visible, whereas maintainability can easily be overlooked since it won't become an issue until after the initial delivery of the system is complete.) Vertical partitioning allows parallel streams of design and build to take place. This partitioning provides rapid development at low risk without increasing costs.

Cut the Politics and Get Serious

**The culture acts against quality—"pass the buck" or "shoot the messenger"
managers are playing politics, for example, holding back the bad news,
hoping other projects will fail first....**

Project review

The early stages of a project often bring into focus internal and external politics that can cause project failure. You need to cut through the politics to get the job done right. Challenge inertia and self-interest. If you want to maintain your integrity, this is better than playing politics. But it's just as unsafe. Cutting through politics requires a project manager with guts—preferably one who is financially secure!

Most projects will have some requirements that are relatively simple and don't require great user involvement to achieve. These are ideal deliverables for the early stages of a project. The team is able to demonstrate what it can achieve. The challenge is then to get the right level of user commitment to ensure the same productivity when a high level of user involvement is needed.

To achieve technical objectives, you might have to bypass IT procedures and common practice. You can often circumvent the system like this when you do it on a limited scale. To deliver major projects, however, such practices and procedures might need to be changed.

Dare to Choose Staff Who Have the Right Stuff

Everyone has talent. What is rare is the courage to follow the talent to the dark place where it leads.

Erica Jong

Those who really care about quality and want to do a good job are often considered mavericks by the organization they work for. They don't fit in, they don't play the political game, and they don't strive to move into the management hierarchy.

Staff who argue their points, don't accept decisions at face value, and insist on doing things the right way can be difficult to manage. They can be a thorn in the manager's side. They might insist on being paid more than their manager. They do build better systems, though; they build systems that are maintainable, meet business needs, and are less costly. They *are* probably worth more than their manager.

See the Big Picture, Plan for Change

You can observe a lot just by watching.

Berra's law

Most experienced developers have at some point felt frustrated because the applications they are maintaining or having to extract data from have not been designed for change. They have probably also experienced this frustration from the other side—frustration that they are not provided with the time or resources to develop a system that provides a flexible but sound foundation for future work.

Data from one application is often reused in multiple applications. The second and subsequent uses are often unanticipated, resulting in a range of problems. For example, data quality might be poor or new databases with gross data transformations between the new and the old databases might be required. (See Figure 16-6 for examples of bad and good data management planning.) The problems arise because the original application was not designed in the context of a corporate long-term view. Without a forward-looking view, some data is not captured and overoptimized structures are used. A business architecture provides a logical view of function and data and attempts to anticipate future needs. To design an application successfully (where success is viewed over the

Figure 16-6

Design for the future

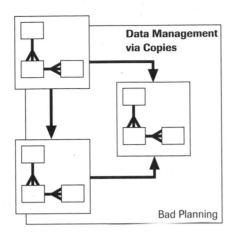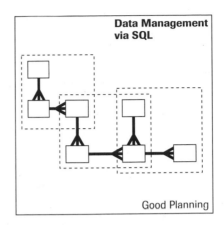

lifetime of the application), you must take the bigger picture into account. A well-planned application can grow organically as new requirements emerge. To plan and design solely for the current application creates problems for the future. For example, databases might not be structured flexibly to support future queries; designs might be highly optimized for a particular application but prove to be inadequate for a subsequent application or after maintenance. Producing reusable business rules and generic code tends to take a low priority if the focus is only on the current project. Designing logically, based on a high-level view of core business operations, tends to produce a reusable design that will support multiple applications at the database and code levels.

WAYS OF ENSURING QUALITY

We started this chapter wondering about a Visual Basic quality crisis. As you've seen, many good practices seem to have been ignored. People who should have known better have gotten caught up in the productivity trap made so obvious by this special development tool. So how can you avoid the same trap? The old adage about an ounce of prevention being better than a pound of cure applies to Visual Basic systems development—there's no better way of eradicating problems in a system than by not putting them into the code in the first place.

The best way to improve the quality of Visual Basic team developments is to introduce a formal review process. Reviews are also known as walkthroughs or inspections—nothing new, but rarely found in the Visual Basic world. We believe that defining standards is not enough: the standards also need to be policed, preferably by an independent QA team. Some excellent tools on the market automate this procedure.

The objectives of a review process must include these:

- To ensure standards are adhered to
- To improve the quality of software
- To improve communication between developers
- To improve code reuse

From experience, we've found that a review process is worthwhile only if it has total management backing; that is, implementation should be blocked until all reviews have passed in all circumstances, regardless of the business pressures to go ahead. Essential documents are a style guide (or user interface guide) and a set of standards, both of which should be second nature to all developers.

At TMS, we use a three-stage review process:

1. **Requirements.** This review gives the designer and developer an opportunity to ensure that the quality of the requirements specification document produced by the analyst is high enough and that it accurately and unambiguously describes the system.

2. **Design.** This review is further segmented into two reviews:

    - A first design review is carried out about 20 percent of the way through the design phase. This review is informal and normally involves the designer explaining the outline of the design on a whiteboard. This review verifies that the proposed design approach is sound. (It's better to catch any design flaws early on, rather than waiting until a detailed design specification has been produced.) At this point, the team can agree on which reviews should follow; a modified review process can be appropriate depending on the project circumstances.

    - A second design review is carried out at the end of the design phase. This review is much more formal than the initial design review and involves careful scrutiny of the design and the design documents produced.

3. **Code.** This review is also further segmented into two reviews:

    - A first review is carried out 20 percent of the way through the coding phase. This review verifies that the proposed coding approach is sound and that standards are being followed.

    - A second review is carried out at the end of the coding phase. This review is more formal than the initial code review.

While it probably seems that this review process will cause a lot of extra effort, we have found that it actually saves a tremendous amount of time and cost in the long run.

There are, of course, many more ways to improve quality. For example, testing properly, maintaining metrics so that Visual Basic projects can be measured, and doing postimplementation reviews are just a few additional ways of monitoring quality.

Demand More Rigor, Not Less

It's a funny thing about life; if you refuse to accept anything but the best, you very often get it.

Somerset Maugham

A desire for quality and technical purity encourages a rigorous approach to development. Formal methods such as VDM (Vienna Development Method), Z, and B are rarely used in commercial development. But methods that promote rigor (such as SSADM) continue to have a high level of use. Do they work? They can work well in the hands of skilled project managers who know what to use and what to leave out for a specific project. In unskilled hands, the level of rigor applied tends to be higher than necessary, project costs soar, and schedules slip.

In some organizations, the consequence of the failure of rigor is that business managers decide to do their own development. In others, hacking takes over. Visual Basic 3 was one of the main tools of the hackers. To continue to use this approach with Visual Basic 5 is at best a waste and at worst a disaster. The development process for a project should be decided by the project manager with the guidance of the analysts and designers. Prescribing a method from outside the project does not work. A Pathfinder approach provides a mechanism for understanding major projects before you commit large numbers of staff to them.

Teach the Fundamentals

As far as the code is concerned, there appear to have been several passes through it. The later passes introduced several bugs. The person or people involved do not appear to understand the Visual Basic event model.

Code review

Tools and methods are only as good as the people who use them. They are no substitute for training. Staff must know *why* as well as *how*. The *why* comes first.

The basics of computing—how chips work, how memory is used, what operating systems and algorithms do—are all essentials for IT professionals. The lack of this fundamental knowledge means that developers cannot use powerful tools such as Visual Basic 5 effectively. They need to understand exactly what the tool is doing and how it works. This knowledge is even more important as the tools become more powerful because they hide so much. To use distributed objects effectively, for example, one has to understand how the technical mechanisms that create the objects work, not just how to make them work. How is a local call turned into a remote call? What is the effect on the network? How does it perform with high transaction rates? What is the impact of other network traffic?

The fundamentals of software engineering must be taught to staff. The principles of data management, security, configuration management, project control, and so on apply to all development approaches. The divisions and disciplines of separate development, test, and production environments are critical to successful implementation. The ability to produce code quickly in Visual Basic 5 doesn't relieve developers and managers of the duty to produce the right code and to use the technical infrastructure correctly and efficiently.

Commit to Staff

Good people are good because they've come to wisdom through failure.

William Saroyan

Good software developers are infinitely better than average ones. The only people worth having on the team are those who are very good and those who are very eager to learn. You can tell people who are good at their jobs a mile off. A team of people who are proud of their work is a thousand times better than a team of average people. High-quality teams lead to real team spirit. At TMS, our hiring process includes a strictly monitored 2½-hour written Visual Basic examination. We never rely on just résumés, references, and interviews. We firmly believe in small, highly skilled teams.

In Visual Basic teams, there is a danger of everyone "doing it all." The Visual Basic 5 box is deceptively small, but there's an awful lot in there (like Dr. Who's TARDIS). Most Visual Basic programmers become jacks-of-all-trades but, of course, masters of none. We therefore believe in specialists across the teams.

Because of Visual Basic's high productivity, it's possible to reach a productivity saturation point long before achieving competency. "Productive incompetent" programmers are the result. Visual Basic programmers need much better education and training. Most employers seem to think that sticking their mainframe programmers in a five-day introductory course is enough. Wrong, wrong, wrong. So many times, we've seen people with inadequate training— for example, with no understanding of the workings of the Microsoft Windows operating system—building mission-critical Visual Basic applications. They assume that they are working in a protected environment with "limitless" resources, just as in the mainframe world. Visual Basic programmers should have a thorough understanding of Windows as well as Visual Basic functionality and syntax. They should also spend at least six months working alongside an experienced Windows/Visual Basic mentor before being let anywhere near an important development project.

Visual Basic 5 client/server development requires that developers have a broad range of technical skills and understanding that covers front-end, middleware, and back-end technologies. Products such as Visual Basic are getting bigger and more sophisticated. Rapid development means shorter analysis, design, and coding stages. Effective staff utilization dictates that the same staff are used across all stages. The implication is that higher-caliber, better-trained, and better-paid staff are needed. Visual Basic 5 client/server development requires stronger analysis because of the more competitive business environment. Design, testing, deployment, and support skills need to be stronger because of the more complex technical environment.

Project managers must be technically competent and have strong business and interpersonal skills. Their management of the users and their own teams has grown more difficult. With the breadth of skills required and the pace of technical change, it is unlikely that team members will have a full set of the required skills. Working together to solve problems, to experiment, to learn, and to cover skill gaps is essential to Visual Basic 5 client/server development. Project managers must build time for learning into the schedules. If overall development costs are not to rise, greater productivity must be achieved. The quality of project management is the key issue in building teams and commitment. A project manager must be a good team builder and team leader.

Some of us have had the rare experience of working in highly cohesive, effective, productive, supportive, and fun teams. From a management perspective, productivity and effectiveness are the only important factors. But these two factors don't come without the others; in fact, they are a result of having developed a supportive, cohesive, and fun environment. Unfortunately, such teams often break down after a short period. Few managers have the skills or support to build and maintain such teams. The best organizations have human resources departments that provide management training and facilitate team development. Some managers treat team building with cynicism. They are fools who are making their own jobs much harder.

Many organizations build teams successfully and then destroy them. Staff must be motivated by training, advancement, recognition, involvement, and money. They must not be demotivated by lack of respect, unreasonable pressure, long hours, or lack of consultation on matters that affect them.

In the case study, we recommended a resource pool—but beware. You can have a resource pool of laptop computers, of cars, of overhead projectors, or of any inanimate objects. You can manipulate them with little thought. People deserve better. They are not things to be moved about on a whim. The resource-pool concept needs to be handled carefully. A good team is more important, more productive, and more effective than the best methods, the best tools, or the best organizational structure. The priority must be on building and maintaining a good team. This investment provides the greatest payoff.

If you commit to staff, they are more likely to commit to you. And successful Visual Basic 5 client/server development requires high levels of commitment from staff. They need to spend their own time researching their tools, and they need to be encouraged to do so. Their commitment must be reciprocated in terms of salary, holidays, working hours, personal development, training, respect, and fun. Good staff can command high contract rates and are mobile. Reward them or lose them. The value of providing appropriate rewards outweighs the costs of poor productivity and poor quality.

Project teams using Visual Basic for client/server projects are often weak in their server-side skills. This is particularly serious where this extends to the project management and designers. Project managers might not schedule the time or resources to carry out physical design or be aware of the risks inherent in their project. It is essential for successful completion of any project that a realistic view of the skills required and those possessed be taken.

There are no experts

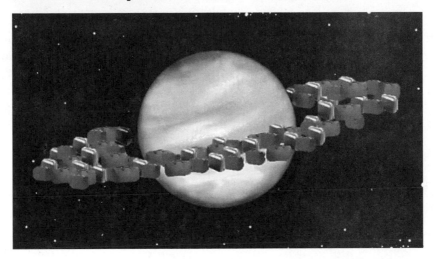

The scientific theory I like best is that the rings of Saturn are composed entirely of lost airline luggage.

Mark Russell

The rate of change in hardware, system software, and development tools means that there are no experts. Visual Basic 3 or Visual Basic 4 gurus are not Visual Basic 5 gurus. With lack of expertise and rapidly changing environments, it's difficult to build a stable and effective technical infrastructure. It's even harder to get good advice on how to use that infrastructure.

A development project is unlikely to have teams with all the skills required in sufficient depth to deliver the project. A realistic assessment of the skills required and those possessed should take place. Any deficiency should be filled for the project and a longer-term solution developed. A good approach is to employ external consultants who have skills transfer as part of their experience. It makes no sense to incur extra expense by continually running to outside resources for core skills.

Three roles are essential in designing Visual Basic 5 client/server systems:

- The system architect creates the overall conceptual design.
- The system designer carries out the detailed specification of the executable code and the implementation.
- The DBA is the database technical expert.

Other experts, such as language or network gurus, might be required to solve particular problems. In addition to these roles, the complexity of the systems demands external review.

You can learn a lot from those who have more experience, so form a partnership to learn more. The problems are complex, and so are the solutions. You might never know whether you have the best solution because the technology is moving on before it is proved. We repeat, there are no experts!

WHY ARE YOU PROTOTYPING?

Spend sufficient time confirming the need and the need will disappear.
Specification Dynamics

Beware of the prototyping trap. If you ask two programmers on the same Visual Basic team what a prototype is, you're likely to get two different answers. Often the team is unclear whether or not the prototype is a throwaway. Ensure that the term "prototype" is well defined and that everyone (including the users) is familiar with this definition. You might even choose to define different types of prototypes. The big trap is to leave the prototype ill defined. We have seen this lead to much grief on many Visual Basic projects. Prototyping in general has been given a bad name because of frequent misuse.

Delivering quickly is often the justification for a prototyping approach to development. But without control, the "what" that is delivered usually fails to meet the business needs for robustness and maintainability.

To be successful, prototyping must have specific goals, such as these:

- Goals to demonstrate feasibility
- Analysis goals to discover or confirm requirements
- Design goals to prove the technology or an approach to implementation
- Implementation goals to evolve a working system with user involvement within a predefined technical architecture

Uncontrolled prototyping, without goals, without a development strategy to produce an application architecture, is doomed. It is hacking with respectability.

Prototyping can be used at various stages during development. The key principle that will ensure prototyping is used correctly is to precisely define the objectives of the prototype and then ensure that appropriate disciplines are used to deliver these objectives. Rules such as "Prototypes must be thrown away" are unnecessarily restrictive.

Creating a Foundation with a Pathfinder Project

If you have built castles in the air, your work need not be lost; that is where they should be. Now put the foundations under them.

Henry David Thoreau

You might not have the luxury of being able to start with a small noncritical project to learn about Visual Basic 5 client/server development. If this is the case, start with a Pathfinder project. The concept of the Pathfinder project was developed to handle the risks in large-scale Visual Basic 5 client/server development. It is aimed primarily at the technical risks, but it does provide an opportunity to address business and people risks. It provides a good foundation from which you can build a successful application. (See Figure 16-7.) Such a project is a significant undertaking, usually requiring the full-time attention of three to five of the best development staff for three to six months. This time frame is dictated by the volume of work to be performed and the high caliber of staff needed to perform it. But it is time and effort well spent.

Figure 16-7

In the absence of architecture, components, and patterns, initiate a Pathfinder project to produce them.

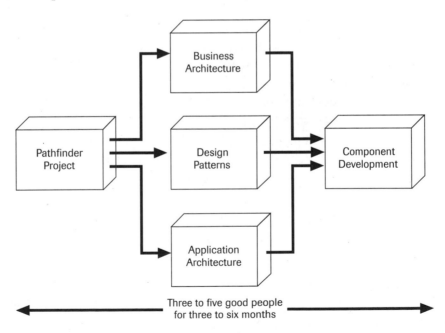

You need to ensure that the application will fit with other applications and will reuse components and ideas. You need to gain appropriate user involvement and commitment. You need to determine team structures and skill requirements and work out the project management approach and the development process. The objectives of the Pathfinder development must be considered nearly impossible to achieve in order to ensure that only commitment from the top and the elimination of politics will achieve them. The Pathfinder project will tackle the difficult things first. It will prove the infrastructure and the techniques for exploiting it. A Pathfinder project kick-starts the process of ongoing research. This process should stop only when the technology stops changing.

Usually some of the work will have been done as part of other projects. This will reduce the workload, but it will still be necessary to bring the various strands of work together to meet the Pathfinder objectives.

A Pathfinder project will include the following objectives:

- Developing a logical business architecture (This architecture is best expressed as a high-level logical business object model.)
- Developing a technical system architecture that will adequately support all the technical requirements, such as database updates, maintainability, and performance
- Developing design patterns and frameworks to address anticipated design problems, such as bulk data movements, locking strategies, and error handling
- Demonstrating that the technical architecture can deliver at least one significant business requirement to a production environment
- Providing an initial knowledge base
- Developing a core team of technical experts who can provide technical supervision and mentoring to other staff
- Identifying the skills required to complete the project

With a new development tool, it is essential that these areas be revisited and fully understood. The people carrying out the investigation need to be among the best developers. They need to be in touch with day-to-day development issues. They need to know what is important.

Proving the Technical Architecture

The doctor can bury his mistakes, but an architect can only advise his client to plant vines.

Frank Lloyd Wright

Can you describe simply how an application is partitioned into a number of discrete components, each of which has a specific purpose? Can you describe how these components interact? Can you describe how and why each component uses the technical infrastructure? Can you describe how a change to a component or to the technical infrastructure will affect the performance of the application? If you have difficulty answering these questions and the system architecture seems to look like that in Figure 16-8, the application probably doesn't have a coherent and efficient underlying structure to it. Maintenance is likely to be a major problem. An application requires a sound technical foundation that has been proved.

FIGURE 16-8

A technical architecture?

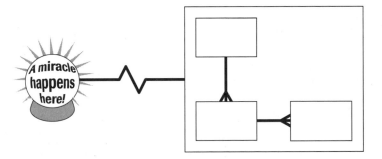

Typically, a layered architecture will be adopted to improve maintainability by isolating different implementation technologies from one another and from the core business logic of the application. It is vital that the technology for building components and for communicating among components be thoroughly tested and benchmarked. The robustness and performance characteristics must be understood so that sound designs can be created and technical risks managed.

Layering insulates an application from change. If used appropriately with an object-based approach, layering can reduce dependencies in project scheduling by insulating one part of an application from another.

The layering model can be as simple or as complex as required for the technical environment. For example, at TMS, we have used a 10-layer model to describe and categorize the elements of a complex Visual Basic client/server system. The model shown in Figure 16-9 on the next page is for a much simpler system.

FIGURE 16-9

A layered architecture

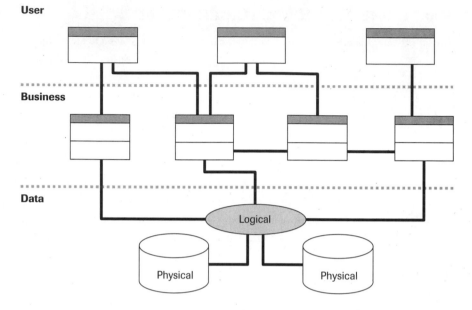

Where the application will be physically partitioned, the deployment mechanisms should be understood. In particular, you should assess the process and the impact of repeated deployment. Operations staff who deploy systems should be aware of possible version conflicts and any special installation requirements. In particular, they should understand how the registration database is used by all the applications that they install.

In the short time between Visual Basic 3 and Visual Basic 5, relatively few major projects were completed using a fully object-oriented approach to developing a distributed Visual Basic 4 application. Some that attempted it produced poor results because the technology was not adequately proved before the project began. With any new product, it is essential that you establish how it works.

Proof of Concept

As mentioned earlier, a key objective of the Pathfinder project is to prove to the business managers and to the IT teams that a business function can be delivered using the application architecture. Using the Pathfinder reduces the perceived risk substantially.

The proof of concept must include thorough testing of the application architecture. Such testing will cover, for example, stress testing the architecture. The architecture should be proven to be a viable basis on which to develop the entire application. Proof of concept includes delivery of the business function into a simulation of a live environment by those who would normally deliver the application. It should be delivered to the user for testing. Difficulties in managing rapid development in the IT department and in the business will be highlighted. Prove that you can deliver. Prove it to the business management, to the technicians, and to the skeptics!

FOCUSING ON DESIGN

Imagination is more important than knowledge.

Albert Einstein

When challenged, most Visual Basic developers would claim they design their applications. Unfortunately, we see little evidence of this. Technical specifications are becoming historical curiosities. It seems that most Visual Basic programmers cannot resist the temptation to start coding on Day 1 and then code, code, and code some more. What's wrong with using pencil and paper and applying a little thought up front to get a handle on a problem? By contrast, tackling, say, a large C++-based development is not easy at the best of times, and developers quickly learn that unless they invest some time in designing carefully, they will waste a lot of time and their development will almost certainly fail. How does this attitude compare with that of Visual Basic developers? We feel that Visual Basic is often abused. It's so easy to build an application that, rather than choose to design, developers build instead; that is, they take the "try it and see" approach to software development. In the Visual Basic 5 enterprise environment, this kind of approach spells disaster.

We recommend that not only must you create a design, you must make sure it fits in with an overall corporate architecture. The application design should be objectized, by building common objects and designing them for reuse. Error handling and debugging aids must be designed in from the start. When it comes to external components and objects, be careful not to include them in your design without properly assessing their quality and their potential impact on your application and on Windows. For example, at TMS, we run all potential custom controls under the Windows debugging kernel—it's often very revealing! Measure the effect on Windows resources of using a particular control, especially if your design means the control has to be multiply instantiated. More broadly, we recommend that external components and objects be assessed, procured, and controlled centrally—and with much care and thought.

What Is Design?

Design is the process of taking a business requirement and applying the constraints of technology, finance, and time. It is a compromise between the needs of a business and the limitations of the computer. It is a mixture of art and science; it is engineering. Design requires its participants to be masters of business and technology in order to draw the appropriate compromise. Designers need to be communicators and influencers. They need to be leaders.

Designers must possess current business and technical knowledge. The introduction of Visual Basic 5 demands that designers work to understand the new technical environment. A design is a specification for building an application. It applies architectural principle to a specific system. The strategy for implementation must be determined as part of the design. The system must function within the technical infrastructure of a business.

A logical model specifies what is required. For the model to be implemented, it must be tempered with reality. The design model has to be accurate to be implemented. The design model might be very different from the logical model. Rarely can the logical model be implemented directly; unfortunately, many try to do just that. For example, it is well known that a third normal form database design often performs poorly, but it's often tried because a logical database design doesn't take performance into account. A design model has to include all the data, not just the data that was thought of. It has to include all the processing, including the housekeeping and the audit trails. It has to account for peculiarities in database query optimization. It should consider the skills of the team, the build strategy, configuration management, and a host of other things that the analyst who creates the logical model can safely ignore.

Logical modeling should occur at the start of the design—and a long way from the end. Design requires detailed technical knowledge of the implementation environment. That environment includes not just technology but people too. The conversion of a logical data model to a robust and efficient physical design is a complex process that must be performed by the system designer in conjunction with the technical specialists. Only together can they make the appropriate compromises between business needs and technical constraints. The system designer from the application development team is unlikely to have the technical knowledge to make best use of the technology. The technical specialist is unlikely to understand where the business can compromise and where it cannot (or will not).

The process of design starts during the feasibility stage and continues throughout the life of a Visual Basic 5 client/server project. Design does not follow analysis; it is more likely to precede it. Design is then a process of gradual refinement from high-level strategies to detailed specification that is continually influenced by and influences analysis. Requirements are generally unstable. They might be specified differently by different people. The software crisis is not in requirements gathering and specification, but in design. Designs must be able to cope with change and uncertainty. A successful system will change, but only a well-architected system will cope effectively with this change and at low cost. The focus of a project must be on design.

What Is *Not* Design?

Never play leapfrog with a unicorn.
  Confucius on gamesmanship

Certain common techniques can create the illusion of design. Each technique has its proper place in development but does not constitute design in its own right. The importance of design must be considered and acknowledged in project planning. There are no alternatives to design if robust and maintainable systems are to be delivered. In some situations, you can use valid shortcuts, but they must be considered carefully and planned. Design is a compromise between business needs and technological capabilities. This means that design decisions are management decisions and that designers need to be aware of business requirements.

A thin GUI produced from evolutionary prototyping might be placed in front of a set of cooperating business objects derived from a business-object model. But prototyping alone is unlikely to produce a coherent design for business objects. These must be designed separately. Prototyping is not design.

A logical model is not design. It is abstract. A design needs to take into account the implementation environment. In Visual Basic 5 client/server development, the environment and potential impacts on other systems are complex. You need to adopt a benchmarking strategy to test and refine a design.

Data modeling is not design. Data modeling approaches to development assume that processing consists of simple inquiries and updates. GUI interfaces enable highly complex transactions to be built (for example, hierarchies and networks built as a single unit of work). The physical design to achieve performance and data integrity can be complex and can require separate modeling.

CASE tools do not guarantee good design. A mass of diagrams and dictionary prints can give the impression of detailed consideration. CASE tools improve productivity regardless of quality and talent, but they should be given only to those capable of doing the job without the tools. Few CASE tools provide adequate support for physical design. To do so, they would have to incorporate a model of the physical infrastructure and its performance characteristics.

Developing Design Patterns

It might not be possible to capture a generic solution in code effectively, but it might be possible to describe an approach or some techniques that will address the problem. Patterns document design experience. They distill design knowledge and allow it to be reused. Visual Basic 5 client/server systems require that considerable thought be given to software and data architecture. You can understand the nature of some of the problems by using simulation and benchmarking, which can help you evaluate potential solutions. Design guidance can be documented. Solution frameworks can be built to encapsulate partial solutions.

Patterns for the solution and demonstration of layering, partitioning, deployment, locking, database access, error handling, application structure, and so on should be developed using Visual Basic 5. Such patterns will then form the foundation for successful future development. If a preexisting design fits the architecture of the solution, the move from requirement to implementation can happen very quickly, making it seem as if there is no design phase.

When software houses come up with seemingly unrealistic estimates for delivering systems and subsequently achieve them, they are often using preexisting designs. They judge carefully whether their client's requirement fits the architecture of their solution. They work with a limited range of applications. They move from requirement to implementation quickly, beginning with a rapid design assessment to ensure that preexisting designs fit the requirements. Design patterns and application frameworks provide architectures for building applications. Much of the thinking has been done. Provided the new application is a close fit to the pattern or framework, rapid conversion of the requirements to code can be achieved with relatively little effort spent on design.

The application must be judged to fit the design. Careful thought must go into those parts of the application that fall outside the scope of the pattern or framework. But with a close fit, the design process can be shortened.

Examples of design patterns

Consider these four uses of design patterns:

- Front end to back end bulk data movements
- Error handling schemes
- Name and address deduplication
- Executive information systems

These are examples in which design patterns have been derived and used to reduce development costs and project schedules. The first two examples are generic technical problems, and the second two are business problems. In each, a completely coded generic solution cannot be produced, but a large amount of the design work can be reused in a subsequent application. Much of this design work can be captured in templates or libraries of classes.

Visual Basic 5 provides facilities for capturing patterns through two new mechanisms: the introduction of a form of inheritance through the use of the *Implements* keyword; and templates, which provide a starting point for custom code. This starting point can capture the key design ideas without the rigidity of finished and working code.

Benchmark-Driven Design

When choosing between two evils, I always like to try the one I've never tried before.

Mae West

Benchmarking is critical to successful physical design. You should carry it out early using representative models of the system to determine what strategies you should employ for different classes of problems (for example, moving large amounts of data from the front end to the back end or locking). Testing with models should include stress testing in such areas as high transaction rates, multiuser testing, and impacts on other systems. Designing the system incorrectly for these types of problems is expensive once the system has been written. With representative benchmarking carried out early, you should be able to upgrade servers and networks if required. Benchmarking will also give you an early indication of whether the application should be distributed over multiple servers or whether the design can remain simple. Where benchmarks show potential problems, you should evaluate alternative solutions. A set of solutions with varying performance characteristics, costs, and complexities will emerge. This process will enable the designer to select the most appropriate solution from a menu of solutions. These solutions are design patterns.

Benchmark-driven design is essential in Visual Basic 5 client/server applications in which there is a mix of technologies and a large potential for bottlenecks. The aim is to ensure that the technical infrastructure and the approach to using the infrastructure in the application will meet business needs for performance and reliability. To do this, you'll need to develop a model of the system. The performance characteristics and options for Visual Basic 5 are very different from Visual Basic 3 or Visual Basic 4. On the whole, version 5 has great improvements—improvements that provide opportunities. For example, developing ActiveX components for remote activation sometimes had to be ruled out under Visual Basic 4 because of poor performance of the interpreted code. Using compiled code under Visual Basic 5 provides a massive performance boost and allows you to use Visual Basic where C or C++ was previously used.

UNDERSTANDING OBJECTS

When the plane you are on is late, the plane you want to transfer to is on time.
The Airplane Law

Visual Basic has gradually become more and more object oriented, and Visual Basic 5 has continued this trend. Whether Visual Basic 5 is fully object oriented according to some academic's definition is irrelevant. However, it is vital to recognize that the only way to build successful systems using Visual Basic 5 is to develop them from an object-oriented design. An object-oriented design can be developed successfully only from an object-oriented analysis. Object-oriented analysis revolves around the identification of business objects. Identifying business objects responsible for data and function eliminates duplication of data and function.

Using business objects allows you to design incrementally. It also forms a basis for reuse. Using business objects in analysis and design provides traceability and allows the specification to evolve seamlessly by the addition of implementation detail rather than by going through translations from one form of model to another.

Business objects encapsulate data and function and form a natural basis for identifying business-oriented components. Analysis approaches that separate function and data make it more difficult to build a comprehensive component architecture. You will want to package the classes that are developed into larger components, ActiveX servers. These can be considered large objects. The message is that if you are to adopt Visual Basic 5 successfully, you must adopt object orientation.

Business objects are inherently traceable to business concepts and requirements. Implementing business objects through Visual Basic 5 class modules carries through this traceability into applications. Using a business-object–based application architecture allows the design and coding of objects to be carried out independently of the design and coding of the application. This allows a large amount of flexibility in developing project plans and is the basis of high levels of reuse.

Investing in Reuse

After things have gone from bad to worse, the cycle will repeat itself.
Farnsdick's corollary

As you saw in Chapter 15, reuse is an obvious source of medium- and long-term benefits to an organization. Visual Basic 5 provides a series of new features to help in this area. These new features require investment of time and, as a result, money for a business to benefit from them. This is where we hit the tired old argument about "Who will pay for reuse?" It should be recognized that reusability is a function of good design. This is true regardless of whether or not reuse is a design objective. A good design supports change, it supports the unknown future, and it is flexible. These characteristics give reusability.

The required investment in many major organizations is in design and designers. This is often an unpalatable truth to be faced. You need to actively look for things that can be reused from other applications. Each project should have a task attached to it for "trawling" or "scavenging" for reuse. If the organization has an organized reuse catalog of components and patterns, this is an obvious starting point. However, few organizations appear to have done such cataloging well, if at all.

An effective approach is to schedule a series of short meetings with the design leaders in other projects. At these meetings, discuss the existing application and the new application both technically and from the business point of view and identify similarities. These areas of similarity should point to reuse. Then take a guided tour of the similar parts of each application. Reuse any applicable code, ideas, or good practices. Generally speaking, one workweek should be sufficient for trawling.

Contribute to the reuse catalog, or start one. Reuse comes for free with good design. Duplication is a product of politics.

FINDING THE RIGHT TOOLS

Many a time we've been down to our last piece of fatback. And I'd say, "Should we eat it or render it down for soap?" Your Uncle Jed would say, "Render it down. God will provide food for us poor folks, but we gotta do our washin'."

Granny, *The Beverly Hillbillies*

Basic data modeling tools are adequate for small-scale development. If application development is extended to large-scale Visual Basic 5 client/server development, a sophisticated CASE tool is required that supports object modeling and partitioning the application into components that can be distributed among processors. Such a tool will require a higher level of expertise to use. A source code control system will be required to manage the software and documentation when applications become of significant size or complexity.

An essential part of managing the risk in Visual Basic 5 client/server development is testing performance under realistic stresses. Load-testing tools are available to assist in this process. Other classes of test tools test the user interface and the code structure.

To use such tools effectively, you must first understand them and then use a method to guide their use during development. Most tools and methods are not mature; some might not exist. Test the methods with the tools. Old methods might not be appropriate or might need adapting.

CONFIGURATION MANAGEMENT: JUST DO IT!

The greatest pleasure in life is doing what people say you cannot do.

Walter Bagehot

Configuration management is one of those tedious details that are often not implemented or are poorly observed. The problems caused by the lack of good configuration management become apparent only when it's too late to do the job properly. A project manager must ensure that code versions are managed across all implementation environments. Yes, that does include the mainframe JCL, the SQL, and the documentation. The structure of the database, the versions of any DLLs, ActiveX servers, operating system and network components, documentation, and procedures should also be under configuration management. Does your source code control software make it easy to manage the configuration of the entire system? Has anyone figured out how to do it? Probably not, so you'll have some work ahead of you to work it out and get it right. Do it now!

A Visual Basic 5 client/server application can have many interacting pieces of software. Changes in the configuration of each piece can cause ripple effects into other components. Code effects can be managed by maintaining consistent interfaces. Changes in loads and performance characteristics might require changes in other components. New versions should always be extensively tested before implementation. The potential for changes being required or imposed in interfaces grows with the number of interacting components.

Dependencies among components might be disguised. (For example, the query "Select * from X" includes an implied column ordering.) Rolling out an application or a new version can be a nightmare. Configuration management controls need to be handed over at the end of development to those carrying out support. It makes sense to involve support staff early so that their requirements are included in the configuration management plan.

One of the biggest challenges in configuration management is to make the controls supportive to the developer. If they are not, creative talents will be turned toward breaking the system.

DOCUMENTATION

When all else fails, read the instructions.
> **Cahn's axiom**

Documentation might be boring, but it's vital. The following (minimal) documentation set works well for Visual Basic applications:

Functional/Requirements Specification

The requirements should be written down, and this specification should reference a Visual Basic prototype rather than embed screen shots in the document. As a result, the document and the prototype together constitute the signed-off requirements. This combination provides a much more realistic representation of the requirements and leads to a solution that is much closer to what the users really want.

Design Specification

A concise design specification should be produced (and maintained). It should describe the key design points.

Excellently Commented Code

This form of documentation is key. In our experience, other forms of documentation invariably become out-of-date. How many times have you been asked to make a change to someone else's code? Do you trust the documentation, or do you review the comments and the code itself to find "the truth"? High-quality module and subroutine headers, excellent block and in-line comments, and good naming conventions are the best types of documentation possible. At TMS, we have tools that build "documentation" from the source files—it's a good test of the standard of commenting.

Test Plan

Testing within Visual Basic teams is generally too informal and ad hoc. Writing a test plan forces some advance thought and planning.

TESTING

Any nontrivial program contains at least one bug. There are no trivial programs.
Seventh Law of Computer Programming

Historically, testing complex team-based applications has been broken down into two main areas: unit testing and system testing. In unit testing, the modules of the system are tested as individual units. Each unit has definite input and output parameters and (often) a definite single function. In system testing, the system is tested as a whole; that is, intercommunication among the individual units and functions of the complete system is tested.

Many of the problems experienced with testing Visual Basic applications occur because testers are trying to apply these conventional methods to systems for which they aren't appropriate. There are fundamental differences in the ways that Visual Basic applications work compared with old-style applications. In Visual Basic applications, you can do things that have no equivalent in a non-GUI application—use a mouse and Visual Basic constructs such as check boxes, option buttons and command buttons, and menus, to name just a few. There are many ways of doing the same thing in a GUI application that would have only one equivalent way in a non-GUI application. An example of this can be found in Microsoft Word, in which you can save a document in at least four ways. To properly test this new type of application, you need to break the old testing methods into four test streams: destruction, window design, navigational, and functional.

Destruction Testing

In this type of testing, the application is tested until it does something it's not supposed to—often in a totally unstructured fashion. You need to come up with a happy medium of what is appropriate. For example, you had 20 days allocated for this testing, and you could let 1 person do this for 20 days or you could let 40 people do this for half a day each. Ideally, about 5 or 6 people for 3 or 4 days each is the best proportion to get the maximum benefit.

Window Design Testing

This kind of test proves that each individual window (such as primary, secondary, pop-up, dialog box, message box) that the system consists of has been designed and built according to the project standards. The best method of ensuring this is in the form of a checklist—that is, points to be checked and signed off by the test reviewer. An example of such a checklist is shown in Table 16-2, but each project should come up with its own checklist for its own project standards and circumstances.

TABLE 16-2

EXAMPLE WINDOW DESIGN CHECKLIST

Checkpoints	Checked
The form positioning is correct relative to other forms on the screen.	
The form has the correct border style.	
The form has the Max, Min, and Control box set on or off as required.	
The control tabbing order is set and is logical to the user (upper left to lower right).	
Correct colors (foreground, background, fill, and so on) are applied to all controls per project standards.	
The first character of each word of text labels and menu choices is in uppercase text.	
Controls are aligned correctly.	
The text and captions of all controls are in the correct font and size.	
All menus, command buttons, check boxes, and option buttons have mnemonics set.	
All mnemonics are unique.	
Ellipses (...) are included for all routing menu choices.	
Shortcut keys for menu options are set if relevant.	
Command button and menu bar choices are unique.	
A Help menu option or Help command button exists if relevant.	
Command buttons are positioned appropriately on the form.	

>>

TABLE 16-2

Checkpoints	Checked
A command button is set to be the Cancel default.	
A command button is set to be the Enter default if appropriate.	
Option buttons have a frame or group box.	
A default option button is set for each group.	
Combo box and list box entries are ordered appropriately.	
Enabled and/or Visible control properties are set where relevant.	
Date fields are formatted correctly.	
Image control is used rather than picture control where appropriate.	
3D and non-3D controls of the same type are not used on the same form.	

Navigational Testing

This test determines whether each window can be navigated to by initiation (via all the multiple ways of initiating) of all the different functions from any other appropriate window in the system, without necessarily performing any of the detailed processing that might be required when it gets there. Again, the best format for this test is a checklist, as shown in Table 16-3. Each list is unique to the particular window that is being tested. The list of navigational actions and results can be easily retested and verified by the test reviewer.

TABLE 16-3

EXAMPLE NAVIGATION DESIGN CHECKLIST

Navigation Action	Navigation Result	Checked
File : New	Entry fields reinitialized for new input	
File : Open	Windows Open dialog box displayed	
File : Delete	Customer details deleted after confirmation	
File : Print	Windows Print dialog box displayed	
File : Exit	Application terminated	
View : Customer Orders	Customer Orders screen displayed	
Options : Toolbar	Toolbar display toggled	
Help : Contents	Application Help file contents displayed	
Help : Search	Application Help file search displayed	
Help : Using Help	Windows Help file displayed	
Help : About	Application About box displayed	

Functional Testing

Having now tested that an individual window (or group of windows) is designed correctly, contains all the functions it should, contains the required methods for initiating those functions, and can navigate via those functions to all the places it has to go, you can now proceed to the "real" testing of the system. Functional testing ensures that the nuts and bolts functions of the system are actually tested. For example, when you initiate the Save function for a document (regardless of how you do it: via the mouse, the keyboard mnemonic keys, or a keyboard accelerator key), does the document get saved to disk correctly? The list of such tests will be a smaller list once the window design and navigational aspects of initiating a function are separated out. This part of the testing is probably the one that equates most closely (although perhaps not definitively) with the old concept of unit testing.

You would have one of each of these checklists per window in the application. Remember also that automated testing tools can be very useful for testing Visual Basic applications.

You should investigate many other forms of testing, among them these:

- Regression test at check-in
- Automated testing
- Usability testing
- Lots of pure pounding

Also, remember that bug tracking and the collection of metrics are very important. A properly thought-out test strategy is vital for any Visual Basic 5 enterprise development. Shorten this phase at your peril!

BUILD PLANNING

Visual Basic 5 client/server development would appear to restrict the options for build and integration planning because of the dependencies among different elements of the development. However, by developing components and using layering, you can manage dependencies.

Your build should take advantage of the layered architecture (as shown in Figure 16-10) so that builds can start earlier. Because the layers obviously interact, moving ahead in one area might require you to make assumptions that could prove to be false and result in rework. Part of the project manager's job is to understand the risk and balance it with the benefit of producing quicker results.

FIGURE 16-10

Build planning

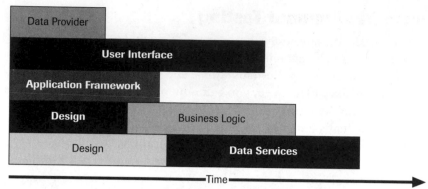

A thin user interface layer can be built as soon as requirements settle down and can emerge from prototyping. The business logic can be attached behind this layer when that logic is written. The design and build of the data services are likely to be the longest-running tasks. But provided a logical data provider is built to insulate the application from changes in database design, the data provider can be written to interface to a dummy database to provide a test harness for the application. The application will usually be written within a framework that handles generic interface services, error handling, persistence, and so on.

YEAR 2000

Year 2000 will cost in the region of $600 billion worldwide to correct.

Gartner Group, 1996

Year 2000 is a well-defined maintenance project—the specification is about as simple as you can get. It is the first project in IT history with an immovable deadline. The consequence of slippage is not just a missed deadline, but the total and catastrophic failure of the organization. The alternative to addressing the problem is to go out of business.

Visual Basic developers are in denial: 90 percent of all applications are affected, not just mainframe code. One bank we know of has developed many Visual Basic systems through the use of freelance contractors. Its own IT department has no support for the language. Today 8 million lines of Visual Basic code are under maintenance by managers. About 5 percent of this code will have to change, and 100 percent will have to be thoroughly tested (incidentally, testing is about 60 percent of the effort). It's really scary.

For a thorough discussion of this topic, refer to Chapter 9.

Concluding Thoughts

**If builders built buildings the way programmers wrote programs,
the first woodpecker to come along would destroy civilization.**

Weinberg's Second Law

This chapter has drawn together a series of ideas that you should take into account when developing a large-scale Visual Basic 5 client/server system. The introduction of Visual Basic 5 means that Visual Basic developers have to change their attitude toward developing higher-quality and more easily maintainable applications. The pursuit of quality must become the prime objective of every member of the team, from the most junior programmer to top management.

You can, of course, improve quality in many different ways, as described early in this chapter. In our discussion, we have touched only on the very basics:

- **Commitment.** Every person involved in a project must be totally committed to the success of the project.

- **Technical excellence.** Insist on the best, and provide support in the form of proper training and the allocation of sufficient hardware and software resources.

- **Communication.** Ensure that the right hand knows what the left is doing. The "mushroom syndrome" must be abandoned forever.

Several basic commonsense steps will help to ensure that quality is maintained in any Visual Basic development:

- **Manage it:** Manage risk carefully.

- **Plan it:** A formal project plan is essential.

- **Design it:** A poorly designed interface to a poorly designed technical infrastructure will invariably result in a very poor system.

- **Test it:** And then test it again. Then get someone else to test it.

- **Review it:** Careful monitoring throughout the development cycle will help to prevent eleventh-hour disasters.

- **Document it:** There is simply no such thing as not having enough time to comment the code properly as you are writing it.

Visual Basic 5 is one of the most powerful tools available to the Windows developer today. And like any powerful tool, in the wrong hands the results can be disastrous. Used correctly, however, Visual Basic 5 can provide unprecedented levels of productivity and sophistication.

Coding **C**onventions

PETER MORRIS   MARK HURST

This appendix describes the coding conventions we used in preparing most of the source code for this book. These conventions are based on extracts from our in-house (TMS) Visual Basic programmer's manual, *VB Vogue*. You can use this appendix purely to look up type or scope prefixes you don't understand, but you might also want to use our conventions in your own code. Or you might decide to adapt them. The important thing is that you have coding conventions and you apply them uniformly across your code. (If your company is interested in purchasing *VB Vogue*, please send e-mail to the TMS *info* alias requesting details and availability.)

NAMING **C**ONVENTIONS

We use a simplified form of Hungarian notation to attach both type and scope information to various object names. Hungarian notation uses character prefixes to denote type, aggregation, and scope, and the full system gets rather complicated. The subset we've chosen for our purposes is defined in the following sections and in the tables that appear at the end of this appendix.

Type Information

Hungarian type prefixes have two parts: a *base type* to represent the base data type and a *modifier* to denote an aggregate type. An example of a base-type prefix is *n*, which denotes an integer, while adding the *a* modifier to the base type denotes an array of integers. An example should make this clearer:

```
Dim nCounter              As Integer
Dim anCounters (1 To 10) As Integer
```

Notice that the variable name itself starts with an uppercase letter, which shows us where the prefix stops and the variable name starts. Sometimes we need to use more than one modifier, such as a multidimensional array:

```
Dim aanStateTable (1 To 10, 1 To 10) As Integer
```

The base types and modifiers we use are listed at the end of this appendix. In fact, we use only one aggregate modifier since arrays are the only single-type aggregates that Visual Basic supports.

Where calls are made to Windows API functions, you might see type prefixes such as *LPSTR* and *sz* that don't appear in our tables: these prefixes are used in the Microsoft Windows documentation. We've found that changing these to match our Visual Basic data types can often conceal errors in the declarations. You might also see *p* used as a modifier to denote a pointer and *pcb* to denote the address of a callback function.

For variables defined with user-defined types and classes, the special base-type prefixes *t* and *C* are used. Although *C* breaks the lowercase rule, we've adopted it because it's used throughout the industry.

Menus are named with the type prefix *mnu*, but the names are aggregated to show the menu structure. For example, the Open item on the File menu is called *mnuFileOpen*. Here are some more standard menu names:

```
mnuHelpAbout
mnuFileExit
```

Scope Information

We also use prefixes to denote an object's scope. Our scope prefixes come between the type prefix and the object name, so we need to make sure they start with an uppercase letter and end with a lowercase letter. This way, the scope prefixes stand out from both the type prefix and the object's name. For example, a private integer variable (scope prefix *Pi*) defined at the module level would be named like this:

```
Private nPiCounter As Integer
```

Variables

Variables are named like this:

```
<type><scope><name>
```

The *name* part is simply the variable name written in mixed case, and the *type* part is a Hungarian type as defined earlier. We don't use type and scope prefixes when naming properties and methods of classes and forms.

The base types and modifiers are given in a table at the end of this appendix. The *scope* part is defined in the following sections.

Local variables

Local variables do not have a scope prefix. Here are some examples of local variable definitions:

```
Dim nCounter   As Integer
Dim sMessage   As String
Dim tThisCell As tTableEntry  ' A user-defined type
ReDim anLookupTable (1 To 10) As Integer
```

Private variables

Private variables defined at the module level have *Pi* as a scope prefix. Some examples follow:

```
Private nPiCounter  As Integer
Private sPiMessage  As String
Private tPiThisCell As tTableEntry  ' A user-defined type
Private anPiLookupTable () As Integer
```

Global variables

Public variables defined at the module level of a standard module (that is, a BAS file) have the module identifier as a scope prefix. The module identifier is a unique two-character prefix that suggests the module name. For example, we might choose *Er* for an error handling module or *Db* for a database module. You'll find some examples at the top of the next page.

```
Public nErCounter As Integer        ' Er for "error handling"
Public sErMessage As String
Public anTbLookupTable () As Integer  ' Tb for "table functions"
Public tTbThisCell As tTableEntry    ' A user-defined type
```

Form and class properties (unprotected)

Public variables defined at the module level of classes and forms are properties and do not have scope or type prefixes.

Functions and Subroutines

Public functions and subroutines have scope prefixes in the same way that variables do. Public and private functions also have a type prefix that reflects the type of value returned. The rules for choosing the type prefix are the same as those for variables.

Private

Private subroutines and functions do not require scope prefixes. Here are some examples of private subroutines:

```
Private Sub OpenLogFile()
Private Sub ClearGrid()
```

And here are some private functions:

```
Private Function nGetNextItem() As Integer
Private Function sGetFullPath(ByVal sFileName As String) _
    As String
Private Function CGetNextCell() As CTableEntry
```

Public subroutines

The rules for choosing scope prefixes for public subroutines are exactly the same as those for variables, as shown here:

```
Public ErReportError()
Public TbInsertTableEntry()
Public DbDeleteItem()
```

Form and class methods

Public functions and subroutines defined in classes and forms are properties and do not have type or scope prefixes.

Form and class properties (protected)

Property Let, *Property Set*, and *Property Get* routines do not have type or scope prefixes.

DLL procedures

When declaring Windows API functions, we use the *Alias* keyword to add the prefix *Win*. For example, *CallWindowProc* becomes *WinCallWindowProc*. When declaring functions in other DLLs, we use the prefix *Dll*.

Parameter lists

Formal parameters are named as local variables but with *i* or *o* added in place of a scope prefix to denote whether the parameter is an input or an output:

```
Sub CrackURL(ByVal siURL As String, ByRef soProtcol, _
    ByRef soPath, ByRef soPath, ByRef noPort)
```

For parameters that are both inputs *and* outputs, we use *io*.

Controls and Forms

We also use type prefixes when naming Visual Basic controls. The prefixes are given at the end of this appendix. Forms are named as if they were controls, even though a form name can also act as a class name. For example, we would name a form *frmPublication* instead of *CPublication*, even though we could create new instances of the form:

```
Dim frmNewPub As New frmPublication
```

Constants

Constants are named in uppercase letters, with no type or scope prefixes. Arbitrary prefixes can be used to group sets of related constants:

```
Const TABLE_SIZE            As Integer = 100
Const DEFAULT_LOG_FILE      As String = "log.txt"

Const ERR_GENERIC           As Integer = 32767
Const ERR_LOGON_FAIL        As Integer = 32766
Const ERR_COMPONENT_MISSING As Integer = 32765
```

Type and Class Definitions

Type names are prefixed with *t*, and class names are prefixed with *C*. These prefixes are also used as the base-type prefixes when naming instances. The rest of the name is written in mixed case:

```
Type tTableEntry
    nNewState As Integer
    lAction   As Long
End Type
```

And in use:

```
Dim tCell        As tTableEntry
Dim CSymbolTable As New CTable
```

Source Files

Source filenames are restricted to the traditional 8.3 format. The first three characters are reserved for a project identifier, and the default file extensions are retained. The remaining five characters are used to distinguish files in whatever way seems appropriate.

CODING CONVENTIONS

This section outlines a number of conventions we have found useful when writing code. It isn't comprehensive—our in-house manual, *VB Vogue,* contains much more detail than we have space for here. We suggest you use this section as a basis for designing your own coding standards.

Principles

Always code for clarity, not efficiency. Choose variable and function names carefully. Be verbose rather than terse, and parenthesize expressions to make them clearer. Write your code for the reader.

Limit the scope of constants, variables, functions, and subroutines as much as possible. If you have the choice, always use a local object in preference to a global one.

Use explicit type conversions (*CInt*, *CStr*, and so on) when assigning between different variable types.

Some Specifics

Follow these guidelines when you write code:

- Define all variables explicitly. Checking the Require Variable Declaration option under Tools/Options/Editor enforces this. Define variable-length arrays explicitly. (Visual Basic will not enforce this.)

- Always specify the upper and lower bounds in an array definition.

- Define constants, and use them in place of numbers in the code.

- Always use the *ByVal* and *ByRef* keywords in parameter lists. Use *ByVal* where you have a choice.

- Always use the *Private* keyword on functions and subroutines that are not exported from a module.

- Define the types of all variables and function and subroutine parameters explicitly. For example, use *Dim nBufSize As Integer* instead of *Dim nBufSize*, and use *Function nGetChars(nBufSize As Integer) As Integer* instead of *Function nGetChars(nBufSize)*.

- Do not use implicit type suffixes (such as ! and &) in variable definitions.

- In *For* loops, use *Next <Index>* instead of just *Next*.

IN-LINE DOCUMENTATION

One of the best sources of documentation is the code itself. When you follow a specific coding format and thoroughly comment your code, you're making your program more readable and providing valuable information to yourself and to other programmers who might have to make modifications to the code later.

Formatting

Follow these rules when formatting your code:

- Punctuate your code with blank lines.

- Keep your procedures to a manageable size—preferably not much more than a single screen.

- Keep indentation under control. If you're having difficulty remaining within the right margin, you're probably nesting too deeply.

- Use parentheses to enhance the readability of your code. No one reading your code should have to wonder what you meant when you wrote it.

- Preserve screen real estate wherever possible. For example, when creating a long string, it might be better to build up the string with multiple assignments:

```
Dim sMsg As String

sMsg = "This is a paragraph that is to appear "
sMsg = sMsg & "in a message box. The text is "
sMsg = sMsg & "broken into several lines of code "
sMsg = sMsg & "in the source code, making it easier "
sMsg = sMsg & "for the programmer to read and debug. "

MsgBox sMsg, vbOkOnly, "Text"

Dim sQRY as String

sQRY = "SELECT Customer.CustomerName, Orders.OrderValue "
sQRY = sQRY & "FROM Customer, Orders "
sQRY = sQRY & "WHERE Customer.CustomerId = Orders.CustomerId"

ReportQry1.SQL = sQRY
```

End-of-Line Comments

End-of-line comments should be used to annotate variable or constant definitions:

```
Const MAX_ROWS = 2147483647 ' (2^31)-1 (Max value for long integer)

Const ICONIZED = 7    ' For starting up applications
                      ' with Shell().
```

In-Line Comments

End-of-line comments are rarely suitable for annotating code. Where a function or subroutine contains a number of logical blocks, introduce each block with a separate comment indented to the same level as the code. Use as many lines as necessary, and don't use surrounding ***** lines to delimit comments unless something really important is about to happen. Keep comment lines short so that the entire comment can be viewed on a VGA display without scrolling left and right.

Use comments to explain the code, not to echo it; if your comments become very involved, consider restructuring the code. Complicated explanations can also be moved into the function header. The following code shows some examples of appropriate in-line comments:

```
MaxCol = nColumn - 1
XL_NewRow stDataBlock
XL_NewRow stDummyRow

' The dummy row now holds the long form of the column headings.
' Appending this to the main data block gives us both long and
' short headings, one below the other.

XL_AppendBlock stDataBlock, stDummyRow

' We now need to step through the data array and extract the
' records for each row in turn. Records corresponding to a
' single row all have the same code and description and are
' contiguous in the array (which is sorted on description).
' The row description array returned by GetNextRow is sorted
' on column number.

nDataIdx = 0
Do While nDataIdx < nNumRecs
```

File Headers

Every module should have a header that sits as a comment in the module's definitions area. The header identifies the module and summarizes the external interfaces to it. Here is an example module header:

```
' *************************************************************
' Module          Startup
'
' Filename        tabstart.bas
' Module Prefix   St
'
' Author          Mark Hurst
'                 The Mandelbrot Set (International) Ltd.
'
' Description
'
' Startup module for the table-driven FSM sample application
'
```

```
' Revisions
' 11-12-96, Mark Hurst
' Added instance checking.
'
' 08-12-96, Mark Hurst
' Moved global FSM object out of here.
' **********************************************************
```

The module prefix is a two-letter code used as a scope prefix that uniquely identifies this module in the project. Module prefixes are significant only for standard (BAS) modules.

Function and Subroutine Headers

A function header is a comment that describes what the function does and summarizes its interface. The description should focus on what the function does, although for complicated or longer functions it might be appropriate to summarize the *how* as well. All nontrivial functions should have function headers, and headers are also recommended for nontrivial event handlers.

Here is an example function header:

```
' **********************************************************
'
' Synopsis       Create the event queue, and attach
'                an event handler to it.
'
' Parameters
'
'   pcbiNewWinProc            (I) Address of the event
'                                 queue callback function
'
' Nonlocal Data
'
'   hwndPiEventQueue          (O) Event queue handle
'   pcblPiEvQueueOldWinProc   (O) Event queue default
'                                 window procedure
'   lPiFSMEventMsg            (O) Event message number
'
' Description
'
' This is where we create the event queue and attach a
' callback function to it to handle our FSM events.
'
```

```
' The event queue is built around a private window that
' we create here. We subclass the window to hook
' pcbiNewWinProc onto it and then register a custom
' message number that we will use to send messages to it.
' The pcbiNewWinProc parameter is a pointer to a VB
' function obtained with the AddressOf operator.
'
' *************************************************************
```

TYPE PREFIXES

In this section, you'll find tables that include prefixes for various data types and control types.

TABLE A-1

VARIABLES PREFIXES

Prefix	Data Type
byt	Byte
b	Boolean
cur	Currency
d	Double
dte	Date
f	Single
hf	File handle (Long)
hwnd	Window handle (Long)
h(... lowercase)	Handle to something (Long)
l	Long
n	Integer
o	Object
s	String
v	Variant

TABLE A-2 | MODIFIERS AND SPECIAL TYPES PREFIXES

Prefix	Data Type
a	Array <of another type>
C	Class or class instance
t	User-defined type or instance
e	Enumerated type or instance
p	Pointer (used with API calls)
pcb	Pointer to a callback function (used with *AddressOf*)

TABLE A-3 | DATA OBJECTS: DAO PREFIXES

Prefix	Visual Basic Data Type
bk	SelBookmarks
ct	Container
db	Database
dc	Document
ds	Dynaset
er	Errors
fd	Field
gp	Group
ix	Index
pa	Parameter
pr	Property
qd	QueryDef
rs	Recordset
rl	Relation
ss	Snapshot
tb	Table
td	TableDef
us	User
wk	Workspace

TABLE A-4

Data Objects: RDO Prefixes

Prefix	Visual Basic Data Type
rdoEng	rdoEngine
rdoEnv	rdoEnvironment
rdoConn	rdoConnection
rdoTbl	rdoTable
rdoCol	rdoColumn
rdoPrepS	rdoPreparedStatement
rdoParam	rdoParameter
rdoRS	rdoResultset
rdoErr	rdoError

TABLE A-5

Controls Prefixes

Prefix	Control Type Description
ani	Animation button
bed	Pen BEdit
cbo	Combobox/Dropdown Listbox
chk	Checkbox
clp	Picture Clip
cmd	Command Button
com	Communications
dat	Data Control
dir	Directory Listbox
dlg	Common dialog
drv	Drive Listbox
fil	File Listbox
fra	Frame
frm	Form
gau	Gauge
gpb	Group Pushbutton
gra	Graph
grd	Grid

>>

TABLE A-5

Prefix	Control Type Description
hed	Pen HEdit
hsb	Horizontal scroll bar
img	Image
ink	Pen Ink
key	Keyboard key status
lab	Label
lin	Line
lst	Listbox
mci	MCI
mnu	Menu
mpm	MAPI Message
mps	MAPI Session
ole	OLE Client
opt	Option Button
out	Outline Control
pic	Picture
pnl	3D Panel
rdc	Remote Data Control
shp	Shape
spn	Spin Control
tab	SS Tab Control
tmr	Timer
txt	Textbox
vsb	Vertical scroll bar
iml	ImageList
lvw	ListView
pbr	ProgressBar
rtf	RichTextBox
sld	Slider
sbr	StatusBar
tab	Tabstrip
tbr	Toolbar
tvw	TreeView

TABLE A-6

DATA-BOUND CONTROLS PREFIXES

Prefix	Control Type Description
dbcbo	Databound Combobox/Dropdown Listbox
dblst	Databound Listbox
dbgrd	Databound Grid

Changes in the DAO Structure

Visual Basic 3 to Visual Basic 5

KEVIN HOUSTOUN

Method Used Under Visual Basic 3	Method Used Under DAO 3 and Later
All *CreateDynaset* methods	*OpenRecordset* method
All *CreateSnapshot* methods	*OpenRecordset* method
All *ListFields* methods	Fields collection
All *ListIndexes* methods	Indexes collection
CompactDatabase statement	*DBEngine.CompactDatabase* method
CreateDatabase statement	*DBEngine.CreateDatabase* method
DBEngine.FreeLocks method	*DBEngine.Idle* property
DBEngine.SetDefaultWorkspace method	*DBEngine.DefaultUser* and *DBEngine.Password* properties

>>

Method Used Under Visual Basic 3	Method Used Under DAO 3 and Later
DBEngine.SetDataAccessOption method	*DBEngine.IniPath* property
Database.BeginTrans method	*WS.BeginTrans* method
Database.CommitTrans method	*WS.CommitTrans* method
Database.Rollback method	*WS.Rollback* method
Database.DeleteQueryDef method	*Delete* method
Database.ExecuteSQL method	*Execute* method
Database.ListTables method	TableDefs collection
Database.OpenQueryDef method	QueryDefs collection
Database.OpenTable method	*OpenRecordset* method
OpenDatabase statement	*DBEngine.OpenDatabase* method
Querydef.ListParameters method	Parameters collection
Recordset.Indexes collection	Indexes collection
Snapshot object	Recordset object
Dynaset object	Recordset object
Table object	Recordset object

Windows 3.11 API Calls

Without Windows 32 Equivalents

KEVIN HOUSTOUN

The following API calls are declared in the Microsoft Windows 16-bit API file shipped with Visual Basic 4. (Some functions are said not to have equivalents in the Win32 API because of a loss of functionality.)

AccessResource	*AnsiUpperBuff*	*DlgDirSelectComboBox*
AllocDStoCSAlias	*Catch*	*DlgDirSelectComboBoxEx*
AllocResource	*ChangeSelector*	*DlgDirSelectEx*
AllocSelector	*CloseComm*	*EnableCommNotification*
AnsiLower	*CloseSound*	*EnableHardwareInput*
AnsiLowerBuff	*CountVoiceNotes*	*EndDocAPI*
AnsiNext	*CreateFont*	*ExitWindowsExec*
AnsiPrev	*CreateScalableFontResource*	*FlushComm*
AnsiToOem	*CreateWindow*	*FreeModule*
AnsiToOemBuff	*CreateWindowEx*	*FreeSelector*
AnsiUpper	*DlgDirSelect*	*GetAspectRatioFilter*

GetAtomHandle
GetBitmapDimension
GetBrushOrg
GetCommEventMask
GetCurrentPDB
GetCurrentPosition
GetCurrentTask
GetCurrentTime
GetDCOrg
GetDesktopHwnd
GetDOSEnvironment
GetDriverInfo
GetEnvironment
GetFontData&
GetFreeSpace
GetFreeSystemResources
GetGlyphOutline&
GetInstanceData
GetMetaFileBits
GetModuleUsage
GetNextDriver
GetNumTasks
GetObjectGDI
GetSysModalWindow
GetSystemDebugState
GetTempDrive
GetTextExtent
GetThresholdEvent
GetThresholdStatus
GetViewportExt
GetViewportOrg
GetWinDebugInfo
GetWindowExt
GetWindowOrg
GetWindowTask
GetWinFlags
GlobalLRUNewest

GlobalLRUOldest
GlobalPageLock
GlobalPageUnlock
IsTask
LimitEmsPages
LocalInit
LockInput
LockSegment
LogError
MoveTo
OemToAnsi
OemToAnsiBuff
OffsetViewportOrg
OffsetWindowOrg
OpenComm
OpenSound
PostAppMessage
ProfClear
ProfFinish
ProfFlush
ProfInsChk
ProfSampRate
ProfSetup
ProfStart
ProfStop
QuerySendMessage
ReadComm
ScaleViewportExt
ScaleViewportExtEx
ScaleWindowExt
ScaleWindowExtEx
ScrollWindowEx
SetBitmapDimension
SetBrushOrg
SetCommEventMask
SetDIBitsToDevice
SetEnvironment

SetMetaFileBits
SetMetaFileBitsBetter
SetSoundNoise
SetSwapAreaSize
SetSysModalWindow
SetViewportExt
SetViewportOrg
SetVoiceAccent
SetVoiceEnvelope
SetVoiceNote
SetVoiceQueueSize
SetVoiceSound
SetVoiceThreshold
SetWinDebugInfo
SetWindowExt
SetWindowOrg
SpoolFile
StartSound
StopSound
StretchBlt
StretchDIBits
SwapRecording
SwitchStackBack
SwitchStackTo
SyncAllVoices
Throw
UngetCommChar
UnlockResource
UnlockSegment
ValidateCodeSegments
ValidateFreeSpaces
WaitSoundState
WriteComm
wvsprintf
Yield

Microsoft **P**roduct **D**ate **L**imits and **F**ormats

MAYES

The following table shows Microsoft's products and the life expectancy of the date formats used within them. Unless otherwise noted, Microsoft's products rely on the system-supplied date formats.

Product Name	Date Limit	Date Format
Microsoft Access 95 (assumed date)	1999	assumed "yy" dates
Microsoft Access 95 (explicit date)	9999	long dates ("yyyy")
Microsoft Access 97	2029	assumed "yy" dates
Microsoft Excel 95	2019	assumed "yy" dates
Microsoft Excel 95	2078	long dates

>>

Product Name	Date Limit	Date Format
Microsoft Excel 97	2029	assumed "yy" dates
Microsoft Excel 97	9999	long dates
Microsoft Project 95 (and previous versions)	2049	32 bits
Microsoft SQL Server	9999	"datetime"
Visual C++ (4.x) run-time library	2036	32 bits
Visual FoxPro	9999	long dates
FAT16 file system	2108	16 bits
Windows 95 file system (FAT32)	2108	32 bits
Windows 95 run-time library	2099	16 bits
Windows NT file system (NTFS)	future centuries	64 bits
Windows NT run-time library	2099	16 bits

Is There
Madness in Methods?

Though this be madness, yet there is method in't.
William Shakespeare

DEREK PEARCE

Thus spake Shakespeare; but then again, he was the Bard of Avon and not an IT professional. My own view tends toward the more appropriate:

Though this be method, yet there is madness in't.   *D. W. Pearce*

PART ONE:
WHEREIN THE AUTHOR MEETS METHOD

I first came across method (it had not at that point taken on the pretentious and spurious *-ology* that it would later sprout in imitation of the true sciences) a long time ago when I was working at a large life insurance company. Our IT manager had assembled the more senior members of the development departments and wheeled in a consultant to tell us all about a data-oriented method for the analysis and design of computer systems. Being a well-behaved and good-mannered bunch, we developers sat and listened in silence—but come question time, it was a different matter. We asked masses of questions, but two obvious categories of question dominated.

PART TWO: WHEREIN QUESTIONS ARE RAISED AND ONLY SOME OF THEM ARE NOT ANSWERED

The first category asked, basically, "So what else is new?" Most of us in the audience had been developing large corporate systems for more than a few years, and nothing in this "new" method came as a surprise—not the rigor nor the techniques.

The second category involved design. At the beginning of the presentation, we had been told that the "new" method addressed both analysis and design, but it seemed to us that analysis dominated the discussion. In fact, the design process had somehow been magically assimilated into the analysis process, or at least it seemed so to the practiced and experienced developers in the audience. We never did get a good answer to our questions about why the method always proceeded from an analysis of the "existing system." The questioner asked, "What about systems to support business that the company doesn't currently engage in? What if we want to create a system to support our company's entry into the retail banking arena? What should we analyze under those circumstances?" Given the subsequent diversification and expansion of financial services companies like the one I was then working for, the questions look remarkably prescient. No satisfactory response was forthcoming, however forcibly the question was pursued.

PART THREE: WHEREIN THE GENUINE MOTIVATION BEHIND THE METHOD IS REVEALED

In the discussion period, our IT manager and the consultant revealed that, yes, it was probably true that much, if not all, of the "new method" was in fact a simple formalization of what was considered good practice and that the formalization of such practices would, if religiously enforced, allow the mediocre (present company obviously excluded) members of the industry to produce mediocre systems. The method was not, they averred, aimed at professionals such as themselves, but meant to address the question of how an increasing demand for reliable computer systems was going to be met by an industry with a small number of experienced developers available.

I would guess that if you had polled that audience, you would have found that though most of them had trained in scientific subjects—math, electronics, and physics were the most widely held areas of qualification—they regarded what they did as a craft rather than an art, and certainly not a science.

PART FOUR:
WHEREIN OUR HISTORICAL VIEW IS UPDATED

Since that day long ago, there have been many methods, even more methodologies, and, of course, many, many systems: structured methods, soft systems methods, rapid methods, engineering methods, information methods, prototyping methods, object-oriented methods, and dynamic methods. This proliferation is inextricably linked with the rapid advances of the technology base on which practical computing was founded. However, the outcome of all these methods has not changed: mediocre systems. Likewise, and as important, in a fulfillment of their own prophecies, neither have the inputs changed: mediocre staff. The false public promise of methods and methodologies (the private message was never made public) ensured that no special premium or reward would be vouchsafed to the exceptional practitioners and that the truly gifted would find no eager welcome. Methods homogenized the development of both systems and practitioners, actual and prospective.

Yet more worrisome and damaging than this pervasive mediocrity is the neglect that design as a discipline has been subject to. Find a methodology book and look in the index for "design." Now read all the topics mentioned. You'll find that analysis is still confused with design and still overwhelms it as a topic. You will be hard-pressed to find a life cycle or a method that lists design as a separate stage—it will be either the analysis and design stage or the design and code stage in which you find design mentioned at all. Books and methods addressing design as a sole topic are equally rare.

PART FIVE:
FOR IN THE BODY OF THESE
METHODOLOGIES LIE THE SEEDS OF THEIR FAILURE

If we accept that computing methodologies are formalizations of best practice, we must also concede that the methodologies must, by definition, be obsolete or at least anachronistic by the time they are published, given the conditions under which they are used: the speed with which the problems we tackle with computerization change, the progress made in base technologies, and the pace at which businesses change.

PART SIX:
IN WHICH THE NEWER METHODS AND THEIR PREDILECTIONS
ARE EXPLICATED AND THE NATURE OF THEIR FAILINGS NOTED
(ALSO, A SAVING GRACE IS FOUND BY ACCIDENT)

Now we must address one of the concomitants of methodologies that has given rise to newer methodologies that manage ironically to build on one of the base failings of the earlier methodologies and to use, unwittingly, one of the things omitted from all methodologies to make it appear as if they've succeeded. If this sounds like a convoluted riddle or some Zen koan, bear with me and all will be revealed.

The most noticeable effect of the widespread acceptance of more traditional methodology-based development has been an ever-increasing devotion of project time to analysis at the expense of requirements gathering, design, and delivery dates. And this last—increasingly delayed delivery dates—is the effect that in turn gave us the rapid, prototyping, and dynamic methods.

All of these "new methods" have in common the delivery of code and function as their prime motive—and delivery at the earliest possible opportunity. Notice that I used the word "possible" rather than "appropriate," for it is speed of delivery that is of the essence to these methods.

To ensure the early delivery of code, analysis tends to be dovetailed within coding and user feedback in such methods. Where design has fled, I know not.

So now we know what gave rise to the "new methods": ill-timed delivery. We know what failing of the earlier methods they perpetuate: lack of design attention and time. So what is "one of the things omitted from all methodologies" on which they base their supposed success? It is that thing that was in the presentation room all those years ago together with the "new method" but unnoticed in the light of its so-called novelty and science: talent, or more specifically, talented and committed practitioners. These new rapid and dynamic methods tend to be deployed in smallish team settings, and the best staff are often chosen to populate these teams. When they succeed, therefore, these methods do so not so much because of the method but almost in spite of it. It is only the iterative nature of development that these methods permit—the constant latitude to make mistakes and to correct them—that differentiates them from their ancestors. True, the propinquity of the user community and access to them, the emphasis on rapid delivery of functionality, and the implicit admission that such systems are ever incomplete in the old sense of the word, all contribute. But they contribute only inasmuch as they remove some of the more traditional obstacles to good development, which were not themselves intrinsic to the methodologies.

PART SEVEN:
IN WHICH THE NOTION OF DEVELOPMENT SUCCESS AS POSITED IN PART FIVE IS EXAMINED AND SOME OF THE PRECURSORS TO THE NEW "NEW METHODS" ARE DOCUMENTED

Before prototyping, iterative, and dynamic development projects, the notion of a successful project was largely defined by its completeness. If a system was delivered to the business in the declared schedule, was within budget, and functioned according to the specification, it was a success.

In those days of what I call "static development"—when a system was described, specified, coded, tested, and then delivered—the measure of completeness was initially the correlation between the functional specification and the system as implemented—functional equivalence, if you will. In an age in which complete and detailed requirements could be expressed and documented at the start of the project, functional equivalence implied or equated to requirements equivalence.

"Requirements equivalence" is the state whereby the system delivers all the functionality the business required. In the early days of the methods camp, functional equivalence and requirements equivalence were effectively identical, but as businesses became more dynamic in both their nature and behavior and as developers started to tackle and computerize those less well understood and less well documented requirements, a divergence occurred.

This desire for functional equivalence gave us such wonders as change control warfare—whereby the developer spends huge amounts of time making sure that as the initial statement of requirements is clarified and expanded by the analyze and specify stages, those changes don't get into the functional specification. In this way, systems developers either achieved functional equivalence and missed requirements equivalence by a great distance or achieved requirements equivalence but missed deadlines and budgets repeatedly.

A new way was needed. IT looked toward the engineering community for an answer. In particular, this problem of slowly emerging requirements was identified by the early workers in commercial artificial intelligence and knowledge-based systems. These people were tackling systems of unknown complexity, and they knew that the complexity was unknown, in fact was initially unknowable. These were the people who pioneered prototyping and what have now become known as dynamic development methods. Not only do we owe a debt to these people, but we also need to understand what they hoped to achieve with prototyping; for, as you'll see, prototyping didn't have the same emphasis as do the current crop of formalized dynamic methods.

These knowledge engineers used a word that has unfortunately slipped from the mainstream IT vocabulary—elicitation. They understood that they needed to draw out gradually the detail and the breadth of the problem domain as it had initially been stated. They also realized that feedback was essential to this process of elicitation. It was with these knowledge-based–systems (KBS) practitioners that the practicalities of iterative developments with scheduled deliveries and critique sessions were worked out.

Keep in mind that these knowledge engineers were among the best and most gifted among the IT staff. They knew best practice, and they knew when it wasn't best for them and their projects. And when that was the case, they knew how to create new best practices.

- They developed practices and processes that focused on drawing out requirements and understanding both from the business and from themselves and used them throughout the project along with well-structured feedback cycles.

- They allotted design its own part in the cycle; they learned to iterate through designs and to evaluate them as requirements emerged.

- They started using timeboxes to better manage and balance the needs of the developers and the business.

- They developed relationships with the business that avoided the constant bickering and change warfare that they saw in traditional IT. They developed ways of managing KBS projects that guaranteed that by the end of a project everyone involved could see some successes. Even failure to solve a problem did not constitute the traditional type of failure—it was in fact a kind of success because of the lessons learned.

- They learned, in effect, to define and run projects that did not focus fixedly on either functional equivalence or requirements equivalence. They taught themselves how to define success in an entirely cooperative way.

- They regularly juggled timeliness, budgetary constraints, user satisfaction, and requirements equivalence. And in so doing, they filled their toolboxes with a legion of tricks, techniques, and methods from which they could assemble best practice on the fly for a multitude of project types and shapes.

When the KBS bubble burst, these pioneers went back into mainstream development and tried to take with them all that they had learned. Alas, the culture of mainstream development had changed, and they found a development community polarized between the IT department's interest and that of the business—as if these could somehow be at odds! The IT departments they returned to were obsessed with managing the business requirements. Such practices were enshrined in their methods—central even, to IT's concept of success. Consequently, the tools they brought back were adopted largely to wage the same war.

Timeboxing was applied to requirements gathering in order to close off scope-creep. Prototyping of functionality was used to get sign-off on the user interface. Feedback cycles were introduced to pacify business and again to get sign-off. But at heart the war still raged. The IT developers didn't learn the lessons of cooperative development. They didn't really learn to deal with the slow process of emerging requirements—at best, they learned to control it.

And then, of course, they formalized what they had taken—what they could see from their warped perspective—and they turned it into a variety of "new methods." They took the flexible and made it inflexible. They took a way of working that had to do with learning, changing, refining, and adapting, and they froze it in place.

Consequently, the rapids, the prototypings, and the dynamics of the new "new methods" share the same adversarial model of development inherited from the traditional development world while seeming to wear the clothes of the cooperative development world of KBS. The fundamental problem of fixing and formalizing best practice in a fast-moving world had struck again. However, the concept of development success had changed forever, and the disparity between functional equivalence and requirements equivalence was now more widely understood.

Part Eight:
In Which the Consequences
of Design Deficit Are Detailed

These days it seems that almost every widely observed and yet poorly understood symptom or set of symptoms is labeled as some pseudoscientific "syndrome." I would therefore like to nominate "design deficit syndrome," or DDS, as the official nomenclature for the wealth of mediocre and poor systems that as an industry we regularly deliver to our customers and that achieve their mediocrity or paucity from a simple lack or impoverishment of design.

Having come up with a new name, I'll next identify the symptoms of systems suffering from DDS:

- Don't scale
- Don't perform
- Don't flex
- Are difficult or inelegant to use or they don't get used
- Are difficult and costly to maintain

And now come the descriptions of the symptoms.

Scaling

The system has difficulty coping or copes badly with the volumes, rates, and pressures of the regular business in diametric opposition to the elegance and slickness with which it performed during the development with small volumes of "representative" data. A classic symptom: I once saw a daily system go into production that took 27 hours to run—when there was only an 8-hour batch window in which it was to run every night.

Performance

Performance is often intertwined with scaling—and sometimes mistaken for it. Many performance inadequacies show up only when the system is required to perform under increased loading. The poor performance is often algorithmic: the system was too slow to start with, but nobody noticed (or maybe nobody looked) because we were concentrating on the build and impressing the users during the feedback cycle.

Flexibility

When the business changes ever so slightly, as it does regularly, the original design cannot cope and a new design or another system is required. Many organizations have multiple payment systems simply because the existing payment systems could not flex when slight variations to the type of business undertaken were made.

Usability

We have all seen systems so difficult or frustrating to use that users avoid them at every opportunity. We have all worked with systems whose user interfaces make it difficult to do what we want to do; most of us work with such software daily. Some of the best-selling software in the world today has this problem.

The manner in which this aspect of systems behavior has been systematically overlooked should be a source of daily shame to the computing profession. I still hear professionals intoning the familiar mantra that anyone can design a user interface. It isn't true. It's never been true. It's less true in the age of GUIs than it's ever been.

The World Wide Web offends in an entirely novel fashion with respect to interface and usability design. Much of the Web has been designed by graphics artists, and while these people have highly developed visual senses and personally based aesthetics, those talents do not contribute significantly toward the goal of usability in information-based computer systems. We are now discovering that the obverse of the computer systems developers' obsession with function over form—the graphic designers' preference for form over function—delivers systems every bit as unusable.

Maintenance

At least 80 percent of the costs incurred for any computer system are incurred postdelivery. An error detected during testing costs four times as much to correct as one caught at specification stage.[1] How much does an error detected during production running cost? How much more an error that is never detected? Like the classic "lemon" car first off the line on Monday or the last one off on Friday, some of our rapidly developed systems seem to spend more time being fixed than "on the road."

Finally, failure in any or all of the above aspects indicates the presence of DDS. These symptoms are to be taken only as indicative and not prescriptive.

PART NINE:
WHEREIN THE FOLLOWERS OF DYNAMIC AND PROTOTYPING METHODS ARE COMPARED WITH JOBBING BUILDERS OF THE VICTORIAN AND EDWARDIAN ERAS

Vast swaths of our cities would look very different today had it not been for the jobbing builder. Reaching prominence in the Victorian and Edwardian eras, the jobbing builder built houses. He was not an architect, nor was he a designer. He would buy some sets of plans for houses, usually from an architect or drafter, and would then offer house building to all and sundry. And although his houses were both economically and, in most cases, structurally appropriate, he was careful not to take on the building of structures that did not fit his basic plans. In this way was constructed much of the residential property we see in present-day city centers in England. The jobbing builder fulfilled a genuine need at a competitive price.

Today many software systems are being constructed in a similar fashion. How, after all, could it be otherwise when many of the major methods have no separate design stage? How could it be otherwise when there is no specific training for designing systems? Dynamic or prototyping methods encourage this jobbing approach; in fact, they rely on it.

Perhaps it is reasonable to think of the current crop of rapid-development advocates as software jobbing builders; but at this point, the metaphor is strained. Admittedly, software jobbing builders have their basic sets of designs.

---

[1] From *Software Engineering Economics*, by Barry W. Boehm (Prentice-Hall, 1981).

Admittedly, they provide cost-effective solutions. Where though, is the evidence that they know the limitations of the plans they carry in their heads? That they won't build systems whose capacities and features are far beyond the capabilities of those basic plans? Whether by using simple arithmetic extrapolations where geometric ones are required or by treating something novel as though it were known (gas and water were plumbed in very much the same way, but electricity was something significantly different, and many jobbing builders failed to appreciate this, as anyone who has rewired such a house could tell you), major mistakes are becoming common in software systems these days. These errors might indicate a lack of humility on the part of jobbers or even a total ignorance of the very existence of limits.

PART TEN:
WHEREIN THE AUTHOR TAKES
A CLOSER LOOK AT A METHOD WITH A DIFFERENT GENESIS

To date, almost all methods (especially the "new methods") that have garnered significant support have originated from the custom software development community. Be they inspired or guided by government organizations such as the CCTA (Central Computer and Telecommunications Agency, the British agency responsible for SSADM, the Structured Systems Analysis and Design Method) or be they guru-inspired by the likes of James Martin and his Information Engineering, they come almost exclusively from custom developers. IBM has tried, over many years, to produce methods that they could persuade their customers to use but with a shocking lack of success.

The latest and most widely respected method from such quarters is of course the Dynamic Systems Development Method (DSDM), which was conceived by major commercial organizations who develop their own internal software systems and has, since it started, collected a large crop of software houses with an eye to the main chance as supporters. DSDM is one of the crop I have called "new methods" and is well regarded among its adherents. By looking at the founders of DSDM and the very checkered history of development success that they share, however, we will discover that DSDM did not in fact have to produce spectacular results to show large improvements. Perhaps we should look elsewhere for methods that succeed.

One place we can look to is the producers of shrink-wrap software. Of the major producers, Microsoft provides a ready and sound source for examination because it publishes its methods for the benefit of its Solution partners. Microsoft refers to its method as a framework rather than as a method, and this choice of wording is instructive. "Framework" connotes flexibility and general approach rather than the rigidity and prescriptive nature of traditional methodologies, and the documentation regularly emphasizes the overhead associated with such prescriptive methods. Rather than dissect the Microsoft Solutions Framework (MSF), however, let's look at some elements of the framework to get a feel for its similarities to and differences from existing methods, particularly the popular DSDM.

Like DSDM, MSF is very articulate regarding the flaws of methodologies. Also like DSDM, MSF uses the regular production of prototypes (especially user interface prototypes), but it does so for a different reason. Rather than use the prototype to confirm and extend the agreement about functionality, MSF uses prototypes to ensure usability of the eventual system. To cover the constant emergence of requirements, MSF advocates a consensual change-control process (although personally I consider this an oxymoron).

Although MSF wisely acknowledges the tension between requirements and functionality delivered, one has to question the severity of the disputes in this area that might arise in a shrink-wrap producer. After all, the customer didn't ask for this software and isn't explicitly paying for its development while it's in progress. I do, however, approve of Microsoft's description of the topic as the vision/scope dichotomy. To quote the documentation, "…Vision…articulates the ultimate goals…. Scope is the opposite of Vision: it defines the limits…." Still more enlightening is, "Further development may come in future versions."

MSF is particularly interesting for the emphasis it places on what it calls the Team Model. It is, I believe, fairly unusual in paying such service to the valuable contribution that people make to software development. This acknowledgment of human ingenuity and skills is long overdue and possibly one of the keys to Microsoft's success. Within the team model, MSF advocates small teams—another sound principle.

Two other points in MSF warrant mention: risk-driven scheduling, which advises developing the elements with most risk involved first, and component-based solution design. Together with the design for usability focus already mentioned and the emphasis given to team models, MSF comes out as a thoughtful, nonprescriptive approach to software development.

However, there have been times when Microsoft and other shrink-wrap software producers have experienced problems that affected delivery schedules and product functionality. It is likely that these companies experience some of the same problems as custom developers do: contradictions, a constant to-ing and fro-ing of likely functionality, and continually shifting delivery dates.

It's also possible that frameworks didn't scale up. Perhaps the size and complexity of the project undertaken, the time frames announced, and a more adversarial position result in some of the method not being heeded.

PART ELEVEN:
IN WHICH THE AUTHOR DISCUSSES WHERE SUCH METHODS CAN AND CANNOT SUCCEED—AND WHY THOSE ARE THE CASES

I contend that there is a strong likelihood that systems built using these methods will suffer from the aforementioned DDS. Notwithstanding Jennifer Stapleton's[2] assertions that DSDM, for instance, has a strong quality focus, I believe that while such projects might have appropriate regard for the quality of the individual deliverables, the quality of the overall system might well be neglected by the emphasis on iterative delivery of parts of the functionality within short schedules.

Any such design or quality deficiency might not be evident, or at least might not be readily observed within the individual components of a systems solution, but might be manifest in the behavior of the system in production. For these reasons, I make the following recommendations:

- Follow these approaches only where the deliverable system is not required to scale far to achieve production status and volumes.
- Maintain the small-team ethos where such methods are used. I don't believe that the methods themselves scale to large projects (30 or more project members). As I have already implied, much of the success of rapid methods comes from the team members being selected from the very best.

---

[2] Jennifer Stapleton is chairman of the DSDM Consortium's technical work group.

- Question the suitability of the method before undertaking systems with high processing complexity relative to their interface requirements. The feedback demands made by short iterative feedback cycles are difficult to partition in such systems.

- Make sure that the controlling bodies of these methods look very carefully at the purposes for which these techniques were originated and try to mirror the original set of motives.

- Do your part to ensure that our industry begins to recognize the true value of design and encourages design excellence and the provision of training for this sadly overlooked discipline.

INDEX

Italicized page references indicate figures, tables, or program listings.

B

C

INDEX

D

H

I

The Mandelbrot Set
(International) Limited

TMS is a British "Windows only" software house that specializes in the Microsoft Visual tool set—that is, Visual Basic, Visual J++, and Visual C++. It is also a Microsoft Solution Provider.

TMS was the company behind the successful TMS Tools developer's toolkit for Visual Basic 3 and Micro-Help's Code Complete Visual Basic 4 developer's toolkit, which was widely acclaimed as one of *the* developer tools of the year in 1996.

TMS has an excellent reputation for creating innovative solutions and technologies and is recognized as one of the most technically proficient companies in the industry today. The company provides a wide range of development and consulting services to a mainly blue-chip client list. For full details, take a look at the TMS Web site at:

> http://www.TheMandelbrotSet.com

You can also contact TMS directly at:

Mandel House, West End
Northleach, Gloucestershire
GL54 3HG England

Telephone: 44 (0)1451 861212
Fax: 44 (0)1451 861122
E-mail: info@TheMandelbrotSet.com

The manuscript for this book was prepared and submitted to Microsoft Press in electronic form. Text files were prepared using Microsoft Word 97. Pages were composed by Microsoft Press using Adobe PageMaker 6.5 for Windows, with text in Melior and display type in Imago Extra Bold. Composed pages were delivered to the printer as electronic prepress files.

COVER GRAPHIC DESIGNER
Tim Girvin Design

COVER ILLUSTRATOR
Glenn Mitsui

INTERIOR GRAPHIC DESIGNER
Kim Eggleston

INTERIOR GRAPHIC ARTIST
Michael Victor

PRINCIPAL COMPOSITOR
Jeffrey Brendecke

PRINCIPAL PROOFREADER/COPY EDITOR
Shawn Peck

INDEXER
Hugh Maddocks

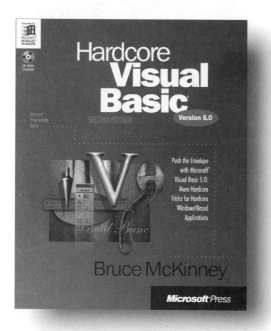

Get active!

ACTIVE VISUAL BASIC® 5.0 introduces the features and capabilities of Visual Basic that allow for the creation of Internet-enabled applications and interactive Web content. After a technical overview of the Internet and the Internet-related capabilities of Visual Basic, the book covers the Internet Control Pack, ActiveX™ control creation, and creating Doc Objects. Advanced topics in the final section include overviews of developing Internet servers and accessing the Windows® Internet API. If you're entering this exciting growth area for Visual Basic development, you'll want this book.

U.S.A.   **$39.99**
U.K.   £37.49 [V.A.T. included]
Canada $54.99
ISBN 1-57231-512-1

Microsoft·Press

Direct *from the* creators *of* **Visual Basic** 5.0.

The two-volume MICROSOFT® VISUAL BASIC 5.0 REFERENCE LIBRARY is the ultimate resource for developers at all levels. It is identical to the authoritative material presented in the Visual Basic 5.0 Help files—presented in the open-book form that many find indispensable. Guided by dictionary-style headings at the top of each page, you can quickly find just the information you need.

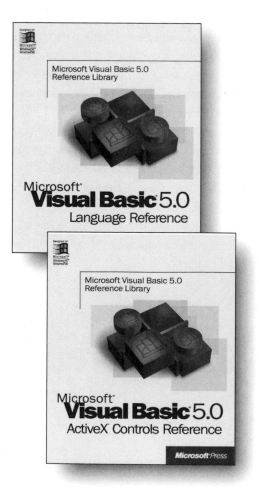

The LANGUAGE REFERENCE contains A–Z listings for the objects, functions, statements, methods, properties, and events encompassed by Visual Basic 5.0. Additional appendixes supply reference information about the ANSI character set, Visual Basic data types, operators, and derived math functions.

U.S.A.	**$39.99**
U.K.	£37.49
Canada	$53.99
ISBN 1-57231-507-5	

THE ACTIVEX™ CONTROLS REFERENCE has two parts: The first provides A–Z entries for the custom controls that ship with Visual Basic. Then, for each control, the relevant properties, events, and methods are described alphabetically.

U.S.A.	**$24.99**
U.K.	£22.99
Canada	$33.99
ISBN 1-57231-508-3	

The **hottest** *guide ever*

to data access with

Microsoft® Visual Basic® 5.0

and **Microsoft SQL Server™ 6.5.**

U.S.A. **$49.99**
U.K. £46.99 [V.A.T. included]
Canada $69.99
ISBN 1-57231-567-9

This indispensable bestseller is known as the missing link in information about client/server programming. And the newest edition is better than ever. Greatly expanded and updated, it gives you a ton of "how it works" and "how to work it" information for using Visual Basic to design, code, debug, and tune front-end applications for SQL Server. Plus, you get thorough coverage of the new possibilities that Microsoft Visual Basic 5.0 offers through powerful RDO enhancements. There's also full coverage of ODBCDirect, the new programming model that lets you use DAO to bypass Jet. Finally, the companion CD-ROM is packed with new and fully updated software tools. Encyclopedic in breadth and filled with deep practical insight, this is industrial-strength information—all in Bill Vaughn's reader-friendly style.

Microsoft® *Press*

IMPORTANT—READ CAREFULLY BEFORE OPENING SOFTWARE PACKET(S). By opening the sealed packet(s) containing the software, you indicate your acceptance of the following Microsoft License Agreement.

MICROSOFT LICENSE AGREEMENT

(Book Companion CD)

This is a legal agreement between you (either an individual or an entity) and Microsoft Corporation. By opening the sealed software packet(s) you are agreeing to be bound by the terms of this agreement. If you do not agree to the terms of this agreement, promptly return the unopened software packet(s) and any accompanying written materials to the place you obtained them for a full refund.

MICROSOFT SOFTWARE LICENSE

1. GRANT OF LICENSE. Microsoft grants to you the right to use one copy of the Microsoft software program included with this book (the "SOFTWARE") on a single terminal connected to a single computer. The SOFTWARE is in "use" on a computer when it is loaded into the temporary memory (i.e., RAM) or installed into the permanent memory (e.g., hard disk, CD-ROM, or other storage device) of that computer. You may not network the SOFTWARE or otherwise use it on more than one computer or computer terminal at the same time.

2. COPYRIGHT. The SOFTWARE is owned by Microsoft or its suppliers and is protected by United States copyright laws and international treaty provisions. Therefore, you must treat the SOFTWARE like any other copyrighted material (e.g., a book or musical recording) except that you may either (a) make one copy of the SOFTWARE solely for backup or archival purposes, or (b) transfer the SOFTWARE to a single hard disk provided you keep the original solely for backup or archival purposes. You may not copy the written materials accompanying the SOFTWARE.

3. OTHER RESTRICTIONS. You may not rent or lease the SOFTWARE, but you may transfer the SOFTWARE and accompanying written materials on a permanent basis provided you retain no copies and the recipient agrees to the terms of this Agreement. You may not reverse engineer, decompile, or disassemble the SOFTWARE. If the SOFTWARE is an update or has been updated, any transfer must include the most recent update and all prior versions.

4. DUAL MEDIA SOFTWARE. If the SOFTWARE package contains more than one kind of disk (3.5", 5.25", and CD-ROM), then you may use only the disks appropriate for your single-user computer. You may not use the other disks on another computer or loan, rent, lease, or transfer them to another user except as part of the permanent transfer (as provided above) of all SOFTWARE and written materials.

5. SAMPLE CODE. If the SOFTWARE includes Sample Code, then Microsoft grants you a royalty-free right to reproduce and distribute the sample code of the SOFTWARE provided that you: (a) distribute the sample code only in conjunction with and as a part of your software product; (b) do not use Microsoft's or its authors' names, logos, or trademarks to market your software product; (c) include the copyright notice that appears on the SOFTWARE on your product label and as a part of the sign-on message for your software product; and (d) agree to indemnify, hold harmless, and defend Microsoft and its authors from and against any claims or lawsuits, including attorneys' fees, that arise or result from the use or distribution of your software product.

DISCLAIMER OF WARRANTY

The SOFTWARE (including instructions for its use) is provided "AS IS" WITHOUT WARRANTY OF ANY KIND. MICROSOFT FURTHER DISCLAIMS ALL IMPLIED WARRANTIES INCLUDING WITHOUT LIMITATION ANY IMPLIED WARRANTIES OF MERCHANTABILITY OR OF FITNESS FOR A PARTICULAR PURPOSE. THE ENTIRE RISK ARISING OUT OF THE USE OR PERFORMANCE OF THE SOFTWARE AND DOCUMENTATION REMAINS WITH YOU.

IN NO EVENT SHALL MICROSOFT, ITS AUTHORS, OR ANYONE ELSE INVOLVED IN THE CREATION, PRODUCTION, OR DELIVERY OF THE SOFTWARE BE LIABLE FOR ANY DAMAGES WHATSOEVER (INCLUDING, WITHOUT LIMITATION, DAMAGES FOR LOSS OF BUSINESS PROFITS, BUSINESS INTERRUPTION, LOSS OF BUSINESS INFORMATION, OR OTHER PECUNIARY LOSS) ARISING OUT OF THE USE OF OR INABILITY TO USE THE SOFTWARE OR DOCUMENTATION, EVEN IF MICROSOFT HAS BEEN ADVISED OF THE POSSIBILITY OF SUCH DAMAGES. BECAUSE SOME STATES/COUNTRIES DO NOT ALLOW THE EXCLUSION OR LIMITATION OF LIABILITY FOR CONSEQUENTIAL OR INCIDENTAL DAMAGES, THE ABOVE LIMITATION MAY NOT APPLY TO YOU.

U.S. GOVERNMENT RESTRICTED RIGHTS

The SOFTWARE and documentation are provided with RESTRICTED RIGHTS. Use, duplication, or disclosure by the Government is subject to restrictions as set forth in subparagraph (c)(1)(ii) of The Rights in Technical Data and Computer Software clause at DFARS 252.227-7013 or subparagraphs (c)(1) and (2) of the Commercial Computer Software — Restricted Rights 48 CFR 52.227-19, as applicable. Manufacturer is Microsoft Corporation, One Microsoft Way, Redmond, WA 98052-6399.

If you acquired this product in the United States, this Agreement is governed by the laws of the State of Washington.

Should you have any questions concerning this Agreement, or if you desire to contact Microsoft Press for any reason, please write: Microsoft Press, One Microsoft Way, Redmond, WA 98052-6399.